GLOBAL STUDIES

INDIA
AND SOUTH ASIA
FOURTH EDITION

Dr. James H. K. Norton

OTHER BOOKS IN THE GLOBAL STUDIES SERIES
- Africa
- China
- Japan and the Pacific Rim
- Latin America
- The Middle East
- Russia, the Eurasian Republics, and
  Central/Eastern Europe
- Western Europe

Dushkin/McGraw-Hill
Sluice Dock, Guilford, Connecticut 06437
Visit us on the Internet—http://www.dushkin.com

STAFF

Ian A. Nielsen	Publisher
Brenda S. Filley	Production Manager
Lisa M. Clyde	Developmental Editor
Roberta Monaco	Editor
Charles Vitelli	Designer
Cheryl Greenleaf	Permissions Coordinator
Lisa Holmes-Doebrick	Administrative Coordinator
Lara M. Johnson	Design/Advertising Coordinator
Laura Levine	Graphics
Michael Campbell	Graphics
Tom Goddard	Graphics
Juliana Arbo	Typesetting Supervisor

Library of Congress Cataloging in Publication Data
Main Entry under title: Global Studies: India and South Asia.
    1. India—History—20th century. 2. India—Politics and government—1947–.
    3. Asia, Southeastern—History—20th century. 4. Asia—History—20th century.
I. Title: India and South Asia. II. Norton, James H. K., *comp.*
ISBN 0–07–024954–7   954   91–71258

We would like to thank Digital Wisdom Incorporated for allowing us to use their Mountain High Maps cartography software. This software was used to create the relief maps in this edition.

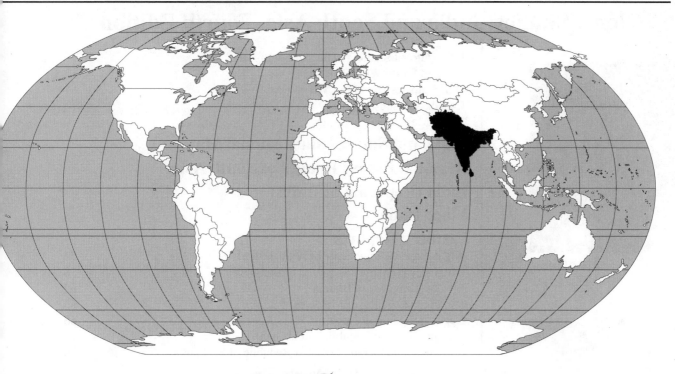

AUTHOR/EDITOR
Dr. James H. K. Norton

The author/editor of *Global Studies: India and South Asia* received a B.S. degree from Yale University, B.A. and M.A. degrees in Sanskrit from Oxford University, and a Ph.D. in Indian philosophy from the University of Madras in India. He taught for 10 years at the College of Wooster, where he was associate professor of religion and chairman of the Department of Indian Studies. While at Wooster, Dr. Norton initiated a junior-year study program for college students in Madurai University, India, now part of the University of Wisconsin College Year in India program. He has also taught at Madurai University, Boston University, and Oberlin College. He is currently farming in Massachusetts, conducting continuing-education courses, and serving on the school committee for Martha's Vineyard. Dr. Norton spent 5 years in India as a Ford Foundation scholar while doing graduate work at the University of Madras as a teacher and as a Senior Research Fellow of the American Institute of Indian Studies. He is a member of the American Academy of Religion, the Association for Asian Studies, and the Conference on Religion in South India, and has served on the executive committee of the Society for South Indian Studies. His articles on Indian philosophy and on comparisons of Eastern and Western thought appear in a number of books and journals.

SERIES CONSULTANT
H. Thomas Collins
PROJECT LINKS
George Washington University

Contents

Global Studies: India and South Asia, Fourth Edition

South Asia   Page 4

South Asia   Page 9

India   Page 19

Using Global Studies: India and South Asia   **vi**
Selected World Wide Web Sites   **vii**
U.S. Statistics and Map   **viii**
Canada Statistics and Map   **ix**
World Map   **x**

2 | **India and South Asia Regional Map**
3 | **Regional Essay: Images of South Asia**
37 | **India (Republic of India)**
Map: India   36
54 | **Country Reports**
Afghanistan (Islamic State of Afghanistan)   **54**
Bangladesh (People's Republic of Bangladesh)   **58**
Bhutan (Kingdom of Bhutan)   **62**
Maldives (Republic of Maldives)   **65**
Nepal (Kingdom of Nepal)   **68**
Pakistan (Islamic Republic of Pakistan)   **71**
Sri Lanka (Democratic Socialist Republic of Sri Lanka)   **78**
82 | **Articles from the World Press**
Annotated Table of Contents of Articles   **82**
Topic Guide to Articles   **84**

Regional Article

1. **Competing Nationalisms: Secessionist Movements and the State,** Raju G. C. Thomas, *Harvard International Review,* Summer 1996.   86

India Articles

2. **India: The Imprint of Empire,** Roderick MacFarquhar, *The New York Review of Books,* October 23, 1997.   90
3. **Gandhi and Nehru: Frustrated Visionaries?** Judith Brown, *History Today,* September 1997.   97
4. **Partition, the Human Cost,** Mushirul Hasan, *History Today,* September 1997.   101
5. **The Muslims and Partition,** Francis Robinson, *History Today,* September 1997.   106
6. **Bengal and Punjab: Before and Beyond,** Jean Alphonse Bernard, *History Today,* September 1997.   110
7. **What Does India Want?** Payal Sampat, *World Watch,* July/August 1998.   114
8. **India's Problem Is Not Politics,** Marshall M. Bouton, *Foreign Affairs,* May/June 1998.   123
9. **Still a Cold War,** Maleeha Lodhi, *The World Today,* May 1998.   128
10. **India's Socioeconomic Makeover,** Richard Breyer, *The World & I,* August 1998.   132
11. **India: Globalized Economy, Victimized Workers?** Sharmila Joshi, *Populi,* June 1998.   135
12. **Life in the Slow Lane,** Dan Biers and Shiraz Sidhva, *Far Eastern Economic Review,* August 21, 1997.   137
13. **Enduring Stereotypes about Asia: India's Caste System,** Joe Elder, *Education About Asia,* Fall 1996.   140

dia   Page 43

ngladesh   Page 59

Lanka   Page 80

14. **Ancient Jewel,** T. R. (Joe) Sundaram, *The World & I,* October 1996.   143

15. **Though Illegal, Child Marriage Is Popular in Part of India,** John F. Burns, *New York Times,* May 11, 1998.   147

16. **India's Misconceived Family Plan,** Jodi L. Jacobson, *World Watch,* November/December 1991.   149

17. **Women in South Asia: The Raj and After,** Tanika Sarkar, *History Today,* September 1997.   154

18. **In India, Men Challenge a Matrilineal Society,** Kavita Menon, *Ms.,* September/October 1998.   158

19. **Oldest Prophetic Religion Struggles for Survival,** John Zubrzycki, *The Christian Science Monitor,* May 13, 1998.   160

20. **Dire Warnings of Environmental Disaster,** Taani Pande, *India Abroad,* December 6, 1996.   162

21. **India's Low-Tech Energy Success,** Payal Sampat, *World Watch,* November/December 1995.   164

22. **A Celluloid Hall of Mirrors,** Somi Roy, *The World & I,* October 1996.   167

23. **Community Radio in India,** Frederick Noronha, *Cultural Survival Quarterly,* Summer 1998.   171

24. **Making Something Out of Nothing,** Pierre-Sylvain Filliozat, *The UNESCO Courier,* November 1993.   175

25. **Ancient Hindu Festival Thrives in Computer-Age India,** John F. Burns, *New York Times,* April 16, 1998.   178

South Asia Articles

26. **The Succession,** Richard Mackenzie, *The New Republic,* September 14 & 21, 1998.   180

27. **A Bank for the Poor,** Muhammad Yunus, *The UNESCO Courier,* January 1997.   184

28. **Pakistan at Fifty: A Tenuous Democracy,** Samina Ahmed, *Current History,* December 1997.   186

29. **The Crumbling of Pakistan,** *The Economist,* October 17, 1998.   191

30. **Sanctions: Lift 'em,** Pervez Hoodbhoy and Zia Mian; **Modify 'em,** David Cortright and Samina Ahmed; and **Hang Tough,** Thomas Graham Jr., *The Bulletin of the Atomic Scientists,* September/October 1998.   192

31. **War in Sri Lanka Feeds on Itself,** John Zubrzycki, *The Christian Science Monitor,* August 12, 1998.   198

32. **After Decades, Tibet Won't Bend to Chinese Ways,** Kevin Platt, *The Christian Science Monitor,* July 29, 1997.   200

33. **Tibet: Communist China and Human Rights,** Tenzin Gyatso, *Vital Speeches of the Day,* May 1, 1997.   201

Credits   204
Sources for Statistical Summaries   204
Glossary of Terms and Abbreviations   205
Bibliography   208
Index   211

Using Global Studies: India and South Asia

THE GLOBAL STUDIES SERIES

The Global Studies series was created to help readers acquire a basic knowledge and understanding of the regions and countries in the world. Each volume provides a foundation of information—geographic, cultural, economic, political, historical, artistic, and religious—that will allow readers to better assess the current and future problems within these countries and regions and to comprehend how events there might affect their own well-being. In short, these volumes present the background information necessary to respond to the realities of our global age.

Each of the volumes in the Global Studies series is crafted under the careful direction of an author/editor—an expert in the area under study. The author/editors teach and conduct research and have traveled extensively through the regions about which they are writing.

In this *India and South Asia* edition, the author/editor has written introductory essays on the South Asia region and country reports for each of the countries included.

MAJOR FEATURES OF THE GLOBAL STUDIES SERIES

The Global Studies volumes are organized to provide concise information on the regions and countries within those areas under study. The major sections and features of the books are described here.

Regional Essays

For *Global Studies: India and South Asia,* the author/editor has written a narrative essay "Images of South Asia" focusing on the religious, cultural, sociopolitical, and economic differences and similarities of the countries and peoples in the region. A detailed map accompanies the essay.

Country Reports

Concise reports are written for each of the countries within the region under study. These reports are the heart of each Global Studies volume. *Global Studies: India and South Asia, Fourth Edition,* contains eight country reports, including India.

The country reports are composed of five standard elements. Each report contains a detailed map visually positioning the country among its neighboring states; a summary of statistical information; a current essay providing important historical, geographical, political, cultural, and economic information; a historical timeline, offering a convenient visual survey of a few key historical events; and four "graphic indicators," with summary statements about the country in terms of development, freedom, health/welfare, and achievements.

A Note on the Statistical Reports

The statistical information provided for each country has been drawn from a wide range of sources. (The most frequently referenced are listed on page 204.) Every effort has been made to provide the most current and accurate information available. However, occasionally the information cited by these sources differs to some extent; and, all too often, the most current information available for some countries is dated. Aside from these difficulties, the statistical summary of each country is generally quite complete and up to date. Care should be taken, however, in using these statistics (or, for that matter, any published statistics) in making hard comparisons among countries. We have also provided comparable statistics for the United States and Canada, which can be found on pages viii and ix.

World Press Articles

Within each Global Studies volume is reprinted a number of articles carefully selected by our editorial staff and the author/editor from a broad range of international periodicals and newspapers. The articles have been chosen for currency, interest, and their differing perspectives on the subject countries. There are 33 articles in *Global Studies: India and South Asia, Fourth Edition.*

The articles section is preceded by an annotated table of contents as well as a topic guide. The annotated table of contents offers a brief summary of each article, while the topic guide indicates the main theme(s) of each article. Thus, readers desiring to focus on articles dealing with a particular theme, say, the environment, may refer to the topic guide to find those articles.

WWW Sites

An extensive annotated list of selected World Wide Web sites can be found on the facing page (vii) in this edition of *Global Studies: India and South Asia.* In addition, the URL addresses for country-specific Web sites are provided on the statistics page of most countries. All of the Web site addresses were correct and operational at press time. Instructors and students alike are urged to refer to those sites often to enhance their understanding of the region and to keep up with current events.

Glossary, Bibliography, Index

At the back of each Global Studies volume, readers will find a glossary of terms and abbreviations, which provides a quick reference to the specialized vocabulary of the area under study and to the standard abbreviations used throughout the volume.

Following the glossary is a bibliography, which lists general works, national histories, and current-events publications and periodicals that provide regular coverage on India and South Asia.

The index at the end of the volume is an accurate reference to the contents of the volume. Readers seeking specific information and citations should consult this standard index.

Currency and Usefulness

Global Studies: India and South Asia, like the other Global Studies volumes, is intended to provide the most current and useful information available necessary to understand the events that are shaping the cultures of the region today.

This volume is revised on a regular basis. The statistics are updated, regional essays and country reports revised, and world press articles replaced. In order to accomplish this task, we turn to our author/editor, our advisory boards, and—hopefully—to you, the users of this volume. Your comments are more than welcome. If you have an idea that you think will make the next edition more useful, an article or bit of information that will make it more current, or a general comment on its organization, content, or features that you would like to share with us, please send it in for serious consideration.

Selected World Wide Web Sites for India and South Asia

GENERAL SITES

BBC World Service—**http://www.bbc.co.uk/worldservice/ sasia/**—The BBC, one of the world's most successful radio networks, provides the latest news from around the world and in South Asia at this site. It is possible to access the news in several languages.

CNN Online Page—**http://www.cnn.com**—U.S. 24-hour video news channel. News, updated every few hours, includes text, pictures, and film. Good external links.

C-SPAN ONLINE—**http://www.c-span.org**—See especially C-SPAN International on the Web for International Programming Highlights and archived C-Span programs.

International Network Information Center at University of Texas—**http://inic.utexas.edu**—Gateway has pointers to international sites, including South Asia.

Penn Library: Resources by Subject—**http://www.library. upenn.edu/resources/subject/subject.html**—This vast site is rich in links to information about Asian studies, including population and demography.

Political Science RESOURCES—**http://www.psr.keele. ac.uk**—Dynamic gateway to sources available via European addresses. Listed by country name.

ReliefWeb—**http://wwwnotes.reliefweb.int**—UN's Department of Humanitarian Affairs clearinghouse for international humanitarian emergencies.

Social Science Information Gateway (SOSIG)—**http:// sosig.esrc.bris.ac.uk**—Project of the Economic and Social Research Council (ESRC). It catalogs 22 subjects and lists developing countries' URL addresses.

Speech and Transcript Center—**http://gwis2.circ.gwu.edu/~ gprice/speech.htm**—This unusual site is the repository of transcripts of every kind, from radio and television, of speeches by world government leaders, and the proceedings of groups like the United Nations, NATO, and the World Bank.

United Nations System—**http://www.unsystem.org**—This is the official Web site for the United Nations system of organizations. Everything is listed alphabetically. Offers: UNICC; Food and Agriculture Organization.

UN Development Programme (UNDP)—**http://www.undp. org**—Publications and current information on world poverty, Mission Statement, UN Development Fund for Women, and more. Be sure to see Poverty Clock.

U.S. Agency for International Development (USAID)—**http:// www.info.usaid.gov**—U.S. policy toward assistance to Asian countries is available at this site.

U.S. Central Intelligence Agency Home Page—**http://www. odci.gov/cia**—This site includes publications of the CIA, such as the World Factbook, Factbook on Intelligence, Handbook of International Economic Statistics, and CIA Maps.

U.S. Department of State Home Page—**http://www. state.gov/index.html**—Organized alphabetically: Country Reports, Human Rights, International Organizations, etc.

World Bank Group—**http://www.worldbank.org/html/Welcome. html**—News (i.e., press releases, summary of new projects, speeches), publications, topics in development, countries and regions. Links to other financial organizations.

World Health Organization (WHO)—**http://www.who.ch**—Maintained by WHO's headquarters in Geneva, Switzerland, this comprehensive site includes a search engine.

World Trade Organization (WTO)—**http://www.wto.org**—Topics include foundation of world trade systems, data on textiles, intellectual property rights, legal frameworks, trade and environmental policies, recent agreements, and others.

GENERAL INDIA AND SOUTH ASIA SITES

ASEANWEB—**http://www.asean.or.id**—This official site of the Association of South East Asian Nations provides an overview of Asian Web sources, Summits, Economic and World Affairs, Publications, Political Foundations, Regional Cooperation.

Asia Web Watch—**http://www.ciolek.com/Asia-Web-Watch/ main-page.html**—Here is a register of statistical data that can be accessed alphabetically. Data includes Asian Online Materials Statistics and Appendices about Asian cyberspace.

Asian Arts—**http://asianart.com**—Here is an online journal for the study and exhibition of the arts of Asia, which includes exhibitions, articles, and galleries.

Asian Studies WWW Virtual Library—**http://coombs. anu.edu.au/WWWVL-AsianStudies.html**—Australia National University maintains these sites, which link to many other Web sources, available at each country's location.

Asia-Yahoo—**http://www.yahoo.com/Regional/Regions/Asia/**—Specialized Yahoo search site permits key-word searches on Asian events, countries, and topics.

History of the Indian Sub-Continent—**http://www.stockon. edu/~gilmorew/consorti/1aindia.htm**—As part of Stockton's World Wide Web Global History Research Institute, the history of the Indian subcontinent has been arranged chronologically at this site. This excellent resource contains maps, pictures, short writings, and scholarly writings.

South Asia Resources—**http://www.lib.berkeley.edu/SSEAL/ SouthAsia/wsaresou.html**—From this University of Berkeley Library site there is quick access to online resources in Asian studies as well as to South Asian specialists and other special features.

See individual country report pages for additional Web sites.

The United States (United States of America)

GEOGRAPHY

Area in Square Miles (Kilometers):
3,618,770 (9,578,626) (slightly larger than China)

Capital (Population): Washington, D.C. (567,100)

Environmental Concerns: air pollution resulting in acid rain; water pollution from runoff of pesticides and fertilizers; desertification; habitat loss; other concerns

Geographical Features: vast central plain, mountains in the west; hills and low mountains in the east; rugged mountains and broad river valleys in Alaska; volcanic topography in Hawaii

Climate: mostly temperate; wide regional variations

PEOPLE

Population

Total: 270,312,000

Annual Growth Rate: 0.87%

Rural/Urban Population Ratio: 24/76

Major Languages: predominantly English; a sizable Spanish-speaking minority; many others

Ethnic Makeup: 83% white; 12% black; 5% Asian, Amerindian, and others

Religions: 56% Protestant; 28% Roman Catholic; 2% Jewish; 14% others or no affiliation

Health

Life Expectancy at Birth: 73 years (male); 80 years (female)

Infant Mortality Rate (Ratio): 6.44/1,000

Average Caloric Intake: 138% of FAO minimum

Physicians Available (Ratio): 1/381

Education

Adult Literacy Rate: 97.9% (official) (estimates vary widely)

Compulsory (Ages): 7–16; free

COMMUNICATION

Telephones: 1 per 1.6 people

Daily Newspaper Circulation: 228 per 1,000 people; approximately 63,000,000 circulation

Televisions: 1 per 1.2 people

TRANSPORTATION

Highways in Miles (Kilometers): 3,906,960 (6,261,154)

Railroads in Miles (Kilometers): 149,161 (240,000)

Usable Airfields: 13,387

Motor Vehicles in Use: 200,500,000

GOVERNMENT

Type: federal republic

Independence Date: July 4, 1776 (from United Kingdom)

Head of State: President William ("Bill") Jefferson Clinton

Political Parties: Democratic Party; Republican Party; others of minor political significance

Suffrage: universal at 18

MILITARY

Military Expenditures (% of GDP): 3.8%

Current Disputes: none

ECONOMY

Per Capita Income/GDP: $30,200/$8.08 trillion

GDP Growth Rate: 3.8%

Inflation Rate: 2%

Unemployment Rate: 4.9%

Labor Force: 136,300,000

Natural Resources: metallic and non-metallic minerals; petroleum; natural gas; timber

Agriculture: food grains; feed crops; oil-bearing crops; livestock; dairy products

Industry: diversified in both capital- and consumer-goods industries

Exports: $625.1 billion (primary partners Canada, Western Europe, Japan, Mexico)

Imports: $822 billion (primary partners Canada, Western Europe, Japan, Mexico)

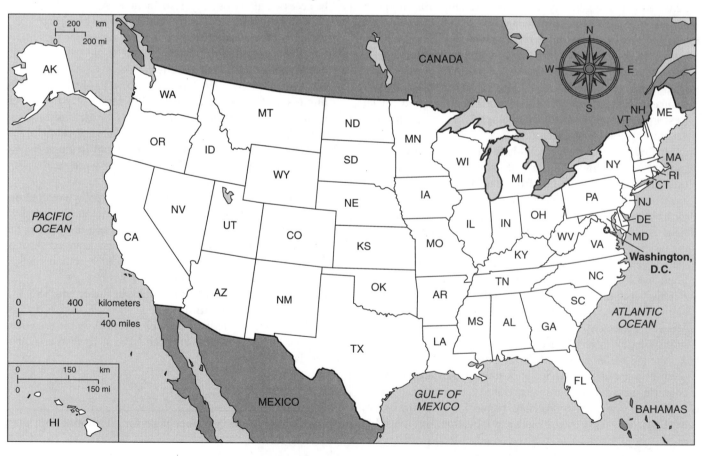

anada

GRAPHY

in Square Miles (Kilometers):
50,790 (9,976,140) (slightly larger
n the United States)
al (Population): Ottawa (1,000,000)
onmental Concerns: air pollution and
ulting acid rain severely affecting lakes
d damaging forests; water pollution
raphical Features: permafrost in the
th; mountains in the west; central
ins
ate: from temperate in south to
arctic and arctic in north

PLE

lation
30,676,000
al Growth Rate: 1.09%
/Urban Population Ratio: 23/77
r Languages: both English and French
official
c Makeup: 40% British Isles origin;
% French origin; 20% other European;
% indigenous Indian and Eskimo;
5% others, mostly Asian
ions: 46% Roman Catholic; 16%
ited Church; 10% Anglican; 28%
ers

th
xpectancy at Birth: 76 years (male);
years (female)

Infant Mortality Rate (Ratio): 5.59/1,000
Average Caloric Intake: 127% of FAO
minimum
Physicians Available (Ratio): 1/464

Education
Adult Literacy Rate: 97%
Compulsory (Ages): primary school

COMMUNICATION
Telephones: 1 per 1.7 people
Daily Newspaper Circulation: 189 per
1,000 people
Televisions: 1 per 1.5 people

TRANSPORTATION
Highways in Miles (Kilometers): 637,104
(1,021,000)
Railroads in Miles (Kilometers): 48,764
(78,148)
Usable Airfields: 1,139
Motor Vehicles in Use: 16,700,000

GOVERNMENT
Type: confederation with parliamentary de-
mocracy
Independence Date: July 1, 1867 (from
United Kingdom)
Head of State/Government: Queen Elizabeth
II; Prime Minister Jean Chrétien

Political Parties: Progressive Conservative
Party; Liberal Party; New Democratic Party;
Reform Party; Bloc Québécois
Suffrage: universal at 18

MILITARY
Military Expenditures (% of GDP): 1.53%
Current Disputes: none

ECONOMY
Currency ($U.S. Equivalent): 1.53
Canadian dollars = $1
Per Capita Income/GDP: $21,700/$658
billion
GDP Growth Rate: 3.5%
Inflation Rate: 1.8%
Unemployment Rate: 8.6%
Labor Force: 15,300,000
Natural Resources: petroleum; coal; natural
gas; fish and other wildlife; minerals;
cement; forestry products
Agriculture: grains; livestock; dairy prod-
ucts; potatoes; hogs; poultry and eggs;
tobacco
Industry: oil production and refining;
natural-gas development; fish products;
wood and paper products; chemicals;
transportation equipment
Exports: $208.6 billion (primary partners
United States, Japan, United Kingdom)
Imports: $194.4 billion (primary partners
United States, Japan, United Kingdom)

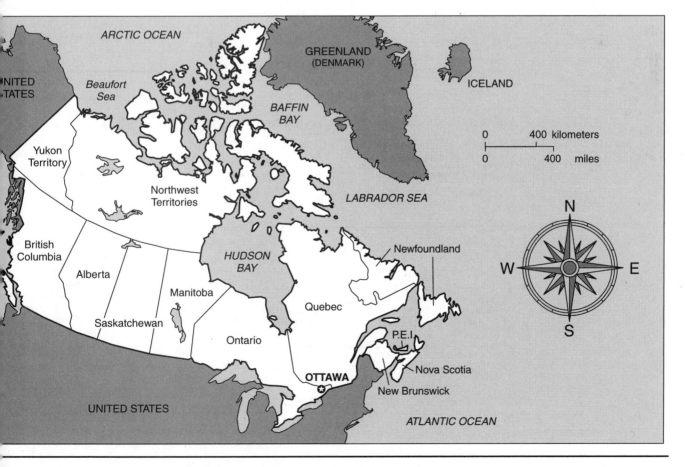

GLOBAL  STUDIES

This map is provided to give you a graphic picture of where the countries of the world are located, the relationships they have with their region and neighbors, and their positions relative to the superpowers and power blocs. We have focused on certain areas to illustrate these crowded regions more clearly.

Scale: 1 to 125,000,000

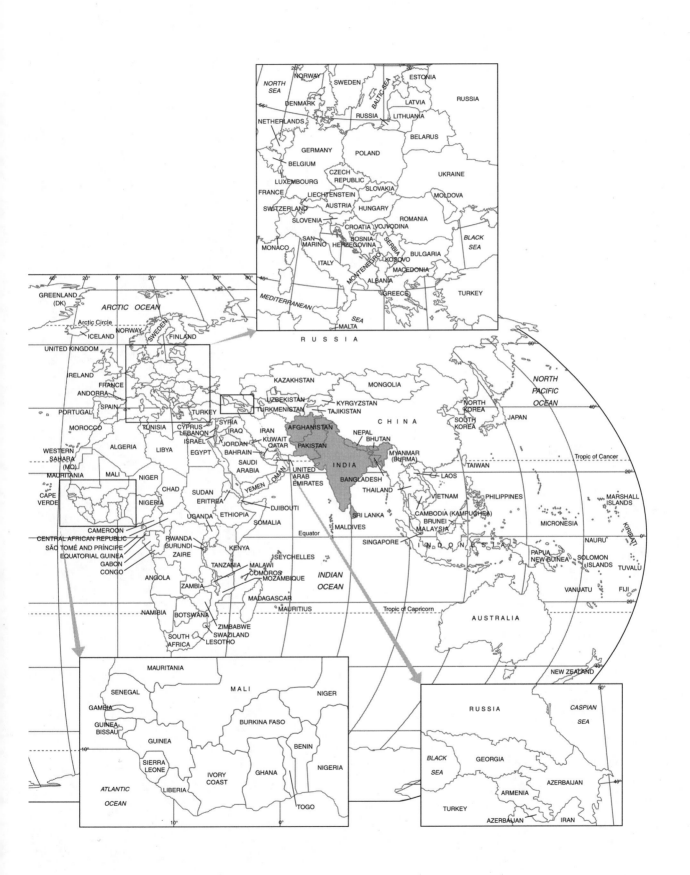

India and South Asia

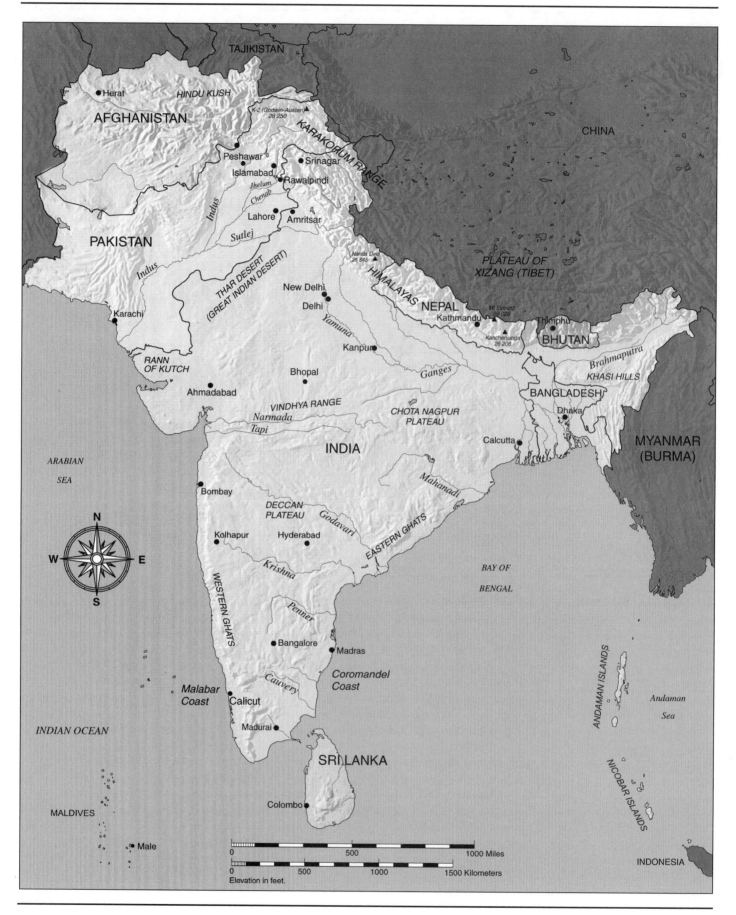

TAJIKISTAN

Herat •
HINDU KUSH

AFGHANISTAN

K-2 (Godwin-Austen)
28 250 ▲

KARAKORUM RANGE

CHINA

Peshawar •
Srinagar •
Islamabad •
Rawalpindi •
Jhelum
Chenab

Lahore •
Amritsar •

PAKISTAN

Indus

Sutlej

Indus

Karachi •

THAR DESERT
(GREAT INDIAN DESERT)

New Delhi •
Delhi •

Nanda Devi
25 645 ▲

HIMALAYAS

NEPAL

PLATEAU OF
XIZANG (TIBET)

Mt Everest
29 028 ▲

Kathmandu •

Kahchenjunga
28 208 ▲

Thimphu •

BHUTAN

Brahmaputra

KHASI HILLS

RANN
OF KUTCH

Ahmadabad •

Yamuna

Kanpur •

Ganges

Bhopal •

VINDHYA RANGE

Narmada

Tapi

CHOTA NAGPUR
PLATEAU

BANGLADESH

Dhaka •

ARABIAN
SEA

Bombay •

DECCAN
PLATEAU

INDIA

Mahanadi

Calcutta •

MYANMAR
(BURMA)

N
W   E
S

Kolhapur •

Hyderabad •

Godavari

EASTERN GHATS

Krishna

BAY OF

BENGAL

WESTERN GHATS

Penner

Bangalore •

Madras •

Cauvery

Coromandel
Coast

ANDAMAN ISLANDS

Andaman
Sea

Malabar
Coast

Calicut •

Madurai •

INDIAN OCEAN

SRI LANKA

NICOBAR ISLANDS

Colombo •

MALDIVES

• Male

0   500   1000 Miles
0   500   1000   1500 Kilometers
Elevation in feet.

INDONESIA

2

Images of South Asia

South Asia is a distinct area, set apart from the rest of the globe. We recognize women from there because they may wear a distinctive dress, called *sari* or *salwar-kameez,* and apply the cosmetic red mark called *bindi* on their foreheads. Men might wear *dhotis, jodhpurs,* or trousers and notched-collar Nehru jackets, and some wrap turbans about their heads. Indian cooking, with its delightfully spicy curries, has a flavor all its own. And Indian music, played on the *sitar, vina,* or *sharod,* does not sound like any other. We experience these sights and tastes and sounds as unusual, yet they identify what is normal for the people of South Asia. Even their attitudes and assumptions about such elemental realities as truth, life, time, and life after death are not the same as understood in other regions of the world.

Some contributions that the world has received from the Indian subcontinent identify the uniqueness of the traditions by which the South Asian people live. The number zero—the most symbolic and elusive of all numbers—was added to the number system of the West only after it had been brought from South Asia by Arab traders (which is why we call them Arabic numbers). Linguistics—the study of the structure of language—also had its origin in South Asia. *Yoga,* a very ancient approach to spiritual discipline, and *satyagraha* (nonviolent resistance), an alternative to power politics developed in this century by India's Mohandas Gandhi, indicate the extent and the variety of creative ideas that were developed in South Asia and that have benefited all humankind.

There are also some common challenges that the peoples of this region share in a different way, in some instances with even greater intensity, than in other parts of the world. These include high population density and growth, environmental degradation, national identity, economic development, social equality and women's rights, child labor, illiteracy, poverty, and disease. How the peoples of South Asia respond to these challenges affects the well-being of everyone in the world.

OUT OF MANY FRAGMENTS, A PORTRAIT
This essay focuses on five images of South Asia. They are not exhaustive descriptions but, rather, impressions that, taken together, give a picture of what we can learn from this distinctive part of the world.

The first image is that South Asia is significant as a distinct geographical and cultural region. The subcontinent is inhabited by almost 1.3 billion people—one fifth of Earth's total population. These people live in a clearly defined space, about a quarter of the size of North America, separated by nature from the rest of the world by high mountains and ocean waters. In this space they have experienced a unique and ancient history that has shaped their lifestyles, languages, social patterns, institutions, and religious traditions in ways that are quite different from those found in other parts of the world. Study of the setting of their lives and traditions provides a basis for mutual respect and understanding, where a lack of such awareness may lead to stereotyping and mistrust. In our increasingly interconnected world, ignorance of such

a significant portion of the world's population is not only deplorable, but it can also be dangerous. A recent example is the portrayal in the West of the nuclear bomb testing done by the governments of India and Pakistan in May 1998 as being militant rather than self-protective and deterrent in nature. The alarmist American response to these tests did not take into account the U.S. government's inability to assure either its own—or, more unsettling, China's—compliance with the Nuclear Non-proliferation Treaty, which both have signed.

The second image is that South Asia is an incredibly diverse as well as crowded multicultural environment. The enormous population is divided among eight countries: Afghanistan, Bangladesh, Bhutan, India, Maldives, Nepal, Pakistan, and Sri Lanka. Only two of these countries—Maldives and Sri Lanka—are clearly defined by geography, because they are islands. But the political boundaries among them, even when natural, do not enclose peoples of common language and ethnic origin. Rather, they separate significant groupings of shared ethnicity, language, and religion into different nationalities. The Pathans, for example, were so divided by the drawing of the border between British India and Afghanistan in 1907. In 1979, at the time of the Soviet invasion of Afghanistan, about 6 million Pathans—more than a third of the total population of that country—lived on the Afghan side. Another 10 million lived on the other side of the border, constituting the dominant population in the Northwest Frontier Province of Pakistan.

The ethnic identities of the people in South Asia do not correspond with their political identities as nation also because, within all but the smallest of these countries, there is within their borders a wide diversity of social groups who speak different languages and follow distinct customs and religious traditions.

India, by far the largest country in South Asia, with more than 75 percent of the total population and occupying approximately 64 percent of the land of the subcontinent, is, in social and linguistic terms, the most diverse. At least 18 major languages, each with innumerable dialects, are spoken in different regions of the country. (English, spoken by fewer than 6 percent of the people, serves as the link language among all of the regions.) People living in the same place, who all speak the same language, are also divided into extended kinship groups called caste *(jati)* communities. These communities sustain accepted norms of behavior, dress, and diet for all their members. They are also endogamous, which means that families are expected to find marriage partners for their children among other families within this group. Many are identified by a traditional occupation, from which each derives its name, such as *kumbhar* (potter), *mali* (gardener), *gujar* (goat herder), *dhobi* (washerman), or *jat* (farmer community). There are thousands of such kinship groups throughout the country. In a normal village setting, individuals will interact on a daily basis with others from about 20 different *jatis.* The locally accepted position of their *jati* in a social hierarchy, generally called the "caste system," determines the socially expected norms of their interactions. One's position in the immediate family is also highly prescribed by traditional expectations, maintained in most instances by the patriarchal structure of the family. All of these bases for identity are much more immediate and meaningful than being the citizen of a nation.

In all of the countries of the subcontinent, there are much larger percentages of rural populations than urban. Those who live in villages contrast vividly with those who are thriving or are crowding and overburdening the available spaces and services in the cities. Striking in both the cities and villages, however, is the stark contrast between those who are very wealthy and the multitude of the poor.

That such diverse peoples live in such crowded circumstances, all drawing upon limited resources, is both a great achievement and a constant challenge. There are many causes of strife among the socially diverse groups in South Asia. Outbursts, rampaging, and rioting do occur among competitive factions and differing religious communities, as well as outright warfare among militant nationalist organizations and between nation-states.

The next two images amplify the first two images of South Asia as a distinct, diverse, and crowded cultural region of the world. The third image looks toward the past, at the classical heritage of the peoples of the subcontinent, known as the "Great Tradition," to see how it underlies and sustains the complex and persistent social diversity in the region. The fourth image looks at the impact of democracy in the subcontinent today, especially among peoples whose primary sense of identity is ethnic, religious, and linguistic (as sustained by one's *jati* community) rather than political (as a nation).

The third image, the Great Tradition of South Asia, has its earliest discernible roots in two vastly different sources. The first is the Harappan city culture, of which archaeological remains reveal organizational and commercial skills developed in the Indus River Valley urban centers more than 4,500 years ago. The second is the Vedic tradition, recorded in a sacred literature that contains the religious musings of a robust, cow-herding people called Aryans, who drove their horse-drawn war chariots into the subcontinent from Central Asia a thousand years later. Over the course of many centuries, these heritages were coalesced, elaborated, appended, and refined into classical forms that became normative for the way civilized people in that region of the world should perceive and participate in life. These forms provided the structure for immense intellectual and artistic creativity, which produced many outstanding works of thought and art.

Because of the skill, discipline, and depth of insight achieved by South Asia's classical thinkers and artisans, their accumulated works are intellectually challenging. Yet the tradition that they created provides an enduring perspective on our world that is broadening and self-affirming for us, and gives some definition to the uniqueness of South Asian culture. An awareness of this Great Tradition provides a context for understanding the introduction of democracy as a political

(UN Photo 153428/John Isaac)

The sheer multitude of people who live in South Asia is mind-boggling: 1.3 billion crowd the subcontinent, and despite some successes in family planning, that number is climbing rapidly.

force among the nations of South Asia. It also provides alternative paths to realize the goals of democracy in a world torn by ethnic violence and warfare.

The fourth image is that the introduction of democracy into the subcontinent as a primary instrument of political modernization is having a profound impact not only on the form and goals of governments in the countries of South Asia but also on how people are interacting. Democratically elected representative government is a modern Western institution, introduced by the British colonial government during the nineteenth and early twentieth centuries. Its introduction has raised a number of far-reaching issues. All of the countries have had to deal with challenges of national identity, of the relation of religion to nationalism, of refugees, and of political stability. These issues have produced unanticipated, sometimes traumatic, consequences for many millions of people.

Yet today, more people live under democratic rule in South Asia than in any other part of the world. There is much that we can learn about democracy by examining the various ways it has come to function in that very different cultural setting.

Finally, we focus attention on Mohandas Gandhi, known as the *Mahatma,* the "great-souled one." During the early twentieth century, Gandhi evolved an effective process of nonviolent political resistance. He also developed a style of leadership that drew upon a unique combination of the classical norms and modern aspirations described in our previous two images of South Asia. He articulated in enviable simplicity the profound perspective of the classical tradition in committing himself not just to the removal of colonial domination, to independence, but to true freedom for an oppressed people. He thus empowered those who today are citizens of the republics of India, Pakistan, Bangladesh, and Nepal to participate in the destiny of new, democratically ruled nations in the modern world.

To understand Gandhi and his leadership role is to realize how much he embodied what is unique about the peoples of South Asia whom he led. Yet it is in the particularity of his uniqueness as an individual among a specific people that he speaks to us all. No one else in the twentieth century has had so wide and positive an impact on the political awareness and empowerment of oppressed peoples all over the world.

IMAGE 1: SOUTH ASIA, A DISTINCT LAND AND UNIQUE CIVILIZATION

A. K. Ramanujan used to tell the story of a Mongolian conqueror who had a certain species of nightingale brought to him from Kashmir because he had heard that this bird sang the most beautiful song in the world. But when the bird arrived, it did not sing. It was explained to the enraged conqueror that it sang only when perched on the branch of a chinar tree and that the chinar tree grows only on the hillsides of Kashmir. Raman concluded this story of what the conqueror needed to do to get his captured nightingale to sing with these words of St.-John Perse:

> We know the story of that Mongolian conqueror, taker of a bird in its nest, and of the nest in its tree, who brought back with the bird and nest and song the whole natal tree itself, torn from its place with its multitude of roots, its ball of earth and its border of soil, a remnant of home territory evoking a field, a province, a country, and an empire. . . .
>
> —St.-John Perse, *Birds*
> (cited in A. K. Ramanujan, *Poems of Love and War*)

A DISTINCT GEOGRAPHICAL AREA
The land on which the people of South Asia live is clearly set apart from the rest of Asia as a geographical area. Geologically speaking, it is a recent addition to the continent. It was originally attached to the east coast of Africa. About 100 million years ago, it broke away from that continent and drifted slowly on a separate geological plate east and north, until it collided, about 28 million years ago, into the southern edge of the continental landmass of Asia. The immense power of this impact scrunched up the south coast of Asia. It pushed the Tibetan Plateau more than 3 miles into the air and created a high ridge of snow-clad peaks that today mark the line of impact. This Himalayan mountain range is the highest in the world, and it is still rising (at a rate of about 10 inches per century) as a result of the massive collision that began so many millions of years ago.

The perimeters of the subcontinent are still clearly delineated by nature—on the north by the high, forbidding Himalayas, and on the south by the vast expanse of the Arabian Sea, the Bay of Bengal, and the Indian Ocean. The high mountain peaks and vast ocean waters clearly dominate the landscape. They also produce the annual monsoons, seasonal torrents of rain upon which the livelihood of the people of South Asia depends.

Within these natural borders is a wide range of geographical conditions, of topography and climate, that divide into four distinct regions. First, farthest to the north, are the frigid, arctic heights of the south face of the Himalayan Mountains. All of Afghanistan and Bhutan, most of Nepal, and small portions of India and Pakistan fall within this region.

These mountainous Himalayan lands fall precipitously and dramatically toward the south into a second region—the wide, alluvial river valleys that stretch across the north-central portion of the subcontinent. Three river systems—the Indus, Jumna–Ganges, and Brahmaputra—begin within 100 miles of one another in the Himalayas but flow in three different directions through the mountains and down into the expanse of the north-central plains. The Indus flows to the west through Pakistan to the Arabian Sea. The Jumna–Ganges Rivers flow to the south and then join to flow east across the great northern plain, to where they merge with the Brahmaputra River. This river flows to the east from its Himalayan source and then south into Bangladesh. Both river systems then flow together through many tributaries into the Bay of Bengal.

All three river systems provide the north-central plains region with a steady, if uneven, flow of melting snow. Because of this flow through the temperate northern plains, this region is the most widely irrigated and has the most productive agricultural lands of the subcontinent.

To the south of the northern plains region, entirely in India, are the highlands of the peninsula, which projects out into the Indian Ocean. The highlands rise to a wide plateau, called the Deccan, which is bordered to the east and west by smaller, but older, mountains than the Himalayas. The central portion of Sri Lanka also rises to highlands, which, together with the Deccan, form the third geographically distinct region of the subcontinent. Because these highlands are not high enough to be snow-covered, farmers in this region are entirely dependent upon the seasonal, monsoon rains for sufficient water to cultivate the land.

From these highlands the land slopes down into the fourth region, the coastal plains and tropical beaches of India, Pakistan, Bangladesh, Sri Lanka, and Maldives. Most of South Asia's largest cities, which developed as trading posts during the seventeenth century and are now great centers of commerce, fall within this coastal region.

These four distinct regions, which also include desert and rain forest, present as wide a range of topography and climate as exists anywhere in the world. Together, appended to the southern side of Asia, they form a varied and isolated geographical space.

MARITIME COMMERCE

The earliest evidence of a distinctive South Asian culture is found in the archaeological sites of the world's earliest-known urban civilization. This Harappan city culture flourished in the Indus River Valley, in the northwestern portion of the subcontinent, from 3000 to 1500 B.C. Excavations of these ancient Harappan sites have revealed that the early city dwellers produced enough surplus, primarily in cotton and grains, to carry on trade well beyond their own region. Their commercial activity extended into the developing civilizations in the Fertile Crescent, Africa, and Europe to the west, and Southeast Asia and China to the east.

This trading shows that, from earliest times, the ocean waters into which the subcontinent projects have been not so much a barrier as a vital concourse. Maritime commerce has continued to be a major activity along the shores of the subcontinent from the days of Harappan mercantile enterprise, through the era of silk trade, to the fiercely competitive activity of European trading companies in the seventeenth and eighteenth centuries, into the present day.

As a result of this crucial location on international trade routes, the peoples of South Asia have interacted with the major currents of human civilization since very ancient times. This interaction brought peacocks out of the subcontinent to embellish the throne of King Solomon in ancient Israel, the number zero to Europe during the Renaissance to change the way mathematical computations were done in the West, and Buddhism to East Asia and the rest of the world.

Because of the extent and intensity of this interaction, it is difficult to trace the origin of many of the concepts and practices that came the other way—that entered the subcontinent and now form a part of South Asian daily life. We do not know, for example, the origin of the Harappan city builders, whose layout of streets and water use reveal a clear understanding of urban planning. We have no earlier instances of city dwelling to learn how or where these skills were developed. The practice of spiritual discipline called *yoga* is also of unknown origin, as is the Dravidian culture of the south of India. Both are old enough to have developed within the Harappan city culture, and attempts have been made to establish demonstrable links between them. But they could have arisen out of totally separate interactions that have been lost and of which they are the only trace.

AN ANCIENT CIVILIZATION

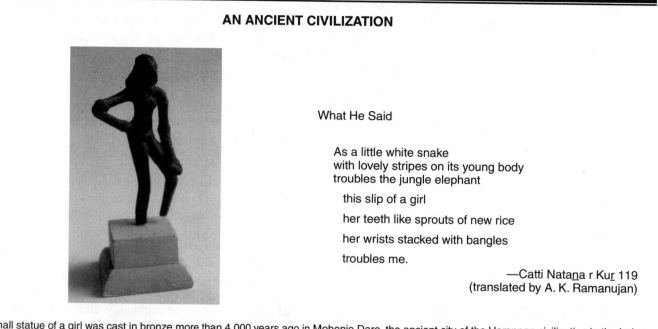

What He Said

As a little white snake
with lovely stripes on its young body
troubles the jungle elephant

   this slip of a girl

   her teeth like sprouts of new rice

   her wrists stacked with bangles

   troubles me.

—Catti Natana r Kur 119
(translated by A. K. Ramanujan)

This small statue of a girl was cast in bronze more than 4,000 years ago in Mohenjo Daro, the ancient city of the Harappan civilization in the Indus River Valley. Lost in the sands that buried that city so long ago, her image was captured 2,000 years later by a south Indian poet at the other end of the subcontinent, some 2,000 miles away, in this love poem found in the classical Tamil Sangam anthology called the *Kuruntokai*. Recovered in the twentieth century from the excavations of the ancient city and in the translations of the classical Sangam poetry, we, too, are tantalized by this tiny yet enduring image from South Asia.

Adding to the difficulty in understanding the impact of this interactivity on the peoples of South Asia is the persistence of so many different indigenous cultural threads that have continued to evolve into such a variety of patterns. So much has been added—yet nothing ever appears to be thrown away. Large slabs and rolling stones, called saddle-querns, were used more than 6,000 years ago by the earliest agrarians on the subcontinent to grind grain into flour. Even though that grinding is now done in mills, the implement is still in use in village kitchens to pulverize condiments to season food. Many old traditions, sometimes intertwined in a variety of ways with other traditions, or appearing in new garb, are still recognizable as significant elements in the heritage of this distinct region of the world. In the Western world of planned obsolescence, such tenacity is hard to imagine. Geeta Mehta, in *Snakes and Ladders,* describes this contrast in a slightly different way: Whereas Westerners have a great struggle to recover their past, the problem for Indians is to discover their present.

THE ARYAN MIGRATION

In contrast to the more elusive impact of maritime commerce, migrations of peoples from other parts of the world are a clear source of new life and perspective in South Asia. They have come, for the most part, overland, across the Central Asian trade routes between China and the Middle East, down into the northwestern approach to the north-central plains region of the subcontinent.

Of the many migrations over the centuries, the two of greatest impact were the Aryan settlement, beginning around

(United Nations/MB/jr)

Hinduism has evolved over the millennia in many different ways, and today it is intricately woven into the social fabric. Siva is one of the two main sects of Hinduism tracing their roots back to the ancient Harappan cities in the Indus River Valley. Pictured above is the gateway of a Siva temple in Tanjore, in the state of Tamil Nadu. The huge *gopuram,* or ornamental tower, is characteristic of south Indian temple architecture.

1500 B.C., and the Moghul invasion, which began in the sixteenth century A.D. The Aryans—tribal, martial, and pastoral in background—brought with them into the subcontinent an Indo–European language, which later evolved into Sanskrit, the classical language of ancient India, and the many contemporary languages that are spoken throughout the northern portion of the subcontinent and on Sri Lanka and Maldives. They also brought collections of religious songs, which formed the basis of a tenth century B.C. anthology of 1,028 poems called the *Rg Veda*, the oldest-surviving religious literature in the world. The *Veda* is still considered *sruti*—that is, inspired, literally, "heard by ancient seers"—the most sacred of all Hindu religious texts. And the Aryans either brought or soon developed a mythic understanding of the world as a sacred reality: that everything is part of a universal, cosmic sacrifice. This perspective blossomed during the time of their settlement in the subcontinent as Vedic culture.

During the era of the Aryan settlement, the Brahmin priests, who were responsible for developing, celebrating, and interpreting Vedic sacrifices as expressive of the total sanctity of all being, asserted a dominant role in restructuring Aryan society around their religious activity. One of the later Vedic hymns sets forward the earliest celebration of the *varna,* or classical, model of the caste system:

When they divided the Man [in the primordial sacrifice], into how many parts did they apportion him? What do they call his mouth, his two arms and thighs and feet?

His mouth became the Brahmin; his arms were made into the Warrior, his thighs the People, and from his feet the Servants were born.

—*Rg Veda* 10.90, 11–12
(translated by O'Flaherty)

This hierarchical structuring of society divided people into these four groups—which, significantly, placed the Brahmins, the priests, at the top. Next in order of preference on the scale were the *Kshatriya,* warriors or rulers by might; then the *Vaisya,* citizens, with landholding or commercial status; and the *Sudra,* laborers or craftspeople. Grouping of people on this scale was done primarily on the basis of an extended family's, community's, or tribe's inherited occupation. The ranking was based on a combination of the ritually purifying–polluting status in a sacrifice of a group's traditional occupation, as determined by the priesthood, and the ability of that social group to maintain social order. Maintaining social order was everyone's responsibility, but it held a specific and elevating prerogative for the priests because they had unique recourse to sacred power, which emanated from their performance of sacrificial rites. This scale clearly envisioned a Brahmin-dominated society.

Subsequent periods in South Asian history and literature do not show general acceptance of this dominant role for the priesthood. In the period between 500 B.C. to A.D. 200, the Sanskrit epics the *Mahabharata* and the *Ramayana,* and early Buddhist literature, give more prominence to the warrior, or princely community, to which the heroes of the epics and the Buddha belonged. Social and world order were not based on the rite of sacrifice, nor were they maintained by the Brahmin priests. It was based, rather, upon princes' strict adherence to their chivalrous obligations, called *dharma.* Rama, the hero of the *Ramayana,* is portrayed as a prince who is severely righteous in order to assure the peace and well-being of the people over whom he is called to govern. In that same tradition, Siddhartha Gautama, who was to become the Buddha—the "enlightened one"—taught to his religious community an eight-fold path of righteousness, which he called *Dhamma,* the "Way," to lead them to realize their Buddha nature and, ultimately, to attain *nirvana.*

The high point of Buddhist expansion came upon the conversion of the Mauryan emperor Asoka to the Buddha's Way in the third century B.C. Struck by the devastation caused by his military defeat of a neighboring kingdom, Asoka determined in the eighth year of his reign to conquer by morality rather than by might. His new policy to shun aggression and to seek "safety, self control, justice and happiness for all beings" gave a wide legitimacy across the span of his empire in the northern plains region of the subcontinent to the Buddhist *Dhamma,* upon which it was based. He also sent his son, Mahinda, to bring the teachings of the Buddha to Sri Lanka. Mahinda's arrival in 246 B.C. marked the beginning of the Theravada Buddhist tradition on that island.

Brahmin religious authority continued to spread and to be recognized through the northern plains and peninsular regions of South Asia. But its full cultural impact was not realized until the beginning of the Gupta imperial dynasty, in the fourth century A.D. Sanskrit, the sacred language of the priesthood, had by then become accepted as appropriate for the royal court and all of the intellectual and artistic endeavors that the court supported. But, also by that time, the influence of other religious communities, such as Jainism and Buddhism, and especially a great surge of popular religious lore, long practiced but unrecognized in courtly circles, infused courtly life with new perspectives and theistic fervor. The austere righteousness and the intricate, sacrificial purity of the earlier eras were augmented by a sense of divine playfulness, spun out in recitations of exemplary cosmic exploits of unnumbered gods and goddesses, heroes and heroines from a mythic past. The Gupta Era, from A.D. 300 to 650, was a time of great creative activity, drawing upon and affirming the Sanskritized models devised by the Brahmin priesthood. The poetic works of Kalidasa, the philosophical writings of Shankara, and the artistic creations found at Ajanta, Ellora, and Elephanta all portray the imaginative insight, excitement, and refinement achieved in that eclectic, yet highly disciplined and politically stable, era.

In the centuries following the Gupta era, the Brahmin community gained economic dominance in addition to their

(United Nations/WT/jr)

The greatest period of Muslim influence in South Asia began in the sixteenth century, when the Moghuls dominated the northern plains. The age was a period of grandeur and elegance; the Taj Mahal in Agra is one of the most famous monuments of this period.

intellectual and religious authority, which had been enhanced during that classical period. In reward for their courtly and religious services, they received land grants—even entire villages—as gifts from Hindu monarchs. Their increasing prominence in all these aspects of courtly life established a pattern for social change in those regions of the subcontinent where Hindus predominated. Today, to achieve higher status in the hierarchical caste structure, other communities must emulate the patterns of behavior practiced by high-caste Brahmins. This process is now called Sanskritization, which indicates how developed and pervasive have become the pastoral religious traditions of the ancient Aryan cow herders in the central portion of the subcontinent over the many centuries since the Vedic Age.

THE MOGHUL MIGRATION

The second migration to have a significant impact on the peoples of South Asia is more recent and reveals a different pattern of acceptance. This migration was of militant Turks from Persia, called the Moghuls, who were forced to move into South Asia by the Mongols' triumphant marches across Central Asia. Babur was the first, when he established a tenuous foothold by the capture of the city of Kabul, in what is now Afghanistan, in 1504. Competition for control of the north-central plains was fierce; and not until the reign of his

grandson, Akbar, which began in 1556, did Moghul rule begin to establish firm imperial control in that commanding region of the subcontinent. Akbar ruled for 49 years, during which time he imposed an extremely effective administrative network to maintain his authority over the realms he conquered. He also maintained a luxurious court, which supported an extensive creativity in art, music, architecture, and literature. Akbar's rule was a magnificent time, driven by his own desire to synthesize the best of the wealth of traditions—Persian, Indian, and even European—that he welcomed into his domain.

The fruits of Akbar's attempts to achieve cultural synthesis remain in the arts. The greatest is architectural: the Taj Mahal, the exquisitely beautiful mausoleum built in Agra by Akbar's grandson, Shah Jahan, in memory of his beloved wife, Mumtaz Mahal, who died in 1631. Miniature painting and Hindustani music continue to reveal the integration of art forms that were introduced under Akbar's imperial patronage. And remnants of his administrative structure, which was adopted by the British colonial government, continue.

Moghul domination in the political realm and its inherent patronage did not, however, lead to mass conversions to Islam. Nor did it lead to the synthesis of their religious faith within a common South Asian culture. It did not even achieve a lasting accommodation among the different religious communities in the subcontinent. During the centuries of their political control, religious leaders like Kabir entertained visions of religious unity. But distinct religious communities have retained their separate identities up to the present day.

The Moghuls, upon their arrival in the sixteenth century, were not the first Muslims to enter South Asia. Arab traders plying the coastal ports had introduced the new Islamic faith as early as the eighth century. They were followed by itinerant Sufi teachers, who settled in villages throughout the subcontinent. Their commitment to a religious life drew respect and veneration from a number of indigenous peoples who were receptive to spiritual insight and leadership. The more mystical quality of the faith of these masters converted large numbers to Islam, mostly in the northwest corner of the region, called the Punjab, and the northeast, known as Bengal—areas in which Buddhists had previously been the most numerous. Further conversions took place during the militant rule of the Sultans, who dominated portions of the Gangetic plain for three centuries prior to the arrival of the Moghuls. The mosque, the daily calls to prayer, Muslim festivals, and Islamic law became an authentic part of the social fabric of South Asian life. They were accepted, even though Muslims were a small religious minority in most regions of the subcontinent.

The imperial stature, administrative acumen, and grandeur of Moghul rule did give immense institutional status to Islam as a distinct religious faith and political legitimacy to a significant, already extensive Muslim community. Even today, Pakistan's aspiration to identify the nation as a modern Islamic republic builds upon this heritage of that Moghul imperial presence. But an immense issue remained during the time of the Moghul emperors: What was to be the status of the much larger Hindu population that resided in the central and southern portions of their empire?

Akbar's response was to try to synthesize his more refined, imperial Islamic faith within a common South Asian culture. His hope was that all his subjects might share in a single, universalist religion. But, because of the diversity that existed even within these faiths, he was not successful. Their separations were emphasized during the nineteenth century, under British colonial rule, and became the basis for the creation of Pakistan and, later, Bangladesh as independent countries, separate from India, with the departure of the British Raj in 1947. These differences have been at the heart of the outbreaks of war between Pakistan and India since their independence and are the source for communal riots throughout the subcontinent to this day. Muslims and Hindus remain two distinct, culturally diverse religious communities.

The Aryan and Moghul migrations reveal two very different experiences of incorporating foreign peoples into the social fabric of the subcontinent during the long course of South Asia's civilization. But they also identify a single pattern of cultural integration. The early Aryan culture, through continuing interaction and adaptation over a long period of time, came to dominate the social realm—not by political force but by intellectual and religious authority,

which set the norms that define the culture. One of those norms is to maintain the integrity of differing linguistic, religious, and ethnic groups who live in the subcontinent by isolating them as discrete cultural units within an abstract, hierarchical framework. The Moghul migration reveals that even extensive political domination, both military and administrative, is not sufficient to create or coerce cultural assimilation in a social environment that accepts cultural pluralism as normal. Both of these migrations contributed significantly to the development of South Asian civilization. They also demonstrate that diversity of language, religion, ethnic community, and social status is very deeply rooted in South Asia.

THE BRITISH RAJ

Another, more recent, interaction of significant impact was with the British Empire. It was not a migration; and, unlike the Moghul experience, it had little impact on the creative arts on the subcontinent. The British Raj was primarily political, imposing colonial rule over the subcontinent from the mid-nineteenth century until the 1940s. Its impact lay largely in the introduction of democracy, industrial development, and technology.

The origin of the British presence on the subcontinent goes back to the early seventeenth century, when the East India Company, with head offices in London, England, began to establish trading centers, first in Indonesia, and then along the Indian coast. In this activity, British entrepreneurs were following a pattern of maritime commerce in this region that goes back to the Harappan cities during the third millennium B.C., back to the earliest days of South Asian civilization.

This British commercial interest, which became dominant in South Asia during the eighteenth century, had no intention of establishing any political authority in the subcontinent. The British were there primarily for economic advantage, and they spent much of their time and effort trying to curry favor and exclusive licenses for trade from whatever local authorities would receive them. But their continuing involvement, especially as they struggled to diminish competing European interests in the region, did bring the peoples of the subcontinent increasingly under their political control.

In the early 1800s, increasing British colonial rule stimulated a concern to bring social reform to the subcontinent as well. The character of this reform movement was most strikingly expressed in the famous "Minute on Education," written by an East India Company Supreme Council member, Thomas Macaulay, in 1835. Macaulay urged that the British administrators create a special class of South Asian people who would be "Indian in blood and colour, but English in taste, in opinions, in morals, and in intellect." These people would bring the new ideas of individualism, technology, democracy, and nationalism, which were then evolving in Europe and America, to usher South Asia into the modern world.

This energizing—but ethnocentric—reform movement received a resounding jolt in British India in 1857, when an isolated British Indian Army unit rebelled because 85 soldiers were jailed for refusing to use ammunition greased with animal fat. Initially, it was a minor incident. But, among other things, it revealed a British insensitivity to Hindu religious attitudes toward the use of beef fat—because, for Hindus the cow is sacred—and Muslim religious attitudes toward pork— that it is polluting. The mutiny became the stimulus for a popular uprising throughout the north-central region of the subcontinent. People took it as an opportunity to express a shared and growing sense of dissatisfaction with British domination. It grew from a minor incident to become the "Great Mutiny" of 1857.

The spontaneity of this revolt contributed to its lack of organization and direction, and it was soon subdued by British military might. But its spontaneity revealed that, for all the enthusiasm and goodwill that the British rulers felt toward their South Asian subjects, their intentions—which appeared appropriate in their Western context—were not going to be readily accepted. The cultural context of South Asia was too substantial, too complex, and too different to be easily reformed.

The reform movement of the early nineteenth century gave way to a more blatant colonial domination of the subcontinent during the late nineteenth century. In 1858, the British Crown assumed direct control of British India. Queen Victoria became the first to bear the title "Empress of India."

The impact of the British Raj is still evident in the setting of the dividing lines that established the boundaries between the nations in the northern part of the subcontinent. It established the northern borders of Bhutan and Nepal with Tibet by a line drawn along the peaks of the Himalayan Mountains—the McMahon Line. The other borders of these two countries were established earlier, before British rule, by Gurkha and Tibetan conquests, but they were secured as national boundaries by the British Raj. In affirming these boundaries, the Raj used existing natural and political realities to assert its own political authority within them.

By contrast, the setting of the borders of Afghanistan do not appear to have recognized any indigenous factors. They were determined by treaty between Czarist Russia and Great Britain in 1907 with other concerns in mind: The British objective, in response to competing colonial interests, was to create a buffer to contain any Russian aspirations to gain access to the Arabian Sea.

The border determination of greatest impact was the decision by the Raj in 1947 to grant independence not only to a large portion of British India as a new republic but also to establish a separate Islamic country, called Pakistan ("Land of the Pure"). At that time, those administrative districts under direct British control that had a majority Muslim population were assigned to Pakistan, and those with a Hindu majority to India. The accession of the princely states that were not under direct British control—about 40 percent of the subcontinent—into either India or Pakistan, was to be based on the preference of the ruling *maharajas.*

There were two major exceptions to this process of accession. The princely state of Hyderabad, in the Deccan, which had a Muslim leader and a Hindu majority population, was absorbed into India when Indian troops rushed into the state to quell riots that came in the wake of the partition of India and Pakistan in 1947. The princely state of Kashmir, on the other hand, with a majority Muslim population and a Hindu *maharaja,* was nominally acceded to India by the maharaja when Pakistani forces began to enter Kashmir at that time. The result of this process of border determination was a Pakistan divided into two sections, East and West, on the shoulders of the subcontinent, separated by 1,000 miles of India; and a Kashmir still divided between the unresolved claims of both India and Pakistan and a United Nations (UN) resolution to encourage the people of Kashmir to have a choice.

Even with the setback experienced in the Great Mutiny of 1857, Western political ideas of democracy, social reform, and freedom of expression continued to pervade the subcontinent. The Indian National Congress was formed in 1887 to seek opportunities for South Asians to shape and to participate in a growing body politic. In 1919, Mohandas Gandhi emerged as the leader of this movement. Through the power of his example and his great organizational skills, he was able to build grassroots support for the Congress throughout British India. Enlivened by a spirit of democracy and of political freedom, this movement first paralleled and then superseded British colonial rule.

The British imperial presence also brought to this part of the world the concept of a modern nation. An independent, democratically elected government was the goal—certainly for those who were under foreign colonial domination; but also for those who had been under the traditional, autocratic rule of hereditary *maharajas,* tribal leaders, and vestigial imperial domains. With the attainment of independence, South Asian peoples awakened from a long era of unrepresentative leadership. Forceful ideas were beginning to take on relevance: of liberty achieved through democracy, prosperity through economic growth, and individual human rights sustained by law. These have become the standards by which the success of a nation's quest for modernization are being measured. Such is the case because the British colonial government set these standards as its expectation of the countries to which it granted independence in the middle of the twentieth century—to India and Pakistan in 1947 and Sri Lanka in 1948. The other, smaller nations—Afghanistan, Bhutan, Maldives, Nepal—which trace the origin of their governments to more autocratic traditions of long standing in the subcontinent, are challenged to hold these same standards to their performance for recognition as modern states. They are all seeking new opportunities for expression, for economic growth, and for taking control of their destiny as politically free peoples among the nations of the world.

The British colonial interaction with the subcontinent is now over. Yet, it continues, like the Aryan and Moghul experiences, to have a discernible, if distinctly different, impact in the region. Significant changes are occurring in the political and economic life there because of the British Raj, just as the artistic and Islamic influences of the Moghul era are also evident in contemporary South Asia. And the religious and intellectual heritage shaped by the evolution of Aryan culture continues to be profoundly present.

All of these threads, each discernible in its own distinctive character, yet interwoven among themselves, have also interacted with the many influences brought by centuries of maritime commerce. All have made a significant, lasting contribution to the long, rich, and varied civilization that is the heritage of the peoples who belong to South Asia.

IMAGE 2: A DIVERSE SOCIAL ENVIRONMENT

It is the endurance of this civilization, despite its encounter with a host of other cultures and other political influences, that has led many observers to conclude that the Hindu style is absorptive, synthesizing, or tolerant. What they see is something quite different, namely, Indian civilization's ability to encapsulate other cultures and make it possible for many levels of civilization to live side by side. But encapsulation is neither toleration, absorption, nor synthesis.

—Ainslie T. Embree

The sheer multitude of the 1.3 billion people who live in South Asia is impressive. They already represent more than a fifth of the total population of the world—and they are growing in numbers at an alarming pace. According to projections prepared by the World Bank, at the current rate of growth, the population of the subcontinent will exceed 1.8 billion by the year 2025. Each of the countries of the subcontinent has developed policies to try to limit this rate, with varying degrees of success. The most effective effort has been in Sri Lanka, where analysts relate this achievement to the high level of literacy that the country has attained. Education, especially of women, appears to them to be the key.

South Asia is not only crowded, but it is also a land of immense human contrasts. There are many different social groups from different parts of the subcontinent, each displaying a distinctive variety of belief and custom, language and culture. Sikhs and Buddhists and Jains; fishermen and pit weavers along the tropical shores of the coastlands; elegant, urban aristocrats and naked, religious mendicants; archaic tribal peoples and computer engineers; beggars, film stars, and Kathakali dancers; and many more—all are woven into the multistranded fabric of South Asian life. It is a rich panoply of colors, activities, and conditions of humanity. This array is always impressive, in almost every context.

The distinctiveness of most of these social groups, especially the caste communities called *jatis,* must be delineated by very small strokes to retain their diversity. To the unfamiliar

eye, many may look the same. Their distinguishing characteristics can be more readily identified in broader sweeps that identify people in regional, religious, and linguistic categories. Each group retains discernible characteristics of the part of the subcontinent in which its members live, of the religious faith to which they belong, and the language that they speak.

Regional differences are the most obvious. Those belonging to a common religious faith tend to concentrate in specific regions of the subcontinent. The same is true of those speaking the same language. But there are so many more languages than religions, and people of the language groups do not always share the same religion.

Differences of region, religion, and language are also important because they are the most general groupings into which the peoples of South Asia have long been separated into social enclaves. To belong to a religious community in a separate language area in a particular region of the subcontinent clearly sets one apart from others and establishes one's distinctive sense of identity as a person. As traditional sources of identity, firmly rooted in their heritage, they remain persistent and vital descriptors of who the people of South Asia are.

MANY RELIGIONS

South Asia is home to several of the world's religions, some of which originated there. Hinduism and Islam—one indigenous, the other imported—are by far the largest, followed, respectively, by approximately two thirds and one fifth of the people of the region. Hinduism is the dominant religion in Nepal (90 percent of the population) and India (80 percent). Islam is dominant in Maldives (100 percent), Pakistan (97 percent), Afghanistan (99 percent), and Bangladesh (83 percent). Buddhism, although not so large—constituting 1.8 percent of the total population—is nonetheless the predominant religion in Sri Lanka and Bhutan.

Jains are another, even smaller, religious community that originated in the subcontinent. Jains, like Buddhists, trace their faith to a religious leader who lived in northern India in the sixth century B.C. There are the Sikhs, whose religion was founded by Guru Nanak during the sixteenth century, A.D. in the northwestern part of South Asia known as the Punjab. Other religious communities include Christians, Jews, and the Parsis, whose Zoroastrian faith had its origin in ancient Persia at the time of the Vedas, more than 3,500 years ago.

All of these faiths evolved in the South Asian context as distinct, structurally integrated expressions of different communities' religious experiences. Although aware of and interacting with peoples of other religious faiths, they have retained an essential sacred identity in their lives as a distinct community. Even when influencing one another, these many religious communities in South Asia continually reaffirm the structural integrity of their own faith as separate from the faiths of others. This accounts for the acceptance of the Sufi religious authority among those who became Muslims during the early years of Islamic influence in the subcontinent. Where Sufi teaching and practice were consistent with the

In South Asia, individuals often identify with societies and religions rather than with a specific country. Modern national boundaries imposed over historically diverse language and religious populations result in weak political identification. This pluralism complicates the establishment of a workable political base as minorities strive to find a legitimate place and voice in their national life. This religious allegiance is exemplified by this Sikh teacher addressing some of his followers at the Golden Temple in Amritsar, India. What he tells people is likely to be more relevant to social and political change than what any politician may say.

religious values and experience of the indigenous communities they were readily co-opted. The Islamic faith of the Sultans and the Moghuls who followed the Sufis into South Asia was recognized, but not so readily followed.

This persistence of the structural integrity of many different religious communities' sacred identity also accounts for the immense variety of Hinduism. *Hinduism* is really a composite term to describe a multitude of quite diverse religious groups. They do share some common teachings and perspectives. They all, for example, affirm the transmigration of the soul after death to some other form of life. This belief they share with Buddhists and Jains, which is why many Hindus consider Buddhists and Jains to be within the inclusive umbrella of Hinduism. But these many different communities practice their separate religious traditions in an immense variety of forms, each the result of an evolution of a distinct path over many centuries.

The earliest record of the Hindu religious tradition is the *Rg Veda,* 1,028 poems that were collected into their current form around the tenth century B.C. The poems themselves were composed earlier, and they presuppose an even earlier history of religious belief and practice. Traditionally the sacred pre-

serve of the Brahmin priesthood, the *Veda* is not widely known or understood among Hindus today. And the Vedic sacrifices around which the collection of sacred poems was initially created and remembered—and upon which the religious authority of the Brahmin priesthood was initially established—are rarely performed. More characteristic of Hindu life today are the rituals, traditions, and festivals celebrated at the innumerable temples and shrines that dot the countryside, daily worship called *puja,* and the sanctity of an epic fragment called *Bhagavad Gita* ("The Song of the Lord"). All of these have been added to the religious traditions of the Hindus since Vedic times (1500–500 B.C.).

These accretions to Vedic religion reveal that Hinduism has evolved over the centuries. Yet, as we have seen, it has evolved not as a single religious tradition but in many different ways, incorporating and encompassing many diverse strands to become the intricate interweaving of schools and sects and disciplines that are encompassed by that religion today. Among these sects are the Vaishnavites, who worship God as first revealed in the *Rg Veda* as Vishnu but recognize His manifestation in a number of *avatars* (incarnations), which include Krishna, the Buddha, and Kalki (the "One who is to come"). Shaivites belong to a separate sect that traces the origin of its faith even further back, to representations of Shiva as Pasupati (the "Lord of animals"), found in the remains of the Harappan civilization, and as *Nataraj* (the "Lord of the Cosmic Dance").

In addition, Hinduism includes worshippers of Krishna and Rama and of the Goddess in a variety of manifestations: as Kali, Durga, or Devi.

There are also innumerable regional and local deities around whom traditions of religious festivals and beliefs are celebrated. And there is *yoga,* which does not affirm the existence of any deity. Any description of Hinduism must attempt to contain all this array of different forms and practices, each with its own history, tradition, and authority, for a vast number of religious groups who consider themselves Hindu.

Buddhism also originated in South Asia and has evolved as a separate religion since the sixth century B.C. Siddhartha Gautama, the founder of the faith, was born a prince in a remote north Indian kingdom not under the sway of a Brahmin priesthood. He renounced his royal inheritance to seek an ultimate meaning for his life. After many years of diligent search, he received the enlightenment of the "Four-fold Truth," upon which this religion developed and eventually expanded throughout the subcontinent.

Buddhism was originally the faith of a monastic community called the *sangha*. It was composed of those who, attracted by the Buddha's example and teaching, abandoned their worldly activities to commit themselves to following his path, or *Dhamma*, in communal, and meditative, isolation. The conversion of the Mauryan emperor Asoka to the Buddha's teaching in the third century B.C. brought about a significant change in the Buddhist tradition. His political authority gave greater currency to the Buddha's *Dhamma* throughout the society. He also endowed the community with royal patronage, which encouraged not only its growth but also spawned a creative outburst of Buddhist art, literature, and philosophy. Tributes to this heritage have survived in the exuberant carvings and frescoes in the caves at Ajanta and in the majestic tranquillity of the exquisitely beautiful sculpture of the Buddha teaching at Sarnath. It was this highly expressive and energetic Buddhism that, during the centuries following Asoka, burst forth into the far reaches of Asia—to Sri Lanka, China, Japan, Mongolia, and Tibet.

As in the case of Islam under Moghul rule, Buddhism, even though indigenous, remained among a dominant Hindu soci-

(United Nations/JL, 80478)

Because of changing circumstances, the Hindu majority of India are continually adjusting themselves to maintain the allegiance and participation of their members. These children are saying their Hindu prayers before the midday meal at their school.

ety an encapsulated religious community, albeit one under imperial patronage for several centuries after Asoka. It even introduced vegetarianism as a social virtue to be observed by Brahmins among the Hindus. Unlike Hinduism, it declined dramatically in the north-central region of the subcontinent, following upon the inspiration of Sufi teachers and under the military attacks and religious zeal of Islamic potentates from Central Asia during the eleventh century A.D. It survives today in enclaves along the borders of South Asia: in Ladakh, the section of Kashmir closest to China; in Bhutan, also along the Himalayan border, next to Tibet; and in Sri Lanka, off the southeastern coast of peninsular India. It has recently been revived in India as a separate religious faith by the Mahar community in Maharastra, under the leadership of Dr. Ambedkar, who converted to Buddhism in 1956 in protest against the Hindu attitude of abhorrence and discrimination toward communities designated by Hindus as "untouchable."

Today, Islam is another significant religious community in South Asia; it was sustained through past generations under the political dominance of Moghul Islamic leadership. The predominance of their numbers on the western and eastern ends of the north-central plains region led to the creation of the separate—western and eastern—arms of the original nation of Pakistan in 1947. Although several million Muslims migrated from India to Pakistan at the time of independence in 1947, more than 112 million still reside in India today, forming a significant religious minority (14 percent). The population of all Muslims in the Indian subcontinent—more than 345 million—is the second-largest Muslim population in the world, second only to Southeast Asia.

The persistence of the various strands of traditions that develop independently, interacting with but not being assimilated into other strands, is also revealed in the evolution of Christianity in South Asia. According to legend, it was first introduced in the subcontinent by the Apostle Thomas during the first century. It was certainly known to silk traders from Egypt passing through northwest Pakistan to China during the second century. Evidence of Syrian Christians having migrated and living along the southwest coast of the subcontinent dates from the fourth century. This religious community continued for a long time, but it did not increase significantly until the arrival of Western colonial powers.

The Portuguese first brought Roman Catholicism to the western coast of India during the 1400s. And, under the restraining eye of the English East India Company, Protestant missions began to work in the subcontinent in the early 1800s. Still today, Christians comprise less than 3 percent of the total population of South Asia. They have become significant as a group in the political life of the subcontinent only in the state of Kerala, in southwest India, where they form nearly one third of the population of that state.

The many different religious minority communities have tended to concentrate in specific regions, where they have become significant political forces. But they are evident and generally accepted everywhere throughout the subcontinent. All of these different religious traditions are distributed across the subcontinent like colors in a patchwork quilt.

MANY LANGUAGES

English visitors to the growing commercial city of Calcutta during the late 1700s would immediately be struck by the immense diversity of languages that they would encounter there. The language of the Calcutta marketplace was Portuguese, a vestige of Portugal's early domination of East Indian trade. The language of government was Persian, also a vestige, in this case of the Moghul imperial past. By contrast, the languages of the courts were Sanskrit and Arabic (depending upon which tradition of law those who were pursuing legal redress belonged). Though each had a specific context in which it was considered appropriate, none of these languages belonged to that area; none was the common tongue, or vernacular, of the people who lived in Calcutta.

Had the visitors wandered into the streets or into homes, they would have discovered another variety of languages. Different tongues spoken by the common people reflected the different places of origin of those from various parts of the Indian subcontinent who moved to Calcutta to take part in the growing activity and prosperity there. Because most of these people came from the immediately surrounding area, the most prevalent vernacular was Bengali.

Today, the English language has replaced the many foreign languages used in the more formal aspects of contemporary urban life, and Bengali remains the most prevalent language of the people. But there is still a wide diversity of indigenous languages spoken in the streets and homes of the city.

The many different vernaculars spoken throughout the subcontinent today belong to four distinct families of languages. These are broadly distributed across specific regions of South Asia. The major dialects in the northernmost, Himalayan region are Tibeto–Burmese, related to the languages across the northern and eastern borders of the subcontinent. Their presence reveals more extensive cultural interaction of those living in the remote valleys through the rugged and forbidding mountains and jungles of that region than with the more settled plains areas to the south.

The prevalent languages of the northern plains region, Sri Lanka, and Maldives belong to the Indo–European family of languages, distant cousins of Latin, Greek, and the Germanic tongues of the West. They were introduced in their earliest form by Aryans—the migrating cattle herders from Central Asia who wandered into the subcontinent more than 3,500 years ago. A second, totally separate family of languages is spoken among the tribal peoples who still inhabit the remote hill regions of peninsular India. These are generally called Munda languages. They are related to those spoken by the Aboriginal peoples of Australia to the southeast. These two families of languages exhibit far-reaching interconnections that existed thousands of years ago among peoples who are now widely separated.

There is yet another family of languages of independent structure and origin, called Dravidian. Its roots can be traced only to the South Asian subcontinent itself. Today, the Dravidian languages are spoken mostly in the south of India and the northern part of Sri Lanka, but they are not confined to the subcontinent. They have been carried to East Africa, Singapore, the Fiji Islands, and the West Indies by immigrants who continue to affirm their South Asian heritage in these many parts of the world.

Each of the numerous languages that belong to these four language families has a specific area in the subcontinent in which it is spoken by the vast majority of the people. It is easy to see where these languages predominate in India and Pakistan, because state borders within these countries have been drawn to enclose specific dominant-language groups. Afghanistan and Sri Lanka are also clearly divided into language-area sections.

The integrity of these languages is retained even beyond the region where they are predominant. They extend as minority linguistic pockets in other language areas. Thus, a variety of languages may be found anywhere, especially in cities, where migrants from many parts of the country tend to gather in sections of the city with others who share their native language.

That so many different dialects, languages, and language families are still spoken in the subcontinent is a primary example of *encapsulation* as a way of describing the social dynamic of the people of South Asia. All of these languages have evolved over time. Some have developed literary and classical forms of expression. But all are most widely familiar as colloquial dialects, which, like accents, reflect common usage among specific groups of people in particular places. Colloquial dialects would seem to be the form of language most subject to assimilation with other languages that are spoken around it. Because of the diverse social context in which they are spoken, these languages do interact and influence one another. But this interaction has not led to their becoming assimilated into a common tongue. Each continues distinct in its integrity as a separate language.

The language that one first learns in childhood, of whichever of the families of languages to which it belongs, is called one's "mother tongue." This way of describing one's native language reveals that, for the people of South Asia, one is born into a language community that is intrinsic to one's identity as a person, even when residing in countries far away from the subcontinent. The same is true for one's caste community and religion. One is born into them, and they remain inherently descriptive of who one is.

A map that delineates the predominant language areas throughout the entire subcontinent, like a map of the religious communities described earlier, looks like an intricate patchwork quilt. The pattern of the language quilt, however, is not the same as for religions. Generally speaking, people belonging to different religions in the same place speak the same language—but those belonging to the same religion speak many different languages. Only in the smaller countries of the subcontinent—Bhutan, Maldives, and Sri Lanka—do religious identities and language identities tend to correspond with each other. And only in Maldives, the smallest of the countries of the subcontinent, do these categories coincide with the national boundaries by which the subcontinent is also divided; only there does being a citizen of the country generally mean that one speaks the same language and worships in a common faith.

RELIGIOUS NATIONALISM
Differences in religious and language identities play an important role in South Asian life. Because of their persistence as distinct social groups, they are a continuing basis for conflict due to the density of the population and the high level of competition among the groups for limited resources. Social unrest, communal disputes, and outright rioting occur frequently in India and South Asia. Even when disputes originate between individuals, they rapidly become characterized by the religious or linguistic identity of the participants.

The Sikh nationalist movement in the Punjab during the 1980s, even though it was pursued by an unrepresentative splinter group led by the headmaster of a rural Sikh school—a young religious zealot named Bhindranwale—was a war that engaged large segments of the Sikh community. Newspapers reported almost daily on what appeared to be random, indiscriminate strafing of buses along the highways and shootings into wedding parties by snipers on passing motor scooters. These acts of violence were sanctioned by the Damdami Taksal militants and the All India Sikh Students Federation because they had Hindus—as well as Sikhs unsympathetic to their cause—as their targets. Bhindranwale's death in 1984 at the hand of Indian Army troops in the Golden Temple, the sacred center of Sikhism in Amritsar, led to the assassination of Indira Gandhi, then prime minister of India, by Sikh members of her bodyguard. Her death was followed by massive riots in the streets of Delhi, India's capital, and the murder of many Sikhs throughout the country. It was a "holy war."

In neighboring Kashmir, the quest for independence is also expressed in religious terms. It is a battle for the freedom of a predominantly Muslim population from what is experienced as an oppressive Hindu India. Heavily armed bands of militants ambush, burn, and kidnap throughout the mountain valleys and in the once placid Vale, all in the name of their religion. Thousands of Hindu families have fled their homes in fear of this violence.

The issue of whether India is, in fact, a Hindu or a secular nation was put to the test in 1992 in the northern city of Ayodhya. An old mosque, built there at the time of the first Moghul emperor, Babur, in the sixteenth century A.D., was identified by a Hindu nationalist political party as the site of an earlier Hindu temple claimed to be the birthplace of Lord Rama. Destruction of the Babri Masjid mosque by a band of Hindu pilgrims on December 6, 1992, led to widespread communal rioting across India and retaliatory destruction of Hindu temples in Pakistan, Bangladesh, and even Great Britain.

This event made evident that the religious identity of the peoples of South Asia is a decisive, immediate, and intense component in the political life of the subcontinent. India especially is a land of many religious strands in which the quest for a unifying political identity is severely challenged. (The results of state and national elections since the 1992 destruction of the mosque reveal that Hindu nationalist sentiment is a formidable force, but does not command a majority.) The ideal of a secular national identity, inclusive of all of a country's religious minorities, is still a viable objective. By contrast, Bhutan and Pakistan are deliberately seeking to affirm modern religious national identities—Bhutan as a Buddhist nation and Pakistan as an Islamic one.

Sri Lanka represents a different configuration; there, linguistic identity reinforces the separation between the regions of the country where different religions are predominant. Most Sri Lankans are Buddhists who speak the Sinhalese language. In the northeast region of the country, however most of the people are Hindu, with significant Muslim enclaves, and are Tamil-speakers. The regional basis of this separation has allowed these communities to coexist for centuries, but the quest to achieve a single national identity since the independence of the country in 1948 has resulted in intense warfare between nationalist groups. Because of the importance of their language differences, these militant groups see the conflict more as cultural—as tigers against lions—than as religious.

LINGUISTIC NATIONALISM

Language plays a much more important role than religion in the distinction in Pakistan between the *muhajirs*—those whose families migrated from India at the time of Pakistan's independence in 1947—and the indigenous peoples of the country. The *muhajirs* retain and cultivate the use of Urdu, the language they brought with them. They are also primarily an urban community, living mostly in the city of Karachi. To maintain their distinct identity in the independent Republic of Pakistan, about 20 million *muhajirs* formed a political party, the Mohajir Quami Movement (MQM), to represent their interests as a group in the affairs of state. Members in this party have been subjected to severe political harassment in Karachi, a city that recorded 1,800 people killed on its streets in 1995. The imposition of federal rule and the creation of military courts in the city in November 1998 is understood by the MQM as an effort to destroy the movement as a political force. The leader of the party now resides in self-imposed exile in London.

Afghanistan, which, like Pakistan, is predominantly Islamic, also has many different language groups separated in different regions of the country. The distinct ethnic identity of these language groups has played a significant role in the inability of the many resistance leaders who joined to fight the Soviet invasion of their country in 1979 to unite to form a

(United Nations/A. Hollmann)

Educating children is something that cannot be delayed if a cohesive social structure and heritage are to be saved. These refugee children are striving for an education in a makeshift school in a land that is not their own.

government since the Soviet withdrawal in 1989. A further distinction between urban and rural Afghanistan was at the base of the rift between the two wings of the People's Democratic (Communist) Party that existed from the party's formation in the early 1960s. In 1979, when the government led by the Communists ruled the city of Kabul, if not the country, this rift gave occasion for the Soviet forces to invade to reestablish order in the country.

The distinction between the more cosmopolitan environment of Kabul and the conservative countryside is also evident in the impact of the reforming zeal of the Taliban movement, which has recently emerged out of the provincial city of Kandahar and has enveloped most of the country. The further devastation brought upon the city of Kabul by this movement is indicative of the disdain in which the Taliban holds those urbanites who do not share their reactionary religious agenda.

AN ENCAPSULATED SOCIETY

There are many significant bases of social distinction in the subcontinent: regional, religious, linguistic, and urban–rural. The distinction between urban and rural is important because the subcontinent has a much greater rural population than urban. The average urban population is only about 24 percent, as compared with 74 percent in the United States. India has the fourth-largest urban population in the world, but urban dwellers still constitute less than a quarter of the total population of the country. Thus, rural ways and the rural voice still have a significant role in the priorities and direction of South Asian life.

There is also a vast disparity between the wealthiest and the poorest of the poor. Recognition of this distinction has led to the development of the Grameen Bank in Bangladesh, an institution that has created effective methods for providing for capitalization of assets among the poor. Women's cooperatives have been set up throughout the subcontinent on the same model as the tremendously successful Grameen Bank.

All of these bases of social distinction reflect the immense diversity and variety in the social fabric of South Asia. And the violence that often results from their interaction reveals the depth and the extent of these differences in establishing the uniqueness and the identity of the many social groups who are defined by them. Each, affirmed in the integrity of its own identity, has coexisted, sometimes in harmony, sometimes at odds, with other distinct groups for many centuries. Social pressures toward conformity within each group are immense. But these groups are not expected to assimilate or fit in with the distinguishing characteristics of other groups. This process functions among the smallest of social groupings, even on the level of the jati caste communities. Extended kinship groups, tribes, migrant peoples, and even highly mobile social classes are accepted as they are simply by placing them as a distinct community within a stratified social hierarchy. Every community, no matter how different its values and character, has a place. They thus remain a distinct yet integral part of the fabric of South Asian society.

This second image of South Asia is one of many people living very close together yet displaying an immense variety of cultural attributes. All of these socially distinct groups are encapsulated in enclaves, which has allowed them to exist in the integrity of their own traditional identities among a large number of culturally different peoples. Even though there have been periods of great confrontation, discrimination, and violence, there is also the acceptance that such wide diversity among so many different peoples is both inevitable and normal. Like the four-fold layering of humanity set forth in the Vedic hymn celebrating the creation sacrifice of primordial man, it is a cosmic reality.

IMAGE 3: THE GREAT TRADITION

THE WORLD AS SYMBOL

The first function [of a symbol] is the representative function. The symbol represents something which is not itself for which it stands and in the power and meaning of which it participates. . . . And now we come to something which is perhaps the main function of the symbol—namely, the opening up of levels of reality which otherwise are hidden and cannot be grasped in any other way.

Every symbol opens up a level of reality for which non-symbolic speaking is inadequate. The more we try to enter into the meaning of symbols, the more we become aware that it is the function of art to open up levels of reality; in poetry, in visual art, and in music, levels of reality are opened up which can be opened up in no other way.

But in order to do this, something else must be opened up—namely, levels of the soul, levels of our interior reality. And they must correspond to the levels in exterior reality which are opened up by a symbol. So every symbol is two-edged. It opens up reality and it opens up the soul. There are, of course, those people who are not opened up by music or who are not opened up by poetry, or more of them who are not opened up at all by visual arts. The "opening up" is a two sided function—namely reality in deeper levels and the human soul in special levels.

—Paul Tillich, *Theology of Culture*

During the long evolution of civilization in South Asia, creative patterns of thinking about the world gradually formed out of the earliest stages of Vedic musings during the second millennium B.C. into a classical tradition. From very early times, Vedic priests looked at the world as a cosmic sacrifice, as an experience of sacred celebration, rather than as a natural reality. Their intellectual pursuits to describe the world as sacrifice created opportunities to see and understand what is beyond the empirical world of objects. They sought to identify a deeper level of reality that gives the things of this world the quality of being sacred. They expressed this level of reality in things as symbols, as what they represent, rather than just the fact of their being. They saw the world as an arena for the refinement of human experience, to realize not just what is but also what is beyond, to deeper levels of their experience.

We understand the world around us in many different ways. Some things, like our hereditary traits, we experience as natural. Others, like our languages and patterns of behavior, we experience as cultural. Because of the great diversity of cultures in the world, those things that we experience culturally are understood in very different ways, depending on the cultural context in which things are experienced. One way to distinguish some of these differences in understanding is to describe them as experienced in different dimensions. For example, an object or experience can be perceived in the natural dimension. That perception tells us what it is, what we call the facts of its physical existence.

The pervasive authority of scientific thinking in Western culture encourages the perception of things primarily as experienced in the natural dimension. Things are acknowledged to be as they are observed, and our understanding of the world is built around relationships revealed and confirmed by such perceptual data. These relationships are called *models*, whether they be of things observed directly, like gravity, or of abstract patterns, like atomic structure or galaxies. All of these descriptions are based on, and authenticated by, what we perceive as the natural world.

(UN Photo 153,017/Oddbjorn Monsen)

These young women of Pushkar, India, are part of the vast cultural mosaic of peoples in South Asia.

Human experience can also be understood in historical dimension. Perceiving an object or experience in this dimension reveals something more than the facts of its existence. It represents by pointing to a special meaning, or interpretation for a significant group of people. For example, a flag can be seen naturally, as a piece of colored cloth. If the pattern of the colors does not represent something to us, it remains a natural object. But if we recognize the pattern of the flag as belonging to a specific group of people, like a tribe or a country, it becomes more than a thing. It stands for something. In understanding what it stands for, we look at it from the historical dimension to see what defines the people for whom it is their flag.

What defines a people historically is events, things that actually happen but that also have a special, even exclusive significance to them as a distinct group. In this dimension, people are defined by their understanding of what happens to them, not by what they are as natural beings. Such events in American experience include the landing of Pilgrims at Plymouth; the Battle of Yorktown, which ended the Revolutionary War and brought freedom from British control to the American colonies; and the assassination of President John F. Kennedy. They also include something as far away as the escape of a group of slaves from ancient Egypt, known as the Exodus experience. They are events because they affirm as real something more than just that they happened. They identify by their significance as having happened to us who we are as a people.

People identify the significance of what happens to them in innumerable ways to express their impact, their identity-defining meaning, and their authority. Thus, by expressing allegiance to their flag, in celebrating Thanksgiving, or the Fourth of July, in parades, and in elections, Americans experience the world in the historical dimension, as giving shared meaning and direction to their lives as a people who have an identity and a destiny. All of these things that Americans recognize or do to affirm this historical reality point beyond what they are as things to this level of experience. In this power to point beyond, to represent something else, they are more than facts; they are symbols.

A language is itself a symbol system. Particular sounds articulated in a distinct way represent a specific meaning to those who share in understanding that language. Its symbolic character is especially expressive in revealing levels of experience beyond the physical world. Words, sentences, stories, even myths not only express, they create the significance of what has happened to make real for us the historical dimension of our experience. They allow us to enter into things that happen as events—even as they happen and long after they have happened. Through language, we become part of, celebrate whole new worlds.

The development of the "Great Tradition" in South Asia pursued yet another dimension of human experience. People looked at their world not only as it is experienced naturally, nor also as it is revealed in symbols, historically. In their concern to identify their experience as sacrifice, as having sacred significance, they entered into a religious dimension of human experience. They sought to discover the world itself as symbol.

This religious dimension shares with the historical dimension in that it is expressed in symbols, in what things *represent* rather than what they are. It is different from the historical, in that its symbols point to and identify levels of reality that transcend the natural and cultural worlds in which we live. When religious rituals and narratives express for a people what is ultimately real and absolutely true for them, then they function as symbols of transcendence. If they are reduced to a natural description of what they are, such as dance patterns or interesting stories, they simply cease to be religious symbols.

The pursuit of the religious dimension of human experience appears first in an anthology of religious poems called the *Rg Veda,* collected some 3,000 years ago during the period of the settlement of the Aryan people in the subcontinent. The men of wisdom during those early times—the Brahmin priesthood—understood their experience of living in the world as participating in an act of cosmic sacrifice. They took upon themselves the exclusive task of developing and giving authenticity to this perception of the world, not only by asserting their social priority, as in the Vedic passage that described them as the mouth of primordial man. They also created an elaborate system of rituals that, as religious acts, as symbols, reenacted, expressed, and celebrated this transcending reality of the created world as a sacrificial event.

This commitment of the scholar–priests to affirm their experience as religiously symbolic led during the classical period of South Asia's history, from the fifth century B.C. to the tenth century A.D. to a number of impressive analyses of various aspects of human experience. These analyses, though based on careful observation, were not so much descriptions of the natural world around them as they were reflections on what this world might be as expressive of a different level or order of being. A remarkable treatise on social structure, the *Laws of Manu,* set forward rules of appropriate behavior for a society as though it were divided and ranked into the four *varna* or classical castes, groups set forward in the *Rg Veda*: Brahmin (priests), Kshatriya (rulers), Vaisya (citizens), and Sudra (laborers). It also divided one's life into four stages, called *ashramas*, which were each to take one quarter of an entire lifetime: that of being a student, a householder, a mendicant, and an ascetic. The *Laws,* rather than assuming that a single behavioral norm can apply to all of life, prescribed a distinct set of rules appropriate for each stage. A clear structure was thus imposed upon people's lives that placed upon them specific expectations of how they ought to act in a wide variety of conditions of class and of age. It was a comprehensive and authoritative model for social behavior, not because it described what actually happens but because it expressed a vision of cosmic social order. It was something to live up to.

Other works of similar magnitude, called *sastras*, or sciences, focus on such topics as statecraft, poetics, philosophy,

music, ritual, and the arts. These works are remarkable for the depth and precision of analysis that their authors undertook. They reveal that the classical scholar-priests who composed them did not find order or ultimate meaning immediately in the natural world about them. They had too strong a sense of the flux and uncertainty in their normal human experience. They sought consistency in, rather, more abstract intellectual patterns, in the refinement rather than the description of what was about them, of what their experience pointed to as symbol rather than what it was as fact. It was out of this refining analysis that the concept of the number zero emerged—it was in the classical South Asian way of looking at things that the idea arose that there is something in our number system that is to be counted even if it is not here.

Of all of the works of analysis during the classical tradition, none is greater than the earliest: the description of the structure of language by Panini, the classical grammarian of the Sanskrit language. Panini probably lived during the fourth century B.C. His achievement was to analyze how sounds, as the basic structural units of a language (morphemes), fit together to form a word or a sentence. Only specific combinations of sounds form words, and specific combinations of words form sentences. When we use them to communicate, words and sentences reveal patterns that are related to their meanings, to what we are trying to say. But these patterns are not established by the meaning; rather, the patterns are established by the structure of language itself.

Panini, in his analysis of the Sanskrit language, sought to discover those patterns that were revealed by the way words and sentences were used—not in ordinary, colloquial language but in the highly refined, classical form of the language of the priesthood. (The word *sanskrit* means "refined," or "perfected," and identifies the level of abstraction to which the formal use of that language had progressed among the intensively trained scholar–priests during the late Vedic period.) In his quest to discover the structure of this highly refined language, Panini identified its abstract form as a profound source of order in human life that is presupposed of any attempt to use words to describe it. He perceived language as an intricately developed symbol system capable, because of its own, self-generating power of expression, of giving expression to a transcendent level of being. Its greatest potential as language was not to describe what is, but, rather, to point to and affirm what is ultimately real in human experience.

Panini's analysis of the Sanskrit language, which he reduced to eight concise chapters of grammatical rules, wherein each successive rule was an exception to all the rules that preceded it, was an impressive intellectual achievement. It is even more remarkable that he achieved this structure without the use of writing; he did it all in his head.

Panini's achievement was matched by other important intellectual quests during the classical period. Elaborations of the concept of cosmic time, or time that is ceaselessly revolving, are quite mind-boggling because of the vast span of the cycles proposed. They were described in the Puranic literature as extending through four eras, called *yugas*, of from

432,000 years to 1,728,000 years long. One thousand of these four-era periods add up to a *Kalpa*, or a day of Brahma. At the end of a 4,320,000,000-year day of Brahma, the created universe comes to an end or is dormant during Brahma's night, of equal duration, before the cycle begins again.

> Brahma is now in the first *kalpa* of his fifty-first year. Six Manus of that *kalpa* have passed away. We are living in the Kaliyuga of the twenty-eighth four-age period *(caturyuga)* of the seventh *manvantara* of Brahma's fifty-first year. The Kaliyuga began on February 18, 3102 B.C. This would seem to indicate that we have a little less than 426,933 years to go until the Kaliyuga with its twilight comes to an end, and we have to face dissolution!
>
> —W. Norman Brown, *Man in the Universe*

This concept of time generated many imaginative images in Sanskrit literature, such as the account of an *apsara,* an angel who lived in the realm of heaven within a different time frame. One heaven day, while at play with her friends in a garden, she fell off a swing and fainted. While unconscious, she went to Earth to be born as a child, reached adulthood, married, gave birth to children, attended her eldest son's wedding, and saw her grandchildren before she died, to return to her friends in the garden. They had anxiously gathered around her upon her fall from the swing and were fanning her to help her recover herself. Upon reviving, she told of her earthly experience to her friends. They were astounded that so much could have happened to her in so short a span of their time.

Imaginative intellectual effort was also devoted to find an adequate understanding of self—an answer to the question "Who am I?" And again, the analysis pursued not the question "What am I?" but "Of what is my being a symbol?"

This philosophical tradition distinguished early on between the self who acts, the agent—"I am the one who does, thinks, feels things"—and the self who observes this agency—the witness. The active self was called *jiva,* (the living thing), the aspect of self to which the acts of *karma,* (acts having moral consequences) become attached. It is this *karma* that determines into what form of life the *jiva* transmigrates in lives after death.

Careful analysis by these early scholar–priests revealed another aspect of one's experience of self as standing apart from oneself as doing, that aspect which is aware of and observes oneself as doing. That aspect they called the *witness.* Because it stands apart, it transcends the activity in which the *jiva* is involved. This aspect of self is called *atma.* The *atma,* because it transcends the natural self, is affirmed as more real, as the ultimate self, of which the natural, active self is a symbol.

The Vedanta philosopher Shankara, who lived during the eighth century A.D. and who ranks with Panini as an intellectual giant among the classical scholars of South Asia, identified the experience of consciousness as the primary designation of the *atma.* It is in understanding our consciousness of being conscious as a symbol that we gain some insight into who we really are, of that self that is ultimately real.

This way of thinking is not available to those who have become literalists, who think that what they see is all that there is to human experience. In the classical world of South Asia, they did not think like that. Rather, they opened up immense avenues of awareness and expression that were realized in creative works of classical art, music, dance, sculpture, and literature. They also discovered and affirmed a transcendent unity in human experience in the world that can be realized through a vast multitude of symbols. It can even be discovered in the spiritual dimension, in the transcendent experience of our own, isolated, individual selves, if we can discover the "ultimate beyond" within.

This heritage helps to explain why encapsulation as a social process is such an integral part of the culture of this region of the world. The classical scholars of South Asia understood that languages and religions are cultural constructs. No language or religion is natural in the sense that it has to be what it is, or that what it is can be fully explained in natural terms. Different peoples express their experience of identical things, even the same event, in very different ways. They even experience them in different ways.

Thus, attempts to construct a universal language, religion, or nationality have failed because the cultural contexts in which the necessary claims to absolutism are expressed, be it truth or allegiance, are not shared by all peoples in common. We see things, experience them, and talk about them in different ways, based upon the cultural context in which we are raised.

This understanding of the cultural relativity of language and religion, which is so evident in the pluralistic social context in which the peoples of South Asia live, does not negate the absolute claims to meaning and truth of the many separate languages and religions around them. Each is recognized as having a functional integrity that distinguishes it from all other languages and religions. They have evolved as structural abstractions among groups of people to reflect the uniqueness of their experience as a group. In this structural integrity as a language or religious faith, however, they become symbols that point beyond what they are as a specific language or religion to the identity and the integrity of those who speak and worship together as a community. This structural integrity is self-validating in the communities in which they are spoken and affirmed.

Among the Brahmin community, for example, it is not the colloquial or even ritual use of the Sanskrit language that makes it sacred. It is, rather, the structure of that language, because it is the most refined of all linguistic structures, that makes it symbolically expressive of the ultimate meaning of the universe.

A Brahmin teaching states that, when God came to create the universe, He did not create objects and then allow Adam, a human being, to invent language by naming them. Instead, He went to the ultimate meaning of what is universally expressed symbolically in the language of the *Rg Veda* to find out what He was to create. That level of reality is for the classical tradition

(World Bank)

The crush of peoples and cultures poses significant challenges to democracy in South Asia. Here, afternoon traffic builds near the India Exchange in Calcutta, India.

more real than the reality of the natural world. Nothing can be literally true in the *Veda* unless it be ultimately true.

Recognition of structural integrity as characteristic of differing languages and religions is the basis for understanding them, as symbols, not as absolutes in themselves but as pointing to a transcendent level of reality that is. One can accept the ultimate claim to universality of others for their religious faith to the degree that one understands the ultimacy of that universal reality to which one's own faith is a symbol. It is not a matter of accepting, or even tolerating, another's religion. It is, rather, the challenge of discovering the transcending beyond, of which one's own is a symbol. To people of great faith, that ultimate reality is one.

Encapsulation as a social process in South Asia is based on this recognition of many different, structurally integrated, cultural abstractions as expressions of another level of being than that defined within the natural and historical dimensions of human experience. Each language and each religion, as a symbol in its structural integrity as a language and a religion, is expressive of what is ultimately true. They are isolated and preserved, then, not for what they are, but for what they represent to those for whom they are authentic symbols.

This heritage continues in contemporary South Asia in the existence of so many mother tongues and so many religious communities as integral to the identity of so many different social groups of people. That is why the pluralistic social environment is so resilient and why language and religion play such an important role in the unfolding of democracy as a way of affirming a political identity for the peoples of South Asia.

IMAGE 4: DEMOCRACY IN SOUTH ASIA

The spirit of democracy is not a mechanical thing to be adjusted by the abolition of forms. It requires a change of the heart.

—Mohandas Gandhi

The road to democracy in South Asia has been arduous. Many obstacles have impeded the progress of all of the nations of the subcontinent toward democratically elected representative governments following the departure of British colonial rule during the middle years of the twentieth century.

Even before the nations of the region were freed from British colonial domination, the leaders whom the British Raj was training to receive the mantle of government were faced with the challenge of creating a sense of political identity for their people. This task has not been easy first of all because the concept of modern nationality is a political abstraction. A nation-state is not a natural entity; it is a cultural construct that developed in the experience of particular groups of people within a European cultural context. Specifically, the formation of nations in Western Europe and the Americas took place among dominant groups of culturally homogeneous people. Those of different cultural backgrounds, those who spoke different languages, and even women, were simply ignored in this process. Because this assumption of a dominant male ethnicity was unchallenged, it was taken for granted that a shared sense of identity as a nation would take precedence over any cultural differences among residual minority groups within the nation—that is, that all people would blend into the culture of the politically dominant.

Such a concept of nationality did not transfer easily into the experience of the peoples of South Asia, because the concept retained many of the assumptions inherent to its European cultural context. In particular, the assumption of dominant ethnicity as determining the distinctive character of a nation could not be easily transposed into the diverse, multicultural environment in South Asian society.

A second reason why the creation of a sense of political identity has been difficult in South Asia is that the people were simply not prepared to think of themselves as having a nationality. Rather, they recognized themselves as belonging first to a traditional community, a *jati,* that lies within a specific language group and affirms a shared religion. All of these bases of group identity set them apart from other peoples living in the same place. They have lived in such a multicultural environment for a long time; they do not see citizenship as something that would expect greater allegiance than the community identities that separate them from all the other linguistic, religious, and social groups among whom they live.

A third reason why the concept of modern nationality was not easily transposed to the subcontinent is that the democratic models of government introduced by British colonial rule did not enter a political vacuum. Patriarchal authority structures within the family served as the model for leadership roles among various levels of the political, economic, and linguistic groupings to which families belonged. Even today, almost all of the women who have served as prime ministers in India, Bangladesh, Pakistan, and Sri Lanka since these countries' independence have gained prominence in national political life primarily because of the dominant roles of their fathers. The Great Mutiny of 1857 demonstrated the resiliency of these established bastions of public power on the regional and local levels. Efforts in the 1900s to encourage public participation in the political process, to make a government of the people, reveal the adaptability of village, caste, and language institutions as well. Established patterns of grassroots governance are significant factors in both imple-

menting and shaping the transition from traditional to democratic power structures. They do not relinquish their authority easily, if at all.

On the national level, the British Raj effectively removed the vestiges of Moghul imperial power from the lands that became Bangladesh, India, and Pakistan. The British also united Sri Lanka under their colonial rule during the 1800s. Afghanistan, during the 1920s, and Nepal, in 1991, moved away from absolute monarchies, Maldives from a sultanate in 1968. Ironically, in 1903, the British Raj established the current dynasty of one of the two monarchies that still function in the subcontinent: the "Dragon Kings" in Bhutan. In this instance, the established patterns of governance were simply reinforced.

Following the example set by the British, four of the new nations—India, from the beginning, and Pakistan, Bangladesh, and Nepal, following several modifications—now have constitutions that use the British parliamentary form of government. In it, the prime minister in the legislature is the chief executive of the nation. He or she is not elected to that office directly by the people but, rather, by a majority of the legislators who are voted into office in general elections. The prime minister must retain the confidence of that majority to remain in office. Should he or she fail to do so, another member of the legislature may be invited to try to form a government. Should no one be able to gain support of a majority of the legislators, the legislature is than dissolved and a new general election is called to select a new one. In India, Pakistan, and Bangladesh, the president, who functions as head of state rather than as chief executive (head of government), is also elected by the legislature; in Nepal, however, as in England, the royal dynasty remains the head of state.

Sri Lanka has a presidential form of government, wherein the chief executive and the legislators are voted for directly by the people in a general election, as in the United States. This form replaced an earlier parliamentary structure by constitutional amendment in 1978 in order to give the chief executive more independent power.

Two of the smallest countries in the subcontinent, Maldives and Bhutan, are making more gradual transitions to democratic forms of government. Maldives does elect a president every five years, but this process represents little change from the absolute power previously held by the sultan. This presidential election is actually a referendum vote by the people for a single candidate who has been selected by secret ballot by the Maldives' Legislature. It is not surprising that the current president has been reelected three times—in 1993 by 93 percent of the voters—and that he belongs to a clan that has ruled these islands for eight centuries.

In Bhutan, the monarch continues as absolute sovereign. However, in 1952, in a move toward modern representative government, the king established a national Legislature with limited authority. A third of its members are appointed by the king. The other two thirds are elected by the village headmen, who are the wielders of power on the local level. In 1998, the

(United Nations/BP)

With the partitioning of India and Pakistan, masses of people migrated because of their religious affiliations. More than 12 million people fled, including these refugees, making it the largest migration in history.

king initiated further reform by establishing a cabinet elected by the Legislature to replace his council of ministers to administer the government.

Afghanistan is a special case. It was one of the first countries of the subcontinent to attempt to introduce democratically elected representative government, during the 1920s. But reform was resisted from the beginning by the many autonomous warlords who held absolute control over isolated regions of the country. In 1979, cold war politics brought Soviet military forces into the country in hopes of maintaining it as a satellite state. Afghan resistance led to a devastating Soviet "scorched earth" policy and a military stalemate. Soviet intervention ended in 1989. But efforts to restore some kind of order in these war-ravaged lands and among the diverse ethnic constituencies of the country led only to intense infighting among rival groups. The emergence of a new, militant Islamic revolutionary force, called the Taliban, has reduced Afghanistan to a state of oppressive religious autocracy.

With the exception of Bhutan and Afghanistan, the other nations of South Asia have held full and free national elections since 1994, with high levels of voter participation in all cases. Except in Maldives (which forbids by law the existence of opposition political parties), these elections have resulted in the civil transfer of power form one political party to another. In Nepal, since the national elections in November 1994, five different coalitions of parties have been called to form governments without having to hold another general election. In Pakistan, the president dismissed the majority government of the Pakistan People's Party in November 1996. Elections held in February 1997 were won by the Pakistan Muslim League Party, which had been the opposition party during the previous session. In India, a constitutional requirement that national elections be held at least once every 5 years led to elections in 1996; this resulted in the transfer of control of the government from the Congress Party to a United Front coalition with support from the Congress Party. Withdrawal of that support in December 1997 led to the fall of the United Front coalition and the need for new elections for the national Legislature. These elections, held in March 1998, led to the transfer of power to a new coalition government, headed by the Bharata Janata Party (BJP).

Clearly, the nations of South Asia still face many challenges in implementing democracy. Yet it is taking hold, and it is today the basis of governance among more people than anywhere else in the world.

RELIGION AND NATIONAL IDENTITY

Nationality is a cultural construct that, like language and religion, needs to develop a sense of corporate identity among particular groups of people. Like them, it also has a structural integrity, expressed in institutions and symbols of public power or authority, which distinguishes it from the domain of other nations. Unlike religion, however, its institutions and symbols are identified almost entirely within the historical dimension of a community's experience. Nationalisms even create their own histories.

Because of this similarity of language, religion, and nationality as creating self-authenticating corporate identities, the leaders of the freedom movements in South Asia during the twentieth century drew upon established language and religion community identities to generate a sense of participation in public authority and thereby create a national identity for their peoples. Especially convenient for this purpose were the traditional affiliations of dominant religious groups. The partitioning of those districts of the British Raj in which the majority of the population were Muslims as belonging to the nation of Pakistan, and Hindu majority districts to India, is the most explicit example of this exploitation of religious identity to attempt to create political cohesion among diverse and encapsulated groups of people.

Religious constructs must have a creative, dynamic, and active bonding process to affirm their life and identity as communities. They are continually adjusting themselves in changing circumstances to maintain the allegiance and participation of their members.

The danger in using the bonding dynamic of religious communities as a way of bringing people together as nations is that it essentially changes the nature of the relationship it affirms among the people. The effective working of the multicultural social environment in South Asia is based on the understanding that different religious communities are symbolic expressions of a transcendent, unified reality. Each community's life is an authentic, symbolic expression of this ultimate truth. The political use of a religious community's bonding dynamic tends to reduce it from a symbolic expression of ultimate truth to something historically concrete, literally true, and both socially and geographically exclusive. At its worst, it has sought to absolutize the nation-state itself.

In the American experience, for example, there are a number of instances where a religious symbol has been reduced to an historical truth, which was then absolutized. One such case is the understanding of the Founders of the United States that the European settlers' crossing of the Atlantic Ocean to start new lives was a sacred act. It had its prototype in the crossing of the Red Sea by the early Israelites to enter into a promised land and a new relationship as a people with God. This image was vital to the framers of the Declaration of Independence as giving sacred meaning and direction to the establishment of a new nation on the western shore of the Atlantic Ocean. The Founders perceived a divine mandate to fulfill as a newly independent people that pointed beyond who they were, to whom, under God, they might become.

The formation of the United States as a religious symbol affirmed a sacred destiny with democracy, which it was the duty and challenge of succeeding generations of citizens to seek and fulfill. That destiny has to do with expectations of freedom, equality, and social justice for all. This symbol is reduced into the historic dimension when U.S. citizens take the promise not as an anticipation of a sacred destiny, not as

pointing beyond itself to another level of reality, but as fulfilled by the historical existence of the country. The United States becomes defined as historically concrete and geographically specific. Expressions like "America first" and "Love it or leave it" reflect this literal rather than symbolic understanding of the national identity. At its worst, the nation becomes sanctified as it is, and citizens begin to demonize other peoples who do not inhabit the land, or who do, but who do not live the "American way," or who are poor.

The reduction of religious identity to national identity is pervasive throughout the world today and has led to severe violence and suffering. It has left an unhappy trail of human misery in many countries in the Middle East and Africa, in Northern Ireland and the former Yugoslavia, in South Asia, and in other regions.

THE PARTITION OF BRITISH INDIA IN 1947

The ethnic, linguistic, and religious groupings used in Western Europe to build the political identity of nations became especially divisive in the socially pluralistic environment of South Asia. The creation of the new nations of India and Pakistan out of the British Indian Empire isolated vast numbers of people not included in the dominant religious identity around which the national borders were drawn. Literally millions of Hindus and Sikhs living in areas of the subcontinent that became Pakistan, and Muslims finding themselves in India, felt threatened as minorities in these newly established nations. Communal violence erupted across the subcontinent, and many thousands were killed.

Children of many different faiths and backgrounds who had grown up together, had learned and played together in the same classes in school for years, suddenly, on the day of the independence of their countries, became enemies. They thought that they were going to be free. But what they experienced, inexplicably, was severe division and hatred. Still dazed and mystified, those of minority faiths were whisked away during the night to seek asylum across the border. Many did not make it.

More than 12 million people fled—the largest refugee migration ever experienced in the world. Homeless and threatened in their own lands, they were forced to flee in haste, destitute, to cross the new national borders in a quest for survival. As Hindus and Sikhs moved toward India and Muslims toward Pakistan, in opposite directions across the border drawn between the two countries, many hundreds of thousands were senselessly killed.

Kushwant Singh wrote movingly of the devastating impact of that violent confrontation on a Sikh village near the border in his novel *Train to Pakistan*:

One morning, a train from Pakistan halted at Mano Majra railway station. At first glance it had the look of trains in the days of peace. No one sat on the roof. No one clung between the bogies. No one was balanced on the foot-boards. But somehow it was different. There was something uneasy about it. It had a ghostly quality. . . .

[That evening] the northern horizon, which had turned a bluish grey, showed orange again. The orange turned into copper and then into luminous russet. Red tongues of flame leaped into the black sky. A soft breeze began to blow towards the village. It brought the smell of burning kerosene, then of wood. And then—a faint acrid smell of searing flesh.

The village was stilled in deathly silence. No one asked anyone else what the odour was. They all knew. They had known it all the time. The answer was implicit in the fact that the train had come from Pakistan.

That evening, for the first time in the memory of Mano Majra, Imam Baksh's sonorous cry did not rise to the heavens to proclaim the glory of God.

Rather than experiencing the exhilaration of political freedom, those who survived this massive migration found themselves bewildered refugees. They were homeless in the lands of their birth, unwelcome in the lands to which they came.

THE INDEPENDENCE OF BANGLADESH

Islamic religious identity had been essential to the creation of a single, independent Pakistan in 1947 for Muslims in the two sections of the subcontinent where they were in the majority. Yet their shared Islamic faith did not prevent the uprising of the peoples of the eastern region of Pakistan in 1971, some 24 years after the partition of British India, to seek their own independence from Pakistan. That movement revealed that the ethnic and linguistic identities of the Bengali people of East Pakistan were stronger than their religious identity as Muslims in a larger country dominated by an ethnically and linguistically different, and financially advantaged, Muslim population in the west.

National identity based on ethnicity rather than religion proved to be no less of a human tragedy. The reign of fury brought on the Bengali people by the Pakistan government to try to preserve the union of its eastern wing with West Pakistan by military repression caused more than 200,000 deaths. According to a news report at that time:

People have killed each other because of race, politics, and religion; no community is entirely free of guilt. But the principal agent of death and hatred has been the Pakistani Army. And its killing has been selective. According to reliable reports from inside East Pakistan, the Army's particular targets have been intellectuals and leaders of opinion—doctors, professors, students, writers. . . .

—*The New York Times* (June 7, 1971)

Eight million people fled across the East Pakistan border during the spring and summer of 1971 into the squalor of refugee camps in the neighboring states of India. That number included more than 1,500 physicians and 10,000 teachers.

The news report explained:

. . . With the closure of the borders by the Pakistani military, large numbers are continuing to infiltrate through the 1,300 mile border with India through forest and swamps. These groups, with numbers sometimes up to 50,000 in a 24 hour period, have for the most part settled along major routes in India. They are found wherever there is a combination of available ground and minimal water supply. . . . The refugee camps may vary in size from small groups to upwards of 50,000. There has been an extraordinary effort on the part of the West Bengal and Indian government to organize these camps and supply them with at least minimal amounts of food and water.

The refugee diet . . . consists of rice boiled in open clay pots, some powdered milk which is occasionally available, and dall, which is a lentil type of bean used for a thin soup. . . . At this point the diet would be classified as barely adequate. . . .

Because uncertain conditions, both political and natural, continue to plague the people of Bangladesh, the flow of refugees from that country into India since its independence in 1971 has continued. It is estimated that anywhere from 7 million to 12 million Bangladeshis are living in India today. The continuing existence of such a large number of refugees illustrates what a heavy toll in human displacement and suffering has resulted from the imposition of religious nationality as a way of grouping the culturally diverse peoples of the subcontinent.

This pattern is not unique to the partition of British India into districts of Hindu and Muslim majorities. Large numbers of people have become refugees in both Sri Lanka and Bhutan, where the large majority of the populations belong to the prevailing traditions of Buddhism. The dominance of these religious majorities is further strengthened by their speaking the same language—Sinhala by almost all Buddhists in Sri Lanka, and, to a lesser degree, Dzongkha in north-central Bhutan.

THE SRI LANKAN EXPERIENCE

Sri Lanka has had the longest experience with democracy of all the nations of South Asia. Free and general elections for political office were first held there in 1935. The country also has the highest levels of education and literacy, an accomplishment that helps to account for its maintaining the lowest birth rate and rate of population growth in the subcontinent. Yet, despite these achievements, the country has experienced a severe refugee problem due to the creation of a national identity based on the religious and linguistic identity of a Sinhalese-speaking, Buddhist majority. This national identity has caused insecurity to develop among various religious and linguistic minority groups.

Within the island nation of Sri Lanka is a large minority of mostly Tamil-speaking and Hindu peoples. They comprise about 17 percent of the total population. Though ethnically the same as the Buddhist majority, they are geographically separate, living mostly in the northern part of the country, where they constitute a plurality, if not an outright majority, in the political districts of that region. Still, the political repression they have experienced in other regions of the country and on the national level led in the early 1980s to outbursts of communal violence. They were followed by a militant and bloody separatist movement, which persists even to this day.

The example of the creation of India and Pakistan would have suggested the division of the island into two countries, based on the majority populations in each of the districts of the British Crown colony, then called *Ceylon*. But at the time of independence, it was hoped that the political identity of a unified island nation would take precedence over the religious and linguistic identities of its constituent regions. It was also hoped that such a unifying political identity would prevail over any cultural and linguistic affinity of the minority Tamil population of Sri Lanka with the larger neighboring state of Tamil Nadu, across the Palk Strait in south India. In 1948, all districts were included under a single, democratically elected, parliamentary government. Under it, a commanding majority was assured for the larger Buddhist, Sinhala-speaking population, without specific safeguards to assure the protection of the rights and safety of its minorities.

At the time of independence, 800,000 Tamils who were not part of the distinct, indigenous Tamil community of the north but had been imported by the British from Tamil-speaking south India during the ninteenth century worked on the coffee, rubber, and tea plantations in the southern hills of the colony. The solution to their presence as an ethnically distinct minority with strong ties to the large Tamil population in south India was for the Ceylonese government to declare them stateless and to push for their repatriation to India. In 1964, and again in 1974, the government of India agreed to receive 600,000 "plantation Tamils" back into India. To the north Ceylonese Tamils, for whom the island had been homeland for more than 2,000 years, these decisions were ominous.

Tensions between the Sinhalese majority and Tamil minority increased during a period of uneasy accommodation, until 1983, when anti-Tamil riots broke out throughout the country. The defense of the linguistic identity and political freedom of the Tamil people was then seized by a militant separatist group called the Liberation Tigers for Tamil Eelam (LTTE). And guerrilla warfare broke out in the predominantly Tamil-speaking areas of the north and east. Thirty thousand Tamils fled to India that year, to be followed by almost 100,000 more refugees in 1984.

Since then, many thousands have been killed in the attacks and counterattacks of the LTTE and the Sri Lanka Army. In 1987, at the invitation of the Sri Lankan government, India sent a strong "Peace Keeping Force" to attempt to bring order to the troubled country. The deployment of this military presence was not able to bring the two sides together, and the invitation was withdrawn in 1990.

Between 1990 and 1995, fighting between the LTTE and the Sri Lanka government increased in intensity and devastation. With the destruction of their means of livelihood and homes, even entire villages, more than 1 million people became refugees.

Because ocean waters and navy ships surround Sri Lanka, escape has been extremely difficult. Fewer than 20 percent have been able to afford the expense and risk of crossing the Palk Strait to India. Saraswathi Sevakam, a refugee in a camp in India, testified in 1991:

In July 1990, I left my village and got into a boat for India. There were 45 of us, all civilians. We were about to leave the cove when a navy gunboat came at us, shooting. We jumped into the shallow water. Some people were waving white flags to show we were not militants. We lay in the water for two hours before the navy boats came back and took us to shore. They threatened that if they found any LTTE in the area, we would be killed. We were taken to a navy camp. My husband was taken away. I have not seen him or heard from him since.

By May 1991, approximately 210,000 refugees were reported to have made it to south India. Another 200,000 had sought asylum in Europe. But most of those who have suffered the ravages of Tamil and Sinhalese militancy have been dependent upon relief efforts set up within Sri Lanka itself. They are refugees in their own land.

Since the election of the Chandrika Kumaratunga government in 1995, there have been renewed efforts to find paths toward a political solution for the divisions among these opposed religious communities in Sri Lanka. The government launched a major military offensive that has wrested control of the Jaffna Peninsula, the Tamil militants' stronghold in the north, from the LTTE. Yet the fighting and the killing and the destruction continue. And those who survive are desperate for food and shelter.

Sri Lanka's experience in seeking an inclusive national identity has taken a heavy toll among its people. Although they remain hopeful, those who have been ravaged by this warfare do not see an early end to their plight.

BHUTAN: A GROWING REFUGEE PROBLEM

Even the small country of Bhutan, tucked away in the high Himalayan Mountains on the northeast side of the subcontinent, has not been immune from a refugee crisis. And the shape of the issue appears discouragingly familiar: Can the identity of the nation include all those living within its borders who belong to distinct ethnic, religious, and linguistic minorities?

The gradual move toward modernization in this mountain kingdom has led to the migration of laborers, some from India, but most from Nepal. The Nepali immigrants have settled almost entirely in the more productive, southern part of the country, where they live as a distinct minority. In recent years, their number has grown to about 28 percent of the population of the nation.

The trend toward modernization has also challenged the traditional way of life of the Bhutanese people. In the face of this challenge, made more intense by the awareness that other Buddhist kingdoms in that region—Tibet, Sikkim, and Ladakh—have not survived, the government of Bhutan has taken a number of actions to create a national identity based upon its Buddhist heritage. These actions include adopting Dzongkha as the national language and mandating wearing a national dress for formal occasions. These actions were not specifically aimed at the Nepali population. However, they were taken with the clear recollection that it was the agitation of Nepalis living in the neighboring kingdom of Sikkim that led to its absorption into India in 1974.

In 1985, the government allowed citizenship to only those Nepalis who could claim residency since 1958. In 1988, this "Citizenship Act" was enforced by a census in southern Bhutan, carried out to identify those immigrants who were not legal residents. The rigor of this census became a direct assault on the Nepalis, threatening both their heritage and their status as citizens in the country. The deportations, social unrest, and terrorist acts that followed this census led to the flight of many Nepalis from the country. By mid-1993, approximately 85,000 had made their way into refugee camps set up by the United Nations in eastern Nepal. Since then, a number of protest marches to Bhutan have been staged from these camps, but with little noticeable impact.

The governments of Bhutan and Nepal have been seeking to work out an agreement on this refugee problem since then. Yet the issue of who is legitimately a citizen of Bhutan remains unresolved.

POLITICAL CRISIS IN AFGHANISTAN

The quest for a common political identity for the people has been shared by all of the nations of the subcontinent. It has been difficult for the people of Afghanistan for many of the same reasons. It is a country divided by a formidable natural barrier, by differing ethnic and linguistic groups, by a modernizing urban population and conservative rural petty states and tribes, fractured among themselves into militant factions. Attempts to unify these disparate groups of people have had to confront the reality that there is little in their traditional way of life to bring them together beyond their allegiance to their own clans. Even the indigenous sources of political stability have depended more on internecine stalemate than a sense of common cause or shared identity.

Yet even more devastating has been the burden of cold war politics. Soviet support for economic development and modernization in Afghanistan began during the 1920s, when Vladimir Lenin sought to extend the provenance of his communist philosophy beyond the border states of the Soviet Union into Mongolia, Finland, and Afghanistan. The U.S. policy to contain the expansion of communism following the World War II led to military support to the shah of Iran and

the government of Pakistan as well as to direct economic development competition in Afghanistan itself. In 1977, with Soviet encouragement, the Afghan People's Democratic (Communist) Party staged a coup in Kabul, and took over the government. In order to protect its influence and investment in Afghanistan, in 1979 the Soviet government sent a military force of 85,000 troops to subdue reactionary forces in the country.

This invasion of the Soviet Army into Afghanistan forced some 400,000 Afghans to flee to Pakistan. Over the next 10 years, the number of refugees grew to nearly 5 million—eventually, one third of Afghanistan's total population were living in refugee camps in Pakistan and Iran. Support for these Afghan refugees came from many sources. The U.S. government, eager to contain further Soviet expansion, contributed supplies, medical assistance, and encouragement to those who fled the devastation of Soviet attacks on their lands. The Pakistan government, finding support for its own military government by assisting the United States in its objectives, took up the Afghan cause. The refugee camps became not just places of refuge for those displaced from Afghanistan but also staging and rehabilitation areas for those returning to fight against Soviet forces in their country.

The withdrawal of Soviet forces from Afghanistan in 1989 left a wide swath of devastation and impoverishment—from Afghanistan and miles of land mines throughout wide, unmapped areas of the country. These conditions, combined with intense internal fighting among the rival *mujahideen* (resistance) groups that opposed the Communist government, offered no inducement to the refugees to return to their former homes. The refugee camps, when they had strong international support, also provided new opportunities for education, social reform, health care and employment—more than the Afghan people had ever received in their home lands. Thus, even with diminishing international aid, close to 2 million Afghan refugees chose to remain in Pakistan and Iran.

The intense fighting around Kabul among the rival *mujahideen* groups and with the new Taliban revolutionary force, all competing for control of the country, led an additional 1.2 million to flee the city and countless others to abandon their blown-up villages. In order to prevent any new influx of refugees, the Pakistan government closed its border with Afghanistan. Many of those refugees are now living in camps in Jalalabad, the closest city to Pakistan within Afghanistan itself. These camps, initially maintained with the help of the UN High Commission for Refugees, are finding it very difficult to operate with the restriction on the activity of women imposed, in its reforming zeal, by the militant Taliban across the 85 percent of the country that it now controls.

With the country so divided by fully armed, opposing religious and ethnic forces, the Afghan people continue to be adrift, in need, uncertainty, and unrelenting anxiety, on both sides of the borders between Afghanistan, Pakistan, and Iran. In such circumstances, there is little opportunity to discover their identity as a people, let alone exercise any instruments of a stable, democratic government.

OTHER REFUGEES

Refugees, by definition, are aliens in the lands in which they live. They remain outside the perimeters of the identity of those who form the nation; and, unless they assimilate into that identity, they cannot participate in government. The presence of so many refugees in the South Asian subcontinent is indicative of a state of political upheaval in which democracy cannot function.

Not all of these refugees are South Asian. The bloody Chinese takeover of Tibet in 1950 led to the flight of the Dalai Lama, the religious and temporal leader of the Tibetan people, into India in 1959. Hundreds of thousands of his followers also fled into India and into neighboring Nepal and Bhutan, seeking refuge from the repression of Chinese domination in their homeland. In their adoptive homes, these refugees continue to search for ways to maintain their identity as a Buddhist people in exile.

And the military repression that followed the thwarting of elections in Myanmar (Burma) in May 1990 has caused many Burmese to flee across its border into Bangladesh and the states of eastern India. Some 280,000 Burmese refugees are now reported to be in camps along the border of eastern Bangladesh. They remain hopeful that the courageous Nobel Laureate Aung San Suu Kyi and her National League for Democracy will succeed in their quest to achieve a stable, democratically elected government, accountable to all the people of that country and protective of their human rights.

The extensive presence of refugees throughout the subcontinent bears witness to the challenge in every country in South Asia to achieve a basis for its political identity as a nation that is both true to and expressive of the unique, multifaceted character of all of its people, inclusive of all their cultural, linguistic, and religious differences. All have had to be responsive to the long-standing multicultural diversity within each of their borders. Yet, indicative of the diversity among the nations themselves, none of them have responded to this challenge in the same way. How each of these countries has progressed on its separate course toward democracy is discussed in the individual reports that follow in this book.

A common thread among these responses has been the attempt to achieve a political solution to adversarial relationships among peoples that are based on more traditional and profound expressions of human identity than that of the nation state. A political solution to human strife was the assumption and the promise in the formation of nations in Western Europe during the 1700s and 1800s. But the experience of two world wars and the continuing presence of refugees throughout the world in the 1900s suggest the inadequacy of nationalism based on self-determination as a way to achieve unity and peace among the many diverse peoples who inhabit our world.

The independence of nations and freedom of the individual are worthy political goals. But the South Asian experience reveals to us that they are not ends in themselves. Nor can they be imposed.

Alexis de Tocqueville observed in the early years of the ninteenth century that the long-term success of democracy in the United States depended not upon the structure and institutions of the government, but upon the habits of the heart of the American people. Mahatma Gandhi, on the threshold of political independence for the people of India, also realized that democracy is not just a matter of form. Rather, it is a matter of the heart and the soul of a people.

IMAGE 5: MAHATMA GANDHI

> Generations to come, it may be, will scarce believe that such a one as this ever in flesh and blood walked upon this earth.
> —Albert Einstein

The name of Mohandas K. Gandhi comes up in a number of contexts in looking at the uniqueness of South Asia. His role in shaping the freedom movement on the subcontinent in this century was immense. He identified himself with India's common people; he adopted their dress and simplicity of life and traveled to village after village to spread his message of reform. He encouraged everyone to use the spinning wheel and to wear clothes made of the hand-spun cloth called *khadi*. He called for national boycotts. And he fasted. He managed to get everyone involved in the political process of becoming a new nation.

Gathering such widespread awareness and involvement, together with his great organizational skills, he was able to restructure the Indian National Congress so that the power base of the movement no longer resided among the elitist group of intellectuals at the top, who had shaped its policies toward achieving independence since 1887. Gandhi brought the power base to the village level, to where the people are. Removing the oppression of colonial rule was something that was happening to everyone, in every corner of the land.

Of greater international significance is the method of non-violent protest against social injustice that Gandhi developed during his years in South Africa and applied with such confounding consistency in leading the peoples of British India to freedom in 1947. Its effectiveness was partly the result of his ability to discipline people in the deployment of his method. He was also able to command accountability from those who were the oppressors. In this way, he established a viable alternative to power politics to achieve historic goals. Gandhi called this method *satyagraha*, or "Soul Force." And he encouraged its use to empower all who are oppressed and powerless, if they have but the courage, the discipline, and the vision to become free.

In the time since his death in 1948, a number of important events have changed the course of history. The rise of the Solidarity movement in Poland initiated the crumbling of the

Soviet Union and its grasp on Eastern/Central Europe. The civil-rights movement in the United States, under the inspiring leadership of Dr. Martin Luther King, Jr., initiated a national policy on race relations to correct historic injustices to minority students and workers. And the election of Nelson Mandela and his African National Congress to political leadership in 1994 brought the end of apartheid in South Africa. These events released new energy and a vision of hope for positive change in the world. They also share a common source: They all trace their inspiration for how to disarm oppressive political power with nonviolent public protest to Mohandas Karamchand Gandhi—the man who came to be called the *Mahatma*.

EARLY YEARS
Gandhi was born in Porbandar, a small seaport town along the western coast of the Kathiawar Peninsula in western India, on October 2, 1869. His father was a *Diwan*, or prime minister, in the employ of local *maharajas* in that region. Although Mohandas was the youngest, the fourth child of his father's fourth wife, it was expected that he would continue his father's—and grandfather's—political careers; he was groomed from an early age for leadership.

Yet Gandhi proved to be an indifferent student. He found mathematics particularly difficult. When he was 13, his parents arranged for his marriage to a young woman his same age, named Kasturbai. In spite of her gentle and accepting nature, he accounted himself an immature, jealous, and domineering husband. He was later to credit her example as a patient and devoted wife in leading him to see the virtues of a life committed to nonviolence.

Gandhi's mother also had a deep influence on his life. She was a devout Hindu who revealed to him by her life of devotion the power of religious faith and fasting. When, at age 18, Gandhi went to England to study law, he made a vow to her that he would abstain from consuming meat and wine while he was away. His determination to honor this vow set a pattern of persistence and discipline in keeping commitments for the rest of his life.

Gandhi stayed in England for just three years. He proved an able enough student to pass the London matriculation examinations in Latin, French, and chemistry, and, a year later, his law examinations. He was admitted to the bar on June 10, 1891, enrolled in the High Court on June 11, and sailed for India on June 12.

Shy and sensitive, Gandhi was not able to establish a law practice in Bombay, nor with his brother back in Porbandar. He therefore leapt at an opportunity with a local firm of Muslim merchants to work on a case in South Africa. The original assignment was for 1 year. But in the course of that year, he became so involved in the plight of Indians living there that he stayed for more than 20 years and changed the course of history in two continents.

IN SOUTH AFRICA
Gandhi's first dramatic encounter with racial discrimination came when he was thrown out of a first-class compartment in a South African train. This episode led him to work to bring a diffuse group of Indians living in South Africa together to protest the many abuses perpetrated against them. Finding the work of organizing demonstrations and campaigns for Indian rights both demanding and effective, Gandhi established a law practice, which eventually became successful enough to support his family and his reform efforts. He also set up a weekly newspaper, *Indian Opinion*, and purchased a farm at Phoenix on which to set up a commune to maintain the paper's publication.

As the South African government began to impose more and more restraints on the Indian people living in the country, Gandhi orchestrated a series of nonviolent protest demonstrations in which increasing numbers of Indians participated. His last protest march involved more than 2,000 men, women, and children, and it was joined "in sympathy" by 50,000 miners and indentured laborers. That action led, in 1914, to the passage of a new law in South Africa to prohibit offensive discriminatory practices against all Indians living there. This movement was so ordered and disciplined by his own character, so shaped by his own commitment to effective nonviolent resistance, that Gandhi emerged from his South African experience a leader of immense stature.

However, the direction of Gandhi's growth in South Africa was, in a significant way, thrust upon him. He could have been treated there with polite respect, done his job, and returned to India unnoticed. That he was physically thrown out of the railway car was not a deliberate act of his own doing. In responding to this immediate experience of social injustice, he gained a sense of something much greater than just what was happening to him. He was discovering a personal mission that he felt compelled to fulfill: to bring together an oppressed people in a quest for social justice.

Being by temperament introspective, deliberate, even fastidious, Gandhi searched for the resources to meet this challenge within himself. This quest brought him to affirm intuitively—for he had no formal training in its conceptual intricacies—two precepts drawn from the classical heritage of South Asia. First, and more consciously, Gandhi identified his mission with the ancient concept of *dharma*, of cosmic moral order. This concept was set forward in the early Sanskrit epics, the *Mahabharata* and the *Ramayana*, as the proper behavior for ruling princes, not only as the moral foundation of their authority to rule but also as the source of the well-being and prosperity of their subjects.

Gandhi pursued the private aspect of *dharma*, the moral foundation for leadership, with determination from his youth. His autobiography, *The Story of My Experiments with Truth*, written mostly in 1926, is replete with descriptions of his attempts to discipline his personal life around issues of celibacy, vegetarianism, purification, and self-control. This pattern of moral exploration and testing he continued throughout

Mohandas Gandhi spent more than 20 years in South Africa as a result of becoming so involved in battling the prejudice against Indians living in that country. Gandhi is pictured above (center) sitting in front of his office In South Africa. On the left is his friend H. S. L. Polak. On the right is his secretary, and standing behind him are two office clerks.

his life, always seeking to be better prepared—by which he meant morally adequate—to undertake the public tasks he felt compelled to perform. Even toward the end of the long struggle for national independence, he questioned not whether the British would grant freedom to the people of the subcontinent; his greatest concern was, rather, whether he personally was morally pure enough to bring the people of India to this goal.

Equally important to Gandhi was the public aspect of *dharma*, that it was to be realized in concrete situations of public benefit. The cosmic dimension of *dharma* is realized not in the abstract, nor just in one's personal life, but in the public affairs of humanity. It was this aspect that made his personal experience with abuse in South Africa a public offense that would be righted only when discrimination would not be practiced against any Indian residing there. His awareness of the epic precept of *dharma* made him aware not only of the moral demands of his mission but also of the magnitude of its objective.

The second precept of the classical heritage that Gandhi affirmed by his experience in South Africa was an awareness of a truer, deeper reality of "self" than he normally experienced in the everyday world. He experienced glimpses of a more ultimate reality of being, what in the classical heritage of South Asia was called *atma*. In his quest for this higher being of self, Gandhi intuited that a vital quality that distinguishes it from the ordinary experience of self is that it is by nature nonviolent. "Non-violence is not a garment to be put on and off at will. Its seat is in the heart, and it must be an inseparable part of our very being." It was this deeper, more refined self that was to define the distinctive character of the mission to which he had been called—that only the means could justify the end. Above all else, it had to be nonviolent.

Gandhi's concern to reduce the level of violence in people's everyday lives and in the world around us reinforced his moral image of *dharma*. Joined with an intimation of the *atma*, he believed that nonviolence requires a discipline that identifies and refines our awareness of our true self:

The acquisition of the spirit of nonviolence is a matter of long training in self-denial and appreciation of the hidden forces within ourselves. It changes one's outlook on life. . . . It is the greatest force because it is the highest expression of the soul.

Gandhi's living out these important concepts of *dharma* and *atma* drawn from his South Asian cultural heritage identified him on a profound level with the people from India who were then living in South Africa. He spoke to them out of a context to which they were uniquely prepared to respond as a distinct group of people. It is also significant that his initial steps to leadership took place a great distance away from India. V. S. Naipal, based upon his own upbringing as an Indian in Trinidad, described an important social dimension to Indian life that Gandhi would have experienced only outside of India:

These overseas Indian groups were mixed. They were miniature Indias, with Hindus and Muslims, and people of different castes. They were disadvantaged, without representation, and without a political tradition. They were isolated by language and culture from the people they found themselves among; they were isolated from India itself. In these special circumstances they developed something they never would have known in India: a sense of belonging to an Indian community. This feeling of community could override religion and caste.

Naipal went on to add that it was essential for Gandhi to have begun his freedom movement among the Indian peoples in South Africa. "It is during his . . . years in South Africa that intimations came to Gandhi of an all-India religious-political mission."

Had Gandhi begun in India, he would not have known for whom he was seeking independence. In South Africa, Gandhi discovered a destiny for a people to become a free nation. As in the case of his own sense of mission, Gandhi returned to India with the conviction that it would not happen until that people had discovered its soul.

RETURN TO INDIA

Gandhi returned to India in 1915, at age 45, recognized as a national hero to a people without a nation. Soon afterward he was widely acclaimed as the *Mahatma*, the "great souled one."

Gandhi continued his work toward the removal of British colonial domination in India much as he had worked to overcome discrimination in South Africa: by addressing particular instances of oppression that were thrust upon him. Initially, these did not involve the government but were between English plantation owners and peasants (in the eastern province of Bihar) and Indian mill owners and mill workers (in the western city, Ahmadabad). Feeling that Indian independence from British colonial rule should not replace one oppression with another, he attacked the subservient role placed upon women in Indian society. He also took up the plight of "untouchable" communities, what he called "the ulcer of untouchability" in Indian life. Between 1915 and 1948, he initiated hundreds of nonviolent protest actions against a wide range of social injustices and abuse.

One of Gandhi's most important achievements during the independence movement of India was his ability to lead the diverse people of the subcontinent to a shared vision of what it was to be free. Drawing upon the importance of symbolic thought as developed in the classical heritage of his people, he insisted that people of all stations and walks of life weave and wear *khadi*, hand-spun cloth. This action not only freed them from the economic tyranny of dependence upon cloth manufactured in England, but, more important as an expression of individual independence, it encouraged them to become self-reliant even while being under the burden of British colonial rule.

Gandhi's most dramatic act of *satyagraha* was in 1930, when he led his followers from Ahmedabad on a 200-mile walk to collect salt from the sea in protest against the salt tax imposed by the British government. What began as a march of 78 men and boys specially trained to undertake the journey with him gathered more and more people as it made its way through the countryside. By the time the column reached Dandi on the shore, the company had grown to thousands. (The Oscar-winning film *Gandhi* gives a vivid picture not only of the energetic figure of Gandhi himself leading the march but also of the dramatic swelling of the crowds who joined behind him to make the salt march such a powerful expression of public support.) Gandhi compared it to the Boston Tea Party, which anticipated the war for independence in America. His march was the culminating act of a series of nonviolent protests against British rule that led to the beginning of home rule in 1937 and the total withdrawal of British colonial government in 1947.

These are just two examples of Gandhi's immense power to draw people into the modern political process by creating powerful symbolic actions. In performing them, people in all reaches of British India began to assert and discover the qualities of freedom among some of the simplest and most immediate elements of their lives: their clothing and their food. These simple acts were symbolic, in the classical sense, in pointing beyond themselves to express what it is to be truly free.

Fasting became another aspect of Gandhi's leadership role in India. In all, he conducted 17 fasts "to the death." The first happened as a part of his efforts to resolve the dispute over wages between the mill workers and the mill owners in

(UN/DPI Photo by Evan Schneider)

Despite widespread poverty, a severe refugee problem, and intense internal conflicts among different religious and linguistic groups, Sri Lanka's democratic political system endures. Here, President Chandrika Bandaranaika Kumaratunga addresses the United Nations General Assembly in September 1998.

Ahmedabad in 1918, soon after his return from South Africa. Like his earlier actions, it was not premeditated but, rather, grew out of the circumstances in which he found himself in that dispute. The drawing out of the strike that he was urging the workers to sustain was exhausting their resources and their resolve. To encourage them to continue, Gandhi decided to subject himself to the same threat of starvation that the strike was imposing upon them; he could not demand of the striking workers more than he would demand of himself. And so he began a fast on March 15, 1918, that would continue until the workers received the wage they were demanding of the mill owners.

Unlike later fasts, this event did not occasion wide public awareness or concern. Nor was Gandhi himself totally comfortable about the coercive elements of his action. But the mill owners were moved by this dramatic placing of himself on the line; after 3 days, they agreed to terms that accepted the workers' demand for a day and the mill owners' offer for a day before subjecting the dispute to arbitration for a long-term settlement. It was a compromised outcome in which all parties could feel some gain. More important, it thrust Gandhi into the decisive mediating role by not allowing the workers to abandon their commitment to improve their lot. He was teaching them, by example, to become empowered by their own inner strength.

In 1932, Gandhi began a series of fasts based on his concern for the plight of the "untouchable" communities in India. His initial protest was against the attempt on the part of the British government to set up separate untouchable electorates in a provisional government in British India, a move that was supported by Dr. Ambedkar and other leaders of the untouchable communities. Gandhi's objection was that giving those groups separate political identity removed from the Hindu community as a whole the imperative to reform itself by eliminating the scourge of discrimination and oppression based on caste. Dr. Ambedkar saw it, however, as an attempt to keep untouchables under oppression. But Gandhi was adamant and, on September 20, he began a fast to raise Hindu consciousness and alter the British proposal. Resolutions against discrimination and intense discussions with the untouchable's leaders immediately ensued. Five days later, a compromise pact was achieved and sent to London, where it was accepted by the prime minister. Thus, by his fasting, Gandhi made a significant impact, for the first time, on British policy in India. And, as fate would have it, it happened while he was imprisoned in Yeravda Prison, where he had been detained since January of that year under a century-old regulation that allowed the government to hold him without sentence or trial.

During the spring of 1933, Gandhi fasted again on behalf of the untouchable communities, not to achieve a specific political objective but as an act of purification. He described it as "an uninterrupted twenty-one days' prayer."

Gandhi fasted twice during the final year of his life, in Calcutta from September 1 to 5, 1947, and in New Delhi beginning on January 13, 1948. In both instances, he was responding to the communal rioting between Hindus and Muslims following the partition of British India and the independence of India and Pakistan on August 15, 1947. By this time, as Gandhi entered his 78th year, people throughout the subcontinent were caught up in daily reports on the state of his health during the fasts. And they were stirred to meet his expectations of amity between the two new countries and among the religious communities that resided in both. In January, Gandhi specifically demanded as a condition of ending his fast the reparation to Pakistan of its share of British India's assets retained by the Indian government. When that was done, the Pakistani foreign minister, before the United Nations Security Council, directly attributed to Gandhi's fast a "new and tremendous wave of feeling and desire for friendship between the two Dominions."

Through the development of his leadership style, by creating symbolic acts of freedom and by fasting, Gandhi was able to command enormous authority among the people—without the benefit of any political office. During his many years of leadership of the independence movement, he held only one elective office—as president of the Indian National Congress in 1925. He held this post for only a year. (He stepped down to give place to Sarojini Naidu, the first woman to be elected to that office.) Being out of political office seemed to increase the impact of his singular, moral basis for authority. It was even more commanding when he took moral positions in direct confrontation with the institutional authority structures of this time. He spent 2,049 of his politically most active days, more than 5½ years, in jail.

Because of this leadership role in the independence movement, which, as in South Africa, was thoroughly shaped by his character and his commitment to nonviolence, Gandhi is recognized as the "Father of the Republic of India."

Any sense of achievement that Gandhi might have felt because of India's achieving independence in 1947 was negated by the scourge of communal rioting and bloodshed that swept across the subcontinent as the specter of partition of British India into two separate countries loomed. As the time of independence approached, Gandhi did not go to the capital to see the reins of power passed. Rather, he walked from village to village in the Noakhali district of East Bengal, seeking to quench the flames of violence that scorched the land. Gandhi himself was shaken, doubting his effectiveness in bringing the message of nonviolence to the people. Lord Mountbatten, who was in New Delhi as the governor general of the newly independent India, described Gandhi's effectiveness in a very different way: "In the Punjab we have 55,000 soldiers and large scale rioting is on our hands. In Bengal our forces consist of one man, and there is no rioting."

GANDHI'S TRUTH

Gandhi remained convinced that Muslims and Hindus could live at peace together in a single, secular nation. For him, truth was not the exclusive possession of any religious community but, rather, what revealed the transcendent unity of all people.

This conviction was to cost him his life. A young Hindu, passionately afraid that Gandhi was threatening Hinduism by being too accommodating to Muslims, assassinated him at his evening prayer meeting on January 30, 1948.

That evening, Jawaharlal Nehru, Gandhi's long-time friend and protégé, and the prime minister of the newly formed government of India, announced his death over the radio:

> Our beloved leader, Bapu, as we call him, the father of our nation is no more . . . The light has gone out, I said, and yet I was wrong. For the light that shone in this country was no ordinary light. The light that has illumined this country for these many years will illumine this country for many more years . . . and the world will see it and it will give solace to innumerable hearts.

Coming from a remote corner of India, through an improbable series of events that included more than 20 years in South Africa and more than 5½ years in prison, without ever holding any official position of state, Mahatma Gandhi rose to become the conscience of an empire and the father of a new nation.

In leading the vastly diverse peoples of India to their independence through the early years of the twentieth century, Mahatma Gandhi learned that political power is normally based on oppression and the use of force; such power leads only to bondage, violence, and suffering. It became his conviction that political freedom cannot be achieved by force—it can be realized only in discovering within ourselves a more profound and demanding quality of human identity and relationship, a quality that is characterized by nonviolence. Only when we become genuinely nonviolent in ourselves and in our relationships with others, he believed, can we become truly ourselves. Nations also must become genuinely nonviolent. Then they, too, will discover their identity as a people that is inclusive of all who live within their borders. Only then can we begin to think about achieving peace among nations.

Eric Ericson, in his perceptive biography called *Gandhi's Truth*, described this insight as a profound source of hope for the survival of the human race on Earth:

To have faced mankind with nonviolence as the alternative to [such policing activities as the British massacre in Amritsar] marks the Mahatma's deed in 1919. In a period when proud statesmen could speak of a "war to end war;" when the super policemen of Versailles could bathe in the glory of a peace that would make "the world safe for democracy"; when the revolutionaries in Russia could entertain the belief that terror could initiate an eventual "withering away of the State"—during that same period, one man in India confronted the world with the strong suggestion that a new political instrument, endowed with a new kind of religious fervor, may yet provide [humanity] with a choice.

India Map

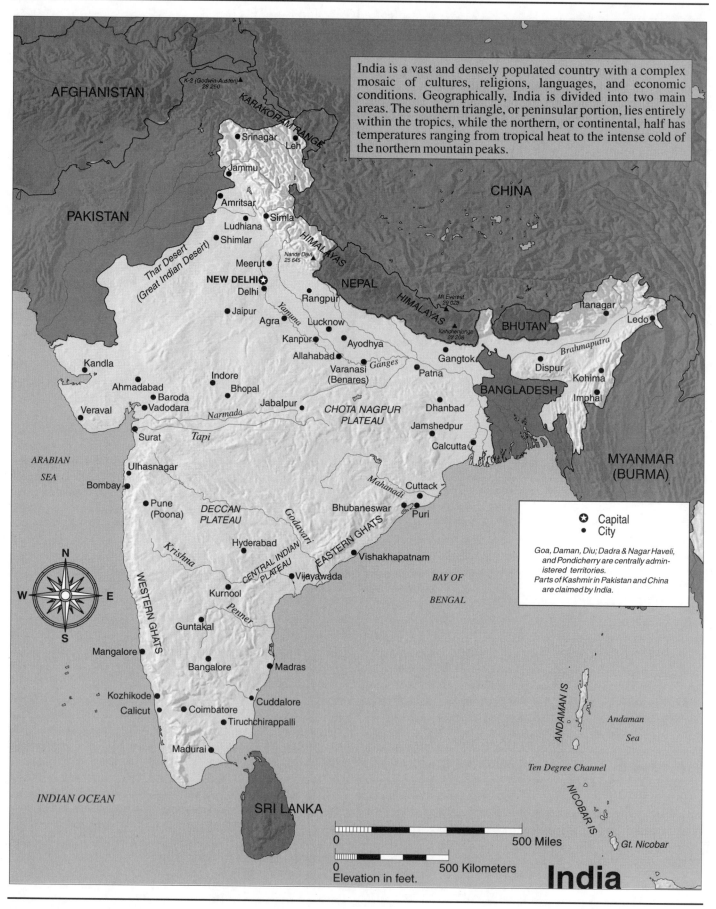

India is a vast and densely populated country with a complex mosaic of cultures, religions, languages, and economic conditions. Geographically, India is divided into two main areas. The southern triangle, or peninsular portion, lies entirely within the tropics, while the northern, or continental, half has temperatures ranging from tropical heat to the intense cold of the northern mountain peaks.

AFGHANISTAN

K-2 (Godwin-Austen)▲
28,250

KARAKORAM RANGE

• Srinagar
• Leh

Jammu

CHINA

PAKISTAN

• Amritsar

• Ludhiana
Simla

• Shimlar

Meerut

Thar Desert
(Great Indian Desert)

NEW DELHI ✪
Delhi

HIMALAYAS

Nanda Devi
25,645 ▲

NEPAL

Mt Everest
29,028 ▲

HIMALAYAS

Kanchenjunga
28,208 ▲

BHUTAN

Itanagar
Ledo

• Rangpur

• Jaipur

Agra

Yamuna

Lucknow

Kanpur
• Ayodhya

Allahabad
Varanasi
(Benares)

Ganges

Gangtok

Brahmaputra

Dispur

Kohima

Patna

BANGLADESH

Imphal

Kandla

Ahmadabad
• Baroda
• Vadodara

Indore

Bhopal

Jabalpur

Narmada

CHOTA NAGPUR
PLATEAU

Dhanbad

Jamshedpur

Veraval

Surat

Tapi

ARABIAN
SEA

Ulhasnagar

Calcutta

MYANMAR
(BURMA)

Bombay

• Pune
(Poona)

DECCAN
PLATEAU

Godavari

Mahanadi

Cuttack

Bhubaneswar
Puri

Hyderabad

Krishna

CENTRAL INDIAN
PLATEAU

EASTERN GHATS

Vijayawada

Vishakhapatnam

BAY OF
BENGAL

WESTERN GHATS

Kurnool

Penner

Guntakal

✪ Capital
• City

Goa, Daman, Diu; Dadra & Nagar Haveli,
and Pondicherry are centrally administered territories.
Parts of Kashmir in Pakistan and China
are claimed by India.

Mangalore

Bangalore

Madras

N
W E
S

Kozhikode
Calicut

Coimbatore
Tiruchchirappalli

Cuddalore

ANDAMAN IS

Andaman
Sea

Madurai

Ten Degree Channel

INDIAN OCEAN

SRI LANKA

NICOBAR IS

Gt. Nicobar

0   500 Miles

0   500 Kilometers
Elevation in feet.

India

36

India (Republic of India)

GEOGRAPHY
Area in Square Miles (Kilometers):
1,269,010 (3,287,590) (about one third
the size of the United States)
Capital (Population): New Delhi
(8,300,000)
Environmental Concerns: soil erosion;
deforestation; overgrazing;
desertification; air and water pollution;
lack of potable water; overpopulation
straining natural resources
Geographical Features: upland plain
(Deccan Plateau) in south; flat to rolling
plain along the Ganges; deserts in West;
Himalaya Mountains in north
Climate: varies from tropical monsoon in
the south to temperate in north to arctic in
Himalayas

PEOPLE

Population
Total: 966,800,000
Annual Growth Rate: 1.72%
Rural/Urban Population Ratio: 72/28
Major Languages: Hindi; English; Bengali;
Telugu; Marathi; Tamil; Urdu; others; 24
languages each spoken by 1 million or
more persons; numerous other languages
and dialects
Ethnic Makeup: 72% Indo-Aryan groups;
25% Dravidian; 3% Mongoloid and others
Religions: 80% Hindu; 14% Muslim; 2%
Christian; 2% Sikh; 2% Buddhist, Jain,
and others

Health
Life Expectancy at Birth: 62 years (male);
63 years (female)
Infant Mortality Rate (Ratio): 65.5/1,000
Physicians Available (Ratio): 1/2,173

Education
Adult Literacy Rate: 52%
Compulsory (Ages): theoretically
compulsory in 23 states to age 14

COMMUNICATION
Telephones: 1 per 78 people
Daily Newspaper Circulation: 21 per 1,000
people
Televisions: 1 per 25 people

TRANSPORTATION
Highways in Miles (Kilometers): 1,205,760
(2,009,600)
Railroads in Miles (Kilometers): 37,477
(62,462)
Usable Airfields: 290
Motor Vehicles in Use: 6,550,000

GOVERNMENT
Type: federal republic
Independence Date: August 15, 1947
Head of State/Government: President K. R.
Narayanan; Prime Minister Atal Behari
Vajpayee

Political Parties: Congress Party; Bharatiya
Janata Party; Bahujan Samaj Party;
Communist Party of India/Marxist;
Janata Dal Party; Samajwadi Party;
All-India Forward Bloc; United Front;
many regional parties
Suffrage: universal at 18

MILITARY
Military Expenditures (% of GDP): 2.7%
Current Disputes: communal unrest;
militant nationalist movements; claims to
Kashmir with Pakistan; border disputes
with China; refugee repatriation and
water-sharing disputes with Bangladesh

ECONOMY
Currency ($ U.S. Equivalent): 36.15 rupees
= $1 (Oct. '97); Rs 42.31 = $1 (Oct. '98)
Per Capita Income/GDP: $1,600/$1.538
trillion
GDP Growth Rate: 6.9% (1993–97) (With
the economic crisis in Asia, growth rates
are declining, less so in South Asia than
in the rest of Asia; UN Survey estimates
4.6% [1998–99] and 5.5% in 1999–2000.)
Inflation Rate: 8.5%
Labor Force: 370,000,000
Natural Resources: coal; iron ore;
manganese; mica; bauxite; titanium ore;
chromite; natural gas; diamonds;
petroleum; limestone
Agriculture: rice; wheat; oilseed; cotton;

jute; tea; sugarcane; potatoes; livestock;
fish
Industry: electronics; textiles; chemicals;
food processing; steel; machinery;
transportation equipment; cement;
mining; petroleum
Exports: $30.5 billion (primary partners
United States, Japan, Germany)
Imports: $34.5 billion (primary partners
United States, Germany, Saudi Arabia)

http://www.wcmc.org.uk/igcmc/main.
html#APP
http://www.odci.gov/cia/publications/
factbook/country-frame.html
http://www.economictimes.com
http://www.economictimes.com/
today/pagepoli.htm
http://www.indiacurrentaffairs.com
http://www.indiaserver.com/
thehindu/thehindu.html
http://www.newsindia-times.com/
http://www.gorp.com/gorp/location/
asia/india/np_into.htm
http://www.ubcnet.or.jp/jin/ind_gen.
html
http://www.indnet.org
http://www.123india.com
http://southasia.net/India/

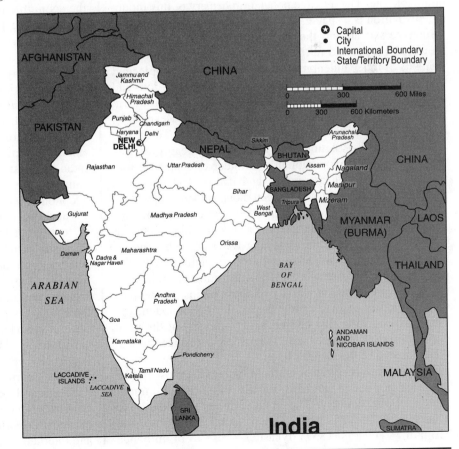

India

INDIA

Of all the countries of South Asia, India is the largest. It is also the land of greatest contrasts, in both topography and people. It is the only country that extends through all the subcontinent's geographical regions, from the frigid snowy peaks of the Himalayas, more than 25,000 feet high, down to the hot tropical beaches of the Malabar Coast on the Laccadive Sea.

India is a very crowded country and is getting more so every day. Only about one third the size of the United States, India has 3½ times as many people. The nearly 967 million people who live there represent about one sixth of the entire population of the world, and their number is increasing at a rate of 1.72 percent per year. The country is also phenomenally diverse—divided by languages, religions, and cultures, by cities and villages, by extremes of poverty and wealth, India is a land of many contrasts.

India reaches farthest to the north among the high peaks of the Karakuram Range in the western Himalayan Mountains, beyond the glacial plateau of Ladakh. There, west of Tibet, India shares a (contested) border with China. Its boundary then extends east along the high ridge of the Himalayas, skirting the mountainous kingdoms of Nepal and Bhutan to the hill country of the northeast frontier, where it again meets the southern border of China.

Because of the high altitude and the unrelenting arctic cold of the barren glaciers coursing the steep, southern slopes of the Himalayas, much of this northern border area of India is uninhabitable. The average population density of this mountainous region is a sparse 70 people per square mile.

Interspersed among the high peaks and the foothills are protected gorges and fertile valleys that sustain isolated settlements of independent mountain peoples. Most people tend flocks of sheep, yak, and goats or work the tea plantations and orchards that cover the lower hills. In other seasons, they form small bands of traders and bearers and make their weary treks through the snow-clad passes over the divide into Tibet. The extreme height, isolation, and breathtaking beauty of this region have found expression in a multitude of distinctive folk traditions of colorful art, music, and dance. And numerous Buddhist monasteries dot the rugged mountain landscape.

This remote Himalayan region is the source of a great river system: the Jumna–Ganges. These rivers provide an uneven but unbroken flow of life-sustaining water down the mountain valleys and through the great northern plains that are the breadbasket of northern India. The cultivation of grains and rice is the predominant activity on these plains, by peoples who live closer and closer together as this region extends to the east toward the Bay of Bengal. The density of the rural population rises to more than 2,000 people per square mile in the delta area of the Ganges River.

The great central plain of northern India is the most arable, the most populated, and historically the most prominent region of the country. The great empires of India—the Mauryan (320–125 B.C.), Gupta (A.D. 250–500), and Moghul (A.D. 1508–1857) dynasties—rose to prominence in this region. New Delhi, the capital of India, is located at the upper end of the central plains region, on the Jumna River. Although it became the capital of British India only in 1911, it is on the site where the Islamic sultans of the thirteenth century and the Moghul kings of the sixteenth century controlled the plains to the east and the Deccan Plateau to the south. Farther south on the Ganges are the even more ancient cities of Varanasi and Patna, known before the time of the Buddha in the sixth century B.C. as the cities of Kasi and Pataliputra, renowned for their commerce and learning. Much of India's wondrous classical tradition in art, literature, music, and philosophy evolved during the times of imperial dominance and patronage. Even today, the Gangetic plains retain their traditional importance in the political and cultural life of India.

Rising to the south of the Gangetic plains, in peninsular India, is a wide plateau flanked by two mountain ranges. These ranges, though smaller and warmer than the Himalayas, are also sparsely populated. They have long provided refuge for renegade princes, slopes for coffee and tea plantations, shelters for wild game, and homes for most of India's tribal population.

As in the central plain, most of the people in the Deccan live in small villages and are dependent upon agriculture for their subsistence. Because the only sources of water for farming are the seasonal, and unpredictable, annual rains brought by the southwest monsoon, this region has not had the economic base for political domination experienced in the Gangetic plain. Only when the great empires of the north have swept south has this region shared in a common history with the rest of the country. Otherwise, separated by geography and language, the Deccan has supported many local kingdoms and developed its own traditions and distinctive cultures.

Hyderabad, Ahmadabad, and Bangalore, three of India's larger and most industrial cities, are in this region. Ahmadabad, long known for its textile mills, is today capital of India's fastest-growing industrial state. Bangalore has become the center of the nation's high-technology industries—telephones, jet engines, and computers.

The fourth region of India is the coastal plain, a narrow strip of low-lying, tropical land around the edge of the Indian Peninsula. During the rainy monsoon seasons, this plain is filled with luxuriant growth, especially along the southwest Malabar Coast. Its rich harvests of rice and fruits support the highest rural population density in the entire country—more than 4,000 people per square mile.

India's two largest urban centers, the port cities of Calcutta and Bombay (Mumbai), and Madras (Chennai), the fourth-largest city, are in this coastal region. All three of these cities were built during the expansion of European commerce in the sixteenth and seventeenth centuries. They became thriving hubs of commerce under British colonial rule. Today, they are the most important centers for banking, investment capital, and international trade for all India.

(United Nations)

The central plains are the most arable region of India and account for much of the country's grain production. This rice field produces a large quantity of grain, which is harvested by traditional labor-intensive methods.

Although India's most important cities are spread throughout the different regions, except in the Himalayas, most of the country's people do not live in cities or even towns. About three quarters live in small, agricultural villages. Most people are tied to the countryside, in geographic environments that are strikingly different in terrain, temperatures, rainfall, food production, and population densities.

THE SOCIETY

The differences among the geographic regions of India and between urban and rural life within these regions are not the only sources of contrast in this diverse country. Even within a single region, people may be profoundly divided in many other ways—by language, by religion, and by complex social groupings called castes. The differences in geography from region to region contribute to, but do not account for, the complex mingling of distinct languages and religions and communities that are found in such wide array throughout India today.

Language

A recent comprehensive ethnographic study, "Peoples of India," identified 324 distinct languages spoken in the country.

Among these are the major languages spoken in the northern plains region (Hindi is the most prevalent, but others spoken widely include Bengali, Punjabi, Bihari, and Urdu), which belong to the Indo-European family of languages. Other languages with Indo-European roots (Oriya, Marathi, and Gujarati) extend beyond this region into the northern parts of the Deccan and the coastal plain. The languages of the people of the southern part of peninsular India (Tamil, Telugu, Kanarese, and Malayalam) belong to a totally different family of languages, called Dravidian.

The Constitution of the Republic of India recognizes 18 different Indo-European and Dravidian languages in the country. This list does not include English, which is still the link language—the language of higher education, the professions, and national business and government in most parts of the nation. Nor does it include the many tongues spoken by the mountain and tribal peoples who live in the remote regions of north, east, and peninsular India. These languages belong to the very different families of languages that are spoken by Tibetans, Burmese (people of Myanmar), and even the Aboriginal peoples of Australia.

The people of India have long been separated into distinct language groups—or, looking at it in their terms, they share a unique identity with those who have the same mother tongue.

These language groups are predominant in particular parts of the country, a native place toward which those language speakers have a sense of social roots, even when they have traveled far afield. The government of India recognized the importance of this language identity when, soon after the country's independence of Britain, it established the boundaries of new states. The old British colonial province of Bombay, for example, was divided in 1956 into the states of Maharashtra and Gujurat. A political boundary was then set between those who speak predominantly the Marathi language and those for whom Gujurati is the mother tongue.

The political divisions in these instances were based on language, and not the other way around, for each individual's identification with a particular language is through the family into which one is born—by one's mother, not by one's location. Adjusting the boundaries of a new state to coincide with the predominance of a language group did not change the linguistic identities of those who speak other mother tongues in that state. These other-language speakers live as minority groups, many times in enclaves in order to preserve the distinctive ethos of their linguistic identities. These different linguistic groups are clearly identifiable in the cities, for example, as Bengalis and Tamils in Bombay, as Malayalis and Telugus in Madras.

India is a nation of linguistic minorities. No single language is spoken or understood by more than 40 percent of the people. There have been efforts since India became independent to establish Hindi, the most prevalent language among the states in the north-central region of India, as the national language. The states of the other regions of the country have resisted this status for any language other than their own. Peoples of other mother tongues cannot easily accept having their political identities defined, nor their primary education taught, in any other language than their own.

Religion

India is divided also by religions, but in a different pattern and in a slightly different way. Unlike the Hindi language, which is nationally a minority language in spite of its predominance in several of the northern states, the Hindu religion is predominant throughout the country. Hindus comprise some 80 percent of the total population and command a majority in almost every region. Islam is the largest of the minority religions. There are well over 100 million Muslims in India—close to the total populations of the neighboring Islamic countries, Pakistan and Bangladesh. But Muslims nevertheless are only about 14 percent of the total population of India. All other religious minorities—Sikhs, Jains, Christians, Buddhists, and others—together add up to only 6 percent.

The minority religious groups tend, however, to concentrate in specific regions of the country in large enough numbers to be politically significant. Muslims are an overwhelming majority in Kashmir and are a sizable minority in the north-central state of Uttar Pradesh. Sikhs comprise approximately 62 percent of the population in Punjab. And the Jains are in sufficient

numbers in Gujarat, and Christians along the southwest Malabar Coast, to have an impact on the cultural, educational, and political dimensions of life in those areas.

India is a land of so many contrasts that one wonders how it holds together. From the day of its independence as a nation in 1947, India has been challenged to find a political identity as a multiethnic, multireligious, multilanguage country.

Economic Disparity

A four-year-old girl with her legs crippled by polio drags herself to the nearest open drain in Bombay's shantytown Dharavi. She cups the foul-smelling water and pours it on her body. That is her daily morning bath, a ritual repeated by children in thousands of slums across the country.

Some 15 miles south of Dharavi in the expensive neighborhood of Altamount Road, the six-year-old son of a wealthy businessman has a massive birthday bash on the manicured lawns of his father's palatial villa as similar rich children from the neighborhood ride around on camels and ponies supplied for the occasion.

What bonds these two children are the extremes of life that India's 350 million children face every day. By all accounts, the children in the condition that the Dharavi girl finds herself grossly outnumber those who can afford the lifestyle of the boy on Altamount Road.

—Neelish Misra, in *India Abroad* (November 1, 1996)

Another challenge in modern India is the extent and the visibility, especially in the urban areas, of poverty. It is estimated that about 20 percent of India's urban population live in slums. And in Calcutta, India's largest city, it is estimated that, beyond the slum dwellers, some 700,000 people sleep on the streets each night.

The scope of India's urban poverty is hard to imagine. V. S. Naipaul wrote this vivid description of his visit to the Bombay slum called Dharavi:

Back-to-back and side-to-side shacks and shelters, a general impression of blackness and greyness and mud, narrow ragged lanes curving out of view; then a side of the main road dug up; then black mud, with men and women and children defecating on the edge of a black lake, swamp and sewage, with hellish oily iridescence.... [It] was also an industrial area of sorts, with many unauthorized businesses, leather works and chemical works among them which wouldn't have been permitted in a better regulated city area.... Petrol and kerosene fumes added to the stench. In this stench, many bare-armed people were at work: gathering or unpacking cloth waste and cardboard waste, working in grey-white dust that banked up on the ground like snow and stifled the sounds of hands and feet, working beside the road itself or in small shanties: large scale rag-picking.

—From *India, A Million Mutinies Now*

In all India, about 30 percent of the population live in poverty. But because the village economy is based upon the production and distribution of food in exchange for craft services or labor—the *jajmani* system—low income does not necessarily mean starvation. As a result of the so-called Green Revolution, which led to the introduction of new, hybrid strains of rice and wheat in the late 1950s, there has been an immense increase in grain production. Since 1970, India has imported these grains only once, in 1987, when monsoon rain failure diminished the yields enough to create a shortage. Other times of famine have occurred in different parts of the country, and many millions of people in both cities and villages live on the edge of subsistence. Without some reduction in India's birth rate and an increase in urban planning and control, it is hard to imagine how the nation's considerable economic progress will be able to reduce the anguish of poverty and environmental decay for an increasing number of its population. All the gains now have to be distributed among too many additional needy people.

Remarkable in this context has been the emergence during the past decade of a significant middle class, of households that are earning more than is necessary for simple survival—food, clothing, and housing—and have money to spend. A recent survey by the National Council for Applied Economic Research identified nearly 300 million people, almost one third of the total population in India, with household incomes above the amount (then calculated at $1,000) needed to live comfortably. This segment of the population, numbering more than the entire population of the United States, has for the most part risen out of the throes of subsistence and is increasing the level of household incomes at impressive rates. As eager consumers, they are creating a vast new market, new opportunities, and new objectives for a population long characterized as austere and protected by very restrictive economic planning and import controls. National economic policy began to change in 1985, before the collapse of the socialist economy in the Soviet Union, so that, today, India is already well on its way to being a consumer-driven economy. Change is in the air.

A COUNTRY OF CHANGE
Change in India is expected. It has to do with the dramatic, annual anticipation of the monsoon, when flood-producing

(United Nations/Jongen)

Poverty is very pronounced in India's urban areas. An estimated 20 percent of India's urban population live in slums. These squatters are preparing a meal in the only home they have, the streets.

torrents of rain end an intolerably hot, dry season each spring; with the unanticipated terror of disease and sudden death; with the rise and fall of fortunes and of transient petty kingdoms and even mighty empires. The people have a conscious heritage of many thousands of years.

The word for "life" in India is *samsara,* which literally means "flowing," like a river. Sometimes, like a river in flood, change can be traumatic. Such was the partition of India and Pakistan at the time of their independence in 1947, when literally millions of people were displaced from their homes and close to 1 million lost their lives in senseless, random massacres. For the most part, life in India flows in a single direction, never at quite the same pace, but usually within its banks. It is never quite predictable, but there are sufficient patterns to give a sense that, in India, even in times of great change, everything is very much the same.

Another significant change in India today—comparable to the emergence of a middle class—is the growth of the urban population. This increase is due as much to in-migration from the villages by the lure of urban opportunity as to the high birth rate and increasing life expectancy of the urban population itself. With this dramatic increase, the pressure on urban lands and services is staggering, the ability to cope near—many people would say past—its limit.

This limit was certainly passed by an outburst of urban rioting, with widespread destruction and bloodshed, that erupted in Bombay for 10 days in January 1993. It began in a climate of communal tension between Hindus and Muslims throughout the nation following the destruction of a Muslim mosque in Ayodhya, in north-central India, on December 6, 1992. Mobs, roused to violence, swept through the slum areas of the city, burning, stabbing, and looting. According to Human Rights Watch, more than 1,000 people were killed and thousands wounded; many more fled, homeless, to other parts of the country in the wake of this devastation. While revealing tensions of national scope, the Bombay riots also expressed the latent social unrest and uncontrollable violence that lurk amid the increasing economic hardship and oppression that afflict such a fast-growing urban population.

The future of urban development in India is extremely challenging. The average projected increase in population of India's five largest cities, from the year 1980 to 2000, was more than 103 percent. At that rate, it was projected that, by the year 2001, India's *urban* population would number from 340 million to 350 million. India would then have the largest urban population in the world.

Yet, even with this staggering urban growth, India's cities would then hold only 35 percent of the total population of the country. Thus, India will be for the foreseeable future primarily a rural country, a nation of villages.

INDIA SINCE INDEPENDENCE
Another change of immense and far-reaching magnitude was India's achievement of independence in 1947. As a new nation, it had first to establish an independent, sovereign government, free of colonial domination. This task was done by the transition of the Indian National Congress—which had, since 1885, led the movement for India's freedom—to the majority political party in a Constituent Assembly that had been set up by the British Raj in 1935. At the time of independence, the Congress Party formed an interim government, with its leader, Jawarhalal Nehru, serving as prime minister.

The formal beginning of the Republic of India as a democratic, secular nation took place with the adoption of its Constitution in 1950. This Constitution incorporated many concepts from Western political theory. Its framers, under the leadership of Dr. B. R. Ambedkar, deliberately drew upon the American, French, and Irish Constitutions as viable models for a modern democratic republic. Its Preamble has a familiar sound: It is the responsibility of the Republic to ensure that all citizens enjoy

> JUSTICE, social, economic, and political; LIBERTY of thought, expression, belief, faith and worship; EQUALITY of status and opportunity; and . . . FRATERNITY assuring the dignity of the individual and the unity of the nation.

And it granted to every adult in the country, male and female, the right to vote.

The Constitution of India separates the powers of the government into three branches: legislative, executive, and judicial. This pattern is familiar to Americans, though the relationship between the legislative and executive branches follows the parliamentary model of Great Britain. The initiative and responsibility for executive leadership rests in Parliament, in the office of the prime minister, not with the executive-branch president. Neither of these offices is gained by direct popular vote.

The president is elected to a 5-year term by a majority of all the elected and appointed representatives to the two houses of the national Legislature: the *Lok Sabha* (House of the People), with 545 members, and the *Rajya Sabha* (Council of States), with 12 members appointed by the president and 238 members elected proportionately by the legislative assemblies in each of the country's 31 states. The role of the president is so severely limited by the Constitution that he or she rarely has an opportunity to determine national policy. But the president can, upon the advice of the prime minister, declare a state of emergency and suspend both national and state governments, an executive tool that has been used far more frequently than the framers of the Constitution envisioned. In general, the president serves more as a symbolic head of state.

The prime minister, as the one primarily responsible to lead the country, is officially invited by the president to form a ministry and conduct the business of government. But he or she must enjoy the support of a majority of the Lok Sabha in order to remain in power. The president therefore looks first to the leadership of the majority party to nominate its candidate for this position. In most national elections since 1952, the Congress Party has either won a majority of the seats in the Lok Sabha or

(United Nations)

In 1950, India adopted its Constitution, thus formally establishing itself as a democratic, secular nation. The first prime minister of this new country was Jawarhalal Nehru (above left), the head of the Congress Party.

has been able to hold together a ruling coalition of parties. The selection of the prime minister has been made largely within the ranks of this party. In recent elections, with the Congress Party no longer winning a majority of seats in the Legislature, the process has become more complex and tenuous.

In the spring of 1991, the Congress Party won the most number of seats, but it fell 37 short of a majority. President Ramaswamy Iyer Venkataraman still felt that the leader of the Congress Party, P. V. Narasimha Rao, even though he did not at that time hold a seat in the Lok Sabha, was the person best able to serve as prime minister. The president invited him to form the government. Narasimha Rao was able to win the support of the Lok Sabha and subsequently won a seat in a November by-election. In further by-elections in February 1992, the Congress Party won enough seats to command a majority in Parliament, which it held for 5 years. Because of Narasimha Rao's effective leadership and growing support, President Venkataraman's confidence in him to become an effective prime minister was well placed.

In the spring elections of 1996, the Bharatiya Janata Party (BJP) and its allies won 186 seats, mostly from the north-central plains states, with Narasimha Rao's Congress Party coming in a distant second, with 136 seats. President Shankar Dayal Sharma initially invited Atal Behari Vajpayee, leader of the BJP, to become prime minister. But he was not able to garner the support of the 269-seat majority needed to gain the confidence of the Lok Sabha. He resigned even before the newly elected Legislature convened. President Sharma then invited the chief minister of the state of Karnataka, Deve Gowda, to form a government. Gowda was the leader of one of six political parties that formed the National Left Front coalition to enter the 1996 elections, which together won 112 seats—the third-largest number in the Legislature. As prime minister designee, even though not elected to a Lok Sabha seat, Gowda was able to bring together 13 parties into a United Front coalition, and, with the support of the Congress Party, to win the support of a majority of the house. In November, he was elected to a seat in the Rajya Sabha, or Upper House, by the Karnataka State Legislature, in order to become a sitting member of Parliament.

Deve Gowda's United Front coalition government was not expected to survive very long because of the tenuous alliance among so many parties and its dependency upon the support of the Congress Party. Yet he managed to steer a sufficiently inclusive and moderate course in Parliament to hold the reins of power for almost a year.

In the spring elections of 1998, the BJP won the most legislative seats, as it had in 1996. But its 176-seat victory fell short of commanding a majority. This time, however, Vajpayee was able to bring together a coalition of 19 parties to form a government, and he has managed to hold together this coalition together enough to remain in office as prime minister.

Since the Nehru era, when that man's charismatic leadership and commitment to democracy brought together many disparate interests into the Congress Party, many of the country's social and regional factions have become more politically savvy while gaining representation in the national Legislature. The Lok Sabha has thus become more representative of the diversity of the country, but its institutional authority as a national Legislature has diminished, with regional, ethnic, and special interests more dominant. As a result, only those parties with the ability to keep these groups to a common political agenda are able to form a stable majority. Maintaining such coalitions tends to have a moderating impact on what can be accomplished in the Legislature. The BJP's move early in its term to test the country's nuclear capability was, among other things, a dramatic attempt to establish a national awareness and agenda for its parliamentary leadership role. An event of such international consequences reveals the extent to which the party felt it had to go to gain legislative initiative. Yet it was the only plank on its election platform to which its coalition partners could readily agree.

(United Nations)

In India, religious identity often takes precedence over the idea of belonging to a nation. Many religious sects demand political recognition. In 1984, the Indian Army stormed the Golden Temple in Amritsar (pictured above), the sacred shrine of the Sikh community. This action was in response to Sikhs' demand for the establishment of an independent state in Punjab. In retaliation, a group of Sikhs assassinated Prime Minister Indira Gandhi.

Should the prime minister lose a vote of confidence (a motion attached to almost all major legislation), he or she would be forced to resign. Because the ruling Congress Party held a majority in the Lok Sabha from the first national election in 1952 until 1977, there were no votes of no-confidence during those years. In 1979, when in-fighting in the then-ruling Janata Party eroded Prime Minister Moraji Desai's support, and again in 1990, when Prime Minister V. P. Singh committed himself to an unpopular affirmative-action policy, votes of no-confidence carried, and the prime ministers were forced to resign.

In such circumstances, if the president feels that someone else can gain the support of a majority of the Lok Sabha, he or she may invite that person to form a government. If no one else is able to command such support, the president must then dissolve the Parliament and declare a new national election. In 1979, following Prime Minister Desai's defeat by a no-confidence vote, President Reddi invited Charan Singh to form a government. Charan Singh's inability to gain the necessary support led to national elections in 1980. Similarly, upon the resignation of Prime Minister V. P. Singh in 1990, Chandra Shekar was invited by President Venkataraman to serve. He managed to maintain a fragile coalition government for several months, largely with the support of the Congress Party. When it

floundered, the president dissolved the Lok Sabha and called for the 1991 elections.

When Deve Gowda was forced to resign in April 1997, frantic negotiations began among the United Front parties and the Congress Party to find a new prime minister in order to avoid the necessity for new national elections. They agreed to accept I. K. Gujral, who had been very successful as external affairs minister in the Gowda government, as the new leader of the United Front. With still tenuous Congress Party support, the United Front was able to continue in power. Seven months later the Congress Party withdrew its support for Gujral's government. With no further compromises in the offing, President Sharma dissolved Parliament and called for new elections in March 1998.

According to the Constitution, an election must be held at least every 5 years. If none is called before that time, Parliament is automatically dissolved. All 545 members of the Lok Sabha must then stand for reelection in an electoral district in each of the states of India. Five uninterrupted years in office was the rule during the early years of the republic, when the government was firmly under the control of Prime Minister Jawarhalal Nehru.

The prime minister may ask the president to dissolve Parliament at any time within the 5-year interval. Indira Gandhi, Nehru's daughter, who succeeded Lal Bahadur Shastri as prime minister in 1965, made this request in 1970, and the next national election—the nation's fifth—took place a year earlier than required. Because many thought that Indira Gandhi's popularity was beginning to wane at that time, the large victory of the Congress Party in that election proved the wisdom of her choice.

Democracy in a parliamentary form of government, as implemented by the Constitution of the Republic of India in 1950, has worked well. The creation of political parties and the ballot box have been effective in establishing the public will and determining the direction of policy in the Lok Sabha on the national level, even for some of the most secessionist-minded groups in the country. The ballot box has also worked to determine the membership and agendas of the similarly structured, though less orderly, legislative assemblies on the state level and municipal governments in the cities.

CHALLENGES TO DEMOCRACY

A great challenge to the democratic system of government in India came in 1975, when Prime Minister Indira Gandhi, in order to protect herself from a legal challenge to her office, had an "Emergency" proclaimed by the president, under the President's Rule Provision in the Constitution. That act suspended for 2 years the normal function of government and the civil liberties protected by the Constitution. National elections were postponed, opposition leaders were put in prison, and press censorship was imposed. When national elections were reinstated in 1977, the people of India, the electorate, voted her and the Congress Party out of office. They were not going to have their political freedom eroded. And theirs was the final say.

A second great challenge, though of a different sort, came with the destruction of a Muslim mosque in the northern city of Ayodhya on December 6, 1992. Hindu nationalist forces—sanctioned, if not actually led, by the popularly elected state government—roused communal religious antagonism among Hindus and Muslims throughout India and in surrounding countries. The riots that followed led to great misgivings about the ability of the government to maintain order and protect its people from uncontrolled violence. It also raised questions, because of the communal tensions that were unleashed, about India's viability as a secular nation.

Both of these crises reveal the depth of the challenge that democracy in India, after half a century, still faces. Its future is not assured, for many different reasons. One basic problem is that democracy in India has been implemented in political structures—Constitution and Parliament—that are not indigenous to India but were instead imposed from the West. The effectiveness of these structures presupposes the existence of a nation as a unified sovereign entity, recognized and respected by the people. Indians' political awareness of themselves as a nation did not previously exist; the people have had to create for themselves a viable concept. And that challenge has not been easy.

In India, in contrast to the United States, there is no awareness of a total, inclusive community defined by a political event. In one sense, there are simply too many events, too much history in India to be affirmed. So many kingdoms and empires have been experienced so differently by so many different groups of people that they are not understood as shared. In addition, there are so many more immediate and compelling bases of their identities as communities of people. Thus, their existence as a nation, even since 1950, is more of an abstraction than an immediate reality.

The writer V. S. Naipaul, during his travels across India, rediscovered this obstacle to national identity among the peoples of this disparate land. His awareness of being an Indian, which was engendered among those of many different languages and religions who had migrated from India to Trinidad, where he grew up, was not shared at all by the people who lived in India itself:

When I got there I found [the idea of an Indian community] had no meaning in India. In the torrent of India, with its hundreds of millions, that continental idea was no comfort at all. People needed to hold on to smaller ideas of who and what they were; they found stability in the smaller groupings of region, clan, caste, family.

—From *India: A Million Mutinies Now*

The most pervasive of these smaller ideas of identity are not based on political groupings. They are, rather, linguistic, religious, and, as Naipaul suggests, social—such as caste, into which the people of India are grouped not by events, but by birth.

Language, because it was used to define the borders of states in India, has become the basis for regional political identity. It has also contributed to an awakening of political awareness. Being grouped together by language has identified other causes that various peoples share and can seek to achieve for their common good. But because there are so many languages, each predominant in a separate region of the country, and none commanding a majority in the country as a whole, language identity has not contributed to a sense of national identity. As in Canada and in Europe, differing languages have generated forces of disintegration rather than of unification.

Religious identity has also been a major factor in the unfolding of India's political experience since independence. The partition between India and Pakistan, at the very beginning, in 1947, was done on the basis of the majority religion on the district (county) level in those regions of the subcontinent administered by the British Raj. Those districts that were predominantly Muslim went to Pakistan; those predominantly Hindu were apportioned to India.

Eighty percent of India's people are Hindus, yet they are so divided among themselves that they do not think of themselves as a political bloc. Their predominance, however, is a source of great concern to those who find themselves a religious minority. These include Muslims, Sikhs, Parsis, Buddhists, Jains, Christians, and Jews. The partition between India and Pakistan was due in large part to just this anxiety among the Muslim community in British India. How could such a predominantly Hindu society, determined to meet its own objectives in a democracy, not discriminate against, if not actually oppress, people of other religions who are in a minority?

The response of the leaders of the Indian National Congress, which for more than 50 years worked constructively and diligently for the independence of India from British rule, was to define the Republic of India as a secular state. Their contention was that the government must recognize the presence and the integrity of the many different religious communities in the nation. It must not promote and interfere with them. In the words of India's Constitution, "all persons are equally entitled to freedom of conscience and the right freely to profess, practice, and propagate religion." The separation between the secular objectives of the nation-state and the religious identity of its peoples has not always been clear, revealing again that religious identity has taken precedence over the more abstract idea of "belonging" to a nation.

Political secularism is being attacked today in two very significant ways. First is the outright demand by a militant wing of the Sikh community for an independent state, called Khalistan, to be established in the current state of Punjab, in northwest India. A number of events have contributed to the vehemence and intensity of this demand, which was expressed for a time in almost daily random terrorist attacks and kidnappings, which led to the suspension in Punjab of the elections that took place in most of the rest of India in the spring of 1991. Most provocative was the storming of the Golden Temple in Amritsar, the sacred shrine of the entire Sikh community, by the Indian Army in 1984. This attack, called Operation Blue Star, was meant to rout out of the temple's protective walls a militant Sikh separatist leader who had sought sanctuary there. The outrage felt by the Sikh community over this assault was expressed in the assassination later that same year of Prime Minister Indira Gandhi by two members of her bodyguard who were Sikhs. Her death in turn stirred reprisals against the Sikh community, leading to the killing of some 3,000 in riots across the north of India. Political order was restored in Punjab under the leadership of a more moderate Sikh, Prakash Singh Badal, who was appointed chief minister of the state after the delayed elections were held in February 1992. His assassination in August 1995 reveals that tension still exists between the Sikhs and surrounding Hindu communities. Yet stable government continues, and both the 1996 and 1998 elections were conducted with a remarkable reduction of violence in the region.

Indira Gandhi's response to Sikh militancy had been secular in intent: to hold India, with all its religious differences, together as one nation. But the participants in this confrontation were defined by their religions rather than their political identities. The drastic consequences were the result of their greater allegiance to their religious communities than to the political state.

Less clear in the subservience of political identity to religion has been the revival of Hindu nationalist sentiment in the country. The man who assassinated Mahatma Gandhi in 1948 did so in the name of Hindu nationalism—he felt that Gandhi's attempts to accommodate the Muslim communities in an independent India were compromising his Hindu faith too much. By this action, he affirmed the greatest fears of those Muslims advocating an independent Pakistan: that they would not receive equal status as a religious minority in the new nation of India. As a consequence of Mahatma Gandhi's example and his death, the quest to achieve a truly secular nation took on great urgency during the early years of India's independence.

But as political awareness and participation have increased among India's peoples, their religious identities have also been stimulated. One impetus was a television extravaganza. Its impact, which is a direct result of the emergence of a middle class in India, reveals just how subtle and complex the manifestations of change in the modern world are. In 1987, a film producer, at the invitation of the national government, created a television series based on the *Ramayana,* a classical Indian epic. The original Sanskrit account of the ideal Indian prince, Rama, recognized by Hindus as an incarnation of the Supreme God Vishnu, was composed around 2,000 years ago. But the story is more popularly known and celebrated among the Hindi-speaking population in a translation of this epic done by a religious poet, Tulsidas, in the sixteenth century. The modern television serial, described as "a mixture of soap opera and national mythology," was broadcast in 104 half-

hour episodes by Doordarshan, the national television channel, on Sunday mornings. During its broadcast times, almost all India came to a halt. A viewership of more than 100 million people were glued to whatever television set (some 25 million of them) they could find. The serial was an immense success, both in telling the story and in spreading the virtues of television among millions of new viewers.

The intent of the government and the serial's producer had been to extol India's ancient, albeit Hindu, heritage as a way of encouraging a greater sense of national pride. The result was to stir religious sentiments of both Hindus and the minorities who had reason to fear the arousal of such passion. The television serial coincided with the rise of a new political party committed to Hindu nationalism, the Bharatiya Janata Party. In a country where many have risen to political prominence through the film industry, it is not difficult to ascribe the increasing popularity of this new party directly to the broadcast of *Ramayana.* Even more did the BJP gain from a sequel, the broadcast of India's other, older, and longer epic, the *Mahabharata,* as a television serial in 93 hour-long episodes from October 1988 to July 1990. This epic also extols the virtues of an ancient Hindu past. It includes the original recitation of the most revered text of contemporary Hinduism, *Bhagavad Gita* ("The Song of the Lord").

The Bharatiya Janata Party had won only two seats in Parliament in the elections of 1984. In 1989, its holdings jumped to 89. In the 1991 elections, they rose to 118 seats, second only to the Congress Party, which won 225 seats, briefly diminishing the Congress Party's hopes for a majority in the national Legislature, the Lok Sabha. Even more impressive, the BJP won a slim majority in the legislative assembly of India's largest state, Uttar Pradesh, long a Congress Party stronghold.

In this rise to political prominence, the Bharatiya Janata Party tied its fortunes directly to another incident that is also related to Rama, the hero of the *Ramayana,* and that also received extensive television-viewing attention, but this time as national news. The BJP leadership became actively involved in a campaign to build a temple to Rama on the site of his legendary birthplace, in the city of Ayodhya, in eastern Uttar Pradesh. Through a number of public demonstrations, including a chariot procession across northern India, it was able to rouse a large amount of public support for the building project and for the leadership itself as a political force. Such a mingling of religion and politics was effective, but potentially dangerous.

What made the building campaign particularly volatile was that the specific location for the proposed temple to Rama was on the site of the Babri Masjid, a mosque. This mosque was built in 1528, purportedly on the site of a temple that had been destroyed, for Babur, the first of the Islamic Moghul emperors who ruled in India from the early sixteenth century until 1857. Because the Muslim community is as eager as the Hindu community to preserve the vestiges of its glorious past in India, the project placed the BJP and its followers in direct conflict with the Indian Muslim minority. In hopes of working out a political compromise that would not stimulate further religious antagonism between Hindus and Muslims, Prime Minister Narasimha Rao placed the dispute over the ownership of this land in the hands of the Supreme Court of India.

The BJP, in control of the Uttar Pradesh government on the state level, became impatient with the maneuvering by the prime minister on the national level. The BJP thus supported a rally on December 6, 1992, at the Babri mosque/proposed Rama temple site in Ayodhya; its aim was to keep national attention on its objective to promote the interests of the Hindus and to urge approval to build the temple. A crowd of more than 700,000 people from across the country gathered for the rally in that city of some 70,000 residents. Even though the national government had assigned 15,000 troops there to maintain order, the situation got out of control, and a small group of enthusiasts scaled the Babri mosque and demolished it.

The response throughout the entire country was immediate and devastating. Dormant feelings of anger, fear, frustration, and hatred erupted into communal riots across the country. Hundreds of people were killed; vast numbers of shops and homes were destroyed, from Assam to Kashmir to Kerala. The violence quickly spread into neighboring Pakistan and Bangladesh, where Hindu temples and homes were destroyed in reprisal. A tinderbox of communal resentment based on religion had exploded.

Realizing its complicity in the far-reaching violence caused by the mosque's demolition, the BJP government of Uttar Pradesh resigned. Narasimha Rao, the prime minister of India, imprisoned the national leaders of the BJP and urged India's president to dismiss the governments in the three other states where the BJP held power: Madhya Pradesh, Rajasthan, and Himachal Pradesh. And, recognizing the challenge to his own government that this unrest and destruction created, Narasimha Rao called for the resignation of his entire cabinet.

There were few aspects of the democratic Republic of India that were not shaken by the Babri Masjid episode. The secular ambitions of the founders of the republic were severely challenged by the outburst of communal rioting that followed upon the demolition of the mosque and the increasing strength and impact of the BJP as a political party. These events suggested that the Hindu religious identity of the majority of the Indian people was continuing to define their national character more powerfully than the political institutions established by the Constitution in 1950. The dawn of *Ram Raj,* an idyllic age of government led by the power of God, was being proclaimed, and the specter of Hindu religious fundamentalism was on the rise.

In the 1996 elections, the BJP continued to gain popular support, winning 160 seats, 42 more than in the 1991 elections, to outstrip all the other parties. But its victories did not achieve a majority. In 1998, the BJP fared slightly better, winning 176 seats, and with allied parties a potential total of 264. The vote of confidence for the A. B. Vajpayee government held in March 1998 was a narrow victory of 274 to 261; this was achieved largely through the last-minute support of a regional party from the state of Andhra Pradesh that, during the previous term of the legislature, had been a major player in the United Front.

In order to assuage the fears of opposition groups and to gain majority support in the Lok Sabha, the leaders of the BJP claim to have tempered their extremist Hindu positions. *Hindutva* (Hindu-ness), they assert is a cultural, not a religious term. And its defining characteristics for them are significantly selective, to sound more like patriotism than symbols of transcendence. They are striving to build a national political party, not to establish a new religious cult.

The BJP's continuing rise to national prominence indicates its success in engaging people in the historical process of becoming a people with the political image of India as being exclusively a Hindu nation. Its success has been particularly strong among an emerging rural middle class throughout north India. This constituency will continue to have a significant voice in determining India's political future. Their support suggests, however, that the real power of the BJP may not be religious but, rather, the conservative forces of the privileged who dominate India's agrarian society.

Other factions in the political spectrum are also having a growing impact. The interests of minorities and the underprivileged received greater voice through the by-elections of 1993 and in the 1996 and 1998 general elections. Coalitions were formed among parties representing Muslims (14 percent of the nation's population) and Dalits (traditional untouchable communities; 16 percent of the people), especially in Uttar Pradesh, the country's largest state, where these two groups are the most numerous. Mayawati, leader of the Bahujan Samaj Party (BSP) and Mulayam Singh Yadav, of the Samajwadi Party (SP), have become particularly prominent, although they aligned themselves in opposition in the 1996 national elections—Mayawati with the Congress Party and Yadav with the United Front. After those elections, Mayawati entered into a coalition agreement with the Bharatiya Janata Party leadership in Uttar Pradesh and became the first woman Dalit to hold the office of chief minister of an Indian state. Political wrangling in the state assembly blunted the effectiveness of her Bahujan Samaj Party in the 1998 national elections. But the Samajwadi Party gained enough seats to become the second-largest delegation from Uttar Pradesh, limiting the BJP's dominance of the election in that state and preventing it from winning a majority in the national Legislature. Analysis of the election results suggests that, if the BSP and the SP had joined forces, they might even have routed the BJP in its greatest stronghold in India. The success of these parties in representing the "underclasses" reveals a growing awareness on the part of the disadvantaged communities of the political process of democracy and of how it can be used for their advantage.

(World Bank)

India is struggling to improve the quality of life for its people. A doctor visits this neighborhood regularly as a part of a local health service in Calcutta.

There are other, more long-term grounds for optimism that Hindu nationalist sentiment will not undermine democracy in India. The thrust of the BJP's assertion of quasi-religious symbols has been to increase its power within the constitutional structure of government—to receive more popular support for its political agenda, not to undermine it. This thrust has been divisive and has generated a great deal of animosity particularly against the Muslim community as ostensibly subversive to the national interests of India. But this opportunistic use of communal politics has been exposed by judicial review and has not won majority support on the national level. Even the political capital that the BJP had hoped to garner by the nuclear testing it initiated in May 1998 did not translate into gains in local elections for political offices and by-elections for state and national seats in June. The BJP and its allies won just 38 percent—18 of 48—state assembly seats in the June 3 elections. In four state-level bi-elections in November 1998, the Congress Party soundly defeated the BJP in Delhi and Rajasthan while retaining its leadership in Madhya Pradesh. The Congress Party, the BJP's only national rival, made the most impressive gains.

The BJP has been restrained both by the electorate in general and by its own ethnic and regional coalition partners, who are essential to its leadership because the BJP has not been able to win a national mandate on its own. Both of these constituencies affirm religious pluralism as a reality of their life together as an Indian people.

India's history is replete with religious strife. The communal outburst in Bombay in 1993 and the continuing terrorist acts of Sikh, Assamese, and Kashmiri militants and repressive counter-measures by the government form another gruesome chapter. But the more normal pattern is one of acceptance of a wide variety of forms of religious practice and expression,

even within Hinduism itself. Overwhelming to the outsider are the myriads of gods and goddesses who populate Hindu mythology. Hinduism can also be described as a collection of many different religious communities who all worship one God (or, as Mahatma Gandhi would say, one Truth) in very different ways. Writes Indian author Shashi Taroor:

It pains me to read in the American newspapers of "Hindu fundamentalism," when Hinduism is a religion without compulsory fundamentals. That devotees of this essentially tolerant faith are desecrating a place of worship and assaulting Muslims in its name is a source of both sorrow and shame. India has survived the Aryans, the Mughuls, the British; it has taken from each—language, art, food, learning—and outlasted them all. The Hinduism that I know understands that faith is a matter of hearts and minds, not bricks and stone.
—From *Indian Express* (January 20, 1993)

An example of India's religious acceptance is the Jewish community in Cochin. Jews have lived in that city on the Malabar Coast for many centuries, maintaining the distinctive practices of their faith without any experience of abuse or persecution. Their survival in India is in striking contrast to the experience of Jewish people who have lived in China, where they have been forced to assimilate into Chinese society in order to survive.

Another basis for optimism regarding democracy in India is the amazing capacity for adaptation that Indian social institutions display. Many factors have contributed to the success that democracy has enjoyed in India since the country's independence. Some people will point to the example and the many years of preparation promoted by British colonial rule. Others look to the inspiration of Mahatma Gandhi and his leadership of the Indian National Congress, which brought the independence movement to the people of the subcontinent. Also important has been the Constitution and the vital leadership and vision of Jawarhalal Nehru and the Congress Party in implementing its guarantees. Other factors include the remarkable restraint of the Indian Army, the dedicated service of the Indian Administrative Service, and an enlightened press.

THE CASTE SYSTEM

All these factors have certainly contributed significantly to the continued strength of democracy in India. But even more important has been the accommodation of the principles of democracy in the traditional pattern of social organization in India: the caste system.

Many have the impression that the caste system in India is a rigid structure that divides people into distinct social groups that are ranked in a fixed hierarchy. We are used to hearing that it is a social evil that has no place in a democracy and ought to be abolished. The reality is that the caste system has provided the indigenous social context that has made it possible for democracy to be introduced into India and to work. As with so much about India, the caste system is much more complex and more flexible than it appears on the surface.

Because of its hierarchical structure, the caste system is by definition inequitable, and thus a contradiction to democracy, which assumes everyone to be equal. Yet to many Indians, the system is seen as not separating basically common people apart but, rather, as what holds very diverse groups of people together. And its hierarchical structure, rather than fixing people into permanent levels, provides them with opportunity for social mobility. Nevertheless, it is true that those who find themselves of lower rank feel the tremendous weight of its oppression, whereas those whose rank level is high or improving are not so troubled by its inherent inequality. One's attitude toward the caste system thus depends a great deal on one's place in the system.

The Indian caste system is based upon a social group for which Westerners do not have a counterpart. In the north of India, the caste community is generally called a *jati,* as an extended kinship group. This definition means that one is born into one's *jati* (the word is based on a verbal root meaning "to be born"), just as one is born into a family. But the perimeters extend beyond the natural family. The *jati* is also endogamous, which means that it includes those relations to whom one expects to get married. Natural family members are excluded from this group by generally accepted rules of incest. A *jati* thus extends the idea of a family to a larger social group of cousins and potential in-laws. This group is further defined by a traditional occupation, which has been passed on from generation to generation and which gives each *jati* its name. There are several thousand separate *jatis,* or caste communities, throughout India, most of them confined to a single linguistic region. There may be as few as

two or three *jatis* in the remote mountain valleys of the Himalayas; generally, in the more densely populated areas of India, a villager will interact with about 20 different such caste groups in normal daily life.

Jati has an important role in an Indian's self-identity. Whereas Westerners tend to think of themselves in society primarily as individuals, in India, one is more apt to think of oneself primarily in society as the member of one's *jati.* It provides a context for all of one's interactions with other people, especially as regards marriage. One is expected to marry someone of one's own *jati.* And in India, where marriages are mostly arranged by one's parents, this expectation is generally the rule.

The most important characteristic of the jati is that it is the social unit that is placed in the hierarchical rank called caste. Here is where the possibility of flexibility, or mobility, arises. That one belongs to a certain jati is fixed by birth. But where that jati is ranked in the hierarchical caste order is not. Its rank is based on some general rules that are accepted by almost everyone. For example, those belonging to Brahmin, or traditional priestly, jatis are placed at the top of the caste hierarchy. It is a significant feature of this system that those who are traditionally given this highest rank are expected to abjure wealth, practice asceticism, and revere learning. It does not hold in as high esteem those who hold political power or pursue money and become conspicuous spenders.

The hierarchical ranking of this system demeans in rank those jatis that are responsible for performing menial tasks such as cleaning latrines, sweeping streets, and removing the carcasses of dead animals. People belonging to these jatis are called "untouchables," a designation that reveals the ancient priestly caste's understanding of its own supremacy in rank. Brahmins as a community had to remain ritually pure in order to retain the efficacy and respect for their priestly functions. Those who performed "polluting" functions in the society— dealing with human waste and animals—had to be avoided for fear of their diminishing the priests' sacred power. They were thus placed the lowest on the hierarchical scale and declared "outcastes." Mahatma Gandhi, in his crusade to remove the scourge of the demeaning term "untouchable," called them Harijans, "children of God," and encouraged members of his religious community to perform the "polluting" functions for themselves. In many parts of India today, people in these jatis prefer to be called Dalits (the "oppressed") and are seeking recognition as equal members of Indian society. Their quest, however, still meets a great deal of resistance throughout the country.

For those *jatis* that fall in between the high-ranked Brahmins and the low-ranked Dalits, even though every *jati* has a rank, the basis of ranking is not so clear or consistent. Some occupations, such as land cultivators or carpenters, are generally accepted as higher than potters, herders, and washermen. Land or industrial ownership, and thus control over production in a village, called dominance, is a very important determinant in caste rank. Social practices, such as ritual observance, dress, vegetarian diet, and with whom one eats, may also determine rank. Different rules apply in different situations. As norms and conditions change, so is the rank of one's *jati* open to change.

Many examples illustrate this fluidity of ranking. The *jati* names of several ancient emperors betray an absence of royal blood or, at least, of earlier royal rank for their caste. Such did not prevent them from becoming kings. A striking, more contemporary example is the Nadar community in south India. It was considered an untouchable community in the nineteenth century, but now it is accepted as a merchant caste. Even Mahatma Gandhi's family was not fixed in *jati* rank. The family name (*gandhi* means "grocer") identifies a *bania,* or merchant, background. But both Gandhi's grandfather and father served as chief ministers for *maharajas* of small Indian states, a role traditionally reserved for Brahmins. Gandhi was himself thrown out of his *jati* by the elders of his community when he went to England to study law. He stepped out of the caste system altogether when he was accepted as a person committed to a religious life, when he became the *Mahatma.*

Although normative rules of ranking in the caste hierarchy generally apply, the position of any specific *jati* is based primarily on the acceptance of its claim to rank by members of the other *jatis* with which it interacts. Because of this need to convince others, change in rank does not happen quickly. But there is nevertheless a social dynamic that asserts a claim to higher rank and encourages its acceptance by others.

The Caste System and Political Change

The flexibility that this dynamic allows in the caste structure provided the opportunity in that traditional social context for democracy to work. The role of democracy is to establish and distribute public power, by the vote of the majority of adults in a society. The right of individuals to vote to determine their government was a new phenomenon in India. But in the presence of a system in which rules of ascendency were continually being worked out, the role of the vote to grant public power, emerged as an acceptable way to establish rank within the village hierarchy. The system did not have to change; it simply had to adapt itself to an additional way to determine ascendency: Those who could command the greatest number of votes maintained the position of rank of their *jatis* in the village social hierarchy.

The winning of democratic elections by commanding votes found a place in the traditional caste structure in two important ways. First, because *jatis* extend as distinct social groups throughout a linguistic region, they provide a cohesive base for region-wide associations formed to promote their political causes, as voting blocs in elections and as lobbies in the halls of government. Another strong factor in determining within a single village which *jati* is of highest rank has been dominance, the control of the production and distribution of the food that is harvested from village lands. Those villagers in positions of dominance were quick to adapt into votes for them the allegiances created by the dependency of those of lower jati rank. Democracy thus became a way to support traditional patterns of social life, rather than a way to reform them.

Clear evidence of this adaptation has been the slow pace of land reform in India, in contrast to the rapid acceptance of new methods of agriculture that produced the Green Revolution. Large land estates have been broken up and absentee landlordism reduced. But politically active regional landholder *jati* associations have been able to block legislative action on some of the most difficult village problems: landlessness and underemployment, the inequities of wealth and privilege, and landowner–laborer relations. Disputes between landowners and their laborers are still mostly resolved by force, with little interference by the police or protection from the courts.

Because of the inherent flexibility and adaptability evident in the *jati* caste structure, democracy has not been the cause of as much social change as initially was expected. Such is true also for economic development. While Americans have tended to view economic improvement and prosperity as direct consequences of political democracy, the developing world in general and India in particular have shown that the two are not necessarily connected—that prosperity is the result of many other factors than just political structure. Population density and population growth, for example, have had a greater impact on economic growth than form of governance. Cultural factors, geocommercial considerations, international economic forces, and specific economic policies of the government of India have also contributed to its continuing struggle to provide well-being for all its people.

To the extent that democracy has not lived up to its economic promise nor contributed to radical social change, those most oppressed and disadvantaged in India today are becoming more disenchanted. Ironically, as they become more politically aware, they become less hopeful about the effectiveness for them of ordered, democratic institutions. The continued burden of poverty itself has become another real threat to democracy in India. Yet hope for more effective government for the disadvantaged is suggested by the results of the 1993 mid-term elections in four Indian states and the 1996 and 1998 general elections, where the voices of the Dalits and other minorities have begun to be heard at the polls.

And so there are new levels of violence: violence caused by the very struggle to become a democracy and at the same time to negate it. In the general elections in 1991, voter turnout was only 54 percent. That is high by North American standards, but it was the lowest participation in a national election in 40 years of democracy in India. Most attribute this decline to the increase in violence and terror that has surrounded the election process itself. By mid-June 1991, more than 800 deaths had been recorded as a result of people going to the polls. In the state of Punjab, elections were postponed because 23 of the more than

1,000 candidates who were running for public office had been killed while campaigning. It was not until February 1992 that enough confidence was restored to hold the elections there. Even then, they were boycotted by five Sikh political parties, and the turnout was less than 22 percent of the voting-age population.

The 1996 national elections showed a significant turn away from the violence that surrounded the 1991 elections. The large turnout of 530 million voters was a record high. The elections in Punjab recorded the highest level of voter turnout in the country. The number of election-related deaths fell dramatically from more than 800 in 1991 to 50 in 1996, those mostly due to some electoral feuds in the state of Bihar. State elections were held for the first time in 6 years in September in Jammu/Kashmir, with some foreboding because of the activity of militant separatist movements in that state. Yet more than 53 percent of the electorate took part in those elections, and that war-torn part of the country is now being ruled by a democratically elected state government.

National elections have become an important part of Indian life. Among the many villages in the country, they have even taken on the character of a festival, as reported under the headline "Joy and Order as India's Voting Starts":

> What seemed important was not so much which of the dozens of political parties was up or down, or which local candidate from among the 15,000 running across India was likely to win. What permeated the mood was something as old as independent India itself—the sheer pleasure of taking part in a basic democratic rite, the business of appointing and dismissing governments, that has survived all of the disappointments that Indians have endured in the past half-century. In a troubled land, democracy means there is hope.
>
> —*The New York Times* (April 18, 1996)

REGIONAL POLITICAL CONCERNS

Dominance, a primary factor in village life, also characterizes India's relationship with its closest, South Asian neighbors. By far the largest country on the subcontinent, in both size and population, India is an overbearing presence to those who surround it.

The nations of Nepal and Bhutan, and the tiny kingdom of Sikkim, before it was absorbed into India in 1974, are isolated by India against the Himalayan Mountains to the north. They are particularly aware of India's dominant presence. Bhutan's economic development is almost totally dependent upon Indian investment. And its foreign relations are, by long-standing treaty, handled by the government of India. Nepal maintains a fragile neutrality, circumscribed by its economic ties to India.

Sri Lanka is geographically separate from India and, except for infrequent discussions about some small islands that lie between them, has had generally peaceful relations with it. In the years following their independence, the government of

India agreed to help Sri Lanka by repatriating half of the 1 million Indian Tamils whose forebears were taken to Sri Lanka by the British during the nineteenth century to work on rubber, coffee, and tea plantations. This agreement helped to ease the unemployment created by the breakup of plantations at that time. An increase in discrimination during the 1980s felt by the remaining Indian Tamils and Sri Lanka Tamils (about 17 percent of the total population of the country) strengthened their language and cultural ties with the nearby Indian state of Tamil Nadu. The subsequent rise of militant Tamil separatist and Sinhalese nationalist movements led to outright warfare in Sri Lanka. About 70,000 refugees fled to South India from the rampant violence in their homelands in 1983. That number increased to more than 200,000 in 1991.

In 1987, Rajiv Gandhi, then prime minister of India, made an agreement with the Sri Lankan government to send a peacekeeping force of 70,000 Indian army troops to contain the Tamil violence. When this force proved ineffective in putting down what was a guerrilla war in a foreign country, the Sri Lankan government asked them to withdraw. Rajiv Gandhi's international initiative became to Sri Lankans an overbearing display of military power imposed upon them. Yet the forces were there long enough to win sufficient enmity of the Tamil militants in Sri Lanka for them to plot his death. The consequences proved dire for all involved, most particularly for Rajiv Gandhi himself, when he became the victim of a suicide bomb attack in south India during the 1991 general elections.

Pakistan and Bangladesh also have their own access to the sea, to the west and east of India, and to the world. Yet they are both aware that they are much smaller than India and that their large neighbor, by attacking Pakistan in 1971, determined that they are two nations instead of one. Even more important, rivers, which are the major source of water for irrigation in both of these countries, originate in and are controlled by their powerful neighbor.

Negotiations with Bangladesh over the distribution of the waters of the Ganges River through the Farakka barrage near the border between the two countries began in 1977. A dramatic resolution was achieved in December 1996, assuring Bangladesh of at least half the available flow. This agreement came partially as an act of goodwill toward the new government of Bangladesh with the electoral victory of Sheikh Hasina Wazed, daughter of Mujibur Rahman. India had helped Rahman win independence for Bangladesh in 1971. But it also reflected a growing understanding among India's leaders that India's emergence as a modern industrial nation depends upon constructive economic relationships with its neighbors.

Another major issue of contention between Bangladesh and India has been the repatriation of undocumented refugees. Millions came into India during the military repression leading up to the independence of Bangladesh in 1971 and have remained because of lack of agreement between the two countries on a process for their transfer. Some progress on this issue was realized in a recent settlement with insurgent tribal groups in eastern Bangladesh that included repatriation

						The founding of the Indian National Congress; start of the independence movement	Mohandas Gandhi returns to India from South Africa
Harappan city culture 3000–1500 B.C.	Aryan Vedic culture 1500–500 B.C.	Buddhist civilization 500 B.C.–A.D.300	Classical Hindu civilization 200–1000	Medieval Islamic civilization 1200–1857	British East India Company 1602–1857	The British Raj era 1857–1947	1885	1915

of more than 60,000 Chakmas from refugee camps in the Indian state of Tripura.

Efforts toward greater cooperation among the nations of South Asia began with the creation of the South Asian Association for Regional Cooperation (SAARC) in 1985. Although progress has been slow, the member nations did initiate a South Asian Preferential Trade Agreement (SAPTA) in December 1996, which established some modest, mutual tariff concessions. Impatient with the pace of SAARC, India also set up two subregional cooperation groups: one with Nepal, Bhutan, and Bangladesh, and another with Sri Lanka and Maldives. A further step is a free-trade agreement signed between Sri Lanka and India in December 1998. These agreements isolate Pakistan, the seventh member of SAARC, and identify a history of altercation and restrictive trade between India and Pakistan.

The long-standing dispute between Indian and Pakistan over Kashmir, which led to outright warfare between the two countries in 1948, 1965, and 1971, has sustained a high level of tension between the two countries since the time of independence. And it has served as a constant drain on the resources that both need for social services and economic development. Pakistan has recently intensified its diplomatic efforts, especially since the nuclear testing in May 1998, not just to call international attention to this issue but to internationalize Kashmir itself. India has continued to assert that Kashmir is an integral part of its country. To internationalize that one part would dismember itself as a nation. High-level bilateral discussions began following a meeting of Prime Ministers Sharif of Pakistan and Vahjayee of India at the United Nations in October 1998. Attempts were made to declare a cease-fire on the Siachen glacier and increase the flow of Jhelam River waters through the Pulkal Barrage and to increase trade and people-to-people contacts. These talks have yet to produce substantive results.

Nuclear proliferation is another major issue in Pakistan–Indian relations. The world was shocked when both India and Pakistan tested nuclear devices in May 1998. In spite of extensive election rhetoric about such testing in India during the months leading up to the national elections in February–March, it came as an unexpected surprise to all but a very few in the newly elected Bharatiya Janata Party–controlled government. The United States was especially outraged by these tests because they represented an unqualified failure of U.S. policy to contain nuclear weapons capability throughout the world. India, and subsequently Pakistan, had unleashed expanding nuclear armament, which threatened the stability of the South Asian region and gave precedence for the develop-

ment of nuclear arms in other volatile areas of the world. The U.S. government responded by imposing sanctions on India; these have turned out to be small in terms of foreign-aid support for India, and largely ineffective. Its greatest impact appears to be on American investors and farmers.

Ironically, this horrified response to these nuclear tests did not acknowledge that U.S. policy itself contributed to India's growing need to acquire what its strategic planners called "credible minimum nuclear deterrence." In the absence of binding international disarmament or control over nuclear weapons development, India's security depends upon its developing sufficient second-strike capability to have a credible response to a nuclear attack. Such deterrence combined with its unilateral commitment not to make a first strike using nuclear arms are the two pillars of India's nuclear policy.

The government of India has long been concerned that U.S. nuclear policy is not committed to a workable timetable to eliminate nuclear weapons, as part of its compliance with the Nuclear Non-Proliferation Treaty, which the United States signed in 1968. Nor does the United States appear effective in enforcing the compliance of other signers of that treaty not to provide nuclear know-how and fissionable materials to other nations. Specifically, India does not have any confidence that U.S. policy can restrain China's ability to destabilize South Asia by providing nuclear materials to Pakistan. In the absence of such assurance, India's own security needs have required it to retain its nuclear testing option. It, therefore, in spite of immense diplomatic pressure, has refused to sign the U.S.–sponsored Comprehensive Test Ban Treaty.

Because of its history of stable, civilian government, India does not see developing its nuclear arms capability, which began in 1974, as threatening to its South Asian neighbors. Pakistan, on the other hand, because it recognizes that some factions in India see its very existence as an Islamic nation as a judgment on India's credibility as a secular state, does not feel secure with India having an overwhelming nuclear advantage. The rise to power of the BJP as a Hindu nationalist party has added to Pakistan's apprehensions. It therefore felt compelled to answer India's test with tests of its own 2 weeks later. India did not react to these tests in any dramatic way. For its own need for nuclear deterrence, even since 1974, has not been to defend itself from Pakistan; India's apprehensions have to do with China.

India's one attempt to confront its large Asian neighbor, China, with conventional arms was to settle a border dispute in 1962. This confrontation led to a humiliating rout of India's

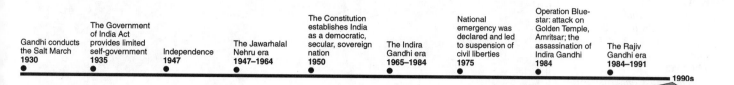

Gandhi conducts the Salt March
1930

The Government of India Act provides limited self-government
1935

Independence
1947

The Jawarhalal Nehru era
1947–1964

The Constitution establishes India as a democratic, secular, sovereign nation
1950

The Indira Gandhi era
1965–1984

National emergency was declared and led to suspension of civil liberties
1975

Operation Blue-star: attack on Golden Temple, Amritsar; the assassination of Indira Gandhi
1984

The Rajiv Gandhi era
1984–1991

1990s

Rajiv Gandhi is assassinated; Congress Party leader Narasimha Rao becomes prime minister

The Babri Masjid is destroyed and leads to riots nationwide; the United Front gains power in the 1996 elections

The Bharatiya Janata Party wins the 1998 elections; nuclear tests startle the world

border forces. Relations with China since then have been formal, and largely inconsequential, due in large part to a lack of interest on China's part. But India cannot help feeling that its nuclear capability has been an important protection and is reluctant to participate in any regional nuclear agreement from which China is excluded. Its preference would be to have all the major powers, including the United States, join in an enforceable nuclear disarmament treaty.

India continues to pursue avenues of wider economic and diplomatic cooperation. It maintains an active role in the 113-nation Non-Aligned Movement, which met in Durban, South Africa, in September 1998. It also became a full dialogue partner in the Association of Southeast Asian Nations (ASEAN) in January 1997. This status in ASEAN is shared with the United States, the European Union, Australia, Japan, and South Korea. India's admission overcame the concerns of Southeast Asian leaders that they not be drawn into such South Asian issues as the Kashmir dispute. And Indian remains hopeful, even after its recent nuclear tests, of becoming a permanent member of an expanded United Nations Security Council.

During the cold war, India sought to remain nonaligned by negotiating with the United States and Europe for economic aid, and with the Soviet Union for military aid to match the military assistance offered by the U.S. government to Pakistan. With the collapse of the Soviet Union, the government of India has sought to open its economy to greater Japanese and American industrial investment. Because of its earlier, restrictive import policies, which forced IBM and Coca-Cola to withdraw during the 1970s, the country established a good industrial base of its own. Its growth since independence has been significant. A rapidly developing middle-class market, decreasing restrictions on foreign investment, and government divestment of its public sector industries create opportunities for even faster growth. This promise was affirmed by the commitment of more than $6 billion in assistance to India over the previous 4 years by the AID India Consortium, international aid agencies, and industrialized countries.

such optimism for growth. The U.S. sanctions imposed on India following its nuclear tests in 1998 reduced foreign-aid assistance by a little less than $1 billion. The government of India hopes to make up for this loss by increases in foreign direct investments, which have grown dramatically with the liberalizing of its economy since 1991. These investments reached $3.5 billion in 1997. But with the uncertainties created by the Asian economic crises since 1997, these investments have slowed to an estimated $3.1 billion. India receives increased investments of $4.2 billion by nonresident Indians and others in more economically prosperous regions of the world to assist it in sustaining an encouraging rate of growth during these troubled times.

Promises for the economic future of India are tempered by the overwhelming demands of contemporary life in India: teeming population, extensive poverty, environmental degradation, and strife. "Excess," V. S. Naipaul calls them, recognizing that so much of the conflict and violence is the result of an awakening of a new political consciousness. "A million mutinies supported by twenty kinds of group excess, sectarian excess, religious excess, regional excess." Yet he finds even in this awakening a vision of hope: "the beginnings of self-awareness . . . the beginning of a new way for the millions, part of India's growth, part of its restoration."

DEVELOPMENT

India has the most diversified industrial economy in South Asia and ranks among the world's top 10 industrial powers. Industry now equals agriculture in its share of GDP. Agriculture still employs two thirds of the labor force. The government has recently moved to sell state-run industries and limit restrictions to encourage more private growth and foreign investment.

FREEDOM

The largest democracy in the world, India has maintained stable parliamentary and local government through elections and rule of law since the adoption of its Constitution in 1950. Frontier territories have been brought into full statehood, and separatist movements have been held in check. Amnesty International has cited some human-rights abuses by security forces and militant separatist groups in Kashmir, Punjab, and Assam.

HEALTH/WELFARE

India's commitment to village development and universal education has improved diet, hygiene, medical services, and literacy. Birth-control policies remain difficult to implement, and urban slums need continuing attention. The awarding of the Nobel Peace Prize to Mother Teresa indicates the magnitude of both the challenge and the vision of health care in India.

ACHIEVEMENTS

Through its Green Revolution, India has been self-sufficient in grain production since 1970. Its high-tech industrial capability and growing middle class attracted increasing direct investment in the economy. Its leadership among nonaligned and developing countries and the world popularity of artists like musician Ravi Shankar reveal the vitality of India's ancient tradition of creativity in language, art, and human relations.

Afghanistan (Islamic State of Afghanistan)

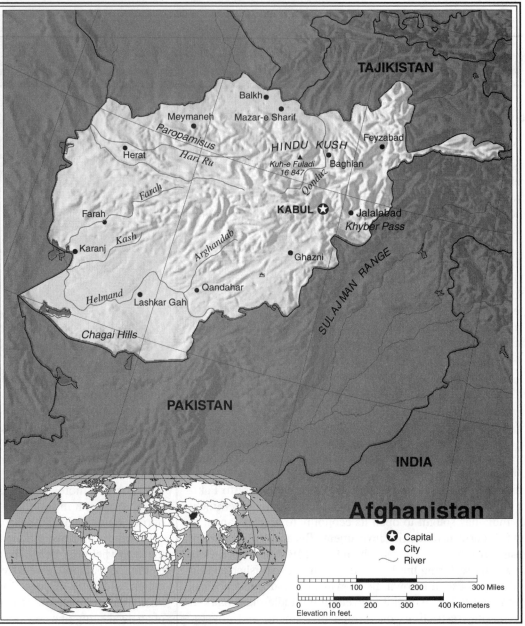

GEOGRAPHY
Area in Square Miles (Kilometers): 249,935 (647,500) (slightly smaller than Texas)
Capital (Population): Kabul (2,029,000)
Environmental Concerns: soil degradation; overgrazing; deforestation; desertification
Geographical Features: mostly rugged mountains; valleys in north and southwest
Climate: arid to semiarid; cold winters and hot summers

PEOPLE

Population
Total: 24,792,400 (including refugees in Pakistan and Iran)
Annual Growth Rate: 4.48% (reflects return of refugees)
Rural/Urban Population Ratio: 80/20
Major Languages: Pashtu; Dari; Turkic languages; 30 minor languages; much bilingualism
Ethnic Makeup: 38% Pashtu; 25% Tajik; 19% Hazara; 6% Uzbek; 12% others
Religions: 84% Sunni Muslim; 15% Shia Muslim; 1% others

Health
Life Expectancy at Birth: 47 years (male); 46 years (female)
Infant Mortality Rate (Ratio): 146.7/1,000
Average Caloric Intake: 73% of FAO minimum
Physicians Available (Ratio): 1/6,690

Education
Adult Literacy Rate: 29%
Compulsory (Ages): 7–13

COMMUNICATION
Telephones: 1 per 694 people
Daily Newspaper Circulation: 11 per 1,000 people
Televisions: 1 per 102 people

TRANSPORTATION
Highways in Miles (Kilometers): 13,640 (22,000)
Railroads in Miles (Kilometers): 15.4 (24.6)
Usable Airfields: 33
Motor Vehicles in Use: 65,000

GOVERNMENT
Type: transitional government
Independence Date: August 19, 1919 (from United Kingdom control over Afghan foreign affairs)
Head of State/Government: no functioning government at this time

Political Parties: Taliban; others
Suffrage: currently undetermined

MILITARY
Military Expenditures (% of GDP): no national military
Current Disputes: severe internal conflicts; border disputes with Pakistan and Iran

ECONOMY
Currency ($ U.S. Equivalent): 17,000 afghanis = $1 (bazaar rate)
Per Capita Income/GDP: $800/$18.1 billion (1996 est.)
Inflation Rate: 204% (1996 est.)
Unemployment Rate: 8%
Labor Force: 7,100,000

Natural Resources: natural gas; petroleum; coal; copper; talc; barite; sulphur; lead; zinc; iron ore; salt; precious and semi-precious stones
Agriculture: largely subsistence; cash products: wheat; fruits; nuts; karakul pelts; wool; mutton
Industry: small-scale production of textiles, soap, furniture, shoes, fertilizer, and cement; handwoven carpets; natural gas; oil; coal; copper
Exports: $80 million (primary partners former Soviet Union, Pakistan, Iran)
Imports: $150 million (primary partners former Soviet Union, Pakistan, Iran)

 http://www.rockbridge.net/personal/bichel/afghan.htp

AFGHANISTAN

Afghanistan is a rugged, mountainous country nearly the size of Texas. It is a nation divided by a high mountain ridge, ethnic conflicts, political ideologies, old superpower strategies, and war.

The natural terrain of Afghanistan has never supported an easy or affluent life for its people, nor has its history provided a basis for their common identity as a nation. Two important imperial powers originated in this land, one in the twelfth century and another in the eighteenth century. But neither lasted more than a generation. In the modern era, global confrontation between European colonial powers, and more recently between the United States and the Soviet Union, has transformed Afghanistan into an international battlefield. The victim of superpowers' quest for political advantage, the country has been ravaged by forces of devastating destruction, with much of its population displaced by war. Since 1996, most of the country has come under the military control and religious fervor of the Taliban, an extreme Islamic fundamentalist group. Yet a vestige of the anti-Soviet resistance forces, called the *mujahideen,* continue to hold out in the northern corner of the country. Their support from the bordering former Soviet republics and from Iran threatens to expand this conflict into international warfare. With such tension, political stability and a sense of national unity in which democracy and social welfare can develop continue to elude the people.

The western extension of the high Himalayan mountain range known as the Hindu Kush is an imposing, 600-mile-long barrier right through the middle of the country. The land slopes away from this range in three different directions into jagged foothills and stark river valleys. Only 12 percent of this land is arable; even more challenging to agricultural subsistence, the area receives an average rainfall of less than 12 inches a year. Toward the south, the land becomes inhospitable desert, racked by seasonal sandstorms that have been known to bury entire villages. The mountainous terrain in the north, which has unexploited (but hard-to-obtain) mineral resources, primarily iron ore and natural gas, experienced a severe earthquake in February 1998; it destroyed more than 20 villages, killing several thousand people. Nowhere in the country can life be characterized as comfortable or abundant.

Afghanistan's traditional importance and wealth was based upon its strategic position along the ancient silk route between China and Europe, from which it extracted a significant bounty of customs fees, commissions for protection, or loot.

The marauding and opportunistic character of this heritage, preserved by independent tribal warlords scattered across the rugged landscape, is evident in the prominent role of drug trafficking and arms dealing in Afghan life today.

The three-way slope of the landscape down from the high, forbidding ridge of the Hindu Kush divides the country into separate ethnic and linguistic regions. On the northern slope, the people lean toward the ethnic groupings of Turkmenistan, Uzbekistan, and Tajikistan—all former republics of the Soviet Union. Northern Afghans are predominantly Uzbeks and Turkmen, who share a strong sense of identity as well as the Turkic language with the peoples who live across that northern border. Sloping to the West are the Tajik and Hazara peoples, who belong to different Islamic traditions (the Tajik are primarily Sunni Muslim, the Hazara Shia Muslim) but share a common language, Dari, which is a dialect of Farsi, the language of Iran. To the south and east, the land is occupied by Pathans, who, like the Tajik, are predominantly Sunni Muslims. But they speak a different language, Pashto, which they share with the people across their southeastern boundary in the Northwest Province of Pakistan.

When Soviet military forces invaded Afghanistan in 1979, hordes of refugees fled across those borders of the country that placed them among neighboring peoples with whom they felt a strong sense of kinship. More than 3 million Afghans crossed the border into Pakistan, where they lived in refugee camps; 1½ million are still awaiting a time of sufficient peace and political stability for them to return home. Another 2 million fled across the Iranian border, where they have been largely assimilated into that country. Although the Iranian government speaks occasionally of deportation, fewer than half of those refugees have returned from Iran since the departure of the Soviet Army in 1989. Together, these two groups of refugees comprised approximately one third of the total population of Afghanistan.

Equally dramatic was the large influx of the rural population into the capital city of Kabul during the time of Soviet occupation, to seek protection there. The population of Kabul grew from about 500,000 in 1970 to more than 2.2 million in 1989. Since the overthrow of Communist rule in April 1993, this trend has been totally reversed. The periodic assaults and bombings due to the infighting among rival political parties seeking control of the city as the seat of power over the entire country have reduced the city's size to its pre-1970 level.

MODERN HISTORY

The increase in maritime commerce across the Indian Ocean, which began in the sixteenth century, replaced the inland silk route through Afghanistan. This part of the world was then reduced to a pawn in what, during the nineteenth century, was called the "Great Game" among European powers for control over the "uncivilized" parts of the world. The borders of modern Afghanistan were established in 1907 by a treaty between Czarist Russia and Great Britain, to contain each other's colonial ambitions. Dost Amanulla Khan, then the emir of Kabul, used the recognition he received by their accord to try to lead the peoples within these borders into a modern nation state. Following the 1917 Communist Revolution in Russia, Vladimir Lenin's government encouraged and aided this effort in what it considered potentially satellite regimes in both Afghanistan and Mongolia. But the emir's attempt at consolidation and reform was thwarted by local chieftains, jealous for their own estates. He was forced to abdicate in 1929, and the countryside reverted to its traditional tribal ways, under the benign leadership of Emir Mohammad Zahir Shah.

A more moderate consolidation effort was undertaken in the 1950s by Emir Zahir Shah's brother-in-law, Prime Minister Sadar Mohammed Daud Khan. Under his leadership, a constitutional monarchy was adopted in 1964, which established a National Assembly under the sovereign power of the emir, Zahir Shah. As an indication of Daud's reforming zeal, women participated for the first time in the elections that took place the following year. Also participating in that election was a newly formed, but already fractious, Communist Party, led by Nur Mohammed Taraki, son of a nomadic Pathan family, and Babrak Karmal, an upper-class intellectual from Kabul. Elections were held again in 1969; but this time, local tribal leaders, who were conservative both religiously and socially, better understood the electoral process. They gained control of the Assembly in order to preserve their traditional authority and effectively limited further reform.

Impatient with this resistance, Prime Minister Daud, with the help of the army, overthrew the government in 1973. He sent Zahir Shah into exile and set himself up as the military dictator of the country. He strengthened the army and the bureaucracy to secure his rule, and with Soviet-government aid, strove to build an industrial sector to replace traditional agriculture and handicrafts as the primary source of the country's wealth. By encouraging the growth and loyalty of these sec-

(Photo: United Nations/A. Hollmann)

Millions of refugees who fled to Pakistan and Iran during the Soviet occupation of Afghanistan have been reluctant to return to Afghanistan. This is due, in no small part, to the constant fighting among the *mujahideen* and today's problems with the Taliban. Afghanistan women and children are a particularly vulnerable group of refugees.

tors, he hoped to have their support to establish a more independent nation and to usher in even broader reforms. To assert this independence, in 1977, he promulgated a new Constitution, which outlawed all political parties other than his own, including the largely urban and intellectual Communist Party. A new Assembly then elected Daud president of the Republic of Afghanistan.

The Soviet Invasion

Resistance to Daud's nationalist reform program came from both sides of the political spectrum, from the leftist, modernizing groups in the city of Kabul and from the more conservative elements in the countryside. A zealous group of militant tribal leaders called the *mujahideen* emerged at this time, armed and trained by Pakistan, which attacked sporadically to harass his government. But Daud was more concerned about the growing influence (encouraged by the Soviets) of the urban forces of the left, and he began to purge suspected Communist Party members from the military and the bureaucracy. Within a year of the formation of his new government, Daud was overthrown by army officers threatened by his purge. Nur Mohammed Taraki, leader of the People's Democratic (Communist) Party, took over the reins of government.

Infighting among the Communist Party leadership led to President Taraki's assas-

sination in 1979 and the rise to power of his former associate and arch rival, Hafizullah Amin.

Both leaders were encouraged by the Soviet Union to reform Afghanistan into a socialist industrial state. But they adopted such a vigorous campaign to break up the landholdings of the local chieftains and to teach literacy among the people that conservative resistance throughout the countryside intensified to a point where President Amin sought Soviet military force to protect his government in Kabul. The Soviets feared that continuing civil strife caused by Amin in Afghanistan would diminish their influence and investment there and threaten the security of the adjoining Soviet states to the north. Thus, Soviet troops were sent in force in December 1979—not to protect, but to depose Amin and his radical faction of the Communist Party. They installed in his place an early factional leader in the Communist Party, Babrak Karmal, to undertake a more moderate approach to socialist reform.

Soviet military intervention continued to increase, climbing to 120,000 troops by 1986. But forces of resistance in the countryside, now being called upon to oppose foreign intervention as well as the movements toward centralization, industrialization, and social modernization, intensified. The *mujahideen* were a disparate collection of warlords. But, strengthened by a rising Islamic fundamentalist zeal and en-

couraged by Pakistani, Iranian, Arabic, and American support, many gathered their families into the safety of Pakistan and prepared to fight back. Wrote one observer:

Most came across in groups of fifty or one hundred, villages or nomad clans led by maliks, the local tribal chieftains. They brought more than 2 million animals with them—goats, sheep, buffalos and camels. It was a timeless sight. The men in turbans or woolen or embroidered caps, baggy pants and vests or robes like academic gowns, bandoliers of cartridges across their chests, old rifles or new machine guns on one shoulder. Their sons were dressed the same way, miniatures of their fathers. The animals and the women walked behind. When they stopped, they sometimes took the tents offered by the United Nations or, sometimes, just re-created their katchi villages on the other side of the mountains. Then the men, many of them, went back to kill Russians.

—Richard Reeves, *Passage to Peshawar*

This conflict took a heavy toll, destroying 12,000 of the 22,000 villages in the country and more than 2,000 schools. It left more than 1 million Afghans and 13,000 Soviet troops dead.

Timeline:

Loose tribal federation A.D. **1747–1973**	The British and Russians establish the boundaries of modern Afghanistan **1907**	Military dictatorship **1973–1978**	Communist Party rule **1978–1992**	Soviet military occupation **1979–1989**	A *mujahideen* resistance is formed in Pakistan; the new Constitution is adopted **1980s**

1990s

The Najibullah government falls to *mujahideen* forces; Burhanuddin Rabbani is installed as the interim president

A political stalemate is created with Rabbani as president and his political and military rival, Gulbuddin Hekmatyar, as prime minister

Taliban forces capture Kabul and control nearly of the country

The Soviet Withdrawal

In 1986, Babrak Karmal resigned and was replaced in 1987 by his associate, Sayid Muhammed Najibullah. In 1988, the leaders of nine Sunni Muslim rebel groups joined in Pakistan to form an interim government-in-exile. Faced with this more united resistance, the Soviet Union became unwilling to sustain the losses of the intensifying military stalemate. It entered into an accord with the United States to withdraw all of its forces by February 15, 1989. On September 13, 1991, the United States and the Soviet Union further agreed to stop providing arms to the warring factions in Afghanistan on January 1, 1992, and to urge a cease-fire in that troubled land.

Warfare between President Najibullah's government and mujahideen continued unabated for more than 3 years after the Soviet troop departure. The *mujahideen* had tried to adopt a common strategy and combine their military forces. But a lack of cohesion—religious, ethnic, and military—thwarted their attempts to overthrow the Kabul government. President Najibullah offered to form a joint government with the leaders of the resistance, but these leaders could agree only that they did not want the Communists to share in any part of a new government.

In March 1992, Najibullah was overthrown by his army, and *mujahideen* forces, under the command of Ahmad Shah Masood, a Tajik Afghan, overtook the city of Kabul. In June, a "national council" of *mujahideen* leaders elected Burhanuddin Rabbani as interim president. But rival *mujahideen* groups, particularly the forces led by Gulbuddin Hekmatyar, a Pathan, continued to contend for recognition and power in Kabul and the surrounding countryside.

In December, a "Council for Resolution and Settlement," consisting of 1,400 delegates, met in Kabul to elect Rabbani to another 18 months as president. It also set up a 250-member Parliament to draw up a new Constitution in anticipation of nationwide elections in 1994. But that council was not supported by all the rival *mujahideen* groups, and the country continued to be ravaged by the residual firepower of the competing political forces of President Rabbani and Prime Minister Hekmatyar, leaders of the two strongest factions.

In 1994, as it appeared President Rabbani was beginning to gain the upper hand in the *mujahideen* infighting, a new force arrived to intensify the conflict. The Taliban ("seekers of religious knowledge") started as a group of Pathan religious students from the southern city of Kandahar who rose up in indignation to oppose the corruption of local warlords in that area of the country. Their reforming fervor spread rapidly among a people weary of the militancy and corruption of the *mujahideen*. By the fall of 1996, their forces, supplied by arms from Pakistan, had won a following and were in control of the southern two thirds of the country. In September, they drove the *mujahideen* government out of Kabul and established a reign of reactionary religious terror in a city that had aspired to become modern. By 1998, the Taliban controlled 85 percent of the country.

AN UNCERTAIN FUTURE

During the time of the fighting among the *mujahideen,* and with the rise of the Taliban, peoples throughout the land continue to suffer the ravages of war. Many of the millions of refugees who fled to Pakistan and Iran during the time of Soviet occupation are hesitant to return. The destruction of their villages and the depletion and the mining of their lands also makes the prospect of their return far less secure than the stark but adequate support they receive in refugee camps. And some refugees, especially women, express fear of repression in their homeland because of the Islamic fundamentalist fervor of both the *mujahideen* and Taliban leaders who are competing for control of their country.

Attempts to resolve the conflict between these warring parties have been undertaken by Afghanistan's neighbors and most recently by Pakhdar Brahim; the UN secretary general's special envoy to Afghanistan. His negotiations have defused tensions between Afghanistan and Iran but have not resolved the more intractable internal disputes. The country has been torn by too many levels of conflict: between modernization and traditional ways of life; between democratic and socialist ideals; between fundamentalist and reform Islam; between ethnic and linguistic groups; between tribes and factions within parties and religious sects; between the interests of Iran and Pakistan. Perhaps the most devastating conflict of all, because of the level of destruction, arms trading, and terrorist training it introduced into the country, was the conflict between the global agendas of the United States and the Soviet Union. It is no wonder that many people in Afghanistan find comfort even in the severe control of the Taliban, which now extends to almost all of the country. The Taliban's religious zeal and military domination has at least stopped the fighting in most of the land.

DEVELOPMENT

In the 1980s, the Soviet government made a concerted effort to establish an industrial base, particularly in mining and processing Afghanistan's natural resources. With the increasing intensity of the warfare between the Afghan rebels and the Soviet occupying forces, these efforts collapsed. Agricultural production declined an estimated 45% to 50%.

FREEDOM

Afghanistan is in a time of political period recovery following the Soviet military occupation. Millions who fled into Pakistan and Iran as refugees are slowly making their way back to their devastated lands. Rival groups among the resistance forces, the *mujahideen,* and the Taliban continue to fight for power in and around the capital, Kabul.

HEALTH/WELFARE

The family and tribe have been the traditional sources of welfare in Afghanistan. Because of continuing warfare and limited access to safe water supplies, disease is prevalent, and the overall life expectancy is about 46 years, the lowest in South Asia. Literacy is also among the lowest on the subcontinent. The ban on woman's activities by the Taliban is severely limiting health and social services in the country.

ACHIEVEMENTS

Given the warfare and devastation to their country that the Afghan people have been through during the past 2 decades, their greatest achievement may be simply their survival.

Bangladesh (People's Republic of Bangladesh)

GEOGRAPHY

Area in Square Miles (Kilometers): 55,584 (144,000) (slightly smaller than Wisconsin)

Capital (Population): Dhaka (8,545,000)

Environmental Concerns: water pollution; soil degradation; deforestation

Geographical Features: mostly flat alluvial plain; hilly in southeast

Climate: tropical; cool, dry winter; hot, humid summer; cool, rainy monsoon

PEOPLE

Population

Total: 125,340,000

Annual Growth Rate: 1.82%

Rural/Urban Population Ratio: 81/19

Major Languages: Bangla; English

Ethnic Makeup: 98% Bengali; 2% Biharis and various tribes

Religions: 83% Muslim; 16% Hindu; 1% others

Health

Life Expectancy at Birth: 56 years (male); 56 years (female)

Infant Mortality Rate (Ratio): 100/1,000

Average Caloric Intake: 85% of FAO minimum

Physicians Available (Ratio): 1/5,505

Education

Adult Literacy Rate: 38%

Compulsory (Ages): 5–11; free

COMMUNICATION

Telephones: 1 per 418 people

Daily Newspaper Circulation: 6 per 1,000 people

Televisions: 1 per 172 people

TRANSPORTATION

Highways in Miles (Kilometers): 101,108 (168,513)

Railroads in Miles (Kilometers): 1,796 (2,892)

Usable Airfields: 15

Motor Vehicles in Use: 223,000

GOVERNMENT

Type: republic

Independence Date: December 16, 1971

Head of State/Government: President Shahabuddin Ahmed; Prime Minister Sheikh Hasina Wajed

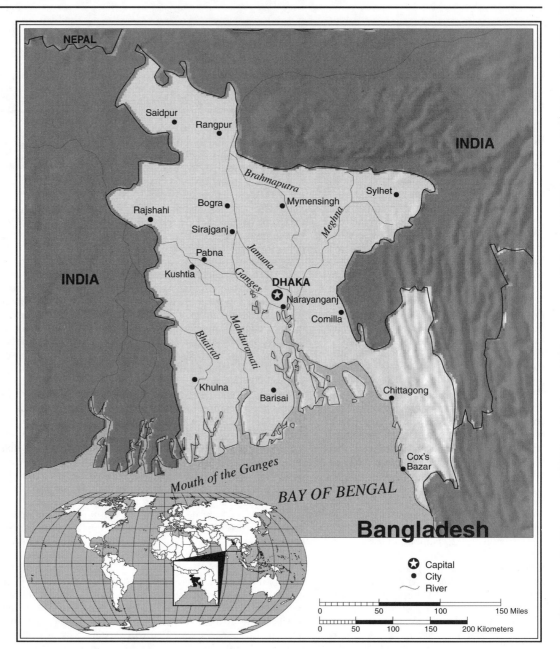

Political Parties: Bangladesh Nationalist Party; Awami League; Jatiya Party; Jamaat-e-Islami; Bangladesh Communist Party

Suffrage: universal at 18

MILITARY

Military Expenditures (% of GDP): 1.7%

Current Disputes: boundary dispute with India

ECONOMY

Currency ($ U.S. Equivalent): 40.25 taka = $1

Per Capita Income/GDP: $1,260/$155.1 billion

GDP Growth Rate: 4.7%

Inflation Rate: 4%

Unemployment Rate: 35.9%

Labor Force: 50,100,000

Natural Resources: fossil fuels; lignite; limestone; china clay; glass sand

Agriculture: rice; jute; tea; wheat; sugarcane; potatoes; beef; milk; poultry

Industry: jute manufacturing; cotton textiles; food processing; steel; fertilizer

Exports: $3.9 billion (primary partners Western Europe, United States, Hong Kong)

Imports: $6.8 billion (primary partners India, China, Western Europe)

 http://www.virtualbangladesh.com
http://southasia.net/Bangladesh

BANGLADESH

Bangladesh is the youngest nation of South Asia, having won its independence from Pakistan in 1971. Although it is one of the smaller countries of the subcontinent, it is also the most densely populated. More than 125 million people, almost half the population of the United States, live in an area smaller than the state of Wisconsin, at an average density of more than 2,000 per square mile. Only 15 percent of these people live in cities. Even in the rural countryside, the land is very crowded.

Bangladesh also has the most cohesive population in South Asia. Almost all citizens share a common Bengali ethnic and language identity, and the majority are Sunni Muslims. But even with so much going for it upon which to build a democratic nation—language, religion, culture, and a successful fight for its independence—the country has had extensive struggles to achieve political stability. And because of its rapidly growing population, its limited resources, and a continuous succession of floods and cyclones, it has also had to struggle to achieve economic well-being for its people. It remains one of the poorest countries in the world—61 percent of the urban population, according to a recent Asian Development Bank survey (some estimates say 80 percent of the total population), live below the poverty line.

CULTURAL DIVERSITY ENDURES

Isolated among the hills and jungles in the eastern regions of Bangladesh, approximately 300,000 tribal peoples continue to live in much the same way as they have for thousands of years. Their cultures show little impact from the more dominant Muslim and Hindu populations, which make up the vast majority of the country. The languages spoken by the tribal peoples are obscure in origin; some have never been studied. Some of these groups, such as the Lushai, Murung, and Kuki, still practice slash-and-burn agriculture and the rite of bride capture.

COLONIAL HISTORY

The origin of Bangladesh as a separate political entity goes back to 1905, when Lord Curzon, the British viceroy in India, attempted to divide the Colonial Province of Bengal into a predominantly Muslim East Bengal (which then included Assam) and a Hindu West Bengal. In the 1947 partition of the subcontinent, when India and Pakistan received their independence of the British Raj, a truncated yet predominantly Muslim province of East Bengal became the eastern wing of Pakistan.

East Pakistan had the larger population of the two wings of the new country, but

(United Nations/Wolff)

Bangladesh is often challenged by devastating cyclones that wreak havoc with rice production, not to mention the loss of life. This farmer planting rice in the paddies near Dhaka has no guarantee that the crop will survive the violent weather that will, in all likelihood, arrive in the months ahead.

economic and political power resided in the western wing. Attempts to impose the Urdu language as the national language of Pakistan, and favoritism toward the western wing in economic development, led during those early years to a sense of isolation and discrimination among the East Pakistanis. In 1970, when the first popular national elections were held, the Awami League Party, led by Sheikh Mujibur Rahman, won a majority of seats in the Pakistan national Legislature. Because this result was not acceptable to the political leaders in West Pakistan, President Yahya Khan suspended the Assembly. The people of East Bengal immediately began to riot in protest. President Yahya Khan tried to suppress this public outcry by military force. Within 8 months, as resistance mounted, the Pakistan Army repression left many hundreds of thousands dead and 10 million people fleeing over the border as refugees into India.

INDEPENDENCE

In December 1971, India attacked Pakistan in support of the Bengali resistance (*Mukti Bahini*). Within 2 weeks, the people of East Bengal were free of Pakistan military rule. A government of the nation of Bangladesh was then established, with Mujibur Rahman as prime minister.

Although he was a popular, charismatic leader, Mujib did not prove an effective

administrator of a new nation facing severe overpopulation, poverty, and natural disaster. In 1974, flooding left millions of people homeless and more than 400,000 dead. Mujib's increasingly authoritarian rule in the face of such crises led to a military coup in 1975, in which he and most of his family were killed.

General Ziaur Rahman, army chief of staff, became martial-law administrator in the political turmoil that followed Mujib's death. As an officer in the Pakistan Army in East Pakistan in 1971, Zia faced opposition from younger officers who were a product of the revolution. But he was equally committed to the establishment of Bangladesh as a separate, independent state and used his office to return the country to the path toward democracy.

During this martial-rule period, General Zia created his own political party, the Bangladesh Nationalist Party (BNP), and encouraged others to participate in national elections to elect 300 members to the national Legislature. (An additional 30 members were to be women subsequently elected by vote of the Legislature.) He also developed an economic policy to increase agricultural production, education, and health care. To assure control of the process, Zia retained the independent executive presidency that had been established by Mujibur Rahman, to which office he acceded in the presidential elections held in 1978. In the legislative elections of 1979, his BNP won two thirds of the seats in the national Legislature.

Zia was well on the way to establishing popular, democratic government when, in 1981, he was assassinated by some dissident military officers. The power vacuum created by his death led to a dispute over the role of the army in the government. This dispute was resolved in 1982, when General Hussain Muhammed Ershad, chief of staff of the army, seized the reins of government.

Ershad wanted to further General Zia's policies of economic development and social reform. But at the same time, he reduced the role of the Legislature by instituting direct military participation in public affairs in an influential "National Security Advisory Council." This favoritism toward the military stirred political unrest among the people and eventually led to his downfall. Although he won the presidential election in 1986, his party won only a very slim and questioned majority in the parliamentary elections that followed.

Two new leaders, each related to Ershad's more charismatic predecessors, came onto the national scene during the 1986 election campaigns. Begum Khaleda Zia (the widow of General Zia), the head of the Bangladesh National Party (BNP), and Sheikh Hasina Wajed (the sole surviving daughter of Mujibar Rahman), leading the Awami League, jointly initiated a public protest soon after Ershad's election, calling for his resignation and new elections. The rivalry between these two has been setting the political agenda ever since.

President Ershad first attempted to suppress their protest. Then, in December 1987, he dissolved the Legislature and called for new elections. The BNP and the Awami League called upon the electorate to boycott these elections. Even though Ershad's party won, voter turnout was very small, and public opinion began to rise against him. In 1990, in response to the public outcry, Ershad was forced to resign. He was replaced by Justice Shahabuddin Ahmed of the Supreme Court as acting president. National elections were held in February 1991, and Begum Zia's BNP, polling 31 percent of the votes, won 140 seats in the 300-member Legislature. The Awami League, although gaining almost the same percentage of the votes, came in a distant second, with 84 seats.

A national referendum in September 1991, supported by both the BNP and the Awami League, voted to reduce the power of the president by placing the executive power in the hands of the prime minister of the national Legislature. Begum Zia

(United Nations/Wolff)

After the Persian Gulf War in 1991, many Bangladeshis who were working in the region were forced to move back to their homeland. As these unemployed workers flooded back into urban areas, the cities rapidly became overcrowded. This teeming city street in Dhaka shows the results of the influx.

then stepped down as president to become the prime minister of the new government.

Because Begum Zia's government did not command a majority of Assembly seats, it depended upon the help of the Jamaat-e-Islami, a conservative Islamic party, which won 18 seats. Even though that party represented a small minority, its vital role emboldened it to condemn and seek the execution of a young doctor-turned-author, Dr. Taslima Nasreen, for alleged "blasphemy" in her novel *Lajja*. The government responded by arresting Nasreen, as much for her protection, one suspects, as her prosecution for "outrag[ing] the religious feelings" of the people of Bangladesh. Having posted bail, Dr. Nasreen escaped to live in exile in Sweden, Germany, and the United States. The episode raised international concern, not only on behalf of the right of freedom of expression but also as an indicator of the strength of religious fundamentalism in the political life of Bangladesh. In sub-

sequent elections, the Jamaat-e-Islami's legislative strength was reduced to three seats.

The closeness of the split of the popular vote between Begum Zia and Sheikh Hasina Wajed in the 1991 elections led Sheikh Hasina's Awami League to continue protests and, in 1994, a total boycott of the Legislature, with a call for new elections. The resultant political turmoil created a breakdown in government. New elections were held in June 1996, in which the BNP's standing was reduced from 140 to 116 seats. With the support of the 18 seats won by General Ershad's Jatiya Party, Sheikh Hasina became prime minister. This time it became the BNP's turn to boycott the Legislature. Because of the fierce rivalry between the Awami League and the BNP, political stability is still not assured for the government of Bangladesh.

Even without the participation of the BNP, the Legislature enacted an important initiative for women in government in

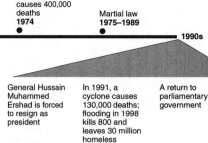

| British control over Bengal A.D. 1757–1947 | East Pakistan 1947–1971 | The birth of Bangladesh 1971 | Mujibur Rahman's presidential rule 1972–1975 | Severe flooding causes 400,000 deaths 1974 | Martial law 1975–1989 | 1990s |

General Hussain Muhammed Ershad is forced to resign as president

In 1991, a cyclone causes 130,000 deaths; flooding in 1998 kills 800 and leaves 30 million homeless

A return to parliamentary government

September 1997. This law reserves three directly elected seats for women in the 4,298 local councils (each with 10 members) that form the lowest tier of government in Bangladesh. Elections started in December 1997 with immense excitement and participation among the women of the country for whom this new opportunity had been opened. More than 45,000 women became candidates for these reserved council seats. This local initiative is an important step toward increasing the place of women in a country where traditional religious teachings and social custom have advocated their repression. Women leaders are now calling for direct elections of women to the national Legislature and urging that the number of reserved seats be increased from 30 to 110 in that 330-member body.

CHALLENGES

Economic problems have also continued to grow during the recent years of political unrest, presenting immense challenges to Sheikh Hasina's government. Among these problems are a diminishing world market for jute, the country's largest export product, and the lack of sufficient natural resources and energy sources to broaden its industrial base and create new employment. The already high unemployment was increased by the loss of jobs for many Bangladeshis who worked in the Persian Gulf prior to the Gulf War in 1991. Skilled workers, who had earlier returned more than $500 million in remittances to Bangladesh each year, flooded the country's already overcrowded job market. Domestic rice production—barely sufficient to feed Bangladesh's large and growing population even in good times— is severely reduced by the devastating cycle of cyclones and floods that ravage the

country. One cyclone, in May 1991, killed 130,000 people. And the worst flood of the century during the summer of 1998 paralyzed the central part of the country, killing 800 people and leaving almost 30 million homeless. Natural disasters remain a constant threat to all aspects of life in Bangladesh. Yet the population continues to grow, though at a decreasing rate (1.8 percent per year).

Another challenge has been the need to receive from India a more favorable distribution of Ganges River waters through the Farakka Barrage into Bangladesh. India has a stranglehold through its control of this major source of vital water for irrigation and commerce in northwestern Bangladesh. Indicative of a new spirit of cooperation among India and its neighbors, a major agreement was signed by the prime ministers of Bangladesh and India on December 12, 1996, to assure Bangladesh of at least half the water flow through the Barrage.

The Bangladeshi people have shown outstanding initiative in meeting the many challenges caused by population growth and rural poverty through grassroots, voluntary organizations, such as the Bangladesh Rural Advancement Committee. Such efforts have built local schools, improved farming practices, and reduced the average number of births per Bangladeshi woman from more than seven in 1975 to less than four today.

Another important initiative to improve the plight of the poor from the ground up is the Grameen Bank. It was founded in the 1970s by economics professor Mohammed Yunus to provide small loans without collateral to help the landless poor in a country where more than half of the population live in poverty. It has been successful in creating credit for more than 1.4

million borrowers, 90 percent of whom are women. It also trains them in management skills, public health, and family planning. Its effectiveness among the impoverished in Bangladesh has established it as a model for economic empowerment in many other countries.

Bangladesh has also been fortunate in the support it has received from many government and independent agencies in response to its great needs. In 1992, such donors provided $1.9 billion, of which the United States, the fourth-largest bilateral donor, provided $99 million targeted to reduce population growth and increase food availability. With continued grants of humanitarian and economic aid, and with stable, democratically elected leadership, a resilient and responsive people remain hopeful for their health and well-being as a nation.

DEVELOPMENT

Bangladesh is an agricultural country with a very small industrial sector, few natural resources, and 40% unemployment. Bangladesh's per capita income has grown an average of only 0.4% per year since 1960. The country continues to rely heavily on relief aid from the international community.

FREEDOM

Bangladesh has reverted to martial law in order to maintain social order several times since its independence in 1971. With reports of an estimated 3 million children in the workforce, their abuse is also a source of concern. In 1994, novelist Taslima Nasreen was prosecuted on charges of blasphemy and fled the country, raising an international outcry.

HEALTH/WELFARE

In spite of many obstacles, overall life expectancy has increased from 27 to 56 years over the past 20 years. Forty-five percent of the population have access to health care, and the number of hospital beds per population has doubled. Literacy has also increased, from 20% to 38%. The country has made significant strides in reducing the rate of population growth, from 3.3% to 1.82% per year.

ACHIEVEMENTS

Surviving extensive flooding in 1975 and the typhoon in 1991, the resilient people of Bangladesh continue to develop their wealth of human resources, mostly through volunteer and nongovernment agencies such as Grameen Bank. In 1991, a national referendum to restrain the military and restrict the power of the executive branch of government made a strong commitment to parliamentary democracy.

Bhutan (Kingdom of Bhutan)

GEOGRAPHY

Area in Square Miles (Kilometers): 18,142 (47,000) (about half the size of Indiana)

Capital (Population): Thimphu (30,300)

Environmental Concerns: soil erosion; limited access to potable water

Geographical Features: mostly mountainous; some fertile valleys and savanna

Climate: tropical in southern plains; cool winters and hot summers in central valleys; severe winters and cool summers in the Himalayas

PEOPLE

Population

Total: 1,865,200 (some estimates as low as 600,000)

Annual Growth Rate: 2.3%

Rural/Urban Population Ratio: 94/6

Major Languages: Dzongkha; various Tibetan dialects; Nepalese dialects

Ethnic Makeup: 50% Bhote; 35% ethnic Nepalese; 15% indigenous or migrant tribes (estimates vary widely)

Religions: 75% Lamaistic Buddhism; 25% Indian- and Nepalese-influenced Hinduism

Health

Life Expectancy at Birth: 52 years (male); 51 years (female)

Infant Mortality Rate (Ratio): 114/1,000

Physicians Available (Ratio): 1/5,335

Education

Adult Literacy Rate: 42%

COMMUNICATION

Telephones: 1 per 160

TRANSPORTATION

Highways in Miles (Kilometers): 1,326 (2,210)

Railroads in Miles (Kilometers): none

Usable Airfields: 2

GOVERNMENT

Type: monarchy; special treaty relationship with India

Independence Date: August 8, 1949

Head of State/Government: King Jigme Singye Wangchuk is both head of state and government

Political Parties: none legal

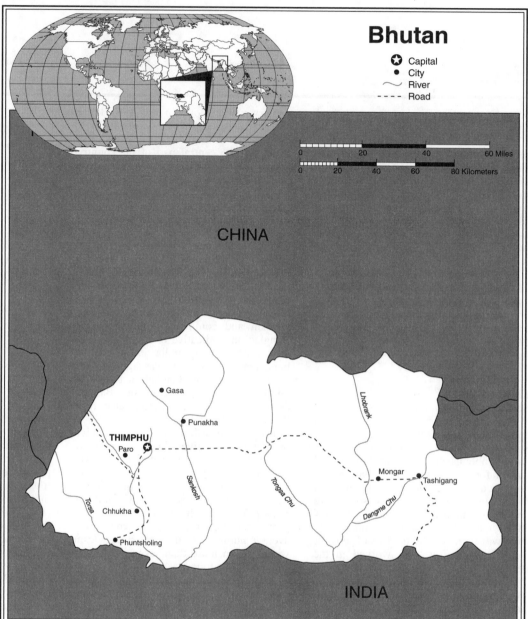

Bhutan

- ⭐ Capital
- ● City
- ∿ River
- - - - Road

Suffrage: each family has one vote in village-level elections

MILITARY

Current Disputes: internal unrest

ECONOMY

Currency ($ U.S. Equivalent): 31.37 ngultrum = $1

Per Capita Income/GDP: $730/$1.3 billion

GDP Growth Rate: 6.9%

Inflation Rate: 8.6%

Natural Resources: timber; hydropower; gypsum; calcium carbide

Agriculture: rice; corn; root crops; citrus fruit; food grains; dairy products; eggs

Industry: cement; wood products; distilling; food processing; calcium carbide; tourism

Exports: $70.9 million (primary partners India, Bangladesh)

Imports: $113.6 million (primary partners India, Japan, United Kingdom)

 http://www.amherst.edu/~amshrest/
bhutan_hist.html
http://www.odci.gov/cia/publications/
factbook/country-frame.html
http://bhutan.org
http://southasia.net/Bhutan/

BHUTAN

Bhutan is a small, Mahayana Buddhist kingdom high in the Himalayan Mountains. (Mahayana is one of the two major forms of Buddhism.) It is the smallest nation on the South Asian subcontinent. It reaches 24,783 feet at its highest point, along the Himalayan ridge border with Tibet, and falls through a series of cascading river valleys down the southern slopes toward Bangladesh, on the eastern side of the subcontinent. Its southern border, barely 100 miles away yet more than 24,000 feet down, touches the edge of the Brahmaputra River plain, through narrow, humid, gorgelike valleys of bamboo jungle. Most of the people in the country (population estimates vary widely, from 600,000 to nearly 2 million) live in the broader, fertile, pine-filled valleys of the central region, which lie from 5,000 to 9,000 feet above sea level. Isolated by its terrain and eager to preserve its unique Buddhist heritage, the country has moved very cautiously into the modern world.

Culturally, religiously, and linguistically, 75 percent of the people of Bhutan are closely related to Tibet. Dzongkha, the most common language, is spoken in the northern and western regions; it is also the official language of the country. Other Tibetan dialects are spoken in the eastern regions, where the people are more closely related by custom to Assam. The remaining 25 percent are Nepali- and Hindi-speaking peoples who have recently migrated into the country, mostly as laborers, and have settled in the southern region closest to India. Several thousand Tibetans fled into Bhutan following the Chinese takeover of their country and subsequent repressions during the 1950s.

The Buddhist religion, which is predominant in Bhutan, also traces its origin to the earliest tradition of Buddhism in Tibet: the Nyingmapa school of the Red Hat sect. Important monasteries, such as at Taktshang, celebrate the advance of the learned Indian monk Padma Sambhava, who introduced Buddhism into Tibet in the eighth century, as the heroic *Guru Rinpoche* ("Precious Teacher"). He is described as coming on a flying tiger to drive the forces of evil out of *Druk Yul,* "Land of the Thunder Dragon." The oldest recorded consolidation of the remote valley peoples under a single authority was in the 1600s by a Tibetan lama, Shabdrung Ngawang Namgyal. He established a tradition of autonomous religious leadership over the entire country that was sustained by the identification of the embodiment of his mind reincarnation (*Dharma Raja*) through successive generations. The religious authority of his *Dharma Raja* was fi-

(Reuters/Bettmann)

King Jigme Singye Wangchuk took over the monarchy of Bhutan in 1972, at the age of 17.

nally subsumed during the 1930s under the temporal authority of a dynastic monarchy that was established in 1907 under British colonial rule.

COLONIAL RULE

British military forces advanced into Bhutan in 1864 to repel Tibetan and Chinese claims of control over the Himalayan Mountains. In gratitude for his help in their successful attack of Tibet in 1903, the British rewarded Ugyen Wangchuk, then feudal lord (*Penlop*) of the north-central district of Tongsa, by assisting him to become *Druk Gyalpo,* the hereditary "Dragon King" of Bhutan in 1907.

The British continued to oversee the external affairs of the country but allowed the new king to rule independently in domestic matters. In 1949, with the end of the British Raj, Bhutan extended this

agreement "to be guided in regard to its foreign relations" with the government of India. India has allowed Bhutan latitude in establishing international agreements, including support of Bhutan's admission to the United Nations in 1971. But it remains the largest investor in the development of Bhutan's economy.

THE MONARCHY

In 1952, Jigme Dorji Wangchuk, grandson of Ugyen Wangchuk and successor to his throne, instituted a number of reforms to bring his country cautiously into the modern era. The king remained the religious head and chief executive of the nation.

To encourage more public participation in government, he established a National Assembly, the Tshoghdu. The Assembly has 151 members, 31 of whom are appointed by the king. The remainder are elected by hereditary village headmen in the districts, who also serve as local judges in a judicial system in which the king remains the chief justice.

In 1968, further reform granted the Assembly powers to limit the absolute authority of the king. No longer can he veto legislation passed by majority vote of the Assembly. Also, by a two-thirds vote, the Assembly can force the king to abdicate. But in that case, he can be succeeded only by the next claimant in his hereditary line. This provision reproduces on the national level the traditional family expectation that a landholder will pass on his lands to his eldest son as soon as the heir comes of age.

Jigme Dorji Wangchuk's reforms have included the elimination of serfdom by granting public lands to landless servants. But he did not break up large private landholdings, so as not to disrupt traditional social patterns and create unemployment. He also, in the face of Chinese threats of invasion during the 1950s, opened the country to the outside world by allowing the Indian government to build a road from its southern border with India to the capital, Thimphu. It took 112 miles of winding roadway to cover this straight-line distance of 45 miles. In 1996, the government of India undertook a project to extend this roadway into eastern Bhutan.

THE CHALLENGE OF MODERNIZATION

Jigme Dorji Wangchuk died in 1972 and was succeeded by his 17-year-old son, Jigme Singye Wangchuk. He has continued his father's policies of cautious change. He proposed during the summer of 1998 to expand and make more representative the powers of the National Assembly by replacing his royal Council of

Dharma Raja of
Tibetan lamas
A.D. 1616–1950

Tongsa Penlop
becomes
hereditary king
1907

British control
over Bhutan's
external affairs
1910–1947

Indian control
over Bhutan's
external affairs
begins
1949

Constitutional
monarchy is
established;
national authority
has power to limit
authority of king
1953

King Jigme
Singe Wangchuk
becomes the
fourth-generation
monarch
1972

Cautious
modernization
efforts begin; the
Citizenship Act
aims at limiting
citizenship
1980s

1990s

Census
enforcement
denies many
Nepali
immigrants
citizenship

Demonstrations
occur in protest
of government
policies toward
Nepalis

More than
110,000 Nepali
residents of
Bhutan remain in
refugee camps in
eastern Nepal

Ministers with a cabinet elected by the Assembly and "vested with full executive powers to provide efficient and effective governance of our country." The Assembly, with some reluctance to adopt the change, carried out his wishes by electing a cabinet from a list of candidates that he provided. In a further step toward modernization, the Assembly voted in November 1998 to impose an income tax on all citizens who earned more than an equivalent of $100 per month to supplement its industrial tax revenues.

With India's help, Bhutan has increased the country's energy potential. The largest of six new hydroelectric generators, the 336-megawatt Chuka Hydroelectric Project, financed by the Indian government, was completed in 1987 and now exports $25 million worth of electricity to India annually. Bhutan's forestry reserves are also extensive but remain virtually unexploited. Even the potential for tourism is being developed on a very modest scale.

The policy of the government is to develop the country's economy so as not to undermine the traditional Buddhist life of the majority of its people. It is also concerned about maintaining Bhutan's dramatically beautiful environment. Twenty percent of the country has been set aside for preservation. The Royal Manas National Park, a 165-square-mile sanctuary, was established along the southern border of Bhutan to protect the natural wildlife of South Asia. Many of the species that find refuge there are endangered.

The emphasis on preserving Bhutan's heritage has slowed the impact of modern advances on the lives of the people. The educational system, with the guidance of Canadian Jesuit Father William Mackey, has increased to provide 180 schools and a national college. Still, only 21 percent

of school-age children attend, and the literacy rate today is less than 15 percent, the lowest in Asia. Health services are also meager; the expectation is that the family unit will remain the primary source of social welfare. Because of the strong monastic tradition, the annual birth rate is also low, at 2 percent. But the level of infant mortality is very high, and average life expectancy is only about 51 years.

Bhutan is facing many severe challenges as it seeks to adopt the virtues of a modern industrial society while maintaining the values of its rich natural and religious heritage. Part of the problem is that greater industrialization requires more labor. Ninety-five percent of the workforce of Bhutan are employed in subsistence farming on the 16 percent of the land that is available for cultivation and pasture. Because this sector is self-sufficient, the country has had to import workers from neighboring Nepal and India to provide the labor needed to develop its industry. But their very presence challenges the indigenous peoples' attempt to create a Bhutanese national identity out of the exclusive cultural characteristics of the dominant community. Rather than recognizing the integrity and richness of the diversity of the many peoples who live within the nation's borders, the government has promoted distinctively northern traditions of language and custom as being nationally correct.

This nationalistic policy has been particularly hard on the Nepali population, who, as noted earlier, have settled mostly in the southern part of the country. Although the government's intent is to promote political unity, its efforts have led to political unrest, terrorist attacks on schools and other public buildings, and deportations. Tens of thousands of people

have fled Bhutan and are now living in refugee camps in the eastern part of Nepal. The governments of Nepal and Bhutan are seeking a solution to this difficult situation. Significantly, in this age of democracy, the role of the enlightened monarch, King Jigme Singye Wangchuk, appears to be the most promising in resolving the cultural and political tensions created by modernization.

DEVELOPMENT

Bhutan's economy is based on agricultural self-sufficiency and barter. More than 95% of the workforce are in the agricultural sector. Bhutan is among the poorest countries in the world. The government is cautiously developing the country's vast hydroelectric power potential and a modest tourist industry.

FREEDOM

In this traditional society, thinly dispersed across rugged mountain slopes, the king instituted political reform in 1952 by creating an advisory National Assembly, the Tshoghdu. This Assembly has enacted laws that repress Nepali and Indian residents.

HEALTH/WELFARE

The family and the village have the primary responsibility for the welfare of the people. In the 1950s the king instituted a program of social work for monks living in the country's numerous state-supported monasteries. The government has recently undertaken an education program, but literacy is the lowest in South Asia.

ACHIEVEMENTS

Twenty percent of the country has been set aside for the preservation of its vast forest and natural wildlife reserves. Efforts at reform are done in the context of maintaining Bhutan's unique and distinctive Buddhist cultural heritage.

Maldives (Republic of Maldives)

GEOGRAPHY

Area in Square Miles (Kilometers): 186 (300) (about 1½ times the size of Washington, D.C.)

Capital (Population): Malé (63,000)

Environmental Concerns: depletion of freshwater aquifers threatens water supplies

Geographical Features: flat, with white sandy beaches

Climate: tropical; monsoon

PEOPLE

Population

Total: 280,400

Annual Growth Rate: 3.47%

Rural/Urban Population Ratio: 73/27

Major Languages: Divehi; English is spoken by most government officials

Ethnic Makeup: Sinhalese; Dravidian; Arab; Black

Religion: 100% Sunni Muslim

Health

Life Expectancy at Birth: 65 years (male); 69 years (female)

Infant Mortality Rate (Ratio): 44.1/1,000

Average Caloric Intake: 83% of FAO minimum

Physicians Available (Ratio): 1/5,297

Education

Adult Literacy Rate: 93%

COMMUNICATION

Telephones: 1 per 18 people

Televisions: 1 per 40 people

TRANSPORTATION

Highways in Miles (Kilometers): 6 (9.6)

Railroads in Miles (Kilometers): none

Usable Airfields: 2

GOVERNMENT

Type: republic

Independence Date: July 26, 1965 (from the United Kingdom)

Head of State/Government: President Maumoon Abdul Gayoom is both head of state and head of government

Political Parties: none; the country has been governed by the Didi clan for 8 centuries

Suffrage: universal at 21

MILITARY

Current Disputes: none

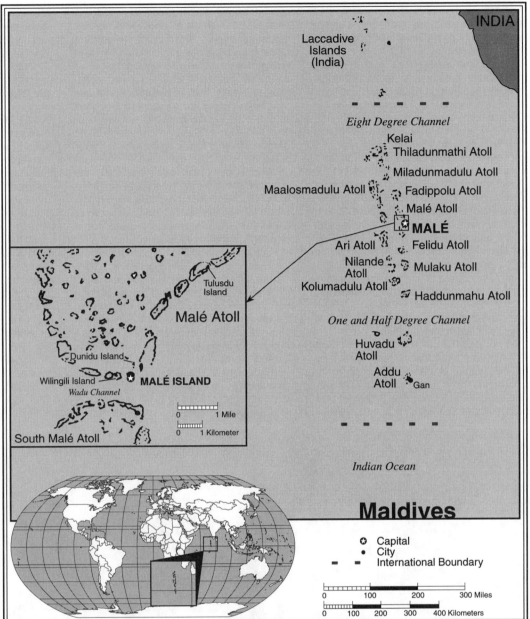

Maldives

- ✪ Capital
- • City
- ▬ ▬ International Boundary

ECONOMY

Currency ($ U.S. Equivalent): 11.77 rufiyaa = $1

Per Capita Income/GDP: $1,620/$423 million

GDP Growth Rate: 5.8%

Inflation Rate: 7.7%

Unemployment Rate: negligible

Labor Force: 56,435 (1990 est.)

Natural Resources: fish

Agriculture: fish; corn; coconuts; sweet potatoes

Industry: tourism; fish processing; tourism; shipping; boat building; coconut processing; garments; woven mats; rope; handicrafts; coral and sand mining

Exports: $50 million (primary partners Sri Lanka, United States, Germany)

Imports: $268 million (primary partners Singapore, India, Sri Lanka)

 http://www.maldive.com/hist/mhisto.html

http://www.odci.gov/cia/publications/factbook/country-frame.html

http://www.undp.org/missions/maldives

http://southasia.net/Maldives/

MALDIVES

Maldives is a string of 1,190 tiny tropical islands grouped into 26 atolls in the Indian Ocean. Located about 400 miles southwest of India and west of Sri Lanka, the island chain stretches for some 510 miles north to south across the equator. The largest of the islands is less than 5 square miles in area, and the highest elevation is only 80 feet above sea level. Most of the islands are much smaller, rising barely 6 feet above sea level. They are easily submerged by tidal waves and storm swells. These are very fragile, remote, but enticingly beautiful.

Most of the islands are covered with lush scrub growth, some have coconut-palm groves, and all are surrounded by coral reefs and clear waters laden with fish. The mean daily temperature remains at 80°F year-round. The climate is humid, especially during the rainy monsoon season, from June to August. Yet because of a shortage of fresh water and arable land on most of the islands, only 200 of them are inhabited.

About one fifth of the total population of 280,400 people live in the capital city on the island of Malé, which is only seven tenths of a square mile in area. An increasing population, due to longer life expectancy and a high birth rate, is rapidly draining the island's limited resources. Its freshwater supply is diminishing, both by the draw upon its aquifer, faster than it can be replenished by rainfall, and through contamination.

The inhabitants of Maldives appear originally to have come from south India and Sri Lanka. There are remains of Buddhist shrines which date from the second century B.C. The prevailing language of the islands, Divehi, also suggests an early relationship with the mainland of the subcontinent. It is derived from Pali, the classical language of Buddhism in India, from which the Sinhalese language of Sri Lanka also comes. But Divehi is now written in the Arabic script, with the addition of many Arabic and Urdu words.

Because the Maldive islands lie across the maritime trade route between Africa and eastern Asia, they were often visited by Arab traders. The arrival of an Islamic Sufi saint in A.D. 1153 led to the Islamic conversion of the peoples of the islands. The Moroccan explorer Ibn Battuta stopped there during his extensive travels through North Africa and Asia in the fourteenth century. Because of his Islamic scholarship, he was invited to stay on Malé as a judge. During his 8-month stay, he was married and divorced six times.

His accounts provide us with a colorful description of island life at that time.

The people of Maldives continue to affirm their Islamic faith. Citizenship is restricted to Sunni Muslims, and the country's legal system is based on Shari'a, the Islamic law.

A HISTORY OF INDEPENDENCE

Strongly united under the authority of a sultan (an Islamic monarch), the Maldivians remained fiercely independent through the centuries. A local leader, Bodu Muhammad Takurufanu, repulsed a brief Portuguese colonial intrusion in 1573. Maldives became a protectorate under the British Crown in 1887. Even then, however, the Maldivian leaders did not permit British interference in their governance. The southern island of Gan became a British military base during World War II and, in 1956, the site of an air base. But strong antiforeign sentiment forced the closing of the base in 1976, some 14 years before the end of a 30-year lease with the British. The following year, Maldives rejected a Soviet offer to lease the base for $1 million per year.

In 1953, the sultan, Muhammad Amin Didi, declared Maldives a democratic republic, with himself as the president. But

(Reuters/Bettmann)

The fragile character of Maldives' environment and the economic reliance of its inhabitants on it make international cooperation an important element in future development. Regional associations and international organizations are important forums for communication. One such organization is the South Asian Association for Regional Cooperation. Pictured above are representatives of the member governments who met on November 21, 1990, in Malé. From left to right were Prime Minister Krishna Prasad Bhattaria of Nepal, India's Prime Minister Chandra Shekhar, Bangladesh's President Hussain Muhammed Ershard, Pakistan's Prime Minister Nawaz Sharif, Bhutan's King Jigme Singye Wangchuk, Maldives' President Maumoon Abdul Gayoom, and Sri Lanka's President Dingiri Banda Wijetunge.

The earliest evidence of Indian Buddhist civilization
300 B.C.

Maldives' conversion to Islam
1153

Maldives is an Islamic sultanate; Bodu Muhammed Takurufanu repulses brief Portuguese intrusion to the islands in 1573
1153–1968

Maldives is a British protectorate
1887–1968

Maldives becomes an independent democratic republic without political parties
1968

An attempted coup is put down by the Indian Army
1988

1990s

The government seeks to improve social services, incurring substantial debt in the process

Maumoon Abdul Guyoom elected to a fourth term as president

Maldives agitates for global environmental responsibility

the power of governance remained with an appointed Regency Committee. In 1968, Amin Ibrahim Nasir, who had served since 1957 as prime minister in the "Committee," successfully instituted a new Constitution with an elected legislative Parliament (*Majlis*). This body selected him as nominee to run for president of the country. The new Constitution also did not allow for the existence of political parties.

During his tenure as president, Ibrahim Nasir abolished the post of prime minister and increased the power of the presidency to quasi-sultan status. He won a second 5-year term in 1973. Nasir decided not to run for a third term and was succeeded in 1978 by Maumoon Abdul Gayoom.

President Gayoom was reelected by large majorities in the elections of 1983, 1988, 1993, and 1998. In 1993, he received 93 percent of the popular vote as the single candidate in a referendum to approve his nomination by a majority vote of the 48-seat Citizen's *Majlis*. An opposition candidate who won 18 votes in the parliamentary election was subsequently charged, according to an Amnesty International report, with violating the Constitution and was sentenced to banishment from the country for 15 years.

In November 1998, the *Majlis* amended the Constitution with a view to assuring citizen's guarantees of civil rights and decentralizing government administration among the many islands of the country. But it did not change the electoral process for the presidency. On October 16, 1998, 90.9 percent of the voters approved President Gayoom's nomination by the *Majlis* to a fifth 5-year term.

An attempted coup, thought to have been instigated by Sri Lankan Tamil militants, was put down in 1988 by an Indian military unit called in by President Gayoom. Ties with the Indian government have become increasingly strong since that time.

QUALITY OF LIFE

The major industries of Maldives are fishing and tourism, both of which are heavily supported by the government. Almost half the country's workforce are employed in fishing, mostly using traditional offshore craft called *dhonis*. In the 1980s, government funds were used to construct canning and cold-storage facilities, as well as more than 200 modern fishing boats, in order to expand the catch—and the markets—for this valuable resource. In 1981, an international airport was constructed on the island of Malé to serve an increasing number of tourists. It, together with the airports on the islands of Hulule and Gan, receive the 395,000 visitors who vacation in the more than 60 new hotels spread over the various atolls in 1998.

These industries, even with a reviving coconut crop and a modest shipping fleet, do not balance the import needs of the country, especially for food. The country receives more than 20 percent of its revenue as foreign aid, and it continues to accumulate debt. Like most regions of the world that are strongly dependent upon the tourist industry for their economic health, Maldives' fortunes are based upon the prosperity of the wealthier nations. In recent years the country has sustained an impressive economic growth rate, rising to a 7.2 percent increase in 1995, and 6 percent in 1997, leading to the highest per capita income in South Asia. Still, because of its fragile environment and economy, the government of Maldives objected very strongly to its removal from the United Nations list of the world's poorest nations to the developing countries category during the meeting of UN General Assembly in 1998.

In spite of setbacks, the Maldivian government has extended education and health services throughout the inhabited islands in the archipelago. The number of primary schools has increased. Adult literacy has also increased, from 82 percent to 93 percent, a result of the outreach of the educational programs to the outer islands. There are now some 42,000 primary students in schools on many islands.

Maldives has no institutions of higher learning. Medical facilities are also limited. There are only four hospitals in the entire country, plus an emergency medical rescue service among the outlying islands. The government, however, continues to work to improve water supplies and to eliminate water-borne diseases through water-purification and other public-health measures.

Although the country does not function as a totally free, modern democracy, the government has retained the confidence of its independent, peace-loving people through its policies to encourage economic growth and expand social services. Because of the fragile character of its environment, upon which so much of the economy depends, Maldives is eager to stimulate increasing international concern for the preservation of the global environment. It also appears to be making progress in its appeal to its neighbors to establish the Indian Ocean as a nuclear-free zone.

DEVELOPMENT

The major economic activity of this nation of islands is fishing, which provides about 20% of its gross domestic product and employs 25% of its workforce. Tourism has also gained tremendously in importance and is attracting foreign investment. Maldives' gross domestic product per capita, though still very low, has increased dramatically since 1960.

FREEDOM

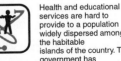

Maldives became a democratic republic in 1968. It adopted a popularly elected unicameral Legislature and made provisions for an independently elected president; but it prohibited the formation of political parties. Rights of citizenship in Maldives, an Islamic nation, are restricted to Sunni Muslims.

HEALTH/WELFARE

Health and educational services are hard to provide to a population widely dispersed among the habitable islands of the country. The government has developed an emergency rescue service that is able to reach 97% of the population. The average overall life expectancy is 67 years.

ACHIEVEMENTS

Maldives has resisted superpower attempts to place a naval base on its territory. To preserve its fragile environment and its peace-loving character, the country has become a strong advocate to make the Indian Ocean an arms-free, and particularly a nuclear-free, zone.

Nepal (Kingdom of Nepal)

GEOGRAPHY

Area in Square Miles (Kilometers): 54,349 (140,800) (slightly larger than Arkansas)

Capital (Population): Kathmandu (535,000)

Environmental Concerns: widespread deforestation; soil erosion; water pollution

Geographical Features: flat river plain in the south; central hills; rugged Himalayas in the north

Climate: cool summers and severe winters in the north; subtropical in the south

PEOPLE

Population
Total: 23,107,500
Annual Growth Rate: 2.53%
Rural/Urban Population Ratio: 89/11
Major Languages: Nepali; 20 languages divided into numerous dialects
Ethnic Makeup: Newar; Indian; Tibetan; Gurung; Magar; Tamang; Bhotia' Rais; Limbu; Sherpa; many smaller groups
Religions: 90% Hindu; 5% Buddhist; 3% Muslim; 2% others

Health
Life Expectancy at Birth: 58 years (male); 57 years (female)
Infant Mortality Rate (Ratio): 78.4/1,000
Average Caloric Intake: 88% of FAO minimum
Physicians Available (Ratio): 1/12,623

Education
Adult Literacy Rate: 27.5%
Compulsory (Ages): 6–11; free

COMMUNICATION
Telephones: 1 per 276 people
Televisions: 1 per 213 people

TRANSPORTATION
Highways in Miles (Kilometers): 4,618 (7,400)
Railroads in Miles (Kilometers): 63 (101)
Usable Airfields: 43

GOVERNMENT
Type: parliamentary democracy
Independence Date: 1768 (unified)
Head of State/Government: King Birendra Bir Bikram Shah Dev; Prime Minister Girija Prasad Koirala
Political Parties: Communist Party of Nepal/Unified Marxist-Leninist Party;

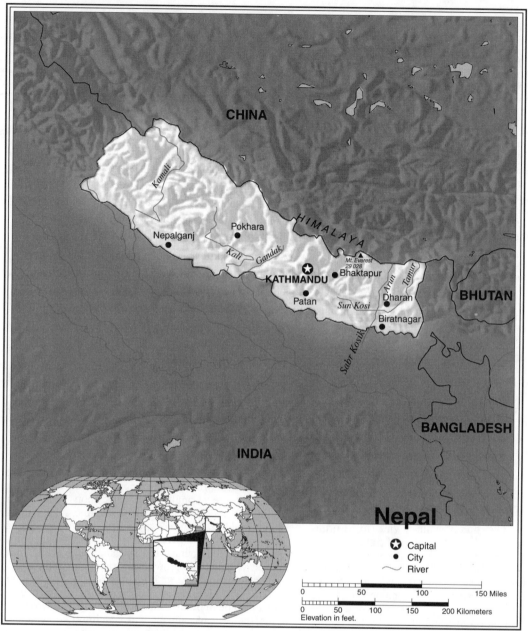

Nepal

- ⊕ Capital
- • City
- ∿ River

0 ... 50 ... 100 ... 150 Miles

0 ... 50 ... 100 ... 150 ... 200 Kilometers
Elevation in feet.

Nepali Congress Party; National Democratic Party (also called Rastriya Prajantra Party); Sadbhavana (Goodwill) Party; Nepal Workers and Peasants Party; many small groups
Suffrage: universal at 18

MILITARY
Military Expenditures (% of GDP): 1.2%
Current Disputes: none

ECONOMY
Currency ($ U.S. Equivalent): 49.88 Nepalese rupees = $1
Per Capita Income/GDP: $1,200/$26.5 billion
GDP Growth Rate: 2.9%
Inflation Rate: 9.2%

Labor Force: 9,200,000
Natural Resources: quartz; timber; hydropower potential; small deposits of lignite, copper, cobalt, and iron ore
Agriculture: rice; corn; wheat; sugarcane; root crops; milk; water buffalo meat
Industry: carpets; textiles; small rice, jute, sugar, and oilseed mills; cigarettes; tourism; cement and brick production
Exports: $343 million (primary partners India, United States, Germany)
Imports: $1.3 billion (primary partners India, Singapore, Japan)

http://rip.physics.unk.edu/Nepal/NPD.html
http://www.catmando.com/nepal.htm

NEPAL

Nepal is like a Tantric mandala: colorful, dramatic, intense, intricate, mystifying. The country is breathtaking, like the magnificent Mount Everest—awesome to behold, confounding to ponder. Everest's peak, the highest in the world, dominates a majestic row of 10 Himalayan mountains over 26,000 feet high that marks the imposing, formidably high boundary between Nepal and Tibet. The land falls steeply, dramatically, from this arctic height into the lush Kathmandu Valley, some 20,000 feet below. It then rises again over the smaller, barren Mahabharat range, up to 11,000 feet, and drops down once more through the foothills into a marshy plain (of the Ganges River), about 900 feet above sea level. Nepal is a land of immense natural contrast, covering a descent from the highest point on Mount Everest down more than 28,000 feet in less than 100 miles. Habitat for a wide variety of species, from the elusive snow leopards to elephants, monkeys, tigers, and crocodiles, the land fills one with a sense of wonder.

Nepal is also home to an immense variety of people. In the broadest of terms, they can be divided by region, religion, and language into three distinct groups. The high mountainous regions to the north are sparsely inhabited, mostly by people of Tibetan descent and language who follow the Lamaist, or Tibetan, Buddhist tradition. Their dress and many customs are from Tibet. Some, for example, practice polyandrous marriage, wherein the wife of the eldest son is also married to his younger brothers. In such families, their lands are not usually subdivided. The brothers also share in the few seasonal occupations that the frigid terrain allows: cultivating in spring, herding in summer, and trading in winter. Because of these practices, even though arable land is scarce and trade has been drastically reduced by the Chinese takeover of Tibet, the people of the northern mountain region are more prosperous than those living in the more fertile valleys to the south. The alternative to family life presented by the Buddhist monastic tradition also restrains their growth in population. Although they occupy almost half of the total land area, they constitute only about 3 percent of the total population of Nepal.

About 31 percent of the population live in the Terai, the low-lying, southernmost region of the country that is in the Gangetic plain. These people are mostly Hindu, although some are Muslim. They speak dialects of Hindi and are ethnically and culturally very close to their Indian neighbors. Because the land is flat, fertile,

and nurtured by the snow-fed rivers flowing out of the mountains, agriculture is the primary activity. Although it is a narrow strip of land, only about 20 miles wide and occupying only 17 percent of the country, it produces more than 60 percent of Nepal's gross national product.

Two thirds of the population live in the interlying hill region, which is also predominantly agricultural, although most of the countriy's urban population live in this region. Arable lands are scarcer than in the Terai and are terraced for farming. Because of the altitude, the growing season is shorter and the yields are lower.

At the center of this region is the Kathmandu Valley, a lush alluvial plain 15 miles long and 12 miles wide. Nepal's three largest cities—Kathmandu, Patan, and Bhaktapur—lie in the valley. These cities threaten to absorb most of the valley as they continue to expand. Dominant among the people of the valley are Newars, who have lived there as a distinct community for many centuries. They were known in ancient times for their skill as artisans and merchants who interacted with the many surrounding cultures to create a distinctive artistic style and to fuse an overwhelming multiplicity of religious expression. The Nepali language, spoken by about 60 percent of the total population, is itself a combination, based on the Indo-European languages of India infused with extensive Tibeto–Burman borrowings. There is a wide array of ethnic and cultural identities as well as urban/rural and rich/poor contrasts in this central valley region of Nepal.

SOCIAL DIVERSITY

Nepali social diversity is partly due to the rugged terrain, which has kept many small groups isolated east to west in the several river valleys that descend down the steep southern slopes of the mountains. Also important, Nepal has been since ancient times on the main trade routes from India north up the river valleys, through the high mountain passes into Tibet, and on into China. Nepali traders along these routes have maintained distinct ethnic identities, whether their primary interaction has been with the Tibetan culture to the north or with the Hindu culture to the south. The success of their mercantile activity with such very different partners has reinforced the cultural contrasts between Tibet and India within the central region of Nepal itself.

The influence of the hierarchical social structure known in India as the caste system has also contributed to Nepal's social diversity. This system, in ranking rather than assimilating differing social and vocational groups, affirms the unique cus-

toms of each group. As the Nepalese criteria for ranking appear more flexible than in India, ethnic identity and adaptive behavior to form distinct social groupings appear to change readily and to add to the diversity of their configuration. The Gurkhas, for example, famous for their military prowess and courage, have been recruited from three different Tibeto–Burman language communities, from different parts of Nepal, who have grouped together because of the opportunity for military employment that a shared identity as Gurkhas affords. Similarly, several distinct tribal groups in the Terai have claimed a single ethnic identity as Tharus in order to gain strength as a political force not available to them as separate minority groups. In contrast, Thaksatae villagers have distanced themselves from other Thakalis, with whom they share ethnic, linguistic, and religious identities, in order to maintain the trading privileges that they have achieved as a distinct community within that group.

POLITICS

The immense and confusing diversity of Nepal's population has contributed to the country's struggle with democracy. For many years it was felt that only a strong, absolute monarchy would be able to hold it together.

The unity of present-day Nepal was forged in the eighteenth century A.D. by Prithvi Narayan Shah, king of the western province of Gorkha, who conquered the surrounding kingdoms and established his dynasty in Kathmandu, the capital of the defeated Newar ruler. His family's reign was circumscribed first by the British East India Company, in 1815, and later, in 1845, by the Kathmandu Rana family, which established a powerful and hereditary prime ministry to rule the Shah domain.

In 1950, with the departure of British support from the subcontinent, a national movement, led by the Nepali Congress Party, overthrew the Rana family. King Tribhuvan Vir Vikram Shah, because of his support for the anti-Rana movement, became a national hero. Upon his reinstitution as full monarch in February 1951, he worked to bring constitutional democracy to Nepal. In 1959, under a new Constitution that set up a national Parliament and limited the powers of the king, elections were held. The Congress Party won 74 of the 109 seats in the Legislature.

King Tribhuvan died in 1955 and was succeeded by his son, Mahendra. In 1960, King Mahendra, in a surprise move to assert his power as absolute monarch, dismissed the Congress government and banned all political parties. In 1962, he ventured to establish a new legislative As-

The Shah dynasty's expansion of the Kingdom of Gorkha A.D. 1742–1814	The British East India Company reduces the Gorkha domain to the Kingdom of Nepal 1815	Rana family domination of the Shah dynasty 1845–1950	The founding of the Nepali Congress Party 1949	Constitutional monarchy 1959–1960	Absolute monarchy; constitutional monarchy established with a multiparty, democratically elected Parliament 1960–1991

1990s

The first national democratic elections in 32 years are held in 1991

Nepal continues to struggle with widespread and severe poverty

sembly—but not one based on nationwide elections; rather, elections were held on the local level for the village council (*panchayat*). Members of the local *panchayat* then elected representatives to an 11-member district *panchayat,* which in turn elected members to the National *Panchayat.* The National *Panchayat* elected its own prime minister. However, the king reserved the power to appoint all the Council of Ministers, who oversee the operation of the different departments of government. In this way, he was able to reinforce the traditional seats of local power, among the landlords, throughout the diverse regions of the country, who, in turn, reaffirmed the authority of the king.

Upon the death of King Mahendra, in 1972, his son Birendra became king. In 1980, in response to growing public concern for greater democracy, he held a referendum to see whether the people would prefer a multiparty electoral process or a continuation of the party-banned, tiered elections to determine membership in the National *Panchayat.* The tiered *panchayat* system won by a 54.7 percent vote. In response, King Birendra retained the ban on political parties, but the electoral process was amended to have the National *Panchayat* representatives elected by direct vote of the people.

Elections were held in 1986, and a majority who favored limiting the power of the king were elected. Encouraged by these results, the combined leadership of the banned Nepali Congress Party (NCP) and the Nepal Communist Party organized public demonstrations for greater democracy. Their agitation found support among a growing middle class, disaffected by economic hardship and bungling, opportunistic *panchayat* leadership. In response to this popular outcry, King Birendra removed the ban on political parties in the spring of 1990. On November 8 of that year, he proclaimed a new Constitution, which he had worked out with the party leaders that limited his absolute sovereign power and marked the beginning of a multiparty, democratically elected, parliamentary government.

National democratic elections—the first in 32 years were held on May 12, 1991, with the Nepali Congress winning 114 of the new 205-seat Parliament. But the Nepali Congress Party continued to struggle with its diversity. In July 1994, some 36 dissident members of the Congress refused to attend the prime minister's annual address. Their absence led to a no-confidence vote in Parliament, its dissolution, and new elections, set for November 1994.

The 1994 elections were won by the major opposition party in the previous Legislature—the Unified Marxist-Leninist Party (UMLP), which took 88 parliamentary seats. But the fragile coalition that it formed to preside in Parliament lasted for less than a year. When it was forced to step down, in September 1995, the Nepali Congress Party, with 86 seats, formed a coalition with two other parties, thereby gaining a bare majority support. In March 1997, this fragile coalition also fell apart. Not wishing to face a new general election, the UMLP formed yet another coalition with a fragile majority. It supported Lokendra Bahadur Chand, a monarchist whose leadership harked back to the days of King Mahendra, who led a party that held only 10 seats in Parliament. Prime Minister Chand was ousted 6 months later by Surya Bahadur Thapa, a member of his own party who managed to form a new coalition with Nepali Congress Party support. After a stormy 6 months, during which the UMLP split and the NCP demanded that it lead the coalition, Thapa first sought to have King Birendra dissolve the Parliament and call for new elections. Unsuccessful in this strategy, he resigned, and on April 12, Girija Prasad Koirala, leader of the NCP, was appointed the fifth prime minister of Nepal since the national elections in November 1994.

CHALLENGES

Each new Nepalese government has been faced with demanding parliamentary struggles to maintain its leadership. Yet beyond the walls of government, the ruling party is more substantively challenged by the country's staggering problems of poverty, high population growth, and illiteracy. More than 90 percent of the workforce barely survive by subsistence farming, and, according to a recent World Bank report, 40 percent of the people live in absolute poverty. The incidences of malnutrition-related retardation and blindness are also high. And HIV, the virus that causes AIDS, is beginning to take its toll. In education and in medical and social services, the country struggles with limited resources, isolation, and ethnosocial diversity.

The country needs a consistent, stable, and purposeful government if these problems are to be solved. Nepal's industrial potential has long been restrained by trade agreements tying the country to India's development policies, and its commerce has been severely limited by the difficulty in traversing the trade routes to Tibet. There is immense potential for improvement in Nepal's social conditions, but among such an incredibly awesome array of peoples, even contemplating this challenge leaves one with a sense of wonder.

DEVELOPMENT

Most of Nepal's economy relies on subsistence agriculture, which involves more than 90% of the labor force. The successful ascent of Mount Everest has introduced a thriving tourist industry. Tourism is up by 20% in recent years. Yet per capita income has increased at an annual rate of only 0.1 percent, placing Nepal among the poorest nations in South Asia and the world.

FREEDOM

The Kingdom of Nepal became a constitutional monarchy in 1959 but reserved executive power with the king and preserved the traditional powers of local chieftans in tiered elections to the Legislature. In 1991 popular elections were held for the first time in 32 years. Limits on royal authority were also established.

HEALTH/WELFARE

In education and social services, the country struggles with limited resources, isolation, and diversity. Malnutrition, caused by a limited growing season and urban crowding, has led to high levels of retardation and blindness. Adult literacy is only 27.5%, while overall life expectancy is but 57 years.

ACHIEVEMENTS

Democracy is beginning to take root in this mountain kingdom long ruled by an entrenched establishment. Tourism has introduced environmental degradation, but it has also brought the stimulus to develop industry based on its large hydropower potential and to undertake social-service and educational reforms.

Pakistan (Islamic Republic of Pakistan)

GEOGRAPHY

Area in Square Miles (Kilometers): 310,320 (803,940) (about twice the size of California)

Capital (Population): Islamabad (201,000)

Environmental Concerns: water pollution; deforestation; soil erosion; desertification

Geographical Features: flat plain in the east; mountains in the north and northwest

Climate: mostly hot, dry desert; temperate in the northwest; arctic in the north

PEOPLE

Population

Total: 132,185,000

Annual Growth Rate: 2.22%

Rural/Urban Population Ratio: 65/35

Major Languages: Punjabi; Sindhi; Siraiki; Pashto; Urdu; Balochi; Hindko; English; others

Ethnic Makeup: 63% Punjabi; 12% Sindhi; 10% Pathan; 8% Urdu; 10% others

Religions: 97% Muslim; 3% others

Health

Life Expectancy at Birth: 58 years (male); 60 years (female)

Infant Mortality Rate (Ratio): 95.1/1,000

Average Caloric Intake: 100% of FAO minimum

Physicians Available (Ratio): 1/2,064

Education

Adult Literacy Rate: 36%

COMMUNICATION

Telephones: 1 per 61 people

Daily Newspaper Circulation: 21 per 1,000 people

Televisions: 1 per 53 people

TRANSPORTATION

Highways in Miles (Kilometers): 129,938 (216,564)

Railroads in Miles (Kilometers): 4,898 (8,163)

Usable Airfields: 102

Motor Vehicles in Use: 1,045,000

GOVERNMENT

Type: federal republic

Independence Date: August 14, 1947 (from the United Kingdom)

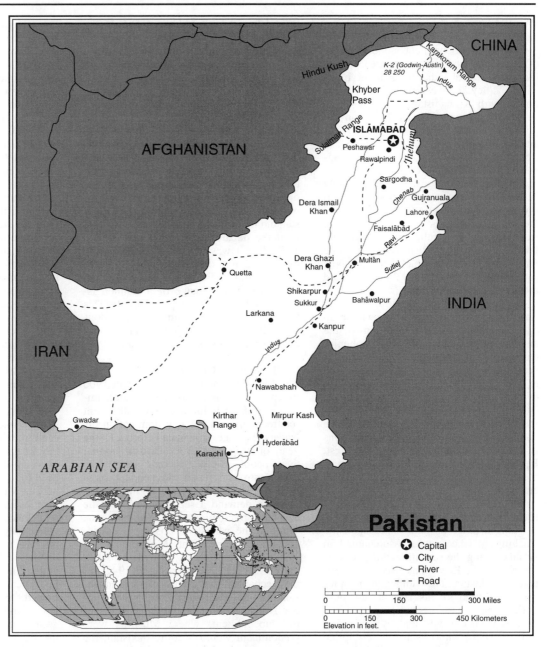

Pakistan

- ✪ Capital
- ● City
- River
- Road

Head of State/Government: President Sardar Farooq Leghari; Prime Minister Mohammad Nawaz Sharif

Political Parties: various government and opposition parties

Suffrage: universal at 21; separate electorates and reserved parliamentary seats for non-Muslims

MILITARY

Military Expenditures (% of GDP): 5.3%

Current Disputes: border disputes with Afghanistan; disputes over Kashmir and water-sharing problems with India

ECONOMY

Currency ($ U.S. Equivalent): 39.68 rupees = $1

Per Capita Income/GDP: $2,300/$296.5 billion

GDP Growth Rate: 5.5%

Inflation Rate: 10.8%

Labor Force: 36,700,000

Natural Resources: natural gas; petroleum; coal; iron ore; copper; salt; limestone

Agriculture: cotton; grains; sugarcane; fruits; vegetables; livestock

Industry: textiles; food processing; construction materials; consumer goods

Exports: $8.3 billion (primary partners United States, Japan, Hong Kong)

Imports: $12.0 billion (primary partners Japan, United States, Germany)

 http://www.clas.ufl.edu/users/gthursby/pak/

PAKISTAN

Pakistan is the second-largest nation of the South Asian subcontinent, about the size of Texas and Louisiana combined, or one fourth the size of India. It lies in the Indus River Valley, between the mountainous border with Afghanistan—through which comes the famous Khyber Pass—on the northwest, and the Great Indian Desert and the Rann of Katch, on the southeast. Long a land of transition between the rugged steppes of Inner Asia and the plains of India, it is today a new nation caught between the heritage of a glorious imperial past and the poetic image of an ideal theocratic future. Its goal to become an exemplary modern religious state, a truly Islamic republic, is affirmed by the name *Pakistan,* given by the Muslim poet Muhammed Iqbal in 1930. The word means "Land of the Pure."

The heritage of the people of Pakistan traces back to the earliest-known urban culture in South Asia. Excavations of the ancient cities of Harappa and Mohenjodaro, discovered in 1922, reveal an impressive civilization that dates from 3000 to 1500 B.C. Distinctive for its knowledge of hydrologics and its use of irrigation to cultivate the valley with the rich waters of the Indus River, it developed an extensive commerce with the emerging civilizations in the Mesopotamian Valley to the west. Patterns of agriculture, craft, and commerce that began during that early urban era have continued to evolve. Those patterns persist in the social and economic life of the country to this day.

Islam, a religious faith based upon the teachings of the prophet Muhammad in Arabia during the seventh century A.D, as revealed in the Koran, has also a long heritage in Pakistan. The indigenous peoples were converted to this vibrant new faith during the eighth century by invading princes from the west and by wandering Sufi mystics, whose spiritual discipline and religious teaching attracted their veneration and submission to the will of Allah (God). This faith has strengthened in the fabric of the people's lives through the centuries and was reaffirmed as the basis for the creation of Pakistan as an Islamic republic in 1947. Today, 97 percent of the 132 million people in the country are Muslim. Of these, 77 percent belong to the Sunni tradition.

The invasion of Moghul princes, who marched their conquering forces across the northern plains of South Asia to the Bay of Bengal in the sixteenth century, marked the period of greatest glory in the heritage of the Pakistani people. The Moghuls were militant Turks refined by the elegance of Persia and energized by their Islamic faith. Akbar (1556–1605), the greatest of these emperors, is remembered for the opulence and splendor of his court; for the far-reaching administrative control of his empire; and for his elaborate building projects, which still stand as massive tribute to his commanding wealth and intellect. The Taj Mahal, built by his grandson, Shah Jahan, is the crowning architectural achievement of this magnificent imperial past. Although the Moghul Dynasty declined in its later years, it continued to dominate northern South Asia until the middle of the nineteenth century, when it fell to British colonial rule. Pakistan did not become an independent nation until the departure of the British Raj in 1947. But it was created then, especially by the 7.2 million people who migrated from central India at the time of independence, in the image of a staunch Islamic and glorious imperial past. This heritage has been both a tremendous strength and a challenging obstacle to its evolution as a modern nation state.

INDEPENDENCE MOVEMENT

The Muslim League was formed in 1906 to represent the interests of the Islamic minority in British India in the movement for freedom from colonial domination. Its leaders became convinced through the years of struggle with the British Raj that their people would become oppressed, even destroyed, in an independent India dominated by Hindus. In 1940, the League voted to demand a separate state for the Muslim population of South Asia. Through the persistent, unswerving leadership of its president, Muhammad Ali Jinnah, this objective was realized when the British Raj, in departing in 1947, set the mechanism to establish two nations instead of one. Those districts that were under British control (about three fifths of the subcontinent) where Muslims were predominant would become Pakistan; the districts where Hindus were in the majority would become India. The remaining areas—princely states not under direct British administrative control—would accede by their own determination to either country.

This scheme to provide a separate Islamic state created two wings: a smaller but more populous East Pakistan, and a larger, dominant West Pakistan, the two separated by 900 miles of India. It also created a number of disputes over the appropriate process for accession of the princely states of British India into the new nations. The most strenuous of these disputes has been over Kashmir, a former princely state on the border between India and Pakistan that had a Muslim majority,

but a Hindu *Maharaja.* The dispute over which country it belongs to has led to two wars between India and Pakistan, an unresolved UN resolution for a plebiscite, and continuing tension. Even today, military units of the two countries fire artillery rounds at each other on the Siachen Glacier, a small, uninhabited Himalayan plateau, 20,000 feet high, at a cost of $6,000 per soldier per year, with 80 percent of the casualties "environment-induced," to assert their mutual claim to control of a divided Kashmir.

Pakistan commits a quarter of its annual budget to the military, in large part to defend its claim to Kashmir. The high expenditure also reflects the dominant role the military establishment has in Pakistan's national life—a role that feeds upon the pervasive fear of a life-threatening attack from India. This fear contributed to the government's decision to test its nuclear capability immediately following India's nuclear tests on May 11 and 13, 1998, even at the high cost of U.S. economic sanctions.

The British scheme for dividing India and Pakistan in 1947 had severe consequences. Those Muslims in British India who most feared Hindu oppression lived in the Hindu-majority districts, in north-central India, not those who had at least the local security of living in a Muslim-majority district. In order to affirm the need for a separate Islamic state, some 7.2 million Muslims who found themselves in independent India moved from their homelands into Muslim majority districts, where they were received as *mohajirs* (immigrants). And Hindu minorities in those districts who feared for their lives migrated the other way, to become refugees in Indian The partition of British India caused the migration of more than 14 million people. And the clashes of these two groups in the border areas, especially in the Punjab, which was split in half between Muslim and Hindu districts, led to the killing of hundreds of thousands of bewildered people. It was a huge human catastrophe that has left an abiding scar on the surface of the subcontinent.

The homelessness and bloodshed of partition taxed to the limit the meager human resources of the new nation of Pakistan, which, lying on what had been the outer edges of British India, lacked adequate administrative services to pull itself together. Muhammad Ali Jinnah took upon himself the chief executive duties as governor general in the interim government. Unfortunately, he became seriously ill and died 13 months later. Liaquat Ali Khan, who became his successor as prime minister, was assassinated 3 years later, in

1951. The Muslim League, which had been imported from British India, lost control of a unifying national agenda to the indigenous traditional sources of provincial power: wealthy landowners and tribal leaders. Even though a constitution was adopted in 1956 that affirmed the common sovereign identity of the two wings of Pakistan as an Islamic republic, the country was in political disarray.

STRIVING FOR POLITICAL STABILITY

In a move to develop political stability in 1958, the commander-in-chief of the Pakistan Army, General Mohammad Ayub Khan, was appointed martial-law administrator of Pakistan. In hopes of stimulating economic growth among a people "not yet ready for democracy," Ayub Khan instituted a new Constitution with extensive executive power. This Constitution established a tiered representative structure built on local elections to elect a National Assembly, which was to be controlled by the president. In 1965, Ayub Khan was elected president by a limited electorate of "Basic Democrats," 80,000 locally elected council members, whom he accepted as prepared to exercise a vote on the national level.

War broke out between India and Pakistan over the Kashmir issue in that same year, resulting in a military stalemate and a renewed UN cease-fire. The peace settlement with India in the Tashkent agreement of 1966 was a tremendous political setback for Ayub Khan. Growing discontent spawned two new political leaders, one in each of the wings of Pakistan, who developed followings in their respective regions sufficient to bring down Ayub Khan's government and divide the one nation in two.

Mujibur Rahman, leader of the Awami League in East Pakistan, capitalized on the perception among the people of that region that they were second-class citizens of the country. His charismatic leadership won immense popular support for greater regional autonomy. At the same time, Zulfikar Ali Bhutto, a Western-educated diplomat from a large landholding family in the province of Sindh in West Pakistan, formed the Pakistan People's Party. Adopting the campaign slogan *Roti, Kapra aur Makon* ("Bread, clothes and shelter"), he mobilized a wide popular following in the western region toward a policy of democratic socialism. Committed to creating a political base in the west, he did not attempt to generate a following of his own nor to accept the rise of the even more popular movement of the Awami League in East Pakistan.

President Ayub Khan was not able to contain either the Bhutto or the Rahman political movements, and, in 1969, he was forced to resign. General Yahya Khan, his successor, in a quest to bring order, declared the first popular national elections to be held in Pakistan since its independence, on December 7, 1970. In that election, the Awami League won 160 of the 162 seats in the National Assembly assigned to the more populous East Pakistan. Bhutto's Pakistan People's Party won 81 seats (58.7 percent) of the 132 assigned to West Pakistan. Bhutto felt that, by winning a majority of the seats in the Assembly from West Pakistan, he was the rightful leader of the country. He therefore refused to join the newly elected national Legislature until he was assured a position in the government. In response to Bhutto's boycott, President Yahya Khan suspended the Legislature. This suspension led to a vehement cry for independence in East Pakistan. The president sought to suppress the freedom movement by severe military repression. Resistance of the people in East Pakistan mounted, and millions fled across the border to find refuge in India. After several months of unrelenting bloodshed, the Indian government launched a military attack in support of the Bengali rebels, who won independence for their country on December 17, 1971.

The separation of East Pakistan to become the independent nation of Bangladesh left the Pakistan People's Party with a majority in the National Assembly, and Bhutto became the president of Pakistan. He set out immediately to bring what was left of the country together by nationalizing banking and such major industries as steel, chemicals, and cement. Bhutto thereby expanded an already cumbersome civil-service bureaucracy. His policy created employment opportunities in the central government but discouraged investment and led to a decline in industrial production.

Zulfikar Ali Bhutto was more successful in restoring parliamentary government. He created a new Constitution, the nation's third in 26 years; it was adopted in 1973. It established a National Assembly of 207 members and four provincial assemblies of proportionate size. (Baluchistan has 40 members; North-West Frontier, 80; Punjab, 240; and Sindh, 100.) All representatives were to be elected directly for 5-year terms. Under its provisions, Bhutto became prime minister, the chief executive of the government, elected by majority of the National Assembly.

National elections were again to become the nation's undoing. Bhutto called for elections in 1977 in hopes of getting endorsement for his leadership and his socialist economic policies. This call spurred an unexpected and virulent opposition of nine parties, which united to form the Pakistan National Alliance (PNA). Although Bhutto's Pakistan People's Party won the election, the PNA, which won only 36 of 207 seats in the National Assembly, charged that the elections had been fixed; the party took to the streets in protest. In the political turmoil that followed, Bhutto called in the army to restore order and sought to negotiate with the PNA to hold new elections. Before agreement could be reached, Mohammad Zia-ul-Haq, chief of staff of the army, seized control of the government. He promised to hold elections within 90 days but cancelled them 2 weeks before they were to be held. He continued to hold out the promise of elections for the following 11 years, during which time he maintained firm military control. Part of that control was to bring charges against Bhutto of complicity in a political murder, which led to Bhutto's trial and execution on April 4, 1979.

In the fall of 1979, Zia took the country further away from democracy by banning all political parties and imposing censorship on the press. The following year, he removed from judicial review the actions of his government and the decisions of the military courts that he had set up to enforce his martial rule. Many of these measures were cloaked in a policy of "Islamization," through which his military regime sought to improve the religious quality of the people's public life by an appeal to traditional laws and teachings of Sunni Islam. Once again, Pakistan's measured steps toward a stable, popularly elected government were thwarted by entrenched divisions, political turmoil, and strong repression more reminiscent of Moghul imperialism than expressive of modern representative democracy.

Zia's consolidation of power in Pakistan coincided with the collapse of the rule of the shah of Iran, the rise of Saudi Arabia as a huge power in the Middle East, and the Soviet invasion of Afghanistan. All of these developments gave Pakistan a place in the U.S. government's policies to contain Soviet expansion and protect Western sources of oil. These vital interests placed a higher priority on the stability of the Zia government in Pakistan than on the suspension of the rule of law and the erosion of democracy that was taking place under his rule. Increasing U.S. support for his repressive military rule had a negative impact not only on the quest for democracy among the people of Pakistan but also on the strength of the Zia government. In the words of Mubashir Hasan, finance minister in the Bhutto government:

> A government without a popular base can't really take a stand against anyone else. Dictatorships have the power to impose the policies demanded by outsiders in the short term. What they don't have is the power to say "No" to the U.S. or the [international] banks. The "strong" are actually weak because they are not being pushed by local interests and constituencies.
>
> —Quoted by Richard Reeves in *Passage to Peshawar* (p. 184)

A spirit of democracy did survive, if only partially, in a hasty referendum called in 1985 by General Zia to affirm his policy of Islamization by electing him president for a 5-year term. The Constitution of 1973 also survived, in an amended form, setting the stage for new elections, unexpectedly announced by Zia to be held in November 1988. They did take place, in spite of his death in a plane crash in August. A ruling of the Supreme Court removed the ban on political parties, and Bhutto's Pakistan People's Party, led by his daughter, Benazir Bhutto, won 93 seats in the 217-member National Assembly. Although not commanding a majority of the Legislature, she was invited to become prime minister. Then just 35 years old, she was the youngest person and the first woman to lead an Islamic nation.

Benazir Bhutto's government was formed by a very uneasy balance within the Legislature itself. In order to keep the support of a majority of the Legislature, necessary to continue as prime minister, she had to keep her opposition at bay by cultivating supporters from other political parties to her cause. Her tenure was fragile at best. But it was further complicated by competing claims to her authority outside the Legislature, by the other large power brokers in the nation—the army leadership and the president.

The leaders of the army had by this time a long tradition of standing in judgment on the conduct of the government—and intervening if they found it lacking. Such had been done by General Ayub Khan in 1958, by General Yahya Khan in 1970, and by General Zia-ul-Haq in 1977. Pakistan had been under military rule for 24 of its 44 years of existence. Even though General Beg, appointed army chief of staff in 1985, advocated restraint from involvement, the army remained a presence to contend with.

All of these military leaders, when they intervened in the government, established

their political role as independent presidents, not as prime ministers answerable to the Legislature. Thus, even though the Constitution of 1973 established a parliamentary form of government, it was modified by Zia in 1985, by the Eighth Amendment, to give the president (normally a formal position in parliamentary government) more power.

Benazir Bhutto tried in 1989 to get the full authority of the prime minister's office restored by having the Eighth Amendment repealed. Her lack of success in getting the necessary two-thirds vote of the Legislature led to the end of her first tenure as prime minister. Because the opposition in the National Assembly was not able to muster a no-confidence vote against her, President Ghulam Ishaq Khan issued a decree in August 1990, under the Eighth Amendment, to have her government dismissed. He then appointed a caretaker government, which brought charges of corruption and nepotism against the former prime minister in a bid to remove her as a candidate for reelection to the legislature by court decree. New elections were then set for October 1990.

ELECTORAL SHIFTS

In the 1990 elections, a coalition of eight parties, led by Mian Nawaz Sharif, chief minister of Punjab and head of the Islami Jamhorri Ittehad (IJI), or Islamic Democratic Alliance, won a decisive margin of 105 seats in the 217-member National Assembly, a jump from 55 seats in the 1988 elections. In the provincial elections in Punjab, the IJI fared even better, winning 208 of the 240 seats. And in the North-West Province it won a commanding 33 of 80 seats. All of this was accomplished by winning 36.86 percent of the popular vote. Benazir Bhutto's People's Democratic Alliance (PDA) was severely reduced, from 93 to 45 seats in the National Assembly, although it won 36.8 percent of the popular vote. Supported by the second-largest number of members, Bhutto joined the National Assembly as the leader of the opposition, a position her father had refused to accept in 1970.

Mian Nawaz Sharif is a member of a successful industrial family who migrated from Amritsar in East Punjab to Pakistan in 1947. Their large foundry business had been nationalized by Zulfikar Ali Bhutto in the 1970s. Its return to his family by General Zia established both his stature and his leanings as a political figure. Based on the results of the national elections of 1990, he was invited by President Ghulam Ishaq Khan to head the new government.

The 1990 elections revealed the fragile nature of Pakistan's political parties and the necessity of their coalition on the national level. The financially conservative IJI was able to bring together the Communist-leaning Awami National Party, dominant in the North-West Frontier Province, and the fundamentalist Jamiat-Ulema-i-Islam party in its bid to win the elections. Without their support, Sharif's party would not have succeeded.

Islamization is still a politically potent issue, and the fundamentalist convictions of the Jamiat-Ulema-i-Islam, although in the minority, are a significant force in Pakistani politics. In order to fulfill a promise made during the campaign to bring the fundamentalist Islamic groups into his coalition, after the elections, Prime Minister Sharif introduced a law to make the Islamic code of Shari'a the supreme law of Pakistan. At the same time, he asserted that he would not present a Shari'a bill that would stand in the path of modernization in the country. The Jamiat-Ulema-i-Islam Party later objected to the Shari'a bill passed by the National Assembly, arguing that it was too vaguely worded and not being implemented, and the party withdrew from the ruling coalition.

Variously interpreted, Islam still serves as a force holding Pakistan together and in harmony with its neighboring countries to the west. The public has come to expect renewed political emphasis on Islamization during times of crisis; blasphemy laws and efforts to amend the Constitution to make the Koran "the supreme law of land" have recently been implemented to divert attention from increasing economic instability in the country.

Nawaz Sharif was not so successful in his attempt to limit the martial-law powers of the president granted by the Eighth Amendment to the Constitution. In response to Sharif's attempt to repeal the amendment, President Ghulam Ishaq Khan invoked it, for a second time, to dismiss the Sharif government on charges of corruption and nepotism, in April 1993. This time, the Supreme Court overruled the president and reinstated the Sharif government. The army chief of staff, General Abdul Waheed, then felt called upon to step into this political deadlock and broker the resignation of both the prime minister and the president. The National Assembly and state legislatures were then dissolved, and new elections were set for October.

In the fall 1993 elections, Benazir Bhutto and her Pakistan People's Party were returned to power by a very slim margin. The PPP won 86 seats in the 217-

(UN/DPI Photo by Evan Schneider]

Pakistan struggles to develop its economy and foreign investment is declining. Prime Minister Mohammad Nawaz Sharif is shown here addressing the UN General Assembly in 1998.

member Legislature, to 72 for Sharif's party. Her position was further strengthened by the election a month later of Farooq Leghari, deputy leader of the PPP, to the office of president. Equally important, her party's nominees for chief minister of the states of Punjab and Sindh were also elected to office.

Benazir Bhutto did not do well in her second term as prime minister. She pursued policies that destabilized the nation's economy, compromised foreign investment, and produced 20 percent inflation. In response, she imposed a sales tax that proved very unpopular among the people.

An image of rampant corruption in government, together with an attempt to appoint sympathetic judges to the high courts, added to the erosion of her popular support. Her political stature was further compromised by accusations of complicity in the death of her brother, Murtaza Ali Bhutto, her most aggressive political rival, in a shoot-out with the police in Karachi in September 1996. All of these factors led to her dismissal on charges of corruption and nepotism under the Eighth Amendment by President Leghari in November and a call for new elections on February 3, 1997.

Even though voter turnout was low, Mian Nawaz Sharif and his Pakistan Muslim League Party won a strong mandate in this election. They garnered a two-thirds majority in the national assembly and 215 of the 240 seats in the Punjab assembly. His government was joined by Benazir Bhutto's opposition party to repeal the Eighth Amendment to the Constitution.

PAKISTAN IN THE MODERN AGE
The topsy-turvy period in Pakistan's political life following the end of General Zia-ul-Haq's martial rule raises questions

Harappan city culture 3000–1500 B.C.	The Moghul empire A.D. 1526–1857	The founding of the Muslim League 1907	The Muslim League adopts the demand for the separate state of Pakistan 1940	The partition of British India; the creation of Pakistan 1947

whether the electoral process as set forth in the Constitution of 1973 can work on the path to becoming a modern democracy. There are many obstacles even beyond the working of the structure of government itself.

Foremost among these obstacles is an inherent regional division of the country into four provinces. Because the regional identities of these provinces have been the primary basis of the formation of the political parties that have brought the people into the political process, the differences between these regions have been strengthened on the national level.

Each of the four provinces is defined not only by a distinct geography and ethnic group; each also has a distinct language that takes precedence in their region over the declared national language of Pakistan—Urdu. It is spoken by only about 8 percent of the population, mostly the families of *mohajirs,* who brought the language with them when they came from India in 1947 and live today primarily in the major cities of the country.

These regional identities further challenge the political future of Pakistan because one province, Punjab, is so clearly dominant. Punjabi speakers comprise about two thirds of the total population. Their lands, considered the granary of the country, are the most heavily irrigated and agriculturally the most productive. The greatest industrial development and most of the wealth is also concentrated there. And because Lahore, the capital city of Punjab, was the administrative center for the region under the British Raj, Punjabis have dominated the ranks of the army and the civil services.

Sindh is the next-most-important province, sharing with Punjab about 90 percent of the industrial production of the country. Karachi, Pakistan's largest city, with a population of 9 million, is the country's only port and a center of commerce. Yet only 12 percent of the country are Sindhi-speakers.

Even smaller in population are Baluchistan and the North-West Frontier Province, which lie to the west and north along the arid desert and mountainous borders with Iran and Afghanistan. The Baluchi language is spoken by less than 5 percent of the population. Pashto is the language of the Pathans, who live in the rugged

mountains of the North-West Province. They also are a small percentage of the total population (about 10 percent) of Pakistan, although their number was increased by the influx of more than 3 million Afghan Pathans forced across the border as refugees by the Soviet invasion of Afghanistan.

The recent rise of the Taliban movement across the border in Afghanistan is stirring new concerns—and opportunities. The shared Pathan identity of the people of the North-West Province with the Taliban challenges the quest for the allegiance of the people of the Province region to Pakistan. And the radical Islamic fervor of this new Afghan leadership also challenges the quest in Pakistan for a more moderate, modern expression of their Muslim faith. At the same time, Taliban control of Afghanistan opens the opportunity to extend a natural-gas pipeline into the former Soviet republics bordering Afghanistan to the north and to increase not only trade but also other alliances with those Islamic countries.

Together with language and ethnic differences among the regions of Pakistan, religious minorities have become a source of significant division within the country. Members of the Ahmadiya Sect of Islam, because their faith is considered heretical by the orthodox, are being imprisoned and committed to death sentences under newly imposed blasphemy laws enacted in response to political pressure for continued Islamization. Hindu and Christian communities also are not secure as minorities among such a highly dominant Sunni Muslim population.

There is also a striking contrast between the needs and expectations of the urban (32 percent) and rural (68 percent) populations, extenuated by the large influx of *mohajirs* from India into the cities of Pakistan in 1947. In the early years of independence, these immigrants comprised 46 percent of the urban population of the country. Today, the Muttahida Quami movement (until recently the Mohajir Quami movement and now divided into two hostile camps), although limited to Karachi for its political base, is the third-largest political party in the country.

Another challenge to a stable, democratically elected government in Pakistan is the wide division between the rich and

the poor: between the traditionally entrenched, wealthy landholders and tribal leaders over the landless peasants and herders in the countryside; between the industrialists and the slum dwellers in the cities. The extent of this urban disparity was revealed in a 1970 study that found that 80 percent of the capital wealth in Pakistan was owned by just 22 families.

New wealth and a new class were created in Pakistan during the 1980s by jobs in the Persian Gulf oil fields. At the peak, more than 2 million young people from all parts of the country were sending home more than $4 billion a year, or about 10 percent of the country's gross domestic product. These monies stimulated conspicuous consumer buying, which led to a number of local enterprises using pickup trucks and video equipment. The loss of jobs during the Persian Gulf War had a double impact on Pakistan's economy, in cutting in half the remittances from overseas Pakistanis and increasing the number of unemployed within the country.

With the Soviet withdrawal from Afghanistan and loss of Western support, international forces have continued to have immense impact on Pakistan. The government has struggled to develop the nation's economy. Prime Minister Nawaz Sharif has made significant strides by encouraging private industrialization through tax benefits and foreign investment. But the weakening of Asian economies beginning in 1997 and the imposition of sanctions by the United States following Pakistan's nuclear tests on May 28, 1998, have led to a decline in the country's economic growth.

Foreign investments are reported to have decreased by more than 50 percent and its foreign reserves by 67 percent during the months immediately following the nuclear tests as compared with the same months a year earlier. The U.S. government has since removed many of the sanctions imposed on Pakistan, and the International Monetary Fund has restored $575 million of a $1.5 billion loan to finance Pakistan's international debts in efforts to stave off a financial crisis.

Under terms set by the IMF, the government has imposed drastic austerity measures, which have coincided with increasing power struggles, splits, and violence among political parties. Violent

| War with India over Kashmir **1948** | The first Constitution establishing Pakistan as an Islamic republic **1956** | Military rule of Ayub Khan **1958–1969** | War with India over Kashmir **1965** | Military rule of Yahya Khan **1969–1971** | First national popular elections; Mujibar Rahman's Awami League wins majority of National Assembly; Zulfikar Ali Bhutto's Pakistan People's party wins West Pakistan majority **1970** | War with India; the breakaway of East Pakistan to become Bangladesh; Zulfikar Ali Bhutto becomes president of Pakistan **1971** | A Constitution establishing parliamentary democracy is adopted; Bhutto becomes prime minister **1973** | Military rule of Zia-ul-Haq; national elections set; helicopter accident kills Zia; Benazir Bhutto becomes prime minister **1977–1988** |

1990s

Parliamentary democracy is restored; Benazir Bhutto becomes prime minister but is subsequently suspended by presidential decree

New elections; Mohammad Nawaz Sharif becomes prime minister; his government is suspended by presidential decree; Benazir Bhutto again becomes prime minister but is dismissed; Sharif wins anew

Pakistan tests its nuclear capability in the wake of Indian tests in May 1998

attacks among opposing factions in Karachi have led to many murders and to a breakdown of law and order. In response, Prime Minister Sharif imposed martial law in the city in November 1998.

Although Pakistan's plight has been extenuated by international forces and events, most of these crises have their origin within the country itself. Observers of Pakistan's plight point to several areas of internal concern: a disproportionately high defense budget (more than $4 billion per year), a high rate of population growth (2.22 percent), the loss of human rights through the imposition of religiously sanctioned blasphemy laws, and the need for human-resources development. In the 1996 World Bank report on Pakistan, economist Hugo Diaz found "Pakistan's performance in important human development indicators has been the Achilles heel of the country's development effort. Without sustained gains in health status and accumulation of skills, continuing growth in labor productivity and incomes will not be possible." The report further identified the fertility rate among women to be 65 percent higher, infant mortality to be 30 percent higher, and literacy 25 percent lower than the average among the world's poorer nations. A more recent report, entitled "Improving Women's Health in Pakistan," identified an extremely high rate of one in every 38 women dying from pregnancy-related causes.

The limited—and elitist—opportunity for education in Pakistan is a significant indicator of the need for human-resources development. The 1998 Census placed the level of literacy in the country at 36 percent—a small improvement over the level, according to UNICEF officials, when Pakistan received its independence in 1947. The Educational Grants Commission estimated in 1983 that fewer than 8 percent of the nation's children went to school. Only a quarter of this number went on to secondary school. And half of the secondary students were educated in private schools, the only place they could get instruction in English, still the language of opportunity in the professions, technology, and trade.

Women are excluded even more from education: their level of literacy is around 16 percent—half that of the men. And girls comprise just a third of the total student population. This lack of education reflects the traditional expectation of their subservience and seclusion in Islamic society. This attitude was expressed as national policy by General Zia-ul-Haq in 1983, when putting forward the "manifesto of this government" and its commitment to Islamization.

In conflict with this traditional attitude is the assertion made at the same time by the economic planners in General Zia-ul-Haq's government in the formulation of the Sixth Five-Year Plan, who found that:

> In Pakistan today, the profile of women is simply shocking. The following cold statistics are a sad commentary on the legacy of neglect. . . . The participation of women in the compensated labour force is only 5 percent . . . less than 3 percent of civil service jobs . . . crippling handicaps of illiteracy, constant motherhood, poor health.

"In all societies," the document declared, "women's development is a prerequisite for overall national development; indeed no society can ever develop half-liberated and half-shackled."

Opportunity for women to share in the national life of Pakistan was encouraged by Zulfikar Ali Bhutto when he became prime minister in 1973. The Constitution of 1973 reserved 27 seats for women in the 217-member National Assembly. That Bhutto's daughter was able to hold the office of prime minister gave encouragement that new roles and responsibilities would be available to women as the country moved toward a more secure democracy.

Even so, the challenge to her position from her brother, Murtaza, who, as Zulfikar Ali Bhutto's son, claimed to be the more legitimate heir to their father's mantle, was instructive. Because her example is on such an elite level of Pakistani society, the need to "unshackle" and develop the vital resources of its female population in more normal and traditional walks of life remains an immense challenge to Pakistan in its quest for modernization.

Pakistan continues in a period of transition. It is still apprehensive about its survival as a unified, sovereign state; it is threatened by political, social, and religious forces and economic challenges both within and without the country. It is concerned about its integrity as an Islamic republic as it seeks ways to become less traditional and yet remain faithful to the teachings of Islam. And it continues to struggle to become a stable, prospering democracy.

DEVELOPMENT

Pakistan's per capita income has grown substantially since 1960. Agricultural industry, primarily cotton textiles and food processing, has grown at an impressive 8.8 percent average annual increase since 1980. This sector now produces more of the GDP than the agricultural sector, although agriculture still employs more than 50 percent of the labor force.

FREEDOM

Pakistan has experienced long years of martial law since independence in 1947. The first popular elections were not held until 1971, and not again until 1988. With the increasing political power of religious conservatives, women are held to their traditional, subservient role in Islamic society. Human-rights abuses are charged against the government, particularly against Hindus in the province of Sindh.

HEALTH/WELFARE

Emphasis on the military budget has slighted government attention to education and social services. Because of increasing agricultural production through the Green Revolution, life expectancy has doubled since 1960. The literacy rate among women is half that of the adult male population.

ACHIEVEMENTS

Pakistan has experienced political instability, warfare with India, the loss of East Pakistan, and the incursion of 3 million refugees from Afghanistan. Yet there has still been substantial industrial growth, and the Constitution, adopted in 1973, is working. The country continues to seek a government that is adequate to the needs of its peoples in the modern world and that is consistent with its Islamic faith and tradition.

Sri Lanka (Democratic Socialist Republic of Sri Lanka)

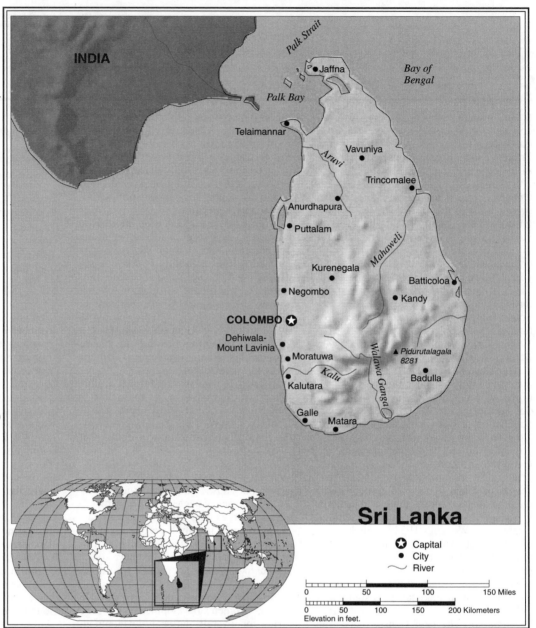

Sri Lanka

⭐ Capital
● City
〜 River

GEOGRAPHY

Area in Square Miles (Kilometers): 25,325 (65,610) (about the size of West Virginia)

Capital (Population): Colombo (2,000,000)

Environmental Concerns: deforestation; soil erosion; poaching; coastal degradation; water pollution

Geographical Features: mostly plain; mountains in the interior

Climate: tropical monsoon

PEOPLE

Population
Total: 18,721,000
Annual Growth Rate: 1.14%
Rural/Urban Population Ratio: 78/22
Major Languages: Sinhala; Tamil; English
Ethnic Makeup: 74% Sinhalese; 18% Tamil; 7% Moor; 1% others
Religions: 69% Buddhist; 15% Hindu; 8% Christian; 8% Muslim

Health
Life Expectancy at Birth: 70 years (male); 75 years (female)
Infant Mortality Rate (Ratio): 16.5/1,000
Average Caloric Intake: 101% of FAO minimum
Physicians Available (Ratio): 1/5,203

Education
Adult Literacy Rate: 90.2%
Compulsory (Ages): 5–15; free

COMMUNICATION
Telephones: 1 per 90 people
Televisions: 1 per 20 people

TRANSPORTATION
Highways in Miles (Kilometers): 59,185 (98,642)
Railroads in Miles (Kilometers): 890 (1,484)
Usable Airfields: 13
Motor Vehicles in Use: 442,000

GOVERNMENT
Type: republic
Independence Date: February 4, 1948 (from the United Kingdom)
Head of State/Government: President Chandrika Bandaranaike Kumaratunga; Prime Minister Sirimavo Bandaranaike; in Sri Lanka, the president is considered to be both head of state and head of government
Political Parties: All Ceylon Tamil Congress; Democratic United National Front; People's Alliance; Sri Lanka Freedom Party; Sri Lanka Muslim Congress; People's United Front; Eelam People's Democratic Party; Tamil United Liberation Front; others
Suffrage: universal at 18

MILITARY
Military Expenditures (% of GDP): 5.7%
Current Disputes: civil war

ECONOMY
Currency ($ U.S. Equivalent): 50.11 Sri Lankan rupees = $1
Per Capita Income/GDP: $3,760/$69.7 billion
GDP Growth Rate: 6.4%
Inflation Rate: 15.9%
Unemployment Rate: 13.1%

Labor Force: 6,200,000
Natural Resources: limestone; graphite; mineral sands; gems; phosphates; clay
Agriculture: tea; rubber; coconuts; rice; sugarcane; grains; pulses; oilseeds; root crops; spices; milk; eggs; hides; meat
Industry: processing of rubber, tea, coconuts, and other agricultural commodities; clothing; cement; petroleum refining; textiles; tobacco
Exports: $4 billion (primary partners United States, United Kingdom, Germany)
Imports: $5 billion (primary partners Japan, India, South Korea)

 http://www.cm.cf.ac.uk/Slanka/clickable_map.html

SRI LANKA

Sri Lanka is a small island nation that hangs like a pendant off the southeast coast of India. Stretching 270 miles from north to south, it expands to 140 miles in width toward its southern end. In total area, it occupies just 1.5 percent of the total landmass of the South Asian subcontinent.

The nation is divided by nature into two distinct zones: the northern, low-lying dry zone, and the mountainous wet zone to the south. At the center of the southern zone are the lush Kandyan Highlands, site of extensive tea and rubber plantations, watered by abundant rainfall, especially during the southwest monsoon season. Tea grown in the Highlands, considered to be among the finest in the world, and rubber and coconuts account for most of the country's exports.

The northern plains are devoted mostly to rice cultivation for domestic consumption. This agriculture is sustained by extensive irrigation systems from artificial lakes to provide water during the long dry spells between the annual northeast monsoon rains. The construction of these irrigation systems dates back to the earliest record of settlers arriving from India, in the fifth century. B.C.

Because of its pleasant tropical climate and natural beauty, Sri Lanka once was known as the "Pearl of the Orient." In recent years, due to the ravages of social unrest, which has rocked its idyllic image of tranquillity, the country has come to be called the "Lebanon of South Asia."

Sri Lanka's population, now 18.7 million, has long been divided between two distinct language and religious identities. Speakers of the Sinhalese language are a dominant majority—74 percent of the total population of the country, of whom most are Theravada Buddhist. Seventeen percent of the total population are Tamil-speakers, a significant minority; of them, two thirds are Hindu, mostly belonging to the Shaivite tradition.

Contemporary Sinhalese trace their origin to fifth-century B.C. Indian settlers. Legend describes their leader, Prince Vijaya, as of the race of the lion, a Sinhal, a symbol of royalty adopted from ancient Persian culture. He was sent away from north India by his father and, according to tradition, arrived on Sri Lanka on the very day of the Buddha's death, in 483 B.C. He established a kingdom around the city of Anuradhapura, in the north-central region of the country.

Theravada Buddhism, as distinct from the Mahayana Buddhist traditions of Tibet, China, and Japan, was brought to Sri Lanka in the third century B.C. by Mahinda, the son and emissary of the Indian emperor Asoka. This tradition reveres the teachings of the earliest elders (*thera*) as contained in the Pali Canon. These sacred writings were produced in north India in the years following the death (entering nirvana) of the Buddha. They were carried throughout South and Southeast Asia by missionary monks during the early years of expansion of the Buddhist faith.

Marauding forces from south India arrived after the early period of Buddhist expansion. Most devastating was the Chola invasion, which destroyed Anuradhapura in the tenth century A.D. These attacks, together with the infestation of malaria, borne by mosquitoes bred in the still waters of the artificial irrigation lakes, drove the population of the north-central region to the coastlands.

The Portuguese arrived on the south coasts of Sri Lanka in the early sixteenth century and forced many of the Sinhalese people of the south into the mountains. There the Sinhalese established a kingdom around the city of Kandy. This dominant Sinhalese Buddhist language/religious group is today divided between the Kandyans, who live in the Highlands, and the "Low Country" people. The latter are more numerous (60 percent) and more prosperous, living in the more urban, coastal rim of the south.

Tamil-speakers are also divided into two groups: the Sri Lankan Tamils (70 percent) and the Indian Tamils (30 percent). The Sri Lankan Tamils are found mostly on the north and east coastlands, the dominant group belonging to a Sri Lankan Vellalar, or land-holding caste. Almost half of this Tamil community live in the northernmost district of Jaffna, where they make up 95 percent of the population. They have lived on the island since ancient times and share its long history with the Kandyan Sinhalese, with whom they have the most in common culturally and ethnically.

The Indian Tamils were brought to Sri Lanka in the nineteenth century by the British colonial government to work as field laborers on the plantations that the British fostered in the Kandyan Highlands. The number of Indian Tamils has been reduced by half since Sri Lankan independence, primarily by their repatriation to India. Only during the 1960s did those who remained, about 5 percent of the total population of Sri Lanka, receive status as citizens of Sri Lanka.

There are also significant Christian and Muslim communities, belonging to both language groups. The Tamil-speaking Muslims live mostly along the east coast; they are a distinct minority caught between the Sri Lankan Tamil and the Kandyan Sinhalese communities.

The British were the first to unify these diverse peoples under a single government administration, in 1815. They introduced the rudiments of a national government in the port city of Colombo, on the southwest coast, and democratic institutions throughout the country. The first general elections were held in 1931, to select representatives to a National Assembly under strict colonial control.

INDEPENDENCE

On February 4, 1948, Sri Lanka, then called *Ceylon,* achieved its independence as a dominion in the British Commonwealth. In 1972, the government adopted a new Constitution as an independent republic, with a single Legislature of 168 members. A further constitutional change, in 1978, endowed the presidency with extensive executive authority. Junius Jayewardene, who had been appointed prime minister in 1978, following a sweeping victory of his United National Party (UNP) in 1977, was elected president in 1982.

The development of new lands for rice cultivation in the earlier malarial-infested and abandoned north-central region started during the British colonial period. Since independence, the cultivation of these lands has become an increasing priority of the government. Jayewardene pursued the development and resettlement of the region, not just to increase rice production but also to provide homes and jobs for an increasing homeless population of Kandy Sinhalese, victims of land reform in the Highlands. He sought also in this way to defuse the impact and the appeal of a militant, Marxist youth group called the People's Liberation Front (JVP), which had been launching devastating attacks on villages throughout the south since 1971.

Jayewardene's primary focus was on the Mahaweli River Project, an ambitious proposal of dams and irrigation works along the 207-mile course of the Mahaweli River from the central Highlands to Koddiyar Bay on the east coast. First proposed in 1968 as a 30-year development scheme, the plan was to clear, resettle, and irrigate 900,000 acres of land in the north-central region of the country. In 1977, the Jayewardene government sought to speed up the project to an intensive effort of 6 years. Since then, four of the five major dams in the initial proposal have been built, largely with foreign aid, and 390,000 acres of "new" land have been prepared for settlement and cultivation. The results in terms of new production, employment, and electrical power have been impressive.

As great as the economic benefits have been, such government resettlement proj-

(UN/DPI Photo by Evan Schneider)

Despite widespread poverty, a severe refugee problem, and intense internal conflicts among different religious and linguistic groups, Sri Lanka's democratic political system endures. Here, President Chandrika Bandaranaika Kumaratunga addresses the UN General Assembly in September 1998.

ects have had severe political consequences.

CIVIL WAR
In the years following the full independence of Sri Lanka, Tamil leaders sought to protect their people from the tyranny of the majority in two ways. On the national level, Tamil legislators, as a solid political group (the Federal Party), were able to hold a balance of votes between rival Sinhalese political parties. With that leverage, they were able to maintain a hearing for their concerns as a minority. They were

also advocates for greater autonomy at the district level, which gave them greater freedom and protection in those northern districts where they were in the majority.

The Tamils lost their leverage as a critical minority group on the national level with the landslide victory of the United National Party in the 1977 elections. And when the UNP enacted resettlement and redistricting policies that placed more Sinhalese voters in redrawn regional districts, they found themselves in danger of losing what political power they had at the district level.

Tamil despair of attaining political accommodation at the national level and retaining control at the local level, combined with the increasing economic potential of the development projects in the north of the country, have fanned the fires of a militant secessionist group, the Liberation Tigers of Tamil Eelam (LTTE). Youthful, and eager for social as well as political change, the LTTE has organized and carried out a sustained reign of terror throughout the northern regions.

Unable to control such violence, President Jayewardene entered into an agree-

Migration of
Sinhalese Indians
500 B.C.
●

Mahinda
introduces
Buddhism
247 B.C.
●

British
colonial rule
A.D. **1815–1948**
●

A Constitution
establishes a
democratically
elected but
limited Legislature
1931
●

The
independence of
Ceylon, as a
British
Commonwealth
dominion
1948
●

A new
Constitution
establishes Sri
Lanka as a
democratic
republic
1972
●

The United
National Party
wins elections by
wide margin
1977
●

The Constitution
is modified to
establish an
independent
president
1978
●

Junius Jayewardene
serves as president;
anti-Tamil riots break
out; Indian Peace
Keeping Force
restores order in
north and east
provinces
1982–1988
●

1990s

Efforts to achieve
cease-fire
between LTTE
and Sri Lankan
military forces
and to negotiate
settlement
dispute between
Tamil minority
and Sinhalese
majority fail

Ranasinghe
Premadasa
becomes
president; he is
assassinated
in 1993

Chandrika
Kumaratunga
is elected
president; efforts
are renewed to
restore order in
Sinhalese
and Tamil
communities

ment with the government of India to send an Indian Peace Keeping Force (IPKF) to neutralize the conflict between militant Tamils and Sinhalese. But the IPKF failed to rout the LTTE, and as the battles continued, the IPKF began to take on the appearance of an occupation force. Faced with its unpopularity and growing violence by the Sinhalese youth group JVP, Jayewardene did not seek reelection in 1988. The United National Party did remain in power, and its candidate, Ranasinghe Premadasa, was elected to succeed him. Immediately following Premadasa's election as president, the Indian Army units were asked to withdraw.

The Indian Peace Keeping Force left the LTTE weakened but no less resolved to seek independence for a separate Tamil state at any cost, including through the drug trade and by assassination. This militant group was implicated in the assassination of President Premadasa on May 1, 1993, by a human time bomb, in the same way Prime Minister Ranjiv Gandhi of India was killed by a Tamil separatist terrorist in 1991.

While still in control of the northern Jaffna District, the LTTE called for a boycott of national elections in August 1994; less than 10 percent of the electorate in that district voted. In other parts of Sri Lanka, the voters, looking for new opportunities for a political rather than military solution to the conflict between the Tamil minority and the Sinhalese majority, defeated the United Front Party for the first time in 17 years.

The People's Alliance, a fragile coalition of leftist parties, won 105 seats in the 1994 elections, and the reins of government were handed over to its leader, Chandrika Kumaratunga. With the help of other parties, it has been able to retain majority support of the 225-member Parliament.

Kumaratunga is another illustration of the pattern for women leaders in South Asian national life. She is the daughter of S. W. R. D. Bandaranaike, leader of the Sri Lanka Freedom Party, a coalition of leftist, pro-Sinhala groups that won control of the national Legislature in 1956. He was a popular prime minister; he was assassinated by an extremist Buddhist monk in 1959. His wife, Sirimavo Bandaranaike, then became leader of his SLRP, and she served as the first woman prime minister from 1960 to 1965, from 1970 to 1977, and again since 1996. Kumaratunga's husband, a popular film actor, had also entered national politics, until his assassination while a presidential candidate in 1988.

Mrs. Kumaratunga initiated a number of proposals for talks with the LTTE for a cease-fire and negotiations toward peace. But negotiations have yet to succeed. The Sri Lankan Army then undertook a major offensive, which removed the LTTE from the ravaged city of Jaffna in October 1995. Weakened and further isolated from any political base, the LTTE has continued to carry out guerrilla attacks and conscript youthful replacements for its forces in the northeastern coastal region of the country. It was able to launch a substantial counterattack to recapture the town of Killinochchi on the vital highway to Jaffna in September 1998. And it was also responsible for the bombing deaths in 1998 of the first two Tamil mayors of Jaffna—Sarojini Yogeswaran, in May, and P. Sivapalan in September—in protest against the attempt of a more moderate Tamil United Liberation Front to reestablish civil order in the north.

The future of the Tamil population within the nation, let alone the rehabilitation of the more than 200,000 refugees who have sought asylum in south India,

is unsure. They are caught between the militant forces of the LTTE and the Sri Lankan Army. And they have experienced such extensive destruction throughout their northern homelands over such a long period of time that the opportunity for mediation and the prospect of a return to normal life seem very far away.

STILL A MODEL
Although the Tamil separatist movement has dominated the political agenda for many years and terrorist bombings remain a threat to everyday life in both the north and in the southern cities, the economy of the country has continued to prosper. The International Monetary Fund reports that, at a time when Asian economies in general are declining, Sri Lanka is showing significant growth (from 3.8 percent in 1996 to 6.4 percent in 1997) in all sectors, particularly in services and manufacturing. In spite of all the political turmoil, Sri Lanka remains a model in South Asia for literacy, population growth, and human services, and a productive place for foreign investment.

DEVELOPMENT

Sri Lanka's economy is primarily agricultural, based on extensive plantation farming. Land reclamation for the production of rice has been its most ambitious development project. Stints of bad weather, a decline in the world tea market, and civil war have all hurt the economy in recent years, yet the country has still managed to prosper.

FREEDOM

Since 1983, Sri Lanka, the oldest democracy in South Asia, has been torn asunder by militant Sinhalese and Tamil rebels. Wanton destruction of peoples and lands, mostly in the more heavily Tamil- and Muslim- populated areas, has forced more than 1 million people to become refugees.

HEALTH/WELFARE

Sri Lanka has the most extensive social services in South Asia. Socialized medicine provides health care throughout the country. Literacy and average life expectancy are the highest in the subcontinent, while the rate of population growth is one of the lowest.

ACHIEVEMENTS

Though severe ethnic and linguistic violence is threatening the political stability of this island nation, the fruits of Buddhism and democracy in Sri Lanka have had exemplary results in economic development and social services.

Annotated Table of Contents

INDIA AND SOUTH ASIA

Regional Articles

1. **Competing Nationalisms: Secessionist Movements and the State,** Raju G. C. Thomas, *Harvard International Review,* Summer 1996. All the South Asia states constitute political conglomerations of several ethnic nations, many of which are demanding separate independent states. Granting separatist demands could exacerbate existing tensions and unravel regional security.   86

India Articles

2. **India: The Imprint of Empire,** Roderick MacFarquhar, *The New York Review of Books,* October 23, 1997. The end of the British presence in India was a tumultuous time. The changeover to Indian independence caused enormous shifts of populations, massive slaughter, and a polarization of religious factions.   90

3. **Gandhi and Nehru: Frustrated Visionaries?,** Judith Brown, *History Today,* September 1997. Both Mahatma Gandhi and Jawaharlal Nehru, in their different ways, spoke of the moral, social, and political regeneration of India as the true basis of self-rule. As this essay points out, these optimistic visions have been largely frustrated.   97

4. **Partition: the Human Cost,** Mushirul Hasan, *History Today,* September 1997. When India became independent, the peaceful coexistence of Hindus and Muslims unraveled. The resultant partitioning of India and Pakistan is reviewed in this article.   101

5. **The Muslims and Partition,** Francis Robinson, *History Today,* September 1997. The partition of India in 1947 was the logical outcome of Britain's policies of dividing and ruling. For the Pakistanis it was their founding moment, and it gave the Muslims their separate identity. For the Bangladeshis it was a prelude to their own nation-state, which was realized in 1971.   106

6. **Bengal and Punjab: Before and Beyond,** Jean Alphonse Bernard, *History Today,* September 1997. Jean Alphonse Bernard considers the key provinces of Bengal and Punjab. How they became powderkegs in the nationalist aspirations of both the Hindus and the Muslims is examined in this report.   110

7. **What Does India Want?,** Payal Sampat, *World Watch,* July/August 1998. The Indian government sent a defiant message when it began nuclear testing in May 1998. As Payal Sampat points out, the people of India feel the real threat comes from their own country.   114

8. **India's Problem Is Not Politics,** Marshall M. Bouton, *Foreign Affairs,* May/June 1998. Future prospects for India are threatened by economics and not by their democratic politics. India's population is enormously diversified, and when an election is held, it is the largest organized human activity ever. Their form of government has worked very well for the country.   123

9. **Still a Cold War,** Maleeha Lodhi, *The World Today,* May 1998. While the end of the cold war has provided momentum to resolve worldwide disputes, India and Pakistan remain mired in their own cold war. As Maleeha Lodhi points out, the dispute is over Kashmir.   128

10. **India's Socioeconomic Makeover,** Richard Breyer, *The World & I,* August 1998. As India experiences the pressures of a free market, its society begins to polarize. A strong middle class is emerging, but at the same time enormous numbers of people are still mired in poverty.   132

11. **India: Globalized Economy, Victimized Workers?** Sharmila Joshi, *Populi,* June 1998. Women are not benefiting from the increase in India's industrial base. A recent study indicates that there are more threats than opportunities for women in the current process of liberalization.   135

12. **Life in the Slow Lane,** Dan Biers and Shiraz Sidhva, *Far Eastern Economic Review,* August 21, 1997. According to the authors, India has discarded much of its socialist baggage since 1991. It is, however, also showing signs of reform fatigue and needs to increase its pace to be more successful economically.   137

13. **Enduring Stereotypes about Asia: India's Caste System,** Joe Elder, *Education About Asia,* Fall 1996. In India the word "caste" is applied to at least three different phenomena. Joe Elder defines caste to mean lineages of related families from among which parents arrange their children's marriages. He points out prevalent misconceptions that result from this definition.   140

14. **Ancient Jewel,** T. R. (Joe) Sundaram, *The World & I,* October 1996. India, perhaps the oldest continuing civilization in existence, operates out of three central tenets: The assimilation of ideas and experiences, a belief in cycles, and the coexistence of opposites. Although it has made numerous material contributions to the world, India's spiritual legacy had the most impact.   143

15. **Though Illegal, Child Marriage Is Popular in Part of India,** John F. Burns, *New York Times,* May 11, 1998. Indian law sets 18 as the minimum age for a women to marry and 21 for a man. In spite of legislation to curb it, child marriages still continue in virtually every state in India. Research indicates that child marriages keep India well behind in women's rights.   147

16. **India's Misconceived Family Plan,** Jodi L. Jacobson, *World Watch,* November/December 1991. India's goal of cutting its runaway birth rate in half by the year 2000 will prove elusive unless the government provides women the means to attain higher status—other than by bearing large numbers of children. — 149

17. **Women in South Asia: The Raj and After,** Tanika Sarkar, *History Today,* September 1997. The role of women in India has undergone some changes, but many of the historical problems persist. Tanika Sarkar examines the evolving position of women in India before 1947 and since its independence. — 154

18. **In India, Men Challenge a Matrilineal Society,** Kavita Menon, *Ms.,* September/October 1998. In Meghalaya, a district in the northeast section of India, the Khasi people have one of the largest surviving matrilineal societies in the world. Descent is traced through the mother's line and women have a honored place in their society. — 158

19. **Oldest Prophetic Religion Struggles for Survival,** John Zubrzycki, *The Christian Science Monitor,* May 13, 1998. The Zoroastrian religion dates back to sometime before 600 B.C. and was imported from what is now eastern Iran. However, current social pressures are working to extinguish this ancient religion. — 160

20. **Dire Warnings of Environmental Disaster,** Taani Pande, *India Abroad,* December 6, 1996. India is undoubtedly one of the world's most environmentally damaged countries. Until the environment is made an electoral issue, politicians will not take the idea of social responsibility for its protection seriously. — 162

21. **India's Low-Tech Energy Success,** Payal Sampat, *World Watch,* November/December 1995. A process developed in India, which turns cow dung into a flammable gas that is an excellent source of electric power and turns a byproduct into an excellent fertilizer, may help in the formation of a decentralized energy strategy not only in India but also in other developing countries. — 164

22. **A Celluloid Hall of Mirrors,** Somi Roy, *The World & I,* October 1996. Most of India's large film industry churns out films that contain wildly popular music and dance extravaganzas. A number of films, however, reflect more complex realities. — 167

23. **Community Radio in India,** Frederick Noronha, *Cultural Survival Quarterly,* Summer 1998. The movement toward diversifying India's antiquated radio system is challenged by the fact that the country has 18 officially recognized languages and a total of 1,652 mother tongues. — 171

24. **Making Something Out of Nothing,** Pierre-Sylvain Filliozat, *The UNESCO Courier,* November 1993. The concept of zero was invented in India; in consequence, it can be argued that this was the birth of modern arithmetic. — 175

25. **Ancient Hindu Festival Thrives in Computer-Age India,** John F. Burns, *New York Times,* April 16, 1998. As India rushes into the age of technology, as well as developing nuclear weapons, the passion for the ancient ritual of bathing in the Ganges shows no signs of dwindling. — 178

South Asia Articles

26. **The Succession,** Richard Mackenzie, *The New Republic,* September 14 & 21, 1998. Richard Mackenzie reviews Afghanistan's long and tumultuous history. The takeover by the extremist movement known as the Taliban and changes that have occurred as a result are examined in this report. — 180

27. **A Bank for the Poor,** Muhammad Yunus, *The UNESCO Courier,* January 1997. The Grameen Bank, which became a pioneering institution that has encouraged the social and political emancipation of needy women in Bangladesh, is reviewed by Muhammad Yunus. — 184

28. **Pakistan at Fifty: A Tenuous Democracy,** Samnia Ahmed, *Current History,* December 1997. When Pakistan gained independence in 1947, the people were optimistic about their future. Now at the age of 50, Pakistan still has not established a stable government, and its economy is in poor shape. — 186

29. **The Crumbling of Pakistan,** *The Economist,* October 17, 1998. While Pakistan is in deep economic trouble, its leadership is not doing much to improve its plight. This, coupled with the fact that it has nuclear capability, makes for an uncertain future. — 191

30. **Sanctions: Lift 'em,** Pervez Hoodbhoy and Zia Mian; **Modify 'em,** David Cortright and Samina Ahmed; and **Hang Tough,** Thomas Graham Jr., *The Bulletin of the Atomic Scientists,* September/October 1998. After Pakistan staged nuclear tests in 1998, the international credit community imposed sanctions. These articles review the importance of restoring important credit resources so Pakistan can get out of the economic hole it is in. — 192

31. **War in Sri Lanka Feeds on Itself,** John Zubrzycki, *The Christian Science Monitor,* August 12, 1998. There does not seem to be an end in sight to the 15-year-old separatist war in Sri Lanka. The government and its armed forces opponents are perpetuating the conflict for their own needs. — 198

32. **After Decades, Tibet Won't Bend to Chinese Ways,** Kevin Platt, *The Christian Science Monitor,* July 29, 1997. China has had control over Tibet since 1950, and during this time it has tried to impose Chinese culture on the Tibet people. The struggle continues to the present. — 200

33. **Tibet: Communist China and Human Rights,** Tenzin Gyatso, *Vital Speeches of the Day,* May 1, 1997. In this speech by the 14th Dalai Lama of Tibet, the plight of his country is outlined. Since China made Tibet an "autonomous region" under Chinese control, Tibet has faced only repression. — 201

Topic Guide to Articles

TOPIC AREA	TREATED IN	TOPIC AREA	TREATED IN
Agriculture	7. What Does India Want? 20. Dire Warnings of Environmental Disaster 21. India's Low-Tech Energy Success	Economy	7. What Does India Want? 10. India's Socioeconomic Makeover 12. Life in the Slow Lane 27. Bank for the Poor 28. Pakistan at Fifty 30. Sanctions
Arts	22. Celluloid Hall of Mirrors 23. Community Radio in India	Education	16. India's Misconceived Family Plan
Caste System	13. Enduring Stereotypes about Asia	Environment	7. What Does India Want? 20. Dire Warnings of Environmental Disaster 21. India's Low-Tech Energy Success
Class	13. Enduring Stereotypes about Asia 16. India's Misconceived Family Plan		
Communication	22. Celluloid Hall of Mirrors 23. Community Radio in India	Ethnicity	1. Competing Nationalisms 4. Partition: The Human Cost 5. Muslims and Partition 23. Community Radio in India 32. After Decades, Tibet Won't Bend to Chinese Ways
Cultural Development	24. Making Something Out of Nothing 28. Pakistan at Fifty		
Cultural Roots	4. Partition: The Human Cost 5. Muslims and Partition 13. Enduring Stereotypes about Asia 15. Though Illegal, Child Marriage Is Popular in Part of India 19. Oldest Prophetic Religion Struggles for Survival 25. Ancient Hindu Festival Thrives in Computer-Age India 32. After Decades, Tibet Won't Bend to Chinese Ways 33. Tibet: Communist China and Human Rights	Family	11. India: Globalized Economy, Victimized Workers? 15. Though Illegal, Child Marriage Is Popular in Part of India 16. India's Misconceived Family Plan 17. Women in South Asia 27. Bank for the Poor
		Financial Reform	12. Life in the Slow Lane
		Foreign Investment	11. India: Globalized Economy, Victimized Workers? 30. Sanctions
Democracy	2. India: The Imprint of Empire 4. Partition: The Human Cost 8. India's Problem Is Not Politics	Foreign Relations	9. Still a Cold War 30. Sanctions
Economic Development	10. India's Socioeconomic Makeover 12. Life in the Slow Lane 21. India's Low-Tech Energy Success 22. Celluloid Hall of Mirrors 27. Bank for the Poor 29. Crumbling of Pakistan	Foreign Trade	11. India: Globalized Economy, Victimized Workers?
		Health and Welfare	3. Gandhi and Nehru 10. India's Socioeconomic Makeover 11. India: Globalized Economy, Victimized Workers? 16. India's Misconceived Family Plan 17. Women in South Asia

TOPIC AREA	TREATED IN	TOPIC AREA	TREATED IN
Hindu Nationalism	5. Muslims and Partition 6. Bengal and Punjab	**Religion and Spirituality**	4. Partition: The Human Cost 6. Bengal and Punjab 14. Ancient Jewel 19. Oldest Prophetic Religion Struggles for Survival 26. The Succession
History	2. India: The Imprint of Empire 3. Gandhi and Nehru 4. Partition: The Human Cost 5. Muslims and Partition 6. Bengal and Punjab 14. Ancient Jewel 24. Making Something Out of Nothing 33. Tibet: Communist China and Human Rights	**Rural Life**	21. India's Low-Tech Energy Success
		Science	21. India's Low-Tech Energy Success 24. Making Something Out of Nothing
		Secession	1. Competing Nationalisms
Human Rights	10. India's Socioeconomic Makeover 11. India: Globalized Economy, Victimized Workers? 13. Enduring Stereotypes about Asia 16. India's Misconceived Family Plan 17. Women in South Asia	**Sex Roles**	13. Enduring Stereotypes about Asia 15. Though Illegal, Child Marriage Is Popular in Part of India 16. India's Misconceived Family Plan 17. Women in South Asia 18. In India, Men Challenge a Matrilineal Society
Industrial Development	21. India's Low-Tech Energy Success 22. Celluloid Hall of Mirrors	**Social Reform**	10. India's Socioeconomic Makeover 11. India: Globalized Economy, Victimized Workers? 12. Life in the Slow Lane 16. India's Misconceived Family Plan
Leaders	3. Gandhi and Nehru 4. Partition: The Human Cost 7. What Does India Want? 29. Crumbling of Pakistan 32. After Decades, Tibet Won't Bend to Chinese Ways 33. Tibet: Communist China and Human Rights	**Social Unrest**	2. India: The Imprint of Empire 3. Gandhi and Nehru 4. Partition: The Human Cost 5. Muslims and Partition 30. Sanctions 31. War in Sri Lanka Feeds on Itself 32. After Decades, Tibet Won't Bend to Chinese Ways 33. Tibet: Communist China and Human Rights
Minorities	18. In India, Men Challenge a Matrilineal Society 19. Oldest Prophetic Religion Struggles for Survival		
National Resources	20. Dire Warnings of Environmental Disaster 21. India's Low-Tech Success	**Women**	11. India: Globalized Economy, Victimized Workers? 13. Enduring Stereotypes about Asia 15. Though Illegal, Child Marriage Is Popular in Part of India 16. India's Misconceived Family Plan 17. Women in South Asia 18. In India, Men Challenge a Matrilineal Society 27. Bank for the Poor
Nationalism	1. Competing Nationalisms 2. India: The Imprint of Empire 8. India's Problem Is Not Politics		
Partition	2. India: The Imprint of Empire 4. Partition: The Human Cost 5. Muslims and Partition 6. Bengal and Punjab		
Peasants	10. India's Socioeconomic Makeover		

Article 1   *Harvard International Review,* Summer 1996

Identity and Politics in South Asia

Competing Nationalisms
Secessionist Movements and the State

Raju G.C. Thomas

Raju G.C. Thomas is Professor of Political Science at Marquette University.

South Asia is home to several world religions, over 30 major languages, a thousand dialects, and innumerable castes and subcastes. During the colonial era, princes held nominal rule over more than 580 separate states in India, while a number of other provinces were directly governed by the British. Although only two movements for national independence have succeeded since the departure of the British in 1947—those of Pakistan and Bangladesh—South Asia has experienced countless separatist movements based on religious, linguistic, or ethnic lines, including campaigns for Dravidastan, Assam, Nagaland, Gurkhaland, Kashmir, Khalistan, Pashtunistan, Baluchistan, Sind-hudesh, and Tamil Eelam.

With such diverse national movements continuing to challenge state lines, South Asia faces the question: should the territorial integrity and sovereignty of existing states be maintained, regardless of the history and legitimacy of their origins, or should the state's various ethnic groups or "nationalities" be allowed the right of self-determination and secession?

The recognition of new states in South Asia may lead to consequences even more disastrous than the status quo, just as the recognition of new states in Europe led to the complete disintegration of the Soviet Union and Yugoslavia. First, recognition would generate new problems arising from new boundaries and new minorities. Second, the recognition of some states could cause a chain reaction elsewhere, leading to the disintegration of India and Pakistan, and to a lesser extent, Sri Lanka. Third, the level of interethnic bloodshed and refugee flows would generate a humanitarian nightmare in South Asia surpassing that of Europe in the early 1990s.

Nation-states based on ethnic lines have rarely existed in South Asia. Instead, great multi-ethnic empires, like those of the Mauryans, Guptas, and Mughals, have arisen and disintegrated. The lesser empires and minor kingdoms that replaced them either comprised multiple ethnic groups or were ethnically pure, but rarely included all the members of the ethnic group within their boundaries. South Asia has no equivalent to Germany, Italy, or Japan, states formed by a group of people largely sharing the same race, language, culture, religion, and historical experience. Even Bangladesh, united by the Bengali language, is divided by religion. Bhutan, too, comes close to an ethnic nation but retains a significant Nepali minority.

> With so many complex lines of religion, culture, and language in South Asia, allowing communities to secede would lead to a number of grave consequences. Regardless of the legitimacy or illegitimacy of the separatist demands, granting them could exacerbate existing tensions and unravel regional security.

Since the partition of British India in 1947, the nations that have formed in South Asia have not been ethnic nations but civic nations. The civic nation is based on a community of people who believe they compose a nation and who are willing to commit themselves to common political institutions and processes, regardless of cultural differences. India is the prime example of a civic nation, with Muslims, Sikhs, Bengalis, and other minorities owing allegiance to the country despite the fact that they may not speak Hindi or practice Hinduism. Pakistan, to a lesser extent, fits this broader conception of a nation because of the belief that all Muslims of the Indian subcontinent belonged in the Muslim state regardless of differences in race or language.

Although both India and Pakistan were formed as multi-ethnic nations, their founders espoused competing visions of nationhood. The state of Pakistan grew out of the vision of Muslim nationalist Mohammed Ali Jinnah, head of the All-India Muslim League between 1930 and 1947 and the first president of Pakistan. Jinnah argued that there were two separate nations in the Indian subcontinent, a nation of Hindus and a nation of Muslims, and that the Muslims should have their own state, Pakistan. He argued that Muslims shared religious practices and were expected to obey common laws based on the Quran and the Shariat, the body of Islamic law. Hindus and Muslims could be distinguished often by dress or lifestyle, if not by race or language, and they often lived separately within India.

Jawaharlal Nehru, leader of the Indian National Congress, argued that there was only one nation in India that encompassed all the peoples of the Indian subcontinent whatever their religion, race, language, or culture. Geography, history, and political experience—not religion—defined Nehru's Indian nation. The historical experience of the peoples of the subcontinent, from the coming of the Aryan invaders in 1700 B.C. through the end of British rule in 1947, set apart the people within the subcontinent from those outside it. History and geography had produced a broader Indian world-view and destined the peoples of the subcontinent to live together. Nehru argued that if religion formed the basis of nationhood, then India could easily be divided into many nations instead of two. Jinnah's "two nation" theory also did not explain why only "Indian" Muslims constituted part of this Islamic nation and not those beyond the subcontinent. Indeed, while Islam was the basis for the creation of Pakistan, the real link among all the Muslims of theoretical Pakistan was that they were all Indians. By focusing on the Islamic link between West and East Pakistan and ignoring the Indian link between the two wings, Pakistan may have undermined its unity.

As the partition-era clash continued between the exclusive concept of a Muslim (but multi-linguistic) Pakistan and an inclusive concept of a united, multi-religious, and multi-linguistic India, there were weaker claims for other nations and states. In Bengal, a region in the far east of the Indian subcontinent, nationalists argued that the Bengali language and culture constituted the basis of a single nation in spite of religious differences. Today, Bengalis are divided between Bangladesh and the Indian state of West Bengal, but these Bengali nationalists argued that while Jinnah could have his Pakistan and Gandhi and Nehru their Hindustan, there ought to be a separate independent state of Bengal consisting of Muslims and Hindus. Likewise, briefly in the 1920s, and then again briefly after Indian independence, the Tamils of the extreme southeast ar-

gued that they should have a state separate from the linguistically distinct Indo-Aryans of the north.

These original concepts of nation in South Asia all incorporated multiple identities of some kind, whether religious, cultural, or linguistic. The only one of these independence movements to succeed after 1947 was the Bengali secessionist movement, which triumphed in the creation of Bangladesh from East Pakistan in 1971. Bengali nationalists led by Sheikh Mujibur Rahman argued that Bengali language and culture justified separate statehood for both the majority Muslims and the minority Hindus in East Pakistan. But most post–independence ideas of nationhood have tended to be much more narrow. Nationalists among the Kashmiris, Sikhs, Assamese, Pashtuns, and to a lesser extent, Sindhis, have all pushed for nations based on one language and one religion.

Changing Identities

The paradox behind these and other nationalist movements is that perceptions of nationhood often change or overlap, or result in the creation of states quite different from those envisioned by the ideology that inspired the original movement. National identifications are not constant, but created and shaped through time. The Muslim nationalist movement that led to the establishment of Pakistan, for example, emerged only at the turn of the century, accelerating in the decades immediately preceding the British withdrawal from India. While Muslims ruled Hindus in India for several centuries before British rule, a great deal of political interaction and communal intermingling (through intermarriage or Hindu conversions to the Islamic faith) occurred so that the two religious groups became racially and culturally similar. Cultural and linguistic differences across India became more regional rather than religious, although religion may have dictated some differences in social practices within the same region. For example, while religion differentiated Muslim, Sikh, and Hindu Punjabis, or Muslim and Hindu Bengalis, race, language, and culture also united them.

It was not until the end of the nineteenth century that Indian Muslim political elites began to perceive the Muslims of India as a distinct nation that could find salvation only in the creation of an Islamic Pakistan. The founding of the Anglo-Mohammedan College (later Aligarh Muslim University) in 1877, and then the establishment of the All-India Muslim League in 1906, gave impetus to the development of a separate Muslim identity. Muslim elites, primarily from the Hindi-speaking Hindu heartland of the United and Central Province of British India, then began to emphasize Islamic symbols and identity in order to mobilize support in the 1930s for Jinnah's two nation theory.

Similarly, variations of twentieth century Bengali nationalism point to the shifting nature of national identity, sometimes influenced chiefly by culture and language and other times predominantly by religion. During the Pakistan movement of the late 1940s, some Bengali leaders had toyed with the idea of a united Hindu-Muslim Bengali state, separate from the proposed independent states of India and Pakistan. Underlying this outlook for a greater Bengal state was the belief that language and culture superseded religious differences. Instead, the partition arrangement split Bengalis between East Pakistan and the Indian state of West Bengal. At some point between the creation of Pakistan and the 1971 war that led to the creation of Bangladesh, Muslim Bengalis who had identified with Pakistan shifted emphasis to their Bengali culture and decided that they could accept nothing less than an independent Bangladesh.

A united Bengal concept may have occurred to some Bengali nationalists on either side in East Pakistan and West Bengal during the 1971 struggle for Bangladesh. Although Indian military intervention helped create Bangladesh, the possibility that Hindu Bengali nationalists in West Bengal would also want to join this "Bengal Nation" must have worried Indian policymakers as well. The total Bengali-speaking population of both Bangladesh and West Bengal in India today number almost 180 million, and would have constituted a powerful state if a united independent Bengal had been forged in 1947 or 1971. But reunification schemes for a "Greater Bengal" have not been heard since the creation of Bangladesh in December 1971. This may be because Bengali Hindus prefer to remain in a Hindu-dominated India rather than a Muslim-majority Greater Bengal. Similarly, while Bengali Muslims may want a united Greater Bengal where they form the majority, they do not wish to be part of the Muslim minority in India.

Self-perceptions among Kashmiri Muslims, many of whom are currently calling for independence for Kashmir, or incorporation with Pakistan, have also fluctuated over the last half century. The first of these identities drew from the ideology of the "Kashmiriyat," which perceived Muslims, Hindus, and Ladakhi Buddhists of Kashmir as sharing an identity that justified separate nationhood for the province. At one time or another, Hindus and Muslims alike have sought an independent multi-religious state of Kashmir. A second outlook, articulated by Nehru, himself a Kashmiri Hindu Pandit, and shared by some Muslim leaders at the time of partition, held that Kashmir was an integral part of a secular Indian heritage. A third outlook among Kashmiri Muslims saw Kashmir as a part of Pakistan because of the shared religious heritage, following the reasoning of Jinnah's two nation theory. A fourth Kashmiri identity is emerging from the spread of transnational Islamist values into the state, which makes Kashmiris feel part of the broader Islamic world of Central Asia and the Middle East.

Another important separatist movement in recent years, that of the Sikhs in the Indian state of Punjab, also drew from a history of shifting identities. The Sikh religion was originally classified as a subdivision of Hinduism, a classification that Sikhs only mildly resisted. Later, they categorically rejected Hindu absorption, and eventually they insisted on a separate state. The turnaround was dramatic; before the mid-1980s, Sikhs viewed themselves as staunch Indian nationalists, and Hindus saw the

Sikhs as the "sword arm" of Hinduism. The Hindu-Sikh conflict that emerged in Punjab in the 1980s reveals the transforming nature of ethnicity and conflict in South Asia.

It is important to recall that the relations among Punjabi Muslims, Sikhs, and Hindus were cooperative and cordial under the British Raj. Indeed, Punjabis of all three religious persuasions constituted the bulk and the backbone of the British Indian Army. They fought shoulder-to-shoulder in two world wars. Even during the mass slaughter and migration of Hindus, Muslims, and Sikhs in Punjab that accompanied the partition of the province in 1947, members of these three religious communities in the British Indian Army remained disciplined. Since partition, however, Indo-Pakistani wars have resembled a civil war among the Punjabis: the Indian armed forces are 30 percent Hindu and Sikh Punjabi while Pakistan's forces are 80 percent Muslim Punjabi. From one racial, linguistic, and cultural ethnic group, Punjabis have become three separate communities.

Even where separatist movements do not of themselves imperil regional stability, the domino effect they may create would have implications for the entire region.

These examples suggest that religion is more divisive than racial, cultural, and linguistic ties in South Asia. But past cooperation and goodwill among Hindus, Muslims, and Sikhs in Bengal, Kashmir, and Punjab show that such positive ties may be restored given the right attitudes and political conditions.

Territorial Secession?

All of the states of South Asia constitute political conglomerations of several ethnic nations, many of which are demanding separate independent states. India faces the independence movements of Muslim Kashmiris, Sikh Punjabis, and Hindu Assamese; Sri Lanka faces an insurgency from Hindu Tamils; and Pakistan has had demands for greater autonomy by groups including Sindhis and Muhajirs (immigrants). With so many complex lines of religion, culture, and language in South Asia, allowing communities to secede would lead to a number of grave consequences. Regardless of the legitimacy or illegitimacy of the separatist demands, granting them could exacerbate existing tensions and unravel regional security.

First, the detachment of Kashmir from India could easily lead to a communal bloodbath and national disintegration. Hard core insurgents seem determined to continue with their campaign whatever the outcome, but if Kashmir is dislodged from India, it could lead to the marginalization of the 115 million Muslims left in India. The Hindu nationalist Bharatiya Janata Party has declared on many occasions that a Kashmiri Muslim decision to leave India would reflect adversely on the loyalty of all Indian Muslims. Even some leaders of the secular Janata Dal and Congress party have hinted at such an interpretation. In response, the Imam Sayyid Bukhari of Jamma Masjid in Delhi stated that Indian Muslims can do no more than support the Indian position on Kashmir, and Indian Muslims publicly do not support the secession of Kashmir. However, if Kashmir were to secede, the Hindu-Muslim communal violence that could very likely arise would be beyond the control of any party or leader.

India considers the Kashmir issue integral to the ability of the Indian state to preserve its multi-religious, multi-ethnic, and secular status, and is thus determined to resist indefinitely the Kashmiri independence struggle. On the other hand, any international decision to maintain the status quo in Kashmir will not be acceptable to Pakistan. Pakistan feels that it was cheated at the time of partition when it failed to acquire Muslim-majority Kashmir. Although Pakistan would be willing to maintain the territorial status quo on all other cases of secessionist demands, it will insist on making Kashmir an exception since it believes that Kashmir should have joined Muslim Pakistan in 1947. The more important question today, however, is not what Pakistan considers its moral or legal right to Kashmir, but the probable consequences for the rest of the subcontinent in tampering with existing state boundaries.

The creation of an independent Khalistan out of the existing Indian Punjab, as demanded by many Sikhs, may prove to be as complicated for the region as the separation of Kashmir or the 1947 partition of India. Thousands of Sikhs, especially the business and professional classes, are scattered throughout India outside Punjab. About 45 percent of the population of Punjab—60 percent of most of its major cities—remains Hindu in spite of a 1966 partition which created two new states out of the formerly Hindu-majority areas of Punjab. Since Punjabi Hindus do not want to be part of an independent Sikh state, there would have to be yet another division of Punjab and the inevitable mass migration of millions of Sikhs and Hindus across new borders. These population transfers would lead to extensive communal bloodshed, as in the 1947 division of Punjab between India and Pakistan. In that partition, about 10 million Muslims, Sikhs, and Hindus were caught on the wrong side of the new frontier and forced to migrate within a month, and about half a million civilians lost their lives in the partition of Punjab.

Even where separatist movements do not of themselves imperil regional stability, the domino effect they may create would have implications for the entire region. In India, the northeastern tea-growing state of Assam has pushed for independence, but its loss would hurt the Indian economy and may eventually lead to the separation of the entire northeast sector of India. Assam would also be the first Hindu-majority state to gain independence, and its secession could trigger similar movements in the Hindu-majority states of South India, like Tamil Nadu, Karnataka, and Telengana. Similarly, the partition of Sri Lanka could create a domino effect through South Asia, especially stimulating the Tamil separatist movement in Tamil Nadu. In addition, the highly contested east-central sector which contains both Tamils and Tamil-speaking Muslims will not be easily separated, since the Muslims prefer to remain in Sri Lanka.

In Pakistan, which has experienced a separation movement in Sindh, democratization and decentralization may not resolve the problem of power sharing among the Sindhis, Muhajirs, Pashtuns, and Punjabis, four of the largest ethnic communities in the province. Democratization and greater regional control may instead lead to greater economic and political power for the Muhajirs and Punjabis resident in Sindh. On the other hand, an independent Sindhi state may exacerbate the problem of Urdu-speaking Muslims from India, as in the case of the Bihari Muslims from East Pakistan. Following the independence of Bangladesh in 1971, over four million Muslims from the Indian state of Bihar who had earlier migrated to East Pakistan were accused of having fought with West Pakistan's military against Bangladeshi independence. Bangladeshis considered them to be Pakistanis and asked that they be repatriated. By the mid-1980s, the Pakistan government had repatriated about 1.8 million Biharis to Pakistan, most of whom joined other Indian immigrant communities in Sindh. But Sindhis resisted these new immigrants since this implied a further addition to the Urdu-speaking Muhajirs in Sindh. According to unofficial estimates, there are still some 2.5 million Biharis left behind in Bangladesh who wish to be repatriated. Thus, the existing 10 million Muhajirs are not likely to be absorbed in an independent Sindhi state, nor are they likely to be accepted back into India. Despite a temporary improvement in the situation of Sindh with the coming to power of Benazir Bhutto, the struggle between the Muhajirs and Sindhis has worsened in the mid-1990s.

Prospects for Confederation

To counter the trend of nationalist and secessionist movements in the region, the South Asian Association for Regional Cooperation (SAARC) has since 1984 attempted to build confidence in the region and encourage the growth of economic, social, and eventually political cooperation. The more optimistic, perhaps utopian, supporters of SAARC would like to see the organization grow into a larger confederation or "super-state" like the European Union. Such a development may serve to prevent the spread of nationalist movements and territorial fragmentation in South Asia. It may soften or even resolve issues such as the Kashmir dispute, Muhajir-Sindhi ethnic and territorial questions, the status of Bengali Muslims in Assam, and the Tamil secessionist struggle in Sri Lanka.

However, Pakistan prefers confederal arrangements with the Muslim countries of the Economic Cooperation Organization (ECO) bloc rather than with the multi-religious countries of SAARC. One Pakistani analyst projects the eventual formation of a large Muslim confederation that would stretch from Pakistan to Turkey and encompass the newly independent Muslim states that emerged from the former Soviet Union. In a sense, this would be the logical extension of the concept of Pakistan as a Muslim homeland in the Indian subcontinent. But Pakistan's strategy of linking itself with the states of Central Asia and the Middle East also has some weaknesses. Afghanistan needs to be stabilized in order to establish road and rail communications with the Central Asian states, and the stability of Tajikistan is equally uncertain. There are also other socio-economic and demographic problems that stand in the way of fostering a strong Islamic confederation.

With the ECO fading away and SAARC making little progress, both India and Pakistan are seeking to join the Association for South East Asian Nations (ASEAN). India has already been accepted as a "dialogue partner" of ASEAN. A potentially larger South and Southeast Asian confederation may offset India's natural and overwhelming economic dominance of South Asia. Muslims and Buddhists in South Asia would also have less to fear from Hindu domination in a confederation which includes 300 million Muslim Indonesians and Malays, Buddhist Thais, Vietnamese, Laotians and Cambodians, and Christian Filipinos. However, ASEAN has been unwilling to admit India and Pakistan as full members partly because they are less economically developed than the ASEAN nations and partly because ASEAN does not want to drag Indo-Pakistani confrontations over Kashmir into its regional political arrangements.

If it is premature to establish a confederation in South Asia, perhaps the countries of South Asia should at least agree on two fundamental principles: that the existing international borders, whether good or bad, legal or illegal, are inviolable; and that none of the states in the region will aid and abet each other's separatist movements. India may find these proposals for maintaining the territorial status quo in South Asia to its liking. Pakistan will surely insist on making an exception for Kashmir, but the reality is that India can enforce the status quo in Kashmir by the sheer weight of its military power. It did so in the past and continues to do so during the present crisis. In any case, Pakistan would also have something to lose if Kashmiris had their way, since most of them would like to incorporate the areas of Kashmir currently under Pakistani control into an independent Kashmir. The most feasible solution short of greater confederation is to preserve the status quo—a conclusion that may not satisfy all the underlying national feelings, but one that addresses the reality of South Asian political life today. The alternative, a readjustment of the complex ethnic distribution of South Asia through territorial change, could fragment all the countries in the region into smaller states only at a very high cost in human life and regional stability.

Article 2

The New York Review of Books, October 23, 1997

India: The Imprint of Empire

Roderick MacFarquhar

1.

In 1947, on the eve of Indian independence, my parents arranged for me to fly from Britain for what promised to be our last family holiday in the subcontinent. As a British member of the Indian Civil Service, my father expected to leave with the departing Raj.[1] My mother and I drove up from New Delhi to the Vale of Kashmir. We visited my brother's grave in Srinagar, where he had died in infancy a decade earlier, one of an estimated two million graves the

British left behind. Then we trekked the final 2,000 feet on tiny ponies up to Gulmarg, where my father joined us after attending the Indian independence ceremonies in New Delhi on August 15. It was an idyllic holiday. Raj-style: golf on two of the most beautiful courses in the world, where the ball soared encouragingly far in the thin mountain air; picnics among the firs and pines; bridge in the club; the latest Agatha Christie mystery in the evening before turning in.

But on the plains of the Punjab, where I had grown up, one of the greatest human tragedies of the twentieth century was taking place. The proudest province of British India, which had just been partitioned between the successor states, India and Pakistan, was collapsing into a state of nature. Sikhs and Hindus killed their Muslim neighbors; Muslims killed Sikhs and Hindus. Millions of Hindus and Sikhs fled eastward to India, Moslems westward to Pakistan.[2] Hundreds of thousands didn't make it.

Trainloads of refugees were ambushed and boarded before they reached the border, and their occupants slaughtered to a man, woman, and child.[3] Only the engine driver would be left alive so that he could deliver his grisly cargo across the border.[4]

Rumors began to reach Gulmarg that former comrades-in-arms of the British Indian Army, now divided into the armed forces of the new nations, were about to fall upon each other in the disputed province of Kashmir. Situated on the Indo-Pakistani border, Kashmir was supposed to have its future decided by the maharaja. Since over 75 percent of Kashmiris were Muslims but the maharaja was a Hindu, both countries hoped for his adherence. He procrastinated, then opted for India. No Pakistani leader since has been willing or able to live with the small portion of Kashmir which his country retained after the fighting of 1947–1948. And so, fifty years and three wars later on, a costly arms race continues, nuclear weapons are developed, missiles are deployed, border clashes take place as I write.[5]

I left Gulmarg on an American plane sent to Srinagar to evacuate embassy staff. Flying low over the Punjab, we saw villages burning below. In New Delhi, our house was deserted; the Muslim servants had fled to refugee camps in the capital. Working as a volunteer, I saw the pitiful condition of the wounded in one of the camps. When my parents returned we located our servants and smuggled them out of New Delhi, where killings were still taking place, hiding them in the bathroom of our carriage on the train to Bombay, where things were calmer. I sailed home to school.

In the years that followed, I returned often to the subcontinent, but always to examine some current problem. "What's gone wrong with us now?" my friends used to ask plaintively. Going back to New Delhi for the fiftieth anniversary of independence this summer, however, it was the scenes of 1947 that were uppermost in my mind. How did Indians look back on the bloodshot moment of Partition which marked the end of British rule?

2.

Answers were hard to find; there has not been a German-style soul-searching in the subcontinent. According to the Delhi University historian Gyanendra Pandey, "Indian intellectuals have tended to celebrate the story of the Independence struggle rather than dwell on the agonies of Partition." Pandey lists evident reasons why the Hindu-Muslim violence has had little attention. Bitter conflict between Hindus and Muslims persists in parts of India today; and those who pursue the history of such strife run the real danger of reopening old wounds. In addition, there is no consensus among Indians about the nature of Partition. "We have no means of representing such tragic loss, nor of pinning down—or rather, owning—responsibility for it. Consequently, our nationalist historiography, journalism, and filmmaking have tended to generate something like a collective amnesia."[6]

For the political scientist Ashis Nandy at Delhi's Center for the Study of Developing Societies, "the silence was one way known to the South Asians to start life anew and contain bitterness. It was a means of restoring community life, interpersonal trust and the known moral universe." Many wanted to wipe away the memories, "both what had been done to them or what was done or sanctioned by them." Still, Nandy wrote, it is gradually "becoming obvious that the summer of 1947 brought out the worst in us, so much so that even our imagination of evil failed." Writing of the "psychopathic and sadistic dimensions of the carnage," he concluded that independence meant "genocide, necrophilia, ethnic cleansing, massive uprooting and collapse of a moral universe."[7]

The implication of such an account is that the responsibility for the slaughter has to be borne by "ordinary" Indians and Pakistanis who turned against each other; the manner of the bloodletting allows of no other conclusion. But what about the Partition that sparked it? The "communal" tensions between Hindus and Muslims in the subcontinent date back centuries to the successive waves of Muslim conquerors who swept down through the Khyber Pass and forced their Hindu subjects to convert. In the twentieth century, some Muslims feared religious, cultural, and economic subordination to the Hindu majority, perhaps even revenge for their earlier victories. Their leaders embraced the theory that the subcontinent comprised "two nations," each of which deserved its own homeland; the idea of a unified subcontinent was imposed by the British.

At the same time Indians have long blamed British divide-and-rule policies for exacerbating and entrenching communal barriers. The Raj was certainly Machiavellian from time to time, not to mention blundering and harsh, but closer to the mark was probably the well-known Indian judgment: "We divided and they ruled." In one of the articles for the fiftieth anniversary, Nitesh Sengupta blamed the British for not conceding home rule after World War I when the future founder of Pakistan, M. A. Jinnah, was still a loyal member of the Indian National Congress.[8]

Sengupta, however, blamed the Congress for the political missteps that occurred thereafter. For instance, in June 1946 Nehru told a press conference that the central government of an independent India (which would be dominated by his Congress Party) would reserve its rights to intervene in the component states of the union on issues of planning and economic development. (India was ultimately to be divided into twenty-five states and centrally administered territories.) Since the Congress had earlier accepted a three-tier constitutional arrangement designed to allow Muslims to exercise all powers in their regions except for defense, foreign affairs, and communications, Jinnah regarded Nehru's assertion as treachery. According to Sengupta, only the final nail in the coffin of a united independent India was driven by the British, when Mountbatten arrived as Britain's last viceroy and decided to accelerate Britain's departure by ten months. It is over this issue that British historians have been arguing.

Essentially, the case against Mountbatten, apart from justifiable jibes about his relentless self-glorification—"I was governing by personality," he later told Nehru's authorized biographer—is that he was pro-Indian and anti-Pakistan, pro-Nehru and anti-Jinnah. He put pressure on the supposedly neutral Boundary Commissioner, Sir Cyril Radcliffe, to make critical adjustments in favor of India when drawing the frontier through the Punjab.

A Cambridge don of Pakistani origin has asserted that "if Jinnah is the first Pakistani, Mountbatten is the first Paki-basher." Mountbatten and his wife certainly hit it off instantly with Nehru while the viceroy later made it clear that he had found Jinnah impossible to deal with.[9]

Cyril Radcliffe had no expert knowledge of India. He was given a task of Solomonic proportions to be completed in an irresponsibly short period of time. He was not insulated from lobbying as claimed but was in contact with Mountbatten and his staff. But since Radcliffe destroyed all his papers on returning to England we cannot know if his earlier ideas on the Punjab boundary were modified by common sense or by the Congress Party via Mountbatten. Auden's caustic poem on his performance remains one of the most telling commentaries written on the Partition.

> "Time," they had briefed him in
>   London, "is short, It's too late
> For mutual reconciliation
>   or rational debate:
> The only solution now lies in
>   separation.
> The Viceroy thinks, as you will
>   see from his letter,
> That the less you are seen in his
>   company the better,
> So we've arranged to provide you
>   with other accommodation..."
> Shut up in a lonely mansion, with
>   police night and day
> Patrolling the gardens
>   to keep assassins away,
> He got down to work, to the task
>   of settling the fate
> Of millions. The maps at his
>   disposal were out of date
> And the Census Returns almost
>   certainly incorrect,
> But there was no time to check
>   them, no time to inspect
> Contested areas. The weather
>   was frightfully hot,
> And a bout of dysentery kept him
>   constantly on the trot,
> But in seven weeks it was done,
>   the frontiers decided,
> A continent for better or worse
>   divided.
> The next day he sailed for
>   England, where he quickly
>   forgot
> The case, as a good lawyer must.
> Return he would not,
> Afraid, as he told his Club, that
>   he might get shot.

The second set of charges against Mountbatten is that by deciding in June 1947 to advance the date of independence from June 1948 to August 1947, he left no time for further negotiation and therefore made Partition inevitable. This also ensured that the exchange of populations would be hurried, chaotic, and bloody. He delayed announcing the location of Radcliffe's boundaries until after independence, at which point the responsibility for law and order devolved on India and Pakistan. He did so, it is alleged, because he sensed a PR disaster in the making for himself and Britain. So, disastrously, there was no British-led unified Indian Army to oversee the transfer of populations. It was issues like these that led Kuldip Nayar, a leading columnist and former High Commissioner in London, to suggest holding a joint Indo-Pakistani seminar to mark the fiftieth anniversary entitled "The Trial of Mountbatten."

How he would have emerged from a fair trial remains unknowable. Mountbatten was an energetic and charismatic viceroy, if often guilty of gross errors of judgment. His colleague Field Marshal Sir Gerald Templer once commented: "You're so crooked, Dickie, if you swallowed a nail you'd shit a corkscrew." Yet many knowledgeable British officials with no cause to admire him felt that in the light of the deteriorating communal situation in the spring of 1947, Britain had no alternative but to hand over power as soon as possible; further delay would have spread the massacres beyond the Punjab to all of India. Moreover, although Mountbatten claimed credit for advancing the timetable, the decision was actually taken in the India Office in London.[10]

Whatever the verdict of history, Mountbatten undoubtedly charmed the Indian public. On the occasion of the Mountbattens' departure for England in June 1948, Nehru remarked how struck he had been at the reception given them in old Delhi earlier in the day:

[Used] as I am to these vast demonstrations here, I was much affected, and I wondered how it was that an Englishman and Englishwoman could become so popular during this brief period of time.... Obviously this was not connected so much with what had happened, but rather with the good

faith, the friendship and the love of India that these two possessed....

Obviously, too, that friendship helped Nehru decide to keep India within the Commonwealth even when it became a republic, thus ensuring that most British ex-colonies followed suit and giving post-imperial Britain the illusion of retaining its global stature. Three decades later, long after Mountbatten's friends and contemporaries of the independence era had died, when the IRA blew up his fishing boat, killing him and members of his family, the Indian parliament and state assemblies stopped their proceedings, shops closed, and a week's state mourning was declared.

3.

As India showed, the end of empire is never easy. The older imperial powers were crippled economically by World War II and lost their aura of unchallengeable authority. In the early postwar years, the British were fortunate to be led by a Labour Party committed to decolonization. Some nations learned the hard way that "nerve without muscle," as the historian Lawrence James put it, could not save an empire.[11] In the fifty years that followed the end of the Raj, virtually the entire British empire in Asia, Africa, and the Americas was dismantled, sometimes peacefully, sometimes with bitterness and bloodshed.[12] During the same period, the other European empires—French, Dutch, Portuguese, Belgian, Spanish—also largely disappeared, and the US left the Philippines.[13] Even the Soviet and tsarist empires collapsed. It was the greatest liberation of subject peoples in history.

The process culminated on June 30 this year with the return to China of Hong Kong, the last great jewel in the tattered imperial regalia of Europe. No imperial divestiture had been longer in the making, but probably not since the loss of the American colonies had the British elite been so publicly and venomously divided about a retreat from empire as it took place. And though Britain had certainly never left a colony in as good economic shape as Hong Kong, there was continual wrangling between the outgoing and incoming sovereigns, which readers of *The New York Review* have had a chance to consider in detail.[14] For the student of the end of empire, the question is: Why did Hong Kong 1997 arouse so much sound and fury while India 1947 did not?

In 1947, although disasters were foreseen, there was little time for reflection—even the high priest of the imperial mission, Churchill, finally accepted that there was no alternative to granting independence to the Indian subcontinent. But in 1997, there persisted to the very end, and at the highest levels, the uneasy feeling that Britain was not behaving honorably. Prime Minister Thatcher later said she hated signing the Joint Declaration of 1984 that sentenced Hong Kong citizens to live under a Communist dictatorship. But in 1989, in the aftermath of the Tiananmen massacre, she rejected a proposal made by Governor Sir David Wilson to grant full British passports to the three and a half million people in the colony who ranked as British Dependent Territories Citizens. The specter, however unlikely, of a flood of refugees from Hong Kong was politically intolerable.

After John Major replaced Mrs. Thatcher, Foreign Office experts persuaded him to go to Beijing to sign an agreement on Hong Kong's new airport. He was embarrassed to become the first Western leader to shake hands with Premier Li Peng, widely despised in the West for his role in Tiananmen. Somewhat unjustly, Major decided to make Wilson, not Sir Percy Cradock, his principal adviser on China policy, the scapegoat for the position he'd been put in. By this time, the new foreign secretary, Douglas Hurd, had become convinced that the endgame in Hong Kong demanded the presence of a political heavyweight rather than a Foreign Office mandarin. Out went Sir David in dignified silence and in came the ex-cabinet minister Chris Patten, chastened by his personal electoral defeat, but ebullient about his new job.

Patten, like Mountbatten, had two enormous advantages over his predecessor, a direct line to the prime minister—who attributed his continuance in office after the 1992 general

election to Patten's chairmanship of the campaign—and to the foreign secretary, both former cabinet colleagues, and carte blanche to do what he thought best. By adhering to the letter of the 1984 Joint Declaration and the Chinese Basic Law implementing it, if not to their spirit, Patten set out to further democratize the Hong Kong electoral system. The British ambassador in Beijing, Sir Robin McLaren, warned that the Chinese government would react badly, and it did. The Beijing authorities expected to be handed a cozy, controllable colonial system with which their officials would be quite comfortable. Instead, they would inherit a Legislative Council which they could rightly anticipate would include significant numbers of capable opponents, such as the barrister Martin Lee.

Before long, Patten was denounced by Beijing propagandists as a "clown," a "dirty trickster," a "tango dancer," a "strutting prostitute," a "serpent," an "assassin," and the "criminal of all time." Far more dangerous for Patten was the assault of those whom he called the "Sinologists," the Foreign Office officials who had helped shape the policy of cooperation with China that had produced the Joint Declaration. Clearly it was galling for them to be depicted in the press as pusillanimous appeasers who kowtowed to the Chinese. Cradock denigrated Patten for "incompetence" and self-aggrandizement.[15] But what probably guided the Sinologists most strongly was their conviction that, precisely because the Chinese were "thugs," as Cradock was wont to describe them, the only option was to coax them into the least punitive arrangements for Hong Kong. "Confrontation" would be counterproductive.

Again, there can be no final judgment. But the Sinologists surely underestimated the character of Hong Kong as revealed by the demonstrations of more than a million people there after the Tiananmen crackdown. Hong Kong could no longer be dismissed as an apolitical city, interested only in acquiring wealth. Its citizens were profoundly concerned about the politics of their forthcoming sovereign and deeply worried that the rule of law which had become integral to their political identity might disappear after July 1, 1997. No

governor could have guaranteed their future. The Chinese have duly swept aside Patten's reforms and the legislative body which they produced. But Patten provided Hong Kongers with a sense of what they needed to fight for if they were to breathe reality into Deng Xiaoping's concept of "one country, two systems." One of his leading Hong Kong opponents even conceded that he transformed the political culture by introducing open debate and government accountability.

Unlike Mountbatten, Patten did not have the benefit of a moving and affectionate farewell from the new sovereign power. But Patten, too, seems to have become widely popular. Even in his final months, when he was effectively a lame duck, the leading opinion sampling organization found that 60 percent of the population still supported Patten, a third of them would have liked Hong Kong to remain British or become independent, while 90 percent, the highest percentage ever, admitted to being content with their lives under British rule. The pollsters added that "as the sun sets on British administration in Hong Kong, many aspects of life under [British] rule seem suffused with a 'golden haze.' "[16]

The haze will dissipate. Nobody can long cherish the memory of being a colonial subject.[17] And after the parting comes the reckoning. History will be rewritten in Hong Kong as it was in India, and likely more harshly.[18] China's foreign minister, Qian Qichen, has stated that Hong Kong history texts have to be revised. Though education is supposedly not a matter for the central government under the Basic Law, the new chief executive, C. H. Tung, has confirmed that there would be a need to rewrite the sections on the colonial past.

4.

The celebration in Beijing of the reversion of Hong Kong was long planned and efficiently organized. Soon after their fifteenth party congress this month, the Chinese authorities, if they have not started already, will surely begin planning the celebration of the fiftieth anniversary of the creation of the People's Republic on October 1, 1999. It is crucial for China's Communist leaders that the party-state they created—and major events in the life of the state like the reversion of Hong Kong—should seem all-important to its citizens. India's politicians, on the other hand, are neither appointed nor given legitimacy by the state; they emerge from their party and their community. Faced with the fiftieth anniversary of independence, the coalition government in New Delhi was so preoccupied with ensuring its own survival that its leaders could hardly focus on a date when they might no longer be in power.

The coalition is still shaky. After the 1996 election, when the Congress government fell, the right-wing Hindu, chauvinist Bharatiya Janata Party (BJP), despite having become the largest party, could not get parliamentary backing for its government. A coalition of thirteen small, mainly regional parties opposed to the BJP came to power, and was maintained in office by the Congress's decision to give it general support. However, the first coalition premier, H. D. Deve Gowda, was toppled in April this year by the Congress party leader, Sitaram Kesri. And while the coalition government has stayed in office under a new leader, Inder Gujral, Delhi political observers believe that Kesri will withdraw support and force an election in about a year when he anticipates Congress will stand higher in the public opinion polls. But neither they nor their democratic system were threatened by a low-key approach to the golden jubilee.

In both Hong Kong and Delhi the official ceremonies I attended were hard going. The open-air British farewell in Hong Kong took place in an unceasing downpour. Many were sad, all seemed miserable. In New Delhi, at the "stroke of the midnight hour" on August 14, Nehru's speech about India awakening to "life and freedom" to keep its "tryst with destiny" was replayed in the Central Hall of Parliament, and President Narayanan, the first untouchable to become head of state, inveighed against corruption, which he said was "corroding the vitals of our politics and our society."[19]

Everyone understood what he meant. In a jubilee poll, corruption was rated as the greatest national evil, far above unemployment or inflation. Corruption permeates Indian life: politicians buy votes from citizens (though an unusually determined election commissioner cracked down on this practice in the 1996 election). Companies buy favors and licenses to do business from politicians and bureaucrats (though the hope is that freeing the economy from state control will lessen such bribery). Citizens pay "facilitation fees" to the police and petty officials to get access to services. "Even the wretched homeless in some cities have to pay for the right to sleep on the sidewalks," according to Shashi Tharoor in *India: From Midnight to the Millennium*.[20]

The courtesy displayed to Mountbatten fifty years earlier was recaptured by the presence on the dais of Betty Boothroyd, the Speaker of the House of Commons.[21] Outside, we milled around searching desperately for our drivers among hundreds of identical white Indian-made Ambassador cars, still modeled on the 1956 Morris Oxford, hoping for a few hours' sleep before our next tryst with an early morning speech by the prime minister. This took place at the mid-seventeenth-century Mogul Red Fort in Old Delhi, one of the great architectural masterpieces commissioned by the Emperor Shah Jahan when he moved his capital from Agra and built the city of Old Delhi.

In Hong Kong, one had to go deep into tourist back alleys to find hand-over kitsch, a few crude T-shirts; the most common logo visible on Hong Kong citizens' chests was "DKNY." As the rising emigration figures have shown, Hong Kong Chinese are uncertain about their future under Beijing and presumably were not sure whether they had much to celebrate.[22] In New Delhi, at the last minute, the government urged citizens to rush out and buy Indian flags, lifting the normal legal ban on the flag being flown except officially. But Indians were gloomy about the recent downturn in the economy, the violence and fissiparous tendencies spawned by intercaste and communal tensions, and the increasingly criminal character not merely of state assemblies but even of the national parliament, where one estimate is that 100 out of the 535 members of the lower house have criminal records, for crimes such as bribery, rape, and attempted murder.[23] Indians have an overdeveloped capacity for devastating self-criticism and this came out in the many series of articles published during the anniversary, e.g., in *The Times of India*. A popular account of recent travels in small-town India by Pankaj Mishra made it seem as if the previous fifty years had succeeded only in transforming country and people for the worse, with the author wondering "if much of urban India wasn't simply a horrible mistake."[24] The "real India," Mishra writes, is

> broken road, the wandering cows, the open gutter, the low ramshackle shops, the ground littered with garbage, the pressing crowd, the dust.

And the people are no better. The state of Bihar, the land of Buddha, is where

> . . . medical colleges sell degrees and doctors pull out transfusion tubes from the veins of their patients when they go on strike, where private caste armies regularly massacre Harijans [untouchables] in droves, where murderers and rapists become legislators through large-scale "booth-capturing" . . .

Aged veterans of the struggle against the British expressed their disillusionment to journalists about what had been achieved since 1947 after all their sacrifices.

5.

For a child of the Raj, it is tempting to believe that the special qualities of both ex-colonies must have something to do with their British legacies: the use of English, for Hong Kong as a bridge to international finance and trade, for India as a link within a polyglot state with eighteen official languages; the rule of law and a well-developed legal structure to protect the citizen and provide a workable market for businessmen; a highly trained and efficient civil service and a relatively uncorrupt police force; and a free press. In the case of India, politicians absorbed the British parliamentary model of democracy and began to practice it in a limited way under the Raj; in Hong Kong, the British stimulated the hunger for one which was introduced too late. Some South Asian historians acknowledge this,[25] and perhaps Hong Kong historians—after understandably excoriating the Opium War and the subsequent British imperialist ventures that led to the formation of the colony—eventually will too.

But the impact of the two hundred—year engagement of Britain with the rich and complex society of India cannot be described by a complacent list of inherited institutions. Indeed, ever since India's domestic troubles in the 1970s, when Mrs. Gandhi declared martial law, radical Indian historians have been seeking the roots of their discontent in the colonial era.[26] They have had important insights; but their approach and some findings have justifiably been questioned. A widely acclaimed study, for example, depicts a pre-colonial period in which an ecological balance was maintained by a caste system largely without conflict. The arrival of the British, it is argued, disrupted this relatively successful traditional culture by emphasizing production for the market over subsistence, undermining cooperation within communities, and by encouraging the unrestrained use of resources, especially forests. This picture is disputed by Delhi University economist Bina Agarwal, partly on factual grounds, partly because it tends to glorify a traditional social system that was infused with unequal gender relations.[27]

Still, the pros and cons of the British legacy are less important for outsiders with an affection for India than the ongoing commitment to parliamentary democracy and the rule of law, though these are marred by glaring political problems and social failures. As an American observer put it, "galloping normlessness" characterizes Indian politics. The statistics on social conditions remain dismaying. Infant malnutrition is worse than in sub-Saharan Africa. The ineffectiveness of family planning means that a population that was 350 million in 1947 is now 950 million, will be about 1,580 million in another fifty years, and may not become stabilized for another hundred years. The percentage of people below the poverty line has declined from over 55 percent when the British left, but it is still well over a

third of the much larger population. The neglect of primary health care, especially for women, is attested to by the infant mortality rate of 75 per 1,000, as compared with 31 in China, 41 in Egypt, and 53 in Indonesia, and with a world rate of 63. There is still desperate poverty and not just in Calcutta.[28]

A particularly sad failure is suggested by the fact that no more than 52 percent of the population is literate—as compared with a world rate of 76 percent—with an Indian female rate of only 36 percent. Though 80 percent of Indian children now start primary school, the failure to spread primary education is attested by the fact that only 40.8 percent of Indians are literate at age fifteen as compared with 90 percent of South Koreans, 72.6 percent of Chinese, and 57.3 percent of Ugandans.[29] There were plausible grounds for the pessimism felt by many Indians as they looked back over five decades.

But India's leaders should be credited for trying to deal with fundamental cleavages in Indian society. The Indian caste system has been around for millennia; the Muslim invasions started over a thousand years ago. But the social and communal problems begotten by that history were confronted at the outset of independence, initially through the agony of Partition, and then through rights and safeguards written into the constitution. It abolished untouchability and said that citizens could not be denied access to shops, restaurants, and other public places on grounds of caste and religion.[30] It promised special treatment for the untouchable castes and tribes which it listed in a special "schedule." In fulfilling these undertakings, the Indian government has reserved 22.5 percent of government jobs and 85 seats in the legislature for members of "scheduled" castes and tribes.

But it is worth emphasizing that attempts to help other backward castes (OBCs), people above the level of untouchability, have caused even more political upheavals than affirmative action for minorities in the US—including the collapse of governments. On August 7, 1990, the then prime minister, V. P. Singh, announced that his government would honor the ten-year-old recom-

mendations of an official commission that 27 percent of all federal government jobs should be reserved for OBCs. In the words of Mr. Singh, all hell broke loose: government buses were burned, trains were attacked, public property was extensively damaged, and some upper-caste youths immolated themselves. His government fell.

Religious tensions have also risen since the bloody violence unleashed in 1992 when the Babri Masjid mosque in Ayodhya was destroyed by Hindus who claimed it had been built on top of an ancient temple to the god Rama. The secularism of the founding fathers is under siege.[31]

Still, acting under far greater pressures than ever constrained the officers of the Raj's Indian Civil Service, Indian politicians and bureaucrats have managed to maintain national unity and a democratic polity. We should remember that in the 1950s, there was speculation that India might fall apart or survive only by totalitarian means,[32] and that in the late 1960s, under Mrs. Gandhi, it was confidently predicted that India had held its last election. The problems remain, but India has held together and the democratic system has taken root among the voters, even if they have an understandable skepticism about what the politicians will actually deliver; 59 percent assert that their vote makes a difference and only 21 percent say the opposite; 69 percent reject the idea that governance would be better without parties and elections, even though 63 percent feel that representatives do not care about the people.[33]

From afar, India's problems look insuperable. The benefit of returning there is to be reminded of the talent, resilience, and determination that abound for tackling them. With economic reform taking hold and the growth rate reaching a healthy 7 percent, India at fifty is making progress, still slowly, always painfully, but with gathering momentum. Hong Kong at year zero is of course enviably better off and always hustling. Its citizens have been promised their own "system" for fifty years. But will Hong Kong at fifty be the mature democracy India is today? Only if China is too.

—September 25, 1997

Notes

1. According to Philip Woodruff, *The Men Who Ruled India, I: The Founders; II: The Guardians* (London: Jonathan Cape, 1953, 1954), in 1939 there were 1,384 officers in the ICS, of whom 759 were British expatriates (II, p. 363). After partition, my father went to Karachi to work for the new Pakistani government.

2. According to the 1941 census, the undivided Punjab consisted of 52.88 percent Moslems, 29.79 percent Hindus, and 14.62 percent Sikhs; Indu Banga, editor, *Five Punjabi Centuries: Policy, Economy, Society, and Culture, c. 1500–1990* (New Delhi: Manohar, 1997), p. 243.

3. Philip Ziegler, *Mountbatten: The Official Biography* (Collins, 1985), p. 437, and Larry Collins and Dominique Lapierre, *Freedom at Midnight* (Simon and Schuster, 1975), p. 342, quote estimates of the dead ranging from 200,000 to 500,000; J. S. Grewal, *The Sikhs of the Punjab* (Cambridge University Press, 1990), p. 181, and Patrick French, *Liberty or Death: India's Journey to Independence and Division* (HarperCollins, 1997), p. 349, agree on a million. The highest figure I have seen is "almost" or "over" 2,000,000 in Akbar S. Ahmed, *Jinnah, Pakistan and Islamic Identity: The Search for Saladin* (Routledge, 1997) pp. xi, 166. Estimates of the number of refugees who managed to survive the two-way border crossing in the Punjab and elsewhere range from 8,000,000 to as high as 17,000,000.

4. For recent accounts of the "ethnic cleansing" of Partition, see S. M. Burke and Salim Al-Din Quraishi, *The British Raj in India: An Historical Review* (Oxford University Press, 1995), pp. 609–625, and French, *Liberty or Death,* pp. 342–356.

5. Prem Shankar Jha, *Kashmir, 1947: Rival Versions of History* (Delhi: Oxford University Press, 1996). For a scalding critique of Britain's handling of its treaty obligations to princely states like Kashmir, see Ian Copland, *The Princes of India in the Endgame of Empire, 1917–1947* (Cambridge University Press, 1997).

6. Gyanendra Pandey, "In Defense of the Fragment: Writing about Hindu-Muslim Riots in India Today," in Ranajit Guha, editor, *A Subaltern Studies Reader, 1986–1995* (University of Minnesota Press, forthcoming 1997).

7. Ashis Nandy, "Too Painful for Words," *Times of India,* July 20, 1997.

8. Nitish Sengupta, "Partition need not have happened if . . . , " *Times of India,* August 6, 1997. Sengupta is the director general of the International Management Institute, New Delhi.

9. Nehru and the Mountbattens had similar leftish political outlooks, and there is the imponderable importance of the undeniably affectionate relationship between the Indian premier and Edwina Mountbatten.

10. The case for the defense is given principally by the official biographer, Philip Ziegler, in whom Mountbatten has been fortunate: *Mountbatten,* pp. 349–379, and especially pp. 438–441; Collins and Lapierre, *Freedom at Midnight,* gave Mountbatten the opportunity to state his own case; French, *Liberty or Death,* pp. 305, 443, note 45, takes a more objective

view, but rejects the notion that a premature British departure was a primary cause of the massacres. Andrew Roberts, in a chapter titled "Lord Mountbatten and the perils of adrenalin" in his *Eminent Churchillians* (Simon and Schuster, 1994), pp. 55–136, attacks Mountbatten's character vigorously and presents a caustic exposé of the egregious errors which he contends littered his entire career; the famous quote from Templer is on page 133.

11. See his *The Rise and Fall of the British Empire* (London: Abacus, 1995), p. 555.

12. For an interesting "worm's-eye view" of this process, see Robin Neillands, *A Fighting Retreat: The British Empire, 1947–1997* (London: Coronet, 1997).

13. See John Keay, *Last Post: The End of Empire in the Far East* (London: John Murray, 1997). Kipling's "The White Man's Burden" was written to encourage the American effort in the Philippines; Rudyard Kipling, *Complete Verse: Definitive Edition* (Anchor, 1989), pp. 321–323.

14. Among other articles, see, for example, Ian Buruma, "Holding Out in Hong Kong," *The New York Review,* June 12, 1997, and Jonathan Mirsky, "Betrayal," *The New York Review,* September 25, 1997.

15. For the controversy over Cradock's views and activities, see Jonathan Dimbleby, *The Last Governor: Chris Patten and the Handover of Hong Kong* (Little, Brown, 1997), pp. 10, 161, 166–167, 414–415, 436–437, 444–445.

16. Dimbleby, *The Last Governor,* pp. 417, 435. The understandably schizophrenic feelings of Hong Kong citizens was underlined by this poll, because for the first time a clear majority—62 percent—said they would prefer Chinese sovereignty to any alternative.

17. Dimbleby (in *The Last Governor,* p. 430) quotes the valedictory comment of the publisher Jimmy Lai, whose papers are almost unique in Hong Kong in crusading for democracy: "It is a shame to have your country colonised, but I have never had this sense of shame, because I have been a free man living in this colony. . . . So long, the British. May God bless you.

18. For a comprehensive and subtle history reflecting, if not in thrall to, post-colonial analyses, see Sugata Bose and Ayesha Jalal, *Modern South Asia: History, Culture, Political Economy* (Delhi: Oxford University Press, forthcoming 1997). Auden's poem is quoted in Chapter 16.

19. In a sad sign of diminishing British expertise on India, an editorial in *The Times* ("Light in dark places," August 18, 1997, p. 19) referred to the prime minister rather than the president as the untouchable.

20. Arcade, 1997, pp. 254–269.

21. Nehru's attentiveness to Mountbatten and Britain's sensitivities at the time of independence was detailed by Ajit Bhattacharjea, "The British tilt," *Outlook,* August 13, 1997. It hardly needs be said that correctness rather than sensitivity characterized the Hong Kong handover.

22. Emigration averaged about 20,000 in the 1980s until 1987, when it jumped to 30,000, perhaps because of the dismissal of the "liberal" party general secretary, Hu Yaobang, that

January. After Tiananmen there was another jump, and through 1994 the annual figure was regularly 60,000 or over, except in 1993 when it was 53,000. See Ronald Skeldon, editor, *Emigration from Hong Kong: Tendencies and Impacts* (Hong Kong: Chinese University Press, 1995), p. 57.

23. See Hiranmay Karlekar, "The growth of violence has been phenomenal," *Times of India,* July 31, 1997; the estimate of criminal politicians is given in Tharoor, *India,* p. 266.

24. See Pankaj Mishra, *Butter Chicken in Ludhiana: Travels in Small Town India* (Penguin, 1995), pp. 12, 93, 253. For attempts to provide a more balanced view, see Pran Chopra, "The success side of India," in *The Hindu,* August 5 and 6, 1997. See also Salman Rushdie and Elizabeth West, editors, *Mirrorwork: 50 Years of Indian Writing, 1947–1997* (Henry Holt, 1997), a celebration of Indian writing in English; and Shashi Tharoor's passionate but often agonized avowal of love for his motherland in *India: From Midnight to the Millennium.*

25. See, for example, Ahmed, *Jinnah, Pakistan and Islamic Identity,* pp. 116–117. The most ubiquitous legacy of the British empire is, however, the pipe band.

26. They call their general approach "subaltern studies." See Guha, *A Subaltern Studies Reader,* especially the introduction.

27. The claims about caste and ecological balance, and the effects of the British, are to be found in Madhav Gadgil and Ramachandra Guha, *This Fissured Land: An Ecological History of India* (University of California Press, 1992), pp. 113–116. For critiques of subaltern studies, see C. A. Bayly in *Empires and Information: Intelligence Gathering and Social Communication in India, 1780–1870* (Cambridge University Press, 1996), p. 368, and Sumit Sarkar, *Writing Social History* (New Delhi: Oxford University Press, 1997), pp. 82–108.

28. See Amartya Sen, "How India has fared," *Frontline,* August 22, 1997. It is worth pointing out, in view of the immense publicity that has attended Mother Teresa's good works in Calcutta and her funeral there, that an extraordinary number and range of Indian private institutions try to substitute for government in providing welfare not only in Calcutta but in many other cities and villages.

29. Jagdish Bhagwati, *India in Transition: Freeing the Economy* (Oxford University Press/Clarendon Press, 1993), p. 48. Resources that might have gone into primary education have been invested in higher education. Taking into account differences in population size, India sends six times as many people to universities as China; see Amartya Sen, "Wrongs and rights in development," *Prospect,* October 1995, p. 30.

30. Contrast this with the American race problem. It is 400 years old. It was finessed at the founding of the United States. After fifty years, the problem had still not even been confronted. By its centenary, the US was emerging from a bloody Civil War and an abortive Reconstruction which failed to lay the problem to rest. Only around the time of the country's two-hundredth anniversary was the US civil rights movement able to demand that the state

bring about changes that should have been accomplished by the Civil War.

31. For a discussion of these deeply troubling issues, see Tharoor, *India,* pp. 50–78; for an attempt to provide a new analytical approach with which to understand post-independence ethnic violence, see Stanley Tambiah, *Leveling*

Crowds: Ethnonationalist Conflicts and Collective Violence in South Asia (University of California Press, 1996).

32. The most prominent discussion of these issues was in Selig S. Harrison, *India: The Most Dangerous Decades* (Princeton University Press, 1960).

33. "The maturing of a democracy," *India Today,* August 31, 1996, p. 41. In a less detailed poll a year later, however, 53 percent voted against the "government's policy based on caste"; *India Today,* August 18, 1997, p. 49.

Article 3   *History Today,* September 1997

Judith Brown assesses the curious coupling of sage and politician that achieved much—but not all—for Hindu aspirations.

GANDHI AND NEHRU

FRUSTRATED VISIONARIES?

The observer of India in 1997 is rightly struck by the immense stability of this, the world's largest democracy, in contrast with her South Asian neighbours and many other new nation states which emerged out of the former British Empire. But equally striking is the great dichotomy between the reality of India at the end of the century and the vision of the new nation offered by its two greatest leaders at the time of independence, Mahatma Gandhi and Jawaharlal Nehru.

From 1920 at least, India's growing nationalist movement had stressed through its main organisation, the Indian National Congress, the meaning of independence for the poor and disadvantaged. There was to be a new and more egalitarian society, where the state would have a moral obligation to help the poor and under-privileged and provide opportunities to those who for centuries had been despised and deprived. These ideals were enshrined in the new constitution of 1950, whose preamble committed India to securing for all its citizens justice, liberty, equality and fraternity, and were spelt out in the sections of Fundamental Rights and Directive Principles of state policy.

Gandhi and Nehru had, in their different ways, spoken constantly of the moral, social and political regeneration of the country as the true heart of *swaraj,* or self-rule. But despite the seminal role of these two leaders, amongst the greatest visionaries of the post-colonial world, after fifty years of democratic government and economic development, there is still widespread and desperate poverty in India. With inequalities of status, consumption and opportunity as great as any in the world, the economy, having teetered on the edge of international bankruptcy at the start of this decade, now moves towards an open market policy with little ideological framework to distinguish it from Western economies. Moreover, this secular state has at times been rent by sectarian loyalties and violence, and India's religious minorities remain fearful and often profoundly disadvantaged. Why has this happened in place of the Mahatma's spiritual vision, and despite Nehru's eloquent pledge at the moment of independence that India would keep her 'tryst with destiny'?

Gandhi and the younger Nehru were, of course, very different as people and also in their vision of the new India to be created as imperial rule ended. A generation separated them, as did social origin and political experience. The older man came from a far more provincial and less privileged background, had reached professional competence as a lawyer by strict personal discipline and a regime of self-denial and hard work: and he had spent twenty formative years in South Africa, where exposure to a wide range of cultural influences and the experience of racial discrimination refined both his political skills and his religious sensibility.

The younger man had been brought up with everything that money could buy, educated at Harrow and Trinity College, Cambridge, and inducted with ease into the world of Indian public life by a father who was one of India's most successful and respected lawyers. With an effortless sense of superiority and no experience of hardship or personal challenge, he had no religious beliefs worth the name, and little knowledge of the India of the vast majority of his compatriots. It was little wonder that his father, Motilal, greatly feared what would befall his cosseted son, in personal and material terms, as he came under the influence of the homespun Mahatma.

Yet Gandhi and the somewhat aimless Jawaharlal formed a strong attachment and political partnership which was to last for almost three decades, until Gandhi's assassination in 1948. The attachment was partly personal, founded on mutual attraction between two strong and idiosyncratic personalities. It was partly forged out of mutual need, as both needed the other to further their public aims. To Gandhi, Nehru was the symbol of the younger generation, the heart and touchstone of a younger India whom he needed to weld into the nationalist movement. To Nehru, Gandhi was unique in his ability to sense the mind and mood of the vast numbers of uneducated Indians, and thus essential for the forging of a broad-based nationalist movement to oust the British. But far beyond mutual need the two shared a passionate conviction that India must change radically as independence was won. This was central to the commitment of each man to a public role, and far more than populist rhetoric. Sensing this core of visionary commitment in the other drew them together in a unique way.

Gandhi first worked out his vision of a new India in a small pamphlet published in 1909, entitled *Hind Swaraj* (Indian Home Rule). Here he made plain his belief that true self-rule was far more than mere political independence, or an inheritance of imperial structures of control, but manned by Indians. True *Swaraj* would be founded on a moral revolution of the individual upwards through society as a whole, changing both the pattern of the economy and the nature of political authority. What was needed was a society based on moral individuals who cared for each other and followed spiritual goals, rather than false standards of gain and wealth, imported from the West, along with the means of large-scale production and their potential for the increase of inequality and of violent relations between individuals and groups. After his final return to India in 1915, he never disavowed this early work with its ruthless denunciation of 'modern civilisation' and of Western educated Indians who accepted its values. He persisted in defining *swaraj* in moral and social, rather than political language, affirming that its hallmarks would be a more equal society, mutual tolerance between different religious groups, and a commitment to small-scale economic arrangements which put people before gain.

Above all, the hallmark of new Indians would be a commitment to non-violence in all public and private relationships, as the only moral means of achieving true change. For Gandhi non-violence was the only way to follow after what one perceived as truth without endangering the perception of truth held by others: by its very presence and working it would transform attitudes and relationships, and so begin the process of change at the roots of the individuals who formed the bedrock of society. In this vision a modern state had little role to play. Gandhi was deeply distrustful of the power of the state, and felt that individual self-control was the only true regulatory power which could change society. At the end of his life he advised Congressmen to disband their party, turn their backs on political power and engage in grass-roots social service.

Gandhi drew his inspiration from aspects of Hindu and other religious traditions, and from a wide range of dissenting voices in Western culture who feared for the spiritual and social implications of industrialisation in Western society. Nehru's vision, by contrast, was generated by his contacts with several variants of Western socialist thinking during his years of education in England and later during his European travels (including a visit to the Soviet Union in 1927), and through his wide reading. Despite his 'alliance' with Gandhi, he made plain the differences in their hopes for India's future, for example, in a series of press articles republished as a pamphlet entitled *Whither India?* (1933) and in his subsequent longer writings, including *An Autobiography* (1936). As he wrote in the former:

> India's immediate goal can . . . only be considered in terms of the ending of exploitation of her people. Politically, it must mean independence and the severance of the British connection . . . economically and socially it must mean the ending of all special class privileges and vested interests. . . . The real question before us . . . is one of fundamental change of regime, politically, economically, socially.

The means to this end was first a powerful and broadly-based nationalist movement to oust the imperial ruler; and second, a powerful modern state to redistribute resources more equitably and to manage a modern economy. Nehru had little time for Gandhi's commitments to non-violence and to individual moral 'change of heart' as the route to truly radical change; and he had no sympathy with the Mahatma's religious language and priorities, aiming instead, in more straightforward political terms, for both a secular state and society.

After India's independence the visions of both men were soon dashed on the rocks of reality. In Gandhi's case this was less surprising. He had always known that few Congressmen had shared his very particular moral viewpoint or sympathised with his broad-ranging plans for the reformation of Indians, their society and polity. When Congressmen had begun to gain sufficient power at provincial level under successive constitutional reforms, he had lamented that they were behaving like their imperial predecessors; and he spoke with sad realism of the way they left his 'constructive programme' lying littered on the floor at party gatherings.

Gandhi never held high office in Congress either after the Second World War, when it was clear that independence was imminent, or, later, in the new nation state; he recognised that political power was in the hands of those, like Nehru, who believed in the need for a strong state, both to serve their political ambitions and also to fulfil their genuine hopes for India's economic and social development. After his assassination he was greatly revered: but the only ways in which his vision was even partially enacted was in the legal abolition of the status and practice of untouchability, a gross form of social and ritual discrimination practised against those at the base of Hindu society, and in the encouragement of 'cottage industries' alongside large-scale industrialisation.

Nehru, on the other hand, was India's prime minister without a break from independence until his death in 1964. Yet even his socialist dreams remained unfulfilled. Despite attempts at far-reaching social legislation, he was unable to achieve genuinely radical reform of landholdings on any scale, which would have been a prerequisite for extensive redistribution of resources and abolition of vested interests. He was unable to push through a uniform civil code which would have done much to ameliorate the legal position of women and reduce the entrenched differences between various religious groups. Although there was significant economic development, particularly large-scale industry, planned and partly managed by the state, there was little change in agricultural practices and production, and the incidence of life-threatening poverty, malnutrition and disease remained widespread, making a mockery of the directive principles of the constitution.

Furthermore, India continued to be governed by Nehru in ways which were remarkably similar to those of his imperial predecessors, both in the structure of the state itself, despite the universal adult franchise, and in the style of the administrative services which he had once denounced as anti-national and requiring drastic reform. At the end of his life he was, like Gandhi, frustrated at his inability to achieve so much of his life's dreams. On his desk he kept the words of the poet, Robert Frost:

But I have promises to keep,
And miles to go before I sleep

The reasons for the frustrations of these great visionary leaders lay in part in their different, but unique, pathways into Indian political life. Both were to an extent 'apart from' the ordinary world of Indian professional and business life, or that of the nationalist politician. Gandhi had failed as a lawyer in his native Western India and had achieved professional success and personal maturity in another continent, working among the Indian migrant community. Nehru had been insulated, indeed isolated, by the great wealth of his family and by his prolonged period of education in England. Back home in Allahabad with his family he saw for himself no clear role either in politics or in the profession of the law, for which he was destined. On their return to India both found that they had few natural connections with the world of Indian politics, and no groups of allies or supporters with whom to make their mark.

Perhaps more importantly, their exposure to the world beyond India had created in each of them a distinctive and idiosyncratic vision of the meaning and nature of 'nationalism' and the Indian nation as they thought it should become. By

contrast most of their contemporaries who saw themselves as nationalists thought primarily in terms either of ameliorating British rule and making more room for Indians within the imperial structures of power, or of removing the British altogether. But few thought beyond independence or had visions of radical change grounded in religious belief or a powerful secular ideology as did Gandhi and Nehru.

Their eruption into the politics of nationalism was therefore unpredictable. Gandhi emerged in 1920 as a leader within the Congress because he offered the party a mode of non-violent protest against the British Raj, at a specific juncture in nationalist politics when constitutional politics seemed to have achieved little and when few were willing to resort to the opposite tactic, namely that of violent protest. In the euphoria which followed, Nehru willingly became involved in politics for the first time, sensing that in Gandhi he had met a leader who would address real social and political problems, would lead Indians in fearless resistance to the imperial ruler, and would do away with the parlour politics of an older generation he had so despised. As he wrote in his autobiography of the heady experience of participating in Gandhi's first nation-wide campaign of non-violent non-co-operation with the Raj:

Many of us who worked for the Congress programme lived in a kind of intoxication during the year 1921. We were full of excitement and optimism and a buoyant enthusiasm. We sensed the happiness of a person crusading for a cause.... Above all, we had a sense of freedom and a pride in that freedom. The old feeling of oppression and frustration was completely gone.

However, the Congress party was never transformed into a band of moral Gandhian enthusiasts, committed to the Mahatma's constructive campaign for the renewal of the nation. Although many Congressmen and many more outside the Party's ranks were attracted by his fearlessness, by his personality and by his Indianness, few accepted his religious vision of man and society, and few were converted to his belief in the rightness and transformative nature of non-violence.

The Congress remained what it had become over the forty years since its inception—a loosely organised association of groups of local men (and a few women), many of high educational and professional background, who were politically active on a full or part-time basis, who wished to gain access to the decision-making and executive power of the state which the imperial authority was creating, and who knew that their hands and arguments would be strengthened by an all-India alliance under the umbrella of the national Congress. It had little full-time and effective party organisation, and depended largely on the co-operative stance of local individuals and groups who used its name—a fact which Gandhi and Nehru both recognised and sought to remedy, because they realised how it reduced the Congress's political effectiveness as a party of direct action or of long-term change.

A further consequence was that Congress had little in the way of a defining and driving ideology, apart from its anti-imperial stance. Ideological compromise was more often the cement which held its members together; particularly as so many of them were comparatively privileged and had social and economic interests to safeguard in the future. Consequently those of its declarations which had a socialist ring were generally little more than vote-catching rhetoric.

In this party Gandhi and Nehru were in their own ways unique, and that uniqueness was both their strength and a long-term weakness in terms of their ability to galvanise Congress into action in pursuit of visionary goals. Gandhi was never a 'leader' in any Western sense of the word. His role from 1920 to the 1940s was more that of an 'expert' to non-violence who could be welcomed and to an extent used by Congress when they felt his particular non-violent strategy of opposition and profoundly moral stance and style suited their purposes; to achieve compromises between different groups within Congress when its internal divisions threatened to rend it apart and destroy the vital unity of the nationalist movement.

Nehru's role was similarly not that of a leader with a natural power base in a locality or in a group of like-minded allies. His 'ticket' in Congress was that of Gandhi's protégé and later heir, a fact which at times caused him embarrassment and distress. In the later 1930s his ideological position was so anti-pathetical to many of the more conservative in Congress that the latter would have made his position in the party impossible if it had not been for Gandhi's presence and watchful eye on the internal dynamics.

As independence became imminent after the end of the Second World War, Congress activists recognised Nehru's skills as a negotiator with the imperial authorities—in part because he spoke their language and had inhabited so much of their mental and political world. But even though he became leader of the transitional government which saw the transfer of power to Indian hands, and subsequently prime minister, Nehru was not secure as the party's undisputed leader and ideologue until some years later.

Although Gandhi lived for a brief period in an independent India, it was Nehru who had to wrestle with the problem of trying to enact his vision of change under the new circumstances—when Congress had become the party of government rather than of nationalist rhetoric and protest, and when he was constrained by the structure of the state and the ability of the administration. For him there were a range of seemingly insurmountable barriers to the achievement of radical change. One continuing example was the nature of the Congress party. Even though he was from the early 1950s its undisputed leader, and though it paid lip service to his vision of a socialist transformation of society, it was now a party which even more than before independence represented the interests of those who had no wish for radical social and economic change. Its very success as a nationalist party had attracted into it many who needed access to power. Increasingly it became the party of the businessman, the prosperous farmer and the professional, those with a stake in the India inherited from the raj and being made more prosperous for those with resources by the actions of an independent government anxious to boost the economy. This rootedness in groups of locally influential people was its great strength at election time, but its weakness as an instrument of change. This Nehru learned the hard way when it came to attempts at land reform and social legislation for the benefit of the deprived.

Moreover, the very structure of the state inhibited change. Just as in imperial India the country had been administered through provinces, often the size of small European countries, now these became the basis of the States within the Indian Union, bound together in a federation. Consequently on many issues legislation had to pass through the legislatures of the States rather than through the Lok Sabha in New Delhi. As in the case of the abolition of great landlords and the redistribution of land into moderate holdings below a certain 'ceiling', those with vested interests could either get themselves into the State legislature where they could modify or delay reforming measures, or could use the months while legislation was being passed to hire lawyers and so equip themselves to avoid the law. Or in the case of agricultural improvement and the dire need to grow more food, policy implementation was in the hands of the agricultural ministries of the States: and Nehru found it impossible to chivvy them in the way he would have wished. Added to this, the actual tools of government were frustratingly weak and slow.

Independent India inherited an administration structured on an immensely slow bureaucracy, which had made a specialty of generating endless files and pushing them from one level to another with agonising slowness. It was a system where those at lower levels were neither trained nor accustomed to take responsibility and make decisions. At the top it was manned by élite generalists who, though highly educated, were essentially trained to conserve the status quo, to enable the collection of adequate revenue, but not to innovate or manage a social revolution. Nehru as a young nationalist had distrusted and criticised the élite Indian Civil Service, although over half of them were Indian by 1947. He spoke of the need for a total overhaul of the administration and the evolution of a new people-oriented class of administrators. But no administrative revolution occurred, and he found himself increasingly having to rely on the heirs of the service he had castigated, who remained in ethos, background and modes of operation so like their imperial predecessors. It was little wonder that he became increasingly frustrated, and at times bad-tempered, at his inability to 'get things done', despite his own vision and frenetic energy.

The frustrations of the idealisms of India's greatest nationalists, and the pragmatism of the Congress Party, created a profound ideological vacuum in independent India. Into this vacuum have emerged a host of parties in place of the once-great and embracing party which led the country to independence. Many are regional in origin and orientation, fostering the interests of specific areas within the subcontinent. But they have proved incapable of making a national appeal or providing the base for a stable all-India coalition. Perhaps the one party which has been able to construct a national vision is the revivalist Hindu Party, the BJP, which has emerged as a highly significant political force over the past decade. But this vision of the nation itself endangers the unity of a nation with many religious minorities and cultural diversities, which Gandhi sought to safeguard with his ethical religion and tolerance, and which Nehru hoped to cement and strengthen with a vision of modern secularism and socialism.

India's politicians need to dream dreams and see visions of a tolerant and compassionate India as their nation's fiftieth birthday is celebrated, for their electorate is telling them sober truths about the lack of repute in which they are held, and their need for integrity and a commitment to real change as the country's expanding population grows increasingly sophisticated and aware of the nature of the political system and its departure from the hopes so manifest in 1947. Gandhi and

Nehru may have been frustrated in their hopes for India: but they laid down a marker and a standard by which subsequent leaders and aspirant leaders are judged.

FOR FURTHER READING:
A. J. Parel (ed.), *M. K. Gandhi. Hind Swaraj and other writings* (Cambridge University Press, 1997); B. Parekh, *Gandhi's Political Philosophy. A Critical Examination* (MacMillan, 1989); Judith M. Brown, *Gandhi, Prisoner of Hope* (Yale University Press, 1989); S. Gopal, *Jawaharlal Nehru. A Biography* (3 vols. Jonathan Cape, 1975–1984); J. Nehru, *An Autobiography* (The Bodley Head, 1936); R. L. Hardgrave, *India. Government and Politics in a Developing Nation* (Harcourt, Brace, 1970); Robert W. Stern, *Changing India. Bourgeois Revolution on the Subcontinent* (Cambridge University Press, 1993).

Judith Brown is Beit Professor of Commonwealth History, at the University of Oxford and author of Modern India. The Origins of an Asian Democracy (*Oxford University Press, 1984*).

Article 4

History Today, September 1997

PARTITION

THE HUMAN COST

Mushirul Hasan looks at the reflection of the trauma and tragedy of partition through literature and personal histories.

The sun had risen fairly high when we reached Amritsar... Everytime I visited Amritsar, I felt captivated. But the city, this time, presented the look of a cremation ghat, eerie and stinking... The silence was so perfect that even the faint hiss of steam from the stationary engine sounded a shriek. Only some Sikhs were hanging about, with unsheathed kirpans which they occasionally brandished... The brief stoppage seemed to have lingered into eternity till the engine whistled and gave a gentle pull... we left Chheharta behind and then Atari and when we entered Wagah and then Harbanspura everyone in the train felt uplifted. A journey through a virtual

valley of destruction had ended when finally the train came to a halt at Platform No. 2—Lahore, the moment was as gratifying as the consummation of a dream.

Mohammad Saeed, *Lahore: A Memoir* (1989)

Few writers reveal such poignancy and tragedy of nationally-contrived divisions and borders. India's partition cast its shadow over many aspects of state and society. Yet the literature on this major event is mostly inadequate, impressionistic and lacking in scholarly rigour. Even after fifty years

of Independence and despite the access to wide-ranging primary source materials, there are no convincing explanations of why and how M. A. Jinnah's 'two-nation' theory emerged, and why partition created millions of refugees and resulted in over a million deaths. Similarly, it is still not clear whether partition allowed the fulfillment of legitimate aspirations or represents the mutilation of historic national entities.

Part of the reason for this flawed frame of reference is the inclination of many writers to draw magisterial conclusions from isolated events and to construct identities along religious lines.

As a result, the discussions tend to be based on statements and manifestos of leaders and their negotiations with British officials in Lutyens' Delhi and Whitehall.

The fiftieth year of liberation from colonial rule is an appropriate moment to question commonly-held assumptions on Muslim politics, to delineate the ideological strands in the Pakistan movement, explore its unities and diversities, and plot its trajectory without preconceived suppositions. Was there intrinsic merit in religious/Islamic appeals? Does one search for clues in British policies (which were tilted in favour of the Muslims to counter the nationalist aspirations)—in the ensuing clash between Hindu and Muslim revivalist movements and in violent contests over religious symbols (a dispute recently played out around the Babri Masjid at Ayodhya)? How and why did the idea of a Muslim nation appeal to the divided and highly stratified Muslim communities, enabling Jinnah and his lieutenants to launch the crusade for a separate Muslim homeland?

As a starting point, it is necessary to repudiate Jinnah's 'two-nation' theory. Time and again it has been pointed out that the Hindu and Muslim communities lived together for centuries in peace and amity. In fact, their common points of contact and association were based on enduring inter-social connections, cross-cultural exchanges and shared material interests. Neither the followers of Islam nor of Hinduism were unified or cohesive in themselves. Their histories, along with social, cultural and occupational patterns, varied from class to class, and region to region.

During his tour in 1946–47 the British civil servant Malcolm Darling found, in the tract between the Beas and Sutlej rivers in Punjab, much similarity between Hindus and Muslims. He wondered how Pakistan was to be fitted into these conditions? He was bothered by the same question while passing through the country between the Chenab and Ravi:

What a hash politics threatens to make of this tract, where Hindu, Muslim and Sikh are as mixed up as the ingredients of a well made pilau . . . I noted how often in a village Muslim and Sikh had a common ancestor. It is the same here with Hindu and Muslim Rajputs, and today we passed a village of Hindu and Muslim Gujars. A Hindu Rajput . . . tells me that where he lives in Karnal to the south, there are fifty Muslim villages converted to Islam in the days of Aurangzeb. They belong to the same clan as he does, and fifteen years ago offered to return to the Hindu fold, on the one condition that their Hindu kinsfolk would give them their daughters in marriage. The condition was refused and they are still Muslim. In this area, even where Hindu and Muslim belong to different clans, they still interchange civilities at marriage, inviting mullah or Brahmin, as the case may be, to share in the feasting.

The search for a political explanation of partition must begin with the fluid political climate during and after the First World War, characterised by the drive for power and political leverage that preoccupied all political parties and their followers. This accounts for the swiftness with which the two-nation idea succeeded in becoming actualised; the vocal demand for carving out a Muslim nation summed up the fears of the powerful landed classes and the aspirations of the newly-emergent professional groups in north India and the small but influential industrial magnates of the western and eastern regions.

The bitter and violent contest over power-sharing reveals a great deal about the three major themes that have dominated South Asian historiography—colonialism, nationalism and communalism. What it does not reveal, however, is how partition affected millions, uprooted from home and field and driven by sheer fear of death to seek safety across a line they had neither drawn nor desired.

The history books do not record the pain, trauma and sufferings of those who had to part from their kin, friends and neighbours, their deepening nostalgia for places they had lived in for generations, the anguish of devotees removed from their places of worship, and the harrowing experiences of the countless people who boarded trains thinking they would be transported to the realisation of their dreams, but of whom not a man, woman or child survived the journey.

Most Hindus and Muslims living in harmony and goodwill could not come to terms with the ill-will and hostility that was conveyed through speeches and pamphlets. There were many places in India where the Muslim League's message was received but failed to impress.

Indeed, most Muslims neither understood nor approved of Pakistan, except as a remote place where they would go, as on a pilgrimage. Some left hoping to secure rapid promotion, but not to set up permanent homes there. It did not really matter to the peasants and the millworkers whether they were physically located in 'India' or 'Pakistan'. Interestingly, for example, the Muslim employees of the East India Railway in a north Indian city decided to stay put in India after having opted for Pakistan, while 8,000 government servants returned to their homes in March 1948, just a few months after they had left for Pakistan.

In other words, most people were indifferent to the newly-created geographical entities, and were committed neither to a Hindu homeland, nor to an imaginary world of Islam. They were unclear whether Lahore or Gurdaspur; Delhi or Dacca would remain in Gandhi's India or Jinnah's Pakistan. They were caught up in the cross-fire of religious hatred—the hapless victims of a triangular game-plan masterminded by the British, the Congress and the Muslim League. 'The English have flung away their Raj like a bundle of old straw', one angry peasant told a British official, 'and we have been chopped in pieces like butcher's meat'. This was a telling comment by a 'subaltern' on the meaning attached to the Pakistan movement.

Saadat Hasan Manto, the famous Urdu writer, captures the mood in 'Toba Tek Singh', one of his finest stories:

As to where Pakistan was located, the inmates knew nothing . . . the mad and the partially mad were unable to decide whether they were now in India or Pakistan. If they were in India where on earth was Pakistan? . . .

Pakistan, a prized trophy for many Muslims, was won, but people on both sides of the fence were tormented by gruesome killings, by the irreparable loss of lives, and by the scale and magnitude of an epic tragedy. There can be no doubt that from a purely liberal and secular perspective, the birth of Pakistan destroyed Mohammad Iqbal's melodious lyric of syncretic nationalism—*Naya Shivala* (New Temple)—once the ideal of patriots and freedom-fighters. The vivisection of India severed cultural ties, undermined a vibrant, composite intellectual tradition and introduced a discordant note in the civilisational rhythm of Indian society.

Indeed, the birth of freedom on that elevated day—August 14th, 1947, for Pakistan and August 15th, for India—did not bring India any 'ennobling benediction'. On the contrary, the country was shaken by 'a volcanic eruption'. There was little to celebrate at the fateful midnight hour. In the words of Faiz Ahmad Faiz, the renowned Urdu poet,

> This is not that long-looked-for break of day
> Not that clear dawn in quest of which those comrades
> Set out, believing that in heaven's wide void
> Somewhere must be the star's last halting place
> Somewhere the verge of night's slow-washing tide,
> Somewhere an anchorage for the ship of heartache.

So, which country did poets like Faiz and writers like Manto belong to? Manto, for one, tried in vain to 'separate India from Pakistan and Pakistan from India'. He asked himself: 'Will Pakistan literature be different—and if so, how? To whom will now belong what had been written in undivided India? Will that be partitioned too?'. The uppermost question in his mind was: 'Were we really free'?

Manto's anguish and dilemma was shared by the silent majority on both sides of the fence, including those 1,000 persons who, after eighteen months of separation, met at the Husainiwala customs barrier in February 1949. They did not pull out daggers and swords but affectionately embraced one another with tears rolling down their cheeks. Their sentiments were reflected neither in the elegant exchanges between the Viceroy and Secretary of State, nor in the unlovely confabulations between the Congress and the League managers.

Today the curtain is drawn on the Husainiwala border; small groups from Pakistan and India congregate at Wagah to witness a colourful military parade

that is held every evening to mark the closing of the iron gates on both sides of the fence. Their expressions seem to echo the widespread feeling in the subcontinent that never before in its history did so few divide and decide the fate of so many in so short a time.

'What a world of loneliness lies upon Shabbir (Husain, grandson of the Prophet of Islam) this day!' Everyone who heard these lines in Gangauli village, the setting for the Rahi Masoom Reza's novel *Aadha-Gaon* (Half-a-Village), wept bitterly. They did so to mourn Husain's martyrdom in Karbala centuries ago, but also because 'the cut umbilical cord of Pakistan was around their necks like a noose, and they were all suffocating'. Now they knew what 'a world of loneliness' meant.

Independence and partition brought varied moods of loneliness. Every individual in Gangauli 'had found himself suddenly alone'. All of them turned, just as they did every day of their existence, to Husain and his seventy-two companions for strength, confidence and spiritual comfort. 'There was a desire to dream, but what was there safe to dream about?' The atmosphere was foul and murky all around. 'The blood of one's veins was wandering hopelessly in Pakistan, and the relationships and mutual affections and friendships ... were breaking, and in place of confidence, a fear and deep suspicion was growing in people's hearts'.

> Today we saw for ourselves something of the stupendous scale of the Punjab upheaval. Even our brief bird's-eye view must have revealed nearly half a million refugees on the roads. At one point during our flight Sikhs and Moslem refugees were moving almost side by side in opposite directions. There was no sign of clash. As though impelled by some deeper instinct, they pushed forward obsessed only with the objective beyond the boundary.
>
> *Alan Campbell-Johnson,*
> Government House, New Delhi,
> Sunday, September 21st, 1947

The partition of the subcontinent led to one of the largest ever migrations in world history, with an estimated 12.5 million people (about 3 per cent of undivided India) being displaced or uprooted. In Punjab, the province most

affected by violence and killings, 12 million Hindus, Sikhs and Muslims were involved, and migration of some 9 million people began overnight in an area the size of Wales. In the north Indian state of Uttar Pradesh (UP), nearly 4,000 Muslims a day boarded the train to Pakistan until 1950.

The number of migrants from central and eastern regions was comparatively small, but the proportion of professional emigrants was relatively high. Educational institutions were depleted of students and teachers overnight. Enrolment figures at the famous seminary in the city of Deoband were down from 1,600 to 1,000 in 1947–48. Income dwindled, as large numbers of students and patrons migrated to Pakistan. The Aligarh Muslim University was rudderless without some of its distinguished teachers who searched for greener pastures in Karachi, the eventual homeland of the *muhajirin* (migrants).

In Bihar, emigration began in November–December 1946 as a sequel to rioting in many places. Peace was soon restored and the movement stopped just before partition. There was fresh migration after August 1947 mainly for economic reasons and because of the acute food shortage in North Bihar, which had a common frontier with East Pakistan. Migrants totalled 4–500,000, although some returned to their homes during 1950–51.

The Princely State of Hyderabad had received a continuous migration of Muslims in their thousands, particularly since 1857, from the rest of India. In 1947 the numbers increased to hundreds of thousands. Drawn from both the rural and urban areas, there were traders, artisans, domestic and government servants, agriculturists and labourers. However, the influx came to an abrupt end on September 13th, 1948, the day the armed forces of India moved into the state 'in response to the call of the people'. Almost immediately a reverse movement started: a number of Hyderabadi Muslims left for Pakistan, while others returned to places they had originally come from.

Elsewhere, nearly 450 Muslims a day continued their trek across the Rajasthan-Sind border. From January to November 1st, 1952, 62,467 Muslims went via Khokhropar to Sind in West Pakistan. 'Some hundreds go daily and have been going, in varying numbers, for the last three-and-a-half years', Nehru informed his chief ministers. 'The fact that they go there itself indicates that the conditions they live in are not agreeable to them and the future they envisage for themselves in India is dark'. But quite a number of established and prosperous professionals from UP, Bihar and the Princely States of Hyderabad, Bhopal and Rampur also left.

Men in government and the professions from Delhi, UP and Bihar formed the core of muhajirin. The Delhi police was depleted of its rank and file because of 'mass desertion'. All the three subordinate judges in the Delhi court rushed to Pakistan. People employed with local and provincial governments also opted for Pakistan, although some changed their minds later and returned to India. Poets and writers, Josh Malihabadi being the most prominent, joined the trek at different times. Some landlords, including Jinnah's lieutenant, Nawab Liaquat Ali Khan, were among the muhajirin. The Raja of Mahmudabad left his family behind in the sprawling Mahmudabad House in Qaiser Bagh, Lucknow, to undertake the mission of creating an Islamic state and society in Pakistan.

Many prominent Muslims stayed, including those who headed the Muslim League campaign. Landlords like Nawab Ismail, Nawab Jamshed Ali Khan, the Nawab of Chattari and the Rajas of Salempur, Nanpara, Kotwara, Pirpur and Jehangirabad clung to their small estates. Ismail was elected to the vice-chancellorship of Aligarh Muslim University in September 1947, but relinquished the post on November 14th, 1948. Several others retained their public positions, although they had lost face with their supporters.

Others felt overwhelmed by the climate of hostility, suspicion and distrust. They had a litany of complaints—recurring Hindu-Muslim riots, discrimination in employment and official neglect of Urdu. Syed Mahmud, Nehru's friend and minister in Bihar, protested that Muslims faced harassment and were treated as 'a body of criminals'.

Thirty-one Muslims were jailed for anti-government activities in addition to many more detained under the Public Safety Act. Muslims in Agra were required to register themselves with the district magistrate. Their houses were searched and a former legislative assembly member, Shaikh Badruddin, was arrested for possessing unlicensed arms. Muslims in Kanpur had to obtain a permit before travelling to Hyderabad; their relatives there had to register at a recognised hotel or a police station in order to visit them.

Muslim officers on the railways in Kanpur, some of whom had served for more than ten years, faced suspicion and dismissal. Aligarh's district magistrate was severe on university students and teachers who had already incurred the wrath of the local leaders for their involvement in the Pakistan movement. The university, threatened with closure, was eventually saved by Nehru's intervention. Zakir Husain, the newly-appointed vice-chancellor, placed it on a firm footing with the active support of Azad, free India's first education minister. Liberal and socialist teachers staged a rearguard action to combat the influence of communal tendencies. In general, however, Mohanlal Gautam, the leading Congressmen touring UP, found 'an all-pervading sense of fear' among the Muslims.

The Evacuee Property Laws, which restricted business opportunities and disabled large numbers of Muslims, were most inequitable. Most Muslims could not easily dispose of their property or carry on trade for fear of the long arm of the property law. A number of old Congressmen continued to send small sums of money to their relatives in Pakistan. They were promptly declared evacuees or prospective evacuees. Nehru was personally distressed by all this, as he was by the spate of communal violence in UP:

> People die and the fact of killing, though painful, does not upset me. But what does upset one is the complete degradation of human nature and, even more, the attempt to find justification for this.

By contrast, some of Nehru's colleagues were unrepentant. A powerful section retorted, in answer to the criticism of its murky conduct in handling the civil strife, that the strong anti-Muslim sentiments were generated by bitter and painful memories of partition. These responses angered Nehru and his liberal and socialist comrades, and dismayed Muslims.

The real pinch was felt in Delhi, UP, Bihar and Hyderabad, the area most affected by riots, the exodus to Pakistan and the extensive skimming-off from the professional classes. 'Partition was a total catastrophe for Delhi', observed one of the few surviving members of Delhi's Muslim aristocracy. 'Those who were left behind are in misery. Those who are uprooted are in misery. The peace of Delhi is gone. Now it is all gone'. In UP and Bihar very few Muslims were left in the Defence services, in the police, the universities, the law courts, or the vast Central Secretariat in Delhi. Large-scale immigration of mostly educated upper-caste Hindus in Lucknow— 70 per cent of the total immigrant figure—gradually reduced Muslim influence in government, business, trade and the professions.

In Hyderabad, Muslims constituted 10 per cent of the population before 1947–48. Muslim government servants held, as in UP, a much higher percentage of posts. But their fortunes dwindled following Hyderabad's merger with the Indian Union. Urdu ceased to be the official language. The abolition of *jagirdari* affected over 11 per cent of the Muslim population, three-quarters of whom inhabited about a dozen urban centres. Smaller *jagirdars,* in particular, faced a bleak future due to retrenchment in government departments, recession in industry after 1951, and a sharp fall in agricultural prices. The old nobles and the absentee landowners started selling their remaining lands and spacious houses to make ends meet.

The dissolution of the Princely States impoverished a large percentage, if not the majority, of the upper classes and the bourgeoisie as well as a large number of peasants, artisans and retainers who lost the patronage networks. Nearly half the population of Hyderabad depended on the Nizam for their livelihood, and thus with sources of patronage rapidly drying up this section was worse off.

The rulers of Rampur, Bhopal and Hyderabad were not turned into paupers overnight; they simply lacked the initiative to convert their wealth into more secure and tangible assets. They squandered their inherited resources to maintain their standard of living and allowed properties to be grabbed by unscrupulous land dealers. Their mango orchards, which had yielded vast revenues, were generally converted into uneconomic farm lands. Few ventured into business, trade or industry, or realised which way the wind was blowing. They continued living in their decaying palaces surrounded by a retinue of servants, wives, eunuchs and hangers-on. Wallowing in nostalgia for the bygone era, they cursed the *khadi*-clad politicians for bringing to an end the *angrezi sarkar* (British Raj).

Accustomed to framing their own laws, codes and regulations, they were irked by the presence of local bureaucrats—the district magistrate, superintendent of police and revenue officials—who were visible symbols of political change. Insulated from the populace and blissfully unaware of the changes that were visibly taking place in urban and rural areas, their public contacts were limited to *Id* celebrations at the close of a month's fast or Muharram observances when the *imambaras* were lit up and the mourners turned up at the desolate Nizam's palace in Hyderabad or the Khas Bagh in Rampur. The memory of the suffering of Husain and his companions at Karbala reminded them of their own trials and tribulations.

The abolition of the zamindari (land holding) system in 1951 stripped the large landlords of the bulk of their estates and awarded the land to the cultivators. The rural influence of the former Muslim landlords was reduced, even more than that of their Hindu counterparts. Many former Hindu rentiers and landowners migrated to places like Kanpur, Gorakhpur and Lucknow in search of new sources of livelihood. Muslim zamindars and taluqdars were bereft of such ideas. Muslim immigration was a mere 16.28 per cent between 1947–55 from rural areas as compared to 68 per cent among upper and intermediate Hindu castes.

The bigger Muslim taluqdars suffered more than their Hindu counterparts also because of families being divided, one branch migrating to Pakistan. Such was the fate of the taluqdari in Mahmudabad. The Raja left behind his estates in Barabanki, Sitapur and Ba-

hraich districts to be looked after by his brother. He may have wished to return to his place of birth, but the India-Pakistan war in September 1965 would have thwarted his plans. His huge assets were declared 'enemy property'.

The Awadh taluqdars, accustomed to supporting themselves from the rental income of their estates, were greatly traumatised by zamindari abolition. Some left for Pakistan, and others retired to anonymity in their villages. Those who stayed found the going hard. 'The abolition of zamindari removed our clientele in one fell swoop. All of a sudden the economy changed. And the English customers left. Our shop was "by appointment" to several governors of the province'.

Some of the smaller zamindars managed to keep their status intact by moving into nearby towns and cities in search of better opportunities. A few families in the Barabanki district, living in close proximity to Lucknow, did well. Some reaped the rewards of being close to the Congress. They obtained private and government contracts, licenses and positions. Mubashir Husain (1898–1959), of Gadia and son of Mushir Husain Kidwai (b. 1878), the pan-Islamic ideologue in the early 1920s, was a judge at the Allahabad High Court until 1948. Begum Aijaz Rasul, the wife of the former taluqdar of Sandila in Hardoi district and mother-in-law of the novelist Attia Hosain, did quite well for herself, being elected to the UP assembly and the Rajya Sabha and holding ministerial positions until 1971. There were other successes too.

For the small Awadh taluqdars, however, the overall scene was discouraging. They lost much of their land to the tenants who acquired legal rights over what they cultivated. They were estranged from the 'new men', rustic and entrepreneurial, who thronged their bazaar and streets and disturbed their social poise and harmony.

For the zamindars their universe had suddenly collapsed: they had no 'land left equivalent even to the hub of the great wheels which was once their zamindaris'. In just a few moments they collapsed like the tomb of Nuruddin the Martyr, a familiar landmark in Gangauli village. In their prayers they cursed the Congress Party. The Syeds, who for centuries had made Gangauli their home,

realised that they no longer had any links with the village they had called their own. Whether Pakistan was created or not had no meaning to them, but the abolition of zamindari shook them to the core. Now it was all the same whether they lived in Ghazipur or in Karachi.

The zamindars of western UP, on the other hand, were not too badly off. Many switched allegiances to the Congress, and some enjoyed a measure of local goodwill because they had implemented certain provisions of agrarian legislation. Most moved to Aligarh to educate their children. They built or renovated their mansions, developed an interest in local politics and used the university—which they treated as an extension of their estates—as a political arena. It satisfied their pride to serve on the university court or the executive council, be involved in the selection of senior office-holders and turn up dutifully at the railway station to greet visiting dignitaries. But when they retired to the privacy of their homes they recounted the harsh encounters in a world that was not their own.

By the early 1960s some smaller zamindars were still struggling to eke out a living. There were those who had limited resources to live on; others relied on inherited charitable endowments or even pawned their family jewellry to maintain the façade of high living. Their crumbling houses on Aligarh's Marris Road bear testimony to their steady impoverishment. The luckier ones, such as the Chattari clan, moved out of Aligarh in search of professional careers. The sherwani-clad Nawab lost the vigour and determination which he displayed during his extended public life, now that he had to cope with harsh realities.

Attia Hosain's novel, *Sunlight on the Broken Column,* describes the faded fortunes of the landed aristocracy and captures the sense of an era having passed once and for all:

> He [the Raja of Amirpur] lived in retirement at Amirpur, dignified and aloof, bearing the landslide of adversities with courage. His palace in the city had been requisitioned as a government hospital for legislators, and the huge rambling house at the outskirts, with its ornamental gardens divided into building plots, was the

centre of the new colonies for the refugees.

The last occasion on which he appeared in public was four years after independence, when he welcomed the President of the Republic to a reception given in his honour by the Taluqdars.

There were no illuminations, no fireworks, no champagne, no glitter of precious gems, orders, silks, brocades and ceremonial uniforms. This last reception of the Taluqdars was a staid tea-party given by hosts who were soon to have their 'special class' and 'special privileges' abolished.

Dusty portraits and marble statues of stately ex-Presidents of their Associations, and of Imperial representatives, looked down with anachronistic grandeur on tea-tables bearing tea becoming tepid, cakes tasting stale, and Indian savouries growing cold. Guests in *Khaddar* (loin-cloth) outnumbered those in more formal attires.

With grace and courtesy Amirpur presided over this swan-song of his order, while those who had habitually bowed before authority hovered round their gentle, dignified guests still hoping for manna from Heaven.

FOR FURTHER READING:

C. H. Philips & M. D. Wainwright (eds.), *The Partition of India, Policies and Perspectives* (Allen & Unwin, 1970); Leonard Mosley, *The Last Days of the British Raj* (Weidenfeld & Nicolson, 1962); Ayesha Jalal, *The Sole Spokesman: Jinnah, the Muslim League and the Demand for Pakistan* (Cambridge University Press, 1985); Mushirul Hasan, *Legacy of a Divided Nation: India's Muslims Since Independence* (C. Hurst, 1997) and *India's Partition: Process, Strategy and Mobilization* (Oxford University Press, 1997); and his anthology of fiction and poetry on Partition, *India Partitioned: The Other Face of Freedom* (Delhi, 1997), in two volumes.

Mushirul Hasan is Professor of Modern Indian history at the Jamia Millia Islamia University, Delhi.

Article 5   *History Today,* September 1997

Francis Robinson considers what the Muslims wanted—and what they got—out of the decision to divide the subcontinent on religious lines.

THE MUSLIMS AND PARTITION

The partition of India at independence in 1947 into the sovereign states of India and Pakistan is one of the more important events of twentieth-century world history. It was a shameful end to the most important project in Britain's imperial enterprise. More important it was a tragic experience for the hundreds of thousands of Hindus, Sikhs and Muslims who were killed in the communal slaughter which accompanied the process and for the nearly 15 million who were made refugees. Over the past fifty years India and Pakistan have been in a state of constant hostility, fighting three wars in 1947–48, 1963 and 1971, and during the last decade fighting low-intensity wars over Kashmir and the drawing of boundaries in the high Himalayas.

Approaches to partition depend very much on where the individual is situated. For Indians, in the classic nationalist interpretation, partition was the logical outcome of Britain's policies of dividing and ruling. For Pakistanis it was their founding moment, the glorious outcome of the struggle of Muslims to have their separate identity recognised by both the British and the Indian nationalist movement. For the Bangladeshis, it was a false dawn, but arguably a necessary prelude to their achievement of their own nation state in 1971. For the British it was a regrettable necessity. They did not have the power to impose a solution on their Indian empire which left it unified; partition came to be the only way in which they could extract themselves from a commitment which they could no longer afford.

When an event is bound up with the founding narratives of three of the world's more populous states and the pride in achievement of a fourth, historiographical positions are likely to be hard fought. That said, any explanation of partition must address two issues: (1) why many Muslims were reluctant to join the Congress, the party of the Indian nationalist movement, and (2) why this fact led to a surgical division of the land.

Before addressing these issues some basic points about India's Muslims should be established. Roughly a quarter of the population, they were in no way a united group. Some were descended from, or liked to claim descent from, those who had come to India over the ages to conquer, to trade or seek their fortunes—Arabs, Persians, Turks, Afghans. But the vast majority were Indian converts to Islam. In the north-east and north-west of the subcontinent they formed majorities of the population, in Bengal being largely peasants, and in the Punjab, Sind and the Northwest Frontier Province landowners, yeoman farmers and tribesmen. In the central and souther regions Muslims were rarely more than 5 per cent of the population and often traders by occupation.

In the Gangetic plain in the north, however, especially in a region called the United Provinces (henceforth UP), matters were somewhat different. In this area, comprising many of the old centres of Muslim power—Delhi, Agra, Allahabad, Lucknow, Jaunpur—Muslims were only about 14 per cent of the population but a good half of these claimed descent from those who had come from outside India to rule. These Muslims, with their memories of power, were to play the leading role in insisting that Muslims remain separate from the mainstream of Indian nationalism.

In any explanation of 'Muslim separatism' the following elements should play a part. Some weight should be given to Islamic values. There is a tendency for some Muslims to organise on a community basis wherever they go into politics. At the level of religious belief there are powerful drives for communal action. God told Muslims through the Prophet Mohammad that they were the 'best community raised up for mankind'. God revealed to Muslims the best way to live if they hoped for salvation, and that involved living within the community and being subject to its law. The idea of community action for community ends has a seductive resonance. However, for a good number of Muslims the idea of community was more a rhetorical flourish than a psychological fact.

Weight should certainly be given to Muslim revivalism. From the beginning of the nineteenth century Indian Muslims, in common with Muslims elsewhere in the world, were in the grip of various movements of revival and reform. These came to intersect with the problems of coping with the meaning of Western power and Western knowledge. There was considerable cultural and intellectual ferment as Muslims in different social and intellectual situations fashioned ways forward. Various movements were founded—those of the Deobandis, Barelvis, Ahmadis, Jamaati-Islamis and Tablighi-Jamaatis—which have come to have worldwide significance. In India they tended to draw firmer distinctions between Muslim practice and that of the Hindu world around them; the outcome was to sharpen the Muslim sense of identity.

From a political point of view the most important part of this process was the attempt of the leading intellectual, Saiyid Ahmad Khan, to build a bridge between Islamic learning and Western science on the one hand, and the Muslim landed and professional classes and British rule on the other. This effort had its institutional focus in the Cambridge-style college which the Saiyid founded in 1877 in the form of the Mohammadan Anglo-Oriental College at Aligarh, some ninety miles from Delhi. The students and supporters of this college were to play the leading role in carrying forward the cause of Muslim separatism.

But it was not just Islam which was challenged by Western power and knowledge: so was Hinduism, the faith of the great majority of Indians. Hindus also experienced a cultural and intellectual ferment, and came to have a sharper sense of their identity. Some hailed British rule for supplanting 'Muslim tyranny'. Muslims were accused of robbing Hindus of religion, wealth and women. They were the outsiders in India, not Hindustanis. The relics of Muslim power, such as mosques in Hindu holy places, were 'wounds in the heart'. In northern India Hindus and Muslims began to rub up against each other more abrasively, particularly as the former demanded an end to the slaughter of cows (cheap food for Muslims but holy for Hindus) and the replacement of the Persian script in government by the Hindu

Nagri script. The presence of Hindu revivalists tended to inhibit the nationalist movement when it sought compromise with the Muslim League.

Recent research, much influenced by Edward Said's *Orientialism* (1978), has focused on how the British constructed knowledge about India, and the ways in which this construction not only influenced British governance but also Indian ideas about themselves. From the very beginning of the serious study of India, Warren Hastings and the orientalists around him—Jones, Halhed, Wilkins—thought of India in terms of Hindus and Muslims, tending to seek classical texts to guide them in government and the administration of justice, rather than grappling with the complexities of the Indian present. When the British came to place a framework over India's past, they divided it into Hindu, Muslim and British periods. When from 1871 they began their decennial census of the Indian empire, they tabulated its peoples under religious headings. For much of the nineteenth century, moreover, this tendency to interpret Indian society in terms of religion was reinforced by the committed Christian beliefs of Indian administrators and the presence of many missionary organisations.

That the British understood Indian society in terms of its religious divisions was always an important prop of the nationalist accusation that Indians were divided, and India ultimately divided, by British policies of divide and rule. There is a smidgeon of truth in these accusations, although British policies are better understood as a series of pragmatic responses to a changing political environment rather than a conscious policy to divide. 'Nothing', declared one leading administrator in the late nineteenth century, 'could be more opposed to the policy and universal practice of our government in India than the old maxim of divide and rule . . .'

At this time the British felt Muslims to be the greatest threat to their rule. They had failed to reconcile the former rulers of India to their government; the Mutiny uprising of 1857 was seen to confirm this. In 1870 they decided that the safety of the Raj demanded that they find ways of attaching powerful Muslims to their side. This policy was developed just at the time that Saiyid

Ahmad Khan was striving to reconcile his co-religionists to Western knowledge and British rule. His initiatives received much official encouragement. Arguably his Aligarh College would never have been founded, and may not have survived, but for government support which ranged from land made available at derisory rates to personal donations from viceroys. His All-India Muslim Educational Conference, which from 1886 drew Muslims together from all over India for the first time, operated within a framework of government approval. He himself was given the most unusual distinction, for an Indian at the time, of being knighted.

Aligarh College and the Educational Conference were the institutional bases on which the All-India Muslim League, the spearhead of Muslim separatism, was founded in 1906. The first office of the League was at Aligarh; its first secretary was the College secretary. The League's first major campaign was to demand separate electorates for Muslims, and extra representation in those areas in which they were 'politically important' such as the UP, in the new legislative councils which Viceroy Minto and Secretary of State Morley were developing for India. With some misgivings the British were persuaded and these privileges were granted in the Council reforms of 1909. Thus a separate Muslim identity was enshrined in India's growing framework of electoral politics. When in 1919 and 1935 the franchise was extended and further powers were devolved, separate electorates were continued and the principle of Muslim separateness confirmed.

Many factors—Islamic values, religious revivalism, British understandings of India and British techniques of rule—helped to establish an important step along the road towards India's partition. We should note, however, that such roads rarely run straight and that different groups of Muslims found the platform suiting their interests at different times. Initially supporters were the landed and government service classes, mainly from the UP, the supporters of Saiyid Ahmad Khan. By the First World War they were increasingly young professional men from the same province—lawyers and newspaper editors. In the 1920s the platform was virtually de-

serted; Muslim landlords joined landlord parties, some young professionals joined the nationalist movement, others left politics altogether. Towards the end of the 1920s as further devolution of power came to be discussed, Muslims crowded back onto the platform again. But many soon lost interest when they found it to be dominated by a view of the future favouring Muslims of the Punjab.

In December 1930 the poet-philosopher, Muhammad Iqbal, sketched out this view when, as President of the Muslim League session at Allahabad, he proposed the creation of a Muslim state in the north-west of India. This subsequently inspired a Cambridge student, Rahmat Ali, to give it a name 'Pakistan' derived thus: 'P' stood for the Punjab, 'A' for Afghanistan or the North-West Frontier Province, 'K' for Kashmir, 'S' for Sind and 'tan' for Baluchistan. It translated as the 'land of the pure'.

At this stage, however, no practical politician imagined that it was likely to be able to create such a state either inside or outside India. Indeed, practical politicians seemed to have deserted Muslim separatism; only once between 1931 and 1936 did the Muslim League meet in full session. Between 1930 and 1935 Mohammad Ali Jinnah, the League's leading figure had his main residence in London, where he practised as a barrister and tried unsuccessfully to be adopted as a parliamentary candidate by first the Labour and then the Conservative Party. Even after Jinnah returned to India, matters did not improve. In 1937, in the first general elections held under the Government of India Act of 1935 which brought provincial autonomy, the League won only 22 per cent of the seats reserved for Muslims. Nationalist governments were formed in seven out of eleven provinces.

In 1937 the Muslim League did not appear to be a major player in Indian politics. By 1946, however, it most certainly was. In the general elections of that year it won over 90 per cent of the seats reserved for Muslims. Its President, Jinnah, now known as the Quaid-i-Azam (Great Leader), had the support of the vast majority of India's Muslims. Any explanation of the partition of India must be able to explain this transformation of the League's position.

One key factor was the impact of the Second World War. It meant that the Brit-

ish were eager to seek Muslim support, in part because half the Indian army was Muslim and in part because the nationalist movement was opposed to the war and any Indian involvement in it. The League had little political clout, yet it was the only serious All-India Muslim party, so the British turned to it.

Within a day of the declaration of war, the Viceroy invited Jinnah for talks on an equal footing with Gandhi; the war thus gave Jinnah a prominence in the high politics of the Raj that his party's strength did not merit. Seven months later he announced the League's agenda at Lahore on March 24th, first of all stating the two-nation theory, which meant that Muslims could not live together as a numerical minority in a Hindu dominated state, and then proposing what came to be called the Pakistan resolution. In the darkest days of the war in 1942, when the Japanese were bombing Calcutta, he discovered just how valuable this prominence was. Sir Stafford Cripps on his mission to India offered him a Pakistan state.

Note should be taken of the mistakes made by the Congress. After its great victories in the 1937 elections, it behaved in a triumphalist fashion, asking too high a price of League members to be included in a coalition government in the UP, hurting Muslim sensibilities by forcing Muslim children to sing the song 'Bande Mataram' with its message of hate for Muslims, and threatening Muslim culture in general. Then, it made the further mistake of letting go the levers of power. In 1939 all the Congress governments resigned in protest against the Viceroy's declaration of war on behalf of India. In 1942 the Congress responded to the Cripps offer by launching a full-scale rebellion against the British, the Quit India movement. The outcome was that all the Congress leadership and 60,000 workers were sent to prison for the rest of the war. The League was given a free hand.

Note should also be taken of the drive of Muslims from the Muslim minority provinces to build the League. In their view, if the League was to be heard, and they were to have adequate protection at independence, they had to win the support of Muslims in the majority provinces, most particularly Bengal and the Punjab. Here the cultural leadership of the UP amongst Indian

Muslims had some part to play: learned and holy men from its leading traditional academies toured schools and shrines in the majority provinces to raise support, so too did students from what was now called the Aligarh Muslim University. But the main factors in its success were the League's capacity first to present a vote for the League as one for economic betterment for the Bengal peasant, and second to persuade the Punjab landlords, who controlled most Muslim votes in their province, that a vote for the League would be willy nilly a vote for their future master.

Finally, there was the outstanding leadership abilities of Jinnah. He was masterly as the builder of the League as a political organisation, masterly as a political strategist and without equal as a negotiator. Few liked him; few doubted his integrity; everyone respected him. 'Of all the statesmen I have known in my life—Clemenceau, Lloyd George, Churchill, Curzon, Mussolini, Mahatma Gandhi', declared the Aga Khan, 'Jinnah is the most remarkable'.

All these factors came together to create the League landslide at the polls in early 1946. But we should not think that this made partition inevitable. In its Pakistan resolution, the League had resolved:

> . . . that no constitutional plan would be workable in this country or acceptable to the Muslims unless it is designed on the following basic principles, viz., that geographically contiguous units are demarcated into regions which should be so constituted . . . that the areas in which the Muslims are numerically in a majority, as in the North-Western and Eastern zones of India, should be grouped to constitute Independent States in which the constituent units shall be autonomous and sovereign.

It was not clear whether these 'States' were to be separate from India or formed within a federal India. This was a lack of clarity which Jinnah found helpful and worked to maintain. In 1946 a delegation of Cabinet Ministers to India proposed an ingenious solution to the Pakistan problem. There were to be three tiers of government at independence, the first to be formed out of the existing provinces, the second to be formed out of separate Hindu and Muslim federations of provinces (a Hindustan and Pakistan), and in the third,

the central government, representatives of these federations would come together on an equal basis to deal with defence, foreign affairs and communications. On June 6th, the League accepted the plan. On June 22nd, so did the Congress but at the same time it refused to support the interim government which was to put the plan into effect.

From this point partition became increasingly inevitable. There was deadlock and growing civil disorder. A Labour Government in Britain was keen to leave India as fast as possible; every extra day that British troops remained added to British debt. In February 1947 Mountbatten was sent out as Viceroy with a brief to pressure the politicians into agreement. Mountbatten quickly saw that Britain could only withdraw by transferring power not to one government, but to two. He also saw that it would not be possible to leave the large Hindu and Sikh minorities of the Punjab and the Hindu minority of Bengal under Muslim rule. The partition of India would also mean the partition of these provinces; thus the League had its two-nation theory played back against it. Jinnah was most unhappy to accept what he termed a 'truncated or mutilated and moth-eaten Pakistan', but eventually on June 3rd, 1947, he did, with a nod of the head. On August 14th, in Karachi, he was installed as Governor-General of the British dominion of Pakistan. Whatever his reservations, it seemed he had won a glorious victory.

There are some significant ironies in the making of partition. A common view would be that the Congress bitterly opposed the mutilation of Mother India. However, Congress did have a hand in the process itself. In the complete edition of his autobiography, *India Wins Freedom,* the Muslim member of the Congress high command, Abul Kalam Azad, makes it clear that of its other three members, Vallabhbhai Patel was positively in favour of partition before Mountbatten arrived, Nehru was quite quickly persuaded, and Gandhi accepted the inevitable. Patel and Nehru were keen to take over a strong central government and relatively weak provinces. Patel wanted strong central government to hold the new state together; Nehru was keen to put Soviet style five-year plans into effect. The Cabinet Mission plan patently did not supply strong central government.

A common view of Jinnah, on the other hand, sees him trying to resolve India's Muslim problem within the framework of a united India up to the late 1930s and then, from the Lahore resolution of March 1940, working for a separate state of Pakistan and fighting his way to triumph at partition. But the more recent interpretation of Ayesha Jalal, which is based on much fresh evidence, sees no change in Jinnah's long-term objective in 1940 and only a shift in strategy. The Lahore resolution was a bargaining card to gain recognition of Indian Muslim nationhood and the right to equal treatment at India's political centre; it was also a stick to bludgeon the Muslims of the majority provinces into supporting the League. When the Cabinet delegation made known its May proposals Jinnah's plans were realised; strong Muslim provinces need not feel concerned about a weak Indian centre.

When the Congress in effect rejected the proposals, Jinnah's plans were in tatters. In the remaining thirteen months leading up to independence, he worked to minimise the consequences of his defeat. Partition happened because, in the circumstances, the Congress leaders wanted it, not because Jinnah desired it.

The final irony was that Pakistan was built on a claim for a separate nationality for Muslims. Yet Pakistan's creation left one third of the subcontinent's Muslims in India, where they would have to subsume their Muslim identity within a greater Indian identity.

FOR FURTHER READING:

Maulana Abul Kalam Azad, *India Wins Freedom; the Complete Version* (Orient Longman, 1988); Mushirul Hasan, *Nationalism and Communal Politics in India, 1916–1928* (Manohar, 1979); H. V. Hodson, *The Great Divide: Britain—India—Pakistan* (Hutchinson, 1969); Ayesha Jalal, *The Sole Spokesman: Jinnah, the Muslim League and the Demand for Pakistan* (Cambridge University Press, 1985); V. P. Menon, *The Transfer of Power in India* (Orient Longman, 1957); David Page, *Prelude to Partition: The Indian Muslims and the Imperial System of Control 1920–1932* (Oxford University Press, 1982); Francis Robinson, *Separatism Among Indian Muslims: The Politics of the United Provinces' Muslims 1860–1923* (Cambridge University Press, 1974).

Francis Robinson is Professor of the History of South Asia at the University of London. His latest book is The Cambridge Illustrated History of the Islamic World *(Cambridge, 1996).*

Article 6

History Today, September 1997

BENGAL AND PUNJAB

BEFORE AND BEYOND

Jean Alphonse Bernard considers the two key provinces—
Bengal and the Punjab—and how they became touchstones and then
powderkegs in the nationalist aspirations of both sides.

What happened in 1947 was not so much the partition of the whole of Britain's Indian Empire as the partition of two of its eleven provinces: Punjab and Bengal. If one considers the North East, Orissa, the Central Provinces, the Bombay State and the whole of peninsular India, not much happened there between July and October of this fateful year. Assam itself was little disrupted in spite of having lost the district of Sylhet to East Bengal. Violence, it is true, erupted in Delhi on a large scale and vast migrations of people took place in Uttar Pradesh and in Bihar. There it was clearly a reverberation of what happened in Punjab and Bengal. Even the events in the Princely State of Kashmir—from the rumours running in the Poonch district that Muslims were massacred in East Punjab, to the raid of Pashtun tribes in the Vale—were clearly an effect of what had happened in Punjab a few weeks before. Why were these two partitions so significant?

Bengal, with 50 million inhabitants (at the 1931 census) was no longer the seat of imperial power, but was still immensely important in economic, social and intellectual terms. It was home to a range of industries, from jute mills to mechanical engineering and shipyards. Calcutta was perhaps the busiest emporium from the Suez Canal to the Far East, serving a vast hinterland from Tibet and Nepal to Burma. It boasted a large intelligentsia and the oldest college in the country, so that it was perhaps the most lively intellectual centre in this part of Asia.

As the oldest area of British establishment in India, Bengal society had been submitted to the most thorough process of Europeanisation. This had resulted in the growth of a particular class of men and women known as the *bhadralok,* 'the people of quality', a term which carried complex connotations of elegance, sophistication and arrogance as well as indicating a comfortable income. Living mostly in towns, the *bhadralok* had kept their roots in the countryside and a good part of the income they drew came under the *zamindari* system, from their poor tenants. These were mostly Muslims, particularly in the central and eastern districts.

The zamindari system was therefore a major fault line in the social landscape, which cut across the universal divide between Muslims and Hindus. Meanwhile, a nascent Muslim bourgeoisie was emerging in Dacca as well as in Calcutta, alongside the feudal nawabs of East Bengal and with the moneylenders and businessmen who had flocked to Calcutta from distant Marwar. In workshops, jute mills and industrial plants, most of the workers were immigrants from Bihar and Orissa, often of Muslim faith.

Punjab stood at the opposite end of the spectrum. It was no doubt fortunate that a thousand miles of land had kept Punjabis and Bengalis apart. When they met, it was rarely felicitous. The proud warriors of Ranjit Singh had certainly resented their defeats at the hand of the East India Company army, in which Bengalis—brahmins included—played no small part. Thereafter Punjabi soldiers had had no qualms about enlisting in the British regiments which crushed the mutineers after Meerut.

In the land of the five rivers the social pattern was altogether simpler than in the delta of Bengal: a rugged peasantry tilled a fertile but dry soil which British engineers had succeeded in turning into a surplus area of wheat, rice, cotton, sugarcane and other plantations. Clans and sectarian conflicts had been fierce indeed until Ranjit Singh had established his enlightened despotism, followed up by the bureaucratic impartiality of British rule. In this traditional setting, the policy of recruiting young males into the army, mostly of Punjabi stock, provided a useful outlet to an energetic nation. As an agrarian and military asset, Punjab was crucial for the British, who were careful to despatch there their best 'guardians' to administer a province of 25 million inhabitants, close to the North West gates and to the imperial capital. It was no chance then, that Punjabi politics had evolved during the 1920s and the 1930s into a solid compound of pragmatism and paternal justice based on the conciliation of the landlords' interests, be they Muslim, Hindu or Sikh.

Consequently, Delhi was conveniently placed in between two regions of great value to itself; on one hand the hectic but still thriving Bengal, on the other the prosperous agrarian republic of the Punjab, guarding its western approaches in the same manner as Rome had been poised between the Aegean world of hellenistic cities and the rustic expanses of Spain and Gaul, a good reservoir of slaves, food and soldiers.

The strength of the Raj was to be able to rely on both, to balance one against the other as circumstances warranted, making the most of each and ensuring that they could never conspire against itself. Above all, Punjab and Bengal, for reasons which nature and history had provided for, were far ahead of all other entities of the subcontinent in their being well defined in terms of territory, customs and languages, as if they were nations in their own right. Thus, the land of the turbaned Lions and the country of the swift Tigers were the twin pillars on which the British Raj rested.

The search for origins is the torment of historians but the *raison d'être* of history. At what point in time should we begin to make the tale meaningful? The answer depends on what assumptions we adopt. If we consider decolonisation to be the main causal factor, then we may have to start from the Battle of Plassey, or from the crushing of the great Mutiny. If we consider the advent of Islam in the subcontinent as the major factor determining the distant origin of the two-nation theory, we have to go back to Ghazni's raid in 1000 or Babur's victory over the Sultan of Delhi in 1526. But in this case our inquiry is inspired by the quest to understand why and how India is a democracy, as Tocqueville was spurred by the failure of democracy in France to understand its success in America.

If we choose the Government of India Act of 1935 as a starting point, we can see that the Act set in motion the elections of January–February 1937 which marked the beginning, at least for British India, of modern mass politics. It is wrong to say that before 1937 India was modern. The establishment of responsible provincial governments after these elections marks the transition from an *ancien régime,* where politics are the business of a few, into the modern era where they become the concern of the many.

There is another reason for choosing this date: the role of Gandhi in the Indian National Congress changed after the session of October 1934, when the Mahatma declared that from now on he would 'cease to shape the policy of the Congress organisation' and devote himself entirely to the task of 'village reconstruction'. That Jinnah accepted to take upon himself the presidency of the

Muslim League the same year is another pointer in the same direction: 1935 was a year of great beginnings, great expectations and equally great disappointments.

At the appointed hour 30 million Indians, men and women, went to the polls for the first time in history to elect their legislators and thereby their rulers, albeit in separate electorates. For Punjab and Bengal the results were strikingly different but equally momentous. In Lahore 120 seats out of 175 were won by the Punjab Unionist Party and its allies. The Indian National Congress won eighteen seats, the Akali Dal, ten, the Muslim League, one seat. It was a blow to Jinnah and a defeat for the Congress. In fact the polls gave a clear approval to the work already done by the Unionists to rule over the Punjab in a Punjabi way. The party itself had been founded in 1923 by two lawyers, one Muslim, Mian Fazl-i-Husain, and one Hindu, Chaudhury Chhotu Ram, both equally devoted to what they considered to be the good of their community. The strength of their alliance was that both appealed to the same kind of people: landlords, big and small, but living on, and from, their estate. They belonged to the three communities which made up the Punjab: Muslims (50 per cent), Hindus (35 per cent), Sikhs and others (15 per cent).

As everywhere in India, religion was an important feature of the community you were born into, as it determined to a great extent your way of life. But in the conditions of peace and relative prosperity which prevailed since the Pax Britannica, the Punjabi ruling élite had more in common to defend than differences to quarrel about. The Unionist Party, strongly supported by the British administration, was the political expression of the will to live together which prevailed in the Punjab. The grand old man of the Unionist Party, Mian Fazli-Husain, had died in July 1936, but another notable and a member of the Hayat clan, Sikander Hayat Khan, was elected unanimously as his successor and became premier in March 1937.

For the bright London barrister who had given up his lucrative law practice to lead Indian Muslim politics, the Punjab situation was ominous. Jinnah had no word strong enough to castigate the

rustic notables who had put their own narrow interests before the wider cause of a nationalist and secular India which, no less than Nehru, he dreamed of ruling once the British were out.

Bengal offered, as usual, a perfect contrast. The polls had given fifty-four seats to the Congress and thirty-nine to the Muslim League out of a total of 250. But a new party, the Krishak Praja Party, had won forty seats and 31.5 per cent of the Muslim vote whereas the old established League got only 27.1 per cent. The new organisation had been founded a year earlier by a Muslim lawyer of great talent, Fazl-ul-Huq, nicknamed the Tiger of Bengal, who had spent many years defending the rights of sharecroppers and tenants against their landlords, Hindu zamindaris and Muslim nawabs. Hence the polls reflected an emerging class warfare within the overall context of the communal polarisation. The Congress Party had put on its platform the abolition of the zamindari rights all over North India. It was only natural, therefore, that the KPP and the Bengal Congress, having concluded earlier on electoral pact not to poach into each other's territory, should now make an alliance of government. However, it was not to be. A decision of the 'high command' rejected Fazl-ul-Huq's overture and forced him into the arms of the Muslim League which he had so vigorously trounced. A historic occasion was missed. Why? A young scholar, Ms Joya Chatterji, has given us the answer. She writes:

> By the early 1930s the Bengal Congress had become a party of the towns but one that still retained its connection with landed interests ... The politics of the Bengal Congress reflected the social conservatism of its predominantly bhadralok membership ... Even after the party retreated to the towns in the late 1920s, its leaders had kept intact their commitment to their landed interests in the mofussil which they had left behind but had not abandoned.

In fact the Bengal Congress was far from being united: the moderates followed closely the 'high command' and were often in tune with the Hindu Mahasabha, whereas the left-wing—led by the Bose brothers—tried to impose a socialist and secular line. This brought conflict between the two factions, which was to develop later into a full-scale battle for the unity of Bengal.

At this point in history, the political game which the British set into play did not oppose the two great forces; the Congress and the Muslim League, much less two great religions. In Punjab and in Bengal—the two provinces offering the best reservoir of talents, economic resources and development potential— the provincial arena presented a promising picture of secular politics: in Punjab around a local party geared to the defence of agrarian interests, in Bengal a more open 'market' with three contenders: a Congress dominated by the bhadralok, a non-sectarian party of poor peasants and a pro-zamindari Muslim League. The province of Punjab was neither at the stage of class struggle nor yet a religious battlefield. As for Bengal, class conflicts tended to steal a march on communal antagonisms.

The next great player was war itself. Its effects upon both provinces were equally powerful if quite different. Bengal came to be close to the Pacific theatre of war after the fall of Singapore (February 15th, 1942), and Rangoon (March 8th). Indian refugees from Malaysia and Burma landed in Calcutta by the boat load. In the summer of 1943 a terrible famine left around 2 million dead among the villagers and the poor. The loss of Burmese rice and the disruption of means of transportation by rivers were the direct causes of the disaster. Above all, the war deepened the divide between communities, increased the ill-will of Hindus towards Muslims and vice versa. It undermined the political leadership of all parties as well as British prestige. The KPP did not survive the trial of governing during the war, even if Fazl-ul-Huq remained personally popular. On the Congress side the Bose faction was badly mauled by the fate of Subash C. Bose and of his brother Sarat, jailed until V-Day. The Bengal Muslim League came to rely on Jinnah, for want of other leaders. Bengal came out of the war divided against itself and more than ever prone to violent means to solve its perennial problems. When chaos had shown its ugly face, it was too late. Leaders such as H. S. Suhrawardy and Sarat C. Bose could

find courage enough to plead *together* the cause of a united Bengal, but the jury was out and the Viceroy had made up his mind.

If Bengal suffered directly from the miseries of war, Punjab suffered from its aftermath. As a surplus area, food rationing was unacceptable to the farmers, price rises resented by the consumers and war losses among Indian troops abroad felt by many families. Faithful to the war effort, the Unionist Party paid the price, whereas the Muslim League, free of responsibility, made capital gains out of it. If the Lahore resolution had refrained from claiming Pakistan, the League made it its catchword from 1943 onwards, with great effect. When the pirs and mollahs decided to back it up in the run up to the elections of 1946, Jinnah had won and the Unionist Party disappeared.

The war strengthened the hand of Jinnah at every turn, because he was careful not to oppose the war effort directly as Gandhi and the Congress did, while he could not be associated with its ill-effects in the minds of his people. This was a great opportunity which he played very well. Whatever the real objective he had in mind in promoting the Pakistan idea, he was unable to fulfill it until the crisis of July 1946. Then Congress decided to call for a showdown and chose partition rather than a coalition with Jinnah at the centre. But great leaders seldom achieve their aims. In curbing the lions of Punjab and the tigers of Bengal, Jinnah helped destroy the seeds of political unity in both 'provinces'. The sombre irony of history is that he could not achieve Pakistan without the two most important Muslim majority provinces, but that in so doing he undermined the future of the two entities he had helped create for a long time. India, being left with a rump Punjab, and Pakistan, being left with the poorest part of Bengal, were both losers.

Those who lost the most, however, were the Bengali and the Punjabi peoples. Their forced co-habitation made the one group the masters, the other the servants. Their close encounter made the Pakistan identity collapse almost as soon as it was erected. The sundered pillars had little strength and no purpose, once the imperial structure had gone. Whatever strength was left in them, they

turned against each other with a vengeance.

One can wonder at the enormous pile of books, articles, pamphlets, lectures, which have been written over the last thirty years in places such as Princeton, Harvard, Oxford or Chicago to explain the failure of Pakistan. A sentence such as L. Zirring's 'Pakistan has not been successful at nation-building because it failed miserably in state-building' is all the more admirable as it can be reversed and be as true as it is meaningless. The simple fact, known by every traveller in the subcontinent from time immemorial was that Punjabis and Bengalis, as a rule, do not mix easily. Consequently, putting them together in great numbers was a sure recipe for disaster. That it took twenty-four years to dissolve the bond and to generate Bangladesh by war is a tribute to the virtues of Islam or perhaps . . . to the distrust of Hindustan.

In spite of all their differences, both states proved to be restive and allergic to the rule of the Congress Party. As a result, both turned to regional parties and leaders, the Akali Dal in Punjab, the Communist Party of India (CPI [M]) in Bengal. For this to happen there was no dearth of twists and turns and violence even, in the political battles of the last forty years.

Right after independence, at the first Republic Day of India, the Akali expressed their resentment by refusing to take part in the celebration. This was a harbinger of worse things to come: the Akali adopted a strategy of reducing the size of the state in order to rule it as their homeland. Having suffered terribly from partition, they made another partition to serve themselves, creating what they defined as a 'punjabi subha'. After protracted agitation they succeeded in 1966 soon after Mrs Gandhi had taken up the prime ministership. She was not averse to letting the Akali rule over a smaller state if they wished it. All the more so since it let her carve a new state, 90 per cent Hindu (Haryana), which would be ruled by Congress. By the same stroke she took away the vast northern lands to create yet another state, Himachal Pradesh, which would be controlled by the Centre, i.e. in her hands. Splitting states was no big worry for someone adept at splitting anything which was an obstacle to her imperious will. Thereafter the Indian Punjab was reduced in size to one seventh of its parent body.

Such a shrinkage of their homeland went against the spirit of the Sikhs or for that matter, of the Punjabi people. As a nation the Sikhs were much too energetic, bold and enterprising to be happy confined to an area of 50,000 sq. kms. Non-resident Sikhs were never loath to send money to their narrow-minded clerics, but they continued to roam the West and make good for themselves. Khalistan was never a deeply-felt aspiration but a way of expressing their despair at being led by Mrs Gandhi in Delhi and her appointed agents in Chandigarh.

As for West Bengal, it was run for fourteen years (1948–62) by a well-minded and respected freedom fighter, Dr B. C. Roy, a Bengali of pre-independence political vintage. At the beginning of his long tenure, soon after partition, an episode happened which is worth recalling. While Dr Roy was abroad, a feud developed between three opposed factions of the Bengal Congress. The 'high command', anxious to set it right, decided to call for fresh elections in the PCC and in the Legislative Assembly. Upon his return Dr Roy took no notice of Delhi's orders and set about settling the matter himself. Nehru and Prasad sent an urgent cable for him to come immediately to Delhi. He ignored the order until he had secured a vote of confidence from the Legislative Party, with a large majority. Then he came to Delhi, having won the day. The significance of the episode lies in the fact that Roy had always been close to the high command and obedient to Nehru's wishes. But as soon as he became Bengal's chief he knew he had to stand up to Delhi and the local factions knew it as well.

The period of the 1960s and 1970s saw West Bengal sink ever lower in economic backwardness, urban squalor and rural poverty. The revolutionary Naxalite movement in the countryside and the young urban guerillas of 1968–70 were the products of deprivation and despair as much as of a Bengali nationalism prone to violence. It is only in the last fifteen to twenty years that hope and pride have returned, at least to some extent. Then they came from the least expected quarter: the CPI (M) and its Bengali leader, Jyoti Basu. A variety of reasons explain why the CPI (M) gave up its revolutionary discourse in Bengal, discovered the virtues of parliamentary democracy and took root in the Bengali countryside to carry out the task left unfinished by the Krishak Praja Party of Fazl-ul-Huq.

Born eighty-two years ago in Dacca to a well-off, educated family of kayastha (a Hindu high caste of scribes) the main fount of bhadralok—Jyoti Basu commented in the *Financial Times* in January 1994, with humour:

> I had selfish reasons to welcome the gradual delicensing of industries because when there was licensing, the federal authorities used to discourage entrepreneurs from setting up industries in West Bengal . . .

He spoke pointedly of the *federal* government, and not as every Indian does, of the *central* government. West Bengali politicians and CPI (M) leaders have given more thought to the federal issue than any other politicians in India. This is not the result of deep Marxist thinking nor sheer pragmatism on the part of an old politician, but the result of the bitter experience of a divided Bengal.

Partition was considered by many as an act of unfinished business or a temporary truce before a final settlement. Thus spoke Nehru, Patel, Acharya Kripalani and many others. Today Kashmir speaks louder to proclaim the same truth.

Leaving aside Kashmir, the sulking Punjab and a frustrated Bengal, let us go back to the beginning, i.e. to part II of the Government of India Act (1935), entitled 'Federation of India'. Every student of the period knows how Jawaharlal Nehru as well as Mohammed-Ali Jinnah rejected it outright and in definitive terms. Churchill dismissed it no less categorically, describing it as 'a gigantic quilt of jumbled crochet work, a monstrous monument of sham built by pigmies'. But what then, was, the political map of India? Was it not indeed a 'gigantic quilt of jumbled crochet work', with its 600-odd Princely States, its border areas under military administration and the eleven provinces of British India, the limits of which were hardly justified on rational grounds? Wasn't it a kind of Holy Roman Germanic Empire with its maze of kingdoms, counties, bishoprics and free cities? By giving it a modern name, part two of the Charter of 1935 gave political expression to the unity created by nature and by culture from time immemorial.

However two different principles were embodied in the same Act: the plurality principle which demands accommodation from every party to a conflict and the majority principle which requires the submission of the weaker party. The first had a long tradition, the second was the product of modernity and democracy. Between 1937 and 1946, the two principles clashed against one another, up until the eventual demise of the Federation idea. Partition, therefore, was but a temporary settlement in an enduring struggle. Democracy prevailed and with it a spirit of centralisation. Kashmir is the ever present witness that partition continues to work itself out in the Indian world to which it certainly belongs. But majority rule, carried to its extreme, would break the old Princely State, this 'ramshackle' entity made by the sword. Perhaps the time has come for the federal idea to be revived and given a new lease of life in the area which was once covered by the Raj.

Two recent developments may help to bring this about. One is the spread of economic liberalisation which will necessarily decrease the leverage of the Centre vis-à-vis the states and increase enormously the bargaining power of the state governments. The second development, not unconnected with the first, is the regionalisation of the political parties which was the main feature of the last Lok Sabha elections. All parties, nowadays, are regional. Gone are the days when the Congress Party operated as an integrating machine over the whole of India. As for the BJP, it is making a heroic effort to become a substitute for the old Congress, an alternative all-embracing force. In attempting too much it will probably over-exert itself and fail. The rule of the game at the Centre is to make or break coalitions. In India today coalitions represent not only various social forces but also, and perhaps predominantly, regional claims for power at the Centre; demanding proper representation as regional entities. This problem has been left unsolved by the 1950 Constitution. Why should the political parties of today solve a problem which is basically a constitutional issue?

The one-nation theory was proved wrong by partition. The two-nations theory has been proved wrong by the break up of the old Pakistan. The nation-state option, if pursued too vigorously by the nationalist Hindus, will prove a dangerous enterprise. Recent developments have, in a way, cleared the ground. Who

will be bold enough to cast out the devils of the past and rehabilitate the much abused idea of a Federation of India?

FOR FURTHER READING:

Jean Alphonse Bernard, *De l'Empire des Indes à la République Indienne, 1935–1990* (Imprimerie Nationale, 1994); Paul R. Brass, *The Politics of India since Independence* (Cambridge University Press, 2nd edition) and 'The Punjab crisis and the unity of India' in Atul Kohli (ed.), *India's Democracy* (Princeton University Press, 1988); Joya Chatterji, *Bengal Divided, Hindu Communalism*

and Partition, 1932–1947, (Cambridge University Press, 1994); Ayesha Jalal, *Jinnah, the Sole Spokesman* (Cambridge University Press, 1985); Ian Talbot, *Provincial Politics and the Pakistan Movement* (Oxford University Press, 1988) and *Growth of the Muslim League in N.W. and N.E. India* (Oxford University Press, 1994).

Jean Alphonse Bernard *is a retired French civil servant. He served in India in the 1960s. This essay is an abridged version of a paper presented to the XIth European Conference on South Asian Studies (1996).*

Article 7

World Watch, July/August 1998

What Does India Want?

The government in New Delhi sent a defiant message when it began setting off nuclear bombs in May. But hundreds of millions of Indians, if they had a voice, might have sent a very different message. The threat they feel most acutely—the destruction of their natural support systems—does not come from Pakistan or China but from within their own country.

by Payal Sampat

It's safe to make just one generalization about India—which is that every other time you generalize about India, you're probably wrong. With over 400 living languages, 85 political parties and a 5,000-year-old cultural and intellectual history, India is defined by its heterogeneity. "All the convergent influences in the world run through this society," wrote historian E. P. Thompson. "There is not a thought that is being thought in the West or East that is not active in some Indian mind."

Perhaps the most noted modern representatives of this diversity of thought were Mahatma Gandhi and Jawaharlal Nehru, who worked together in the first half of this century to

get the British to "quit India," but differed sharply in their vision of what an independent nation should look like. At that time, their debate pertained only to the future of a former colony facing the challenges of self-governance. Today, the echoes of that famous debate still resonate—now in the accelerating development of the second-most populous nation, and with large implications for the world as a whole.

Nehru aspired to make India a leading industrial society, a *force to reckon with* in the global economy; it would be powered by modern machinery and giant dams—he called these the "new temples of modern India." Gandhi's hope, in contrast, was to strengthen India's grassroots village economies by pro-

The illustrations for this article were done by artists of the indigenous Warli tribe of Maharashtra, north of Bombay. They illustrate folk stories based on the activities of traditional village life, as identified on each page. Above: Tree of life. Title page: Piper calling villagers to dance.

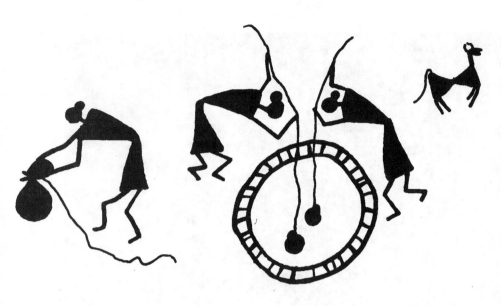

Drawing water from a well

highways, and nuclear power plants. Unlike the Soviet and Chinese regimes, however, the Indian government encouraged private ownership. In keeping with its long tradition of ideological plurality, it embraced a "mixed economy": although the state controlled some key sectors (electricity utilities, telecommunications, aviation, and mining, among them), private enterprise continued to be a vital part of the economy.

While Nehru's vision prevailed most visibly, Gandhi's ideas shaped the economy as well. His idea of *swadeshi,* putting emphasis on things "indigenously produced," played an important role in India's freedom struggle, and has strongly influenced India's economic philosophy—and its citizens' psyche—ever since. The idea was to empower ordinary people by fostering pride in what they produced themselves, and by encouraging self-reliance through activities like spinning cotton and growing food for their own consumption. By extension, *swadeshi* led to a policy of national self-sufficiency in food production. However, the means that were used to enact this policy—the "Green Revolution" with its heavy dependence on mechanization, agrochemical applications and centralized seed banks—had a decidedly Nehruvian spin. While bureaucrats in New Delhi have continued their pursuit of large-scale development, much of Gandhi's legacy has evolved in less conspicuous venues—in the rural villages and in India's 25,000 non-governmental organizations and grassroots movements involved in environmental and social reform.

moting local self-reliance, and by using what would today be called "appropriate technology"—the kind of tool that increases a worker's productivity, but does not devalue or replace him.

In recent years, the intellectual successors to Nehru and Gandhi have polarized the issue in a way those early leaders may never have intended. The debate has taken different forms in the half-century since India's independence in 1947, but the tensions it expresses—over modernism and tradition, globalization and community, economic prosperity and voluntary simplicity—are now as familiar in Mexico, Nigeria, and Japan as they are in India.

Giving added urgency to the debate today is the fact that these issues are matters not only of political philosophy, but also of biological and economic survival. India's physical environment is deeply threatened, and so, as a result, are the one billion people and the economic activities that it supports. At a time when homogeneous prescriptions for economic development are being called into question, the sprawling diversity that has kept people debating for the past half-century may hold answers for India's biggest challenge yet: balancing the needs of its people with the natural systems that sustain them.

Fifty Years in the Making

At the time the British left India in 1947, the newly independent nation faced human deprivation of staggering dimensions. Nehru, as the nation's first prime minister, guided the country's development along the lines of the Soviet Union, a model that suited both his industrial aspirations and the need to overcome this poverty. Like the state planners of China and the Soviet Union, Nehru envisioned development on a grand scale. His government and its successors undertook an ambitious, ongoing campaign to construct dams, transcontinental

Over the past decade, a third voice—promoting free-market policies—has been introduced to the old debate, and has brought rapid changes. The shakeup began in 1991, when India's economy faltered. A weak monsoon that year hit farmers hard. Since agriculture is the backbone of the Indian economy (providing a third of the country's GDP and 70 percent of its jobs), the blow to agricultural growth sent repercussions throughout the economy. Later that year, the Soviet Union disintegrated and India lost its primary export market—and oil supplier. India's GDP, which had grown at about 5.5 percent per year throughout the 1980s, flattened to a growth of less than 1 percent in 1991. At the time, the country owed $90 billion in foreign loans it had taken out to finance its many infrastructure projects. With under $1 billion in foreign reserves, India found itself in a dangerously vulnerable position.

At that point, the International Monetary Fund stepped in with an offer to bail India out—on the condition that the country abandon its socialist planning for free-market policies. Like several other developing countries around the same period—Mexico and Vietnam, for example—India agreed to "liberalize" its economy: to reshape its laws to encourage foreign investment, to privatize certain state enterprises, and to dismantle trade barriers that protect domestic industry. These reforms met with hostility in a nation built on the concept of local self-determination. But economists, who had long complained about the inefficiencies of their country's protectionist policies, were relieved that India was finally poised to become a competitive force in the global economy.

Draining Groundwater

In the 50 years since its independence in 1947, India's economy has grown ninefold. While its population in that time has doubled, its grain production has nearly quadrupled—on the surface, an extremely good ratio. And during the same period, the country's electricity generation capacity has expanded 50 times. But much of its material progress has neglected—and often come at the devastating cost of—the natural resources that have fueled it.

In its efforts to jumpstart industry and agriculture, India offered virtually free access to those natural resources—fresh water, forests, and minerals—that are the basic materials of a modern industrial economy. It offered high energy subsidies for electricity and diesel fuel. (Electricity subsidies amount to 1.5 percent of India's GDP.) It assumed the costs of expanding roads and railways into previously remote areas, making it cheaper and easier still to take out timber and other resources. These subsidies have allowed increasingly wasteful use of these resources.

This imprudence appears particularly costly in the way India has squandered its freshwater. Highly subsidized electricity rates have encouraged the extraction of increasing quantities of water from underground aquifers. During the 1960s, the Green Revolution spurred a huge increase in the use of shallow tube-wells, whose numbers have grown from 360,000 to 6 million in the last thirty years. (Robert Repetto, an economist at the World Resources Institute, has dubbed this development "the tube-well revolution.") With that many punctures in its skin, it's not surprising that India is dehydrating at an alarming rate: the country's National Environmental Engineering Research Institute reports that in several states groundwater is being drawn faster than its rate of recharge. Farmers in semiarid northern Gujarat say they have to lower their pumps by 3 meters every two years to keep up with falling water levels. Most notably, in some parts of Punjab and Haryana, the "breadbasket" of India where almost a third of the country's wheat is grown, water tables have fallen over 4 meters in the last decade.

In some areas, much of the water that is extracted is not efficiently used: according to the Tata Energy Research Institute in New Delhi, 45 percent of all irrigation water (mostly from canals) seeps through unlined field channels. Some of the seepage causes waterlogging, depriving plant roots of oxygen and reducing their productivity. In warm areas, most of the water evaporates, leaving excessive salt deposits in the soil,

rendering it less productive still. As a result, some 10 million hectares are now salinized; another 12 million hectares are waterlogged.

Meanwhile, traditional techniques of water harvesting that were tailored to regional variations in rainfall and water availability have been cast aside. Until about a century ago, the southern city of Bangalore obtained its water from an intricate system of interconnected stone tanks that capture rainfall runoff. These systems also irrigated surrounding farmland. Now India's fastest-growing city and high-technology capital, Bangalore has built football stadiums and apartment buildings over some of its tanks, reports the New Delhi-based Centre for Science and the Environment. The water for Bangalore now has

Hunting

to be carried from the Cauvery River, which means lifting it 1,000 meters in elevation and transporting it a distance of 100 kilometers. It now costs more to supply water to Bangalore than to any other city in South Asia (although Bangalore's residents foot just 5 percent of this bill), and shortages have become routine.

Several other regions also experience chronic water shortages. Every day, diesel-fueled tanker trucks haul water to the city of Madras in the southern state of Tamil Nadu. (Groundwater levels in Tamil Nadu reportedly fell between 25 and 30 meters over a decade due to overpumping.) Even heavier costs have been exacted in western India, where 30 large dams, 135 medium-sized ones, and 3,000 small dams are planned on the Narmada River. One of the primary beneficiaries will be the textile-manufacturing city of Ahmedabad in Gujarat, where the water table fell by over 20 meters in the 1980s. Yet, the project has become one of the world's most notorious examples of a rob-Peter-to-pay-Paul system of resource management. Critics note that 70 percent of Gujarat's drought-affected areas will not receive water from this scheme. The centerpiece of the project—the now-halted Sardar Sarovar dam—has alone displaced some 100,000 tribal villagers, and if completed, its reservoir will submerge some 37,000 hectares of forests and farmland.

Even so, the worst could be yet to come. The International Food Policy Research Institute projects that India will step up its water demand by 50 percent over the next 20 years. Its water demand will grow from just over 600 billion cubic meters in 1995 to over 900 cubic meters by 2020—the highest absolute increase for any nation over that span. Most of this increase will go to industrial and domestic users, with each projected to quadruple its current demand. By that year, it is estimated that most regions in India will be "water-stressed," meaning that water shortages could become chronic and widespread, and that the quantity available to each person will have fallen to 1,700 cubic meters or less—down from 2,200 cubic meters today, already just a third of the global average. (By comparison, the per person availability is 9,200 cubic meters in the United States and 12,800 cubic meters in Indonesia.)

India has prided itself on its self-sufficiency in food production, a task that will be rendered increasingly difficult by projected water depletion. (Although the country is a net exporter of food, on average one-third of its households do not get adequate nutrition.) Declining soil quality could make this task harder still. About half of India's farmland—some 80 million hectares—suffers from some form of degradation. At a conservative estimate, says a World Bank report, soil degradation reduces agricultural output by between 4 and 6 percent a year; other studies have placed this annual loss at as high as 26 percent.

Putting higher prices on water and electricity to cover the real costs of their production could slow the water decline. This would encourage water-intensive industries like steel, fertilizers and textiles to leapfrog to more efficient production practices, and could prompt municipalities to revive local systems of rainwater harvesting and storage. It would also spur farmers to reconsider crop choices (sugarcane, for instance, is very demanding of water, and uses half of Maharashtra's irrigation water, although it is grown on just 10 percent of its cropland). It would also encourage them to maintain and improve bunding systems (barriers built along contour lines that prevent water runoff and spread rainwater evenly across fields), and to shift to more efficient irrigation practices. Since three-fourths of India's 4,000 cubic meters of rainfall is concentrated in 3 monsoon months, irrigation during the dry months is vital. In the northeastern state of Meghalaya, drip irrigation systems are constructed by stringing together split bamboo sticks that carry spring water over hundreds of meters to betel and black pepper orchards. In mountainous Himachal Pradesh, vegetable farmers hope to double their planted area by stretching their water supply with drip systems during the dry winter months. Introduced by non-profit International Development Enterprises, each system costs $100 per acre of land irrigated. And some villages in Maharashtra manage water resources collectively. This motivates individual farmers to use this limited resource frugally rather than assuming that if they don't take as much as they can, some competitor will.

Disappearing Forests

India has one of the world's highest shares of arable land: more than half of its land is cultivated. (By comparison, 20 percent of land in the United States, and 10 percent of China's land—the world's other major food producers—is arable). Unlike other populous countries such as Egypt, Ethiopia, or even China, it does not have vast areas of barren or mountainous territory from which little productivity can be gleaned. Another 20 percent of its land is forested, and 4 percent is pastureland. Although much of rural India lives alongside its farms and forests (3 million people live *inside* its forests), most of the country's people and industries are spread out over a remaining area a little larger than the state of Texas. As India's population and economy swell, and its cities and industries expand into the countryside, it faces critical decisions about how to allocate its land. A key question is what will become of the four-fifths of India's land that is still not urbanized or industrialized.

Of the one-fifth of India's land that is forested, just 40 percent (or 8 percent of the country's land overall) is intact, dense forest. Plantations, which have displaced natural ecosystems with monocrops, cover almost a quarter of the land designated as "forested." (A third of these plantations cultivate eucalyptus, a fast-growing, non-indigenous species that is very demanding of soil moisture.) At 15 million hectares, India has the largest

Climbing for coconuts

plantation area in the tropics. The natural forests that remain are fragmented and consist of more sparsely covered tracts.

Moving—displaced by development

Less than a century ago, 40 percent of India was forested. Large tracts of deciduous and tropical rainforest were destroyed over the past century as the British expanded India's railway network across the country. Then, between 1951 and 1976, some 15 percent of the nation's land area was converted to cropland, and much of this came from natural forest. Today, though most of India's natural forests are protected by national law, 43 of its 521 protected areas are endangered by conversion to industrial uses. In the country's most forested state, Madhya Pradesh, in the very center of the subcontinent, diamond and sandstone mines have taken over parts of the Panna Tiger Reserve, one of the last homes of the tiger. The mines routinely dump contaminated tailings into the Ken River, which flows through the tigers' habitat. And one-third of the Melghat Tiger Reserve in Maharashtra has been "de-reserved" to make way for dam construction and industrial timber harvesting.

Forests are strained by increasing demand for their resources. As human and livestock populations swell and forests shrink, the relationship between rural communities and forests has become increasingly precarious. Nearly 90 percent of the wood taken from the forests is used as fuel. And India's forests provide fodder for some 100 million head of cattle that trample and denude undergrowth as they graze.

According to the U.N. Food and Agriculture Organization, the area allotted to plantations in India has been increasing at an average of 15 percent a year. At that rate, if all the plantations were taken from existing forests, all of India's natural forests—even the sparsely covered tracts—would be destroyed in less than a quarter-century. Yet, India's natural forests provide it with some extremely vital services: they protect topsoil from wind and water erosion, regulate temperatures, replenish aquifers, store genetic diversity, offer recreational relief to an increasingly crowded human population, and provide a number of valuable products other than wood—including medicines and food.

Biologically, India's forests are exceptionally diverse: they range from the world's most extensive mangrove forests, the Sunderbans in West Bengal, to evergreen rainforest in the Andaman and Nicobar Islands, and dry alpine forest in the Himalayan foothills. Together, India's forests house some 45,000 plant species, 372 species of mammals, 1,250 bird species, and 399 species of reptiles. But this diversity is eroding precipitously, as natural habitat is cleared for new plantations or farms, bulldozed for mines or dams, or picked over for firewood. One in four of India's mammal species are threatened, says the International Union for the Conservation of Nature. India is one of ten countries with the highest percentage of threatened mammal, bird, *and* plant species. Endemic species—species that are found nowhere else in the world—are particularly vulnerable. Just 4,000 lion-tailed macaques, 2,000 Nilgiri *tahrs* (a kind of mountain goat), and 300 grizzled mountain squirrels now remain in India's Western Ghats, a southwestern mountain range designated one of the world's 19 "biodiversity hotspots" by Conservation International. Other distinctive fauna, such as the pink-headed duck, are already extinct.

In some areas, local communities have teamed up with state agencies to manage and regenerate forests. In West Bengal, 150,000 villagers tend to 350,000 hectares of *sal* forest (*sal* is a high-value hardwood somewhat similar to teak), some of which was badly degraded before the state Forest Department initiated the project in 1972. No money was exchanged for this service, but it has turned out to be an important economic transaction nonetheless: the revived forests supply the villagers with medicinal products, food and fuel, and officials no longer need to invest in policing the *sal* groves. Similar partnerships, involving some 15,000 villages in all, have been initiated in other states. Since an estimated one-half of India's forest land is degraded to some degree, and the areas bordering forests are often unproductive marginal lands, such projects offer immense potential for regeneration of lost forest cover. Elsewhere, biogas plants (which convert organic waste like cow dung into a methane-based fuel) have offset firewood demand for some 10 million rural Indians—and have reduced the health risks of burning wood and dung cakes indoors.

Increasing Pollution

At current prices, about half of India's economic growth over the past half-century has been concentrated in the seven years since liberalization. Although the nation's notorious bureaucracy has daunted international investors, the prospect of finding hundreds of millions of new customers for their cars, colas, and cosmetics has proved irresistible. Nine of the world's major auto makers have set up shop in India in the last few years, as have Coca-Cola, Kellogg, Revlon and other international vendors of consumer wares. India has now opened up its natural resources to foreign investors, welcoming international oil giants Shell, Exxon and Mobil, and mining companies like Australia's BHP Minerals and South Africa's De Beers Group.

But the years since the new economic boom have also brought a spate of environmental problems—over and above resource depletion—of an enormity that India was unprepared for. Perhaps the most pervasive problem is that the building of productive capacity has run far faster than the building of any accompanying protections for environmental and public health. Where environmental laws do exist, they are largely unenforced: just 7 percent of Indian industries comply with pollution control guidelines, says the Asian Development Bank. The mounting risks that result from this course of action have been compounded by rising consumer demands, and population growth that is now the equivalent of adding the entire population of Australia to India's already crowded land each year.

In the past ten years, the number of vehicles on Indian roads has increased threefold. With vehicles contributing over 70 percent of the country's urban air pollution, the consequences have been alarming: by one estimate, the average resident of Bombay or New Delhi has the lung capacity of a two-pack-a-day smoker. Most of the new automobiles are diesel powered (diesel is cheaper in India than anywhere else in the world), and only a fraction were equipped with pollution control devices when built. Diesel's sooty emissions aggravate asthma and other breathing disorders, and recent studies have linked diesel exhaust with increased cancer rates. Although new gasoline vehicles (1995 and later) are required to have catalytic converters, most are still tanked with fuel that contains lead, since the unleaded variety is hard to find at gas stations. Leaded gasoline damages the catalytic converters—and human nervous systems. According to the Tata Institute, air pollution in India caused an estimated 2.5 million premature deaths in 1997—equivalent to wiping out the entire population of Jamaica or Singapore. In 1995, 25 million people in India's major cities were treated for respiratory diseases like asthma and bronchitis.

Indian cities also churn out rising amounts of solid waste, much of which consists of substances that are hard to compost or return to the environment. In the last decade, for example, plastics consumption has increased ten-fold. Plastic bags litter the last remaining mangroves that line Bombay's western coast, while other inorganic waste clogs the creeks and lakes that supply the city's drinking water. India also generates 48 million tons of solid waste each year, most of which is disposed of in unsafe ways: burned, dumped into oceans and other water bodies, or land-filled. Chemicals leak out of landfills, contaminating agricultural land and groundwater supplies. In a country this densely inhabited, landfill space comes at the expense of valuable cropland or forests.

Another outfall of the widening gap between population growth and the building of suitable environmental protections is that only ten percent of all sewage in India is treated. One result is that about one-fifth of all communicable disease in India is transmitted through contaminated water. And only a fraction of industrial wastewater is treated, although industries contribute half of the pollutant load.

India clearly cannot afford the costs of its continued inaction: a study by the World Bank pegs the health costs from air and water contamination at $7 billion a year. By one estimate, Indian industries will need to spend $3 billion on pollution control equipment by the year 2000. This demand will grow by 25 percent a year as industries expand and generate more waste. And fewer than one in three Indians have access to basic sanitation services. As Indian cities explode in the next few decades, municipalities will be hard pressed to meet these needs without private-sector assistance.

India can channel its influxes of foreign investment in ways that benefit, rather than impose on, its environment and people. In some areas it already has. For instance, with the help of Danish, German and Dutch know-how, India has become the world's fourth largest producer of wind power—forerunner to a decentralized renewable energy system that can help the country begin to phase out its heavily polluting, climate-threatening, and health-damaging dependency on coal. Because coal is abundant and its production heavily subsidized, 70 percent of India's power has come from this fossil fuel. The new market-based economy can help streamline environmentally harmful inefficiencies in the state-controlled model. For example, in the first five years of liberalization, India cut back its coal subsidies from $3.3 billion in 1990–91 to $1.9 billion in 1995–96.

Herding

And Another Kind of Impoverishment

India's ecological self-destruction has drained its key resources and undermined the health of its citizens. But the hardest hit, even though statistics may not always show it, are probably those who live closest to their ecological roots: an estimated 400 to 500 million rural Indians who depend directly on their natural environment for their sustenance. Eco-historians Madhav Gadgil and Ramachandra Guha of the Indian Institute for Science describe these subsistence farmers, herders, fisherfolk, artisans and indigenous communities as "ecosystem people." India's natural resource commons have produced their food, traditional medicines, housing material and fuel. In terms of their sheer numbers—and the vital role they can play in preventing the erosion of India's natural systems—India's ecosystem people may hold an important key to its sustainable future.

Since industrial India has appropriated a large part of the nation's natural resource commons to generate its power, build its skyscrapers and discard its waste, four-fifths of the nation's villages are now not just income-poor, but natural resource-poor. In Kumaun, the hilly region to the west of Nepal, forests and pastureland have been cooperatively managed by local ecosystem communities for centuries. Soapstone and magnesite (magnesium carbonate) quarries have since taken over these commons. Be depriving the local people of large tracts of their forest- and pasture-based livelihoods, the mines have cast them into profound impoverishment.

As the commons diminish and populations increase, a destructive treadmill is set in motion, and the resource-poor are forced to use their limited resources in increasingly unsustainable ways. And some of the most resource-abundant states house the largest numbers of India's poor—coal-rich Bihar, or *sal*-forested Meghalaya, for example, where extractive industries have displaced thousands of resource-dependent communities. Ironically, much of this destruction has been rewarded by the state, as investments in "backward" regions come with enormous tax benefits; of the top ten "zero-tax" payers in India, three are mining companies. As local people are pushed onto unproductive soils and arid hillsides which cannot support their needs, they have to seek out new sources of fuelwood, food, and fodder (livestock feed).

Grassroots movements have long protested the impoverishment of India's ecosystem people. Those movements have included, for example, the widely publicized protests against the Narmada and Tehri dams, and the Chipko opposition to deforestation in the Himalayas. Several of these grassroots groups recently banded together to form a National Alliance of Peoples' Movements. And there are signs that the authorities are listening. The southwestern states of Maharashtra, Goa, Karnataka, and Kerala banned mechanized trawling in their coastal fisheries during the monsoon months when fish breed, after local fishing communities complained that trawling was rapidly depleting fish populations. This has proved to be a

School

sound resource management practice: harvests in Kerala have significantly rebounded since the seasonal ban was introduced in the late 1980s. And the government has seen clear demonstrations, in joint forestry projects like the ones in West Bengal, that traditional knowledge can be an invaluable factor in protecting natural resources and supporting local communities. But these efforts are still largely piecemeal, and the link between natural resource protection and peoples' well-being has thus far been given short shrift by policymakers.

And despite the social spending policies set in motion by Nehru and kept up by his successors, income poverty, not to mention resource-poverty, is still pervasive. Poverty rates have declined slowly in the years since independence—from 45 to 36 percent of the population. In absolute numbers of people trapped in poverty, India is still the world's poorest nation—more than 500 million Indians earn less than $1 a day (many of them less than five or ten cents a day) in purchasing-power terms, says the U.N. Development Programme (UNDP). Meanwhile, the number of "super rich" Indians—those who earn over half a million dollars a year in purchasing power terms—quadrupled from 10,000 to 39,000 in the past 3 years. In short, the benefits of the country's impressive gains in GDP have not been well distributed. In India, the absence of comprehensive land reforms, and persistent inequalities like the legacy of the caste system, have perpetuated these injustices; some government policies have intensified them. Writes WRI's Robert Repetto about the nation's water subsidization policies: "In India, the rights to an immensely valuable resource were distributed gratis in a pattern even more unequal than land distribution, reinforcing rural inequalities in income and wealth."

India needs the benefits—health care, sanitation, education, clean water, and energy—that come with economic prosperity. Yet it also needs to address the inequities that undermine this progress. The *New York Times* quotes a bricklayer who earns less than $1 a day, responding to the promise of India's economic expansion: "I was poor before, and I am poor now. I suppose I will always be poor." And the gap between the urban affluent and rural poor threatens to widen. A study by the New Delhi-based National Council of Applied Economic Research forecasts that in the next decade, the share of India's poor living in its villages will rise from 75 percent to 95 percent.

Mahbub Ul Haq, formerly Pakistan's Finance Minister, and advisor to the World Bank and UNDP notes that "experience in many countries has taught us that economic growth does not translate into human development: a link between growth and human lives must be created through conscious national policies." Policies in the state of Kerala demonstrate the role that good governance—comprehensive land reform, and targeted spending on education, health care, and access to family planning, in this case—can play in overcoming human deprivation and unequal distribution. Almost all its citizens are literate, there is no population growth, it has the highest ratio of working women in all of India, and people live as long as their counterparts in industrial countries—on a seventieth of the income. And Kerala's achievements are relatively recent: from being India's second poorest state in 1960, by 1990 it was ranked among the five most prosperous, according to World Bank researchers Martin Ravallion and Gaurav Datt. Kerala's success provides a powerful model for improving human development and curbing population growth in other regions in India.

What's Next?

India's natural resource wealth—its coal, iron ore, arable land, forests, and freshwater supplies—can be viewed myopically as the fuel that drives its economy. It provides the commodity exports that bring in foreign exchange, and the cheap raw materials needed to build a domestic industrial sector fast. From a longer viewpoint, however, the rapid depletion of these resources is clearly unsustainable. By all indications, India's natural systems are already showing signs of collapse—as seen in falling water tables, deforestation, degraded soils, and dangerous pollution levels. At a conservative estimate, says a World Bank study, the latter three forms of damage alone cost India 4.5 percent of its GDP each year.

India's massive expansion, both human and economic, will place tremendous demands on this already stressed natural resource base. In the next 50 years, its population is projected to increase by 700 million—equivalent to adding the entire population of Africa to its already huge numbers. Almost all of this increase will be in cities, projected to triple in size from today's 250 million to 750 million by 2050, when almost half of India's population will be urban. In the same period, says the Tata Institute, at an estimated 5 percent economic growth a year, industrial production will increase at staggering rates: steel production will grow 10-fold, cement 15-fold, and cotton textiles 8-fold. Without radical changes in the way natural resources are managed, the collective impact of this expansion on air and water pollution, water scarcity, habitat destruction, human health, and rural livelihoods—and the national economy—could be devastating.

If India's grassroots communities and urban victims of pollution—to whom the impacts of this resource destruction are painfully apparent—could frame the national agenda, competing in the international arms race would probably not feature on their list of priorities. They might tell a different story: that the future of this giant nation depends on its ability to protect its natural support systems. India can harness its unique combination of biological and intellectual diversity in this effort, rather than shrink and marginalize it. Its success in this task will have profound implications for the world as a whole.

Payal Sampat is a staff researcher at the Worldwatch Institute.

Article 8   *Foreign Affairs,* May/June 1998

India's Problem Is Not Politics

Marshall M. Bouton

MISREADING THE ELECTIONS

INDIA'S RECENT parliamentary elections aroused fears about its political viability, but not about its economy. The fractured verdict—40 parties won at least one seat, and no party won more than a third of the seats—created a hung parliament incapable of ending the political turmoil at India's center. While Sonia Gandhi stemmed the Congress Party's losses by assuming its leadership, the party that once provided India's stability continued its sclerotic decline. At the same time, the strong showing by the Hindu nationalist Bharatiya Janata Party (BJP), which was asked to form the new government, stirred fears that India would abandon its commitment to secularism in public life, setting the stage for sharper Hindu-Muslim conflict, political unrest, and perhaps heightened tension with Pakistan.

Economic issues, in contrast, stirred little alarm. They played practically no role in the elections, despite the current slump in India's economy and the meltdown in East Asia. Instead, most observers assumed that continued economic reforms, even at a slow pace, would keep India moving forward on the higher GDP growth path of six to seven percent attained in recent years.

The reality of India's prospects is just the opposite of these perceptions. The main threat to India's future is not political but economic. India's political system has for several years been in transition from Congress Party dominance to a more splintered picture in which regional and caste-based parties control most states, alongside a still unclear political pattern at the center. But neither the kaleidoscope of parties nor frequent changes of government nor the rise of the BJP as the preeminent national party should be mistaken for threats to India's underlying stability or its very unity. Rather, they are integral to the latest stage—a messy one, to be sure—of a social and political transformation made possible by democracy itself.

On the economic front, however, India's reforms are for all intents and purposes stalled, and its relatively poor recent performance—GDP was projected to increase by five percent at most in the 1997–98 fiscal year—is more than a passing business-cycle downturn. The unfinished half of the reforms—structural adjustments needed to lower fiscal deficits, improve financial markets, and create labor market flexibility—are nowhere in sight. During the tedious last two years, observers have consoled themselves over the slow pace with the view that the reform process is irreversible. But elements in the business community have soured on the reforms, no foreseeable government in New Delhi will have the strength to take on those who guard the status quo, and support for structural economic changes remains limited to narrow segments of the population.

A slower pace of reform and lower growth rates will not only cause economic pain but will also endanger India's social and political progress. Indian democracy is mobilizing heretofore sidelined classes and castes seeking both group recognition and material benefits. Regional differences in living standards and growth, a long-standing problem now exacerbated by the reforms, are creating new demands from laggard states. A failure to accelerate reform and growth would make the orderly accommodation of these interests, the reduction of poverty, and, eventually, the maintenance of democratic stability and national unity vastly more difficult.

DEMOCRATIC GLUE

THE WEST pays a great deal of lip service to India's democracy, but democracy is just as often blamed for the country's ills, especially the slow pace of economic progress, government ineffectiveness, social turmoil, and frequent challenges to national authority. More recently, the ascent of the BJP has led to fears that democracy could pave the way for an illiberal regime.

This is flatly wrong. India's democratic political system has been the ultimate source of the state's legitimacy, the major avenue of group mobility, and the main ingredient in the glue that has kept the country together. The leaders of India's independence movement are often accused of wrongly choosing democracy in 1947. In fact, they had little choice. Democracy was the only system that could possibly provide political cohesion in a society with little tradition of political centralism, dizzying social diversity, an independence movement built along participatory lines, and limited elections introduced only in the last three decades of British rule.

Today a vibrant, durable democracy is well established in India. India has had 12 general elections and many more state-level contests. Despite an electorate of over 600 million—each time an Indian general election is held, it is the largest organized human activity ever—elections have generally been free and fair. Despite illiteracy and daunting logistics, the average turnout in Indian parliamentary elections, including 1998, has been 57 percent of all adults, as compared to an average turnout of only 56 percent of registered voters in U.S. presidential elections since 1948.

Indian support for democracy was revealed in the largest ever national survey of political attitudes and behavior, conducted in 1996 by the Centre for the Study of Developing Societies (CSDS) and *India Today*. Almost 70 percent of respondents said that governance is better because of parties and elections, up from 43 percent in a smaller but comparable 1971 survey. About 60 percent told the pollsters that voting made a difference, a conviction held disproportionately by poor people. Three-quarters dismissed the proposition that only the educated should have the right to vote. The very poor had a voting rate three percent higher than the national average.

Indian voters have repeatedly demonstrated their independence and sophistication. Since 1947, only a quarter of incumbents have been returned to power. Indeed, anti-incumbency was the only common denominator of the 1998 results. For instance, voters in ten states voted overwhelmingly against parties they had favored only two years ago. The Indian electorate also learned long ago to split its vote among different parties in elections for both state assemblies and the national parliament.

Governmental instability at the center is in fact partly a result of a healthy extension of democracy's reach. The ballot box has mobilized numerous linguistic, ethnic, and caste groups in the states, leading to the emergence of parties to represent them. Indian voters have been quite decisive in choosing among these and other parties at the state level. In the 1998 elections, for instance, voters in 13 of the 15 major states gave more than half of each state's parliamentary seats to one party or alliance. But because so many regional and caste-based parties are now contesting elections, the aggregation of these choices at the center produces fragmentation.

ACTUALLY, THE CENTER CAN HOLD

AMIDST THE much heightened competition in Indian politics today, the moderation embedded in Indian democracy remains a key source of underlying stability. This tendency is largely the result of the interplay of electoral politics and India's diversity. Because the electorate is so segmented by ethnicity, language, caste, and religion, politicians must build coalitions across parochial lines to gain power, which means in turn that they must avoid appeals that exclude or alienate.

The glue of these coalitions is usually only the desire to wield power or prevent others from acquiring it, which also helps explain India's wobbly governments. Once in office, the disparate coalition partners often have little to hold them together. The 1996–97 United Front government, whose constituent parts were united only by their desire to block the BJP, was easily toppled once Congress withdrew its support. Ironically, this syndrome may also be a problem for the new BJP-led

alliance, which showed its fragility almost as soon as the election was over.

But over the longer term, democracy pushes all major political actors, even the BJP, toward moderation and power-sharing. Extremist and separatist appeals almost always wind up being repudiated at the ballot box. India's communists, for instance, moved toward the center and embraced the democratic process soon after independence to stay in the political game. In the Punjab, despite a decade of separatist violence and repression, voters strongly endorsed the moderate Sikh party once the political process was permitted to function.

India's diversity also means that few issues can effectively swing a broad geographic or political spectrum of Indian voters. Class-based politics, for instance, have had much less resonance than many expected in a country with such a gulf between rich and poor. Economic grievances are channeled through segmented social groups such as castes, keeping class in the European sense out of Indian politics.

LIMITS OF HINDU NATIONALISM

THE 1998 GAINS by the BJP constitute an important turning point in Indian politics. At a minimum, Congress has been replaced as the dominant party in Delhi for the first time since independence. Some observers also see in the BJP's Hindu nationalist ideology a dramatic and dangerous shift away from the values that have fostered India's "unity within diversity." But there is no need for panic. The BJP will be constrained by the centrist dynamic of Indian politics. The closer the BJP has gotten to power in recent years, the more it has learned that it must moderate or shed its extremist views if it hopes to seize it.

Voters punished the BJP in the 1993 state elections for its involvement in the destruction of the Babri mosque at Ayodhya in December 1992. From then on, the BJP retreated from the more aggressive version of its Hindu chauvinism. Even so, in the 1996 elections it failed to increase its share of the vote or to widen its geographic base. A post-election CSDS-*India Today* survey helped explain the BJP's poor showing: majorities of both Hindus and Muslims agreed that government should protect minorities' interests. So since 1996 the BJP has assiduously softened its Hindu chauvinism, including its promise to build a Hindu temple on the ruins of the Babri mosque. It also developed preelection alliances with regional and caste-based parties in states where it had little chance of gaining support itself.

The BJP's strategy paid off—but more through its alliances than through its own success at the polls. It increased its share of the vote in 1998 by only 5 percent, to 25 percent, and its seat total by only 16. One reason for this modest gain was the surprising and sobering losses in two key states where the BJP and its allies ran state governments, Maharashtra and Rajasthan. The BJP's allies accounted for 72 seats, giving it the opportunity to form a government by enlisting support from still more regional parties through still more policy concessions.

The BJP took power, then, with a deeply compromised mandate, dependent on the support of almost 100 MPs from 17 other parties. It has already shelved some of its most controversial plans, such as revoking laws that protect distinctive Muslim marriage, divorce, and property practices. Furthermore, having appealed to voters as the party that could bring stable and effective government, the BJP must act cautiously if it is to both preserve its coalition and deliver on its promise. It is unlikely to antagonize Pakistan by curtailing Kashmir's autonomy or the United States by going openly nuclear.

These constraints are no guarantee that the BJP will pursue a moderate course or be able to hold a government together. There are serious ideological and programmatic differences within the party and between moderate figures like Prime Minister Atal Bihari Vajpayee, and the purist leaders of the Rashtriya Swayamsevak Sangh, the BJP's parent organization, to say nothing of its quarrels with its allies. And if the BJP fails, it will almost surely lose support next election.

ATTACKING CORRUPTION

THE GREATEST immediate threat to India's governance is not tottering coalition governments or the BJP but corruption. The combination of a state-run economy and weak political institutions created all too many opportunities for crooked politicos and bureaucrats. The resultant graft was exacerbated by the concentration of power at the center by Indira Gandhi, the former prime minister. Public trust in government has plummeted. In a recent survey, four of five respondents said the country had become corrupt, and only five percent described either politicians or the police as completely honest.

The problems are deep-seated, but India seems to have turned a corner in its public life. Spurred by public discontent, a process of political reform has begun that promises to reinvigorate both India's governing institutions and its citizens' confidence in them. Progress will be slow, but the country's political and governmental ills are being attacked on several fronts at once: electoral reform, corruption, intra-party democracy, and power-sharing between the center and the states.

The attack on corruption has been led by India's judiciary, including a Supreme Court that has rooted out graft at the highest levels. In recent years India's Election Commission, initially led by the maverick civil servant T. N. Seshan, has regulated campaign finance practices and forced political parties to hold more open leadership elections. The corruption issue was probably the most important reason for the Congress Party's electoral debacle in 1996, which sent a powerful message to other parties. Media muckraking has also been vital. For the first time in three decades, there is movement in the right direction.

Another salutary trend is the gradual but inexorable devolution of power from Delhi to state and local authorities. Coalition government at the center has given dramatic clout to regional parties. While state governments may be susceptible to populism and less experienced at policymaking, their increasing importance will bring longer-term benefits: a more open, accountable government and increasingly vigorous political competition at state and local levels, reinforcing both India's democratic process and its economic reforms.

LET'S STAY TOGETHER

THE ABSENCE of a strong party at the center and the growing power of regional parties and state governments have raised fresh doubts about India's ability to remain united. But India's nation-building record is strong. After 50 years, the country's international boundaries have not changed despite several secessionist threats, and the remaining challenges to national integrity are not especially daunting. By comparison, other new multiethnic states, such as Nigeria, Czechoslovakia, and Yugoslavia, have failed, and even older ones like Canada remain at risk.

Several factors explain India's success in forging a multinational state. First, democracy provided a highly effective alternative for disgruntled regions and groups to extremism and violence. Democratic politics let recently mobilized malcontents challenge the Indian state. When a group's demands were effectively accommodated, however, their stake in the political process led them to "buy in." In the mid-1960s, for instance, Delhi drew back from an ill-advised effort to impose Hindi as the official language in the face of fierce resistance from the southern states, especially Tamil Nadu, thereby blunting rising Tamil nationalism. Under the control of regional parties ever since, that state has never had a serious recurrence of separatism, even after India refused to aid ethnic Tamils in neighboring Sri Lanka's civil war.

A second factor is the dynamism of India's federalism. No mere formal division of powers, India's federal system encourages negotiation, compromise, and cooperation. This has been particularly evident in the northeast, where Delhi has sought to accommodate demands for autonomy and co-opt ethnic movements amidst rising violence.

The Indian state, on balance, responds well to separatist crises. In the 1960s, Gunnar Myrdal worried that as a "soft state" India would not be able to manage decisively. Certainly there have been mistakes in India's first half-century of nation-building—the festering Kashmir situation is a result, in part, of such misjudgments—but the government's ability to effectively bring its coercive, administrative, and developmental resources to bear has been amply demonstrated in Punjab and the northeast.

TIGER OR ELEPHANT?

ALL THIS is the good news. The bad is that India's economic reforms are at a crossroads. Although long overdue, the reform process initiated in 1991 brought far-reaching change to India's creaky, largely state-controlled economy in just four years. The removal of the "license raj" system that stifled domestic businesses and the reduction of taxes and tariffs, as well as a new openness to foreign investment, generated rapid growth. India's economy, which had lumbered along at 3.5 percent growth per year from 1950 to 1980, picked up to 5.5 percent in the 1980s and averaged 7 percent growth in fiscal years 1995 to 1997. Some claimed that India had joined the ranks of Asia's tiger economies.

Last year, however, India looked more like an elephant again. Industrial growth in the first three quarters of fiscal year 1998 was half that of the same period the previous year and a third of its peak between 1994 and 1996. Agriculture, which had been a star performer in the previous fiscal year, is expected to have negative growth in 1997–98. Exports increased only 4 percent during 1997, compared with an average of 20 percent from 1994 to 1996. One of the few bright spots was the continued influx of foreign direct investment—up 52 percent in the first 11 months of 1997 over the same period in 1996—despite the mixed signals India continues to send foreign investors. In February 1998, Delhi revised its estimate of GDP growth for 1997–98 from 7 to 5 percent, and some economists thought this optimistic.

India's growth will be slowed unless it makes painful changes.

India's current economic slump has many of the hallmarks of a business-cycle downturn: excess capacity, dropping demand, and weak investor and consumer confidence. The rapid growth of 1993–96 generated high levels of investment and capacity, especially by India's previous standards. In late 1995, the government, worried about inflation before the 1996 elections, began squeezing liquidity and curtailing public investment. Retail investors, scared away by the stock market scams and disappointments of the boom, put their spare cash into bank savings and gold instead. Growth slowed, leading to overcapacity in many industries and cuts in business expenses and investment. Delhi's political instability after June 1996 depressed confidence further. Despite the government's lowering of interest rates and other credit relaxation measures in late 1996, the slowdown continued through 1997.

UNFINISHED BUSINESS

INDIA'S BUSINESS-CYCLE downturn is in one sense heartening: the liberalizing reforms of the last seven years have opened the economy to market forces and thus to boom and bust. Alas, India is unlikely to resume the growth of seven to eight percent a year it needs over the long term without further liberalization and structural adjustments. Like Mexico and others, India faces the quandary of a half-completed reform process: the forces unleashed by the first phase of change are driving it toward

further reform, but the obstacles and pain of the next phase are greater still.

Even so, further reform is critical for several reasons. First, India's financial sector still cannot effectively mobilize and mediate capital to respond to economic changes. The resulting high cost of capital makes Indian industry and exports less competitive. Although much improved since 1991, India's equity markets are still too thin and volatile to inspire great confidence on the part of domestic or foreign investors. Bond markets are practically nonexistent. Liberalization of the insurance industry, which would greatly improve the investing of India's substantial savings, now 26 percent of GDP, has been stymied. India's banking system remains flawed, with the dominant state-owned banks still carrying bad loans amounting to 15 to 25 percent of their total.

Second, India's abysmal infrastructure is a major constraint on growth. Part of the problem is that financing has been difficult. Ambitious plans to improve power generation, telecommunications, ports, and roads have also been thwarted by poor policies, indecision, and corruption. Of eight so-called fast-track power projects initiated in 1992, only two are producing or are close to producing power. Telecommunications reforms were mired first in massive graft and then in battles over regulation; unsurprisingly, many major foreign companies retreated.

Third, Indian trade has been opened enough to expose many companies to greater competition but not enough to provide a strong, sustained impetus for growth. Bankruptcies and near-bankruptcies of noncompetitive Indian companies are on the rise. At the same time, healthy Indian companies that could lower their production costs with cheaper imported goods saw Delhi raise tariffs by three percent in 1997. Export growth might have been a useful counterweight to economic sluggishness at home, but excessive import tariffs, high transaction costs due to bureaucratic inefficiency and corruption, infrastructure bottlenecks, and an appreciating rupee made Indian exports too expensive.

Fourth, uncertainty about Indian macroeconomic policy worries investors and managers. Business plans in India have generally been held hostage to unpredictable cycles of inflation caused by government spending, followed by liquidity squeezes to contain it. Delhi has not yet taken the steps that would break the resulting long-term inflation expectations of investors. It reduced the fiscal deficit from a high of almost ten percent of GDP in the early 1990s to about half that by last year. Much of this progress has been achieved, however, by increasing revenues rather than by reducing government expenditures. Subsidies, which primarily benefit middle-class farmers and cost 15 percent of GDP, have generally not been reduced. Support for public-sector enterprises, most of which lose money, has been cut but remains a major drain on government funds. Government salaries were hiked in 1997, a move that may eventually cost as much as five percent of GDP a year without reducing the size of government. As a result, the 1997–98 deficit is likely to be well above five percent of GDP.

Fifth, India needs greater labor market flexibility to make its companies more competitive and its economy more productive. Politically powerful labor unions have stifled most efforts at serious reform or privatization of India's largest public sector enterprises, including most banks, all insurance companies, and many major industries—even though privatization would probably cost the jobs of no more than 1.1 percent of the urban labor market. India's labor laws hinder efficiency and growth.

Finally, foreign investment in India, while much increased in recent years, remains far too low. Foreign direct investment approvals have soared since reform began, from 5.3 billion rupees in 1991 to 361 billion in 1996, but the cumulative actual flows have been only one-fifth of the amount approved. In contrast, approved FDI to China has been eight to ten times India's in recent years, and actual flows as a percentage of approvals have been twice India's.

This FDI performance has not even met Delhi's goals—a disappointment born of bureaucratic delays, unclear regulations, and investors' fears of inconstancy from the central government. In the past year, a number of high-profile disputes, including a spat between the Indian government and Suzuki over management of their joint automotive venture, have further diminished investor confidence. And now foreign business leaders will be watching closely to see whether a BJP-led government will keep its promise to implement more restrictive policies on outside investment.

ORPHANED REFORMS

THE REFORM agenda faces growing resistance from both right and left. Powerful Indian industries are now feeling the competitive heat and looking for cover, including anti-takeover legislation, a slowdown of tariff reductions, and aggressive antidumping measures. Both the BJP and Congress have said that they favor protecting Indian businesses for at least five years. Meanwhile, the left will continue to defend fiercely its organized labor base, to which the BJP owes little.

Economic nationalism may be regaining its respectability. The combination of the BJP's ascendancy and the lessons of East Asia's economic crisis has given new currency to Indian protectionism, from delaying capital account convertibility to increasing restrictions on foreign investment to slowing tariff reductions. After the election, one BJP leader said India had to liberalize and modernize before it could globalize. A BJP government would no doubt try to be pragmatic on these issues, at least at first; Vajpayee wants foreign investment in some sectors and is loath to renege on India's World Trade Organization commitments. But chauvinist ideology and responsible government are difficult to reconcile.

Political instability and gridlock in Delhi may frustrate restructuring, as they have in Japan. A BJP dependent on more than a dozen parties for its political survival will find it hard to enact even those reforms it favors. Populism remains a staple of state-level politics, and many of the regional and caste-based parties with which the BJP may ally will be wary of policies affecting such key constituencies as civil servants or farmers. Given the current fragmented state of India's national politics, this would be a problem even if Congress and the United Front were to form a government.

So the political base for reform remains narrow. The only significant constituency for reform is the urban middle class, which is at most a quarter of the electorate. By contrast, almost 60 percent of India's electorate is from the rural lower castes, and only a handful of these voters have even heard of the reforms. But the next stage of the reform process, which will create many more losers—notably public sector employees and subsidy recipients—will require a broader base of support than the first stage.

The international environment for reform may be worsening. True, India has been spared the worst of the East Asian troubles because of its lower dependence on exports, healthier current account balance, modest short-term debt, and the limited convertibility of the rupee. But the danger has not yet passed. Currency depreciations in East Asia are forcing the prices of tradable goods down, further threatening Indian producers and fanning protectionist sentiment. If the new government reverses course and lets the rupee depreciate, it will have to deal with higher inflation, especially if it also chooses to prime the pump with increased government spending. Direct investment from East Asia will suffer, and more cautious portfolio investors may shy away from India.

REMEMBER THE POOR

OVERCOMING THE obstacles to further economic reform will be a long and challenging process. Few observers in 1991 would have predicted that India would come as far as it has. But until now, Indian leaders have generally followed a "reform by stealth" strategy to avoid arousing opposition. This is neither desirable nor possible in the next phase. To build support for restructuring, Indian leaders will need to broaden the reforms and sell them to India's people.

The reforms must be seen to benefit India's huge rural, lower-caste population. Without their support, agricultural subsidies cannot be reduced or eventually eliminated. In the end, the most important constituency for the reforms is the rural poor, whose increasing political participation and rising economic expectations must be accommodated to maintain political stability.

The next phase of reform must therefore give greater attention to improving agriculture, which grew at an annual average of only 3.6 percent from 1991 to 1997 despite a series of favorable monsoon seasons. Higher growth and incomes can be attained relatively simply by deregulation and by investing in rural infrastructure. Social spending must also increase. Improvements in health, education, the water supply, and sanitation will have both immediate and long-term payoffs. While public investment here has been growing, it could increase dramatically if other government expenditures were brought under control. Finally, widening economic disparities between India's regions and states, particularly the fast-growing west and south and the slow-growing east and north, could become a ticking time bomb. Market-friendly measures to narrow these gaps without cutting off growth could pay major dividends in support for reform.

As India approaches the close of its 50th year of independence, it has, by any reasonable standard, done quite well

at nation-building. The two most important objectives of Gandhi and Nehru in August 1947—political viability and national integrity—have been met. The recent political and economic reforms will, if successful, strengthen the Indian body politic and improve the living standards of close to a billion citizens. Achieving these goals will require a degree of vision and courage from today's leaders even greater than that of India's founders.

Article 9

The World Today, May 1998

STILL A COLD WAR

Maleeha Lodhi

Apart from the Middle East, South Asia is the world's most daunting challenge to conflict resolution and the promotion of peace. Nearly a fifth of humanity lives on the Subcontinent, and the peace dividend could be enormous, as is the mounting cost of the absence of peace. The threat to international peace and security is all the more ominous since both Pakistan and India are nuclear-capable states, and Pakistan has just countered India's missiles by successfully testing a medium range one of its own.

WHILE THE END of the Cold War has provided momentum to resolve disputes and negotiate peace, South Asia remains mired in its own cold war. Can it break out of fifty years of hostility, conflict and confrontation—is it ready for peace?

By the logic of contemporary global trends, the answer should be yes. The importance of economic development, cooperation and trade in the post cold war world, coupled with the complex challenges of globalisation, should urge India and Pakistan to live together in an increasingly interdependent world. They should try to overcome differences and enter the mainstream of international life, concentrating on trade and economic modernisation rather than political confrontation and low intensity conflict.

DR MALEEHA LODHI, Editor of *The News,* Pakistan's leading English daily paper, was Ambassador to the US (1994–1997).

But this is not going to be easy just because it is politically correct and reasonable. This article seeks to identify factors that can help promote cooperative behaviour and also lists those that can and do fuel confrontation and antagonism. Three possible scenarios are mapped for the future, and steps suggested to realise the most attractive.

PERSISTENT ANIMOSITY

The history of animosity between the neighbours, spawned by the bloody partition of 1947, is too well known to merit detailed elaboration, but a number of factors promote conflict.

The Indian leadership has persistently questioned Pakistan's rationale for existence and viability. It views the country as an unfortunate but temporary breach in the strategic unity of the subcontinent. Compounding Pakistan's sense of vulnerability was the lack of empathy, much less enthusiasm, from the rest of the world.

Pakistan was born during the growing East-West confrontation. While the West lamented the division of India, Soviet leader Joseph Stalin contemptuously dismissed the new state of Pakistan as primitive, since it was created on the basis of religion. This incipient hostility contributed further to Pakistan's sense of being beleaguered.

Pakistan's fear of Indian hostility and domination was reinforced by Delhi's behaviour during and after partition. The incorporation into the Indian Union of several princely states, most notably Kashmir, underscored the tendency to use force.

India's self image as the natural postcolonial inheritor of the British, and its belief in the strategic unity of the subcontinent, fuelled the impulse to regional domination. This in turn generated tensions and exacerbated Pakistan's fears and security anxieties. This antagonism crystallised into the early conflict over Kashmir, the centrepiece of the unfinished business of partition.

Given the imbalance of power, Pakistan looked for allies or alignments outside the region to reduce its acute sense of vulnerability. Its membership of western alliances in the mid-fifties, and links with the United States, were intended to provide a counterweight against India. Close ties to Washington gave Islamabad a sense of strategic belonging and helped mitigate chronic insecurity.

Pakistan's strategic partnership with the US was matched by India's alignment with the Soviet Union and its allies. But this drove the region into the vortex of Cold War superpower conflict, magnifying tensions and rivalry.

The military build up by both India and Pakistan, aided by their great power benefactors, set in train a dangerous and open-ended arms race. The two countries fought three wars—two over Kashmir, while the third in 1971 culminated in the break up of Pakistan. This confirmed Pakistan's worst fears about India, and brought home sharply the limitations of its strategy of borrowing power from external alignments to contain the threat. Pakistan was compelled to find a way to provide its own security.

The arrival of the nuclear factor qualitatively transformed the region's security environment. The international community has had a rather skewed view of the nuclear race, focusing much of its attention on Pakistan's programme. In fact India's pursuit of 'dual use' nuclear capability began at least two decades before Pakistan's programme and was driven by a desire for great power status.

India's nuclear test of May 1974 put the region inescapably on the path of nuclear competition with both countries acquiring nuclear weapons capability. But while there were no international penalties or embargoes on India's efforts to acquire nuclear status, Pakistan repeatedly faced discriminatory sanctions and embargoes by the United States, many of which are still in place.

Pakistan's acquisition, against heavy odds, of what many regard as a strategic equaliser to India's preponderant military strength, brought a degree of deterrence stability to the region by making the costs of conflict unacceptably high. This has made another conventional war virtually unthinkable.

AN OPEN SPACE

Before turning to the sources of conflict and cooperation, it is necessary to consider these in the context of the present political and security environment.

With the end of the cold war, both India and Pakistan have been bereft of the psychological props provided by their superpower patrons. Great power withdrawal has opened political space which India wants to fill to realise its regional ambitions and great power aspirations. This has aggravated Pakistan's security dilemma.

A 'hot' war rages over Kashmir with Indian repression of the Kashmiri people involving heavy military force. There are regular exchanges of fire on the Line of Control which divides Indian controlled Kashmir from Pakistan administered Azad (Free) Kashmir. There is a stand-off on the Siachen glacier, described as the world's highest and most inhospitable battleground.

OPAQUE DETERRENCE

Deterrence prevails, with presumed nuclear capabilities which could be turned into weapons and deployed in a very short time. This unique form of deterrence has variously been described as non-weaponised, shadow, or recessed deterrence. Its special nature lies in nuclear programmes which have moved beyond the mere acquisition of technical capability.

The absence since 1990 of any serious preparations for war by either country is usually ascribed in the subcontinent to the effective operation of 'opaque deterrence'. This raises the question of whether deterrence is sustainable at this non-deployed level, and if this form of deterrence can be managed to prevent escalation to potentially destabilising levels.

In the nineties, there has been an 'on-off', 'start-stumble-stop' pattern to bilateral dialogue. This is produced by a mutual lack of faith in bilateral talks, which have been held more in response to external pressure than a popular, domestic yearning for peace. Small wonder then that, so far, normalisation efforts have been a series of false starts.

India is trying to further develop and enhance its military capabilities. This is evident in the acquisitions of conventional arms from Russia, as well as its ambitious missile development programme and efforts to secure anti-ballistic theatre missile defenses (TMDs). This in turn is creating compulsions for Pakistan to make matching responses.

Lastly, the military build-up has been accompanied by Indian efforts to extend its power into the global arena in seeking permanent membership of the UN Security Council. In Pakistan's perception, these are manifestations of India's long-standing ambition for great power status. Combined with Delhi's inflexibility on outstanding disputes, these assertions of regional dominance are not reassuring signals for Islamabad.

GUJRAL DOCTRINE

The so-called Gujral doctrine applied during former Prime Minister IK Gujral's brief stint in power, marked an effort to extend India's influence in its neighbourhood. This 'good neighbour' problem-solving approach towards Nepal, Bangladesh and Sri Lanka, explicitly excluded Pakistan. It was seen by Islamabad as an effort to isolate it in the region.

The Gujral doctrine was interpreted as part of India's push for power. By extricating itself from troubled relations in South Asia, Delhi was viewed as trying to achieve regional dominance by other means.

In this environment a number of factors have the potential to reinforce confrontation between the two neighbours.

On Kashmir there are mutually exclusive positions. With no solution in sight, escalation remains a clear and present danger. Lack of resolution of the dispute means that the insurgency might be radicalised and the Kashmir political leadership of the APHC (All Parties Hurriyat Conference) marginalised.

The habit of confrontation may allow rivalry and antagonism to spill over into new and multiple arenas. Delhi's current alignment with the anti government coalition in Afghanistan, to counter Pakistan's presumed backing for the Taliban, is a case in point. It is also a classic illustration of the old realpolitik notion of 'my enemy's enemy is my best friend'. Confrontation is also driven by domestic political considerations which use antagonism to retain or augment popular support.

The self images of the two neighbours are produced by history, religion and half a century's experience. India's image as the pre-eminent regional power and its belief in the strategic unity of the subcontinent, leads to expectations of how smaller states should behave. This conflicts with the smaller states' concept of their security, especially when fear of domination drives them to extra regional means to balance India. Counter reactions spur cycles of suspicion and confrontation which are hard to reverse.

Pakistan's self image as the natural leader in the Islamic world and pursuer of transcendental causes mirrors, in some respects, Indian images. These clashing views are seen as mutually threatening.

India's military activism and drive to maintain vast military disparities are interpreted as a means to confirm or validate its dominance over South Asia and beyond. Efforts by Pakistan to incrementally augment its conventional military strength are viewed with alarm by Delhi. This in turn reinforces Pakistan's view of India's ambitions.

There is competition for the new political space that has opened up around the region following the collapse of the Soviet Union. Rivalry for influence in Central Asia is already underway. Pakistan sees Delhi weighing in with Russian efforts to block its access to Central Asia.

At present India is aligned with Russia and other anti-Taliban forces against Pakistan in Afghanistan. In any future Sino-US competition or confrontation, India may offer itself as a strategic partner for Washington. Such a 'checkerboard' pattern of alignments in and beyond the region will obviously intensify not defuse Indo-Pakistan confrontation.

WORKING TOGETHER

South Asia is the only region—other than the Korean peninsula—bucking the trend towards the peaceful resolution of disputes. The end of superpower rivalry is helpful, as is the strong desire of the international community, led by the US, to avoid conflict between India and Pakistan and promote cooperation.

On the nuclear issue, there was cooperation between India and Pakistan at the UN Conference on Disarmament at Geneva in calling for negotiations on universal nuclear disarmament, and opposition to the Fissile Material Cutoff Treaty (FMCT), which was seen to be aimed only at Islamabad and Delhi. The two nations share a feeling of being discriminated against on this issue. They resist what they see as the campaign by the permanent five members of the Security Council to entrench their nuclear monopoly through anti-proliferation arrangements which are promoted as disarmament measures.

Common views are also developing on the imposition of an unequal trade and economic regime through bodies such as the World Trade Organisation and International Labour Organisation. Significantly, at the December 1996 conference of trade ministers in Singapore, it was India and Pakistan which alone held out until the last on such Western-sponsored 'new issues' as linking trade and labour standards and international rules on Investment and Competition Policy. In the North-South context the two nations view 'human rights' as a means of interference in the internal affairs of developing countries.

Regional trade and economics are creating shared interests but the obvious benefits of bilateral trade are offset at present by security considerations. As the smaller state, Pakistan's willingness to expand trade would depend on the creation of a level playing field since India has a much more restrictive import regime. The gains from trade need to be equally shared.

Pakistan is not unique among nations with acute security concerns being prepared to forego trade with its adversary if it is likely to accentuate imbalances of economic and political power. Nevertheless, patient dialogue can identify areas of mutual advantage.

There is a potential common interest in ensuring that Central Asia's resources and trade flow south to Pakistan and India and not west—through Iran, Turkey or Russia. This would need a review of the Indian posture on Afghanistan and a more fundamental revaluation by Delhi of its attitude toward Pakistan.

As both countries accelerate economic reform and liberalisation, there is a shared interest in projecting South Asia as a zone of peace and economic opportunity. With both trying to attract foreign investment, this interest—tempered by competition—will grow.

THREE FUTURES

What kind of future scenarios emerge? Three alternative scenarios can be suggested.

A 'Pax Indiana'—for lack of a better phrase—with a hierarchical regional system dominated by Delhi using its greater power. This would be acknowledged and endorsed by the US-led international community, and would mark a reincarnation of the discredited seventies notion of the 'regional influential' charged with maintaining stability.

At present this scenario appears unlikely. It is also untenable because since the 70s, India's bid to dominate has met with varying degrees of resistance from virtually all its neighbours. The scenario implies a situation of no war, no peace, but would be marked by high levels of tension and chronic instability as smaller states, especially Pakistan, resist and challenge Indian dominance.

A **'Strategic Confrontation'** scenario would be more of the same, with high potential for regional instability. Confrontation would be accentuated by competing coalitions or alignments—Indo-US vs Pakistan-China or Pak-US vs India-Russia. While a degree of balance would be created, it would continue to deprive South Asia of the peace dividend, retard its economic progress, and relegate the region to the backwaters of the global economy.

A **'Strategic Equilibrium and Accommodation'** would be achieved by negotiated solutions to disputes and differences, minimising confrontation while enlarging areas for cooperation. This would involve radical revisions of present perceptions and the self images of both India and Pakistan. It is obviously the most attractive yet most difficult scenario to realise.

India and Pakistan need to focus their energies on promoting the third scenario. The bilateral dialogue that resumed a year ago, after a three year hiatus, can usefully explore this. But as the three rounds of talks in March, June and September last year indicate, there is no fast track to normalisation. It is likely to be a complex, slow and extremely fragile process, critically dependent on domestic political developments in both countries.

To sustain this process and construct the difficult road to peace, differences will have to be resolved and cooperation promoted. This applies especially to three main items of the eight on the agreed agenda: Jammu and Kashmir; Peace and Security; and Trade and economic cooperation.

RESOLUTION OF DIFFERENCES

Given the sharply divergent positions of the two countries on Kashmir, no immediate solution is likely. A graduated approach is necessary. India must recognise that it cannot change Kashmiri minds by repression and force, and the Kashmiri militancy will have to acknowledge that it is not going to produce Indian 'withdrawal' through insurgency.

Efforts are required to promote a *genuine* political solution. Once both sides step back from their positions and recognise the centrality of the wishes of the Kashmiri people, many alternatives are possible. The first steps could be:

- the de-escalation of violence
- reduction of Indian troop numbers
- allowing 'people to people' contact and trade across the Line of Control
- a genuinely free election in Indian controlled Kashmir under international supervision—without the requirement for candidates to swear allegiance to India
- the involvement of 'elected' Kashmiri representatives in ongoing Indo-Pakistan negotiations. The sovereignty issue could be addressed at a second stage.

It is essential to redress the asymmetry of conventional arms capabilities. India would have to restrain its quantitative and qualitative build-up. Embargoes on Pakistan would have to be removed, enabling it to acquire the means to conventionally deter India's conventional superiority. Mutually agreed reductions and restraint to achieve a 'balance' may be explored.

There is a need for confidence building measures such as the redeployment of land, air and missile forces away from borders or forward positions, and the creation of zones free from offensive weapons.

On the nuclear issue, the aim should be to promote continued deterrence at the lowest possible level of capabilities. This implies decisions against weaponisation and deployment of nuclear capabilities. Restraint could encompass:

- a ban on nuclear testing to refine warheads
- no serial production or deployment of short-medium range missiles—those available should not be deployed
- eventual agreement to halt fissile material production when each side is 'comfortable' with its capacity.
- mutual assurance of non weaponisation and deployment of nuclear weapons.

The Indo-Pakistan dialogue can produce cooperation in several areas. It can promote more equitable international economic relations, and the revival of Indo-Pakistan leadership in the Group of 77 and the Non Aligned Movement. Bilateral trade and economic exchanges should be explored, along with transit trade. The South Asian Association of Regional Cooperation (SAARC) should be promoted as a genuine trade/economic bloc and cultural cooperation should be encouraged.

In the final analysis, the ability and will to change the direction and destiny of the region will be a test of leadership in both countries. The challenge of traversing unchartered ground is a daunting one, fraught with risks and fear of the unknown. Political inertia can also impede movement. This is where the international community can play a positive role by offering incentives for the peaceful resolution of the subcontinent's problems. International support can be provided both formally and informally; the UN, in any case, has long-standing formal responsibilities in Kashmir.

Article 10

The World & I, August 1998

India's Socioeconomic Makeover

by Richard Breyer

Namaste, Sony Entertainment Television. Please hold. Namaste, Sony . . ."

It's a hectic morning at the corporate headquarters of one of India's leading cable companies—and New Delhi's recent nuclear test explosions haven't caused the pace of business to miss a beat. Inside, secretaries juggle phone calls. Outside, in the crowded reception area, anxious young producers—men and women in their midtwenties—rehearse their pitches and plan power lunches on their mobile phones.

Off to the side, a large television set shows *I Dream of Jeannie.* Jeannie speaks Hindi, out of sync.

This is the new, post-1992 India— young, ambitious Indians in offices of multinational corporations; mobile phones; cable television; and Hollywood stars dubbed in Hindi.

In the old India, there was no cable television or mobile phones. Multinationals had to play by the government's Byzantine rules. Many stayed away.

And before the 1992 economic reforms, the young and the restless were not rehearsing pitches or doing power lunches. They were at the U.S. Consulate applying for a visa to study in the United States, or at the Ministry of Information meeting an uncle who would introduce them to the subsecretary in whose department there was an opening.

In 1992, India began dismantling its unique brand of socialism—part Soviet-style centrally planned, part British colonial bureaucracy. The country really had no choice. With the fall of the Soviet Union, India lost a major trading partner, political ally, and benefactor.

MIRACLE OF THE FREE MARKET

Before the reforms, most of the pillars of commerce—banks, utilities, airlines, trains, radio, and television—were government owned. High tariffs, inconvertibility of the rupee, limitations on foreign ownership, corruption, and exorbitant taxes kept foreign investors and multinationals away.

Today there are privately owned airlines, phone companies, and television channels. Foreign capital is being invested in India, and foreign corporations are setting up shop. There are more choices, more jobs, more money flowing into the country and into the pockets of the well-educated, well-connected urban middle and upper classes—stockbrokers, airline executives, copywriters, computer programmers, shop owners, and TV producers.

Five years ago it was difficult to find pizzas, jeans and Walkmans in India. Today Domino's, Levi's, and Sony have outlets in most major cities. India's af-fluent can shop at malls and supermarkets, watch cable television, surf the Internet. Their children have Barbie dolls, *Star Wars* action figures, and video and computer games. To put it simply, India appears to be becoming more Western.

Is this good or bad? It depends on whom you talk to. The upper 5 percent, whose horizons are broader and pockets are deeper as a result of this trend, are very pleased. Followers of Mahatma Gandhi give it a thumbs down, arguing that Walkmans and pizza have little to do with self-sufficiency and simplicity.

Others are concerned that a relative few will benefit from these changes. India's population is nearing a billion. A third are poor—some very poor. The saddest cases are in cities, where millions live in, to Western eyes, garbage heaps.

In the new, more open economy, the gap between the haves (200 million at the most) and have-nots (300 million at least) will likely increase. The majority of the poor simply do not have the resources or opportunities to participate in the new order, but the communications revolution will make them more aware of what they're missing.

In Indian cities, at an intersection or stoplight, it is quite common to see a primitive oxcart next to a Mercedes. In the past, the oxcart driver did not envy—and probably did not even see— the Mercedes and its well-dressed owner in the back. If India's consumer-based culture is anything like the West's, however, in the future the poor will want essentially the same things as the rich.

Environmentalists are also concerned about the changes in culture and economy. Currently, Indians consume one-thirtieth of the nonrenewable resources of their counterparts in the West: one-

Up and Coming India

In 1992, with the Soviet apron strings cut, India began to dismantle its socialist system—part Soviet-style central planning, part British colonial bureaucracy.

The advent of the free market has brought an unprecedented expansion of the middle class, which is now over 200 million strong.

Still, at least 300 million people remain mired in desperate poverty.

But while televisions, jeans, pizzas, and Walkmans have proliferated, Indian families remain large and extended, with at least three generations living in one household—and many marriages are still arranged.

thirtieth the electricity, plastics, and paper products.

In rural India, cow dung is used as fuel and fertilizer and oxen for transportation. There is no refrigeration or packaged goods. Most villagers brush their teeth with neem tree branches. The neem tree has a natural antibacterial sap that works just as well as commercial toothpaste.

GROWING PAINS

In the new India, villagers, especially the young, will probably want Colgate, a Honda motor scooter, a John Deere tractor—someday a Ford. But if India's 1 billion—who live in a country a third the size of the United States—begin to consume like America's 260 million, there will be a catastrophe. India does not have the resources to produce the goods and services required to sustain a Western-style consumer economy.

So with development comes problems, new challenges. What else is new? Like other modern countries, India faces explosions of expectations and threats to its traditional culture. The question is not, will India change? It is, how deeply and how rapidly?

Bombay, the economic hub of the country, is a good place to ponder this question. The city has million-dollar condominiums and luxurious five-star hotels. It also has slums with sewage running through them.

And there are millions of middle-class Indians who will never set foot in a five-star hotel or a slum. But, like middle-class Indians throughout the subcontinent, they will set foot in appliance stores, buy a television set, and pay 200 rupees ($6) a month to have it hooked up to "cable."

The viewing habits of this important sector of society offer clues to what post-1992 India is becoming.

Cable television arrived in India at about the same time the government opened up its markets to the West, in the early 1990s. CNN's coverage of the Persian Gulf War was a key factor in cable's expansion. Indians had thousands of relatives working in the Gulf region, and their well-being was of great interest to their families back home.

Bombay, the economic hub of the country, has million-dollar condos and luxurious five-star hotels. It also has slums with sewage running through them

---

After the war, Indians stayed connected. At that time, the only cable channel available in India was Hong Kong-based Star-TV, which offered only English-language programs. After years of being deprived of Western popular culture, urban middle-class Indians could now feast on MTV, *Oprah*, and *Baywatch*.

RESISTING THE HOLLYWOOD CULTURE

The common wisdom among media types was that it would be just a matter of time before English programming, most of it produced in Hollywood, would take over Indian screens and, eventually, its culture—or, at least, the culture of the young. It was just a matter of time, critics warned, before teenagers in New Delhi and Madras would look, sound, and act like VJs on MTV or before young professionals in Bombay and Bangalore would behave like those on *The Bold and the Beautiful.*

However, when Doordarshan, the national broadcasting system, and new cable companies began to offer high-quality programs in regional languages, a different scenario unfolded. Viewers switched to films, musical shows, sitcoms, and soaps in Hindi, Tamil, and other "local" languages.

The only Hollywood-made programs that earn reasonable ratings are those that are dubbed. For example, *Who's the Boss, Dennis the Menace,* and *I Dream of Jeannie* in Hindi have loyal fans, but their numbers are nothing compared with the "channel drivers" produced in Bollywood—the hip name for Bombay, India's film and television capital.

The issue of language is complicated in India. Hindi is the official national language and the tongue of the wealthy north, which includes Bombay and New Delhi, the capital of the country. However, it is only 1 of 14 major languages and hundreds of dialects. Each of the 14 languages is part of a distinct culture with its own traditions and literature, which includes radio and television programs and, in some cases, regional film industries.

There is a Hindi film industry that makes films in Hindi, and there are Hindi cable television channels. There are also cable channels and film industries making and distributing products in other "local" languages—Tamil, Telugu, Gujarati, and so forth.

English is an important linking language, used across the country for business, scholarship, and medicine. Cable companies offer ESPN, CNBC, Discovery, and the BBC in English, but these channels get very low ratings. Most Indians—even those fluent in English—

prefer their music, films, television, and radio in their regional language. Why? Language is the glue that holds together that which is sacred to Indians—family, region, and class.

TRADITIONAL FAMILIES AND MARRIAGES

With few exceptions, Indian families are large and extended, with at least three generations living in one household. Elders have very high status and play central roles in the family. In many cases, they provide the roof over their children's and grandchildren's heads.

It is common for newlyweds to move in with parents rather than go off on their own. "Grannies" raise the young, teaching family traditions and language, while parents pursue their careers.

With one television set per household in India, grandparents also have a great deal of say about what the family watches. This clearly has much to do with the popularity of programs in Hindi, Tamil, and Bengali and the poor ratings of English-language programs.

India's multilingualism is a key ingredient of the nation's rigid class and caste systems—systems that, among other things, help sustain a dependable and inexpensive pool of servants who make the lives of upper-class Indians quite comfortable.

There are few opportunities for members of the lower classes to learn English. Those who attend school are taught only their local language. Employers speak to their cooks, drivers, guards, "tea boys," and nannies in Tamil or Hindi or Bengali. As a result, there is no need or impetus for those in the lower classes to learn English. In fact, in many instances there are pressures for them not to learn a second, "foreign" language, for this would be interpreted as rejecting one's community and culture.

Without English, there is little opportunity for social or economic mobility. A guard, sweeper, or bus driver who speaks only Tamil or Hindi will do the same work all his life. And there is a good chance that his son will do the same work as he.

This is also true for mothers and daughters. A washerwoman, house cleaner, or seamstress who speaks only her regional language has little chance to

India

Official Name: Republic of India.

Capital: New Delhi.

Geography: Area: 1.22 million square miles (about one-third the size of the United States). Location: Occupies the bulk of South Asia's Indian subcontinent. Neighbors: Pakistan on west; China, Nepal, and Bhutan on north; Burma and Bangladesh on east.

Climate/Topography: The highest mountains in the world, the Himalayas, dominate India's northern border. South of that, the wide, fertile Ganges Plain is one of the world's most densely populated areas. Just below is the Deccan Peninsula. About one-quarter of India is forested. The climate ranges from the south's tropical heat to the north's frigid cold. In the northwest is the arid Rajasthan Desert. By contrast, 400 inches of rain fall annually on the northeast's Assam Hills.

People: Population: 970 million. Ethnic groups: Indo-Aryan, 72 percent, Dravidian, 25 percent; Mongoloid and other, 3 percent. Principal languages: Hindi (official), English (associate official), 14 regional languages, hundreds of dialects.

Religions: Hindu, 80 percent; Muslim, 14 percent; Sikh, 2 percent; Christian, 2 percent.

Education: Literacy: 52 percent.

Economy: Industries: textiles, steel, processed foods, cement, machinery, chemicals, mining, autos. Chief crops: rice, grains, sugar, spices, tea, cashews, cotton, potatoes, jute, linseed. Minerals: coal, iron, manganese, mica, bauxite, titanium, chromite, diamonds, gas, oil. Crude oil reserves: 4.3 billion barrels. Arable land: 55 percent. Per capital GDP: $1,500.

Government: Federal republic.

change her status or the status of her children and move up the economic ladder.

WEARING NIKES BENEATH SARIS

Language plays a very different role in the lives of the middle and upper classes—and their children. They have unlimited opportunities. Because 99 percent know English, they can practice their professions or do business in any region of the country or in most parts of the world. They can also live in both traditional and modern India—yuppies with arranged marriages, enjoying pizza as much as chapati, wearing Nikes under their saris.

Language and regional loyalties are not the only reasons upper-and middle-class Indians stay connected to their traditions. Another factor is that they simply don't need many of the things the West has to offer.

At construction sites, it is common for laborers to crush boulders by hand with sledgehammers to make gravel. This would make no sense in the West—too labor-intensive, too expensive, very inefficient. But in India, this way of doing things provides employment for 40 people who need the work.

Western-style supermarkets, and the culture that goes with them, have little appeal to middle-and upper-class Indians living in neighborhoods where street vendors sell high-quality fruits, vegetables, dairy products, and other staples door-to-door. Labor-saving devices—washing machines, dishwashers, power tools, and the like—are of relatively little value in a country with hundreds of millions of people willing and able to do manual labor.

But in some sectors, the old ways are changing. To participate in the global economy, India's banks, investment companies, and media have to modernize. Foreign manufacturers and mutual funds are investing in India because they are convinced that 200 million middle-class Indians are about to become Western-style consumers. They may be correct.

In downtown Bombay, New Delhi, and Madras, shoppers use American Express and Visa cards to pay their bills. Bankers sit in front of computer termi-nals finalizing car loans and home mort-gages. Producers edit Pepsi, Nike, and Honda commercials on digital editing systems, then uplink them to satellites. From there they travel to television sets across the country.

These new technologies are changing India—especially urban India—but not such much as to put street vendors, ser-vants, and grandparents, and the culture they help maintain, out of business.

Stay tuned.

Richard Breyer is chairman of the Television, Radio, and Film Department at the S.I. Newhouse School of Public Communications at Syracuse University. He has been a Fulbright scholar to India twice.

Article 11   *Populi*, June 1998

India: Globalized Economy, Victimized Workers?

by Sharmila Joshi

What does a globalized economy mean for India's women workers? A recent study suggests that there are more threats than opportunities for women in the current process of liberalization. Traditionally an under-paid, exploited and unorganized group, women employees in many Indian industries have found that the restructuring of their workplaces has virtually restructured their lives.

Let us take, for instance, Sushama, a skilled worker in an electronics factory in the Okhla Industrial Area of Delhi. In mid-1995, she found that her job, along with that of many co-workers', had been downgraded to an unskilled, less-paid category. Ratni, Gayatri and Sandhya, from another electronics factory in the area, found themselves locked out, after 20 years of work, along with 200 other workers, some of whom were retrenched with a 'final settlement'.

In the diamond-processing and jewellery industry in Mum-bai, the city formerly known as Bombay, women workers have had to juggle household budgets to live through the 1990s decade of rising prices and reduced real incomes. This has included reductions in medical and food expenditure, at great costs to their health.

"Several studies have pointed out, and our study confirms, that in policies like the Structural Adjustment Programme or the Indian version of it, the New Economic Policy, it is often households, and much more often the women of the household, who have to play the role of a buffer," writes Sujata Gothoskar, co-author of an extensive report on the effects of industrial restructuring on women workers, at home and in the work-place. The report is the outcome of a three-year (1993–96) research project which covered 610 women workers in five industries: pharmaceuticals, plastics, soaps and detergents, gems and jewellery in Mumbai and electronics in Delhi. The four researchers—Ms. Gothoskar, Amrita Chhachhi, Nandita Gandhi and Nandita Shah—also interviewed male workers, employers, managers and trade unionists.

The five industries were chosen from available data from the Factory Inspectorate for National Industrial Classification. The choice was based on several factors: industries with sig-nificant changes in the proportion of women employees over the years and those employing many women affected by in-dustrial restructuring.

The report examines the effects of an increasingly "flexible" market and points out that newer forms of adjustments now overlap older ones such as lax labour regulations and easy availability of labour. The new flexibility encourages changes in the organizational structure of a firm through subcontract-ing.

"A major impetus for subcontracting was lower labour costs and an attempt to avoid dealing with a unionized workforce," writes Ms. Chhachhi, who studied Delhi's electronics industry, which employs 45,000 workers, up to 40 per cent of whom are women. The number is expected to grow, according to Ms. Chhachhi, as labour force flexibility increases and industries seek more "exploitable" workers. New forms of flexibility also promote changes in the pattern of production through the manufacture of customized products, automation and changes in job categories; job rotation; and the training of workers for multiple jobs.

The new policies have changed legal regulations and prac-tices to make it easier for management to hire and fire workers.

They have further casualized labour and restricted workers' rights to organize themselves. For instance, due to economic reform, the electronics industry was opened almost completely to global competition. "By 1996, domestic manufacturers had begun to change their attitudes towards multinational corporations (MNCs)," writes Ms. Chhachhi. "Now, there is talk of foreign friends, partnership and collaboration. Behind the scenes, domestic manufacturers engaged in yet another phase of restructuring to meet the challenge of the MNCs by introducing more 'flexibility' in the organizational structure as well as in the production of items."

The research report reveals that in the five industries, 63 per cent of the workers were non-permanent, with an attendant absence of labour rights. Only 28 per cent had written contracts, while the rest had verbal ones. Besides, 56 per cent had no unions in their workplaces, 14 per cent had some form of informal groups and only 29 per cent worked in unionized units.

In the pharmaceuticals, soaps and cosmetics industries in Mumbai, automation, a ban on new permanent recruitment, the replacement of permanent staff with contract workers, retrenchment and other strategies, have had a direct impact on women workers. "What were earlier stable, well-paying jobs, are now being converted into sweat-shop jobs," writes Ms. Gothoskar.

Who are the women working in these industries? The younger ones are in small- and medium-scale units: women in their 20s, in their first jobs, neither permanent nor unionized. Older women, with a greater degree of unionization and politicization—because of long years of factory work and a strongly developed worker identity—are being phased out.

Some industries are giving more work to employees at home. "This provides a flexible workforce which can be deployed without any overhead cost to the employer," writes Ms. Shah, who studied the plastics processing industry in Mumbai. Such home-based work includes assembly of toys, switches, toothbrushes and scooter parts. Of the home-based workers, 45.8 per cent spend their own money on equipment and part of the raw materials and 41.1 per cent do not take even a single day's break. "The low pay rate forced employees to work as much as they could. The majority of women were working all year round," writes Ms. Shah.

UNFPA/Vivianne Moos

An Indian electronics factory worker.

A casual, unorganized workforce ensures lower wages and benefits, according to the study. In the plastic processing industry, 88.3 per cent of the 180 women surveyed came from families with a per-capita income of less than 950 rupees a month [39.44 rupees:US$1]. As many as 86.7 per cent of the workers received less than the average minimum wage.

"With the tussle between family expenditure and insufficient income, any small or big crises sent these workers over the brink and into debt," writes Ms. Shah. "The price rise has affected 97.8 per cent of households negatively. They had to cut down their expenses."

This included 46.6 per cent who had cut down on food items and 28.3 per cent who were buying cheaper food. In more than 10 per cent of the families, the women were eating less food. All this while coping with work at home and in the factory, and facing an uncertain future.

The three-year study also looks at the job loss experience of 46 workers, men and women, in the electronics industry in Delhi. Most had worked for 10–20 years in the same unit, and 42 per cent were below 30 years of age, contrary to the belief that only older workers are being phased out. Compensation for retrenchment ranged from 9,000 to 65,000 rupees.

"The money for most of the workers disappeared overnight. For over half, it was spent on domestic expenditure," write Ms. Chhachhi and Ms. Gothoskar. As many as 26 per cent of the jobless workers belonged to single-income families. Due to the drastic cut in family income, 43 per cent were buying cheaper food and 48 per cent had reduced the number of meals they ate daily. One worker said: "Earlier, we were two earners, now we can barely get two *rotis* a day."

After two years of job loss, 41 per cent of the workers interviewed were still unemployed, 37 per cent self-employed and 9 per cent had irregular jobs. Only two workers, one man and one woman, had again landed permanent jobs in an electronics factory.

Job loss has also meant loss of identity and dignity. Ms. Gayatri, now in her late 40s, misses the company of other workers and the joy of earning an income. "The future is bleak for us," she said. "Only this house and the tenancy keep us going, and my husband's pension helps. But it's not like working and earning, which had given me so much confidence."

"For retrenched workers from the organized sector, the loss of a regular, stable job with benefits won over years creates a different kind of trauma," write Ms. Chhachhi and Ms. Gothoskar. "They are unable to enter the lower levels of the unorganized sector, given a strong sense of worker identity as organized sector workers."

One worker said: "It is very difficult to run a house with two growing sons. My husband retired at the same time as when our factory closed. I cannot think of working as a domestic servant. After so many years of work experience, I cannot join a new factory only to be dismissed after six months of being a casual worker. I do not know what to do. What is the result of so many years of hard work?"

What, indeed? Years spent labouring, painstakingly juggling incomes and expenditure, hoping for brighter days, have come to nought. Drastic macro-level economic policies have crushed their hopes. For these invisible victims, what are the benefits of a Brave New Economic India, what is the use of better television sets and lipsticks?

Article 12

Far Eastern Economic Review, August 21, 1997

ECONOMIES

Life in the Slow Lane

India has discarded much of its socialist baggage since 1991, but it's also showing signs of reform fatigue. Unless it can pick up the pace, it stands little chance of becoming Asia's next tiger.

By Dan Biers and Shiraz Sidhva
in New Delhi and Bombay

For just a moment, P. Chidambaram puts his mind on fast forward. Midway through an interview in his spacious New Delhi office, India's finance minister is envisioning what his country might look like in 20 years if it follows the path of sustained high growth already travelled by its East Asian counterparts. The India he foresees has a giant economy and modest per-capita income, and is free from the grinding poverty that has haunted it for a century. It leads in two dozen industries—maybe more—and is a centre for research and development. Its farmers feed its billion-plus population while exporting food to scores of other countries.

It's a compelling vision, and not necessarily a pipe dream. After all, the 51-year-old Chidambaram, who holds a Harvard MBA, isn't often given to idle speculation. And if it were up to him alone, his vision would become reality.

"The power is in our hands, the choice is ours," says the bespectacled former lawyer, impatiently twirling a pen atop a desk cluttered with a calculator, a budget-at-a-glance booklet and other tools of his trade. "We have to wait and see whether we exercise that choice wisely."

The core of Chidambaram's strategy is simple: broadening the six-year-old programme of market reforms already responsible for nearly doubling India's notoriously slow "Hindu rate of growth" to a respectable 7% a year. Yet today even Chidambaram puts India's chances of success at only 50–50, longer odds than he would have given a few years back, when the country was enjoying the first flush of rapid economic growth. And he's not alone in making such a reassessment: Throughout the nation there is a growing realization that much still needs to be done if India is to become one of Asia's economic tigers, and there are mounting concerns that the country's fractious coalition government simply isn't up to the task.

For signs of unease, look no further than Suresh Rajpal, head of Hewlett-Packard's India operations. It's been eight years since he returned to India to establish a subsidiary for the big American computer maker, and his self-confessed optimism has made him an articulate cheerleader for India's potential. Today, however, his tone is a bit subdued. "At this stage, I'm concerned," he says. "I expected us to be further ahead today than we are."

The numbers tell the story; progress, yes, but the pep is missing. The Indian juggernaut is moving faster than it was before reforms, but it's still not burning any rubber. Trade growth, for example, fell in the year to March 31 after a run of sharp increases triggered by steep tar-

HALF FULL, HALF EMPTY

India has liberalized significantly since 1991, but it must do more to catch
up with East Asia economies.

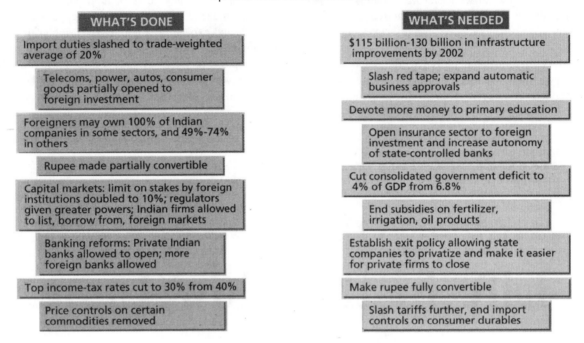

WHAT'S DONE

Import duties slashed to trade-weighted average of 20%

Telecoms, power, autos, consumer goods partially opened to foreign investment

Foreigners may own 100% of Indian companies in some sectors, and 49%-74% in others

Rupee made partially convertible

Capital markets: limit on stakes by foreign institutions doubled to 10%; regulators given greater powers; Indian firms allowed to list, borrow from, foreign markets

Banking reforms: Private Indian banks allowed to open; more foreign banks allowed

Top income-tax rates cut to 30% from 40%

Price controls on certain commodities removed

WHAT'S NEEDED

$115 billion-130 billion in infrastructure improvements by 2002

Slash red tape; expand automatic business approvals

Devote more money to primary education

Open insurance sector to foreign investment and increase autonomy of state-controlled banks

Cut consolidated government deficit to 4% of GDP from 6.8%

End subsidies on fertilizer, irrigation, oil products

Establish exit policy allowing state companies to privatize and make it easier for private firms to close

Make rupee fully convertible

Slash tariffs further, end import controls on consumer durables

iff reductions. Export growth, a pillar of development for the rest of Asia, fell to 4.1% from 21% the year before, according to the World Bank. Other Asian countries have also experienced sluggishness, but have tended to blame poor markets abroad. India's government, by contrast, acknowledges that the initial impact of trade liberalization appears to be petering out.

As for imports, tariff reductions haven't been nearly as dramatic recently as in the early years of reform. The average import-weighted tariff fell from a whopping 87% in fiscal 1990–91 to about 25% four years later. The World Bank estimates it will be 20.3% this year. But that's still well above the norm for East Asia. Some businessmen complain about duties on capital goods, the imported machines that Indian industry needs to make it more competitive. O.P. Lohia, managing director of Indo Rama Synthetics, insists the rates are too high, at about 20%. "That must be abolished immediately," says Lohia, whose family also owns factories in Southeast Asia. "Those goods are needed to make India more efficient."

India would also be far more competitive if it made faster progress reducing the fiscal deficit, which stood at a high 5% of GDP last year. Economists say the government should cut spending on subsidies, which account for up to 15% of GDP and cover everything from fertilizer and electricity to the cheap, rationed food that even wealthy citizens avail of. Many say the state should get out of loss-making public enterprises altogether. These measures would stimulate private-sector investment by lowering interest rates and help free up money for vital infrastructure projects.

From Chidambaram on down, everyone agrees that infrastructure is India's Achilles' heel—from its chronic power shortages to its clogged ports and inadequate road and rail networks. The volume of cargo transported by road has risen more than 60-fold in the past four decades, passenger traffic more than 70-fold. But the road network has grown only five times, and then mostly in rural areas. The national highway system is only 1.7 times its 1951 length.

India's 150 ports are also overburdened. Most handle about 20% more cargo than they were built for, and none has been modernized in decades. The average turnaround time for Indian ports is seven days (queues can last weeks), compared with six to eight hours for modern shipping hubs such as Hong Kong, Singapore and Colombo.

Government officials readily acknowledge the desperate need for more power, but electricity generation is growing at a painfully inadequate pace. New thermal plants added 800 megawatts to the country's 85,000-megawatt total in the last fiscal year, and another 3,000 are to come on-line this fiscal year. But according to the *India Development Report 1997*, published by the autonomous Indira Gandhi Institute of Development Research, India needs an additional 35,000–50,000 megawatts within the next five years if it's to sustain economic growth.

The power situation is grim, and unlikely to improve in a hurry. "India is facing an imminent crisis in infrastructure," warns a World Bank report released in May. "Unless investment in infrastructure expands significantly, India's emerging infrastructure crisis may prevent the country from sustaining the high levels of growth that the last few years have shown to be within reach."

HP is a case in point. It was considering India and several other Asian countries as the site for a new $400 million inkjet-printer factory that would have been the country's largest foreign electronics investment ever. Yet HP dropped India as a contender "mainly because of logistics," says Rajpal. The competitive advantages the country offers, such as cheap and skilled labour, would have been wiped out by costly delays due to road and port bottlenecks. Analysts say such constraints could put off more industries from locating their plants in India, and could even force some to leave altogether.

"Roads, ports and the railway system are so overburdened that freight sometimes sits undelivered for days," says an executive in a large Japanese electronics company with an investment of $100 million in India. "We just cannot afford the delays caused, and it's unlikely we will make any new investment here."

Bureaucratic hassles are another problem bedeviling foreign investors. Sat Pal Khattar, a Sinaporean who has invested millions of dollars in India, notes a cooling of investor sentiment because "projects take too long to take off."

He should know. Just down the road from the international airport is the spanking new Radisson Hotel Delhi, in which Khattar, an ethnic Indian, has more than a quarter share. At first glance, everything seems just fine: There's a liveried doorman at the granite-and-marble front entrance, and waiters in black bow ties standing at the ready in the banquet hall inside. Down the corridor, tables are tastefully set in the I Ching, a Chinese restaurant that looks out onto a beautifully manicured garden, while the latest weight machines fill the fitness centre. The only thing missing is the guests.

They were to have started coming half a year ago, when the hotel was ready for occupancy and a staff of several hundred was hired. "It was supposed to open 12 days after I arrived" in December, says the front-office manager. But a last-minute bureaucratic snafu kept the doors shut. "The last six months have been wasted waiting for approvals that should have come a long time ago," says Khattar. Delhi authorities blame the delays on Radisson's failure to comply with licensing rules and a dispute over the hotel site.

To be fair, such tales are also common in China, but that doesn't seem to

have damped the ardour of foreign investors. China snares up to $40 billion a year in foreign direct investment. Much of the money has gone into factories that have brought in modern technologies and management skills, and made China—like its Southeast Asian

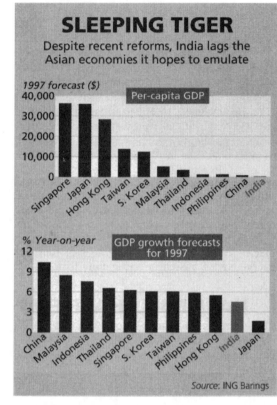

SLEEPING TIGER
Despite recent reforms, India lags the Asian economies it hopes to emulate

1997 forecast ($) — Per-capita GDP

% Year-on-year — GDP growth forecasts for 1997

Source: ING Barings

REVIEW GRAPHIC/RINGO CHUNG

neighbours—an export powerhouse. While India's FDI inflows are increasing, from a paltry $165 million in fiscal 1990–91 to about $2.6 billion in the year that ended March 31, they still pale in comparison with China's.

The Indian government's post–1991 policies have substantially relaxed regulations related to foreign investment, industrial licensing and foreign-exchange controls. Delhi has opened the capital market to foreign investment and largely dismantled restrictions on imports.

But domestic political interests make for occasional backtracking. The latest example came on August 6, when the coalition government withdrew legislation intended to open the insurance sector to foreign competition. The Bharatiya Janata Party, the largest oppo-

sition group, and the Communists, who generally support the government, opposed the bill on grounds that liberalization would jeopardize thousands of jobs in India's two main state-owned insurers.

Still, the government hopes for annual foreign investment of $10 billion by 2000. Some say it should aim even higher. Setting sights too low has not been a failing of other Asian leaders, be it China's Deng Xiaoping, Malaysia's Mahathir Mohamad or the Philippines' Fidel Ramos. Indians now feel they need such can-do leadership to cut through the bureaucracy and special interests that are slowing up reform.

A bolder government could make an immediate impact on the economy. Here's how:

• It could cut through red tape, which delays badly needed infrastructure and keeps foreigners wary of investing in those and other projects. Chidambaram himself recalls one instance when a ministry took nine months to provide a simple letter needed to secure financing for a power project. "This is the kind of delay that is painful and completely inexplicable. I'm not saying there are no delays in my ministry—but I am as impatient with those," he says.

• It could take on vested interests that prevent inefficient companies from dying and managers from reducing bloated work forces. Vested interests also stymie plans to cut subsidies—a World Bank economist estimates that only one-fifth of that money gets to the poor anyway. That would free up money for more-productive programmes such as improving rural irrigation.

• It could make politically difficult but sorely needed policy changes, such as devoting more of the education budget to primary schooling. India's adult illiteracy is far worse than in East Asia—nearly two-thirds of Indian women and about one-third of Indian men were illiterate in 1995, compared with rates of

27% and 10% in China, according to the *World Development Report 1997.* That's also one reason India's population growth rate remains high. One of the country's most prominent business leaders, Hindustan Lever Chairman K.B. Dadiseth, notes that Indonesia has had far greater success in promoting literacy by allocating 90% of its education spending to the primary level, roughly twice the rate in India, where higher education is the big winner of government largesse.

Some Indians, dismayed by the lack of political leadership, wonder if the country needs a forceful figure like Singapore's Lee Kuan Yew to clear the bureaucratic bottlenecks. Yet that would involve substituting a free-wheeling democracy with a more authoritarian system, a trade-off that the vast majority of Indians are unwilling to make. They remember Indira Gandhi's attempt to concentrate power in her own hands in 1977. True, she reined in potato and onion prices and got the trains running on time, but ultimately failed to win popular support.

So Indians will have to look elsewhere for their solutions. One might be strengthening the current government by including the Congress Party. It cur-

rently supports the ruling United Front coalition, which holds only 142 of the all-important lower house's 543 seats. This is a distinct possibility in the coming months. "Any government with more than 300 seats would be able to address the systemic problems," says Chidambaram. "The present government is too weak to push through tougher measures such as the privatization of loss-making public-sector units," admits an official in the Industries Ministry.

Some say another crisis is needed to make the government move faster. It took a balance-of-payments crisis in 1991 to trigger the first round of reforms, which included lowering tariffs, liberalizing foreign direct investment policies, and dismantling what was aptly termed the "licence *raj*" (rule). Bombay consultant Praween Napate says the next crisis is on its way: He believes the economy is already in recession and forecasts big trouble for the fiscal deficit. But that may be just what the doctor ordered. "Only a crisis can expedite the reforms," he says. "I'm ashamed as an Indian to say only a crisis can make us work."

Finally, there are signs that some state governments, unrestrained by the coalition politics found at

the federal level, are taking the lead in deepening reforms. That's why some of those who are disappointed with the pace of development remain bullish on India's long-term prospects. It is often noted that despite the country's revolving-door government, reforms have not been derailed. The HP factory isn't coming to India, but the company's Delhi headquarters keeps on growing anyway: It recently moved to new quarters that doubled its floor space. India will take off, says HP's Rajpal, it's just a matter of when. "That's absolutely in the cards," he says.

Perhaps the reason so many remain upbeat is that the alternative is too depressing to contemplate. Back in the finance minister's office, the walls are adorned with photos of Mahatma Gandhi, Jawaharlal Nehru and Indira Gandhi, leaders who gave India a sense of nationhood and pride but not the policies to escape poverty. Chidambaram says the economy cannot backslide to the days of sub–6% growth. If it does, he says, India will remain "one of the poorer countries in the world, though not the poorest. And South Asia will remain the poorest region in the world," having squandered the chance to follow in East Asia's footsteps.

Article 13

Education About Asia, Fall 1996

Enduring Stereotypes About Asia
India's Caste System

Joe Elder

Joe Elder is Professor of Sociology and South Asian Studies at the University of Wisconsin at Madison. He is also Director of the Center for South Asia.

For decades most United States textbooks dealing with South Asia have contained sections on India's caste system, and most such sections have contrasted India's "immobile caste society" negatively with America's "open and

mobile class society." People in India are seen (presumably) as locked forever in birth-determined positions, while people in the United States can (presumably) rise to whatever levels their abilities and good fortune permit. Caste in India is described as a fatalistically-accepted system of discrimination, an inducer of lethargy, and the generator of a mindset that continues to permit a tiny minority of high-caste brahman priests to exploit a large majority of lower-caste farmers and laborers. Implicit—and sometimes explicit—questions in these textbooks are: "When will Indians treat each other more fairly?" and "When will India get rid of its caste system?"[1]

One difficulty in discussing caste in India is that the term itself is applied to several quite different Indian social phenomena. "Casta" was originally a Portuguese word, used in places such as Brazil to describe groups with different proportions of "racial purity" as the Portuguese inter-bred with local Indians and Blacks. The Portuguese applied the term "casta" (inappropriately) to the inter-marrying groups they found in India. The British changed the word to "caste" and incorporated it into their legal documents, where it continues to be used by the post-independence government of India.

Today in India the word "caste" is applied to at least three different social phenomena

---

1 FOUR MYTHICAL CATEGORIES OF HUMANS THAT EMERGED FROM FOUR DIFFERENT PARTS OF PURUSA'S BODY AT THE DAWN OF CREATION.

According to the *Rig Veda* (X, 90)[2] four categories of humans emerged from four different parts of the body of the primeval man, Purusa when he sacrificed himself on a cosmic funeral pyre at the dawn of creation. In Sanskrit texts, these categories are often referred to by the term *varna*. The dawn-of-creation story had been in circulation for centuries before priestly intellectuals generated different rules for each of the four mythical categories. Such rules were incorporated, for example, in the frequently cited *Laws of Manu*. Central to the *Laws of Manu* were requirements that men and women marry within their category *(varna)* and perform occupations assigned to their category *(varna)*. Thus, members of the brahman *varna* (that emerged from Purusa's mouth) should be priests; members of the ksatriya *varna* (that emerged from Purusa's arms) should be warriors and administrators; members of the valsya *varna* (that emerged from Purusa's thighs) should be producers of wealth; and members of the sudra *varna* (that emerged from Purusa's feet) should serve the other three *varnas*. The *Laws of Manu* describe a fifth "mixed" *Varna*, the candalas. Candalas were, according to myth, the offspring of brahman women impregnated by sudra men—in gross violation of rules prohibiting such inter-*Varna* sexual relations. According to the *Laws of Manu,* candalas were to be dealt with as social pariahs, excluded from sacred places and events, and required to perform the least pleasant tasks of society, including removing human feces and disposing of the carcasses of dead animals. The mythical candalas may have provided a ba-

sis for the more recent identification and segregation of India's "untouchables."

It is unlikely that the mythical four-*varna* society ever historically existed for any extended period of time. However, such a mythical society is described in epics and folk tales, and it serves even today as a point of reference for an idealized harmonious society.

2 HUNDREDS OF PUBLICLY IDENTIFIED KINSHI GROUPS LABELED AS "CASTES" IN CENSUS TRACTS AND OTHER OFFICIAL DOCUMENTS BY PEOPLE IN AUTHORITY.

According to the Government of India, for example, 15 percent of India's population belong to "scheduled castes," and another 7.5 percent belong to "scheduled tribes"—kinship groups, many of them previously considered to be "untouchables" who suffered historic deprivations at the hands of their neighbors—who were often regarded as ritually "polluting," were prevented from using certain temples and wells, and who are now entitled to special governmental benefits.

The government of India's 1960 publication entitled *Scheduled Castes and Scheduled Tribes Arranged in Alphabetical Order*[3] lists 405 scheduled castes and 255 scheduled tribes, for a total of 660 kinship groups (the boundaries distinguishing "castes" from "tribes" are unclear). Indian citizens who can establish their claim to belong to one of these publicly identified "castes" or "tribes" are today entitled to special benefits from the government (e.g., preferential access to government jobs, special representation on elected bodies, etc.). More recently, the government has published lists of "Other Backward Classes"—52 percent of India's population belonging to kinship groups that are also entitled to certain benefits because they are disadvantaged—but generally less disadvantaged than the scheduled castes and scheduled tribes. The government's 1980 publication entitled *Report of the Backward Classes Commission* (also called the Mandal Commission Report) lists on a state-by-state basis a total of 3,743 castes belonging to "Other Backward Classes" above and beyond the "scheduled castes" and "scheduled tribes" included in the earlier government lists.

As one examines the official government lists of castes, it is clear that considerable arbitrariness went into identifying what comprised any given caste. For example, "scheduled caste no. 186" that is listed as jolaha in the region of Jammu and Kashmir is listed as kabirpanthi, megh, meghwal, or keer in other regions of northern India. The government official who identified "scheduled caste no. 186" provided no evidence why he ultimately gave the same single label to kinship groups with different names in different regions of India.[4]

3 LINEAGES OF RELATED FAMILIES FROM AMONG WHICH PARENTS ARRANGE THEIR CHILDREN'S MARRIAGES.

Historically, a major responsibility of parents in India has been to arrange their children's (especially their daughters') marriages. Typically, the caste into which one is born provides the boundaries within which one's parents' marriage partners were selected, one's own marriage partners are selected, and one will select the marriage partners for one's own children. To marry outside of one's caste is usually to invite serious social opprobrium—and possibly even expulsion from one's caste.

The caste made up of one's own intra-marrying lineages forms one's ultimate base of social support. These are the people to whom one is related, whose food one can eat, whose hospitality one can provide (and benefit from), to whom one can go for financial and other assistance, and on whom one will have to depend for aid in one's old age and for proper disposal of one's body after one's death.

When defined as marriage-pool lineages, hundreds of thousands of such castes exist today in India. Strong we–they distinctions are often drawn between the members of one's caste and the members of other castes. What from one perspective is standing by one's relatives, from another perspective is favoritism and nepotism. Also higher and lower social distinctions between castes are often perpetuated—or challenged. Certain lineages fall out of favor, are cut off, and become separate castes. Similarly, mergers are possible between castes that see themselves as near social equals. Castes' standings in relation to one another are constantly being renegotiated on the basis of changing wealth, power, status, ritual behavior, sponsorship by important "others," political mobilization, education, and geographical location. One can see parallels between castes as status determiners and marriage pools in India and racial, religious, and ethnic groups as status determiners and marriage pools in the United States.

True or False?

As a consequence of the term "caste" referring to such different social phenomena in India, misconceptions about caste have frequently arisen. Taking "caste" to mean *lineages of related families from among which parents arrange their children's marriages,* here are seven prevalent misconceptions about India's caste system:

1. *The caste into which one is born determines one's occupation.*

False. People in the same caste engage in (and historically have engaged in) a wide variety of different occupations. Confusion arises from the fact that according to the mythical *varna* system of the idealized Hindu law books, everyone is *supposed to* carry out occupations that match their *varnas.* However, the mythical *varna* system and the current caste system are two very different phenomena. Only a very few caste names listed in official publications refer specifically to occupations. Most caste names are merely designations whereby other castes identify a given caste.

2. *Caste designations are changeless.*

False. There are many historical instances of castes changing (or trying to change) their caste names and behavior in order to receive advantageous treatment. Trying to convince someone in authority to label one's caste more highly in a public document is one well-tried way to change one's status. Some efforts to "move up" have succeeded; others have failed. There are instances of castes moving to new areas and thereby changing their names and status. When members of a caste acquire wealth or political leverage, they can sometimes use such resources to upgrade their caste.

3. *Castes relate to each other in mutually accepted hierarchical patterns.*

Frequently false. In any given locality some castes are likely to differ from other castes in their perceptions of what the "correct" local hierarchical patterns are. Disputes regarding the "correct" local hierarchy occur (and have occurred) frequently.

4. *Everyone called by the same caste name is related to everyone else called by that same caste name.*

False. Castes are assigned names by other castes living around them. Labeling coincidences frequently occur. Thus, there are numerous castes, some of whose members perform priestly functions, that are called brahmans by those around them. However, they are not related to all other castes that are called brahmans. There are castes that are called "patels," "deshmukhs," or "rajputs" (honorific civil titles) by those around them that are not related to all other castes called "patels," "deshmukhs," or "rajputs." There are numerous castes, some of whose members make (or did make) pots, that are called "potters" by those around them that are not related to all other castes called "potters." Every "gandhi" is not related to every other "gandhi."

5. *Castes are uniquely Hindu.*

False. In India castes exist among Christians, Jains, Sikhs, Buddhists, and Muslims. Frequently the rules about marrying within one's caste and avoiding interactions with other castes are as strict among Christians, Jains, etc. as they are among Hindus.

6. *Hinduism legitimizes preferential treatment according to caste.*

Occasionally false. In the idealized *varna* system, being born into a high *varna* was seen as a reward for virtue in a previous life. Being born in a low *varna* was seen as punishment for sins in a previous life. However, throughout India's history, movements have appeared within Hinduism criticizing preferential ranking and treatment according to caste (or *varna*). These movements have included Buddhism, Jainism, *bhakti* poets and saints, the Lingayats, Sikhism, and philosophers and intellectuals such as Mahatma Gandhi and Dr. B. R. Ambedkar, the architect of India's constitution.

7. *Castes have been abolished.*

False. India's constitution declares that "untouchability" is abolished and anyone discriminating against "untouchables" can be prosecuted. In addition, India's government now provides certain benefits to members of the "scheduled castes," "scheduled tribes," and "Other Backward Classes." However, India's constitution says nothing about abolishing castes. That would mean abolishing lineages of related families from among which parents select their children's marriage partners, and that would not be possible.

In the United States, discrimination on the grounds of race and gender has been declared illegal. However, the U.S. has no laws abolishing race or gender. Just as race and gender cannot be abolished by laws (although efforts can be made to end discrimination based on race and gender) so castes cannot be abolished by laws (although efforts can be made—and some are being made—to end discrimination based on caste).

Notes

1. For a review of U.S. textbook presentations of India, see Bonnie R. Crown, "Textbook Images of India," in Barbara J. Harrison (ed.), *Learning About India: An Annotated Guide for Nonspecialists* (Albany: Center for International Programs and Comparative Studies, New York State Education Department, 1977), 21–37.

2. Vedas Rgveda, *Rgveda Samhita,* with English translation by Svami Satya Prakash Sarasvati and Satyakam Vidyalankar, vol. XIII (New Delhi: Veda Pratishthana, 1987), 4483–4487.

3. Census of India, Paper No. 2 (New Delhi: Government of India, Manager of Publications, 1960).

4. For a thorough discussion of the Government of India's efforts to improve the lives of the lowest castes and poorest classes, see Marc Galanter, *Competing Equalities: Law and the Backward Classes in India* (Berkeley: University of California Press, 1984).

Bibliography

India (Republic), Backward Classes Commission. *Report of the Backward Classes Commission.* Vols. I–VII. New Delhi: Manager of Publications, 1980.

Manu. *The Laws of Manu.* Trans. by George Bühler. Vol. 25. Sacred Books of the East; reprint New York: Dover, 1969.

Article 14

The World & I, October 1996

Ancient Jewel

From early Greece to the modern civil rights movement, Indian thought and philosophy have had a wide-ranging influence on Western culture.

T. R. (Joe) Sundaram

T. R. (Joe) Sundaram is the owner of an engineering research firm in Columbia, Maryland, and has written extensively on Indian history, culture, and science.

The very word *India* conjures up exotic images in one's mind. Yet this name for the south Asian subcontinent is of Western making, mediated by the Persians and the Arabs. The name used in ancient Sanskrit texts is *Bharat* (for the land of Bharatha, a legendary king), which is also the official name of the modern republic. Other familiar Western words such as *Hindu, caste,* and *curry* are also totally foreign to India. The general knowledge that exists in the West about India, its early history, philosophy, and culture is, at best, superficial. Nevertheless, since it would be impossible in a brief article to do justice to even one of these topics, I shall provide a brief, accurate glimpse into each.

Embassy of India

Continuous civilization: Excavations at Mohenjo-Daro and Harappa reveal well-planned towns and a sophisticated urban culture dating back to 2500 B.C.

Crucible of Learning

- *India's may be the oldest continuing civilization in existence.*
- *To avoid misunderstanding India, it is essential to appreciate three central tenets of Indian thinking: assimilating ideas and experiences, a belief in cycles, and the coexistence of opposites.*
- *India has made numerous contributions to contemporary Western understanding of mathematics, science, and philosophy.*

India covers about 1.2 million square miles and is home to a population of 895 million; in comparison, the United States covers 3.6 million square miles and has 258 million residents. Thus, the population density of India is nearly 10 times that of the United States. (The size of classical India—which includes modern-day India, Pakistan, Bangladesh, and parts of Afghanistan—is about two-thirds that of the continental United States.)

But statistics about India can be misleading. For example, while only about one-quarter of the population is "literate," able to read and write, this has to be viewed in light of the strong oral traditions present in India since antiquity. Therefore, while a "literate" American may often be unaware of the collective name of the first 10 amendments to the U.S. Constitution, an "illiterate" Indian peasant would be aware of the history of his ancestors from antiquity to the present day.

Not only is India one of the oldest civilizations in the world, being more than 6,000 years old, but also it may be the oldest continuing civilization in existence; that is, one without any major "gaps" in its history. As the renowned historian A. L. Basham has pointed out,

Until the advent of archeologists, the peasant of Egypt or Iraq had no knowledge of the culture of his forefathers, and it is doubtful whether his Greek counterpart had any but the vaguest ideas about the glory of Periclean Athens. In each case there had been an almost complete break with the past. On the other hand, the earliest Europeans to visit India found a culture fully conscious of its own antiquity.

India is a land of many ancient "living" cities, such as, for example, Varanasi. Even at sites like Delhi, many successive cities have been built over thousands of years. Among old buried cities that have been unearthed in modern times by archaeologists are Mohenjo-Daro and Harappa.

Of these cities, the renowned archaeologist Sir John Marshall writes that they establish the existence

in the fourth and third millennium B.C., of a highly developed city life; and the presence in many houses, of wells and bathrooms as well as an elaborate drainage system, betoken a social condition of the citizens at least equal to that found in Sumer, and superior to that prevailing in contemporary Babylonia and Egypt.

Thus, India was the "jewel of the world" long before the Greek and Roman civilizations.

Nor was classical India isolated from developing civilizations in other parts of the world. Clay seals from Mohenjo-Daro have been found in Babylonia and vice versa. Ancient Indian artifacts such as beads and bangles have been found in many parts of the Middle East and Africa. India and Indian culture were known to the Greeks even before the time of Alexander the Great. The Greek historian Herodotus wrote extensively about India during the sixth century B.C. Also, during this period many Greeks, including Pythagoras, are known to have traveled to India.

India was the "jewel of the world" long before the Greek and Roman civilizations.

Sixth century B.C. was a period of great religious and philosophical upheaval in India. Hinduism was already an established, "old" religion, and reform movements were beginning to appear, such as one by a prince known as Siddhartha Gautama, who later came to be known as the Buddha. The religion that was founded based on his teachings spread not only throughout Asia but also to many parts of the world, including Greece, and it helped spread Indian culture in the process.

Embassy of India

A terra-cotta toy cow: Ancient Indian civilizations featured highly talented artisans and craftsmen.

In Alexander the Great's campaign to conquer the world, his ultimate goal was India; he died without achieving that objective. When Seleucus Nicator, Alexander's successor, tried to follow in Alexander's footsteps, he was soundly defeated by Indian emperor Chandragupta Maurya. A peace treaty was signed between the two, and Seleucus sent an ambassador, Megasthenes, to the court of Chandragupta. Megasthenes sent glowing reports back to Greece about India, and he pronounced Indian culture to be equal or superior to his own, a high compliment indeed, since Greece was then near its zenith.

For the next 1,500 years or so, India—rich in material wealth, scientific knowledge, and spiritual wisdom—enjoyed the reputation of being at the pinnacle of world civilizations. Arab writers of the Middle Ages routinely referred to mathematics as *hindsat,* the "Indian science."

And as is well known now, it was Columbus' desire to reach India that led to the discovery of America. Indeed, the explorer died thinking that he had discovered a new sea route to India, while he had merely landed on a Caribbean island. Columbus' mistake also led to the mislabeling of the natives of the land as "Indians," a label that survived even after the mistake had been discovered.

Khorrum Omer/The World & I

Indian music has influenced Western artists, particularly in modern times. The beat of the tabla (above) can be heard in pop music ranging from the Beatles to Michael Jackson.

The Upanishads

Indian philosophy is almost as old as Indian civilization, and its zenith was reached nearly 3,000 years ago with the compilation, by unknown sages, of 108 ancient philosophical texts known as the Upanishads. These texts reflect even older wisdom, which was passed down from generation to generation through oral transmission. A Western commentator has remarked that in the Upanishads the Indian mind moved from cosmology to psychology, and that while most other contemporary civilizations were still asking the question "What am I?" the Indian mind was already asking, "Who am I?"

When translations of the Upanishads first became available in the West in the nineteenth century, the impact on European philosophers such as Goethe and Schopenhauer and on American writers such as Emerson and Whitman was pro-

found. "In the whole world," wrote Schopenhauer emotionally, "there is no study as beneficial and as elevating as the Upanishads." Emerson wrote poems based on the texts.

One of the principal underlying themes in the Upanishads is the quest for a "personal reality." This quest began with the conviction that the limitations of our sensory perceptions give us an imperfect model to comprehend the real world around us; this is known as the concept of *maya.* Since individual perceptions can be different, different people can also have different "realities."

For example, a happy event for one individual may be an unhappy one for another. Recognition and perfection of our personal reality is the quintessential goal of Indian philosophy and is also the basic principle behind yoga. Indeed, the literal meaning of the Sanskrit word

yoga is "union," and the union that is sought is not with any external entity but with one's self. This is, of course, also the principal tenet of modern psychoanalysis.

From a Western perspective, to avoid misunderstanding India in general, and Indian philosophy in particular, it is essential to appreciate three central tenets of the Indian way of thinking. These are:

Assimilation. In the Indian way of thinking, new experiences and ideas never replace old ones but are simply absorbed into, and made a part of, old experiences. Although some have characterized such thinking as static, in reality such thinking is both dynamic and conservative, since old experiences are preserved and new experiences are continually accumulated.

Belief in cycles. Another central tenet of the Indian character is the belief that all changes in the world take place through cycles, there being cycles super-imposed on other cycles, cycles within cycles, and so on. Inherent in the concept of cycles is alternation, and the Upanishads speak of the two alternating states of all things being "potentiality" and "expression."

Acceptance of the coexistence of opposites. Early Western readers of the Upanishads were puzzled by the apparent inherent ability of the Indian mind to accept the coexistence of seemingly diametrically opposite concepts. Belief in, and acceptance of, contradictory ideas is a natural part of the Indian way

Ironically, the culture that taught of the need to renounce materialistic desires also produced some of the most pleasurable things in life. The intricacies and highly developed nature of Indian art, music, dance, and cuisine are examples. And the Kama Sutra is perhaps the oldest, and best known, manual on the pleasures of love and sex.

From Pythagoras to King

Throughout history, India's contributions to the Western world have been

Khorrum Omer/The World & I

Melodic inspiration: Performing traditional dance and music in Orissa.

of life, and the logical complement to the tenets already mentioned. It is an indisputable fact that birth (creation) must necessarily be eventually followed by death (destruction). Creation and destruction are inseparable alternations. Even concepts such as "good" and "evil" are complementary, as each of us may have within us the most lofty and divine qualities and at the same time the basest qualities. We ourselves and the whole world can be whatever we want to make of them.

These three tenets are responsible for the amazing continuity of the Indian civilization, its reverence for the elderly, and the acceptance of the aging process without a morbid fear of death.

considerable, albeit during the Middle Ages they were often felt only indirectly, having been mediated by the Middle Eastern cultures.

After the early contacts between Greece and India in the sixth and fifth centuries B.C., many concepts that had been in use in India centuries earlier made their appearance in Greek literature, although no source was ever acknowledged. For example, consider the so-called Pythagorean theorem of a right triangle and the Pythagorean school's theory of the "transmigration of souls"; the former was in use in India (for temple construction) centuries earlier, and the latter is merely "reincarnation," a concept of Vedic antiquity. There was

also a flourishing trade between the Roman Empire and the kingdoms in southern India, through which not only Indian goods but also ideas made their journey westward.

During the Middle Ages, the Arabs translated many classical Indian works into Arabic, and the ideas contained in them eventually made their way to Europe. A principal mission of the "House of Wisdom" that was established by the caliph in Baghdad in the eighth century was the translation of Indian works.

Among the major Indian ideas that entered Europe through the Arabs are the mathematical concept of zero (for which there was no equivalent in Greek or Roman mathematics) and the modern numerical system we use today. Until the twelfth century, Europe was shackled by the unwieldy Roman numerals. The famous French mathematician Laplace has written: "It is India that gave us the ingenious method of expressing all numbers by ten symbols, each receiving a value of position as well as an absolute value, a profound and important idea which appears so simple to us now that we ignore its true merit."

India's contributions to other areas of science and mathematics were equally important. The seventh-century Syrian astronomer Severus Sebokht wrote that "the subtle theories" of Indian astronomers were "even more ingenious than those of the Greeks and the Babylonians."

The scientific approach permeated other aspects of Indian life as well. For example, classical Indian music has a highly mathematical structure, based on divisions of musical scales into tones and microtones.

In modern times, Indian music has had a considerable influence on Western music. Starting in the 1960s, the famous Indian sitar virtuoso Ravi Shankar popularized sitar music in the West, and now the melodic strains of the sitar, as well as the beat of the Indian drum known as tabla, can be heard in the works of many pop-music artists, ranging from the Beatles to Michael Jackson. The movies of the Indian filmmaker Satyajit Ray have also made a significant impact on the West.

Th contributions of many modern Indian scientists have been important to the overall development of Western science. The mathematical genius Srinivasa Ramanujan, who died in 1920, has been called "the greatest mathematician of the century" and "the man who knew infinity." The discovery by the Nobel Prize–winning Indian physicist Chandrasekhara Venkata Raman of the effect (which bears his name) by which light diffusing through a transparent material changes in wavelength has revolutionized laser technology. The theoretical predictions by the Nobel Prize-winning astrophysicist Subrahmanyan Chandrasekhar on the life and death of white-dwarf stars led to the concept of "black holes."

In the literary area, the poetry of Nobel laureate Rabindranath Tagore and the philosophical interpretations of the scholar (and a former president of India) Sarvepalli Radhakrishnan have inspired the West. Albert Einstein was one of the admirers of the former and corresponded with him on the meaning of "truth."

In terms of our daily dietary habits, many vegetables such as cucumber, eggplant, okra, squash, carrots, many types of beans, and lentils were first domesticated in India. Rice, sugarcane, and tea, *as well as fruits such as bananas and oranges, are of Indian origin. The name orange is derived from the Sanskrit word narangi.* Chicken and cattle were also first domesticated in India, albeit the latter for milk production and not for meat consumption. Cotton was first

> *For all India's material contributions to the world, it is its spiritual legacy that has had the widest impact.*

domesticated in India. The process of dying fabrics also was invented in India. Indian fabrics (both cotton and silk) have been world renowned for their quality since antiquity. The game of chess was invented in India, and the name itself derives from the Sanskrit name Chaturanga.

India's most popular modern exports have been yoga and meditation. Hatha yoga, the exercise system that is a part of yoga, is now taught widely in America, in institutions ranging from colleges to hospitals. Many scientific studies on the beneficial effects of yoga practice are now under way. A similar state of affairs is true of Indian meditation techniques, which people under stress use for mental relaxation.

Finally the Rev. Martin Luther King, Jr., repeatedly acknowledged his debt to Mahatma Gandhi for the technique of nonviolent civil disobedience, which he used in the civil rights movement. For all India's material contributions to the world, it is its spiritual legacy that has had the widest impact. The ancient sages who wrote the Upanishads would have been pleased.

Additional Reading

A. L. Basham, *The Wonder That Was India,* Grove Press, New York, 1959.

———, *Ancient India: Land of Mystery,* Time-Life Books, Alexandria, Virginia, 1994.

Will Durant, *the Story of Civilization: Part I, Our Oriental Heritage,* Simon and Schuster, New York, 1954.

Article 15   *The New York Times,* May 11, 1998

Though Illegal, Child Marriage Is Popular in Part of India

By JOHN F. BURNS

MADHOGARH, India—If a wedding is supposed to fulfill a girl's earliest dreams, Hansa's in this tiny hamlet in Rajasthan State seemed more like a nightmare.

Early in the starlit evening, the smoke from the sacred fire began searing her eyes. The rituals pushed the ceremony deep into the night, in a crucible of heat and haze. After the first two hours, Hansa was quietly sobbing. By midnight, with Hindu priests leading Hansa and her new husband, Sitaram, in the climactic ritual, involving seven purifying circuits of the wood-burning fire, Hansa's wailing was drowning the rhythmic mantras of the priests.

"I want to go to bed," she cried. "Please, Mama, Papa. Let me sleep!"

Bafflement can only have worsened the ordeal, since Hansa, the youngest of six sisters being married in a joint ceremony to boys from other villages, was only 4. Her husband was 12.

Such weddings are common in Rajasthan, a state known for its desert landscapes, hilltop forts and maharajahs' palaces, as well as its persistence in feudal traditions, including child marriages, that have kept Rajasthani women among the most socially disadvantaged in India.

Indian law sets 18 as the minimum age for a woman to marry and 21 for a man. When India's Parliament adopted the Child Marriage Restraint Act in 1978, legislators hoped that the statute would curb child marriages and the social ills they perpetuate.

Concern focused on an arc of populous northern states where child marriages are most deeply rooted: Rajasthan, Madhya Pradesh, Uttar Pradesh, Bihar and West Bengal, with a combined population of 420 million, about 40 percent of all Indians.

According to decades of research, child marriages contribute to virtually every social malaise that keeps India behind in women's rights. The problems include soaring birth rates, grinding poverty and malnutrition, high illiteracy and infant mortality and low life expectancy, especially among rural women.

In Rajasthan, a survey of more than 5,000 women conducted by the national Government in 1993 showed that 56 percent had married before they were 15. Of those, 3 percent married before they were 5 and another 14 percent before they were 10. Barely 18 percent were literate, and only 3 percent used any form of birth control other than sterilization.

Large families and poor health for children and mothers were among the results. The survey showed that of every 1,000 births, 73 children died in infancy and 103 before they reached age 5. Sixty-three percent of children under 4 were found to be severely undernourished. Average life expectancy for women was 58.

In every case, the figures were among the worst for any Indian state.

Social workers say many husbands tire of their marriages after the third, fourth or fifth child, when their wives are still teen-agers. Alcoholism contributes to domestic violence, with sometimes fatal beatings.

In some cases, husbands sell their wives, and even their unmarried daughters, as sexual partners to other men. In scores of cases every year, village women strike back by killing their husbands, only to face long terms in prison.

"It is a tragedy for these little flowers, and for our country, that they are snatched away into marriage before they even have a chance to bloom," said Mohini Giri, 60, chairwoman of the National Commission for Women, a Government agency established in the early 1990's that has become a driving force for raising awareness about the plight of women.

In Rajasthan, child marriages remain so popular that virtually every city, town and village takes on a holiday atmosphere ahead of the day set by astrologers for the annual Akha Teej festival—the moment judged most auspicious for marriages.

On the day of the festival, usually in late April or early May, roads are choked with tractors pulling trailers filled with gaily dressed wedding guests. On the outskirts of every settlement there are open-sided wedding tents in brightly patterned fabrics known as pandals.

Each year, formal warnings are posted outside state government offices stating that child marriages are illegal, but they have little impact.

Three strangers arriving at Madhogarh, the village where Hansa was married, had only to pull off the main road running south from the town of Alwar, 125 miles southwest of New Delhi, and drive a mile to spot a wedding pandal.

Villagers were unhesitating in their welcome, even when one of the visitors was introduced as a reporter.

"Of course, we know that marrying children is against the law, but it's only a paper law," said Govind Singh Patel, a village elder in the cattle-herding Gujjar community, which is among the poorest in Rajasthan and the most resistant to social change.

Sociologists say the Gujjars and similar groups trace the origin of child marriages to Muslim invasions that began more than 1,000 years ago. Legend has it that the invaders raped unmarried Hindu girls or carried them off as booty, prompting Hindu communities to marry off their daughters almost from birth to protect them.

Today, the stories have an echo in the local view that any girl reaching puberty without getting married will fall prey to sexual depredations, some from men imbued with the common belief that having sex with a "fresh" girl can cure syphilis, gonorrhea and other sexually transmitted diseases, including the virus that causes AIDS.

Tradition has been reinforced by necessity. In villages like Madhogarh, a family can be fortunate to have an annual income of $500, less in years when there is drought or flood. Securing early marriages for daughters can mean the difference between subsistence and hunger.

Traditionally, this has meant seeking grooms in neighboring villages, since the fear of inbreeding has generated a taboo against marriage between boys and girls from the same village.

Hansa's father, Shriram Gujjar, 40, works an acre of land beside the family's thatched home of mud and straw, with three cows to supplement his crop of mustard and wheat. Villagers say his troubles were compounded when his wife, Gyarsi Devi, gave birth to seven daughters but no sons.

But Mr. Gujjar's fortunes improved when a network of community contacts found husbands for the first six daughters, ranging in age from 4-year-old Hansa to Dohli, 14. An infant girl of 18 months, and another child on the way, will await another marriage ceremony in the future.

Mr. Gujjar, a fierce-looking man with a handlebar mustache and a luxuriant white turban, said he had borrowed about 60,000 rupees, about $1,500, to pay for the dowries required by the grooms' families and for the wedding festivities. While the loan will be a problem for years, he said, the weddings mean that he can now look forward to growing old without being trapped in penury by the need to support his daughters.

"Tonight I am a free man again!" he said, grinning as he circulated proudly among the scores of wedding guests seated cross-legged beneath the pandal.

After a moment to check the register in which cash donations from the guests were being entered, he returned, thrust his hands into the air in a gesture of release and added, "Thanks to God, the heaviest of my burdens has been lifted."

The brides spend the night of their weddings in their homes, then join their husband's families the next day for a journey to their in-laws' village.

In Hansa's case, this entailed traveling half a day by oxcart and bus to a village 25 miles away. After a few days there, tradition required that she return to her family in Madhogarh and await the onset of puberty, when another ceremony known as the Gauna would mark her fitness to join her husband's family.

But not all grooms' families are prepared to wait for puberty. In many cases documented by sociologists, girls as young as 6 or 7 have been taken away by their husbands' families to begin working as servants or field hands.

"With the addition of a girl to the household, the in-laws get a laborer, someone who will feed the cattle and clear the house, a servant who comes free of cost," said Ratan Katyani, a social worker in the Rajasthan city of Jaipur.

In 1994 the National Commission for Women urged the national Government, then headed by Prime Minister P. V. Narasimha Rao, to consolidate the separate marriage laws that exist for each of the major religious communities—Hindu, Muslim and Christian—and to include a provision requiring that all marriages be legally registered. That, the commission reasoned, could be used to bar under-age marriages.

But the Government rejected the proposal, as did its successor, headed by Prime Minister H. D. Deve Gowda, in 1996.

"It has been the consistent policy of the Government not to interfere in the personal laws of the distinct communities unless the initiative comes from the communities themselves," the Government said in a statement. "The Government is of the view that it is only through social and economic upliftment of these sections of the community that the practice can be eradicated."

Article 16

World Watch, November/December 1991

India's Misconceived Family Plan

India's goal of cutting its runaway birthrate in half by the year 2000 will prove elusive unless the government provides women means to attain higher status other than by bearing large numbers of children.

Jodi L. Jacobson

Jodi L. Jacobson is a senior researcher for the Worldwatch Institute. She recently spent two months working with environmental and women's groups in India.

"If a family is small, all its dreams come true," reads a Hindi slogan painted on the walls of a government-run clinic in Rajasthan. The message is clear: In an overwhelmingly poor and rapidly growing country like India, fewer people means a higher standard of living for all.

Yet, in this glib slogan lies a potentially dangerous myth. Among advocates of "sustainable development"—in India, in the United States, and throughout much of the international community—conventional wisdom holds that slowing population growth is the key to solving a vast array of social, economic, and environmental problems. To be sure, in a world of finite resources, unlimited growth in the number of people requiring food, shelter, and work, not to mention access to natural resources, cannot be sustained. But the increasingly singular focus on demographics simply deflects attention from the fundamental social conditions—poverty, inequity, and the abject status of women—of which population growth is not the cause, but the consequence.

In India, as in much of the world, women are last in line for education, job training, credit, and sometimes even food—despite the fact that raising the status of women is the most effective way both to reduce births and to achieve higher standards of health and economic productivity.

The strategies needed to increase women's access to these basic amenities, however, are complex and require a kind of sustained political commitment not abundantly present in the governments of most developing countries. The rapid pace of population growth, on the other hand, ignites support for political shortcuts. Women, overwhelmingly poor and lacking political clout, too often become the first targets of population "control."

The inevitable conflicts between development policy and women's human rights are nowhere more evident than in India. In the mid-to-late 1970s, for example, Indian women were subjected to compulsory birth control and sterilization programs under a state of national "emergency" [see "A History of Missed Targets"]. Today, pressures are again rising to reduce fertility at all costs.

In India's tradition-bound society, where childbearing is often the only route to status and security, the majority of women have little to gain from having fewer children. The government, by contrast, is bent on cutting birthrates in half over the next decade, but has shown little commitment to meeting women's needs. And so a vicious cycle is perpetuated. As long as the status of women remains low, voluntary family planning efforts will continue to founder, tempting the government to use pressure to meet its demographic goals.

THE CHINA SYNDROME

The Hindi "small families" slogan reflects an acute consciousness in the Indian government of that country's most dubious demographic distinction. Now at 859 million people (more than three times the population of the United States), India is expected to reach 1 billion people within 10 years. It will surpass China as the world's most populous country by the middle of the next century.

At the same time, current trends indicate the world's overall population will nearly double to 9 billion by 2030. Such a scenario, paired with rising levels of resource consumption in virtually every country, rich or poor, makes the prospects for restoring the earth's ecosystems appear increasingly bleak. Meanwhile, each day the number of people who lack access to adequate food, health care, housing, clean water, and education spirals upward.

In response, leaders around the world now regularly voice sentiments similar to those of Sat Paul Mittal, a member of India's ruling Congress party, who states, "This population explosion is no less than an epidemic. We have reached the stage where we can no longer talk only in terms of rights, we have to talk in terms of duties." But such rhetoric brushes aside a simple truth: No population policy alone, however well-designed, can make up for decades of economic and development strategies that ignored the needs of the poor, the limits of the environment, and the overconsumption by the few.

In assigning "rights and duties," the emphasis is too often placed on the obligations of couples to have smaller families, and too rarely on the duties of governments to ensure that their people have the resources required to meet basic needs, despite the fact that poverty is the major cause of rapid population growth. But few of the governments that have become ardent converts to population control are as fervent in their efforts to pursue economically and ecologically sustainable policies, largely because these involve hard choices that may unsettle vested interests.

In India, women are last in line for education, job training, credit, and sometimes food—despite the fact that raising the status of women is the most effective way to reduce births.

In India, for example, a study by World Bank researcher Nirmala Murthy and her colleagues found that, despite continued economic growth and an increase in the supply of food grains, the share of India's population too poor to buy enough food has remained stuck at 40 percent for the past 25 years. From one-fourth to one-half of the inhabitants of the largest cities live in slums without adequate housing or sewage. More than 30 percent of India's children are born at low birth weight; nearly three out of four suffer from stunted growth during their preschool years, due mainly to nutritional deficiencies. Only one-quarter of Indian females are literate, as opposed to one-half of males.

To claim that rampant population growth does not hamper efforts to solve these and other problems facing India— not to mention deforestation, water scarcity, and a host of environmental concerns—would be naive. But it would be equally naive to ignore the effect the government's lack of commitment to reducing poverty and forging a sustainable development path has had on these issues. The World Bank study concludes, for example, that caste- and class-based discrimination, together with corruption and government indifference to the quality of health and educational services offered, have only exacerbated the plight of India's poor. By failing to confront these issues, the Indian government continues to perpetuate the very conditions that keep birthrates high.

THE SCHOOL GAP

Neither the state nor national governments in India have taken the steps necessary to increase women's access to education, despite the fact that, as international experience has shown, female education is the single most influential determinant of both lower birthrates and increasing empowerment for women. The government's eighth Five-Year Plan, published in 1990, states that "spending [is] either the same or a lower amount per [primary school] student today than in the 1950s and 1960s." Indeed, India spends far less on education per capita than do several other countries in Asia with similar levels of personal income. Indonesia and Thailand, for example, invest more in education generally and have made it more available to females, with obvious results. More than two-thirds of all women in Indonesia and more than three-fourths in Thailand are literate. Birthrates in both countries are markedly lower than in India.

Even with so little to give, Indian society manages to devote fewer resources to educating its girls than its boys. At the household level, cultural restrictions on female behavior combined with the need for cheap household labor create a sharp gender gap in literacy. In both the Hindu and Moslem traditions, for example, notions of female "modesty" and "purity" dictate that unmarried females remain separate from unrelated males. Because the bulk of India's teachers are men, and most schools educate boys and girls under the same roof, many traditional families keep their daughters home, regardless of their income. Moreover, parents are apt to invest in educating girls only when they perceive that long-term gains will outweigh immediate costs.

Where Boys Are Better

According to Indian tradition and, until recent years, by law, only males could inherit their parents' property. In an agrarian society, where land is the primary form of wealth, having at least one surviving son is the only sure way of keeping it in the family. Tradition also holds sons responsible for providing their parents, particularly their mothers, with a secure future; widowed or divorced women without adult male sons to support them invariably face destitution.

Moreover, sons accrue another form of economic wealth when they marry. Daughters-in-law move into the homes of their husbands' parents, bringing with them not only dowries but also a form of income in their ability to perform work and produce grandchildren.

Daughters, by contrast, are viewed as a drain on household income. Not only is the work they do in their parents' homes not valued by society, but when they marry they take with them a dowry that their parents may be forced into debt to provide. Although laws governing inheritance and other property rights have been formally changed, government enforcement and judicial support for carrying them out remains weak, posing no match for the strength of cultural practice in denying women access to productive resources such as land and credit.

For the impoverished majority, the expense of sending a girl to school—paying for uniforms, books, and even bribes to take advantage of a "free" education—is prohibitive, especially when young girls are required to work at home and in the fields. Moreover, parents hold little hope for recouping these expenses, since daughters are unable to contribute much to family income later in life, in large part because sex discrimination, combined with low levels of access to education and training, prevents them from earning wages equal to those of men.

Women's lack of knowledge translates directly into poor nutrition and health for themselves and their offspring. In turn, these conditions cause high infant mortality—for which many women compensate by having more babies.

THE FOOD GAP

Nutritional and health status is also marked by gender disparity. Both boys and girls in India are nutritionally disadvantaged, as nearly half of the country's households fail to provide even the minimum daily caloric requirements. But malnutrition is far more prevalent among females than males. From birth, male children consistently receive more and better food than their sisters, even though the nutritional needs of prepubescent boys and girls are virtually identical. Boys, given the same level of illness, are taken to doctors more often than girls. As a result of this neglect, far more girls than boys die in the critical period between infancy and age five.

The pattern continues through adulthood, with working females receiving less protein and calories relative to their labor needs than do their male counterparts. A survey cited by the World Bank of more than 500 households in the state of Karnataka, for example, found that women consumed 100 fewer calories than needed to fuel the work they perform each day, while consumption levels among men represented a *surplus* of 800 calories.

Discrimination in feeding and health care produces one of India's most provocative signs of gender bias: Females have lower life expectancies than males. This pattern is contrary to that found in the majority of other nations. In fact, the ratio of women to men in the country has been declining. Today, there are only 919 women for every 1,000 men, a decline from 972 women to 1,000 men in 1901.

For India as a whole, Indian health scientist and World Bank consultant Meera Chatterjee estimates that deaths of girls under age five exceed those of boys by nearly 330,000 annually. One of every six infant deaths is attributable to gender bias. Older females die at higher rates than males from preventable causes, such as tuberculosis and gastroenteric infections. Dr. Veena Mazumdar, director of the Delhi-based Center for Women's Development Studies, notes that "the declining sex ratio is the final indicator that registers . . . women are losing out on all fronts—on the job market, in health and nutrition, and economic prosperity."

THE MYTH OF FEMALE NON-PRODUCTIVITY

Son preference and the subsequently biased allocation of family resources is based on a series of myths the Indian government has failed to combat [see box above]. One is the notion—not peculiar to India—that females do not contribute to family income. Throughout the world, women bear the "invisible" burdens of unpaid domestic work and childbearing, the economic value of which is rarely reflected by official statistics.

According to conventional measures based on wage labor, for example, government data show that only 34 percent of Indian females are in the labor force, as opposed to 63 percent of males. A survey of work patterns by occupational categories including household production and domestic work, however, reveals that 75 percent of females over age five are working, as opposed to 64 percent of males.

Young girls in India generally work longer hours than boys of the same age. By age 10, girls in low-income families are working eight or more hours a day assisting their mothers by tending siblings, collecting water and firewood, herding small animals, weeding fields, or facing the daily grind of low-paid child labor in the marketplace. By age 15, an Indian girl works more than 10 hours a day. And adult women work 16 to 18 hours a day on average, as opposed to 10 to 12 for men.

The poorer the family, the more vital the economic contribution that women and girls make, especially in the growing number of female-headed households. "Even where there is a male earner," notes World Bank consultant Lynn Bennett, "women's earnings form a major part of the income of poor households." Nevertheless, the lack of official recognition of women's work—what Bennett has termed a "statistical purdah"—both reflects and reinforces cultural patterns of discrimination.

A POLICY OF INDIFFERENCE

The Indian government's response to the debilitating conditions faced by women ranges from apathy to willful neglect. In every sector, according to a World Bank report, "India invests far less in its women workers and they receive a considerably smaller share of what society produces than their male counterparts." The results are most apparent in agriculture, where the majority of women work.

Nearly 40 percent of India's economy is based on agriculture. Few resources reach women, although they comprise a large share of both paid and unpaid (family) agricultural labor. Here again, the government statistics on which investment decisions are based present a misleading picture. Survey data imply that women make up 46 percent of the nation's agricultural labor force. A study by the United Nations International Labor Organization detailing the way rural women spend their time indicates that up to 90 percent of rural women in central India participate in agriculture. This suggests, as Bennett maintains, that "there are very few rural women in India who are not in some sense 'farmers'—working as wage laborers, unpaid workers in the family farm enterprise, or some combination of the two."

Despite the evidence, government attempts to enhance agricultural productivity disproportionately benefit men. The agricultural extension system now largely bypasses the 40 percent of India's self-employed cultivators who are women. The distribution of irrigation outlets, skewed in favor of large landholders, discriminates against the small family farms on which women work and produce food for domestic consumption. And the credit needed to enhance productivity remains out of reach of women, largely because they lack ownership of land as collateral.

Apart from outright official neglect, government funds often are channeled into large-scale projects that exacerbate women's poverty. Massive irrigation projects in the state of Rajasthan and Punjab are notable examples. Expansion of the irrigated area allocated to cash crops, such as groundnut and cotton, has come at the expense of food crops on which women depend to feed their families. And while the mechanization of plowing and leveling that comes with these projects reduces the traditional workload of men, that for women actually increases. Women still must carry out by hand the tasks of weeding, turning soil, and harvesting, but over much larger areas.

The result is to deepen women's poverty and enhance the perceived value of having many children to help with chores. By failing to account for and enhance women's productivity in this and every other sector of the economy, India's leaders undermine their own development goals.

THE GREAT MISNOMER

While women have been ignored as an economic force, they have been zealously pursued by India's family planners, not as clients deserving of good quality health care, but as the bull's-eye in a series of official demographic targets. The agency charged with family planning is the Family Welfare Program, which has been up and running since 1974. In theory, the program is set up to provide universal access to a wide range of health and family planning services for women and children. However, a number of studies by family planning researchers, such as Anrudh K. Jain and Moni Nag, senior analysts at the New York-based Population Council, and discussions with health advocates throughout India, reveal that the Family Welfare Program has acquired a reputation for inefficiency, graft, bribery, and a chilling emphasis on sterilization rather than on improving health.

The Family Welfare Program is supposed to serve its clients through an extensive system of hospitals and clinics. In practice, this chain of health care outlets is more often than not broken by the absence of clinic buildings, staff, and supplies. Millions of women are deterred from seeking preventive health care by the long distances to functioning clinics, the wages and work hours lost due to chronically long delays in receiving care, and the lack of female personnel to attend them.

At the district level, surveys by Chatterjee and others show the low status of women is actually reinforced by the government program. Compared to their male counterparts, female health workers receive lower pay, less training, and are regarded within the system as having low status because they work with "women's illnesses."

Nevertheless, female employees of the Family Welfare Program have a stressful job. Each is charged with carrying out an incredible 47 different health-care strategies among a population of 5,000. And as Chatterjee points out: "One of the foremost problems faced by [female health workers] is having to meet family planning targets. The fact that the failure to do so is punishable results in little other maternal and child health work being done." Female health workers' association with the government population targets—upon which wages and promotions depend—also results in their being mistrusted by the very women they are meant to serve.

Not surprisingly, the share of married couples of reproductive age using contraceptives—now 40 percent—is low, and most of these are older couples who turned to sterilization (counted as a form of contraceptive) only after having large families. The government's obsessive focus on sterilization shuts out the majority of younger potential clients who might like to have fewer children overall but want to space them by using reversible methods such as condoms, diaphragms, intrauterine devices, and oral contraceptives. With the exception of condoms, these generally remain in short supply, however, and are often available only for a high price—even to the poor—from the very government doctors who are supposed to be dispensing them at no charge. Counseling to enhance couples' understanding and effective use of these methods is virtually nonexistent.

This bleak situation is shadowed by an ominous fact of history. Past attempts by the Indian government to reduce births in the absence of social changes enhancing women's status have been accompanied by increases in violence against females—in the beating and abandonment of women who don't bear

A History of Missed Targets

In 1952, India became the first country to establish an official family planning program with the expressed intent of curtailing the size of its future population. Quiescent until the mid-1960s, family planning took off in 1966 with the setting of demographic targets and the proliferation of "camps" for mass insertions of intrauterine devices (IUDs). Negative public reaction to the poor training of health workers and unsanitary camps, among other things, killed the program.

Vasectomy camps came next. Encouraged by one-time cash payments for undergoing the procedure, more than 3 million men were sterilized from 1970 to 1971. This effort, too, soon collapsed under the weight of rumors, administrative bungling, and drastic budget cuts. But just four years later, with economic and political crises threatening her rule, then-Prime Minister Indira Gandhi declared family planning to be part of the "Emergency Drive." Once again, targets were set.

As Indian economist Pravin Visaria and sociologist Leela Visaria point out in a review of Gandhi's program for the Population Reference Bureau in Washington, D.C., "Government administra-tors went far beyond official policy . . . and passed orders down the line that everybody—from teachers and police to government contractors and railway inspectors—must meet monthly quotas [for recruiting sterilization acceptors] or jobs, salaries, [and] contracts would suffer."

On a state-by-state basis, incentives ranged from Andrha Pradesh's guarantee that all government employees undergoing sterilization would get a raise, to harsher measures. The latter included Bihar state's denial of public food rations to families with more than three children, Uttar Pradesh's order that teachers be sterilized or forfeit a month's salary, and legislation passed in Maharashtra calling for compulsory sterilization of couples with three or more children. More than twice the 4 million people targeted by the national government were sterilized in 1976, but a popular backlash forced the government to retrench once again.

Today, the quality of family-planning services remains poor, the level of public mistrust high, and demand for contraceptives low. All conspire to undercut the government's chances for reaching its goal of reducing fertility by half within a decade.

---

sons, in female infanticide and child neglect, and in the rising use of abortion for sex-selection.

THE PATH AHEAD

Like so many other countries today, India faces a series of seemingly intractable problems. Reducing population growth is critical to reversing the deterioration of both human and environmental health. However, development strategies that fail to address the root causes of the population problem render this objective virtually meaningless. The ways in which demographic goals are divorced from other development efforts have serious human rights implications for women lacking access to education, legal rights, income-earning opportunities, and the promise of increasing personal autonomy.

The Indian government can take immediate steps to meet the growing needs for good-quality health and family planning services—and improve women's health—by emphasizing maternal and child health care while at the same time offering couples a wide variety of contraceptive choices. All of these services need to be high-quality, close to home, provided by trusted members of the community, and respectful of women's fears and concerns.

Experience shows that even in India, with its immense tangle of troubles, well-designed programs can produce dramatic improvements in family health while improving women's status and reducing births. The Society for Education, Welfare, and Action-Rural (SEWA-Rural), a non-governmental group founded in 1980, tends to the health and family planning needs of 40,000 people in the 41 villages of Jaghadia, a district of Gujarat state. The organization's centrally located, well-staffed and well-equipped district hospital is linked to villages by a network of community health centers.

SEWA-Rural's doctors, village health workers, and birth attendants—the majority of whom are drawn from the local population and trained by SEWA-Rural—work together in an atmosphere of mutual respect that includes ongoing training and refresher courses, adequate pay, good working conditions, and shared concern for improving the health of all people.

The input of practitioners at every level in SEWA-Rural's operation, from village midwife to surgeon, is solicited. Among the many achievements in SEWA-Rural's first decade was the reduction by half of infant and maternal death rates, and the subsequent fall in birthrates by at least one-third throughout the region. The Indian government might duplicate this success by fostering the creation of similar high-quality, locally sponsored programs.

Increasing young girls' access to education and offering older women a chance for learning are essential to increasing female autonomy. Requisite steps include serious efforts to train and hire more female teachers, to set up literacy and tutoring campaigns in every state, and to encourage the growth of women's empowerment groups to foster changes at the village level. Indeed, the government has a role model for such programs in its own backyard. These strategies already have been proven in the southern state of Kerala, internationally lauded for its dramatic gains in the health and economic status of women and in slowing population growth.

Equally important are broad public education campaigns to raise awareness of the immense value of women's work and welfare to families and societies. An overhaul of the outmoded measures of work and productivity to reflect women's productivity in all government statistics is an imperative. The mass media also could be enlisted in the effort to change dramatically social perceptions of women's roles by depicting positive images of women and their economic contribution to society. Changes in laws and policies affecting women's access to resources are no less critical but will require political commitment to enforce.

Much of the money needed for such a comprehensive development strategy in India, as anywhere else, could be raised by reordering government priorities and improving the efficiency with which resources are now used. International experience already has proven there is no more cost-effective development strategy than investing in women, not only to improve their status, but to reduce population growth and promote equity. For example, it's a fact that Third World women, more often than men, invest their income to improve family welfare.

Much of the battle to win recognition of the importance of women's lives and health to societies will have to be fought by women themselves. Indications are that women are responding to the challenge. Throughout India, community-based groups have been bringing women together to share problems and find solutions on issues ranging from sex discrimination to wasteland development.

One example is the Deccan Development Society (DDS), a group working with women in the villages of northern Andrha Pradesh. DDS acts as a catalyst for indigenous women's groups devising plans workable in their own environs. Within just a few years, DDS and other groups have delivered marked gains in agricultural productivity, water supply, and the area of land forested, as well as in the health of women and children in the participating villages.

Reductions in poverty, increases in social equity for women, and the sustainable use of resources are compatible *and* achievable development goals. Unfortunately, the Indian government—like so many others—has taken few real steps to attain them. Now little time exists for hesitation.

By filling the existing demand for quality voluntary family planning services, the government can make cuts in birthrates of at least 25 percent over the next decade, thereby starting the process toward reducing the country's population. Equally critical to a long-term strategy of sustainable development is a sustained political commitment to improve the status of women throughout India. Only by working toward all of these objectives simultaneously can the dreams of women for full partnership in society come true.

Article 17

History Today, September 1997

WOMEN IN SOUTH ASIA: THE RAJ AND AFTER

Tanika Sarkar examines the evolving position of women in India before 1947 and since independence.

The fiftieth year of Indian independence lends itself to various kinds of stocktaking. It seems almost natural that the history of modern Indian women should be an essential part of this exercise, so when and why did the condition of women become an index to measure the nation's progress?

The nineteenth century started with extensive and anxious debates about the state of gender relations in Indian traditions. The new print culture, journalism and other forms of vernacular prose took up discussions about 'private' family matters and 'intimate' subjects concerning women and the household: suttee or widow immolation, age and forms of marriage, the possibility of divorce, of widow remarriage, education and male polygamy and so on. Social and religious reform associations spent a great deal of time arguing about such matters. Later, with the deepening of popular anti-colonial protest, the possibility of womens' participation in this widened the area of discussion still further.

All this was very new. Not only were the issues of debate unprecedented, so was the amount of talk expended on them. Prior to this gender relations were frozen in sacred laws and in custom. If they were challenged it was within the context of everyday acts of defiance by women, in their secret transgressions, protest masked as sorrowful dirges and tales indicating a sense of the unfairness of the world. Now a qualitative leap was made away from these oblique expressions to a more open interrogation—not only by women, but also by men of liberal reformist persuasion.

The change has been explained in terms of an exposure to a liberal Western education that taught middle-class Indians to question the subjection of women. However, recent interpretations have been more critical of the gender perspective of these liberal reformers, attributing the changes to a desire to emulate Victorian moral codes and aping a bourgeois form of companionate marriage.

The first to question patriarchal traditions came from modern, dissident religious sects—the Brahmo Samaj, the Prarthana Samaj and later, the Arya Samaj. It is argued that their dissent isolated and excluded these reformers from larger networks of kinship and neighbourhood ties. In terrible personal loneliness, they turned to their core family group for social sustenance: wives and daughters suddenly emerged as crucial figures in their lives and this, in turn, brought their problems into focus.

Inspired by an acute sense of the deep social malaise of the country, there was little the reformers could actually hope to change. Their upper-caste, middle-class social moorings prevented a critical engagement with issues of peasant or caste exploitation and before the formation of nationalist associations in the late nineteenth century, there was an unwillingness to reflect on the colonial condition. Given these constraints, and the fact that Indian élites were excluded from administrative and entrepreneurial initiatives, there was little else that they could try to achieve.

The very fact of political subjection, which came to be regarded as a state of humiliation, raised sensitivity to wider issues of domination and subordination. How could it be recommended for one group of people and questioned for another? The subjection of women at home was immediately thrown into the spotlight. Recommended by the highest religious authorities, what had passed as unquestionable prescription suddenly lost its force.

Early women writers—from Kailashbashini Debi in Bengal in the 1860s, to Tarabai Shinde and Pandite Ramabai from Maharashtra in the 1880s—were already identifying the distribution of power in intimate human relationships in gender-political terms. The same vocabulary was often used to describe the subjection of the country as it was the subjection of women.

Since the late eighteenth century, British rule had exempted the domain of personal laws from state intervention, unless customary or scriptural sanction could be cited as a reason for change. Three important historical developments followed from this. First, the domestic sphere, governed by the personal laws, and a site of relative autonomy, became the last bastion of a vanished freedom, as well as the possible site of an emergent nation. Secondly, law as a domain of self activism led to a widespread involvement with the processes of legal

change. The spread of print culture enabled a continuous interaction among various social groups on the everyday lives of ordinary folk. In the Telegu speaking areas of Madras, reformers relied on vernacular journalism to campaign on widow remarriage, in sharp contrast to Tamil speaking areas where reformist campaigns were moderate and dependent on English. As a result of the debates, gender norms were detached from the realm of sacred prescription or commonsense, and their ideological basis was made transparent.

Thirdly, legality now clashed with religious prescription in unprecedented ways. Suttee—hitherto a universally accepted sign of womanly virtue—was now legally classified as a crime. Widow remarriage—previously castigated by all pious Hindus as an entirely illegitimate desire—was now made legal. Not that the laws actually transformed patriarchal practices and prejudices. Iswarchandra Vidyasagar, the chief campaigner for remarriage, died a disappointed man. He often had to bribe men to marry widows and quite a few deserted their wives later. The number of remarried widows remained negligible. The Widow Remarriage Association at Rajamundry under Viresalingam Pantulu achieved a total of forty remarriages in the Telegu speaking areas of the south between 1881 and 1919. Yet the laws opened up a faultline, a tension, between what was becoming illicit practice and what was now legally permissible. Moreover, arguments replaced the unquestioned acceptance of what defined a 'good' woman. In 1870, Vishnu Shastri Pandit initiated a famous debate at Poona, the stronghold of Braham orthodoxy, on the question of remarriage. It went on for ten days. Reformers were defeated, but they had forced the orthodoxy to engage in debate.

Up until the late nineteenth century, there was a powerful customary belief that educated women were destined to be spinsters. Reformist endeavours strained against this. Starting with Calcutta, Bombay and Madras, they were able to make some education available for middle-class girls. This was done in the teeth of orthodox resistance. In colonial India, male claims to power depended very largely on their intellectual achievements, since most other forms of

'manly' and masterful enterprise were closed to them. Educated women, therefore, posed a threat to the very basis of masculinity. Orthodox reactions often took in the form of satirical imaginings of emasculated, effeminate men and masculinised women on top.

The content of women's education tended to be moderate and geared to home management—a fact which has to be separated from the actual social consequences of the act of learning. The pressure for education at least, from women in reformist, élite families was, therefore, persistent. The first girl graduates from Calcutta University received their degrees decades ahead of British women.

Reformers could not always achieve new legislation, however. Malabari's campaign for raising the age of marriage was truncated into a highly modified age of consent. Agitations against polygamy did not produce any legal deterrents. The new laws never really acquired the power and influence that religious prescriptions had enjoyed. Nor were they grounded in a strong or coherent notion of equality or individual rights. Their significance, then, was not so much the creation of a new order as questioning existing practice and rattling the bars. Once suttee, absence of education, remarriage of widows, non-consensual, indissoluble, early marriage for girls were reinterpreted as signs of great oppression, the Hindu home and the family were recast as primary sites for the practice of oppression. So the discussions extended beyond their specific objectives and made porous the divide between the private and the public spheres.

The Petition against the Abolition of Suttee of 1829 had claimed:

> Hindu widows perform of their own accord and pleasure and for the benefit of their husbands' souls and for their own the sacrifice of self immolation called suttee.

Later, the 1856 Bill to remove all legal obstacles to the marriage of Hindu widows stated:

> In the case of the widow who is of full age or whose marriage has been consummated, her own consent shall be sufficient to constitute her remarriage lawful.

The two statements came from two very different positions, one from the orthodox view that defended suttee, and the second from a reformist bill, legalising widow remarriage. Yet both refer to the woman's own consent, pleasure and will as the ultimate arbiter in the decisions. No doubt, the inference is purely strategic, consent meaning something far less than informed and adult assent. But, it was a sign of the new times that the words were used at all on the basis of internal imperative, rather than as a purely externalised prescription. In the case of the Age of Consent controversy of 1891, after a girl of ten died in Calcutta having been raped by her husband, the language of willed consent clashed too obviously with the Hindu revivalist imperative of justifying a state of non-interference and status quo in the Hindu patriarchal order. As a result, in the last decades of the nineteenth century revivalists moved away from the domain of personal laws altogether. Swami Vivekananda gathered around a group of male ascetics who would try to rejuvenate Hindu society through philanthropic service.

In Punjab and in the United Provinces, the revivalist, Vedas-based Arya Samaj of Swami Dayanand marked out a different trajectory. This group introduced quite drastic changes in conventional domestic practices: widow remarriage, an end to child marriage and male polygamy and the introduction of education for women. However, whereas earlier liberal reformers had advocated remarriage by normalising the sexual desires of child widows, Dayanand advised it in the interests of a better growth rate for the community. A widow was permitted only to remarry a widower, and the marriage had to be terminated after procreation. The women was to be educated solely for more disciplined child-rearing. Each change denied individual rights and further provoked the woman to the demographic and pedagogic purposes of an authoritarian community.

It is true that reformers, generally, functioned within a middle-class, upper-caste orbit. Few would support the Act of 1891, curtailing working hours in factories for women and children. There was little concern for the problems that tribal women faced over the encroachments of a modern market economy. Large-scale industrial production severed the earlier links between the household and production and the woman's role therein.

With the commercialisation of agriculture and the emergence of an upwardly mobile peasantry, peasant women were pulled out of farm labour in the interests of social respectability and confined to the household where their labour inputs were relatively invisible. In the new factories, there were practically no government regulations to ensure living wages, security of jobs and welfare facilities. In the tea plantations there was reckless economic and sexual exploitation of coolie women. These developments occasionally produced flashes of concerned, investigative journalistic exposure, but, otherwise, received little systematic attention. Education was largely confined to affluent, upper-caste urban families.

However, the limited reforms had some influence beyond the upper social level. There had been a long-term percolation of Brahmanical orthodoxy among upwardly-mobile low castes. Suttee, for instance, had become fairly common among several low castes in Bengal, even though the custom was meant for upper-caste widows. A prohibition against widow remarriage and the spread of infant marriage had become prevalent among castes whose custom did not prescribe such practices. Reforms that encouraged widow remarriage, womens' education and a higher age of marriage gradually emerged as alternative ways of acquiring social respectability. It is interesting that low-caste reformers like Jotirao Phule in western India knitted up the oppression against high-caste women with the exploitation of low castes to indicate the scope of Brahmanical disciplines.

Much of the nineteenth-century legal and educational reforms were restricted within the Hindu community. Modern education was a domain that even Muslim men entered rather late, after substantial resistance from the orthodoxy. Sayyid Ahmad Khan, who fought a hard battle to legitimise Western education and science, believed that women needed to be shielded from Western innovation like schooling. However, a consensus developed later in the century that women could be given an education befitting to their sex at home. Nadhir Ahmad wrote several best-selling Urdu novels popularising a new ideal for the élite woman: instead of following the typically feminine preoccupations of a leisured class, secluded education at home would turn her into a pious, responsible housewife.

While such literature reflected new patriarchal needs in an embourgeoised household, it also found enormous resonance among women readers. Accessible, fictionalised Urdu satisfied a thirst for reading matter that was at once interesting as well as serious. The narrative of home-based achievements through education created a hopeful blueprint for women whose status so far had depended only on kinship connections. While the new novels did not expand the boundaries of domestic confinement, they conveyed, nonetheless, a sense of self-worth by underlining women's importance both to home and society. They were also sensitive to the problems of seclusion.

Following upon his *Mirat al ars* and its sequels that appeared from the 1870s, and partly as a reaction to their relatively non-denominational and open nature, Maulana Ashraf Ali Thanawi came up with novels within the same format but with a different set of values. His *Bihishti Zewar* (1905) attempted a thoroughgoing Islamicisation of women who shared a lot of female custom with Hindu women. It was also careful to shore up the domestic confines that were now troubled by demands for schools for girls. In 1906, in the face of opposition from the local Urdu press, Begum Abdullah and the Begum of Bhopal had managed to open a girls' school at Aligarh.

While formal education for Muslim girls came late in the day, and legal reforms had to wait until the first few decades of the twentieth century, a different kind of battle over womens' rights was going on in the Anglo-Indian lawcourts throughout the nineteenth century. This laid the basis for the Shariati Act of the 1930s. The British Government was formally committed to privileging Quranic and Shariati regulation over customary norms and practices. The policy provided for larger property entitlements. Widows, for instance, could claim and win the restoration of the full amount of the *mehr* (the sum promised to the bride at the time of the marriage) which customarily was rarely given to her. Despite problems of deposition of evidence in court by women in Purdah, we find them tenaciously fighting out disputes in lawcourts.

The reforms had created great interest in domestic issues and women were the privileged authorities on the subject. The first generations of middle-class women graduates, doctors and teachers were seen as saviours of their sex. Their achievements were celebrated less in terms of economic independence as for proving the innate intellectual abilities of women.

Gradually women began to organise public institutions for reform: mostly, schools and widows' homes. Pandita Ramabai founded the Sharda Sadan at Poona for widows to educate and train them as teachers, doctors and nurses. Sister Subbalakshmi established a school for high-caste widows in Madras.

In the early years of the twentieth century, Begum Rokeya Sakhawat Hussein founded a chain of schools. She also wrote biting satire on the nature of religious sanction for patriarchal double standards. Subbalakshmi and Ramabai had converted to Christianity, although Ramabai's relations with her church were very tense; Rokeya was suspected of Christian leanings. All three were bitterly criticised by the custodians of their respective religious communities.

From public institutions for reform and welfare, women leaders had moved into the corridors of mainstream political activism by the second decade of the twentieth century. Associations like Womens' Indian Association, the National Council of Women in India and the All India Womens' Conference campaigned for suffrage, marriage reform, participation in municipal and legislative politics. The language of reform did not directly challenge the public/private divide, nor did it unambiguously speak about equality. Public activism of a few, however, strained against the domestic confines of most. Also, at a time of worsening Hindu-Muslim relations throughout the country, these associations represented all religious communities and advanced issues that concerned women across religious divides.

There has been considerable debate about whether the militant political activism that the Gandhian Congress offered to women empowered them in the long run. Gandhi himself espoused the ideology of separate spheres for men and women, although he was critical of specific abuses like women's seclusion. The urgent pressures of anticolonial protest made it difficult, in any case, to focus adequately on an agenda of social reform. In practice, however, Gandhi opened up forms of political activism to all women. During the Civil Disobedience movement, peasant women became 'dictators' of underground Congress units at village level while Marwari women from deeply conservative families joined street demonstrations, picketed shops and courted arrest. The principle of non-violence saw to it that women's political activism would not appear as too radically transgressive an act.

The deployment of familial images and kinship terms that described the nationalist community as a family helped women to inhabit the political domain more easily. Bi Amman, the mother of the Ali brothers, could address mass meetings of men whom she called her sons, during the Khilafat movement, reaching a stage when she could publicly unveil herself. The forms of political activism breached the boundaries of feminine domesticity irretrievably. Ordinary housewives transgressed ritual taboo by going to prison, joining street demonstrations, and facing police violence. In this vein, nationalism also created immensely widened networks of female solidarity. The active and creative political struggles of women created some of the authentic sources for Indian democracy, and disseminated a highly informed political understanding despite widespread illiteracy and poverty.

The mass movements of the Left openly repudiated the ideology of separate spheres. Women from tribal and poor peasant milieus joined enormously risky peasant armed struggles. Yet in spite of this they were excluded from decision-making processes, and thrust back into old roles after the collapse of the movements. In working-class movements, women workers joined strikes and demonstrations, and middle-class women trade unionists worked in the slums. Yet, specific problems of women workers were routinely placed at the bottom of general charters of demands and working-class women, for all their militancy, would be absent from union leadership.

When independence came, the liberal premises of Indian nationalism were embodied in the secular-democratic constitution which recognised all adult Indian women as fully-fledged citizens of the country. At the same time, a very different logic of state-sponsored patriarchy unfolded when Hindu women, abducted into Pakistani territory during the riots, were collected by state agencies and returned to their families without their consent being solicited. The tension between a formal commitment to equality and deeply ingrained patriarchal traditions in the organs of the state have remained constant. In the early 1950s, a series of laws modified Hindu marriage, divorce, inheritance and maintenance rights. Though they outraged conservative Hindu opinion, radicals and women politicians felt them to be far too moderate. The state does not interfere in the laws of the religious minorities which remain the preserve of orthodox community leaders.

A new wave in women's movements was evident from the 1970s, in the wake of radical class struggles in the late 1960s and 70s where women had participated on a wide scale, but on somewhat unequal terms. Autonomous organisations developed along with a strengthening of womens' groups within mainstream Left parties. Their radicalism has forced the state to embark upon a spate of fresh legislation, especially concerning rape and dowry.

However, women's radicalism has produced an orthodox backlash that legislative activity failed to contain. Suttee was spectacularly celebrated at Deorala in 1987 when a teenaged widow was publicly burnt to death, with the criminal instigators released by court order this year. Bhanwari Debi, a poor low-caste woman, was gang-raped at Bhateri village in Rajasthan for trying to prevent infant marriage among high-caste landlords. The police brutally humiliated her when she approached them. Law, justice and the police remain deeply implicated in the most unambiguous forms of patriarchal controls.

The recent growth of religious fundamentalism and violent Hindu majoritarianism seeks to compel women to submit to the discipline of community custodians. Majoritarian violence puts a difficult choice before Muslim women since Muslim fundamentalism uses the image of an endangered minority community to reinforce its rule, and opposes reform of divorce and maintenance regulations. The Hindutva movement, which has so far insulated its women from active politics, now offers them leading roles within violent attacks on Muslims.

The New Right divides and separates women into communities, and gender-based commonalities are sought to be undermined. This comes at a most opportune moment for the current phase in Indian capitalism when structural adjustment programmes, with their inflationary plans and their cuts into extremely meagre welfare spending, have created immense hardships for poorer women.

The sectorisation of women and the constant presence of communal violence may sap women's resistance to upper-caste and ruling-class control over the labour force, trade union rights and the bodies of low-caste, peasant, tribal and working-class women.

Have we moved ahead at all, or are we running round in circles, rooted to the same spot? There is no easy answer. The widening mobilisation of élite women for prestigious management and bureaucratic jobs must be set against the increasing vulnerability of large masses of women as employment becomes rare or informal and casual, and as prices continue to rise, cutting into their limited share of domestic resources.

Indian women still live with murders related to dowry demands, suttee, rape—especially of low-caste and labouring women—female infanticide and foeticide. Female morality is much higher and literacy rates are considerably lower in India

than they are in sub-Saharan Africa. The real measure of change lies, perhaps, more in the domain of political activism: the capacity for protest, the understanding and the world view that sustain the protests and the collectivities that enable and embody them.

FOR FURTHER READING:

J. Krishnamurty (ed), *Women in Colonial India* (Oxford University Press, 1989); Gail Minault, *The Extended Family: Women and Political Participation in India and Pakistan* (Chanakya Publications, Delhi, 1981); Sangari and Vaid (eds), *Recasting Women: Essays in Colonial History* (Kali for Women, Delhi, 1989); Zoye Hasan (ed), *Forging Identities: Gender, Communities and the State* (Kali for Women, Delhi, 1994); Tanika Sarkar and Vrashi Butalia (eds), *Women and the Hindu Right* (Zed Press, 1995).

Tanika Sarkar *is Senior Lecturer in History, St Stephen's College, University of Delhi and the author of* Bengal 1928–34: The Politics of Protest *(Oxford University Press, 1987).*

Article 18

Ms., September/October 1998

In India, Men Challenge A Matrilineal Society

By Kavita Menon

Meghalaya, a district tucked away in the remote northeastern corner of India, is home to the Khasi, one of the largest surviving matrilineal societies in the world. In this hill tribe of nearly 650,000, descent is traced through the mother's line and women have an honored place in the society. Here, baby girls are quite welcome, and, some argue, even more highly prized than boys. Since the woman's family holds the

cards when arranging a marriage, the question of dowry—paying a man's family for accepting the "burden" of a wife—would never even arise. No social stigma is attached to women, whether they choose to divorce, remarry, or stay single.

Anthropologists say the Khasi matriliny developed as a practical measure: the men were often away fighting in wars, so it made sense for the women to hold all that was precious to a family.

Money, land, and lineage were passed from youngest daughter to youngest daughter, since it was expected she would be the last to marry.

But a growing number of Khasi men are not interested in the logic of the old system. They say the matriliny has empowered women at the expense of men and the community as a whole. The epicenter of this dissent is a tiny office in a pleasant residential neighborhood in Shillong, Meghalaya's capital city. This is where the Syngkhong Rympei Thymmai (SRT)—which means "organization for the restructuring of Khasi society"—has its headquarters. The SRT, which was formed eight years ago and has a membership of about 400, including a handful of women, aims to dismantle the matriliny. It wants property to be equally divided among all the children in a family, and children to carry their father's surname.

"We believe that children should take their father's name because 90 percent of the blood comes from the male," says Johnny Lyngdoh, an active member of the SRT. Many SRT members, like Lyngdoh, believe it is both a biological and a divine imperative for a man to be the head of the family. They argue that it is the man who plants the seed that becomes the child and that for this reason almost all children resemble their fathers. For many, passing on their titles—or establishing ownership of their children and their wives—is even more important than the matter of inheritance.

SRT members believe the Khasi matriliny has favored the development of Khasi women to the detriment of the men. "Women have all the inheritance and therefore all the power," says SRT vice president Pilgrim Lakiang. "They are making more progress than the men and boys."

Women are indeed prominent in Khasi life. There are more Khasi women doctors than men, more Khasi women graduating from colleges, more Khasi women conducting business in the marketplaces. Women are now even seen in the traditional governing bodies, or durbars, which were once off-limits to them.

In contrast, Khasi men are said to be drinking too much, and are increasingly worried about losing their jobs, their land, and their women to migrants from West Bengal and Bangladesh. "Well-to-do families give their daughters to non-tribals instead of to Khasi boys, and property and other assets that belong to the Khasi society pass to them," bemoans the writer of an article in one SRT booklet.

Others in the community, like Sweetymon Rynjah, a retired civil servant, believe the men have only themselves to blame for their problems. "The males have become degraded in the perform-ance of their duties," she says. "They haven't understood their own customs. They have only read the customs of other people."

By "the customs of other people" Rynjah means Christianity. European missionaries introduced the Christian faith to Meghalaya in the 1800s. Many tribe members have since replaced Ka Iawbei, the original grandmother from whom all Khasi clans trace their ancestry, with the Father, Son, and Holy Ghost. About half the Khasi population is Christian, as against almost the entire SRT membership.

Donakor Shanpru is a single woman in her late forties whose family home is situated on the same block as the SRT headquarters. She lives in the home of her youngest aunt, who is also unmarried, with other members of the extended family including her father, a widower; a brother, who has left his wife and child; and two sisters (whose husbands have both left them, then tried to return, only to be turned away) and their children.

Shanpru, who teaches Khasi literature at one of Shillong's four women's colleges, has no patience with the SRT or its views. As far as she's concerned, it is a minority group expressing a minority position, and she's happy to let you know that its president has been kicked out of her house three times for "talking nonsense." For all the SRT's huffing and puffing, Shanpru says, Khasi men have been invested with important duties, as husbands, fathers, and maternal uncles in the clan. Maternal uncles in particular exercise a lot of clout—though the youngest daughter holds the purse strings and her opinions matter, it is typically the oldest maternal uncle who decides when and how to spend the clan's money.

But while the SRT positions are seen as extremist by some, they do fit into a larger debate within the society and attract some unexpected sympathizers. Patricia Mukhim, a journalist from Shillong, agrees to some extent with what the SRT is saying. She believes that giving boys an equal share of the family property will boost their self-esteem and encourage them to be more responsible, industrious husbands and citizens. Mukhim also blames the matriliny for making Khasi marriages "very brittle." Divorce has become too easy, she says, because husbands and wives can always return to their respective clans.

Men's roles are less of an issue in the villages where the traditional system still serves people's needs.

Where Mukhim disagrees with the SRT is in the speed of change. "We can't turn the system inside out so suddenly," she says. But change must come, she feels, since the problems that the men are facing affect everybody in the end.

A traditional society is being pressured to adjust to a modern world that is increasingly urban, and one in which families are smaller and more distant. Although the men's movement and the anxiety it expresses are city-based—men's roles are less of an issue in the villages where the traditional system still serves people's needs—the debate is widespread. The extent of it was made clear recently when the Khasi Social Custom of Lineage Bill, which seeks to codify Khasi customary law, and maintain matriliny, was put on hold.

The bill stalled following disagreements voiced by various factions that don't necessarily hold to the old way—many of the most respected Khasi intellectuals already use the clan title of their fathers, according to *Grassroots Options,* a magazine that covers the Indian northeast. If the bill is passed, those who don't adhere to all the traditions would have to relinquish Khasi status—and the privileges that go with it. Minorities in India are entitled to special benefits, including quotas for places in universities and jobs in the government.

Even though the matriliny has been the norm in Khasi society, that doesn't mean there are no gendered roles. In one traditional Khasi dance, for instance, the women are required to creep slowly forward by wriggling their toes like inchworms. They move in large groups, chins upturned and eyes downcast, looking very regal in their elaborate headdresses and long gowns. The role of the men is to "protect" the women—and they look like they're having great fun galloping, skipping, and spinning in circles around the women, while madly waving long, feathered whisks.

In the dance, the women are locked into the lines and circles assigned them, a reminder that in addition to being doctors and teachers and shopkeepers, they are still expected to be dutiful daughters, good mothers, and patient wives. And, for all the SRT members' talk of being downtrodden, men in a traditional Khasi home are still served the top of the rice bowl as a blessing on the family—and they very rarely cook or clean.

Kavita Menon, a writer, works at the Committee to Protect Journalists, in New York City.

Article 19   *The Christian Science Monitor,* May 13, 1998

India's Parsi community may have to change customs in order to grow.

Oldest Prophetic Religion Struggles For Survival

By John Zubrzycki

Special to The Christian Science Monitor

BOMBAY

DEEP in the heart of downtown Bombay, a century-old blue-granite building stands like a silent sentinel to an ancient community in rapid decline. The dilapidated building houses the Parsi Lying-in Hospital, established in 1893 as a maternity unit for the city's once-thriving Parsi community. Built to accommodate 40 beds, its wards are almost empty today. "We get only four or five patients a month," says Zarin Langdana, the doctor-in-charge. "And most of them are not Parsis."

As India's population expands steadily, the country's Parsi community faces extinction. Emigration, falling birthrates, the growing tendency to marry outside the community, and an injunction against accepting converts is threatening to erase Zoroastrianism, the world's oldest prophetic religion, and its followers from the map of India. "We are an endangered species, just like the tiger and the lion," says Jamshed Guzdar, chairman of the Parsi Panchayat, or council.

A recent demographic study predicts that by 2021, when the population of India will be 1.2 billion, the number of Parsis will drop from their current level of 60,000 to just 21,000.

Bombay legacy

Parsis once dominated Bombay's commercial life. Almost every major municipal building built in the 19th century had the bust or statue of a Parsi benefactor perched on a pedestal outside. Parsis started the city's first hospital, university, and municipal corporation. The city's best-known landmark is probably the Taj hotel, built by Jamshetji Nusserwanji Tata in 1903 after he was refused entry into the exclusive Green's Hotel because he was a native.

> Zoroastrian activist Smiti Crishna says, 'The religion has to undergo a change in order to protect and propagate the community.'

Mr. Jamshetji's great-grandson Ratan controls India's largest industrial conglomerate, the Tata group. "Now the Parsi population's outlook has changed," laments Mr. Guzdar. "There is on urge to step forward and create for themselves high positions in business and industry. Now they find they cannot meet the competition."

For most communities, the prospect of extinction would unite members, but it has divided the Parsis. In Bombay, the world's Parsi "capital," the gulf between those who refuse to question orthodox Zoroastrianism and those clamoring for reform is breaking apart a once close-knit community.

Perhaps the most divisive issue is whether the children of a Parsi woman who marries outside the community can be considered Zoroastrian. "It's a very emotional issue," says Jehangir Patel, editor of the monthly magazine Parsiana. "As the community gets smaller, your chances of finding a Parsi spouse to your liking are dwindling. More and more families are being touched by this problem."

Questioning Zoroastrianism

With almost 1 in 4 women marrying outside the community and almost as many not marrying at all, the mixed-marriage bias is being challenged. "People are questioning the faith much more," says Smiti Crishna, vice chairperson of the Association of Intermarried Zoroastrians. "The religion has to

undergo a change in order to protect and propagate the community."

A member of the wealthy Godrej family of Parsi industrialists, Ms. Crishna broke the taboo on intermarriages when she wed a Christian businessman. According to the orthodox keepers of the faith, her two daughters cannot undergo a *navjote,* or baptism ceremony, or enter a Zoroastrian fire temple. "Women like us are ostracized," Crishna says. "Why should people look down on us when there is no injunction against intermarriage in our holy books?"

> Dastur Firoze Kotwal, a Parsi high priest, dismisses demands that a ban on conversions be lifted to swell the community's numbers.

That's wrong, retorts Dastur Firoze Kotwal, one of the religion's eight high priests, who leafs through a religious text in his south Bombay flat. According to Dastur Kotwal, the Zoroastrian scriptures outlaw all intermarriages. He also dismisses demands that the ban on conversions be lifted to swell the community's numbers, a stand that has put him at loggerheads with the normally conservative Parsi Panchayat. "Zarathustra never said you can't convert. If you don't allow conversions, how does the community grow?" asks Guzdar of the Parsi Panchayat.

Alarmed by the steady demographic decline of the Parsi population, Guzdar persuaded the Panchayat to sponsor the third child of every Parsi couple to encourage larger families. The Panchayat now looks after the material and educational needs of 45 children. "I thought to myself, I cannot let my community perish," Guzdar says. "I hope that by doing something like this, the population will increase."

A successful businessman who established India's first air freight business in the 1940s, Guzdar plans to set up a venture-capital fund to encourage young Parsi entrepreneurs to start businesses in India rather than moving abroad.

Persian Roots of Zoroastrian Faith

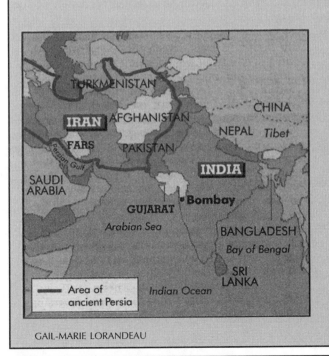

GAIL-MARIE LORANDEAU

BOMBAY

The Zoroastrian religion was expounded sometime before 600 BC by the ancient Persian prophet, Zarathustra, who lived in what is now eastern Iran. Some scholars, however, say the prophet, whose name means "rich in camels," dates back as far as 1200 BC.

Central to the religion is a concept of righteousness or natural law, the notion of a supreme all-knowing and benign God, and the rejection of polytheism. The word Parsi is thought to be derived from Fars, the name of the port in Persia from which the Parsis fled in the 10th century AD to protect their religion from Islamic persecution.

The first Parsi settlers soon arrived on the coast of Gujarat, taking with them the sacred fire that, according to the legend, has

burned continuously in their temples ever since. Like earth and water, fire is sacred to the Zoroastrians and symbolizes *asha,* the concept of truth, order, and righteousness.

When Bombay became a trading center under the British in the 17th century, the Parsis moved to the city in large numbers, quickly establishing a reputation for hard work, entrepreneurship, and honesty. Their ability to adapt to Western ways made them into a colonial elite, and they flourished under British patronage. While the Parsis are unique to India and remain the largest contingent of the Zoroastrians today, pockets of followers remain in Iran as well as in other parts of Asia, the United States, and Canada.

—*J.Z.*

The disappearance of the Parsis would not just be a loss for Bombay. This small but talented community has produced composers like Zubin Mehta, novelists like Rohiton Mistry, and the late rock star Freddie Mercury, the former front man of the band Queen. "Last year when I was asked to become the chairman of the National Foundation for Social Affairs and Family Planning, I was told, 'Do all you can to control India's population but make sure the Parsis increase in number,'" chuckles Guzdar.

Article 20

India Abroad, December 6, 1996

Dire Warnings of Environmental Disaster

Taani Pande

NEW DELHI—Political indifference and a lack of public consciousness may sound the death knell for India's environment, ecological activists warn.

Mounting problems of deforestation, destruction of precious wildlife species, air pollution, dumping of toxic wastes and uncleared piles of garbage in every city are having a deleterious effect on the country's ecological health, environmentalists say.

According to Anil Aggarwal, environmental crusader and director of the Delhi-based Center for Science and Environment (CSE), India is one of the worst environmentally damaged countries in the world.

"We are in the middle of an environmental disaster," he says.

According to a recent World Bank study, environmental damage in the country amounted to a total of $9.7 billion per year, or 4.5 percent of the gross domestic product, in 1992. Titled "The Cost of Inaction: Valuing the Economy-Wide Cost of Environmental Degradation in India," the report puts India's annual environmental costs at higher than China's.

The estimates disclose that the largest share of economic and health costs, about $7 billion a year, emerges from the growing pollution of water and air. Water degradation accounts for the highest health toll across the country, accounting for costs of $5.7 billion, or 59 percent of the total environmental costs. Land degradation and deforestation result in production losses of about $2.7 billion annually, the report said. Total health costs from pollutant levels exceeding WHO guidelines are estimated at $517 million to $2.102 billion.

However, environmentalists feel the study is a gross understatement and does not account for a large number of environmental costs. Health costs arising from pollution due to hazardous wastes, indoor air pollution and rising costs of providing clean drinking water, among others, are some of the things not mentioned in the report, they maintain.

The concept of environmental protection and making it a social responsibility is largely nonexistent in India. This situation is likely to continue till the environment is made an electoral issue, Aggarwal said, remarking, "Politicians are simply not interested because this (the environment) is not an electoral issue as yet."

Environmentalist Sunder Lal Bahuguna, renowned for his espousal of the cause of environmental protection in the Himalayan foothills, lambasted political parties for their callous approach to environmental issues, saying, "The environment does not figure in the agenda of any political party."

"The State of Forest Report (1995)" published by the Ministry of Environment and Forests (MEF) notes an alarming 507 square-kilometer decrease in forest cover in India for the two-year period since 1993. According to MEF data, 16 states and union territories showed a decline in forest cover during that period.

Ten states and union territories showed an increase and in three the forest cover remained unchanged. At present, only 19 percent of India's total geographical area of 1,222,559 square miles is covered by forests. Experts, who maintain that one-third of the country's total land mass should be covered by forests, noted that the present forest cover is only half of what it should be.

Another report titled "Green India 2047" published by the Delhi-based Tata Energy Research Institute (TERI) said that half of the current forest cover was "degraded to a varying extent." "Frequent forest fires and indiscriminate grazing are among the most important causes for degradation of the forests in India. These two factors affect not only the ecology of the area but also decrease the natural regeneration of tree species to a very considerable extent," the MEF report said.

India's forests also have a poor rate of regeneration and this is because of "unregulated grazing over forest lands and the erosion of growing stock due to unsustainable fuel wood demand," the TERI report said, adding, "As against a world average of 2.1 cubic meters per hectare every year, the productivity of India's forests lies between 0.7 and 1.1 cubic meter per hectare every year." The report points out that while fuel wood demand in 1990 was 235 million cubic meters, the amount sustainable was only 40 million cubic meters.

India's forests are under severe pressure from the diversion of forest areas to other uses and through encroachment, the ecologists say. The TERI report estimates that between 1981 and 1994 0.3 million hectares of forest land was diverted to other uses.

Forests in the lower Himalayan region of Uttar Pradesh state have witnessed large-scale timber smuggling. Nearly 15,800 cases of timber theft were reported in the state during the 1995–96, when timber worth nearly a million dollars was reported "stolen" from forests in the state. India, which accounts for 2.4 percent of the world's land area, contributes to 7 percent of the world's agri-biodiversity. The country has two of the world's 18 identified hot spots, one in the eastern Himalayas and the other in the western ghats. Today these areas are under severe threat from poachers.

According to Aggarwal, "Indian wildlife areas and wildlife living in those areas are in a state of crisis. A lot of wildlife is being killed and a lot of poaching is going on and the tiger, the flagship species in the country, is likely to disappear."

Increasing air pollution in urban areas has become a major cause of concern for environmentalists. Studies indicate that six of India's ten largest cities—Delhi, Calcutta, Bombay, Nagpur, Kanpur and Ahmedabad—have recorded average levels of total suspended particulates at least three times as high as the WHO standard.

Delhi and Calcutta are already listed among the seven most polluted cities in the world. A study conducted by the Delhi-based Central Pollution Control Board disclosed that 2,000 tons of pollutants are released into Delhi's air every day. One in every five persons has developed a respiratory disorder in Delhi. Physicians in the city claim that respiratory diseases are on the rise even though the number of smokers has decreased. Health officials in Calcutta have reported an increasing trend of respiratory illnesses like bronchitis, pulmonary edema and dust allergies among the city's inhabitants.

India's urban population has increased from 62 million in 1951 to 217 million in 1991. The rise in population has led to an increase in the demand for mobility, which has led to an explosion in the number of vehicles in the cities. Environ-

mentalists point out that vehicular emissions are the largest contributors to air pollution in urban areas.

Environmentalists maintain that lead is among the most pervasive and toxic of the environmental contaminants that are finding their way into the country. According to Iqbal Malik of the Vatavaran non-governmental organization (NGO), "Lead is one of the most strictly regulated substances in the industrial countries. Most lead recycling plants in the U.S. have been shut down over the past 12 years." Lead is being imported into India in the form of lead acid batteries, which are being phased out internationally, she alleged.

India's trade with developed nations in recyclable and toxic wastes has been increasing, Malik pointed out. "As Western environmental standards tighten and hazardous waste disposal costs soar, producers arelooking to developing countries to get rid of their waste cheaply," she said.

Ecological activists fear that with Africa closing its doors to toxic wastes and China following suit, India is increasingly becoming the world's dumping ground. However, manufacturers do not agree with their contention. Kailash C. Aggarwal of the Chandigarh-based Micronutrient Manufacturer's Association said all manufacturers have to work within the specified laws. Overseas consignments are "imported by regular actual user bona-fide manufacturers" and are tested by various customs authorities, he added.

Serviced by an outdated sewage disposal system, Indian cities continue to be plagued by piles of rotting garbage. According to Dinesh Mehta of the National Institute of Urban Affairs, the present system is not geared to handle the continually increasing amounts of waste from the cities.

Apart from the increasing quantities of waste, the alterations in its composition are also becoming a problem for waste managers, Mehta said, adding, "More paper, metal, plastic and hazardous material is finding its way into the waste discharged in most cities."

Since most cities are either home to, or are surrounded by, industries or industrial units, wastes from here are dumped together with domestic wastes, Mehta said. "Industrial wastes are not treated properly (before release). Most industrial effluents carry toxic chemicals that can travel great distances," he added.

Cities also have a large amount of hospital wastes, which if not disposed of properly can become a major threat, he said. The dumping of untreated wastes into water bodies, which supply drinking water to the cities, is affecting not only the immediate water supply but is also threatening ground-water resources.

A TERI survey of ground-water quality conducted in 22 industrialized zones, with a network consisting of 138 sampling locations, showed that water in none of the areas was fit for drinking. The survey revealed that some samples showed concentrations of toxic metals and toxic chemicals as high as 20 times the safe limit for drinking water.

Ecological activists say India suffers annual losses worth more than Rs. 10 billion from flood and cyclone damage, making it the most disaster-prone area of the world. About 40 million hectares of land area of the country are prone to floods and available date indicates that the frequency of the floods is increasing annually.

Bahuguna said, "As of now, the government has no concrete disaster management policy. Many of the disasters are first created by us and then crores of rupees are spent in relief and rescue operations." Manoj Mathur of the Indian Red Cross Society said the major causes of floods are irregular and unplanned settlements, haphazard development and deforestation.

Meanwhile, NGOs have begun working to change the apathetic attitude toward the environment. Noted environmentalist Medha Patkar, who has been working with villagers at grass-root levels and has launched a campaign to protest the construction of a dam on the River Narmada in Gujarat, has said that such organizations are considering the possibility of entering electoral politics.

A viable option available to NGOs is to form a political party with a distinct identity to contest elections on national issues, Patkar said. This issue will come up for discussion at the next meeting of NGO representatives in December, she said.

Article 21

World Watch, November/December 1995

India's Low-Tech Energy Success

How 2 million power plants are turning cow dung into electric power and cooking fuel—and ending up with even better fertilizer than manure.

Payal Sampat

Payal Sampat was a research intern at the Worldwatch Institute and is currently studying international environmental policy at Tufts University.

Cow dung may not be the first thing that comes to mind when you think of state-of-the-art energy technology. Yet in the tiny village of Pura in south India, this humble waste material is providing people with basic amenities formerly in short supply: electric light, pumped water, and clean cooking fuel. An ingeniously simple process that converts dung into a flammable gas, called biogas, has greatly improved dally life for Pura's 485 inhabitants—and for over 10 million other rural Indians.

Biogas, as its name suggests, is produced by extracting chemical energy from organic materials. This process takes place in a sealed container known as a biogas digester. The digester is usually a squat, cement cylinder two to four meters in diameter, with a duct in the side that allows the dung or other organic wastes to be fed in, along with water. In ambient temperatures of 25 to 35 degrees centigrade, the material soon begins to ferment. This produces a mixture of gases, primarily methane and carbon dioxide, and a nutrient-rich slurry. The gas is drawn out through a valve at the top of the digester,

and the slurry is drained off into settling troughs at its base. (See illustration.)

Methane is the combustible component of biogas. It is piped into homes to be used as a cooking fuel, or used to fire a diesel engine to generate electricity, as in the case of Pura. The slurry is such an excellent fertilizer that it's often more highly valued than the gas—biogas plants are often called "biofertilizer plants."

Biogas dates as far back as the 16th century, when it was used for heating bath-water in Persia, and it has been used in India for almost a hundred years. In 1981, however, the Indian government launched biogas production on a large scale, by embarking on a "National Project on Biogas Development." Close to 2 million digesters have been constructed in India since then, and although the program has had its share of problems, it has made substantial progress. Most plants are located In rural, agrarian parts of the country and are designed to serve the cooking needs of a single household of four to seven people. Over 1,150 large "community" plants—like the one in Pura—have also been installed. These are operated by an entire village, and the cooking fuel or electricity is shared by the community.

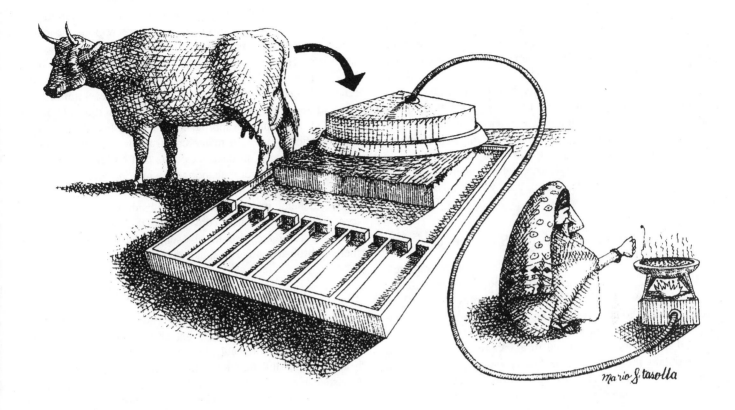

Why Biogas?

Ostensibly 84 percent of Indian villages are connected to the electrical grid, but only 27 percent of their inhabitants actually had access to power in 1991, according to R. K. Pachauri of the Tata Energy Research Institute in New Delhi. That means 435 million people, more than half of India's population, lack electricity. And 80 percent of rural India faces difficulties in obtaining sufficient cooking fuel. Biogas bypasses these shortages and transmission problems by providing a decentralized and locally-controlled fuel supply from a readily available material.

Generating biogas also makes sense in the Indian cultural context. All products of the cow, including dung (or "gobar" in Hindi) are considered purifying agents by Hindus, according to O. P. Joshi, a sociologist at the H. C. Mathur Institute of Public Administration in Rajasthan. In the classical Indian epic, the *Mahabharata,* says Joshi, "gobar is described as the living place of Lakshmi, the goddess of wealth." Traditionally in India, dung is collected and fashioned into dung-cakes, to be burned directly as fuel or composted for fertilizer. Dung accounts for over 21 percent of total rural energy use in India, and as much as 40 percent in certain states.

Usually, dung used for one purpose is lost to the other, but biogas provides a means to both ends. It exploits the caloric content of the waste, while retaining the nutrients as fertilizer—and on both counts, it is more efficient than traditional methods. Direct burning only captures about 11 percent of the

dung's energy value, but biogas generation has a 45 to 60 percent efficiency. In other words, biogas captures approximately 5 times as much energy as does direct burning. And the by-product slurry has twice the nitrogen content of composted dung because open-air composting allows much of the nitrogen to escape in the form of volatile compounds. The slurry also releases its nutrients more readily than composted dung. And unlike decomposing dung, it is odorless and does not attract flies or mosquitoes. Farmers in Pura say it actually *repels* termites, and inhibits weed growth.

In addition to the slurry's nutrient recycling function, the gas itself has important environmental benefits. It offers an ecologically sustainable alternative to fuel wood, which currently provides over half of India's rural household energy. Biogas can help check deforestation; in the 1980s, for instance, when biogas technology was introduced into villages near the Gir Lion Sanctuary in Gujarat, woodcutting within the Sanctuary dropped substantially. And since the conversion process in the digester is anaerobic (it occurs in the absence of oxygen), it destroys most of the pathogens present in dung and waste, thereby reducing the potential for infections like dysentery and enteritis.

The burning of traditional fuels like dung cakes or wood releases high levels of carbon monoxide, suspended particulates, hydrocarbons, and often, contaminants like sulfur oxides. (Dung contains traces of hydrogen sulfide, which is converted to sulfur oxides on combustion.) Exposure to these fumes in unvented cooking spaces increases the risk of respiratory disease. According to a study sponsored by the World Health Organization, Indian women cooking over firewood were inhaling as much of the carcinogen benzopyrene—a combustion by-product of wood—as they would by smoking 20 packs of cigarettes a day. Because it is a gas, biogas burns much more efficiently than these solid fuels. It leaves very few contaminants, although it is true that biogas releases small quantities of sulfur oxides. Biogas offers perhaps the most environmentally benign method for tapping the solar energy stored in biomass. It's a renewable and decentralized alternative to the other methane-based fuel, natural gas, which is commonly used in cities.

The Economics of Self-Sufficiency

But biogas is more than just a renewable energy technology. As a comprehensive rural development tool, it allows villages to meet fundamental needs using local resources. It is a labor-intensive technology, and therefore a significant source of employment, especially for village women who collect the dung and sell the slurry, and for the rural laborers who construct and maintain the plants. Some family biogas digesters even support small-scale enterprises, by providing electricity for agricultural and cottage industries. Community digesters encourage collective responsibility and local participation in decision-making. The role that women play in the operation enhances their social standing. Biogas also helps ease the traditional burdens of women and girls, by reducing the amount of time they have to spend collecting fuel-wood. And with the advent of biogas-powered pumps, it also reduces the time spent fetching water.

A biogas digester with a 2 cubic meter capacity—enough to meet the cooking needs of a family of five—costs approximately $350. The costs of inputs are minimal assuming the household has a water supply and at least five cows—the minimum necessary to supply the digester. Yet despite government subsidies that run as high as 85 percent of total costs, start-up expenses can seem formidable to farmers, whose participation in the cash economy is often limited.

Finding a Strategy That Works

India's biogas plants are generally sound investments, particularly the community digesters, which can achieve greater economies of scale. Yet the biogas program has not yet taken off as some experts expected it to. According to the Tata Institute's Pachauri, only two-thirds of the installed plants are actually functioning (although official figures have placed this figure at 89 percent), and the project is now faced with major funding cuts. Given the technical simplicity and the many advantages of biogas production, what went wrong?

Biogas production is limited by environmental conditions such as the need for warm temperatures and availability of water and dung. In cooler or drought-prone regions, or in villages with insufficient cattle, projects have failed. These and other problems relating to construction and maintenance have been compounded by institutional factors that obstruct most renewable energy projects. As an essentially decentralized energy strategy, biogas has suffered from a far too centralized and topdown planning approach. Across-the-board implementation policies have led to the construction of plants in areas unsuited to biogas production; plants that suffered from technical difficulties were abandoned when project technicians failed to follow up. And although the government introduced many financial incentives such as subsidies and tax benefits to encourage biogas use, conventional fuels like diesel, kerosene and LPG are also highly subsidized in rural areas, so there is little incentive to make the switch.

Tapping into the Potential

Restructuring rural energy subsidies, and bringing the planning down to the local level, would unlock an enormous energy potential. India has more cattle than any other country—262 million head. (It is possible that this immense herd may eventually prove unsustainable, but for the present at least, rural India needs its cows. They do much of the plowing and transporting that is done by tractors and trucks in other parts of the world.) Given the amount of dung available, it has been estimated that biogas could provide cooking fuel to 52 percent of the Indian population during the part of the year when conditions are optimum, and for 25 percent of the population during the lean season, when dung production, water supply, and temperatures are low. According to Amulya Reddy of the International Energy Initiative in Bangalore, harnessing this total potential would conserve some 130 million tons of wood. In theory, that amount of wood could yield enough liquid or gaseous fuel to power every truck, bus, and irrigation pump in the country.

Many other developing nations, primarily in Asia but also in Africa and Latin America, have implemented biogas programs. The Chinese program is the largest. In 1991, it had 5 million digesters; these use human waste as well as animal dung. The United States and several western European countries are interested in the biogas potential of other sources of organic waste, mainly municipal solid waste. It's too early to say how much power this approach will eventually yield, but over the next few years, a number of large U.S. and European biogas plants are scheduled to go online.

The goal of India's biogas program is to construct digesters for the 12 million rural Indian households that have enough cattle to maintain a regular supply of dung. Depending on family size, this would mean a regular supply of fuel for 60 to 85 million people. In a largely agrarian nation where rural electrification is limited and commercial fuels make up only 11 percent of rural energy use, biogas could go a long way toward improving the energy and environmental future. And given the broad availability of dung, crop residues, and other organic wastes, biogas could do the same elsewhere. Along with other renewable technologies like photovoltaics, biogas could help form the foundations of a decentralized energy strategy in many developing countries.

Article 22

The World & I, October 1996

A Celluloid Hall of Mirrors

The world's largest film industry churns out wildly popular music and dance extravaganzas that have roots deep in Indian culture, but a number of films reflect more complex realities.

Somi Roy

Somi Roy is a film curator based in New York City. His articles have appeared in a number of national magazines, including Asian Art, Artforum, *and* Wide Angle.

As filmmakers in countries from France to Japan lament that their country's top-grossing films come from Hollywood, the Indian film industry is more than holding its own. Indeed, it might be ventured that within India itself, the popular Indian film, along with its inescapable music, is perhaps the single most important modern force—cricket being a distant second—that has held together this incredibly diverse nation of 850 million people with well over 200 languages.

Remarkably independent of Hollywood and other major film centers, the popular Indian film has its own body of cinematic conventions and stylistic signatures. If one has seen the spectacular song-and-dance melodrama that is the run-of-the-mill Indian film, one might wonder why these films have such tremendous appeal, not only in India but throughout the geographic area that stretches from Morocco to Indonesia.

To begin with, it is all rather awe-inspiring and numbing. Credits and title music blast your eyes and ears. The hero takes on the food hoarder, dances with the heroine on a hilltop, engages a gang of hooligans in a choreographed fight. There is applause, wolf whistles, singing, and dancing in the aisles. Outside, three-story-high movie posters with film stars painted in poisonous green, neon blue, and lurid pink scream: "Every Sinner Has to Pay the Price!" "A Saga of Love, Hate, and Desire!" and "He Sings, He Dances, He Kills, Too!"

The typical film is a star-studded affair with household names like Amitabh Bachhan, Sanjay Dutt, Sridevi, and Madhuri Dixit. (Some stars, like Bachhan and Rajesh Khanna, are so popular they are elected to political office.)

Structurally, the usual popular film essentially strings together six or seven extended sequences of song and dance with bits of melodramatic plot sandwiched between. Emphasis is not on the linear unfolding of a story line (unlike the popular films of the West, with their novelistic narrative); plots are interrupted by lengthy music, dance, fight, or comedy sequences that may have nothing to do with the plot. In a typically three-hour film, the plot may be introduced at the beginning but may not reappear until after the intermission.

The roots of this burlesquelike approach lie in traditions of folk theater and performance that stretch back 2,000 years, traditions that developed from dances performed at religious festivals. The fact that popular Indian cinema uses these as the basis of its film grammar accounts for the immense popularity of these films in India, but it also may explain their appeal in countries that have similarly ancient yet still vital folk cultures.

Stories and themes are repeated in film after film: good triumphing over evil, the struggle of the poor, the sins of the big city, the destruction of family. Actors declaim stylized dialogue underscored by near-constant background music. The result is a heady mixture of fantasy and exaggerated melodrama that packs in the crowds. In India, every showing of these popular-audience films attracts throngs like *Independence Day* did at its U.S. opening, even though in large cities theaters seat several thousand. The biggest blockbuster, *Sholay* (1975), ran for five years in one Bombay theater alone.

Reflections in Cinema

- Most popular Indian films are music and dance extravaganzas with roots in ancient traditions.
- "All-India" films, made to reach the broadest audience, are a force for cultural and linguistic unity.
- Since the late 1960s, filmmakers of the New Indian Cinema have striven to reflect daily life realistically and to create serious art films.

While the popular Indian film consists of musical extravaganzas, the film industry also produces other kinds by internationally recognized artists like Satyajit Ray, who was awarded a Lifetime Achievement Oscar in 1992 for masterpieces such as *Pather Panchali* (1955) and *Jana Aranya* (1975). Directors including Ray, Shyam Benegal, and Adoor Gopalakrishnan make independent films that, like the independent "art films" in the United States, are seen by smaller, more discriminating audiences.

Films by these independent directors, being the work of individualistic artists, don't fall into easily identifiable genres. But popular Indian cinema, manufactured as commercial entertainment, has enthroned a handful of reigning genres.

This was true from the beginning. Dadasaheb Phalke, an amateur magician and theater buff, made *Raja Harishchandra*, the first Indian feature, in 1912. Released to an enthusiastic audience the following year, it cannily took a story from Indian mythology well known to the national collective mind. It was the beginning of a hardy and perennially popular genre of Indian cinema: the mythological film—usually based on episodes from religious epics such as the Ramayana and the Mahabharata—and its cousin the devotional film, about the lives of Indian saints.

Historical films about familiar figures, like *Razia Begum* (1924), soon followed. And as film came to India at a time when the country was poised to embark on major social and political reforms, a more realistic genre called the social film emerged, with its cautious critiques of social evils like dowries and polygamy.

Thus, Indian cinema was truly Indian from the start. The mythological, devotional, historical, and social genres still

survive, sometimes in new, surprising mutations.

In fashioning their films, Indian filmmakers were basically exercising good business sense. The industry is big business: About $270 million is invested in films annually. It is the largest film industry in the world (almost three times bigger than that of Hollywood), producing over 800 films on average every year. The budget of a film usually runs to about 30 million rupees, or about $1 million.

Superstar actresses work on up to six films a day, in six different shifts, shuttling from one studio to another.

A major film issues only 100 to 150 prints—compared with Hollywood's 3,000 or so for a major release—since there are only about 13,000 cinemas in India, one-third of which are touring cinemas that screen movies in outdoor tents. Still, five billion tickets are sold every year to 300 million moviegoers. Tickets are relatively cheap—a ticket in an air-conditioned Bombay theater may cost as much as 20 rupees, about 80 cents, and in a touring cinema it may be as little as 2 rupees, less than a dime.

The all-India film, also called the Hindi film, is made in Bombay, a city the size of New York, and is seen pretty much throughout India. It also receives international distribution to the geo-

graphic swath mentioned earlier. Yet, in this country of so many different languages and dialects, there are in addition five major film production centers in five different states, each making films in one of five major languages: Tamil, Malayalam, Telugu, Bengali, and Kannada. These generally do not receive international distribution. The all-India film and the five others all follow the formulaic approach outlined above, though some younger regional filmmakers have forsaken formulas for more authentic reflections of local life.

As for the stars, many sign on for up to 20 films at once. Superstar actresses like Sridevi work on up to six films a day, in six different shifts, shuttling from one studio to another—a practice that has earned them the name "taxi stars." Over 600 film magazines, with names like *Stardust* and *Film fare,* breathlessly cover the lives and careers of these stars for hungry fans.

Characteristics and Impact

Because it is such big business, the popular Indian film has evolved several characteristic features. It is these features—formulaic filmmaking (colloquially referred to as *masala* filmmaking, a term derived from the mix of spices that go into an Indian curry), melodrama, nonspecificity as to regional cultures, nonsectarianism, and music and dance—that have made the film industry so powerful in India today.

The perfunctory attention often paid to the script and the resultant formulaic quality of the films is very much a response to India's postindependence economic policies, which financed social programs for education, industry, and agriculture with high taxes and tight controls on industry. As much as 60 percent of all box-office receipts went into taxes of one sort or another. At the time there was no credit financing and, under these heavy taxation rates, producers were forced to turn to distributors to finance films. They would sell distributors regional rights to films, but the distributors in turn demanded tried-and-true formula films: major stars, six dances, seven songs, and so on. Popular stars began working in several films at once, script values began to suffer, and the melodramatic formula film became ascendant. The resulting masala film made for high entertainment values and reliable escapist fare for the average audience.

What the Indian film provides without parallel are Indian dreams based on Indian situations acted out by Indian character archetypes.

('Twas not ever thus. During the time when India was struggling to shake off the British, many Indians felt it was vital to modernize. In the 1930s and '40s filmmakers made movies that, though still melodramatic, took up extremely powerful social themes with solid scripts and strong story lines. Classics such as *Achhut Kanya* (1936) and *Duniya na Mane* (1937) may have had some elements of song and dance, but the result was not the pastiche that is so prevalent today.)

Melodrama itself—with its sensational, emotionally overwrought, romantic, and violent character—is eminently suited to being the prime form for popular entertainment everywhere. The average Hollywood product (especially thrillers), or any soap opera worth its salt in tears, provides as much. What the Indian film provides without parallel are Indian dreams based on Indian situations acted out by Indian character archetypes. In a popular film such as Maui Rathnam's *Bombay* (1994), a Hindu boy and a Muslim girl who fall in love are forced to escape their village for the relative secular anonymity and safety of Bombay, which later explodes in religious riots. The familiar Indian archetypes—such as, in this film, young star-crossed lovers, complaining in-laws, a family ruptured by an intolerant and violent society, and the contrast of intimate village life with the anonymous and decadent city—make it easy for a broad spectrum of people to identify with the characters and situations.

Because the Indian film is designed to attract the largest number of viewers, and mainly in towns and cities, the all-India film shows no regional specificity. Its story, sets, costumes, and language are devoid of the cultural distinctions of the different linguistic and ethnic regions—say Bengal or Kerala—that actually make up the country, although all these aspects in fact tend to be dominated by the numerically dominant culture of northern India. Though generally called the Hindi film, the all-India is actually in Hindustani, a vernacular mix of Hindi and Urdu, effectively making this north Indian hybrid the country's lingua franca. As this film is seen pretty much all over India, it contributes to the linguistic unification of the country.

The fact that the all-India film is made for a national market has resulted in the espousal, in these films, of a near nonsectarianism. This creates a sort of demilitarized zone in a country where religion is extremely important and often divisive. Most all-India films are made by Hindus, but apart from the religious themes of mythologicals, most of the films' characters have only a broad identification with Hinduism, the overwhelmingly predominant religion. Many of these films—such as *Amar, Akbar, Anthony* (1977), about three brothers separated as children to be brought up as a Hindu, a Muslim, and a Christian, making the point that we are all brothers under the skin—espouse communal and religious harmony. This is done to give these films the widest possible reach and ensure a stable environment for business, and it effectively serves as a unifying cultural force.

Music often stands in for the kiss in a society where public displays of intimacy are frowned upon.

The use of music and dance is perhaps the most distinctive feature of the Indian film. Creating songs that dominate the music industry, the film industry is like Hollywood and the rock music industry rolled into one huge behemoth. Because of the absence of differentiation between the two industries, the signing up of singing stars like Lata Mangeshkar and Asha Bhosle is essential to ensure investment in a film. The soundtrack, often released before the film itself, determines to a great extent the film's performance at the box office.

The songs are composed by hot music directors such as A. R. Rahman and Rahul Dev Burman, and are set to lyrics by some of the country's finest poets, such as Kaifi Azmi and Gulzar. The very enjoyment of music and dance in an Indian film is often based on the use of classical Indian dance, traditionally performed in temples or royal courts (where they could not be seen very well by the common people), or the ring of familiarity of a raga-based song. In a masala film today, sitars, synthesizers, pianos, and violins provide a score that moves effortlessly from classical Indian ragas to Mozart to hip-hop and rap music. Every taste is catered to, while creating a bridge between East and West, and between traditional and contemporary cultures.

Music in Indian cinema not only entertains the audience but establishes dramatic development, emotional continuity and emphasis—and often stands in for the kiss in a society where public displays of intimacy are frowned upon. Ironically, to skirt an actual ban on kissing, many Indian films evolved extended "wetsari" sequences and the like, which are infinitely more suggestive. And now that the ban has been revoked, these sequences still persist, as they have become established conventions.

When it comes to using songs to advance plots, director S.S. Vasan's 1948 *Chandralekha,* though it used Busby Berkeley-inspired choreography, actually preceded Hollywood's use of songs in this way, says noted American critic Elliott Stein. When filmmaker Ketan Mehta made his version of *Madame Bovary—Maya Memsahib* (1992)—without songs for non-Indian audiences, a noted critic mused that it no longer had a place for the eyes and ears to rest.

Mirrors Trick and True

Spectacle, music, melodrama, romance, and action go only a little way in explaining the allure of the Indian film, however. A typical Hollywood studio product provides as much.

More to the point, perhaps, popular Indian films tell stories of good triumphing over evil in a distinctly Indian context. Mythological works, like the extra-ordinarily successful *Ramayana* and *Mahabharata* epics on television in recent years, are direct extensions of the ritualistic oral tradition of Hinduism into the medium of the moving picture. But even an average musical melodrama unconsciously but powerfully reflects a basic Indian reality, however distorted. Manufactured as commercial entertainment and based on tried-and-true formulas, the Indian film is inevitably the product of contemporary Indian psyches and is a psychological index of a society.

Ray opened the eyes of young aspiring filmmakers in India to films that were true to an Indian reality and possessed artistic integrity.

Often what is portrayed, however, is a reflection of what simmers beneath the surface. The Indian screen, for instance, often depicts romantic love and alliances, whereas in real life, society severely restricts romantic behavior and most marriages are arranged. In this case film does not so much mirror reality as make an inverse reflection of Indians' desires.

But some films explore both reality and desire quite penetratingly. It is in the internationally better-known cinema

of artists like Satyajit Ray, Ritwik Ghatak, and Shyam Benegal that we see a conscious exploration of these psychological states and social phenomena. Ray's *Devi* (1960), for example, is a richly perceptive and nuanced Freudian tragedy about a wealthy Hindu man who begins to perceive his young daughter-in-law as the incarnation of a goddess. The film was controversial when it first came out because of its depiction of Hinduism and the disturbing effect it can have on individual lives. The man "sublimates" his sexual attraction to his daughter-in-law by venerating her as a deity; the girl takes part in his religious rituals, begins to hallucinate, and winds up losing her mind—a pointed commentary on how Indian women are made to sacrifice themselves uselessly for religious obsessions.

Starting with his famous Apu Trilogy, Ray opened the eyes of young aspiring filmmakers in India to films that were true to an Indian reality and possessed remarkable artistic integrity. For his films, Ray dug deep into the immense riches of Bengali literature, Indian classical music, and international cinema—in particular post–World War II Italian Neo-Realism's humanism, style, and use of outdoor locations, amateur actors, and inexpensive technology. (Other international influences were undoubtedly the lyric realism of Jean Renoir and John Ford's use of sound and straightforward, simple, but well-composed camera angles.)

Yet Ray's films appeal basically to only the urban elite of India. When the commercial film industry was attacked by Ray's disciples for creating trash, the commercial producers replied that they felt Ray's truthful depiction of the realities of Indian society, as in his celebrated *Pather Panchali,* only provided despair for the average filmgoer, who actually needed escapist entertainment.

It was in reaction against popular cinema's escapism and portrayal of a fictional India that this new generation of filmmakers, inspired by Ray, sought to deal directly with the realities of modern India. These filmmakers of the New Indian Cinema strove to portray recognizable but distinctly individual characters with inner complexities in situations close to life. Some chose to work in regional Indian cinema to create films true to specific locales, like Adoor Gopalak-

rishnan in his *Elippathayyam* (1981), set in his native Kerala. Others, like Shyam Benegal, chose a sort of middle way, making classics such as *Bhumika* (1977) in Hindi—the language of popular film—retaining and reworking the familiar elements of song and dance. The difference is that for once there is a conscious effort to weave these elements into the story and characters of the film. And in a third skein, filmmakers like Mani Kaul, with films such as *Siddeshwari* (1986), and Kumar Shahani, whose latest film is *Bhavantaran* (1996), display a consummate experimental style.

The New Indian Cinema, which started in the late 1960s, is basically the cinema of the urban, educated baby boomers of India. Their films, both in form and content, tend to be politically progressive, interpreting and reflecting the world around them through the eyes of the modern Indian. The social critiques in these films—of, say, lingering feudal values or the oppressed status of women—reflect the modernizing ideology of post-independence India. Because many of these filmmakers such as Benegal incorporate elements from the popular cinema, it is no surprise that many of their films get funding from India's state film corporation or state television.

An emerging alternative, especially for New Indian Cinema filmmakers who are based abroad or have been educated in the West, is to secure international financing from Europe, Britain, the United States, or even Japan, to produce films that appeal not only to their traditional urban constituency in India but also to the international art film market.

As might be expected, many of these international coproductions have favored certain subjects and treatments of Indian themes that would be easily recognizable as such by an international audience. The fact that certain images of India are widely prevalent in the West—including poverty, exoticism, and the caste system—was probably not lost on the international financers of Mira Nair's *Salaam Bombay* (1988), about street children, or *Kama Sutra,* her forthcoming erotic fantasy, or Shekar Kapur's *Bandit Queen* (1994), which explores the exploitation of a low-caste woman. The Merchant Ivory team built its early career on the clash of Eastern and Western worlds in *Shakespeare Wallah* (1965), a film about a traveling

English theater troupe in India, and *The Guru* (1969), a satire about Westerners coming to India—a subject that was given an updated spin in Pradip Krishen's *Electric Moon* (1992).

The Indian film industry today is an immensely and increasingly varied world, with filmmakers such as Maui Rathnam and Ketan Mehta at one end of the spectrum, creatively using hallowed conventions of the popular cinema while dealing with actual contemporary political situations (as in Rathnam's *Bombay),* and at the opposite end, thinkers in film like Maui Kaul extending and recreating the boundaries of film. A broad range of styles, conventions, and schools of realism and experimentation now exist, together with the glitter and gloss of the ever-popular musical melodramas, to make up the great Indian film bazaar.

Article 23

Cultural Survival Quarterly, Summer 1998

Community Radio in India

by Frederick Noronha

While Indian radio is shifting from a government monopoly to a highly-commercialized broadcasting network, citizens' groups are also demanding that the media be democratized.

Imagine a country which has 18 officially-recognized languages and a total of 1652 mother tongues in a country nearly a billion strong and spread over an area of 3.2 million square kilometers—that's India.

Given its diversity an expanse, one could well understand the problems that tribal, under-privileged, or minority cultures face in getting their voices heard.

As far as the radio is concerned, long years of official domination by the government, outdated, but existing British regulations, and the rampant commercialization of the airwaves have complicated the problem. Citizens groups and non-profit organizations in India are pushing for a wider representation on the centralized and hierarchical Indian radio network—with some success. Court rulings have recently favored the establishment of new, local stations and campaigners from across India are underlining the importance of radio in shaping the destiny of Indian society. For decades, India's radio stations have been centralized, unable to cater to the regional diversity of India, and lacking editorial independence. Now, citizens' groups are pressuring the government for a community radio model.

Call it by any name—community radio, rural radio, cooperative radio, or development radio—its proponents feel that radio holds the key that will unite India's linguistic and ethnic diversity and improve the economic disparity and the huge rural-urban divide. "Imagine having your own radio station where you can walk in any time to ask for your favorite music, share some important local event or chat with your neighbor who's now become a celebrity," says media advocacy campaigner Ms. Sucharita S. Eashwar from Bangalore, the capital of the Indian federal state.

Decentralizing Indian Radio

Ms. Eashwar leads a non-profit development communication group called VOICES that has lobbied to start community radio in India. Based on the current debate in the national media, interested parties feel India has only developed its urban commercial broadcast facilities while ignoring its public service, community, educational, and developmental broadcast networks. Indian non-profit groups are looking to the more vibrant community radio models like those in nearby Sri Lanka, the Philippines, and other African or Latin American countries.

Media advocacy groups have been pressing policy and decision makers in New Dehli to give broadcasting licenses to universities (particularly agricultural universities, medical institutions, adult and legal literacy organizations), registered cooperatives, women's cooperatives, and suitable public bodies. "Our problem has been a 'Delhi-centric' approach to broadcasting that we, in this country, have taken. One fear is that [community broadcasting and grassroots radio] could become inconvenient for the existing power-structure," says prominent media critic Professor K. E. Eapen of Bangalore.

In India, radio is shifting from being a government monopoly to a highly-commercialized broadcasting service. Media advocacy groups say the media needs to be "democratized" simultaneously as it moves away from official control. Privatization and total deregulation is not enough if the media becomes irrelevant to the vast majority of Indians. Now, while the policies are being developed, is the time for non-profit groups, educational and research institutions, cooperatives, women's groups, and development organizations to seize the

FM announcer at an Indian radio station.

available opportunities created by liberalizing the electronic media.

In September, 1996, in Banglore, VOICES brought together a group of radio broadcasters, policy planners, media professionals, and non-profit groups to study how community radio could be relevant to India and what policies were needed. Initially, one suggestion was that the approximately 76 local radio stations that make up the state-run monopoly, All India Radio, could allocate an hour of air time each day to community broadcasting. The Banglore Declaration for a Media Policy on Community Radio was released at the end of the meeting and aimed to shape media policies in India.

Meanwhile, several non-profit organizations have written to the Information and Broadcasting Ministry showing an interest in establishing low-cost local radio broadcasting facilities to support their community development work. Problems remain since cheap FM receiver sets are not easily available, especially in rural areas.

An official of the state-run Bharat Electronics Limited, Mr. Rajamani, points out that low-cost radio stations are becoming affordable in India too. One low-cost station with a transmitting power of up to 50W that reaches a target audience of square kilometers would cost between Rs 1 to 1.2 million (almost US$ .5 million). Basic equipment for recording, mixing, editing, and a 20-feet high antenna would cost a little more.

Radio has already proven its relevance to Indians. Recent government studies suggest that radio in India could potentially reach up to 98.5% of the population. There are approximately 104 million homes that have radio—nearly double the number of homes that have TV. "Over the last decade, All India Radio has focused more on the rural population and the urban lower middle classes, unlike [TV's] preoccupation with the urban upper middle classes," Ms. Eashwar says. India's population is overwhelmingly poor and over one-third of the population lives below the official poverty line, the equivalent of US$300 a year!

India's Broadcasting Policies

In a recent ruling, India's Supreme Court declared the airwaves public property to be used for promoting public good and ventilating plurality of views, opinions, and ideas. In the context of delivering its crucial 1995 judgment, the Supreme Court of India looked closely at the evolution of the broadcast laws in Europe and the U.S. and stated "Use of the airwaves, which is public property, must be regulated for its optimum use for public good for the greatest number. The rights of the listeners and viewers, and not of the broadcaster, is paramount." The court felt that monopolies in broadcasting—either

India's National Broadcasting Policy: Towards Public Service Broadcasting Through Community Radio

The following mandates were developed from the Bangalore Consultation aimed at developing a national broadcasting policy in India. Over 60 persons, representing a wide cross-section of diverse groups with common concerns in the media, met to share experiences and discuss the formation of a policy framework for community radio. Since the Bangalore Consultation was specifically focused on radio broadcasting, the following statement of policy is limited only to radio broadcasting and its community broadcasting application. It is our hope that this statement would be included appropriately in the National Media Policy which would cover all media—TV, radio, cinema, and print.

The Legislative Imperative

1. Airwaves are public property and must be used for public good. Public good is not served optimally when there is a monopoly by the government over this public resource or when liberalization of broadcasting is confined to commercial use of airwaves. Access to the airwaves by everyone who acts in public interest is the sine qua non of public good in this context. This is also part of the right to information, a guaranteed constitutional right.

Need for Community Radio

2. Centralized one-way broadcasting at various levels of aggregation has limited scope to serve the goals of development, especially in the context of pluralism and diversity which is a singular characteristic of Indian society. As such, the regulatory framework should promote a decentralized system of radio broadcasting.

3. Community broadcasting is a concept relevant to social cohesion, development for conviviality and national integration. Community radio is public service broadcasting in its most decentralized and its most democratic form. A community radio station serves a defined geographical area of a village or groups of villages and is owned and managed by organisations serving a given community.

4. A community radio station would, besides educating and entertaining people, connect people with people through participatory or circular communication, connect with organisations and communities, and finally, connect people with government and public service agencies. These needs are not met under the current framework.

5. In a number of ways, community or public interest broadcasting can be termed Equal Opportunity Broadcasting, which is essential not only for effective democratization of a public resource, viz the airwaves, but also in the context of our plural society with a multiplicity of languages, cultures, and ethnic groups.

Policy Formulation

6. Radio combines the benefits of low cost, and wide reach and access. When used in a community setting with limited area coverage, for example as in FM radio broadcasting, it offers many exciting possibilities for fulfilling the developmental goals and aspirations of the people, and wider choices in accessing information from diverse sources within and outside the community. Its potential for creating social change has been demonstrated in many parts of the world. For these reasons, control for community broadcasting should be vested with the community rather than with the government or private commercial enterprises.

7. The present centralized structure of broadcasting is not conducive to people-centered, participatory methods of communication. The potential of the medium to promote community development is largely unrealized. The involvement of other public bodies, NGOs, professional associations, etc., in the utilization and management of airwaves is essential for realizing this potential to promote the welfare of millions in communities, and therefore the public good. The need for structural changes in airwaves management in order to accommodate localized initiatives is a logical result of this imperative.

8. As recommended in the Paswan Committee (1996), while there can be a single national policy which addresses macrolevel issues common to all media, medium-specific policies are required for each medium, taking into account the coverage, reach, cost structure, technology, administration and, finally, the social application of this medium.

9. Radio broadcasting, like other media, has developed around power centers and power structures in society, resulting in disparity of access and use among different sections of society. Changes in media policy which seek to mitigate, if not eliminate, these disparities require political will and a people-centered, bottom-up approach already contemplated in the 74th Constitutional Amendment. Community radio is an illustration of this evolutionary process; therefore, it needs to be acknowledged and supported.

10. At the operational level, a regulatory structure which is independent of the government and existing broadcasting organisations, public and private, should be set up in order to facilitate and support all licensed broadcasters in the country and their shared use of the airwaves under a fair and reasonable regime, consonant with national interests and priorities. The structure must address a variety of issues such as: licensing criteria for various categories of broadcasting, technical and service standards, technical support and training, social and administrative auditing, funding sources and support, etc.

11. Frequency spectrum resources—particularly in the band allocated for FM radio broadcasting, viz 86–108 MHz—will be made available on a shared basis with existing services for community broadcasting applications. Efforts will be made to evolve a national plan for the allocation of frequencies in this band so that the establishment of a large number of community radio stations across the country, based on a high degree of frequency re-use, is facilitated.

Source: 1997. Consultation on Media Policy and Community Radio. Bangalore, South India: Voices.

by the government, an individual, or organization—was unacceptable.

Oddly, there were no special laws to govern broadcasting in India except the Indian Telegraph Act, a British colonial legislation that dated back to 1885. This law scarcely fit the purpose, since it was developed before the radio was even invented. "Centralized, one-way broadcasting . . . has a limited scope to serve the goals of development, especially in the context of pluralism and diversity which is a singular characteristic of Indian society," read the Bangalore Declaration on Radio.

India has been poised on the brink of broadcasting autonomy for at least three decades. Yet, media policy and implementation continue to remain in the hands of the government. Because of this, Indian radio has grown impressively, but has remained inaccessible to large groups of nonaffluent segments of the population, despite sporadic efforts at innovation. India has been unable to chart out a well-formulated communication strategy to support broadcasting development and there have been lopsided priorities while defining the state's role in the media. Recent economic policy changes in India introduced foreign technology, capital, and the advent of satellite television. This has reoriented broadcasting towards commercialization and the formerly powerful All India Radio has been relegated to a distant second place.

Recently, India has been making efforts to revamp its age-old broadcasting laws. But shaping a new broadcasting policy is turning into a tough job. For the last five years, there has been a hotly argued debate over the social, political, and cultural impact of the electronic media in India. "We have an impressive [radio] infrastructure—one of the best in the world—with broadcasting content that is of limited interest for its listeners," commented journalist Kalpana Sharma in national newspaper *The Hindu*. She blamed government's domination of radio for this.

Examples Across the Border

Meanwhile, broadcasting lessons are being learned from some of India's neighbors. Tiny landlocked Nepal, the Himalayan country that is home to some of the world's highest peaks, is showing the way to south Asia by setting up its first community radio station. Official restrictions have not hindered the arrival of Radio Sagarmatha, the first non-governmental FM station in Nepal. It broadcasts from a transmitter set up by non-governmental organizations (NGOs) with support from the United Nations.

Over the past few months, this station has been filling the airwaves of capital Kathmandu with the sound of long forgotten Nepali folk music mixed with 'development messages.' Sagarmatha, literally meaning the 'forehead of the ocean' is the Nepali name for Mount Everest. The Nepal Forum of Environmental Journalists (NEFEJ), headed this project and is planning to develop Radio Sagarmatha as a prototype station and training and resource center that will expand radio into the

rural areas of Nepal. "Our long term objective is to encourage dozens or more of small stations throughout the Himalayan country," said NEFEJ executive director Om Khadka.

Radio Sagarmatha launched its own test transmissions in early June after getting a license from the Nepali government—a herculean effort. Over a dozen other applications are believed to be pending with the Ministry of Communication and Information in this Himalayan kingdom, but analysts in Kathmandu feel it is unlikely that there will be more private radio stations because of the enormous bureaucratic obstacles one must overcome.

Presently, Nepal only has two FM stations, both operating from Kathmandu. Radio Sagarmatha's 500 watt transmitter has just joined the government-run FM station in Kathmandu. Both stations cover the Kathmandu Valley, an area of around 400 square kilometers.

Radio Sagarmatha is an unusual experiment in other ways. Some of the country's best known media organizations, the Nepal Forum for Environmental Journalists (NEFEJ), the Nepal Press Institute, publishers of *Himal* magazine, and Worldview Nepal (a media related organization), have taken a lead in establishing Radio Sagarmatha.

UN development statistics say 75% of Nepalis live below the poverty line. Average life expectancy is 55 years. One in every 10 infants dies before the age of five, and 40% of Nepali children are undernourished. Environmental problems have been a concern in Nepal for quite some time. Some two-thirds of the country's rural population live in mountains and plateaus with only 30% of Nepal's arable land. Population pressures on the land in these rural areas have caused erosion and deforestation to reach alarming proportions. Low productivity, unemployment, and poverty are some of the concerns staring in the face of the country. Its backers hope that the Radio Sagarmatha experiment will boos pluralism in the broadcast media in the South Asian region, where the scene has largely been dominated by large, sometimes-monolith official organizations. India hopes to follow this example to improve the economic and social well-being of the country's rural inhabitants, as well as to improve the communication between these communities.

Frederick Noronha is an independent journalist in India who writes on the media. E-mail: fred @bom2.vsnl.net.in

References

Mathew, K.M., ed. 1998. Manorama Yearbook 1998. *Kottayam, India, pp. 459–460.*

May 1996. India-1996: A Reference Annual. *New Delhi: Ministry of Information and Broadcasting, p. 211.*

Interview with Professor K.E. Eapen of Bangalore, June, July, 1997.

Interview with NEFEJ Executive Director Om Khadka, June, July, 1997.

Article 24

The UNESCO Courier, November 1993

Making Something Out of Nothing

By inventing the zero, India became the birthplace of modern arithmetic

Pierre-Sylvain Filliozat

Pierre-Sylvain Filliozat, of France, is a specialist in Indian studies. He is a director of studies at the Ecole Pratique des Hautes Etudes in Paris.

In India mathematics has not always been linked to writing. The earliest surviving written document dates from the third century B.C., but India certainly had an advanced civilization many centuries before that, and scientific knowledge formed part of it. Most knowledge was transmitted orally. This ancient learning preserved in human memory makes up the corpus of the great religious texts known as the Vedas, which incidentally contain evidence of mathematical knowledge. The Vedas are written in an archaic form of Sanskrit. Like all Indo-European languages, Sanskrit has decimal numerals and individual names for the nine units, as well as for ten, a hundred, a thousand and higher powers of ten (figure 2).

The names of the tens are derived from those of the units, somewhat modified and with the addition of a suffix. Examples are *vimçati* 20, *trimçat* 30, *catvârimçat* 40. The other numerals are formed from these components. The names for the hundreds, thousands and so on consist of a unit name followed by *çata* or *sahasra. Dve çate* (dual), for example, means 200, and *trini-sahasrani* (plural), 3,000.

In Sanskrit grammar the qualifier in a compound word precedes the qualified. In the case of compound numerals the number of the higher order is regarded as qualified by the lower. Eleven, for example, is ten qualified by the addition of one, giving the compound *ekâ-daça,* and similarly *dvâ-daça* is 12, *trayas-trimçat* 33 and so on. The number is divided into components, with the smallest coming first. Units are followed by tens and so on.

The advent of writing

We do not know when, how or by whom writing was introduced into India. All we know is that as early as the third century B.C. two scripts were in use. One, called *kharoshtî,* was derived from Aramaic. It was used in the extreme northwest of the sub-continent, but soon fell into disuse. The other, known as *brâhmî,* seems to have originated in India itself. It is the forerunner of all the scripts now in use in the Indian sub-continent and in southeast Asia. The earliest records (from between the third century B.C. and the third century A.D.) of figures transcribed into this script reveal a notation system that corresponds fairly closely to the pronunciation system.

There is one sign for each digit, and so there are nine signs for the nine units, an entirely different sign for each of the tens (10, 20, etc.), another sign for 100 and yet another for 1,000. Compound numbers are represented by combinations of symbols. The *brâhmî* script reads from left to right, and combinations of signs are written in that direction, starting with the highest value. Here there is a difference between the written and the spoken language. The scribe starts with the highest component, whereas the speaker starts with the lowest. For example, the number 13 is pronounced *trayo-daça,* or "three-ten", but is written "ten-three".

Combinations of components are usually produced by juxtaposing signs, in some cases by ligatures. Whereas there are

Numerals	Value	Numerals	Value
∝ ⹀	12	—	1
—	1	∝ ⹀	12
T ২म	1700	ToT	21,000
২⊙७	189	—	1
∝ ٦	17	Ʈ	60,000
Ʈ∝ T	11,000	Ʈ∝ —	10,001
T	1,000	২ —	101
∝ ⹀	12	T ২	1,100
—	1	২	100
ToTʒ২न	24,400	২ —	101
Ʈφ	6,000	T ২ —	1,101
—	1	T ২ —	1,101
—	1	২ —	101
—	1	T ⹀	1,002
২	100	T —	1,001

Figure 1
Numeral signs and their values as attested by the Nâneghât inscriptions (first century B.C.)

different signs for each of the tens, for the hundreds there is just the sign for 100 plus the sign for the number of hundreds, and likewise with the thousands.

At this stage we cannot yet speak of positional notation. There is a juxtaposition of the numeral signs which when added together give the desired number. This is exactly in keeping with the structure of the language (figure 1).

The zero and positional numeration

In the decimal positional system of numeration the tens, hundreds and thousands are not represented by different signs but by the same digit signs placed in different positions. Only then does position become significant. It alone shows which are the tens, which the hundreds and which the thousands. Such a system needs only ten signs, the digits from 1 to 9 and a zero—or at least a blank space.

There is no satisfactory documentary evidence as to how and in what exact period this system was discovered in India, and how it developed. The earliest reference to a place-value notation is a literary one. Vasumitra, a Buddhist writer and leading figure at a great religious council convened by King Kanishka (who reigned over the whole of north and northwest India at the end of the first or the beginning of the second

century A.D.), maintained in a book on Buddhist doctrine that if a substance that exists in all three time dimensions (past, present and future) is regarded as something different every time it enters a new state, this change is due to the alterity of the state, not to its own alterity. He illustrated this idea by speaking of a marker which in the units position counts as a unit but in the hundreds position counts as a hundred. He did not specify the nature of the marker.

This may be a reference to a kind of abacus. The marker might have been an object that could be placed in a column or square, where its position gave it the value of a power of ten. Or it could be a mark in the sand, in the case of sums written on the ground. Indian accounts are known to have liked the simplicity of this method. In some parts of southern India village astrologers can still be seen doing calculations by placing cowrie shells in columns drawn in the sand. Whatever the form of the abacus, Vasumitra's reference implies the existence of a notation that took account of positional value.

The same is true of the zero, the use of which in India is known from literary references predating the earliest written examples. The zero forms part of the positional system of numeration. Originally it seems to have been a gap in a column resulting from the absence of a figure or marker in the space reserved for an order of the power of ten. This is shown by the use of one of the words meaning empty, *çûnya* or *kha*. The word *kha* occurs in a treatise on metrics by Pingala, in which he sets forth a rule for turning binary numbers into decimal numbers. Pingala's dates are unknown, but quotations from his works are found from the third century A.D. onwards, and so he must have lived earlier than that.

That a dot came to be used to indicate an empty space we know from a Sanskrit storyteller, Subandhu, who probably lived in the sixth century A.D. To denote the zero Subandhu used the compound noun *cûnya-bindu,* literally "empty point", in other words a dot indicating an empty space in a column.

The zero itself appears in a deed of gift, carved on copper plates, from King Devendravarman of Kalinga (Orissa, in eastern India). The document is dated in letters and figures: "*samvacchara-çatam trir-âçîte* (100) 83 *shravane masi dine vimçati* 20 *utkîrnnam*", literally "carved a hundred and eighty-three years (100) 83 (having passed) the twenty day 20 in the month of *Shravana*". The number 183 is written as three signs, the sign for a hundred and then the figures 8 and 3. The number 20 is written with the figure 2 and a zero in the form of a small circle. The period specified in this document began in 498 A.D., so that it dates from the year 681 A.D.

Positional notation, and the zero in the form of a big dot or small circle, are found in inscriptions in southeast Asia, at Sambor (Cambodia) and Kota Kapur (Malaysia), where the earliest records go back to the seventh century A.D. The scripts used in these countries are all derived from Indian scripts, and their system of writing numbers is undoubtedly the Indian system. All these documents show that by the late seventh century the positional system and the zero were in general use not

Figure 2. Number names in Sanskrit

eka	1	çata	100
dvi	2	sahasra	1 000
tri	3	ayuta	10 000
catur	4	niyuta	100 000
pañca	5	prayuta	1 000 000
shat	6	arbuda	10 000 000
sapta	7	nyarbuda	100 000 000
ashtan	8	samudra	1 000 000 000
nava	9	madhya	10 000 000 000
daça	10	anta	100 000 000 000
		parârdha	1 000 000 000 000

in Indian geographical mythology), ten by "fingers", thirty-two by "teeth", hundred by "human life-span", zero by "empty space", and so on. These words are arranged as they would be in speech, so that in a compound number the lowest numerals come first. In other words, the order is opposite to that used in writing. For instance, the number 4,320,000 is pronounced khaca-tushka-rada-arnavâh, which literally means "tetrad of empty spaces-teeth-oceans," or 0—0—0—0—32—4.

This example is taken from the *Sûrya-siddhânta,* an astronomical text which takes account of data observable in the fourth century A.D. It is one of the earliest records of this mixed notation, which enjoyed great popularity throughout the history of Sanskrit literature. Even among mathematicians and astronomers it seems to have been the preferred method of expressing numbers. Its advantage was that it allowed variation of vocabulary. Sanskrit has ten or so common words for eyes, whereas there is no synonym for the number 2. Sanskrit technical and scientific literature was usually written in verse, so that authors needed to command a wide vocabulary in order to find words to fit the requirements of prosody.

It would be a mistake to regard this mixed notation as a transitional stage between the old oral system and the pure positional system. It was an artificial method adopted by authors who were familiar with both systems and used them in their writings.

only in India but in all the countries to which Indian civilization had spread as well.

Notation using nine digits and a zero seems to have quickly taken the lead for inscriptions, but it never completely superseded the old system, which survived until recently in manuscripts, and in southern India even in early twentieth century-printed books.

Words standing for numerals

A mixed notation, in which features of the old system are combined with or alternate with characteristics of positional notation, was also known and used in India. In this system number names are replaced by words with numerical connotations. For example, two is replaced by "eyes", "arms", "wings", or "twins", four by "oceans" (there being four oceans

Economy and lightness

In 662 A.D. a Syriac writer, Severus Sebokt, wishing to show that the Greeks had no monopoly on science, referred to the inventiveness of Indian scholars. The only one of their mathematical skills that he mentioned was their system of reckoning using nine digits. Severus Sebokt's comment points to the greatest advantage of this system, its economy. By reducing the symbols needed for the notation of all numbers to ten—nine digits and a zero—the system achieves the ideal of economy and efficiency. Indian intellectuals were well aware of the advantages of economy. They had a technical term for it—laghava or "lightness"—and have cultivated it since Antiquity in various fields of thought.

Article 25   *The New York Times,* April 16, 1998

Ancient Hindu Festival Thrives in Computer-Age India

By JOHN F. BURNS

HARDWAR, India, April 14—The rushing grey-green waters of the Ganges were as chilly as they have been in years today as A. K. Sharma stripped to his underwear, plunged into the shallow edge of India's holiest river and raised cupped handfuls of water towards the rising sun.

But Mr. Sharma, a 48-year-old engineer, was jubilant. After journeying 250 miles from his home in Agra, the city of the Taj Mahal, Mr. Sharma, his wife and two children joined millions of Hindu pilgrims who traveled to Hardwar from across India in the last three months to join in what is billed here as the world's biggest religious festival.

After an exhausting day on chaotic roads and a night in a dusty tented camp, Mr. Sharma had timed his bathing well. As he made his way through the dense crowd of worshipers pressing towards the river, less than two hours remained to the most propitious moment of the most propitious day in the Hindu calendar, as determined by astrological calculations that underpin what is known here as the kumbh mela.

The mela, or festival, is a rotating rite chroniclers say has been observed at Hardwar every 12 years since the second millennium B.C.

As India rushes into the age of technology, launching communications satellites, developing nuclear weapons and enthusiastically embracing the Internet, the passion for the ancient rituals among the country's 700 million Hindus shows no sign of flagging.

The Hardwar mela is believed to have drawn the largest crowds ever to converge on this city in the lee of the Himalayan foothills. By some accounts as many as 10 million people have come since January. In 1989, a kumbh mela

at Allahabad, on the lower reaches of the Ganges, drew as many as 30 million.

The phenomenon has delighted many Indians, who yearn to guard their ancient traditions even as they seek to modernize what had been one of Asia's most creaky economies.

"Our technological know-how is very well, but our ancients were understanding things much better," Mr. Sharma said. Motioning towards the hubbub along the Ganges and the dozens of brightly-hued temples dotting the escarpment, he added: "Something is there, something which I am not exactly knowing, something which is hidden; something which I may not be able to prove technically, but which I know to be there in my soul."

Ritual bathing and spiritual renewal at the Ganges.

According to ancient Hindu scriptures, bathing at Hardwar at the time of the kumbh mela, or at Allahabad, Nasik and Ujjain, the other cities on the north Indian plain that host the mela at three-year intervals, is the supreme act of worship, worth 10 million dips in the Ganges at less propitious times.

Some Hindus believe that dipping at a kumbh mela will guarantee eternal salvation, a release from the cycle of birth, death and reincarnation. Others believe that the mela washes away all sins, cleanses the soul, or earns the blessings of the Hindu deities for a marriage or business venture, or for relief from illness.

There were many pilgrims with disabilities here this week. One man in his 30's, paralyzed in both legs by polio, arrived at the most holy spot along the riverbank, known as the brahmakund, after dragging himself by his arms from a camp more than 10 miles away, a journey he said had taken him 20 hours.

The origin of the kumbh melas lies in a Hindu legend involving a struggle between gods and demons for control of a kumbha, or clay pitcher, filled with the nectar of immortality churned from the bottom of the oceans. According to the legend, one god seized the pitcher and circled the earth for 12 days—12 years in earthly time—spilling drops of nectar at four places on earth that are the sites of the kumbh melas and at eight places in the heavens.

According to early records, including an account in the 7th century A.D. by a Chinese traveler, Hsuang Tang, the melas served from ancient times as grand gatherings of Hindu holy men, the sadhus, swamis, sanyasis, gurus and yogis of the time.

"When the stars were in a particular position, the sadhus simply followed the great rivers to their confluence and stayed there until others, from all directions, joined them," according to Rajesh Bedi, who wrote a 1991 book on the sadhus, itinerant holy men who renounce all wordly goods. "Then they discussed the state of the body politic, the economic condition of the people and philosophical and theological questions."

The ascetic sadhus still dominate the festivals, setting up vast encampments near the river where they pray, practice yoga, perform their rites, read from Hindu scriptures, chant mantras and hold discourses with the common pilgrims. For urban Hindus, in particular,

Associated Press

Throngs of Hindus bathed in the Ganges this week during the kumbh mela, a major festival at Hardwar, in northern India. Millions of pilgrims gathered at the holy site, one of four where it is celebrated.

the sadhus, many of whom still live lives of renunciation in the forests and mountains, are a focus of profound fascination and respect.

Although India is instinctively entrepreneurial, Hindu beliefs have engendered an abiding respect for those who abjure the material world; exploiting this politically was part of the genius of Mohandas K. Gandhi, the independence leader, a London-trained barrister who led the struggle against British rule in the accoutrements of the sadhu, with a cotton loincloth and a wooden stave. These days, Indians who once followed Gandhi are as likely to be found at melas chanting the praises of near-naked sadhus, as the crowds did everywhere at Hardwar.

Men like Mr. Sharma, the engineer from Agra, and their wives, lined the riverbanks today as more than 60,000 sadhus, organized into monastic orders called akharas, marched across pontoon bridges to the bathing ghats, terraced areas flanked by temples at the heart of the city. The crowds tossed garlands of

marigolds and shouted "We bow to you, o holy men!" "We kiss your feet!" and "Long Live Lord Ram!".

The sadhus and their leaders, many of them carried to the ghats in gaily-colored palanquins shaded from the sun by gold

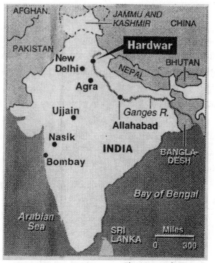

The New York Times

Hardwar is the site of this year's kumbh mela, a major festival.

and crimson parasols, waved back regally.

But not all sadhus, or their supreme leaders, known as shankaracharayas, are what they once were. Few shankaracharayas arrive these days atop richly caparisoned elephants or camels; many came in air-conditioned cars, and were borne to the rivers on thrones mounted atop cars and trucks. According to Indian newspapers, their numbers include many charlatans, more interested in money, power and women.

Not for the first time at a kumbh mela, rivalries between monastic orders known as the akharas erupted in violence. On March 28, a pitched battle flared between two orders, the Niranjani and the Juna, after members of one group delayed evacuating the most sacred of the bathing ghats. The fighting, involving ceremonial swords, staves and trishuls—trident-like staffs—left more than 100 sadhus and policemen injured. Several policemen were thrown into the Ganges, and several ashrams burned down.

Indeed, animosities threatened to scuttle the heart of the festival. Unable to agree on which group should occupy the central ghat at 12.10 P.M. on Tuesday, the moment astrologers had set as marking the correct alignment of Jupiter, Saturn, the earth and the moon, the two orders threatened to fight again. A police force of 30,000 moved special units with automatic rifles, flak jackets and riot helmets in to surround all 13 akharas in their camps, lifting the siege only hours before the astrologically propitious moment.

Even then the Juna, having ceded precedence at the ghat, boycotted the procession to the river, along with three other allied akharas. This left the Niran-jani to march to the river in triumph, headed by hundreds of stark naked Naga sadhus, the warrior-like holy men who constitute a kind of commando force of their own. The Juna leaders charged that India's new Government, headed by the Hindu nationalist Bharatiya Janata Party, had manipulated the negotiations in favor of the party-linked Niranjani.

The festival was rated a success for the Hindu nationalists who control the Government in Delhi and the state government of Uttar Pradesh and were responsible for the management of the festival. Contrary to the state's reputation elsewhere in India as a crucible of the country's ills, Uttar Pradesh ran the event with uncharacteristic efficiency, re-building 100 miles of roads, laying 50 miles of water piping to the tented camps, and re-building bathing ghats. Most important, the police avoided a repeat of the disasters that marred previous Hardwar melas, including a stampede in 1986 in which at least 60 people died.

But not all the warrior-like holy men appreciated the police controls. "We have asked them not to carry pistols and other firearms during the processions to the river," said J. P. Sharma, the official responsible for managing the mela. "We have kindly requested them to carry only religious symbols."

Article 26

The New Republic, September 14 & 21, 1998

The price of neglecting Afghanistan.

THE SUCCESSION

By Richard Mackenzie

Ahmed Shah Massoud, the charismatic resistance fighter whom *The Wall Street Journal* once called "the Afghan who won the cold war," sat cross-legged on the floor of a rambling building in Jabul Siraj, a village at the foot of the Hindu Kush mountain range north of Kabul. A fierce wind blew across the Shomali plains, bending trees in its path, whipping up dust devils, and rattling windows—and adding an appropriate touch of drama to his warning: "We don't need armed Arabs wandering around our country," Massoud said. "They have no place here; they should leave."

Massoud was speaking about a small army of Arab fighting men who had ventured into Afghanistan to witness the jihad against the Soviets, and who had since become embroiled in Afghanistan's ongoing and torturous civil war. It was the late summer of 1993—still five years before the Arabs' leader, Osama Bin Ladin, would become an international household name as a terrorist. Massoud, the strongman behind the Afghan government of the day, was then holding 30 Arabs whom his forces had captured in attacks on his capital—prisoners whom he described as terrorists.

I was there because Massoud was convinced that such terrorism was bad news not only for Afghanistan, but for the United States, as well. I was working on a documentary for CNN called "Terror Nation: U.S. Creation?" and Massoud was hoping to send a message through the broadcast. Yet, though Massoud and his allies would spend months trying to get the attention of American officials—and warn them about the terrorist headquarters being established in Afghanistan—the United States would never show interest. Indeed, the thesis of that CNN special, which aired in 1994, was that the bombing of the World Trade Center was an unintended consequence—what intelligence types call "blowback"—of the CIA's involvement in the Afghan war against the Soviet Union. Among its other revelations were stories of camps in Afghanistan, where new armies of international terrorists were training. But, when it aired, U.S. officials would not even entertain the notion that such camps existed, let alone that they were another form of blowback.

Now, of course, we know that the camps do exist. We also know that the extremist movement known as the Taliban, which eventually drove Massoud out of Kabul to take power, is inexorably linked to Bin Ladin. And we know that U.S. policy blunders played no small part in creating this problem.

In December 1979, American officials responded to the surprise Soviet invasion of Afghanistan by pouring money into the Afghan resistance. Over the next eleven years, the United States would subsidize Afghan rebels to the tune of $3 billion. But, because the United States had been caught off guard, it quickly delegated important decision-making to Pakistan, despite the fact that it was not at all clear Pakistan's interests truly coincided with those of either Washington or the Afghan people.

And that would prove to be a key error. Although the natural leaders in Afghanistan were tribal heads and men like Massoud—who had developed a broad, grassroots infrastructure—Pakistan ignored or abandoned them. Chronically nervous about its front with India to the east, Pakistan has long been determined to keep a weak, nonthreatening regime in Kabul as a counterbalance to the West—and that was the criterion Pakistan used in choosing which rebels to back. In the end, the Pakistanis embraced Gulbuddin Hekmatyar, an anti-Western firebrand, who gained notoriety in Afghanistan for killing more fellow mujahideen than Communists. Human rights groups and Western journalists tried to spread word of his atrocities. But he was obedient to Pakistan, and that was good enough to win him the lion's share of CIA supplies—as well as the endorsement of the United States, which adopted the Pakistani line that he was the most effective and representative mujahideen leader. "You don't understand," a senior U.S. official in Pakistan said at the time. "These Afghans are always killing each other. Hekmatyar gets the most weapons because he deserves it."

By 1992, with the Soviet Union no longer a threat, the United States had ceased supplying the Afghan rebels—and many American officials had simply ceased to be interested in Afghanistan altogether. But Afghanistan was hardly on its way to peace. The puppet regime the Soviets had left behind had withdrawn from its distant outposts and had pulled most of its forces back into larger cities. In April, the mujahideen entered Kabul—this was the time, say Afghans and observers, that Afghanistan needed a new kind of aid from Washington. "After pouring in three billion dollars' worth of weapons, America could have helped us find our way back to civilization and rebuild our nation," says a prominent Afghan leader who, in

light of recent anti-Americanism in the area, asked not to be named. "For more than a decade, we knew only one thing, to settle arguments through the barrels of our guns."

But no aid from the United States came. And international groups could only watch in horror as Hekmatyar began blitzkrieg assaults on Kabul to try to drive out the forces of Massoud. From positions in the mountains surrounding Kabul, Hekmatyar rained daily barrages of rockets into the capital, striking indiscriminately at civilian areas where hundreds of rockets often hit before breakfast, leaving the mangled and the survivors to await the next onslaught. "We are witnessing one of the world's worst humanitarian disasters," a Red Cross official in Kabul said at the time. Again, representatives of Massoud and his party leader, President Burhanuddin Rabbani, made entreaties to Washington—and, again, there was no response. During the first few months of the mujahideen victory in 1992, the U.S. ambassador-at-large for Afghanistan, Peter Tomsen, and his deputy, Richard Hoagland, visited Kabul—but that would be the last of such visits for a half-decade. The two men, both well-attuned to the nation's problems, were promoted and transferred.

As Hekmatyar continued his assault on Kabul, Massoud's forces began to capture increasing numbers of Arabs who said they had come to Afghanistan for training and battlefield experience. Many of them turned out to be followers of Bin Ladin, the wealthy son of a Saudi industrialist who—at the time—was living in Sudan. Bin Ladin had cultivated a reputation as a courageous warrior, although his real contribution may have been simply to bankroll Afghan rebels and their families. He came with a checkbook—and a $300 million balance—thus allowing him to buy his way into the Afghans' favor. "We knew him as one of the Saudi benefactors who took care of widows and orphans," a retired U.S. official who helped fight the anti-Soviet jihad told *The New York Times*.

As Kabul remained mired in civil war in 1994, a new movement appeared on the scene: the Taliban, a motley group of former Islamic theological students. Initially, U.S. officials welcomed their arrival. After all, the Taliban had restored order in Kandahar and other corners of the South—perhaps, it was thought, they could do the same for the rest of the nation. In addition, U.S. officials reasoned, the Taliban could serve as a bulwark against Russian and Iranian interests, while providing Pakistan with an overland link to the lucrative flow of trade through Central Asia. U.S. narcotics officials had their own ideas: they believed, or at least hoped, that the Taliban might succeed in shutting down Afghanistan's blossoming opium trade.

What probably made the most difference to U.S. policymakers, though, was the Taliban's commitment to a particular commercial enterprise. The Taliban had promised to permit construction of giant gas and oil pipelines from Central Asia, down through Afghanistan, to Pakistan. The main contender for that work was an American-Saudi coalition of Unocal and Delta oil companies. The Taliban's "most important function . . . was to provide security for roads and, potentially, oil and gas pipelines that would link the states of Central Asia to the international market through Pakistan rather than Iran," says Barnett Rubin, an analyst of Afghan affairs. Indeed, in the summer of 1996, when U.S. Senator Hank Brown of Colorado held meetings on Afghanistan, the most memorable testimony came not from an Afghan but from Martin Miller, the Unocal vice president in charge of the proposed Afghan pipeline project. From day one, Unocal said, the oil route through Afghanistan could pump a million barrels of oil per day. And, within a few years, once the pipeline reached other oil fields in Central Asia, it could pump five million barrels a day, the company vowed. (Many analysts believe that Central Asia is the next Middle East; one country alone, Turkmenistan, has 21,000 billion cubic meters of natural gas, the third-largest reserve in the world.)

It took a while for many in the West to catch on, but inside Afghanistan the key players were already well-aware of the pipeline's importance—and its potential effect on policy. In 1996, during a conversation in Kabul not long before the Taliban reached the capital, Ahmed Shah Massoud asked me about Unocal, its motives, its methods, and its ties to the U.S. government. When the Taliban finally reached the gates of Kabul, it was well-financed and well-equipped—and it could count upon the acquiescence of the United States.

Kabul fell to the Taliban quickly, and the new rulers brought with them mind-numbing rules for society: women could not venture outside their homes without a male relative—and, even then, not without tentlike clothing called *burkas* that covered them from head to foot. The Taliban also prohibited women from working, attending school, or being examined by male doctors. Religious police squads roamed the streets, beating offenders—such as errant women or men who trimmed their beards or did not pray at mosques when the Taliban said they should. Virtually every form of entertainment was banned, from television to kite-flying; glass windows on private homes were painted black.

But none of this raised the Clinton administration's ire, at least not initially. Hours after the Taliban took Kabul in September 1996, State Department spokesman Glyn Davies said the United States could see "nothing objectionable" about the version of Islamic law the Taliban had imposed in the areas it then controlled. In an address to the United Nations two months later, then-Assistant Secretary of State for South Asian Affairs Robin Raphel conceded international "misgivings" about the Taliban but insisted the Tali-

ban had to be "acknowledged" as an "indigenous" movement that had "demonstrated staying power." U.S. officials spoke of seeking early talks with the Taliban's leaders and discussed reopening the U.S. Embassy in Kabul once the dust had settled. This was entirely in character: in one encounter a few months before the Taliban entered Kabul, a mid-level bureaucrat at the State Department perched on his couch and tried to convince me that the Taliban was really not such a bad bunch. "You get to know them and you find they really have a great sense of humor," he said.

If the administration seemed nonchalant about the Taliban, Unocal was downright gleeful. In a statement to Reuters that the company has worked ever since to retract, a Unocal official applauded the Taliban's arrival and spoke glowingly about the immediate prospects for doing business with the group. Of course, this was hardly surprising, given Unocal's courtship of the Taliban. The company had played host to Taliban clerics on a trip to the United States. Unocal had also hired as "consultants" key Americans involved in Afghan operations during the jihad years. The former U.S. ambassador to Pakistan, Robert Oakley, went on the Unocal payroll. A former official of the U.N. secretary-general's mission to Afghanistan, Charles Santos, was given a far more obscure position—he went to work for Unocal's Saudi partner, the firm Delta.

Eventually, both the United States and Unocal would come to regret their decisions. When Sudan expelled Bin Ladin in 1996 at the behest of Washington, he returned to Pakistan and then ventured into Afghanistan, where he settled in a no-man's-land outside Jalalabad, a city across the Khyber Pass from Peshawar. Upon his return, *The New York Times* recently reported, Bin Ladin personally gave the Taliban $3 million—a vast sum in such an impoverished nation—that helped cement a relationship. Bin Ladin saw he had a common cause with the emerging Taliban; Pakistani military intelligence officers who were helping to create the Taliban saw the wisdom of fostering relations between Bin Ladin and the Taliban's reclusive leader, Mullah Mohammed Omar. The two were introduced, and, after the Taliban took Kabul, Bin Ladin moved to Kandahar—the city the Taliban now calls its headquarters.

The United States knew Bin Ladin had come to Afghanistan, and, when Bill Richardson, then the Clinton administration's U.N. ambassador, visited the Taliban leadership earlier this year, he asked them to expel Bin Ladin. The Taliban refused. (This, at least, is one official version. Other State Department officials have said that Richardson merely asked the Taliban to keep Bin Ladin "under control.") Finally—and quite belatedly—the administration turned. On a visit to a girls' school at an Afghan refugee camp in Pakistan this year, Secretary of State Madeleine Albright angrily denounced the Taliban: "I think it is very clear why we are opposed to the Taliban. Because of their approach to human rights, their despicable treatment of women and children, and their general lack of respect for human dignity . . . [that is] more reminiscent of the past than of the future." Other U.S. hopes had gone unfulfilled,

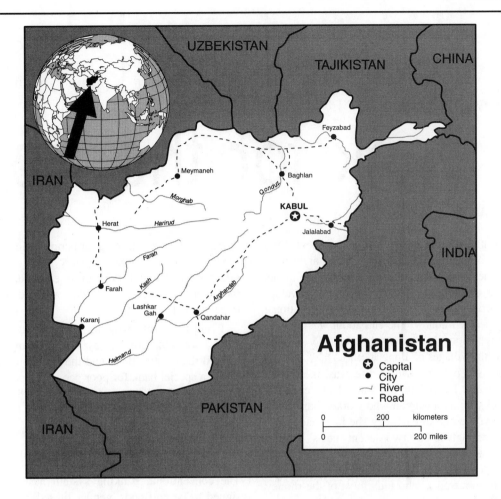

too: rather than destroy the opium trade, a U.S. officials had hoped, the Taliban taxed it, earning millions of dollars in the process.

Unocal, meanwhile, met with similar disappointment. Just this week, it announced that the pipeline project it had worked so hard to promote—the project on which so much U.S. policy had been premised—had become unfeasible. It was, for now,

pulling the plug. Much had been sacrificed for that endeavor—money being the least of it.

RICHARD MACKENZIE is an award-winning independent television producer and writer. He has recently reported on Afghanistan and international terrorism for CNN, the Discovery Channel, The Asian Wall Street Journal, *and* National Geographic.

Article 27   *The UNESCO Courier,* January 1997

The founder of the Grameen Bank describes the genesis of a pioneering institution that has encouraged the social and political emancipation of needy women in Bangladesh

A Bank for the Poor

By Muhammad Yunus

In 1972, the year after Bangladesh became independent, I began to teach economics at one of the country's universities. Two years later the country was hit by a devastating famine. On the campus I was teaching complicated theories of development while outside people were dying in hundreds. Conventional economics suddenly seemed hollow. The classroom was a world apart from the reality of poverty and struggle outside. I left it and stepped out into the villages of Bangladesh.

I started talking to people for whom life was an endless struggle for survival and learned things that I had never encountered in textbooks. I met a woman who worked hard making bamboo stools. At the end of each day she had made only two pennies, hardly enough to buy two decent meals. I could not understand how anyone could work so hard for so long and receive so little. I found out that to buy her raw material she had to borrow from a trader, who took most of the money and left the woman with very little. I realized that if the money she needed were available at normal interest rates the woman would earn enough to reinvest and make higher profits. She could earn a decent living and escape from poverty.

I spoke to forty-two other people in the village who were trapped in poverty because they were dependent on loans from traders and money-lenders. Their total credit requirement was only thirty dollars. I lent them the money out of my own pocket. I thought that if normal banking institutions would do likewise, these people could leave poverty behind. However, conventional banking institutions do not make loans to the poor, especially to rural women.

The bankers I met laughed at me. They did not think it was their business to hand out small amounts of money to the poor. They did not think it was possible to hand out money without collateral. Since poor people by definition had no collateral, the banks refused to deal with them. I went from one bank to another. They all said the same. I offered to act as guarantor for the loans. This was acceptable to them for a few more loans, amounting to a few hundred dollars.

All the poor people who contracted these loans repaid the money. I went back to the banks, showing this as proof that poor people repay their debts and that there was no need to insist on collateral. The bankers said, it may work in this one village but it wouldn't work in many. I tried the same scheme in many villages. All the poor people who borrowed paid back. I went back to the banks. They said it may work in a few villages but it won't work in an entire district. So I extended the scheme to an entire district. It worked. The banks remained unpersuaded.

I said to myself, why am I running after the bankers? Why don't I solve the problem by setting up my own bank? And so I asked the Central Bank and the Government for permission to set up a special bank for poor people. It took a long time but the Government finally gave permission in 1983. Grameen Bank was born as an independent bank, a bank for the poor.[1]

Banks that lend only to the rich

The conventional banking system has been deliberately designed to be anti-poor, gender biased, and anti-illiterate.

The idea of "collateral", which bankers regard as sacred, is to push the poor away from banks. But any good banker who looked at our banking system in Bangladesh would be horrified. Millions of dollars are lent to very rich people who never bother to pay back. The repayment rate of our industrial banks, which lend money to rich people in the name of industrialization, has been less than 10 percent over the past fifteen years. "Why call yourself a bank?" I ask them. "Why not take your signboard down and put up a new one saying something like 'Charity Organization for the Rich'?"

Banks do not like women. They do not want to lend money to women. There are "Ladies' Branches" all over Dhaka city designed to serve women only—i.e., designed to get their money. Lending to them is a very different story. In a Bangladeshi bank, if a woman wants to borrow money, she is asked whether she has discussed it with her husband. If she says "Yes" she is asked, "Is he supportive or your proposal?" If the answer is still "Yes", she is asked to bring him along to talk the matter over. No male borrower is asked whether he has discussed the idea with his wife, or whether she is supportive of it, or whether he would like to bring her along to discuss the proposal. I would think that less than 1 per cent of borrowers in Bangladesh are women. There must be something wrong with the system.

UNESCO AND THE GRAMEEN BANK

In September 1995, UNESCO signed a memorandum of understanding with the Grameen Bank in which the two organizations pledged to combat poverty by joining forces in their specific areas of competence. UNESCO's participation in the co-operation scheme has so far involved:

☛ designing a basic education programme for Grameen borrowers and their families directly related to their economic activities;

☛ providing the Bank with technical assistance in setting up a company which now brings cellular telephones to needy rural women in Bangladesh;

☛ supplying expert advice on the exploitation of solar power and other renewable energy sources;

☛ organizing training programmes and workshops for Member States interested in adopting the Grameen Bank model. A workshop for Central Asian countries was held at Bishkek (Kyrgyzstan) in March 1996 and has been followed up by a study visit of the Grameen banking mechanism in Bangladesh.

☛ producing an information kit explaining the Grameen Bank's philosophy, mechanism and success (published in English, French and Spanish).

Banks demand that clients write everything down. In Bangladesh, where 75 per cent of the people cannot read and write, this is a ridiculous situation. Even when people bring money to deposit in the bank, they have to write down every detail on paper. I asked why banks cannot simply take money and issue a receipt saying "received such and such an amount of money from such and such a person?" Why must the depositor have to do all this writing? When I first challenged this notion, bankers asked me how records could be kept without reading and writing. My reply was that banks could issue receipts for amounts received or disbursed, and that all the necessary accounting could be done by the bank. Why punish the illiterate person?

The Grameen system

Grameen Bank now operates in over half the villages of Bangladesh. It has over two million members, 94 per cent of whom are women. Over $1.7 billion have been disbursed so far, and more than 300,000 houses have been built with Grameen housing loans. Depositors, saving only one or two taka per week, have managed to save over $120 million. This has been achieved because Grameen Bank is pro-poor, pro-women and supportive of the illiterate.

Grameen Bank rejected collateral-based banking as a structural impediment to the participation of the poor, and introduced instead group-based lending and peer monitoring to ensure both the selection of needy clients and the maintenance of high repayments. Groups of five are formed with members from homogeneous backgrounds who know and trust each other. Six to eight groups are integrated in one centre. Each village will generally have one or two centres. Instead of making people come to the bank, Grameen goes to the people. All financial transactions take place at weekly centre meetings. This lowers transaction costs as well as making the banking institution subordinate to people's needs.

Ninety four per cent of Grameen members are women. This emphasis on women is based on the fact that women are the most oppressed within the ranks of the poor and, more importantly, because giving credit to poor women translates into greater welfare within the household. Unlike men, women in rural Bangladesh spend almost all their earnings on the family and plan for the family's future. There is also a social dimension to the emphasis on women group members. Women who had earlier rarely ventured out of their houses now come to group meetings; women who had previously never handled cash now keep accounts and engage in financial transactions; women who had never been visible in public now become assertive and confident.

Most Grameen members have no formal schooling. At Grameen they are taught to sign their names, to count and keep accounts. Banking procedures are simple and transparent. Members discuss among themselves and learn to keep track of their money without having to use difficult forms. Simple receipts are issued so that record keeping is simplified.

Grameen has led to a virtual transformation of rural society. Numerous studies on the Bank have shown that it has increased the economic well-being of its members. Grameen loans have contributed to the building of sturdy houses, to better health and sanitation, and to higher school attendance. Studies have also pointed to the increasing power of women, to their challenging of conventional norms discriminating against them, and to their greater political participation. While much remains to be done to alleviate poverty and end inequality and gender discrimination, microcredit in Bangladesh, as practised by the Grameen Banks, has provided one simple strategy that works.

Poverty alleviation initiatives

We at Grameen, however, are not content to stop here. We dare to dream of microcredit paving the way for poverty alleviation once and for all. The Grameen family is thus working on expanding agricultural productivity through environment-friendly integrated agricultural methods. We are promoting the development of fisheries. We are expanding local markets by linking weavers from the heartland of Bangladesh to retail outlets in the United States and Europe through the export of "Grameen check" clothing.

We strongly believe that the most advanced technology should be appropriated by the poor. We are thus working on harnessing solar and wind energy, and on providing telecommunication facilities to every village in Bangledesh. This will not be organized by wealthy corporations. Access to credit will ensure that poor rural men and women are both the owners and users of such products and services.

1. Muhammad Yunus talked about the Grameen Bank in an interview published in the September 1995 issue of the Unesco Courier. Editor

Article 28

Current History, December 1997

"Successive elected governments have advanced the military's interests in the belief that the military establishment holds the ultimate political veto . . . [U]nless the political leadership realizes that its very survival lies in collaborative efforts to consolidate a representative, pluralistic, and participatory system strong enough to withstand military intervention, democracy in Pakistan will remain vulnerable."

Pakistan at Fifty:
A Tenuous Democracy

Samina Ahmed

When Pakistan gained independence after the dismemberment of the British Indian empire in 1947, the people of the newly independent state were hopeful that their own country would give them the rights and freedoms denied by a colonial order. For most of Pakistan's history, however, the rights of the people have been usurped by authoritarian rulers. Although Pakistan at 50 does have all the trappings of a democratic regime—an elected government, functioning representative institutions, and a formal adherence to constitutional rule—democratic norms and governance continue to elude a weak and fragile state. Not only is the legitimacy of state institutions contested, but linguistic, regional, ethnic, and sectarian divisions threaten Pakistan's fragile national cohesion. Moreover, with the economy in shambles, the managers of the state have proved themselves incapable of providing a better life for Pakistan's citizens.

Democracy was formally restored in 1988 after more than a decade of military rule that had seen state policies fuel ethnoregional and sectarian tensions and widen economic disparities. Nine years later, Pakistan's political leaders and parties have failed to establish a stable democratic order. Economic stagnation and underdevelopment, political infighting, corruption, and ineptitude have led to widespread popular disillusionment and even despair. A public opinion poll published by *The News* (Islamabad) in September 1997 found that a vast major-

ity of respondents believed sectarian conflict and lawlessness would rise; only 5 percent were optimistic that Pakistan would even survive.

As public confidence in the state and its institutions has declined, elements of Pakistan's opinion-making elite have begun to question the democratic system, claiming that an ineffective and irresponsible elected leadership cannot achieve political stability and economic growth. Pakistan's political history, however, reveals that authoritarian state structures, weak democratic institutions, and the absence of democratic values and norms have all contributed to the crisis of the state after 50 years of existence.

MILITARY-GUIDED DEMOCRACY

In its first decade, Pakistan was ostensibly a democratic state. Yet none of the preconditions for a democratic order existed. There was no elected leadership or representative political institutions. The absence of democratic values and institutions was partly the legacy of Pakistan's birth. Political institutions in the former colonial state were weak, while its state apparatus was overdeveloped. Moreover, the Muslim League leadership that had spearheaded the struggle to form the Muslim-majority state lacked mass support in the areas that now constituted Pakistan. Since the political leadership was incapable of or uninterested in attaining popular support, it soon became dependent on the civil and military bureaucracies to retain power and suppress domestic dissent.

The inherited state apparatus at first propped up the political leadership and then supplanted it. As a result, during the so-called parliamentary period between 1947 and 1958, there were no elected parliaments, and governments were formed

Samina Ahmed's *recent writings include "The Military and Ethnic Politics," in Charles H. Kennedy and Rasul B. Rais, eds., Pakistan 1995 (Boulder, Colo.: Westview, 1995) and "Pakistan: The Crisis Within," in Mutiah Alagappa, ed., Asian Security Practice: Material and Ideational (Stanford, Calif.: Stanford University Press).*

and dismissed by the civil bureaucracy with the military's support. When General Ayub Khan decided in 1958 to oust the nominal political leadership, a period of direct military rule followed in which no political dissent was allowed and any pretense of representative rule was discarded.

Internal tensions and popular demands for democracy resulted in Ayub's replacement in 1969 by General Yahya Khan, who held Pakistan's first general elections. The results of the 1970 elections, in which the Awami League, an East Pakistani opposition party, emerged victorious, were rejected by the West Pakistan–based Punjabi-Pakhtun dominated military; civil war, Indian military intervention, and the breakaway of East Pakistan soon followed.

After its defeat in the 1971 Indo-Pakistani war and East Pakistan's secession and recognition as the independent state of Bangladesh, the military withdrew to the background, transferring power to Zulfiqar Ali Bhutto, the head of the Pakistan People's Party (PPP), which had won a majority of seats in West Pakistan in the 1970 election. Authoritarian rule was replaced by a democratic order of sorts, but this new dispensation contained its own contradictions. Although Bhutto had a significant base of popular support, he was unable to challenge the military's dominance. Moreover, encroachments on provincial autonomy and Bhutto's disregard of democratic norms weakened his government's legitimacy. His growing dependence on the military to forcibly suppress political dissent spelled the end of a brief democratic episode. Following allegations of rigging the 1977 elections, the Bhutto government was dismissed and martial law imposed.

Whenever a government has attempted to challenge the military's dictates, it has been removed.

During the next 11 years, General Zia ul-Haq's military regime discarded democracy. Dissent was forcibly repressed and political parties were banned. Since popular legitimacy eluded the military regime, Zia tried to consolidate its domestic hold by co-opting a section of the political leadership, appointing a nominated parliament and prime minister. When Zia died in a plane crash in 1988, the military high command decided, once again, to direct affairs from behind the scenes, ostensibly restoring democracy.

The military's refusal to accept civilian supremacy has distorted and diluted the democratic character of the political order in place since 1988. For example, after the PPP's victory under Benazir Bhutto—the daughter of Zulfiqar—in the 1988

elections, it was not allowed to form a government until it had consented to a power-sharing agreement that ensured that the armed forces' institutional interests and the military's formulation of sensitive internal and external policies would not be challenged. Thus the first Benazir Bhutto government and all those that have followed have relinquished some of their authority in return for military support.

Whenever a government has attempted to challenge the military's dictates, it has been removed. Thus governments may have been formed by the will of the people, but the popular mandate has not been respected. No elected government has survived a full term, and even the electoral process has been tampered with. In 1990, for example, Prime Minister Benazir Bhutto's two-year-old PPP government was removed by the president at the military's behest, and the elections later that year resulting in the victory of Nawaz Sharif's Islamic Democratic Alliance (IDA) were rigged. In 1993, the military's displeasure with Sharif led to his removal. Behazir Bhutto was again elected prime minister, and the military was, once again, instrumental in dismissing her government in 1996. February 1997 saw Sharif, now head of the Pakistan Muslim League-Nawaz (PML-N), elected prime minister again. The military's constant interventions have led to a progressive weakening of democratic institutions, creating doubts about the democratic character of Pakistan's current political dispensation.

DISTORTED DEMOCRACY

Long years of authoritarian rule have left the political leadership unable to work collectively to strengthen and maintain democratic institutions and values. For example, since it came to power this February, Sharif's Muslim League has used its overwhelming majority in parliament to push through successive amendments that have distorted the spirit of the 1973 constitution. The behavior mirrors that of the government's predecessors, since most Pakistani governments have disregarded constitutional governance and norms. Pakistan's founding fathers did not even feel the need for a constitution; the first was drafted as late as 1956 by Iskader Mirza, an unelected president who represented the interests of the dominant civil-military bureaucracies. The declaration of martial law in 1958 led to the abrogation of this document. In 1962 the military regime promulgated its own constitution, which had as little legitimacy as its authors.

Both the 1956 and 1962 constitutions created highly centralized state structures dominated by a strong executive. Nominal legislatures and state intolerance of political dissent retarded the growth of a political party system and perpetuated patron-client relationships. The judiciary, lacking independence and autonomy, was unable to provide justice; thus the rule of law was undermined.

Following Pakistan's breakup in 1971 and the withdrawal of direct military rule, the political leadership, headed by Zulfiqar Bhutto's PPP government, drafted the 1973 constitution. This document created a parliamentary democracy based on a federal structure, the separation of the three branches of government, and the provision of fundamental rights to citizens. While Bhutto's authoritarian style subsequently undermined the fundamental rights guaranteed by the constitution, the existence of a constitutional doctrine formally defining governmental limits and responsibilities did reinforce democratic norms, including the rule of law.

The 1973 constitution was, however, distorted in spirit and form by Zia ul-Haq's attempt to gain legitimacy and suppress dissent and democratic aspirations. While the constitution was not abrogated, a 1985 amendment providing constitutional cover to all acts and ordinances of martial law changed its character. Thus Islamic legislation discriminating against women and minorities became a part of the constitution, directly contradicting the doctrine of fundamental rights. The military regime's political preferences were also constitutionally enshrined. Parliamentary democracy was weakened by Article 52, which gave an indirectly elected president—a position held by Zia himself—the power to dismiss a representative prime minister and national and provincial legislatures.

The distorted constitutional framework inherited by elected governments after the restoration of democracy in 1988 prevented the consolidation of democratic institutions and norms. Since the long period of authoritarian rule had also deeply polarized the body politic, the Pakistani political leadership failed to join hands to remove the 1985 amendment. When in power, the two major political parties, the PPP and the Muslim League, have supported the abrogation of the 1985 amendment; when in opposition, they have advocated keeping the amendment, since it is seen as a device to dismiss the government of their political opponent. With the assistance of willing political partners, successive military chiefs have used the 1985 amendment to remove elected governments, manipulating democratic politics and the direction of political development.

The military has long been deeply hostile to the PPP, which had been the mainstay of organized political opposition during the Zia years. In a military-directed "constitutional coup," the president dismissed the PPP government of Benazir Bhutto in 1990, using his powers under the 1985 amendment. When Bhutto's successor and the military's chosen civilian partner, Prime Minister Sharif, attempted to assert his authority, he too was removed by the president at the military's instigation using Article 52 in 1993. A temporary alliance with the military high command brought Bhutto back to power but not for a full term since she was, as noted earlier, once again removed by the president at the military's bidding in 1996.

Not surprisingly, the top priority of the current Sharif government is survival. Using its overwhelming majority in parliament, the government has pushed through successive constitutional amendments to strengthen its position. This April, with the support of the PPP opposition, the ruling party passed the thirteenth amendment to the constitution, depriving the president of his powers to dismiss assemblies and sack governments. While the passage of this amendment has received strong domestic support, the July 1997 fourteenth amendment—an antidefection bill—has been strongly criticized.

Dissension within the ruling party's ranks prompted Sharif to push through the fourteenth amendment, by which a parliamentarian can lose his or her seat if he or she breaches party discipline, votes against the party line, or abstains from voting in a manner that violates party policy. No judicial recourse will be available to a legislator declared a defector by a party's disciplinary committee.

The fourteenth amendment has led to concerns that members of parliament will be held hostage by their party leadership, unable to voice dissenting opinions or vote their conscience. This emasculation bodies ill for democratic politics, especially in view of the Muslim League's majority and a weak and ineffective parliamentary opposition.

RELYING ON THE JUDICIARY

While the legislature has become increasingly subservient to the executive, democracy has been strengthened by an assertive judiciary. In the past, especially during periods of direct military rule, the judgments of superior courts had undermined democratic norms by condoning authoritarian intervention. Since the restoration of democracy, some judgments of the superior judiciary, such as its decision to uphold the dismissals of PPP governments in 1990 and 1996, have been internally queried; moreover, the judiciary rejected the president's dismissal of Sharif's Muslim League administration in 1993, which led to the restoration of the Muslim League government. (The military high command, however, then forced the prime minister and president to resign, which led to the government's dissolution.)

At the same time, the judiciary has aggressively asserted its constitutional role, upholding the rule of law and reinforcing democratic norms. Superior court rulings and findings have condemned transgressions by state institutions of the fundamental rights of citizens. Judges on the panel examining the circumstances behind the killing of Murtaza Bhutto, Benazir Bhutto's brother, for example, held police and state agencies responsible for acts of premeditated violence.

The superior judiciary has also taken governments to task for resorting to coercive measures to stem ethnic and sectarian conflict. The supreme court upheld the dismissal of the Bhutto government in 1996 partly on the grounds that it had allowed human rights violations and "extrajudicial" killings in Sindh province. In July 1997, the chief justice of the supreme court took suo moto action on "indiscriminate killings," crime, and violence in Karachi, the capital of Sindh. The hearings are under way.

Nor is the judiciary prepared to accept executive interference with its independence. Thus another judicial justification for the dismissal of the Bhutto government was its contempt for the superior judiciary and political interference in judicial appointments. Just as the assertiveness of the judiciary led to a clash between the two branches of government in 1996, there are indications of growing tensions between the superior judiciary and the Sharif government.

Reacting negatively to judicial assertiveness, including the examination of ethnic management policies in Sindh, the Sharif administration has begun to challenge the judiciary's autonomy. In September the government initially decided (though it later reversed itself) to reduce the number of supreme court judges in an attempt to circumvent the chief justice's recommended promotions to the bench. Despite warnings from the bench that executive interference will undermine democratic governance, Sharif has declared that the parliament, in which the ruling party has a large majority, will exercise its constitutional powers to determine the size of the supreme court.

This confrontation between two key institutions of a fragile democratic order bodies ill for political stability. The removal of yet another elected government, no matter how inept, would likely destabilize democracy. Judicial assertiveness in upholding the rule of law and fundamental human rights will promote and maintain democratic norms, but only if democratic governance survives and is strengthened.

INTERNAL SCHISMS

Ethnic and sectarian violence poses a far greater threat to the Sharif government than judicial disapproval since it has rendered elected governments vulnerable to authoritarian intervention. The breakdown of law and order in Sindh—especially ethnic violence in the province's urban areas—was used by the military as a justification for dismissing the PPP governments in 1990 and 1996. Proponents of authoritarian rule claim that the failure of elected representatives to subdue substate extremism proves the ineffectiveness and inadequacy of democratic politics in Pakistan.

But Pakistan's political history reveals that ethnic divisions and sectarian tensions are directly related to the absence of representative rule and democratic norms. Successive regimes have failed to provide institutionalized mechanisms to accommodate ethnic and regional demands in a pluralistic society, transforming the internal competition for political power and socioeconomic benefits into conflict between substate actors.

In pre-1971 united Pakistan, political and economic power was monopolized by a predominantly West Pakistan–based, and mainly Punjabi, civil and military bureaucracy that operated through highly centralized state structures; this resulted in widespread alienation among the Bengalis of East Pakistan. Since Bengalis constituted over 54 percent of the population, the predominantly Punjabi, politically dominant military saw democratic institutions as a threat to its interests. Even in West Pakistan, ethnic grievances mounted as the Sindhi, Baluch, and (to a lesser extent) the Pakhtun populations were deprived of representative and participatory avenues for articulating grievances and voicing demands (In 1971, the Yahya regime's re-fusal to transfer power to the East Pakistan–based Awami League resulted in the bloody civil war and the breakup of Pakistan.)

In present-day Pakistan, Punjabis form a majority of the population and continue to dominate the military and civil bureaucracy. Only superficial attempts have been made to provide adequate representation to ethnic minorities such as the Sindhis and the Baluch. The 1973 constitution did address some ethnoregional demands by creating a federal framework, but it has failed to accommodate regional demands for greater autonomy and control over provincial resources. As ethnic grievances have increased, authoritarian rulers, apparently having learned little from the East Pakistan experience, have relied on coercion to suppress regional and ethnic demands. Even when elected governments have been in power, the military has retained control over sensitive policy areas, including ethnic relations. Its dependence on ethnic manipulation, divide-and-rule strategies, and the use of force have exacerbated internal divisions.

In Sindh, for example, the Zia regime considered the Sindhis a threat since they had spearheaded resistance to military rule. To contain Sindhi dissent, the minority Urdu-speaking Muhajir community—migrants and their descendants from India's west and north—were extended state support. Since Pakistan's formation, Muhajirs, who mainly settled in the urban centers of Sindh, had received state patronage while ethnic Sindhis were neglected. Muhajirs were, for example, over-represented in the civil bureaucracy and provided preferential access to economic resources. During the administration of Zulfiqar Ali Bhutto—himself a Sindhi—attempts to redress the grievances of the Sindhis caused Muhajir estrangement, manifested in language riots. Under Zia's military rule, when Sindhi alienation was at its height, Sindhi-Muhajir relations deteriorated even further as the Muhajirs sided with the military regime. Following the formation of Altaf Hussain's Muhajir Qaumi Movement (MQM) in 1986, Sindhi-Muhajir tensions resulted in periodic outbreaks of violence.

During the first terms of the PPP and PML-N governments, the military continued to dictate ethnic policy in Sindh, based on a combination of coercion and co-optation. When ethnic violence increased, especially in Sindh's capital, Karachi (Pakistan's only port and main industrial and commercial center), the military conducted operations, first against the Sindhis, and then against an increasingly assertive Muhajir leadership. The military-sponsored split of the MQM, which created a splinter group called the MQM-Haqiqi, contributed to ongoing Muhajir infighting that has claimed more than 400 lives in the first six months of 1997 alone.

Thus elected governments have been dismissed for their failure to maintain law and order in Sindh, but democratic governance and democratic politics themselves have been the victims of the military's interventionist policies. Electoral alliances in the Sindh provincial government and in the federal government, such as the coalition between the first PPP government and the MQM, have failed because of direct intervention on the part of the military. In 1997, Sindh is once again ruled by a precariously balanced alliance, this time between the Muslim League and the MQM. As Muhajir infighting engulfs Karachi, MQM leader Altaf believes that the MQM's branch of the Muslim League is incapable or unwilling to address its concerns, including the alleged support extended by military-dominated intelligence agencies to its MQM-Haqiqi rivals.

Democratic governance and democratic politics themselves have been the victims of the military's interventionist policies.

The Sharif government also faces an upsurge of sectarian violence between Pakistan's 80 percent Sunni Muslim majority and 18 percent Shiite Muslim minority, particularly in urban Sindh and Punjab; this has prompted the administration to deploy paramilitary forces in a number of cities. While sectarian tensions have periodically erupted throughout Pakistan's history, communal violence has become endemic since the 1980s, when the Zia dictatorship used religion to legitimize military rule, patronizing selected Sunni religious groups who were then pitted against the regime's political opponents. The confrontation with state-sponsored Sunni religious extremists resulted in a Shiite backlash and the formation of Shiite armed factions. After the restoration of democracy, successive governments have tried to contain sectarian violence with little success, since groups across the sectarian divide are well armed and motivated.

The situation is complicated by the links between Pakistan's internal and external security dilemmas. Ethnic and sectarian groups have easy access to sophisticated arms, a direct result of Pakistan's involvement in neighboring Afghanistan's civil war (yet another legacy of the Zia era). Crossborder traffic in narcotics also provides funds for extremists and has promoted the criminalization of Pakistani politics. A speedy resolution of the Afghan crisis and a strict policy of nonintervention would clearly help elected governments buttress internal stability. The military, however, continues to dictate policy toward Afghanistan.

The Sharif administration's proposed remedy, the Anti-Terrorist Act of August 1997, is unlikely to help the government contain ethnic and sectarian violence, and may have grave implications for democracy. The act gives the military and civilian law-enforcement agencies unprecedented powers to search and enter or arrest without a warrant and to use force against "suspected" perpetrators of violence. It also waives the con-

stitutional bar against self-incrimination. No legal action can be taken against any person for any act committed in good faith under the antiterrorist law. Special courts dealing with criminals charged under the act must dispose of cases within seven days, and appeals can be lodged only in a specially constituted appellate tribunal, which again must give its judgment within a week.

The act has been severely criticized by the political opposition, lawyers, and human rights activists, who fear that granting extraordinary powers to the police, paramilitary forces, and the military will undermine fundamental human rights guaranteed by the constitution and turn Pakistan into a police state. The political legitimacy of the ruling Muslim League is likely to erode as the antidemocratic provisions of the act are applied. And it will not bring an end to sectarian and ethnic strife, which depends on the government's political resolve to address internal grievances and uphold the rule of law.

QUESTIONING DEMOCRACY

A shift from democracy to authoritarianism is unlikely to occur in the immediate future due to a number of internal and external imperatives. In the external sphere, the military establishment is aware of the changes in the international environment. With the end of the cold war and the decline in Pakistan's strategic utility, its main allies, such as the United States, will not approve of a reimposition of military rule, and major aid donors such as Japan could withdraw badly needed assistance and investment.

Internal factors will, however, play a more significant role in preventing direct military rule. The military's ostensible support for democracy has helped democratic governance regain some of its lost legitimacy, and Pakistan's circumscribed democracy has helped strengthen civil society; democratic norms are gradually taking root. In the past nine years a fiercely independent press has critically monitored the government's actions, promoting public awareness of democratic values and the dangers posed to civil society by authoritarianism. Human rights groups such as the Human Rights Commission of Pakistan are playing a crucial role in assisting the democratic process, as are several professional organizations, including those representing lawyers, women, and minorities.

Any attempt to remove the formal infrastructure of representative government is likely to be strongly resisted. Even the judiciary, which in the past accepted the executive's bidding, is unlikely to condone such a change. Yet the present political order's built-in distortions could prevent the consolidation of democratic institutions and norms. The growth of political consciousness among the Pakistani public is not paralleled by a commitment of its elite to democratic ideals. Thus a deeply polarized political leadership has become more committed to sustaining or attaining power, even at the cost of sacrificing democratization.

Successive elected governments have advanced the military's interests in the belief that the military establishment holds the ultimate political veto. In the 1997–1998 budget, for example, social spending has been cut while defense expenditures have increased and formally constitute 26 percent of the budget. At the same time, substate violence continues to threaten the security of Pakistan's citizens but there is little awareness in the political leadership of the urgent need to find sustainable solutions based on accommodation and bargaining as well as strict adherence to the rule of law.

The political leadership's lack of commitment to democratic politics is demonstrated by the Sharif administration's deeply flawed policy of *ehtesab,* or accountability, which is intended to end political corruption but is unmistakably partisan in nature, selectively targeting political opponents with little regard for legal due process. For her part, the main opposition leader, former Prime Minister Benazir Bhutto, has called for the dismissal of the elected leadership and the formation of a "national" government in which the bureaucracy, the armed forces, and the intelligence agencies are given representation. Sharif claims that "We have democracy and we should be thinking of strengthening" it; but unless the political leadership realizes that its very survival lies in collaborative efforts to consolidate a representative, pluralistic, and participatory system strong enough to withstand military intervention, democracy in Pakistan will remain vulnerable.

Article 29　　　　　　　　　　　　　　　　　　　*The Economist,* October 17, 1998

ASIA

The crumbling of Pakistan

LAHORE

Recipe for ruin: a deadbeat economy, nuclear bombs and fundamentalism

ALMOST anywhere but Pakistan the plug would surely be yanked out. With days to go before an IMF mission was due to put the finishing touches to a rescue package, the prime minister, Nawaz Sharif, announced a 30% cut in electricity charges. This is lunancy of a high order: Pakistan's utilities are already losing enough money to sink the foundering economy. The IMF wants charges put up. If neither side budges, the IMF will withhold cash Pakistan desperately needs to service its $42 billion external debt. Trade and the currency will slide, pulling down Pakistan's already low living standards.

But Pakistan is no ordinary deadbeat debtor. It is a nuclear power engaged in a low-level war with another nuclear power, India, over the disputed province of Kashmir. In Afghanistan, its north-western neighbour, it is backing the militantly Islamic Taliban regime, which until recently seemed on the brink of war with Iran. Pakistan's internal politics are hardly more tranquil. Crisscrossing rivalries among sects, regions, tongues and political parties

make Balkan disputes look simple. They have been made more lethal by weapons that have poured into the country since the Soviet Union's invasion of Afghanistan in 1979. Every newspaper carries a litany of murder prompted by greed or group hatred. An economic implosion would make things worse.

So Mr Sharif may reckon that the IMF will, at America's behest, prop up his economy no matter what he does. This is not so, says Mushahid Hussain, Pakistan's information minister. But then he points out that the West has a big stake in the region's stability. The denial suddenly sounds less convincing.

How worried should the West be? The economy has rarely been in such bad shape. Industry and investment are at a standstill; the banks, whose bad assets account for a third or more of their balance-sheets, are trembling. And now courts have begun to cancel agreements with private power companies accused of corruption by the government. Pakistan can forget about having private investment for a while.

Still, Pakistan looks more likely to crumble than to explode. A good harvest this year has so far kept the country's economic tribulations from being a catastrophe for most Pakistanis. If Pakistan fails to pay its debts, trade is likely to slide rather than to collapse all at once. The receding threat of war between Sunni Afghanistan and Shia Iran makes it less likely that Pakistan's militant Islamists will turn on its Shia minority. The militants are few in number; they wield more terror than power. The country's multiplicity of conflicts may spare it a conventional civil war.

Mr Sharif's government looks entrenched. When General Jehangir Karamat, the army's respected chief of staff, last week accused the prime minister of "destabilising" Pakistan and proposed that he should share power with the army, it was the general who had to clear his desk. Nor, after a change to the constitution last year, can the president dismiss the prime minister. Mr Sharif's Muslim League controls two-thirds of the seats in the all-important lower house of parliament.

Yet Mr Sharif's grip is not sure, and it may be about to become less democratic. Few people think that the army has changed its mind about his rule. It regards Pakistan's economic chaos as a threat to its own power and perks (though an IMF-imposed austerity programme might also cut into its budget). In any event, influence may be shifting from the army, which keeps largely to its cantonments, to the Inter Services Intelligence, which orchestrates the proxy wars in Afghanistan and India's part of Kashmir. It may be to placate the ISI's fundamentalist friends that Mr Sharif is seeking a change to the constitution that would enshrine *sharia*—Islamic law— as the "supreme law of Pakistan".

Mr Sharif's friends manage to make the amendment sound innocuously progressive. Its "core point", says Shahbaz Sharif, the prime minister's brother and chief minister of Punjab, the biggest of Pakistan's four provinces, is "speedy and cheap justice". It will "provide people an opportunity to live an honoured and dignified life".

Some people, perhaps. On one reading, the amendment gives the government absolute power by conferring on it the obligation to "prescribe what is right and to forbid what is wrong". Nonsense, retort its supporters, the government will enforce *sharia* but the courts will interpret it. Yet this is small comfort in a country where judges are murdered for verdicts that offend fundamentalist Muslims.

Women and minority groups are terrified of the measure. Already, in the antiwestern mood that has followed America's attack on terrorist bases in Afghanistan, some women feel threatened. Those deemed immodestly dressed have become targets of weird assaults: some have been jabbed with pins labelled "Welcome to the HIV club". Hindus and Christians object that members of their communities will be allowed to serve neither as judges nor as advocates at Islamic courts likely to be set up under *sharia*. Liberals fear that the balance in the constitution between provisions that protect "fundamental rights" and those securing Pakistan's Islamic character will be tipped decisively in favour of Islam.

The amendment may never become law. The lower house has given it the necessary two-thirds backing, but the Muslim League is in the minority in the Senate, where nearly all opposition members say they will vote against it. Even so, now that the hopes of fundamentalists have been raised, the amendment's failure might provoke as much trouble as its enactment.

The Sharif brothers have not wholly turned their backs on modernity. Shahbaz Sharif talks energetically about good governance. He boasts of restoring merit to the admissions procedures at Punjab's medical schools and of shutting down "phantom schools" that were draining the province's education budget. He wants to lift literacy in his province from 35% to 70% within the next five years by luring children back to school with stipends. Since the Sharifs came to power last year, Shahbaz points out, Pakistan's ranking in the leading survey of international corruption has dropped from second place to 15th.

This is all encouraging stuff. Yet the Sharif brothers seem to think that Pakistan can have *sharia* and constitutional democracy, holy wars and a peaceful society, economic populism and an IMF bail-out. Their bet on the bail-out is a long shot. The other gambles are doomed.

Article 30

The Bulletin of the Atomic Scientists, September/October 1998

Sanctions: Lift 'em

By Pervez Hoodbhoy & Zia Mian

CAUGHT BETWEEN A DESIRE TO MATCH INDIA'S NUCLEAR tests and the fear of devastating sanctions, Pakistan vacillated for two weeks before testing. Subsequently, Prime Minister Nawaz Sharif went on television and declared, "This auspicious day is an historic event for us." Anticipating the price the country would have to pay, he urged "sacrifices" and added, "If the need arises be ready to go hungry."

Now, with sanctions imposed by its international creditors and private capital scared away, the specter of Pakistan's economic collapse looms large. The currency has fallen sharply and may well go into free fall, driving up inflation and increasing the difficulty of finding resources to pay the debt. Foreign debt is around $30 billion—small by Western standards, but large for a nation like Pakistan. Debt service was set at 45 percent of government expenditures at the time of the June budget—before the collapse of the currency.

As the economy falters, societal institutions, weak even before the tests, could collapse. Should there be a breakdown of governance, Prime Minister Sharif, as well as the current chief of the army, a moderate, may be replaced by hardliners from Islamist groups. Within the army, fire-breathers such as retired Gen. Hamid Gul, the former head of Pakistan's Inter-Service Intelligence Agency, stand to gain. These groups are the ones who rejoiced most loudly at Pakistan's tests. They are pathologically anti-Indian and determined to settle old scores. What this may mean in the nuclear age is terrifying.

In the months ahead it may become difficult for any government to manage the country. When Muslim-hating Bharatiya Janata Party (BJP hard-liners in India incited and enticed Pakistan into testing—the first time a state has tried to *compel* an adversary to test nuclear weapons—they may have hoped for a repeat of Cold War history. The BJP would like to see Pakistan exhausted and broken by an arms race and, quite possibly, they might get their wish.

Disintegration into civil war could turn Pakistan into a nuclear Somalia.

But unlike the steel cage of the Soviet state, which insured that some crucial structures of governance survived even as everything else collapsed, Pakistan is already fractured by multiple violent ethnic and religious conflicts. Disintegration into molecular civil war with fiefdoms and warlords is a terrible possibility. Should it occur, India will have created a nuclear Somalia for a neighbor.

THE SITUATION THAT PAKISTAN FINDS ITSELF IN PREDATES ITS debut into the nuclear world. The Pakistani state is not able to provide even the basics of education, health care, housing, or jobs for its people. For almost all of its 50 years of independence, the avarice of Pakistan's tax-dodging elite has been allied with a desperate sense of insecurity about India, insuring that the military got the lion's share of what few public resources were available.

This fundamentally untenable situation was sustained for years largely by military and economic aid, especially from the United States in exchange for Pakistan's loyalty in the Cold War. But the collapse of the Soviet Union meant the end of Pakistan's free ride; further, in 1990 the United States imposed sanctions because of Pakistan's nuclear weapons program.

Left to its own resources and never having been able to create institutions to manage them efficiently, Pakistan plunged deeper and deeper into debt. Debt service replaced military spending as the largest item in government spending.

In the past few years, the need to address the economic and social crisis had dawned on some in government and the military. A quiet revolution had begun. Military spending unobtrusively started to decline both in real terms and as a fraction of government spending.

Astonishingly, just weeks before the Indian tests, Gen. Jehangir Karamat, the head of Pakistan's army, publicly identified the state of the economy and internal problems as being more serious threats to the future of Pakistan than India was likely to be. All this changed after India's tests on May 11.

The stock of the hard-liners has risen, India is now back as enemy number one, and the 14 percent increase in India's military budget has led Pakistan to increase its military spending by eight percent. This was only for openers. India's defense minister has promised further large increases in military spending.

PAKISTAN'S DISINTEGRATION WOULD HAVE CALAMITOUS CONSEQUENCES for South Asia and it must be averted. But the situation may be too far gone for Pakistan's leaders to handle it alone. The international community must help.

The first thing the international community must do is insure that the situation is not made worse. Sanctions applied for punitive ends, which take no account of political constraints and possibilities, are part of the problem. The longer they are applied, the more quickly will Pakistan's economic and social structures collapse.

Second, the international community should realize the potential of Kashmir as a flashpoint for nuclear conflagration. Today Pakistan's leaders privately admit they can't win Kashmir but, in the same breath, they stress that they cannot be seen to give up on the issue. They are prisoners of their success in manufacturing public consent to a particular solution to Kashmir. They desperately need a fig leaf.

What can this cover be? An excellent beginning could be to make greater use of the U.N. military observers who have been in Kashmir for almost 50 years. They could be increased in numbers and authorized to separate the two armies and keep them out of each other's artillery range, and they could prevent illegal movement across the border.

But this is only a stop-gap. The international community must try harder to break the impasse between India and Pakistan on Kashmir. At present, the two states cannot even agree on the terms for *talking* about Kashmir. Pakistan believes the basis for discussion must be the 1948 and 1949 U.N. resolutions on Kashmir, agreed to by India, which envisaged the United Nations Commission for India and Pakistan supervising a settlement in Kashmir "in accordance with the will of the people," which was to be determined through a plebiscite.

India argues the 1972 Simla Agreement must be the basis for talks. Signed after the 1971 India-Pakistan war, the agreement makes no mention of the United Nations. Instead, it commits the two states to settle their disputes "through bilateral negotiations or by any other peaceful means mutually agreed upon between them."

An international contact group (which might be, for example, composed of judges from the International Court of Justice) may be able to help the two countries work out the legal basis for proceeding on Kashmir.

Given their vulnerability, Pakistan's leaders also cannot afford to be seen as caving in to pressure on arms control measures such as the Comprehensive Test Ban Treaty, a no-first-use agreement, or a ban on the production of fissile materials.

However, Pakistan's post-test statements about undertaking a strategic review and possibly delinking its policy from India's on these treaties can be positively interpreted as signs of a willingness to move forward.

But the international community should not be blinded by its wish to see progress in this direction. In particular, it must resist efforts to push things along by offering conventional weapons and dual-use technology to Pakistan or India. Such deals would amount to helping South Asia jump out of the nuclear frying pan and into the conventional-weapons fire. This fire has singed both countries three times already.

What Pakistan needs is the time and resources to dig itself out of the hole it is in. The backbreaking sanctions imposed by the international community must be lifted. Instead, Pakistan must be given help to create and manage the urgently needed social infrastructure of schools and hospitals, and to put its economic house in order. Social peace, something Pakistan has rarely enjoyed, can create the basis for peace with India. Nothing else has.

Pervez Hoodbhoy is professor of physics at Quaid-i-Azam, Islamabad. Zia Mian is a research associate at the Center for Energy and Environmental Studies, Princeton University. They are involved in the peace movement and other campaigns for social justice and human rights in Pakistan.

Sanctions: Modify 'em

By David Cortright & Samina Ahmed

U.S. SANCTIONS AGAINST INDIA AND PAKISTAN ARE A classic case of how not to impose sanctions. While the U.S. ban on foreign aid and loans, military assistance, investment and credit support, and technology transfers will cause economic pain to the people of India and Pakistan, it is not likely to force either government to alter its commitment to nuclear weapons development.

Sanctions that ignore the critical distinction between government and civil society and that impose punishments without offering rewards are often counterproductive. Indeed, New Delhi and Islamabad have attempted to use U.S. sanctions to mobilize nationalist fervor and build political support for their nuclear weapons policies. On the other hand, as Washington has shown more flexibility in the implementation of sanctions, India and Pakistan have shown some willingness to consider signing the Comprehensive Test Ban Treaty.

Sanctions are most effective when they are multilateral, targeted, and flexible. Economic statecraft should also include incentives capable of influencing public opinion and persuading officials to accept nuclear restraint. U.S. sanctions meet none of these criteria and are likely to fail.

U.S. unilateral sanctions were mandated by the Arms Export Control Act, approved by Congress in 1994. Also known as the Proliferation Prevention Act, the law is a prime example of a punitive approach to sanctions. It was designed to be draconian in an effort to deter India, Pakistan, and other would-be proliferators from nuclear testing or other overt nuclear weapons activity. Once India and Pakistan crossed the nuclear Ru-

bicon, sanctions became mandatory. Having failed as a deterrent, sanctions became policy.

Doubts about the sanctions emerged soon after they were imposed. When farm state senators realized that the sanctions would block grain exports and thereby harm their constituents, they quickly passed legislation exempting American farmers from the ban on export credits and guarantees.

Concerns were also raised about the lack of a waiver provision. As originally written, the Proliferation Prevention Act contains no sunset clause or mechanism for lifting sanctions. A separate act of Congress is required to remove or modify the sanctions. The president thus lacks the option of easing sanctions as part of carrots-and-sticks diplomacy. That limits the ability of the United States to influence the future direction of Indian and Pakistani nuclear policies.

In response to these concerns, members of the Senate have introduced legislation to provide presidential waiver authority. The Clinton administration also called for the authority to lift or ease the sanctions, arguing that greater flexibility in the imposition of sanctions would enable the United States to negotiate more effectively with New Delhi and Islamabad.

THE SANCTIONS ARE LIKELY TO HAVE NEGATIVE HUMANITARIAN consequences. According to Deputy Secretary of State Strobe Talbott, the United States has attempted to "avoid bringing hardship to the peoples of India and Pakistan . . . especially the poor." But general trade sanctions inevitably cause the greatest harm to the most vulnerable.

In contrast to targeted "smart sanctions" strategies now favored by sanctions experts and many U.N. officials, these congressionally mandated sanctions are blunt instruments that impose their greatest impact on those farthest from the seat of power. The withdrawal of U.S. backing for several power generation projects in India, for instance, will impede economic development and pose special hardships in communities plagued by recurring electricity outages.

The cut in U.S. foreign assistance has already caused postponement of a $21 million housing subsidy project and a $5 million greenhouse gases program in India.

The sanctions require the United States to oppose World Bank funding in India, much of which goes for health care and rural development. Washington lacks the voting power to block these projects, however, and has voted for them on humanitarian grounds.

In Pakistan the impact of sanctions is likely to be more severe. The sanctions, although less extensive than those applied to India, will seriously damage Pakistan's faltering economy, already burdened by huge external debt payments and dangerously low currency reserves.

The sanctions require the United States to vote against International Monetary Fund credits that are keeping Pakistan's enfeebled economy afloat. Recognizing that such action could have devastating consequences, however, the United States has abstained from voting on financial support for Pakistan, thereby allowing IMF funding to proceed.

The sanctions have caused a general lowering of business confidence in both countries. The United States is the largest market for Pakistani exports and the largest trade and investment partner of India. The decline of U.S. investment and trade has combined with the continuing Asian financial crisis and New Delhi's unrealistic budget projections to generate growing economic uncertainty.

The stock market in Mumbai (formerly Bombay) nosedived 22 percent in the month after the Indian nuclear tests. The Indian rupee lost nearly 10 percent of its value during the same period. Perhaps most ominously for India, Moody's Investors Service downgraded India's debt offerings, causing an immediate spike in interest rates and raising the cost of borrowing for all Indian businesses, even those not directly affected by sanctions.

The cumulative impact of these mounting pressures has already caused political difficulty, especially in India. Business executives complain that the government has not acted forcefully enough to counteract the effect of sanctions. Opposition political leaders criticize the Hindu nationalist government for jeopardizing previous economic gains and undermining India's political standing in the world.

If economic and social hardships mount, these pressures could intensify, leading to greater xenophobia and nationalism. Intolerance and Hindu nationalism are on the rise in India; right-wing forces have been active in Pakistan. The greater political polarization resulting from the nuclear tests and sanctions may make it more difficult for New Delhi and Islamabad to compromise on nuclear and security policy.

SANCTIONS CAN BE EFFECTIVE AT TIMES, BUT THEY MUST BE guided by a strategic design. They should exert pressure on decision-making elites while exempting innocent populations and, if possible, empowering reform constituencies.

A targeted sanctions policy would identify the Hindu nationalist leaders of the Bharatiya Janata Party (BJP) in India as the group responsible for precipitating the nuclear crisis. In Pakistan it would target the military leaders and nuclear scientists who have controlled military policy and long championed the nuclear option.

Measures against these elites might include freezing their overseas financial assets, blocking financial transactions, canceling visas and residency permits for leaders and their families, and banning travel. The cancellation of visa and residency permits would be especially onerous, because many Indian and Pakistani leaders send their children to universities in North America and Europe and have business connections there.

Accompanying such sanctions would be a series of incentives designed to influence the political dynamics of the two countries in ways that favor accommodation. Incentives should empower political constituencies most likely to favor military and nuclear restraint. This would involve offering assistance to institutions in civil society that advocate democracy, human rights, and reordered spending priorities.

It would also mean supporting programs for increasing literacy, especially among women, and encouraging a more informed and diverse public debate about the risk of nuclear weapons. One of the most powerful incentives for South Asia would be a "debt for disarmament" swap in which major countries and the international financial institutions agree to forgive portions of the huge foreign debt owed by each country in exchange for a commitment to denuclearize.

Such a policy could have enormous economic and social benefits, especially in Pakistan, freeing vast resources for critically needed human development programs. To work as a denuclearization initiative, a debt-relief policy would have to stipulate that the money saved from reduced debt servicing be directed solely to social development purposes. This would help create a broad social constituency in favor of the debt forgiveness program while empowering constituencies that are more likely to support denuclearization.

WASHINGTON'S EFFORTS TO ENCOURAGE NUCLEAR RESTRAINT in South Asia have been undermined by contradictions in U.S. nonproliferation policy. New Delhi and Islamabad argue that the United States has no moral basis for imposing sanctions when it has conducted more than a thousand nuclear tests of its own, and while it maintains an arsenal of 10,000 strategic nuclear weapons.

Washington would be in a stronger position to pressure India and Pakistan if it were to agree to serious negotiations aimed at the eventual elimination of these weapons. India has said it will give up the bomb as part of a global ban on nuclear weapons, and it has urged U.N. Secretary General Kofi Annan to begin negotiations for a nuclear weapons convention. Meanwhile, Pakistan has said it will abandon the nuclear option if India does. (In 1994 and 1996, public opinion surveys sponsored by the Fourth Freedom Forum confirmed widespread support for nuclear disarmament in India and Pakistan.)

The United States and the other major powers have committed themselves to nuclear disarmament on many occasions, most significantly in the Nuclear Non-Proliferation Treaty. In 1995, when the treaty was made permanent, the United States and the other nuclear weapons states promised "the determined pursuit . . . of systematic and progressive efforts to reduce nuclear weapons globally with the ultimate goal of eliminating those weapons."

It is time for the United States and the other nuclear states to live up to those commitments by putting forward a technically sound blueprint for moving toward the elimination of nuclear weapons. Only if the United States leads by example in eliminating nuclear arms will it have broad political backing for sanctioning other would-be proliferators.

A universal, nondiscriminatory disarmament regime offers the best hope for restraining Indian and Pakistani nuclear ambitions and containing the global proliferation threat. It would also provide a solid foundation for sanctioning countries that violate such a regime.

An initiative by the major powers to begin negotiations for a nuclear weapons convention, and an invitation for India and Pakistan to sit at the table and join the process, would transform the dynamics of nuclear policy in South Asia. It would also lay the foundations for a nuclear-weapons-free world.

Until then, the United States, as well as other states, must demonstrate their collective resolve to oppose nuclear proliferation in India and Pakistan by imposing wisely designed checks on irresponsible governmental behavior and by offering rewards for steps toward nuclear restraint.

David Cortright is president of the Fourth Freedom Forum in Goshen, Indiana. Samina Ahmed is a freelance journalist living in Islamabad. They are co-editors of Pakistan and the Bomb *(Notre Dame Press, 1998).*

Sanctions: Hang tough

By Thomas Graham, Jr.

THE PEOPLE OF INDIA AND PAKISTAN, AS WELL AS THOSE who depend on the nuclear nonproliferation regime the world over for their security, have been endangered by the emerging nuclear arms race in South Asia.

By conducting nuclear weapon tests in May, India departed from its internationalist tradition and its commitment to peace. The tests, followed by Pakistani tests, violated the global norm based on the Nuclear Non-Proliferation Treaty, which had held for three decades.

During the first two decades of the nuclear era, five states—the United States, the Soviet Union, Britain, France, and China—declared their possession of these weapons. In the 1960s, there were predictions that there would be 25 to 30 declared nuclear weapon states by the end of the 1970s.

In response, the international community negotiated the 1968 Nuclear Non-Proliferation Treaty (NPT), in which the 181 non-nuclear weapon states that are now parties to the treaty have forsworn the acquisition of nuclear weapons. Meanwhile, the five nuclear weapon states agreed to engage in negotiations leading to reductions in the numbers of nuclear weapons, with zero being the ultimate goal.

Thus the international norm of behavior based on the NPT that emerged was that there would be no more than five nuclear weapon states, that all other parties of the NPT would pledge not to acquire nuclear weapons, and that there would be three states tolerated outside the regime in an ambiguous posture with potential but not overt nuclear weapon capability.

These reciprocal obligations undergird all subsequent nuclear arms control agreements. If the number of nuclear weapon states had not been held in check, the remarkable arms reductions of recent years would not have been possible. And if the number of nuclear weapon states cannot be held in check in the future, then urgent and desperately needed next steps to reduce the danger posed by the thousands of nuclear weapons that remain at high levels of alert may not be possible.

THE TESTS BY INDIA AND PAKISTAN BROUGHT THE WORLD TO the most dangerous point since the beginning of the nuclear age, with the exception of the Cuban missile crisis in 1962. Far from stabilizing the relationship between these two countries—which have fought three wars since independence—the introduction of nuclear weapons onto the subcontinent has sharply increased the stakes of a potential future conflict.

Some argue that the increased risk will induce caution. This is unlikely because of the tradition of distrust in the region and the proximity of the potential adversaries. Lacking the sophisticated early warning systems of the United States and the former Soviet Union, Indian and Pakistani commanders would not know that an attack was under way until enemy weapons began to detonate on their soil, potentially destroying their capability to retaliate. During times of great tension, the pressure to use the weapons or lose them will be increased. Stable deterrence is very unlikely to exist under these conditions.

The nuclear tests have opened the door to similar actions by Israel and other states like North Korea.

In addition to violating the international norm based on the NPT regime, the nuclear tests in India and Pakistan opened the door to similar action by Israel as well as by other states, such as North Korea. If India and Pakistan fail to reverse course, we can expect others to follow suit.

INDIA AND PAKISTAN CANNOT JOIN THE NPT AS NUCLEAR weapon states, as some observers have suggested, because the treaty defines this term as a state that had tested a nuclear explosive device prior to 1967. The treaty would have to be amended to change that definition; that would be nearly impossible, given the treaty's cumbersome amendment procedure.

But even if amendment were possible, it would not be desirable. The definition of a nuclear weapon state is more than a semantic issue. Limiting the number of nuclear weapon states to five is at the core of the NPT. The treaty did not legitimize the nuclear weapon programs of the five nuclear weapon states, as India has charged for 30 years. Rather, it recognized historical reality, while establishing a legal barrier in an attempt to prevent a bad situation from getting worse.

To preserve the NPT regime, India and Pakistan must forgo their nuclear weapon programs and join the NPT as non-nuclear weapon states—as South Africa did in 1991 after destroying the six weapons it had built.

But this can be done only in the context of the five nuclear weapon states complying with their disarmament obligations as outlined in Article VI of the NPT and in the statement of "Principles and Objectives for Non-Proliferation" associated with the treaty's indefinite extension in 1995. In plain language, the nuclear weapon states obligated themselves to reduce their nuclear arsenals as fast as practicable with the goal of eliminating such weapons.

The five nuclear weapon states must recommit themselves to nuclear disarmament if they are to persuade India and Paki-

stan to rejoin the world community by joining the NPT, and if they hope to persuade other nations that acquiring nuclear weapons does not add to a state's prestige and power.

The United States Senate should promptly approve the Comprehensive Test Ban Treaty to strengthen the consensus against nuclear testing. The nuclear weapon states, however, must do more to reduce the perceived high political value of nuclear weapons. The role of nuclear weapons should be strictly limited to deterring their use by others as we proceed toward deep reductions.

By refusing to join the community of responsible nations as a party to the NPT, the Indian government has repeatedly mischaracterized the regime as discriminatory. This is neither accurate nor useful.

The NPT did not cause the five declared nuclear weapon states to develop nuclear arsenals; in fact, the NPT constitutes the only legally binding obligation the five have to reduce and ultimately eliminate those arsenals. The NPT stopped a dangerous trend toward widespread nuclear proliferation that had, in two decades, ensnared five states in a dangerous and costly nuclear arms race.

INDIA VIEWS THE ACQUISITION OF NUCLEAR WEAPONS AS A LEGITIMATE way to increase national prestige. This attitude, if widely adopted, could cause the world to resume a race down the path toward widespread nuclear proliferation, which was so narrowly averted in the 1960s by the conclusion of the NPT.

More frightening still, in a world filled with nuclear weapon states, keeping these weapons out of the hands of criminals, terrorists, or religious cults will become all but impossible.

The Indian decision to openly declare itself a nuclear weapon state and the Pakistani response constitute a threat to the central security interests of every state party to the NPT. And yet, the world has not reacted accordingly.

Many countries resisted supporting any kind of vigorous response, such as the sanctions imposed by the United States—and even those sanctions have been rendered relatively meaningless by a Congress eager to prevent adverse impacts on American farmers and by the administration's decision to view most World Bank assistance as humanitarian aid immune from sanctions.

As the Senate acted to exclude agricultural products from the sanctions package, long-time nonproliferation proponent Sen. Richard Lugar of Indiana observed that "food should not be used as a weapon of foreign policy. . . . When sanctions are unduly rigid and automatic, they become a roadblock to diplomacy."

While these concerns are real, they were foreseeable. By imposing sanctions it was not prepared to uphold, the United States made its commitment to respond to threats to the nonproliferation regime seem uncertain—perhaps as uncertain, in the eyes of some non-nuclear weapon states, as the U.S. commitment to nuclear disarmament under Article VI of the NPT.

Firm resolve is necessary in both areas, if the regime is to remain strong and the unthinkable is to be prevented.

Thomas Graham, Jr. has represented the United States in negotiating every major arms control and nonproliferation treaty over

the past 30 years. Most recently, he was President Clinton's Special Representative for Arms Control, Nonproliferation, and Disarmament. He is now president of LAWS, the Lawyers Alliance for World Security.

Article 31

The Christian Science Monitor, August 12, 1998

War in Sri Lanka Feeds on Itself

■ Conflict-weary people watch as military seems to flourish on an ethnic war now in its 15th year.

By John Zubrzycki

Special to *The Christian Science Monitor*
JAFFNA, SRI LANKA

At his heavily bunkered headquarters in Jaffna, Maj. Gen. Lionel Balagalle revels in treating correspondents to an eggs-and-toast breakfast briefing on how he is winning the war for the hearts and minds of Sri Lanka's minority Tamils.

Complete with computer-generated graphics, detailed maps, and impressive statistics, the briefing is more public relations than strategic analysis.

"The disappearances, rapes, and other excesses have to stop," says the mustached and portly leader. "But getting the confidence of the people is difficult," he admits.

General Balagalle says the soldiers patrolling the marketplace and manning checkpoints at almost every intersection are there to reassure the Tamils that peace and security have returned.

But people are angry and frustrated by the constant searches, the lack of electricity, and the shortage of telephone lines. The only way out of the city is by

a motley fleet of chartered Ukrainian aircraft booked months in advance.

"We are in a prison. We can't go anywhere, we can't do anything," says a street vendor who asks not to be named.

Growing military forces

With no end to the 15-year-old separatist war in sight, an increasing number of Sri Lankans believe that the government and the armed forces are perpetuating the conflict for their own ends.

Since the Liberation Tigers of Tamil Eelam (LTTE) and other separatists took up arms to demand a Tamil Eelam, or homeland, in the early 1980s, more than 50,000 people have died in this brutal and intractable ethnic conflict.

Last week hopes of a resolution took a step backward when President Chandrika Kumaratunga extended a state of emergency already in force in Jaffna to cover the whole country, citing the threats posed by the ongoing insurgency.

The opposition blasted the move as an excuse by the government to post-

pone provincial elections that they claim would go against the ruling People's Alliance.

Some loyal to rebels

The loyalties of many people in this battle-scarred city are still with the LTTE. For nearly five years, until they were driven out in December 1995, the Tigers ran a de facto state in Jaffna—collecting taxes, dispensing justice, and recruiting fighters for their cause. "LTTE government good. Strict. Understand the Tamil people. No curfew. No problem with food," whispers Kanageratna, a shopkeeper at Jaffna's central market, making sure no soldiers are within earshot.

Whether this former British colony, the former Ceylon, can ever restore the 'emerald isle' image promoted in glossy tourist brochures will depend largely on Balagalle's success in weaning Jaffna's Tamils away from the Tigers, who have retreated to the jungles in the south.

The 45,000 troops under Balagalle's control are drawn entirely from the Sri Lanka's Sinhalese majority and are seen as an occupation force by the peninsula's Tamils. "The majority of our soldiers cannot speak Tamil and there is a vast communication gap," Balagalle says.

From a largely ceremonial force of just 12,000 in 1983, the Sri Lankan military has grown 10-fold and now numbers 120,000 soldiers and 6,000 officers. Defense spending consumes a massive 30 to 40 percent of the annual budget.

In a country where unemployment is endemic, thousands of rural youths are absorbed into the Army every year. And the need to keep the forces equipped with increasingly sophisticated weaponry has increased the opportunity for corruption.

"The youth are not joining the army for patriotic or nationalist reasons. They are joining because they need a job. If there was no war, where would they go?" asks Marwaan Macan-Markar, features editor at the Sunday Leader newspaper in the capital, Colombo. "And yes, you have people who have built empires as a result of the war, particularly those in the upper cadre."

Uncovering evidence of corruption within the military can be risky for journalists who are already subjected to strict censorship when reporting on the war. When Iqbal Attas, an investigative reporter for Colombo's Sunday Times, began closing in on evidence of massive kickbacks in a combat-aircraft deal, armed men broke into his house, pointed a gun at his head while his terrified wife and daughter looked on, and then fled. Mr. Attas later identified one of the assailants as the personal bodyguard of a

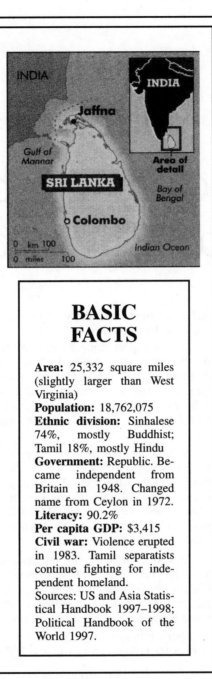

BASIC FACTS

Area: 25,332 square miles (slightly larger than West Virginia)
Population: 18,762,075
Ethnic division: Sinhalese 74%, mostly Buddhist; Tamil 18%, mostly Hindu
Government: Republic. Became independent from Britain in 1948. Changed name from Ceylon in 1972.
Literacy: 90.2%
Per capita GDP: $3,415
Civil war: Violence erupted in 1983. Tamil separatists continue fighting for independent homeland.
Sources: US and Asia Statistical Handbook 1997–1998; Political Handbook of the World 1997.

former Air Force commander implicated in the deal.

"The war has become a very big industry," says Attas. "Look at the sophistication of the Army and the Air Force . . . and yet they claim that the LTTE numbers only a couple of thousand soldiers."

As the military tries to sidestep damaging allegations of corruption, a new controversy has erupted that could jeopardize whatever progress Balagalle has made in Jaffna. In June, a Sinhalese soldier being sentenced to 30 years imprisonment for raping and murdering a school girl at an Army checkpoint made the startling revelation that a mass grave containing 400 bodies of Tamil civilians was located on the outskirts of the city.

Distrust of the government

Balagalle has promised a thorough investigation. But Tamil groups accuse the government of stalling for time so that the Army can tamper with the evidence before a fact-finding mission reaches the site. "Delays of this nature are making the people suspicious," says S. Paramantan, a member of the People's Council for Peace and Goodwill. "It cannot be left up to the Army alone. One person cannot be the prosecutor and the defense."

With a devolution package giving more autonomy to Tamil-dominated areas stalled in Parliament and the Tigers unwilling to come to the negotiating table, a military solution is the only option, says Balagalle.

"Peace will only come through military means. I am saying that because we [the Army] know the LTTE better than anyone else."

Article 32   *The Christian Science Monitor,* July 29, 1997

Beijing promised Tibet autonomy when it took control in 1950. But its actions since then suggest it's trying to 'civilize' this very different culture

After Decades, Tibet Won't Bend to Chinese Ways

By Kevin Platt

Staff writer of The Christian Science Monitor

BEIJING

THE world seems to be watching every step taken by China's new, hand-picked rulers in Hong Kong to gauge whether Beijing plans to live up to its guarantees of freedom and autonomy for the enclave.

But an earlier generation of Chinese communist rulers made eerily similar promises when Tibet was "peacefully liberated" nearly 50 years ago.

Beijing pledged during its takeover of Tibet in 1950, and again in Hong Kong earlier this month, that both regions would be largely self-ruled by local elites, with entrenched customs, social systems, and religious rights preserved.

The "Tibet Autonomous Region" of China, created after Chinese troops crossed into the remote Himalayan region in 1950, was initially ruled by a curious coalition of Communist Party, Army, and Tibetan Buddhist officials.

Mao Zedong and other Chinese leaders said they were committed to protecting Tibet's unique Buddhist culture while reforming its feudal, serf-based economy. To back that policy, they chose the teenaged Dalai Lama, the head of Tibet's Buddhist theocracy, to lead the experiment in joint rule.

Tibet's religious foundations have since been subject to constant attack, first by Communist troops and now by party controls on monasteries. The Dalai Lama, who was forced to flee into exile during a 1959 uprising against Chinese rule, has been branded a secessionist

and the Communist Party is trying to wipe out his influence in Tibet.

Yet few expect Hong Kong to follow in the steps of Tibet's decline. The meshing of a common Confucian culture, language, and ethnicity is likely to help smooth Hong Kong's integration with China, say Chinese and American scholars.

Chinese nationalism is propelling Beijing's peaceful annexation of Hong Kong. But the same trend is sharpening the cultural fault lines that divide ethnic Chinese and Tibetans, says Dru Gladney, a China scholar at the East-West Center in Honolulu, Hawaii.

Chinese Communist rule in Buddhist Tibet has been marked by an unending clash of civilization, says Bhuchang Tsering, a spokesman for the Washington-based International Campaign for Tibet.

Tibet's religion, language, and traditions were isolated from Chinese influ-

ence for centuries by the world's highest mountains, and Indian Buddhism rather than Chinese Confucianism helped build the foundations of Tibetan society.

In the decades following its armed conquest of the region, China tried to impose Chinese culture in the vast Tibetan plateau "through military occupation and the destruction of monasteries and monks," Mr. Tsering says.

Yet religion still pervades nearly every aspect of daily life in Tibet. Every Tibetan makes a pilgrimage, sometimes on hands and knees, to Lhasa, which means "the place of the gods." The Dalai Lama is considered the center of Tibet's spiritual universe and decades after his departure is still fervently revered.

Armed attacks on Tiber have in the last decade been replaced by a much less visible invasion of Tibet's remaining temples: the silent replacement of lead-

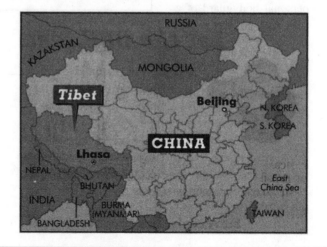

ing monks loyal to the Dalai Lama with pro-Beijing figures, Tsering adds.

The Chinese leadership is attempting to strengthen its political control by "destroying Tibet's religion and civilization from within," Tsering says.

He and other Tibetan exiles say that a "peaceful war" over Tibet's cultural identity and future has replaced the armed conflicts of the past. But the clash continues to claim casualties.

They cite as an example the recent struggle over the search for the reincarnation of the Panchen Lama, Tibet's second highest religious leader. Tibetans believe that high lamas, or monks, like the Dalai and Panchen are able to choose the timing and place of their rebirth.

Days after the 10th Panchen died in 1989, China's State Council, or cabinet, said that it would fund a golden shrine to him and helped organize a search party to track down his new incarnation.

But Chadrel Rinpoche, abbot of the Panchen Lama's Tashi Lhunpo Monastery in eastern Tibet, faced an impossible dilemma when Communist Party officials named him to head the search committee.

Centuries-old Tibetan custom dictates that senior monks consult countless mystical markers on the rebirth, which should then be interpreted by the Dalai Lama.

But the Dalai Lama, who was awarded the Nobel Peace Prize in 1989 for publicizing the plight of Tibet's people and culture, has been branded a traitor and "national splittist" by Beijing for the same actions.

When Mr. Chadrel decided to follow the dictates of his conscience rather than those of the party, he was tried and sentenced to six years imprisonment for treason and espionage some months ago.

During the search for the Panchen Lama, "Chadrel secretly communicated with the Dalai Lama, who has long staged activities abroad aimed at splitting the country," says Li Guoqing, a senior Beijing-based official on Tibet. "In plotting to secretly find the Panchen Lama, Chadrel and the Dalai Lama aimed to usurp the authority of the central committee," he adds.

Eight-year-old Gedhun Choekyi Nyima, the Dalai Lama's choice for the No. 2 spot in Tibetan Buddhism, has been dethroned by China's leaders and replaced with their own candidate. Instead, Beijing selected Gyaltsen Norbu as the "chosen" one.

Mr. Li says the dethroned boy, who is being held incommunicado, "has been placed under government protection to guard against the Dalai Lama sending teams into China to seek him out."

"Dozens of monks at Tashi Lhunpo who protested the arrest of Chadrel Rinpoche or the replacement of the Panchen Lama have been detained," says a Chinese intellectual with high-level government contacts.

"The attacks on Tibet's religion are considered a worse crime than the military occupation of the region," Tsering says. "Religion is at the heart of Tibetan culture, and this act is part of China's plan to destroy Tibet's collective soul."

The Dalai Lama, who says Chinese rule in Tibet is aimed at "cultural genocide," recently asked that the high degree of autonomy promised to Hong Kong be implemented in Tibet.

But a Beijing official scoffed at the notion that the same standards be applied in Hong Kong, a rich economy dominated by ethnic Chinese, and Tibet, one of the poorest regions in Asia. "The Tibetans' poverty has been caused by their superstitious religion and primitive culture," he says. "China wants to help civilize Tibet, and that is its top political goal in the region."

Article 33   *VItal Speeches of the Day,* May 1, 1997

Tibet

COMMUNIST CHINA AND HUMAN RIGHTS

Address by HIS HOLINESS TENZIN GYATSO, *The 14th Dalai Lama*

Delivered on the 38th Anniversary of the Tibetan National Uprising, Dharamsala, India, March 10, 1997

In the closing years of the 20th century, as we commemorate the 38th anniversary of the Tibetan people's National Uprising, it is evident that the human community has reached a critical juncture in its history. The world is becoming smaller and increasingly interdependent. One nation's problem can no longer be solved by itself. Without a sense of universal responsibility our very future is in danger.

Today's problems of militarization, development, ecology, population, and the constant search for new sources of energy and raw materials require more then piecemeal actions and short-term problem solving. Modern scientific development has, to an extent, helped in solving mankind's problems. However, in tackling these global issues, there is the need to cultivate not only the rational mind, but also the other remarkable faculties of the human spirit: the power of love, compassion and solidarity.

A new way of thinking has become the necessary condition for responsible living and acting. If we maintain obsolete values and beliefs, a fragmented consciousness and self-centered spirit, we will continue to hold on to outdated goals and behaviours. Such an attitude by a large number of people would block the entire transition to an interdependent yet peaceful and cooperative global society.

We must draw lessons from the experience we gained. If we look back at the development in the 20th century, the most devastating cause of human suffering, of deprivation of human dignity, freedom and peace, has been the culture of violence in resolving differences and conflicts. In some ways, our century could be called the century of war and bloodshed. The challenge before us, therefore, is to make the next century a century of dialogue and nonviolent conflict resolution.

In human societies there will always be differences of views and interests. But the reality today is that we are all interdependent and have to co-exist on this small planet. Therefore, the only sensible and intelligent way of resolving differences and clashes of interests, whether between individuals or nations, is through dialogue. The promotion of a culture of dialogue and nonviolence for the future of mankind is thus an important task of the international community. It is not enough for governments to endorse the principle of non-violence or hold it high without any appropriate action to promote it.

With these convictions, I have led the Tibetan freedom struggle on a path of nonviolence, and have sought a mutually agreeable solution to the Tibetan issue through negotiations in a spirit of reconciliation and compromise. Inspired by the Buddha's message of nonviolence and compassion, we have sought to respect every form of life and abandoned war as an instrument of national policy. For us Tibetans the path of nonviolence is a matter of principle. And I am convinced that this approach is the most beneficial and practical course in the long run.

As we commemorate this anniversary, we look back at yet another year of escalating repression in Tibet where the Chinese authorities continue to commit widespread and grave human rights abuses.

Under the "Strike Hard" campaign launched by the Chinese authorities in April last year, Tibetans are subjected to increased torture and imprisonment for peacefully expressing their political aspirations. Political re-education conducted by the authorities in monasteries and nunneries throughout Tibet have resulted in mass expulsion, imprisonment and death. I continue to be concerned about the fate of Gedun Choekyi Nyima, the boy I have recognised as the 11th Panchen Lama, and whose whereabouts are still not known.

Last year China dropped all pretense of respecting the ancient religious and cultural heritage of Tibet by launching a large-scale reform of its religious policy. The new policy states that "Buddhism must conform to socialism and not socialism to Buddhism." Under the pretext that religion would have a negative influence on Tibet's economic development, the new policy aims to systematically undermine and destroy the distinct cultural and national identity of the Tibetan people.

New measures to curtail the use of the Tibetan language in schools were introduced. The Tibet University in Lhasa has been compelled to teach even Tibetan history in the Chinese language at the Tibetan Language Department. Experimental Tibetan language middle schools, established in the 1980s with the active encouragement and support of the late Panchen Lama, are being closed down. These schools were very successful and were highly appreciated by Tibetans.

These new measures in the field of culture, religion and education, coupled with the unabated influx of Chinese immigrants to Tibet, which has the effect of overwhelming Tibet's distinct cultural and religious identity and reducing the Tibetans to an insignificant minority in their own country, amounts to a policy of cultural genocide. Today, in most major towns and cities Tibetans are already marginalised. If this population transfer is allowed to continue, in a few decades Tibetan civilization will cease to exist.

Tibetans have reacted to all this repression largely peacefully and I believe all people have the right to peacefully protest injustice. However, recent reports of isolated incidents of bomb explosions in Tibet are a cause of deep concern to me. I will continue to counsel for nonviolence, but unless the Chinese authorities forsake the brutal methods it employs, it will be difficult to prevent the situation in Tibet from deteriorating further.

Being a Tibetan, I have been giving particular importance to reaching out to the Chinese people, whether they are in China or elsewhere. It is in the interest of both the Tibetan people and the Chinese that there be a deeper level of understanding between ourselves. It has always been my belief that the cultivation of human relationships is of great importance in the creation of an atmosphere conducive to human understanding, mutual respect and peace.

In recent times the people-to-people dialogue between the Tibetans and Chinese is fostering a better understanding of our mutual concerns and interests. The growing empathy, support and solidarity from our Chinese brothers and sisters in China, as well as overseas, for the plight and fundamental rights of the Tibetan people is of particular inspiration and encouragement for us Tibetans.

The recent passing away of Mr. Deng Xiaoping is a great loss to China. I have known him personally. Mr. Deng Xiaoping took the initiative to establish direct contact with us to start a dialogue to solve the Tibetan problem. Unfortunately, serious negotiations could not take place during his lifetime. It is my sincere hope that the succeeding Chinese leadership will find the courage, wisdom and vision for new openings to solve the Tibetan issue through negotiations.

The beginning of a new era in modern China presents an opportunity for constructive change and positive development. The recent military clampdown in East Turkestan (Xinjiang), aimed at quelling the Uighur people's demonstrations and the ensuing cycle of violence are tragic and unfortunate. As in the case of Tibet, similarly also in East Turkestan, a lasting and peaceful solution can be found only through dialogue. Another important task ahead for the Chinese government is the smooth transition of Hong Kong and the implementation of the pragmatic and wise concept of "one country, two systems" in spirit and letter. A constructive approach to these issues provides important opportunities to create a political climate of trust, confidence and openness, both domestically and internationally.

The growing international support for Tibet reflects the inherent human empathy for and solidarity with human suffering and universal appreciation for truth and justice. To portray the support for Tibet as a plot of Western anti-China forces is to evade the truth for political convenience. This is unfortunate because such kind of mental bamboo-walling will continue to prevent a constructive approach to solving the problem.

Ultimately, it is for the Tibetan and the Chinese peoples to find a mutually acceptable solution to the Tibetan issue. Bearing in mind this reality, we have consistently pursued a course of dialogue with the leadership in Beijing. However, Beijing's refusal to listen to and recognize the genuine grievances of our people left us with no other choice but to present our legitimate and just cause to the international community.

The Tibetan people have displayed a remarkable spirit of endurance, courage and patience in the face of the most brutal repression. I urge my fellow Tibetans to continue to resist violent acts of frustration and desperation as a means to protest against injustice and repression. If we give in to hatred, desperation and violence, we would debase ourselves to the level of the oppressors. The way of the oppressors is intimidation, coercion and the use of force. Ours is a belief in and reliance on truth, justice and reason. This distinction is our most effective weapon. The call of the time for us in this period of difficulty is to exert ourselves with greater determination, wisdom and patience.

With my homage to, and prayers for the brave men and women who have died for the cause of Tibetan freedom.

Credits

REGIONAL ARTICLE

Page 86 Article 1. Reprinted with permission of *Harvard International Review.*

INDIA ARTICLE

Page 90 Article 2. Reprinted with permission from *The New York Review of Books,* © 1997 NYREV, Inc.

Page 97 Article 3. This article first appeared in *History Today,* September 1997. © 1997 by History Today, Ltd.

Page 101 Article 4. This article first appeared in *History Today,* September 1997. © 1997 by History Today, Ltd.

Page 106 Article 5. This article first appeared in *History Today,* September 1997. © 1997 by History Today, Ltd.

Page 110 Article 6. This article first appeared in *History Today,* September 1997. © 1997 by History Today, Ltd.

Page 114 Article 7. Reprinted by permission of Worldwatch Institute.

Page 123 Article 8. Reprinted by permission of *Foreign Affairs,* May/June 1998. © 1998 by the Council on Foreign Relations, Inc.

Page 128 Article 9. Reprinted by permission of *The World Today.*

Page 132 Article 10. This article appeared in *The World & I,* August 1998. *The World & I* is a publication of The Washington Times Corporation. © 1998.

Page 135 Article 11. From *Populi,* June 1998. © 1998 by WFS, Women's Feature Service.

Page 137 Article 12. From *Far Eastern Eceonomic Review,* August 21, 1997. © 1998 by Review Publishing Company Ltd.

Page 140 Article 13. From *Education About Asia,* Fall 1996. *Education About Asia,* Association of Asian Studies, University of Michigan.

Page 143 Article 14. This article appeared in *The World & I,* October 1996. *The World & I* is a publication of The Washington Times Corporation. © 1996.

Page 147 Article 15. © 1998 by The New York Times Company. Reprinted by permission.

Page 149 Article 16. Reprinted by permission of Worldwatch Institute.

Page 154 Article 17.This article first appeared in *History Today,* September 1997. © 1997 by History Today, Ltd.

Page 158 Article 18. Reprinted by permission of *Ms.* Magazine, © 1998.

Page 160 Article 19. © 1998 by John Zubrzycki. Reprinted by permission.

Page 162 Article 20. © 1996 by India Abroad Publications, Inc.

Page 164 Article 21. Reprinted by permission of Worldwatch Institute.

Page 167 Article 22. This article appeared in *The World & I,* October 1996. *The World & I* is a publication of The Washington Times Corporation. © 1996.

Page 171 Article 23. Reproduced courtesy of Cultural Survival Inc. www.cs.org.

Page 175 Article 24. Reprinted from the *UNESCO Courier,* November 1993, by Pierre-Sylvain Filliozat.

Page 178 Article 25. © 1998 by The New York Times Company. Reprinted by permission.

SOUTH ASIA ARTICLES

Page 180 Article 26. Reprinted by permission of *The New Republic.* © 1998, The New Republic, Inc.

Page 184 Article 27. Reprinted from the *UNESCO Courier,* January 1997, by Muhammad Yunus.

Page 186 Article 28. Reprinted with permission from *Current History* magazine, December 1997. © 1997, Current History, Inc.

Page 191 Article 29. © 1998 by The Economist, Ltd. Distrubuted by the New York Times Syndicated Sales.

Page 192 Article 30. Reprinted by permission of *The Bulletin of the Atomic Scientists.* © 1998 by the Educational Foundation for Nuclear Science, 6042 South Kimbark, Chicago, Illinois, 60637, USA. A one-year subscription is $28.

Page 198 Article 31. © 1998 by John Zubrzycki. Reprinted by permission.

Page 200 Article 32. © 1997 by The Christian Science Publishing Society.

Page 201 Article 33. © 1997 by City News Publishing Company, Inc.

Sources for Statistical Reports

U.S. State Department, *Background Notes* (1998).

C.I.A. *World Factbook* (1997).

World Bank, *World Development Report* (1998).

UN *Population and Vital Statistics Report* (January 1998).

World Statistics in Brief (1998).

The Statesman's Yearbook (1998–1999).

Population Reference Bureau, *World Population Data Sheet* (1998).

World Almanac (1998).

Glossary of Terms and Abbreviations

Asoka   A Mauryan emperor in northern India from 268 to 232 B.C. Overcome with remorse about deaths caused by his military conquests, he abandoned warfare as an instrument of imperial power and adopted the Buddhist Dharma as the standard for his rule. He enforced this expectation in a series of edicts carved into stones and pillars throughout his kingdom. His example is recognized today in the adoption of the lion capital on one of his pillars as the insignia of the Republic of India.

Babur   The first of the Moghul emperors, who engaged in a military conquest of northern India from 1526 to 1529. It was during his brief reign that the Babri Mosque was built in Ayodhya, purportedly on the site of an earlier Hindu temple, the destruction of which, in December 1992, led to communal riots across India. Akbar, the greatest of the Moghul monarchs, who ruled from 1556 to 1605 and completed the Moghul conquest of northern India, was Babur's grandson.

Bharatiya Janata Party (BJP)   "Indian Peoples Party" grew as a Hindu nationalist party out of the heartland of the Gangetic Plain during the 1980s to become the only party to challenge Congress Party hegemony on a national level. It attained leadership in Parliament in 1998, but only through the support of a 19-party coalition.

Bindi   A small, red cosmetic circle in the middle of the forehead, worn by women as a sign that they are marriageable or married. It is not usually worn by girls or by widows.

Brahmin   The priestly community, ranked highest on the varna caste scale.

Buddhism   A religious faith that started in India in the sixth century B.C. by Siddhartha Gautama, who renounced his royal heritage to seek enlightenment for the salvation of all humankind. The attainment of Nirvana (his death) is placed at 483 B.C. This faith extended throughout Asia in two major traditions: Theravada ("Teaching of the Elders") to Sri Lanka and Southeast Asia; and Mahayana ("Great Vehicle") to China and Japan. Tibetan Buddhism is a subset of the Mahayana tradition. Theravada has been called Hinayana ("Lesser Vehicle") by Mahayana Buddhists to distinguish that tradition from their own.

Chola   A Tamil dynasty centered in the Tanjavur District of the current state of Tamil Nadu, which dominated that part of south India from A.D. 880 to 1279. The temples built and the bronzes cast under the patronage of the Chola kings remain some of the most beautiful and cherished works of Indian art.

Congress Party   As the successor of the Indian National Congress in 1935, it led the new Republic of India to independence in 1947 and remained in control of the country for 45 years as the majority party in India's Parliament. The party split in 1969 but has rallied around the descendants of its first prime minister, Jawarhalal Nehru. His granddaughter-in-law, Sonia Gandhi, was elected president of the party in 1998.

Dalits   The "broken" or "oppressed"; this is the name preferred by those traditionally known as scheduled castes, outcastes, or untouchables, members of the lowest-rank communities in the classical caste system, below the four ranks of priests, rulers, citizens, and laborers on the varna social scale. Mahatma Gandhi, deeply concerned about removing their oppression, called them *Harijans,* children of God.

Dharma   Translated as "law, justice, duty, cosmic order," the moral standard by which society and an individual's life are ordered and given meaning.

Dhoti   A single piece of cloth tied as a garment by men around the lower portion of their bodies.

Green Revolution   An upsurge in agricultural production that followed the introduction of high-yielding hybrids of rice and grains, developed by the Rockefeller Foundation in Mexico and the Philippines, into South Asia during the 1950s and 1960s.

Harappa and Mohenjo Daro   The two largest cities excavated during the 1930s in the Indus River Valley to reveal an ancient urban culture that began around 3000 B.C. It flourished for 1,000 years and then inexplicably disappeared.

Hindi   The prevalent language and literature of northern India.

Hindu   One who follows the faith of Hinduism.

Hinduism   The dominant religion of India, emphasizing Dharma, with its ritual and social observances and often mystical contemplation and ascetic practices.

Indian National Congress   An association of educated Indians and sympathetic Europeans who gathered in Bengal in 1885 to seek admission for qualified Indians into the British Indian Civil Service. In the early twentieth century, this association became the bearer of the independence movement of the subcontinent from British colonial rule. Following the establishment of a provisional government in 1935, it evolved into the Congress Party.

Islam   A religious faith started in Arabia during the seventh century A.D. by the Prophet Mohammad.

Jain   A religious faith started in India by Mahavira in the sixth century B.C. Its primary teachings include the eternal transmigration of souls and the practice of nonviolence toward all living creatures.

Jajmani   A barter system of economic activity in the village, in which villagers provide their services on a regular basis to particular land owners—their patrons—in exchange for fixed portions of the annual harvest.

Jati   An extended kinship group, usually identified with a traditional occupation, that defines the parameters of accepted marriage relationships. It is the unit that is ranked in the hierarchical social (caste) structure of a village and that moves within that structure.

Koran   The sacred scripture of the Islamic faith, the teachings of Allah (God) as revealed to His prophet Mohammad in the seventh century A.D.

Ladakh   The easternmost and highest region of the state of Kashmir-Jammu, inhabited mostly by Buddhists.

Lama   A leader of a Tibetan Buddhist monastic community (sangha).

Lok Sabha and Rajya Sabha   The two houses of Parliament in the Republic of India: "The House of the People" has 545 members elected directly by voters on the district level; "The Council of States" has 250 members, 12 appointed by the president and 238 elected by state legislatures.

Mahabharata   The Great Epic of India, with more than 90,000 stanzas, composed around the third century B.C. The longest poem in the world, it is the story of five brothers' struggle to wrest their father's kingdom from their cousins. This epic contains the *Bhagavad Gita,* a discourse between one of the brothers, Arjuna, and his charioteer, Krishna, on the eve of the culminating battle with their cousins, when Arjuna is overcome by concerns about appropriate behavior and quality of life.

Mahar   A depressed (untouchable) community in the state of Maharashtra, who converted to Buddhism in October 1956 as an initiative to free themselves as a community from the social burden of untouchability, under the leadership of Dr. B. R. Ambedkar.

Mahatma   Literally "great souled one"; a title given to Mohandas Gandhi by Rabindranath Tagore in 1921 and adopted by the people of India to express their belief in Gandhi's saintliness.

Mandala   An intricate visual symbol developed in the Tibetan Buddhist tradition, revealing elaborate patterns of many shapes and colors, intended to lead its creator and observer into supranormal levels of consciousness.

Moghuls   Islamic invaders of Turkish descent who established the longest dynastic imperial rule in the Great Central Plain of South Asia, from A.D. 1526 to 1857.

Mohajirs   "Immigrants"; those Muslims who moved from their homelands in India at the time of partition in 1947 to settle in Pakistan. Because they have retained many of the customs as well as the language (Urdu) of their former homes, even today they remain a distinctive community and political force, as the Mohajir Quami Movement (MQM) in Pakistan.

Monsoon   An annual torrential rainfall, which normally begins during the month of June, when the prevailing winds shift to the west, gather clouds with water from the Arabian Sea, and deluge the subcontinent with rain as the clouds rise over the Himalayan Mountains. The dramatic shift from the torrid dry heat of late spring to this stormy wet season and the lush growth that it provides has an immense impact on the economies, the literature, and the consciousness of South Asian peoples. Raja Rao gives a brief, gripping description of the coming of the monsoon on page 50 of his novel *Kanthapura* and in his notes, pages 215–216.

Mujahideen   Militant tribal leaders in Afghanistan who joined in alliance to protect their authority as local warlords from national and foreign (Soviet) incursion.

Muslim   One who submits to the supreme will of Allah (God), as revealed to the prophet Mohammad; one who practices Islam. Sometimes spelled Moslem.

Nirvana   Literally, "blowing out, extinguishing"; the ultimate enlightenment of Buddhism: departure from the relentless transmigratory cycle of births and deaths into nothingness.

Pali   One of many regional Indo-European languages (called Prakrits) spoken in the northern plains region of South Asia following the Aryan Invasion (ca. 1700 B.C.) and before the evolution of the subcontinent's modern languages, following the twelfth century A.D. It was the language in which the earliest documents of the Buddhist faith were composed in northern India.

Panchayat   Literally, "council of five." This traditional leadership of elders in the jati kinship group was adopted in the Panchayat Acts in state legislatures during the 1950s as the appropriate form of democratically elected village government in the Republic of India.

Parsi   A member of the Zoroastrian faith, the ancient religion of Persia. Most of the Parsis in South Asia live in Bombay (Mumbai) and Karachi.

Pathans   Tribal peoples in the northwest corner of the subcontinent who speak the Pushtu language.

Punjab   Translated as *panch* ("five") and *ap* ("water"), designates the land in the western portion of the Great Central Plain through which the five rivers forming the Indus River System flow. The province that had this name during the British Indian Empire was divided between India and Pakistan in 1947.

Purana   "Tradition," a genre of Sanskrit religious texts of different sects of Hinduism from the Classical Period (A.D. 300 to 1200), setting forth their primary myths and teachings; also the accounts in local languages of the sacred significance of religious sites, temples, places of pilgrimage, etc.

Rabindranath Tagore   An outstanding Bengali poet and educator (1861–1941), whose collection of poems, *Gitanjali,* published in English translation in 1912, won the Nobel Prize for Literature.

Raj   Translated as "rule" or "king," a term that designates political sovereignty. (The word *reign* comes from the same Indo-European root.) Raj is used with British to identify the British colonial government in India; it is used with *maha* ("great") to identify rulers of the Indian princely states; and it is used with *swa* ("self") to mean self-rule or independence. Swaraj also has the connotation of self-discipline, which is an important aspect of Mahatma Gandhi's concept of independence.

Ramayana   An epic Sanskrit poem, composed around the second century A.D. and attributed to Valmiki, describing the ordeals of the ideal prince Rama. Most of the text describes his ultimately successful quest for his faithful wife Sita, who was abducted by the demonic King Ravana.

Rig Veda   The first of the four Vedas, which are the earliest and most sacred of the writings of the Hindus. Around 1000 B.C., it was compiled into an anthology of 10 books containing 1,028 hymns.

RSS Rashtriya Swayamsevak Sangh, an organization founded in 1925 to train Hindus to seek independence from the British Raj by whatever means necessary and to further Hindu nationalistic objectives. Recognized as a militant alternative to Mahatma Gandhi's nonviolent movement, it is today a significant political force within the Bharatiya Janata Party (BJP).

Salt March An act of nonviolent civil disobedience (*satyagraha*) led by Mahatma Gandhi in 1930. He and his followers marched from his *ashram* at Sabarmati 241 miles to Dandi on the coast to evaporate salt from the sea, in order to protest the British tax on salt.

Salwar Kameez Salwar is a pajama-like trouser; Kameez is a loose-fitting, long-sleeved blouse that extends below the hips. This attire is more common for women than the sari in the wheat-growing portion of the subcontinent.

Sangha A Buddhist community of holy men and women who follow the Buddha's path called Dharma. The Buddha, Dharma, and Sangha are called the "three jewels of the Buddhist faith."

Sanskrit Translated as "made together, formed, perfected," as descriptive of the classical language of India as structurally perfected.

Sari A woman's garment, a single piece of cloth 6 yards long, which she wraps around her waist, pleats across the front, and drapes over her shoulder. Simple in design and graceful in appearance, it is worn by those of all walks of life, with only the quality of the material and the pattern changing to meet the occasion.

Satyagraha Literally, "holding the truth," the name that Mahatma Gandhi adopted while in South Africa to describe his nonviolent civil protest against the South African government's oppression of the people from India. Gandhi's translation of this term as "soul force" affirms that, even early in his public career, he understood such action to be primarily religious and only secondarily political.

Shiva Literally, "auspicious"; the name of God in one of the two main sects of Hinduism: Shaivism (from Shiva) and Vaishnavism ("followers of Vishnu").

Sitar, Vina, and Sharod Traditional stringed instruments used to play classical Indian music. The vina, upon which south Indian, or Karnatic, music is performed, is the oldest. The other two, more prevalent in the north of the subcontinent, evolved during Moghul times to perform music that reveals the Persian and Middle Eastern influences of that period.

Sufi A person of the Islamic faith who affirms through religious discipline and mystical experience the spiritual union of self with God.

Taliban "Seekers of religious knowledge"; members of a militant and exceptionally conservative freedom force named after the Pathan students of Islam from Kandahar who started a fundamentalist crusade to free Afghanistan from foreign and modern corruptions of their faith and traditional way of life.

Varna Originally translated as "class," later as "color"; the fourfold division of classical Indian society, ranked on a purity–pollution scale: priests, rulers, citizens, and laborers. The untouchables and tribals are a fifth group, known as outcastes, ranked below the laborers.

Vellalas Among Tamil-speaking peoples, the dominant landholding and cultivating communities, similar to the Jat communities in the Hindi-speaking regions of the subcontinent.

Vishnu Receiving somewhat minor attention as a solar deity in the *Rig Veda*, Vishnu became recognized as Supreme Lord of the universe, its creator and preserver during the classical period (A.D. 300–1200). He is worshipped widely throughout Hinduism through His incarnations (*avatars*), of whom Rama and Krishna are the most prevalent.

Yoga A highly disciplined set of exercises to identify, nurture, and develop different parts of one's natural body, breathing, nervous system, and consciousness. Practice of this discipline leads to the integration of one's total self—physical, mental, and spiritual, the unconscious as well as the conscious.

Bibliography

GENERAL WORKS

Bina Agarwal, *A Field of One's Own: Gender and the Land Rights in South Asia* (Cambridge: Cambridge University Press, 1994).

F. R. Allchin et al. *The Archaeology of Early Historic South Asia: The Emergence of Cities and States* (Cambridge: Cambridge University Press, 1995).
A survey of archeological research done in South Asia.

A. L. Basham, *The Wonder That Was India* (Columbia, MO: South Asia Books, 1995).
A comprehensive introduction to classical India.

Ashish Bose, ed., *Population Transition in South Asia* (Columbia, MO: South Asia Books, 1992).

Myron L. Cohen, *Asia, Case Studies in Social Sciences* (Armonk, NY: M. E. Sharpe, 1992).
A Guide for Teaching, Columbia Project on Asia in the Core Curriculum.

W. T. deBary, ed., *Sources of Indian Tradition* (New York: Columbia University Press, 1988).
Translations of primary texts from the Vedic Period to independence.

Joseph Elder, ed., *Lectures in Indian Civilization,* Dubuque, IA: 1970).
A syllabus and supporting materials for a survey course on India and Pakistan.

Ainslie T. Embree and Carol Gluck, eds., *Asia in Western and World History* (Armonk, NY: M. E. Sharpe, 1993).
A Guide for Teaching, Columbia Project on Asia in the Core Curriculum.

Roger Jeffery and Alaka M. Basu, *Girl's Schooling, Women's Autonomy and Fertility Change in South Asia* (New Delhi: Sage, 1996).

Veena Jha, Grant Hewison, and Maree Underhill, *Trade, Environment, and Sustainable Development: A South Asian Perspective* (New York: St. Martin's Press, 1997).

Ann Leonard, *Seeds: Supporting Women's Work in the Third World* (New York: Feminist Press, 1989).
Chapters on Credit Organization in Madras, India; Non-craft Employment in Bangladesh; and Forest Conservation in Nepal.

Todd Lewis and Theodore Riccardi, *The Himalayas: A Syllabus of the Region's History, Anthropology, and Religion* (Ann Arbor: Association of Asian Studies, 1995).

Satu Limaye, *South Asia and the United States after the Cold War* (New York: The Asia Society, 1994).

Barbara Stoler Miller, ed., *Masterworks of Asian Literature in Comparative Perspective* (Armonk, NY: M. E. Sharpe, 1993).
A Guide for Teaching, Columbia Project on Asia in the Core Curriculum.

James H. K. Norton, *The Third World: South Asia* (Guilford, CT: Dushkin/McGraw-Hill, 1984).
A brief introduction to the region.

Gowher Rizvi, *South Asia in a Changing International Order* (Troy, NY: Sage Publishing, 1993).

Francis Robinson, ed., *The Cambridge Encyclopedia of India, Pakistan, Bangladesh, Sri Lanka, Nepal, Bhutan, and the Maldives* (Cambridge: Cambridge University Press, 1989).

Joseph Schwartzberg, *A Historical Atlas of South Asia* (New York: Oxford University Press, 1992).

Robert H. Taylor, ed., *Asia and the Pacific*, 2 vols. (New York: Facts on File Publications, 1990).
Brief articles on every Asian country, with supplementary essays on topics of development, education, communication, etc.

NATIONAL HISTORIES AND ANALYSES

Afghanistan

N. D. Ahmad, *Survival of Afghanistan: A Historical Survey of the Afghanistan Crisis* (Rockwell, TX: KBA Publishing, forthcoming).

Louis Dupree, *Afghanistan* (Princeton: Princeton University Press, 1973).

Edward R. Girardet, *Afghanistan: The Soviet War* (New York: St. Martin's Press, 1986).

Ralph H. Magnus and Eden Naby, *Afghanistan: Marx, Mullah, and Mujahid* (Boulder: Westview Press, 1992).

William Maley and Fazel H. Saikal, *Political Order in Post-Communist Afghanistan* (New York: International Peace Academy, 1992).

Louis Palmer, *Adventures in Afghanistan* (Los Altos, CA: Institute for the Study of Human Knowledge, 1990).

Myron Weiner and Ali Banuazizi, eds., *The Politics of Social Transformation in Afghanistan, Iran, and Pakistan* (Syracuse: Syracuse University Press, 1993).

Bangladesh

Craig Baxter, *Bangladesh: A New Nation in an Old Setting* (Boulder: Westview Press, 1984).

Dilara Choudhury, *Bangladesh and the South Asian International System* (Chicago: Kazi Publications, 1992).

Amiul H. Faraizi, *Bangladesh: Peasant Migration and the World Capitalist Economy* (New York: Apt Books, 1993).

Bosse Kramsjo, *Breaking the Chains: Collective Action for Social Justice among the Rural Poor in Bangladesh* (New York: Intermed Technology Development Group of North America, 1992).

Rokeya Sakhawat Hossain, *Sultana's Dream* (New York: The Feminist Press, 1988).
A Bengali Muslim writer on purdah and her dream of its reversal.

Beth Roy, *Some Trouble with Cows: Making Sense of Social Conflict* (Berkeley: University of California Press, 1994).

Abu N. M. Wahid, ed., *The Grameen Bank: Poverty Relief in Bangladesh* (Boulder, CO: Westview Press, 1993).

Bhutan

Ramesh C. Dogra, *Bhutan* (Santa Barbara: ABC-CLIO, 1991).

Tom O. Edmunds, *Bhutan: Land of the Thunder Dragon* (New York: Viking Penguin, 1989).

A. C. Singh, *Bhutan: Ethnic Identity and National Dilemma* (New York: Apt Books, 1991).

Narendra Singh, *Bhutan, A Kingdom in the Himalayas* (New Delhi: S. Chand, 1985).

India

Bina Agarwal, *A Field of One's Own: Gender and Land Rights in South Asia* (Cambridge: Cambridge University Press, 1994).

Geoffrey Ashe, *Gandhi* (Chelsea, MI: Scarborough House, 1969).

Jonah Blank, *Arrow of the Blue Skinned God: Retracing the Ramayana through India* (Boston: Houghton Mifflin, 1992).

Joan Bondurant, *Conquest of Violence* (Princeton: Princeton University Press, 1988).

Sumantra Bose, *The Challenge in Kashmir: Democracy, Self-Determination and a Just Peace* (New Delhi: Sage, 1997).

Paul Brass, *The Politics of India since Independence* (Cambridge: Cambridge University Press, 1990).

Leslie J. Calman, *Toward Empowerment: Women and Movement Politics in India* (Boulder, CO: Westview Press, 1992).

Sharat Chandra, *Population Pattern and Social Change in India* (Columbia, MO: South Asia Books, 1992).

Barbara Crossette, *India: Facing the Twenty-First Century* (Bloomington: Indiana University Press, 1993).

Dennis Dalton, *Mahatma Gandhi, Nonviolent Power in Action* (New York: Columbia University Press, 1995).

Narendra K. Dash, *Encyclopaedic Dictionary of Indian Culture* (Columbia, MO: South Asia Books, 1992).

Steve Derne, *Culture in Action: Family Life, Emotion, and Male Domination in Banaras, India* (Albany: State University of New York Press, 1995).

Jean Dreze and Amartya Sen, eds., *Indian Development: Selected Regional Perspectives* (Delhi: Oxford University Press, 1997).

———*India: Economic Development and Social Opportunity* (Delhi: Oxford University Press, 1995).

Diana Eck, *Darshan—Seeing the Divine Image in India* (New York: Columbia University Press, 1995).

Ainslie Embree, *Utopias in Conflict: Religion and Nationalism in Modern India* (Berkeley: University of California Press, 1990).

Eric Ericson, *Gandhi's Truth* (New York: Norton, 1970).

Geraldine Forbes, *Women in Modern India: The New Cambridge History of India* (Cambridge: Cambridge University Press, 1996).

Mohandas K. Gandhi, *An Autobiography: The Story of My Experiments with Truth* (Boston: Beacon, 1957).

Zoya Hasan, ed. *Forging Identities: Gender, Communities and the State* (New Delhi: Kali for Women, 1994).

John Stratton Hawley and Donna Marie Wulff, *Devi: Goddesses of India* (Berkeley: University of California Press, 1996).

Thomas Hopkins, *The Hindu Religious Tradition* (Belmont: Dickenson, 1971).

S. M. Ikram, *Muslim Civilization in India* (New York: Columbia University Press, 1964).

India (Alexandria: Time/Life Books, 1988).

Doranne Jacobson, *India: Land of Dreams and Fantasy* (Columbia, MO: South Asia Books, 1992).

Ashok Kapur and A. Jeyaratnam Wilson, *The Foreign Policy of India and Her Neighbors* (New York: St. Martin's Press, 1996).

David Knipe, *Hinduism, Experiments in the Sacred* (New York: Harper, 1990).

Donald Lopez, Jr., *Religions of India in Practice* (Princeton: Princeton University Press, 1995).

David Ludden, ed., *Contesting the Nation: Religion, Community, and the Politics of Democracy in India* (Philadelphia: University of Pennsylvania Press, 1996).

V. S. Naipaul, *India: A Million Mutinies Now* (New York: Viking, 1992).

Kirin Narayan, *Mondays on the Dark Night of the Moon: Himalayan Foothill Folktales* (New York: Oxford University Press, 1997).

Jawaharlal Nehru, *The Discovery of India* (New York: John Day, 1946).

Jean-Luc Racine, ed., *Peasant Moorings: Village Ties and Mobility Rationales in South India,* (New Delhi: Sage, 1997).

Raja Rao, *Kanthapura* (New York: New Directions, 1963).
   A novel describing the impact of Mahatma Gandhi on a south Indian village.

Lloyd and Suzanne Rudolph, *The Modernity of Tradition* (Chicago: University of Chicago Press, 1984).

Jadunath Sarkar, *India through the Ages* (New York: Apt Books, 1993).

Tanika Sarkar and Urvashi Butalia, ed., *Women and Right Wing Movements: Indian Experiences* (London and NY: Zed Books, Ltd. 1995).

S. N. Sharma, *Personal Liberty under Indian Constitution* (Columbia, MO: South Asia Books, 1991).

Thomas Spear and Romilia Thapar, *A History of India,* 2 vols. (Baltimore: Penguin, 1965).

M. N. Srinivas, *Social Change in Modern India* (Berkeley: University of California Press, 1969).

Mark Tully and Zareer Masani, *From Raj to Rajiv, 40 Years of Indian Independence* (New Delhi: Universal Book Stall, 1988).

Peter van der Veer, *Religious Nationalism: Hindus and Muslims in India* (Berkeley: University of California Press, 1994).

John C. B. Webster, *A History of the Dalit Christians in India* (San Francisco: Mellen Research University Press, 1992).

Myron Weiner, *The Indian Paradox: Essays on Indian Politics* (Newbury Park: Sage, 1983).

William and Charlotte Wiser, *Behind Mud Walls* (Berkeley: University of California Press, 1989).
   A classic description of an Indian village in 1930 and 1960, with a new chapter on 1984.

Stanley Wolpert, *India* (Berkeley: University of California Press, 1991).

———*Nehru, A Tryst with Destiny* (New York: Oxford University Press, 1969).

R. C. Zaehner, *Hinduism* (New York: Oxford University Press, 1970).

Heinreich Zimmer, *Myths and Symbols in Indian Art and Civilization* (New York: Harper, 1946).

Maldives

Mark Balla, *Maldives and Islands of the East Indian Ocean: A Travel Survival Kit* (Oakland: Lonely Planet Publishing, 1993).

Camerapix, *Maldives* (Edison, NY: Hunter Publishing, 1993).

Ursula and Luithui Phabnis and Ela Dutt, *Maldives: Winds of Change in an Atoll State* (New Delhi: South Asian Publishers, 1985).

Nepal

Lok R. Baral, *Nepal: Problems of Governance* (New York: Advent Books, 1993).

Monica Connell, *Against a Peacock Sky* (New York: Viking, 1992).

Kirkpatrick, *An Account of the Kingdom of Nepal* (Columbia, MO: South Asia Books, 1986).

Bruce M. Nevin, *The Mountain Kingdom: Portraits of Nepal and the Gurkhas* (Cincinnati: Seven Hills Book Distributors, 1991).

Leo E. Rose and John T. Schulz, *Nepal: Profile of a Himalayan Kingdom* (Boulder, CO: Westview Press, 1980).

Andrea M. Savada, ed., *Nepal and Bhutan: Country Studies* (Washington: Library of Congress, 1993).

Prem R. Uperty, *Political Awakening in Nepal: The Search for a New Identity* (Columbia, MO: South Asia Books, 1992).

Eden Vansittart, *Notes on Nepal with an Introduction by H. H. Risley* (Columbia, MO: South Asia Books, 1992).

Pakistan

Prabha Arun, *Pathway to Pakistan* (Columbia, MO: South Asia Books, 1992).

Benazir Bhutto, *Daughter of Destiny, An Autobiography* (New York: S & S Trade, 1990).

Shahid Javed Burki, *Pakistan: The Continuing Search for Nationhood* (Boulder: Westview Press, 1991).

Attar Chand, *Pakistan: In Search of Modernization* (Columbia, MO: South Asia Books, 1992).

Surendra Chopra, *Pakistan's Thrust in the Muslim World: India as a Factor* (Columbia, MO: South Asia Books, 1992).

Ayesha Jalal, *Democracy and Authority in South Asia: A Comparative and Historical Perspective* (Cambridge: Cambridge University Press, 1995).

Jamal Malik, *Colonialization of Islam: Dissolution of Traditional Institutions in Pakistan* (New Delhi: Manohar, 1996).

Mokhdum E. Mushrafi, *Pakistan and Bangladesh: Political Culture and Political Parties* (Columbia, MO: South Asia Books, 1992).

Richard Reeves, *Passage to Peshawar* (New York: Simon & Schuster, 1984).

Abdul Quddus Syed, *Cultural Patterns of Pakistan* (Chicago: Kazi Publications, 1989).

Sri Lanka

Kingsley De Silva, *Problems of Governing Sri Lanka* (New York: Advent Books, 1993).

Pradeep Jeganathan and Qadri Ismail, *Unmaking the Nation: The Politics of Identity and History in Modern Sri Lanka* (Colombo: Social Scientists' Association, 1995).

E. F. Ludowyk, *The Footprint of the Buddha* (London: George Allen & Unwin, 1958).

James Manor, ed., *Sri Lanka in Change and Crisis* (New York: St. Martin's Press, 1984).

Walpola Rahula, *History of Buddhism in Ceylon* (Colombo: M. D. Gunasena, 1956).

Mohan Ram, *Sri Lanka: The Fractured Island* (New York: Penguin, 1990).

S. J. Tambiah, *Sri Lanka, Ethnic Fratricide and the Dismantling of Democracy* (Chicago: University of Chicago Press, 1991).

Ananda Wickremeratne, *Buddhism and Ethnicity in Sri Lanka: A Historical Analysis* (Columbia, MO: South Asia Books, 1995).

Index

abacus, 176
Afghanistan, 56, 72, 76, 90, 107, 108, 130, 144, 191, 192; overview of, 54–57; and overview of South Asia, 3–35; Soviet Union and, 180–184
Agarwal, Bina, 95
Age of Consent controversy, in India, 156
Aggarwal, Kailash C., 163
Ahmad, Nadhir, 156
AIDS, 70
air pollution, 162, 163
Akbar, Moghul emperor, 9, 10, 72
Albright, Madeleine, 182
Alexander the Great, 145
Ali Khan, Liaquat, 72–73
Ambedekar, B. R., 42
Amin, Hafizullah, 56
Amman, Bi, 157
animal waste, and biogas power plants, 164–166
anti-ballistic theatre missile defenses (TMDs), 130
apsara, 21
art, Indian, 114–122
Aryan people, 4, 7–8, 10, 11, 15, 20, 87
ashramas, 20
Asian Development Bank, 120
Asoka, Mauryan emperor, 8, 14, 79
Assam, 86, 87, 110
assimilation, Indian culture and, 145
Association of Southeast Asian Nations (ASEAN), 53, 90
atma, 21, 31
Attas, Iqbal, 199
Auden, W. H., 92
Aung San Suu Kyi, 29
Australia, 53
Autobiography, An (Nehru), 98
avatars, 14
Ayub Khan, 74
Azad, Abdul Kalam, 109
Azman, Kaifi, 169

Babur, Moghul emperor, 9, 111
Badal, Prakash Singh, 46
Balagalle, Lionel, 198, 199
Baluchistan, 86
Bandaranaike, S. W. R. D., 81
Bangladesh, 51–52, 86, 88, 106, 130, 144; Grameen Bank and, 184–185; overview of, 58–61; and overview of South Asia, 3–35
Basham, A. L., 144
Basu, Jyoti, 113
Battle of Plassy, 111
Bedi, Rajesh, 178
Begum Khaleda Zia, 60
Benegal, Shyam, 168, 170
Bengal, 10, 59, 87, 88, 110–114, 134
Bennett, Lynn, 151
Bhagavad Gita, 13, 46
Bhutan, 38, 51, 52; overview of, 62–64; and overview of South Asia, 3–35; Tibet and, 63–64
Bhutto, Benazir, 74–75, 77, 187, 188
Bhutto, Murtaza, 188
Bhutto, Zulfikar Ali, 73, 74, 77, 187
Bihishti Zewar (Thanawi), 156

Bin Laden, Osama, 180, 181
bindi, 3
biogas, as energy source, 119, 164–166
Birenda, Nepal's king, 70
Bose, Sarat C., 112
Brahmaputra River, 5
Brahmin priests, 8–9, 13, 14, 20, 21, 49, 140–143
Britain: colonialism and, 3, 4, 9, 10–12, 23, 25–26, 31–35, 59, 63, 72, 79, 86, 88, 99, 106, 107, 108, 114, 116, 132, 174, 179, 196, 198; India and, 38, 39, 42, 45, 48, 90–97, 154–158
Brown, Hank, 182
Brown, W. Norman, 21
Buddhism, 8, 10, 12, 13, 14, 17, 26, 28, 40, 45, 63, 64, 66, 142. *See also* Mahayana Buddhism; Theravada Buddhism
Bukhari, Imam Sayyid, 89
burkas, 182
Burkman, Rahul Dev, 169

Cambodia, 90, 176
Campbell-Johnson, Alan, 103
Canada, 125
candalas, 141
castes, 3–4, 8–9, 11, 18, 69, 95, 140–143, 150; in India, 49–51
Chandrasekhar, Subrahmanyan, 147
Chatterjee, Meera, 151
Chhachhi, Amrita, 135, 136, 137
Chidambaram, P., 137, 138, 139, 140
child labor, 3
child marriage, in India, 147–149
China, 3, 14, 48, 52–53, 69, 79, 92–94, 95, 116, 118, 139, 196; Tibet and, 200–201, 201–203
Christianity, 14, 40, 45, 79, 142, 149, 157, 159, 192
Churchill, Winston, 93, 109, 113
citizen caste, 8, 20, 140–143
Clinton, Bill, 183, 194
colonialism, 3, 4, 9, 10–12, 23, 25–26, 31–35, 59, 63, 72, 79, 86, 198; India and, 90–97
communism, 56, 112; in Tibet, 200–201, 201–203
community radio, in India, 171–174
Comprehensive Test Ban Treaty, 52, 194
corruption, political, in India, 125, 126
Cradock, Percy, 93
Cripps, Sir Stafford, 108
Crishna, Smiti, 161
curry, 3, 143
cycles, belief in, Indian culture and, 145–146
cyclones, 59
Czechoslovakia, 125

Dadiseth, K. B., 140
Dalai Lama, 200, 201; on human rights, 201–203
Dalits. *See* untouchables
Dari language, 155
Datt, Gaurav, 122
Daud Khan, Za-Sadar Mohammed, 55–56
Davies, Glyn, 183
Debi, Kailashbashini, 155
Deccan plateau, 5, 11, 38
deforestation, 118–119, 162, 164

democracy, 4–5, 22–24, 111; in India, 44–49, 123–124; in Pakistan, 186–191
Deng Xiaoping, 139
deterrence, opaque, nuclear weapons and, 129–130
Devi, 14
Dhamma, 14
dharma, 8, 30, 31
Diaz, Hugo, 77
Didi, Muhammed Amin, 66–67
Divehi language, 66
divorce, in India, 159
dowry, 158
Dravidastan, 86
Dravidian culture, 6, 16, 39
Durga, 14
Dzongkha language, 63

Eapen, K. E., 171
East India Company, 10, 14, 110
Economic Cooperation Organization (ECO), 90
economy: India's, 40–41, 116–117, 120–121, 123, 125–126, 132–135, 135–136, 137–140; 192–194,194–196, 196–198; Pakistan's, 191–192, 192–194, 194–196, 196–198; Sri Lanka's, 81
education, in India, 150–151, 153, 155, 156
Egypt, 95, 118
Einstein, Albert, 29, 147
elections, in India, 123–128
encapsulation, as social dynamic in South Asia, 16, 17–18
endogamy, 3
English language, 14, 39
environmental issues, 162–164, 164–166
Ericson, Eric, 35
Ershad, Hussain Muhammed, 60
Ethiopia, 118
European Union, 53, 89
Evacuee Property Laws, 104
extinction, species, 119

Faiz, Faiz Ahmad, 103
family, in India, 134
Fazli-Husain, Mian, 111
federalism, in India, 125
Fertile Crescent, 6
Fiji, 16
film industry, in India, 167–170
Finland, 28
Fissile Material Cutoff Treaty (FMCT), 130
foreign direct investment, 127, 138–139
Four-fold Truth, Buddhism and, 14
France, 196
Frost, Robert, 99

Gadgil, Madhav, 121
Gandhi, Indira, 16, 44, 46, 95, 112, 113, 125
Gandhi, Mohandas, 3, 5, 11, 22, 29–35, 46, 48–49, 50, 87, 97–101, 102, 108, 109, 111, 114, 116, 132, 147, 157, 179
Gandhi, Nandita, 135

Gandhi, Rajiv, 51
Gandhi, Sonia, 123
Gautama, Siddhartha, 8, 14, 144
Gayoom, Mamoon Abdul, 67
Ghatak, Ritwik, 170
Ghulam Ishaq Khan, 74
Giri, Mohini, 148
Gladney, Dru, 200
global economy, India and, 135–137
Gopalakrishnan, Adoor, 168
Gothoskar, Sujata, 135, 136, 137
Gowda, Deve, 43, 94, 149
Grameen Bank, 18, 61, 184–185
Great Mutiny of 1857, 11, 23, 111
Great Tradition of South Asia, 4, 18–22
Greece, 146
Green Revolution, 41, 50, 116, 117
Group of 77, 131
Guha, Ramachandra, 121
Gujral, I. K., 44, 94
Gujral Doctrine, 130
Gul, Hamid, 193
Gupta Era, 8, 38
Gurkhaland, 86
Guzdar, Jamshed, 160–161, 162

Harappan city culture, 4, 6, 7, 10, 72, 144
Hasan, Mubashir, 74
Hasina Wased, Sheikh, 60, 61
Hastings, Warren, 107
hatha yoga, 147
Hayat Khan, Sikander, 111
Hekmatyar, Gulbuddin, 57, 181
hierarchy, caste and, 142
Himalayan mountains, 5, 38, 55, 69, 163
Hinduism, 7, 8, 9, 10, 11, 12, 13, 14, 16–17, 25,
    26, 34, 40, 42, 45, 46, 47, 59, 90, 91, 94, 95,
    124–125, 142, 143, 144, 150, 155, 157, 158,
    178–189, 192, 195; and child marriage in In-
    dia, 147–149; and Gandhi and Nehru, 97–101;
    and partition of India and Pakistan, 101–106,
    106–109, 110–114
Hoagland, Richard, 181
Hong Kong, 92–95, 200
Hosain, Attia, 105–106
human rights, 11, 29, 42, 77, 149, 181, 182, 201–
    203
Hurd, Douglas, 93
Husain, Zakir, 104
Hussain, Altaf, 189
Hussein, Begum Rokeya, 157
Hyderabad, 11, 103–104

Ibrahim Nasir, Amin, 67
India, 64, 66, 187, 191, 192; and Bengal and
    Punjab, 110–114; biogas power plants in,
    164–166; caste system in, 140–143; child mar-
    riage in, 149–154; community radio in, 171–
    174; economy of, 123, 125–126, 132–135,
    135–136, 137–140; environmental issues and,
    162–164; future of, 114–122; and Gandhi and
    Nehru, 97–101; influence of, on Western cul-
    ture, 143–147; kumbh mela festival in, 178–

179; matrilineal society in, 158–159; national-
    ism and, 86–90; nuclear weapons and, 129–
    131; overview of, 36–81; and overview of
    South Asia, 3–35; and Pakistan, 72–76, 101–
    106, 106–109, 110–114; Parsi religion in,
    160–161; politics in, 123–128; population
    growth in, 149–154; U.S. sanctions against,
    192–194, 194–196, 196–198; women in, 154–
    158
Indo-European languages, 15, 39
Indonesia, 90
Indus River, 4, 6
infrastructure, India's, 138
International Court of Justice, 193–194
International Labor Organization, 130
International Monetary Fund, 76–77, 81, 116,
    191, 195
International Union for the Conservation of Na-
    ture, 119
intrauterine devices (IUDs), 153
Iqbal, Muhammed, 72, 102–103, 108
Iran, 28, 55, 131, 191
Islam, 9–10, 11, 12–13, 25, 26, 34, 40, 42, 45, 46,
    47, 56, 57, 79, 90, 91, 95, 125, 142, 147, 149,
    150, 156, 157, 158, 193; and Afghanistan,
    180–183; and India, 101–106, 106–109, 110–
    114; and Pakistan, 71–76, 101–106, 106–109,
    110–114. See also Shia Muslims; Sufi Mus-
    lims; Sunni Muslims

Jain, Anrudh K., 152
Jainism, 8, 11, 13, 40, 45, 142
jamjani system, 41
Japan, 14, 53, 79
jati. See castes
Jayewardene, Junius, 79, 80–81
Jigme Dorji Wangchuk, 63
Jigme Singye Wangchuk, 63–64
Jinnah, Muhammad Ali, 72, 87, 91, 92, 101, 102,
    104, 108, 109, 111, 112, 113
jiva, 21
Joshi, O. P., 165
Judaism, 45, 48
Jumna-Ganges Rivers, 5, 38, 51, 61

Kabir, 10
Khan, Saiyid Ahmad, 107–108
Kali, 14
Kalidasa, 8
Kalki, 14
Kapur, Shekar, 170
Karamat, Jenhangir, 191, 193
karma, 21
Karmal, Babrak, 55
Kashmir, 4, 11, 14, 16, 48, 52, 53, 72, 73, 86, 87,
    88, 89, 91, 110, 113, 125, 129, 130, 131, 191,
    193, 194
Katyani, Ratan, 149
Kerala, 14, 121, 122
Kesri, Sitaram, 94
khadi, 31
Khalistan, 45, 86
Khasi, India, matrilineal society in, 158–159

Khattar, Sat Pal, 139
Khilifat movement, 157
Khyber Pass, 72, 91, 182
King, Martin Luther, 30, 147
Koran, 72
Kotwal, Dastur Firoze, 161
Kripalani, Acharya, 113
Krishna, 14
Kumaratunga, Chandrika, 27, 33, 80, 81
kumbh mela festival, India's, 178–179
Kyshatriya. See warrior caste

laborer caste, 8, 140–143
Ladakh, 28, 38, 88
Langdana, Zarin, 160
languages, 8, 14–16, 17, 19, 63, 66, 76, 114, 133;
    in India, 39–40, 45; nationalism and, 86–90
Laos, 90
Laws of Manu, 20, 141
Lee Kuan Yew, 140
Lee, Martin, 93
Lenin, Vladimir, 28, 55
Li Guoqing, 201
Li Peng, 93
"license raj" system, in India, 125
linguistics, 3
literature, Indian, 147
Lohia, O. P., 138
Lugar, Richard, 197
Lyngdoh, Johnny, 159

Macan-Markar, Marwaan, 199
Macauley, Thomas, 10
Mackey, William, 64
Mahabharata, 8, 30, 46, 170
Mahal, Mumtaz, 9
maharajas, 11, 30
Mahayana Buddhism, 63–64, 79
Mahendra, Nepal's king, 69–70
Mahinda, Mauryan emperor, 8
Major, John, 93
Malaysia, 90, 112, 139, 176
Maldives: overview of, 65–67; and overview of
    South Asia, 3–35
Malik, Iqbal, 163
Man in the Universe (Brown), 21
Mandal Commission Report, 141
Mandela, Nelson, 30
Manto, Saadat Hasan, 102
maritime commerce, in early South Asia, 6–7
marriages, in India, 134, 141–142, 147–149, 155
Marshall, Sir John, 144
masala filmmaking, in India, 168
Massoud, Ahmed Shah, 180, 182
mathematics, India and, 3, 6, 145, 146, 175–178
matrilineal society, in India, 158–159
Mauryan empire, 38, 86, 145
Mazumdar, Veena, 151
McLaren, Sir Robin, 93
media, in India, 133–134, 167–170, 171–175
meditation, 147
Megasthenes, 145
Mehta, Dinesh, 163

Mehta, Geeta, 7
Mehta, Ketan, 169
Mehta, Zubin, 162
melodrama, in Indian films, 169
methane, biogas power plants in, 164–166
Mexico, 116
Miller, Martin, 182
"Minute on Education" (Macauley), 10
Misra, Neelish, 40
Mishra, Pankaj, 94
Mistry, Rohiton, 162
Mittal, Sat Paul, 150
Moghul people, 8, 9–10, 11, 15, 23, 38, 72, 86
Mohamad, Mathahir, 139
Mongolia, 14, 28
monsoons, 5, 38, 41–42, 76, 116
Mount Everest, 69
Mountbatten, Lord Louis, 92, 93, 109
movies, Indian, 133–134
mujahideen, Afghan, 28, 55, 56, 57, 181
Mujibur Rahman, 51, 59–60, 73, 87
Mukhim, Patricia, 159
Munda languages, 15
Murthy, Nirmala, 150
music, 3, 146
Myrdal, Gunnar, 125

Nag, Moni, 152
Nagaland, 86
Naidu, Sarojini, 34
Naipul, V. S., 32, 40, 44
Nair, Mira, 170
Najibullah, Sayid Muhammed, 57
Nandy, Ashis, 91
Napate, Praween, 140
Nasreen, Taslima, 60
national identity, religion and, 24–25
nationalism, 4, 16–18; and Bengal and Punjab,
    110–114; Hindu, 124–125; secessionism and,
    86–90
Nawaz Sharif, Mian, 74, 75, 76
Nayar, Kuldip, 92
Nehru, Jawaharlal, 34, 42, 43, 44, 49, 87, 91, 94,
    97–101, 104, 109, 113, 114, 116, 121
Nepal, 38, 51, 52, 86, 130, 174; overview of,
    68–70; and overview of South Asia, 3–35
New Economic Policy, India's, 135
New Indian Cinema, 170
Nigeria, 125
nirvana, 8
Non-Aligned Movement (NAM), 53, 131
nongovernmental organizations (NGOs), 163
nonviolence, Gandhi and, 29–35, 97–101, 147,
    157
nuclear weapons, 3, 52, 125, 128–131, 178, 191–
    192; and U.S. sanctions against India and
    Pakistan, 192–194, 194–196, 196–198

Oakley, Robert, 182
occupation, caste and, 142
Omar, Mullah Mohammed, 182
opaque deterrence, nuclear weapons and, 129–
    130

Operation Blue Star, 46
opposites, coexistence of, Indian culture and, 146
Orientalism (Said), 107

Pachauri, R. K., 165, 166
Pakistan, 2, 52, 56, 122, 125, 144, 157, 181, 182;
    Bangladesh and, 59–61; democracy in, 186–
    191; economy of, 191–192; and India, 91,
    101–106, 106–109, 110–114; nationalism
    and, 86–90; nuclear weapons and, 129–131;
    overview of, 71–76; and overview of South
    Asia, 3–35
Pali language, 66
Panchen Lama, 201
Pantalu, Viresalingam, 155
Parsi people, 45, 160–161
partition, of India and Pakistan, 92, 101–106,
    106–109, 110–114
Pashtun, 86, 87, 89
Passage to Peshawar (Reeves), 56, 74
Patel, Jengahir, 161
Pathan people, 3, 55, 57
patriarchy, in India, 154
Patten, Chris, 93
Pax Indiana, 131
Persian Gulf War, 60, 61, 133
Phalke, Dadasaheb, 168
Philippines, 139
politics: in India, 123–128; in Nepal, 69–70; in
    Pakistan, 73–74
polygamy, 155, 156
population growth, 3, 17–18, 38, 42, 120, 121,
    160, 163; in India, 149–154
Portugal, 14, 15, 79
positional numeration, and Indian mathematics,
    176–177
poverty, 3, 4, 18, 40–41, 95, 121–122, 127–128,
    150, 152, 185
Pradesh, Andra, 153
priest caste, 8–9, 13, 20, 49, 140–143
prophetic religion, Parsi as, 160–161
public service broadcasting, in India, 173
puja, 13
Punjab, 10, 12, 45, 72, 88, 89, 91, 102, 107,
    110–114, 152, 153
Pythagorean theorem, 146

Qian Qichen, 93
quality of life, in Maldives, 67

Rabbani, Burhanuddin, 57
Radcliffe, Sir Cyril, 91–92
Radhakrishnan, Sarvepalli, 147
radio, community, in India, 171–174
Rahman, A. R., 169
raj, British. *See* colonialism
Rajpal, Suresh, 137
Ram, Chaudhury Chhotu, 111
Ram Raj, 47
Rama, 8, 14, 46, 47, 95
Ramabai, Pandite, 155, 157
Raman, Chandrasekhara Venkata, 147

Ramanujan, A. K., 5
Ramanujan, Srinivasa, 147
Ramayana, 8, 30, 46, 170
Ramos, Fidel, 139
Rann of Katch, 72
Rao, P. V. Narasimha, 43, 47, 149
Raphel, Robin, 182
Rathman, Maui, 169
Ravaillon, Martin, 122
Ray, Sayajit, 146, 168, 170
Reddy, Amulya, 166
Reeves, Richard, 56, 74
reincarnation, 146
religion: nationalism and, 86–90; and overview of
    South Asia, 3–35. *See also* individual faiths
renewable energy, biogas as, 164–166
Repetto, Robert, 117, 121–122
Rg Veda, 8, 13–14, 20, 21, 141
Richardson, Bill, 182
Roy, B. C., 113
Russia, 11, 55, 131. *See also* Soviet Union
Rynjah, Sweetymon, 159

saddle-querns, 7
sadhus, 178–179
Saeed, Mohammed, 101
Said, Edward, 107
samsara, 42
sanctions, U.S., against India and Pakistan, 192–
    194, 194–196, 196–198
sangha, 14
Sanskrit, 8, 9, 20, 21, 30, 141, 143, 175, 176
sari, 3
sastras, 20
satyagraha, 3, 29, 32
science, ancient India and, 146, 147
Sebokt, Severus, 177
secessionism, nationalism and, 86–90
Sengupta, Nitesh, 91
Seshan, T. N., 125
Shah, Nandita, 135, 136
Shankar, Ravi, 146
Shankara, 8
shankarachayaras, 179
Shanpru, Donakor, 159
Sharif, Nawaz, 187, 188, 189, 190, 191, 192
sharia, 192
Shekar, Chandra, 44
Shia Muslims, 55, 190
Shinde, Tarabai, 155
Shiva, 13–14
Siachen Glacier, 72
Sikh people, 12, 16, 25, 40, 44, 45, 46, 48, 87, 88,
    89, 90, 102, 106, 111, 113, 142
Sikkim, 28, 51
Sind-hudesh, 86
Singapore, 16, 112, 130, 139, 140
Singh, Charan, 44
Singh, Kushwant, 25–26
Singh, Ranjit, 110
Singh, V. P., 44, 95
Sinhalese people, 17, 26, 27, 51, 79
sitar, 3, 146
Siva Hinduism, 7

Snakes and Ladders (Mehta), 7
social diversity, in Nepal, 69
socialism, 132, 137
South Africa, 30, 34
South Asian Association for Regional Cooperation (SAARC), 52, 89
South Asian Preferential Trade Agreement (SAPTA), 52
South Korea, 53
Soviet Union, 3, 30, 53, 76, 116, 132, 193, 196; Afghanistan and, 56–57, 180–184
Sri Lanka, 51, 88, 130; ethnic war in, 198–199; overview of, 78–81; and overview of South Asia, 3–35
Stalin, Joseph, 129
sterilization programs, in India, 153
Story of My Experiments with Truth, The (Gandhi), 30
strategic confrontation, nuclear weapons and, 131
structural adjustment programs, 135
Subandhu, 176
Sudan, 182
Sudra. *See* laborer caste
Sufi Muslims, 12–13, 14, 72
Suhrawardy, H. S., 112
Sunlight on the Broken Columns (Hosain), 105–106
Sunni Muslims, 55, 57, 59, 66, 190
sustainable development, 149
suttee, 155–156
sweatshops, in India, 136

Tagore, Rabindranath, 147
Taj Mahal, 9, 72
Tajikistan, 55
Talbott, Strobe, 194
Taliban, 55, 57, 76, 130, 181–182, 183, 191
Tamil people, 17, 26, 27, 51, 67, 79, 80, 81, 86, 87, 88, 89, 125, 134, 198–199
Taraki, Nur Mohammed, 55, 56
Taroor, Shashi, 48

Tata, Jamshetji Nusserwanji, 160
Templer, Sir Gerald, 92
Thailand, 90
Thanawi, Maulana Ashraf Ali, 156
Thapa, Surrja Bahadur, 70
Thatcher, Margaret, 93
Theology of Culture (Tillich), 18
Theravada Buddhism, 79
Thompson, E. P., 114
Thomsen, Peter, 181
Tibet, 14, 28, 69, 79; Bhutan and, 63–64; China and, 200–201, 201–203
Tillich, Paul, 18
Train to Peshawar (Singh), 25–26
transmigration of souls, 146
Tribhuvan, Nepal's king, 69
turbans, 3
Turkey, 90, 107, 131
Turkmenistan, 55, 182
"two nation" theory, Jinnah's, 87, 101, 102

Ul Haq, Mahbub, 122
unions, labor, in India, 136
United Nations, 11, 67, 75, 119, 121, 122, 130, 152, 185, 193
United States, 52, 53, 125, 129, 149, 181, 182, 183
untouchables, 14, 32, 47, 49, 95, 140–143
Upanishads, 145–146
Urdu language, 59, 76, 156, 188
Uzbekistan, 55

Vaisya. See citizen caste
Vajpayee, A. B., 43, 125, 127
varna, 141, 142
vasectomy, 153
Vedic tradition, 4, 146, 175
Venkataraman, R. I., 43
Victoria, Britain's queen, 11
Vidyasagar, Iswarchandra, 155

Vietnam, 116
Visaria, Pravin, and Leela, 153
Vishnu, 13–14
Vivekananda, Swami, 156

Waheed, Abdul, 74
warrior caste, 8, 20, 140–143
water pollution, 117–118, 163
Wazed, Sheikh Hasina, 51
West Indies, 16
Western culture, influence of India on, 143–147
Whither India? (Nehru), 98
widow remarriage, in India, 155–156
wind power, 120
witness, self as, 21
women, 3, 18; in Afghanistan, 182; Grameen Bank and, 184–185; in India, 135–136, 147–149, 149–154, 154–158; in Pakistan, 60–61, 77, 192
world as symbol, in South Asia, 18–22
World Bank, 12, 70, 77, 120, 122, 138, 150, 151, 152, 162, 195
World Health Organization, 166
World Trade Organization, 127, 130
writing, introduction of, in India, 175–176

Yadav, Mulayam Singh, 47
Yahya Khan, 73, 74, 187, 189
yoga, 3, 6, 14, 147
Yunus, Mohammed, 61; on Grameen Bank, 184–185

zamindari, 105, 110, 111, 112
zero, invention of, 3, 6, 146, 175–178
Zia-ul-Haq, Mohammad, 73–74, 75–76, 77, 187, 188, 190
Ziaur Rahman, 59–60